CASES AND MATERIALS

PRODUCTS LIABILITY AND SAFETY

THIRD EDITION

1999 CASE AND STATUTORY SUPPLEMENT

by

DAVID G. OWEN
Carolina Distinguished Professor of Law
University of South Carolina

MARY J. DAVIS
Stites & Harbison Professor of Law
University of Kentucky

NEW YORK, NEW YORK
FOUNDATION PRESS
1999

INDEX

COPYRIGHT © 1999

By

FOUNDATION PRESS

All rights reserved

ISBN 1–56662–842–3

[No claim of copyright is made for official U.S. government statutes, rules or regulations.]

PREFACE

This Case and Statutory Supplement accompanies the Third Edition of Products Liability and Safety: Cases and Materials. The new Cases and Notes material includes critical recent cases on the concept of defectiveness, use of expert testimony, preemption and class actions and updated notes in the swiftly evolving areas of tobacco litigation, and toxic causation, among others. This Supplement retains and updates the statutory material from the 1998 Supplement to the Third Edition. Because of the publication of the Restatement Third of Torts: Products Liability, we have retained only the most critical portions of the Second Restatement. This Supplement reproduces much of the Restatement on Products Liability, published in 1998. Retained from the previous Supplement are the Uniform Commercial Code and the various legislative materials included therein. State legislatures continue to enact products liability "reform" acts of various types, and a number of the more important statutes of this type are included. At the federal level, a products liability bill was passed by both houses of Congress for the first time in 1996, but it was vetoed by the President. That bill, H.R. 956, the Common Sense Product Liability Legal Reform Act of 1996, is reproduced here accompanied by the Conference Committee report. The 1997 version of the federal reform effort, the Product Liability Reform Act of 1997, is also reproduced. A portion of that bill has been separately enacted, the Biomaterials Access Assurance Act of 1998, and is reproduced as well.

In order to maximize the materials available to teachers and students, we have erred on the side of over-inclusion, particularly in the selected state statutes. We expect teachers will be selective in their assignments from this supplement and intend that the supplement complement the individual teaching styles and topic preferences of our users.

From time to time we receive comments and suggestions for improvement from users of the book. We consider this information valuable in our ongoing effort to present teachers and students with the most useful and up-to-date materials on the law of products liability. To that end, as in the past, we invite comments and criticisms on the materials in the casebook and the Supplement alike.

DAVID G. OWEN
MARY J. DAVIS

July 1999

*

✱ 2 TYPES of SELLER WRONGDOING:

MISREPRESENTATION	PRODUCT INTRINSICALLY FLAWED	
NEGLIGENCE	DESIGN DEFECT	2-314
STRICT TORT	WARNINGS/INSTRUCTIONS	402A
FRAUD	MISMANUFACTURE	NEGLIGENCE
2-313		
402B		

✱

	NEGLIGENCE	S/L	FRAUD
BASIS	Conduct	Content	Conduct
INTENT?	No	No	Scienter
DAMAGES	Reg	Reg.	Reg. + Punitive
PLEAD SPECIFIC?	No	No	Yes

✱ 4 CATEGORIES:

① MISREP/PIPD : Tort

② MISREP/PEL : K

③ FLAW/PIPD : Tort

④ FLAW/ PEL : K

✱ NEGLIGENCE

- ELEMENTS: Duty, Breach, Causation, Damages
- Neglig. Party liable for FORESEEABLE CONSEQUENCES
- FOR NEGLIG. REPRESENT, Δ must have known or had reason to believe existence of defective condition

✱ (Standard of Conduct for Reasonable Person)

K nowledge

A ttention

M emory

P erception

I ntelligence

J udgement

ACKNOWLEDGEMENTS

We are grateful for the considerable secretarial and administrative assistance of Bonnie Detzel whose professionalism and good cheer is greatly appreciated.

We would also like to acknowledge the following publishers who permitted us to use the materials noted:

American Law Institute, Restatement of the Law (Second) of Torts, selected sections. Copyright 1965 by the American Law Institute. American Law Institute, Restatement of the Law (Third) of Torts: Products Liability, selected sections. Copyright 1998 by the American Law Institute. Reprinted with permission of the American Law Institute.

Uniform Commercial Code, Official Text and Comments, selected sections. Copyright 1987 by the American Law Institute and the National Conference of Commissioners on the Uniform State Laws. Reprinted with permission. All rights are reserved.

Lurking in the background, as ever, remain our spouses, Joan Owen and Stuart Scales.

*

* Warranty by Description

* Express W may arise after transaction if B is free to repudiate at that time

* 3P and Δ may be joint & severally liable IF

   ① They act in concert

   ② They commit separate acts that combine to produce a single indivisible injury

SUMMARY OF CONTENTS

*

TABLE OF CONTENTS

Section

MODEL UNIFORM PRODUCT LIABILITY ACT

Section

＊

TABLE OF CASES

Principal cases are in bold type. Non-principal cases are in roman type. References are to Pages.

1999 CASE AND STATUTORY SUPPLEMENT

CASES AND MATERIALS

PRODUCTS LIABILITY AND SAFETY

*

PART I

THEORIES OF MANUFACTURER LIABILITY

CHAPTER 3

TORTIOUS MISREPRESENTATION

3. STRICT LIABILITY FOR MISREPRESENTATION

REPLACE on page 90 the reference to § 17 of the new Products Liability Restatement with a reference to § 9. The final version was approved on May 20, 1997 at the Annual Meeting of the American Law Institute, and was published in 1998. The final version is included in this Supplement.

Please note that further references in the casebook to the Products Liability Restatement should be cross-referenced to the final version.

CHAPTER 4

WARRANTY

2. IMPLIED WARRANTY OF MERCHANTABILITY

ADD to the end of note **3. Standard of Liability**, on page 108:

The National Conference of Commissioners on Uniform State Laws and the American Law Institute are almost done revising Article 2 of the UCC. See Uniform Commercial Code Revised Article 2. Sales, ALI *Proposed Final Draft,* May 1, 1999. At the Annual Meeting of the ALI in May, 1997, the members discussed the interplay between warranty and tort standards of liability for personal injury and property damage resulting from a defective product. The ALI membership approved the following language that in the May 1999 draft appears as comment 4 to the new implied warranty of merchantability § 2–404: "When recovery is sought for injury to person or property, whether goods are merchantable is to be determined by applicable state products liability law."

If a jury finds a product non-defective in a tort cause of action, does this language mean that the same jury is precluded from finding that the product was unmerchantable for breach of warranty purposes? Reconsider this question after examining *Denny v. Ford Motor Co.*, in ch. 5, which begins on the next page.

CHAPTER 5

STRICT LIABILITY IN TORT

---

1. DEVELOPMENT

ADD **Denny v. Ford Motor Co.,** 662 N.E.2d 730 (N.Y. 1995), as a
principal case in place of the note material on pages 166–67.

Denny v. Ford Motor Co.

Court of Appeals of New York, 1995.
87 N.Y.2d 248, 639 N.Y.S.2d 250, 662 N.E.2d 730.

■ TITONE, JUDGE.

Are the elements of New York's causes of action for strict products
liability and breach of implied warranty always co-extensive? If not, can the
latter be broader than the former? These are the core issues presented by
the questions that the United States Court of Appeals for the Second
Circuit has certified to us in this diversity action involving an allegedly
defective vehicle. On the facts set forth by the Second Circuit, we hold that
the causes of action are not identical and that, under the circumstances
presented here, it is possible to be liable for breach of implied warranty
even though a claim of strict products liability has not been satisfactorily
established.

I.

As stated by the Second Circuit, this action arises out of a June 9, 1986
accident in which plaintiff Nancy Denny was severely injured when the
Ford Bronco II that she was driving rolled over. The rollover accident
occurred when Denny slammed on her brakes in an effort to avoid a deer
that had walked directly into her motor vehicle's path. Denny and her
spouse sued Ford Motor Co., the vehicle's manufacturer, asserting claims
for negligence, strict products liability and breach of implied warranty of
merchantability. The case went to trial in the District Court for the
Northern District of New York in October of 1992.

The trial evidence centered on the particular characteristics of utility
vehicles, which are generally made for off-road use on unpaved and often
rugged terrain. Such use sometimes necessitates climbing over obstacles
such as fallen logs and rocks. While utility vehicles are traditionally
considerably larger than passenger cars, some manufacturers have created
a category of down-sized "small" utility vehicles, which are designed to be
lighter, to achieve better fuel economy and, presumably, to appeal to a

wider consumer market. The Bronco II in which Denny was injured falls into this category.

Plaintiffs introduced evidence at trial to show that small utility vehicles in general, and the Bronco II in particular, present a significantly higher risk of rollover accidents than do ordinary passenger automobiles. Plaintiffs' evidence also showed that the Bronco II had a low stability index attributable to its high center of gravity and relatively narrow track width. The vehicle's shorter wheel base and suspension system were additional factors contributing to its instability. Ford had made minor design changes in an effort to achieve a higher stability index, but, according to plaintiffs' proof, none of the changes produced a significant improvement in the vehicle's stability.

Ford argued at trial that the design features of which plaintiffs complained were necessary to the vehicle's off-road capabilities. According to Ford, the vehicle had been intended to be used as an off-road vehicle and had not been designed to be sold as a conventional passenger automobile. Ford's own engineer stated that he would not recommend the Bronco II to someone whose primary interest was to use it as a passenger car, since the features of a four-wheel-drive utility vehicle were not helpful for that purpose and the vehicle's design made it inherently less stable.

Despite the engineer's testimony, plaintiffs introduced a Ford marketing manual which predicted that many buyers would be attracted to the Bronco II because utility vehicles were "suitable to contemporary life styles" and were "considered fashionable" in some suburban areas. According to this manual, the sales presentation of the Bronco II should take into account the vehicle's "suitability for commuting and for suburban and city driving." Additionally, the vehicle's ability to switch between two-wheel and four-wheel drive would "be particularly appealing to women who may be concerned about driving in snow and ice with their children." Plaintiffs both testified that the perceived safety benefits of its four-wheel-drive capacity were what attracted them to the Bronco II. They were not at all interested in its off-road use.

At the close of the evidence, the District Court Judge submitted both the strict-products-liability claim and the breach-of-implied-warranty claim, despite Ford's objection that the two causes of action were identical. With respect to the strict-products-liability claim the court told the jury that "[a] manufacturer who places a product on the market in a defective condition is liable for injury which results from use of the product when the product is used for its intended or reasonably foreseeable purpose." Further, the court [defined "defective" as "not reasonably safe," explaining that the plaintiffs must prove that a reasonable person who knew of the product's potential for causing injury and the existence of available alternative designs would have concluded that such a product should not have been marketed in that condition. This conclusion should be reached by balancing the risks involved in using the product against its usefulness, and its costs

4

against the risks, usefulness and costs of the alternative designs. With respect to the breach-of-implied-warranty claim, the court instructed the jury that a product must be reasonably fit for the ordinary purposes for which it was intended and that "if it is, in fact, defective and not reasonably fit to be used for its intended purpose, the warranty is breached."] The plaintiffs claim that the Bronco II was not fit for its ordinary purpose because of its alleged propensity to rollover and lack of warnings to the consumer of this propensity. Neither party objected to the content of these charges.

[The jury found that the Bronco II was not "defective" and that defendant was not liable under plaintiffs' strict-products-liability cause of action. The jury also found, however, that defendant had breached its implied warranty of merchantability, that the breach was the proximate cause of Nancy Denny's injuries, and plaintiff was awarded judgment in the amount of $1.2 million. Ford moved for a new trial under Fed. R. Civ. P. 59(a), arguing that the jury's finding on the breach-of-implied-warranty cause of action was irreconcilable with its finding on the strict-products-liability claim. The trial court rejected this argument.]

On defendant's appeal, [the Second Circuit] certified the following questions for consideration by this Court * * *: (1) whether the strict products liability claim and the breach of implied warranty claims are identical; (2) whether, if the claims are different, the strict products liability claim is broader than the implied warranty claim and encompasses the latter; and (3) whether, if the claims are different and a strict liability claim may fail while an implied warranty claim succeeds, the jury's finding of no product defect is reconcilable with its finding of a breach of warranty.

II.

In this proceeding, Ford's sole argument is that plaintiffs' strict-products-liability and breach-of-implied warranty causes of action were identical and that, accordingly, a defendant's verdict on the former cannot be reconciled with a plaintiff's verdict on the latter. This argument is, in turn, premised on both the intertwined history of the two doctrines and the close similarity in their elements and legal functions. Although Ford recognizes that New York has previously permitted personal-injury plaintiffs to simultaneously assert different products-liability theories in support of their claims [citation], it contends that the breach-of-implied-warranty cause of action, which sounds in contract, has been subsumed by the more recently adopted, and more highly evolved, strict-products-liability theory, which sounds in tort. Ford's argument has much to commend it. However, in the final analysis, the argument is flawed because it overlooks the continued existence of a separate statutory predicate for the breach-of-warranty theory and the subtle but important distinction between the two theories that arises from their different historical and doctrinal root.

When products-liability litigation was in its infancy, the courts relied upon contractual warranty theories as the only existing means of facilitating economic recovery for personal injuries arising from the use of defective goods. [Citations.] Citing statutory authority [citations], the courts posited the existence of an implied warranty arising as an incident of the product's sale and premised a cause of action for consequential personal injuries based on breaches of that warranty [citation].

Eventually, the contractually based implied-warranty theory came to be perceived as inadequate in an economic universe that was dominated by mass-produced products and an impersonal marketplace. Its primary weakness was, of course, its rigid requirement of a relationship of privity between the seller and the injured consumer—a requirement that often could not be satisfied, [citation]. Some courts (including ours) recognized certain narrow exceptions to the privity requirement in an effort to avoid the doctrine's harsher effects, [citations]. However, the warranty approach remained unsatisfactory, and the courts shifted their focus to the development of a new, more flexible tort cause of action: the doctrine of strict products liability. [Citations.]

The establishment of this tort remedy has, as this Court has recognized, significantly diminished the need to rely on the contractually-based breach-of-implied-warranty remedy as a means of compensating individuals injured because of defective products, [citations]. Further, although the available defenses and applicable limitations principles may differ, there is a high degree of overlap between the substantive aspects of the two causes of action, [citation]. Indeed, on an earlier occasion, this Court observed, in dictum, that "strict liability in tort and implied warranty in the absence of privity are different ways of describing the very same cause of action." [Citations].

Nonetheless, it would not be correct to infer that the tort cause of action has completely supplanted the older breach-of-implied-warranty cause of action or that the two doctrines are now identical in every respect. [Citation]. The continued vitality of the warranty approach is evidenced by its retention and expansion in New York's version of the Uniform Commercial Code (UCC §§ 2–314[2][c],–318). The existence of this statutory authority belies any argument that the breach-of-implied-warranty remedy is a dead letter [citation].[2]

Although the products-liability theory sounding in tort and the breach-of-implied warranty theory authorized by the UCC co-exist and are often invoked in tandem, the core element of "defect" is subtly different in the two causes of action. Under New York law, a design defect may be actionable under a strict products liability theory if the product is not

---

2. Indeed, the statutory provision for personal injury recovery as an element of "consequential damages" (UCC § 2–715[2][b]) makes it illogical to conclude * * * that the breach-of-implied-warranty theory should be confined to recovery for economic loss [citations].

reasonably safe. Since this Court's decision in Voss v. Black & Decker Mfg. Co., 450 N.E.2d 204, the New York standard for determining the existence of a design defect has required an assessment of whether "if the design defect were known at the time of manufacture, a reasonable person would conclude that the utility of the product did not outweigh the risk inherent in marketing a product designed in that manner." [Citations.] This standard demands an inquiry into such factors as (1) the product's utility to the public as a whole, (2) its utility to the individual user, (3) the likelihood that the product will cause injury, (4) the availability of a safer design, (5) the possibility of designing and manufacturing the product so that it is safer but remains functional and reasonably priced, (6) the degree of awareness of the product's potential danger that can reasonably be attributed to the injured user, and (7) the manufacturer's ability to spread the cost of any safety-related design changes (*Voss v Black & Decker Mfg. Co.*, supra). The above-described analysis is rooted in a recognition that there are both risks and benefits associated with many products and that there are instances in which a product's inherent dangers cannot be eliminated without simultaneously compromising or completely nullifying its benefits. In such circumstances, a weighing of the product's benefits against its risks is an appropriate and necessary component of the liability assessment under the policy-based principles associated with tort law.

The adoption of this risk/utility balance as a component of the "defectiveness" element has brought the inquiry in design defect cases closer to that used in traditional negligence cases, where the reasonableness of an actor's conduct is considered in light of a number of situational and policy-driven factors. While efforts have been made to steer away from the fault-oriented negligence principles by characterizing the design defect cause of action in terms of a product-based rather than a conduct-based analysis (see, e.g., *Voss v. Black & Decker Mfg.*, supra; Barker v. Lull Engineering Co., 20 Cal.3d 413), the reality is that the risk/utility balancing test is a "negligence inspired" approach, since it invites the parties to adduce proof about the manufacturer's choices and ultimately requires the factfinder to make "a judgment about [the manufacturer's] judgment." (S. Birnbaum, Unmasking the Test for Design Defect: From Negligence [to Warranty] to Strict Liability to Negligence, 33 Vand. L.Rev. 593, 610, 648; [citations]). In other words, an assessment of the manufacturer's conduct is virtually inevitable, and, as one commentator observed, "in general, * * * the strict liability concept of 'defective design' [is] functionally synonymous with the earlier negligence concept of unreasonable design." (Schwartz, New Products, Old Products, Evolving Law, Retroactive Law, 58 NYU L.Rev. 796, 803, [citations]).

It is this negligence-like risk/benefit component of the defect element that differentiates strict-products-liability claims from UCC-based breach-of-implied-warranty claims in cases involving design defects. While the strict products concept of a product that is "not reasonably safe" requires a weighing of the product's dangers against its overall advantages, the UCC's concept of a "defective" product requires an inquiry only into whether the product in question was "fit for the ordinary purposes for which such goods are used" (UCC § 2–314[2][c]). The latter inquiry focuses on the expectations for the performance of the product when used in the customary, usual and reasonably foreseeable manners. The cause of action is one involving true "strict" liability, since recovery may be had upon a showing that the product was not minimally safe for its expected purpose—without regard to the feasibility of alternative designs or the manufacturer's "reasonableness" in marketing it in that unsafe condition.

This distinction between the "defect" analysis in breach-of-implied-warranty actions and the "defect" analysis in strict-products-liability actions is explained by the differing etiology and doctrinal underpinnings of the two distinct theories. The former class of actions originates in contract law, which directs its attention to the purchaser's disappointed expectations; the latter originates in tort law, which traditionally has concerned itself with social policy and risk allocation by means other than those dictated by the marketplace.

The dissent takes issue with the foregoing conclusion, arguing, in essence, that any residual distinction that exists between the two causes of action should be eliminated and that the analysis for "defect" in implied-warranty claims should be deemed to encompass the risk/utility analysis that has previously been incorporated in tort causes of action. This argument is predicated on the dissent's view that the common history of the two causes of action and the perceived advantages of risk/utility analysis counsel in favor of the use of a unitary standard. The dissent has even gone so far as to suggest that the breach of implied warranty cause of action should be treated like a tort claim despite the fact that it is based on the provisions of the Uniform Commercial Code.

What the dissent overlooks is that, as long as that legislative source of authority exists, we are not free to merge the warranty cause of action with its tort-based sibling regardless of whether, as a matter of policy, the contract-based warranty claim may fairly be regarded as a historical relic that no longer has any independent substantive value. Rather, we must construe and apply this separate remedy in a manner that remains consistent with its current roots in contract law [citation].

To the extent that the dissent advocates a merger of the common-law and statutory causes of action through the use of a single analytical standard, its argument is undermined by an examination of what other jurisdictions have done. In most of the cases where the courts have pronounced the merger of breach of warranty with the other products liability theories sounding in tort, they were relying on specific state statutory schemes that were enacted to govern products-liability litigation and not only contain preemptive language but also specifically define "product liability claim" as one encompassing breach of express or implied warranty as well as negligence and strict liability in tort (see, e.g., Philpott

v. A.H. Robins Co., 710 F.2d 1422 [applying Or.Rev.Stat. § 30.905]; [citations]). Indeed, the proposed Model Uniform Product Liability Act, which was issued by the Commerce Department in 1979, embodies precisely the kind of doctrinal merger that the dissent advocates. New York, of course, has not adopted the Model Act or any other such unifying measures. [And c]ontrary to the dissent's suggestion, the current version of UCC § 2–318 is not the equivalent of these uniform product-liability provisions, nor does it manifest an intention by our State's Legislature to engraft a tort cause of action onto a UCC article that concerns itself principally with the contract-based obligations. * * * In fact, it is evident * * * that its purpose was to expand the class of plaintiffs who can avail themselves of the Code's warranty remedies and not to transform those remedies into a new tort cause of action [citation].

Moreover, the dissent's novel proposal that the contract-based consumer-expectation test should be abandoned for the tort-based risk/utility approach even for contract-based warranty claims has not been embraced or even suggested by any of the risk/utility advocates that the dissent cites. For example, although the drafters of the Third Restatement have endorsed risk/utility analysis for design defect cases sounding in tort, they also have made clear that claims based on warranty theories are "not within the scope" of the newly drafted section and are, in fact, "unaffected by it" (ALI, Restatement of Torts: Product Liability, Tentative Draft No. 2 [March 13, 1995], § 2, comment m, p 42). Further, the drafters have noted that "warranty law as a body of legal doctrine separate from tort may impose legal obligations that go beyond those set forth" in the Restatement of Torts (id., comment q, p 46). [And though commentators criticize the consumer-expectation based tests for product defect and argue instead for the use of a risk/utility approach, their arguments are addressed to tort causes of action alone. And those criticisms are inconsistent with recent expressions by courts and commentators of considerable support for a threshold test which does not require that the rigorous risk-utility analysis be undertaken in every design defect case.]

As a practical matter, the distinction between the defect concepts in tort law and in implied-warranty theory may have little or no effect in most cases. In this case, however, the nature of the proof and the way in which the fact issues were litigated demonstrates how the two causes of action can diverge. In the trial court, Ford took the position that the design features of which plaintiffs complain, i.e., the Bronco II's high center of gravity, narrow track width, short wheel base and specially tailored suspension system, were important to preserving the vehicle's ability to drive over the highly irregular terrain that typifies off-road travel. Ford's proof in this regard was relevant to the strict-products-liability risk/utility equation, which required the factfinder to determine whether the Bronco II's value as an off-road vehicle outweighed the risk of the rollover accidents that could occur when the vehicle was used for other driving tasks.

On the other hand, plaintiffs' proof focused, in part, on the sale of the Bronco II for suburban driving and everyday road travel. Plaintiffs also adduced proof that the Bronco II's design characteristics made it unusually susceptible to rollover accidents when used on paved roads. All of this evidence was useful in showing that routine highway and street driving was the "ordinary purpose" for which the Bronco II was sold and that it was not "fit"—or safe—for that purpose.

Thus, under the evidence in this case, a rational factfinder could have simultaneously concluded that the Bronco II's utility as an off-road vehicle outweighed the risk of injury resulting from rollover accidents and that the vehicle was not safe for the "ordinary purpose" of daily driving for which it was marketed and sold. Under the law of this State such a set of factual judgments would lead to the concomitant legal conclusion that plaintiffs' strict-products-liability cause of action was not viable but that defendant should nevertheless be held liable for breach of its implied promise that the Bronco II was "merchantable" or "fit" for its "ordinary purpose." Importantly, what makes this case distinctive is that the "ordinary purpose" for which the product was marketed and sold to the plaintiff was not the same as the utility against which the risk was to be weighed. It is these unusual circumstances that give practical significance to the ordinarily theoretical difference between the defect concepts in tort and statutory breach-of-implied warranty causes of action (see, e.g., McLaughlin v. Michelin Tire Corp., 778 P.2d 59, 66–67 [Wyo.]; accord, 1 M. Madden, Products Liability [2d ed.] § 5.11, at 160).

From the foregoing it is apparent that the causes of action for strict products liability and breach of implied warranty of merchantability are not identical in New York and that the latter is not necessarily subsumed by the former. It follows that, under the circumstances presented, a verdict such as the one occurring here—in which the manufacturer was found liable under an implied warranty cause of action and not liable under a strict products cause of action—is theoretically reconcilable under New York law. * * *

Accordingly, certified question No. 1 should be answered in the negative, certified question No. 2 in the negative and certified question No. 3 in the affirmative.

■ SIMONS, J. (Dissenting):

I agree with the majority that causes of action in strict products liability and breach of implied warranty are not identical. In my view, however, the strict products liability claim is substantively broader than and encompasses the implied warranty claim and, thus, the jury's verdict of no defect in the products liability cause of action is not reconcilable with its finding of breach of implied warranty. Accordingly, I would answer the first two questions certified to the Court no and yes and find it unnecessary to answer the third question.

I

* * *

A

Logically, there is no substantive difference for testing liability in the two causes of action. Recovery in each depends upon establishing that the product was defective because improperly designed. But the word "defect" has no clear legal meaning. In this case, the court defined defect in its strict products liability charge but did not attempt to define it otherwise; in the warranty cause of action the meaning had to be found in the court's instructions describing the nature of the cause of action. Nevertheless, the predicate for recovery in both claims was the same.

* * *

When [the jury instructions] are compared, it is apparent that a defect for strict products liability purposes is broader than a defect for implied warranty purposes. The vehicle could not have been defective when used for its ordinary and intended purpose (warranty), but not defective and reasonably safe when used for its "intended or for an unintended but reasonably foreseeable purpose" (strict products liability). As the Court of Appeals observed, foreseeable use "certainly includes all purposes that are 'ordinary' and perhaps some that are not 'ordinary'". The jury having concluded that the Bronco II was not defective for strict products liability purposes, could not logically conclude that it was defective for warranty purposes.

B

Nor is there any legal reason to distinguish the two causes of action in this respect. Breach of implied warranty and strict liability in tort developed from separate legal doctrines but are not materially different when applied to personal injury claims involving design defects. While breach of implied warranty retains its contractual law characteristics when applied to commercial transactions, it has been consistently recognized that it is a tort when applied to personal injury litigation and that tort principles should apply. To introduce a new test of defectiveness into tort litigation—one based on contract principles—can only destabilize the well settled law in this area. Both causes of action are torts and defectiveness for both should be determined by the same standard.

* * *

II

The majority has not attempted to define the consumer expectation standard, nor did the District Court use the phrase in its charge. Under one formulation, however, the standard provides that a product is defective, i.e, it is unreasonably dangerous, if it is "dangerous to an extent beyond that which would be contemplated by the ordinary consumer who purchases it, with the ordinary knowledge common to the community as to its character- istics" (see, Restatement [Second] Torts, § 402A, Comment i; [citation]). The consumer expectation standard originated from the sales notion that a seller could agree, expressly or impliedly, to indemnify a buyer if the purchased product did not satisfy the buyer's purposes. * * * As evolving social policy sought to hold manufacturers and sellers liable for personal injuries caused by defective products, * * * the courts extended liability as far as social policy required. With these developments, it made little sense to think in terms of the buyer's bargain or expectations. In many, if not most, cases the buyer was not litigating.

[New York has never recognized the consumer expectations test for resolving claims of design defect. It has been widely criticized by commen- tators who contend that it is ambiguous because it does not define the relevant expectations, it has been applied inconsistently and, from a social policy standpoint, it produces bad results. If the standard used is the actual buyer's expectations, as in contract law, absolute liability upon manufac- turers and sellers will result. If the test is objective, it is beyond the experience of most lay jurors to determine what an "ordinary consumer" expects or "how safe" a sophisticated modern product could or should be made. The consumer expectation test is unworkable when applied in cases involving design defects because the plaintiff contends that the product has been made precisely as intended but is nevertheless defective because the design is defective.] But unless some external standard, such as available alternative designs and risk/utility analysis is employed, how is the jury to measure the propriety of the design? The consumer cannot reasonably expect a design to be changed if the cost of doing so far outweighs the utility of the product or if there is no alternative design available. Some products are inherently dangerous, * * *, and when that is so, policy concerns mandate that the responsibility for risks that cannot reasonably be designed out of a product should be transferred to the party who has the choice of using them or not, the consumer. The method for determining just what products fall within that group is the risk/utility analysis.

* * *

III

The majority maintains, however, that consumer expectation standard must be applied because breach of implied warranty is a statutory cause of action and the Court is not free to ignore the statute's provisions or draw a distinction between its application to commercial claims and personal injury claims. [The statutory law of implied warranties has existed since 1911], long before any serious attempt was made to base tort liability on them. [Those provisions, and their successors] in the Uniform Commercial Code, were enacted to address problems arising in commercial transactions. For many years they had no significant impact upon personal injury

litigation because of the rules of privity. However, [when privity was statutorily abandoned, the change had no relevance to commercial claims]; it was proposed by the Legislature, and widely supported, because it acknowledged and encouraged the judicial development of a separate category of warranty providing a tort remedy for personal injuries [citations].
* * *

Moreover, no words in the statute either before or after the amendment, provide that the defectiveness of the product in tort claims, or commercial claims for that matter, is to be measured by the consumer's expectations. That standard has been developed by the courts. It may accurately assess the terms and conditions of the bargain between the parties to a sale but it can hardly extend beyond them to address defectiveness in the sense that something is "wrong" with the product. The thing "wrong" with the product in the consumer expectation test is that it has not lived up to the consumer's expectations and this is so even if the design of the product is perfection itself. The standard may retain some vitality when applied to commercial transactions but its individualized concept of injury is entirely foreign to tort doctrine underlying this area of law which is based upon the broad concept of enterprise responsibility to protect the public at large from harm.

* * *

The warranty claim in this case was for tortious personal injury and rests on the underlying "social concerns for the protection of life and property, not regularity in commercial exchange" (see, Restatement [Third], p 46, supra). As such, it should be governed by tort rules, not contract rules. Nothing has prevented us in the past from construing and applying the provisions of the Uniform Commercial Code to supplement and advance the policy concerns underlying strict products liability generally, and we should not construe the statute now to establish a standard for determining defectiveness which is inconsistent with the present law in this area (see generally, UCC § 1–103).

Accordingly, I dissent.

PART II

The Concept of Defectiveness

CHAPTER 6

Tests of Defectiveness

---

1. Consumer Expectations

ADD to the end of note 1, page 242, the following:

The evolution of the consumer expectations test in Oregon illustrates its burdens and benefits as a test of defectiveness. The test was endorsed, with trepidation, in *Heaton v. Ford Motor Co.* (cited in the casebook at note 1, on page 197) and *Markle* (discussing the basis for the test, in note 5 on page 199), abandoned for a risk-utility test in *Phillips v. Kimwood Machine Co.* (cited in the casebook on page 190), and readopted by the legislature which specifically endorsed the tests of comments g and i of section 402A. The Oregon Court of Appeals, for the first time in thirty years, discussed the test at length in McCathern v. Toyota Motor Corp., 1999 WL 247404 (Or. App. 1999). In *McCathern*, plaintiff, a passenger in a Toyota 4Runner sport utility vehicle, was injured when the vehicle rolled over as the driver attempted to avoid collision with an oncoming car. Plaintiff received a jury verdict under the consumer expectations test of defectiveness, alleging that the tendency to roll over defeated the consumer's expectations, and also offering proof of an alternative design in subsequent models of the vehicle. The court of appeals noted two distinct approaches to the consumer expectations test: the "representational" approach, based on the manufacturer's safety representations in which "considerations of cost and utility are immaterial," and the "consumer risk-utility" approach which "proceeds from the premise that ordinary consumers reasonably expect products to be designed in the safest feasible and practicable manner." Are both these tests consistent with the comments to § 402A?

The court of appeals noted that most jurisdictions have opted for one or the other of the two tests, and not both, but concluded that "[t]he two approaches promote distinct, but not conflicting policies; they require different, but not inconsistent, proof. We perceive no reason why a plaintiff, with legally sufficient proof, could not proceed under both approaches." The court of appeals explained its adoption of both approaches:

> First, the 'representational' approach * * * is quite constrictive, requiring a substantial correspondence—albeit not an exact equivalence—between the manufacturer's representations and the conditions of the product's nonperformance. If the representational approach were exclusive, in those cases in which the manufacturer made only general representations—or, indeed, no representations at all—the manufacturer could escape strict liability. Thus, to treat that approach as the sole method of proving product defect would substantially compromise the consumer-protective underpinnings of strict liability. Conversely, the premise of the 'consumer risk-utility' approach—that consumers can reasonably expect a product to be designed in the safest practicable manner—comports with Oregon's articulation of these policies: 'The user has a right to expect a reasonably safe design.' *Heaton.*

Id. at *8. The court of appeals concluded that plaintiff introduced sufficient proof that the 4Runner was defective under both tests. Plaintiff introduced evidence of a safer, feasible alternative design by virtue of a later re-designed model which had a lower center of gravity and a wider wheel base. The court of appeals summarily concluded that such evidence met the "consumer risk-utility" test. In applying the "representational" approach, the court elaborated on the nature of evidence sufficient to satisfy the test.

> A representation that a car is "safe" does not support a reasonable expectation that the vehicle can negotiate and withstand all foreseeable road hazards any more than does a representation that a pick-up is "rugged." [Such was the representation in *Heaton.*] Conversely, to restrict the representational approach to those circumstances where the manufacturer's representations correspond exactly with the circumstances of the accident would effectively insulate manufacturers from liability. The circumstances of accidents are so variable that a manufacturer will rarely, if ever, represent that the product will perform safely under precisely those conditions.

> In truth, it is difficult, if not impossible, to define a principled point of evidentiary sufficiency on that continuum. We also acknowledge that a standard of "substantial similarity" may seem to be so indefinite as to describe a result rather than an analysis. Nevertheless, we believe that is the correct standard: A plaintiff's proof under the representational theory is legally sufficient if a reasonable juror could find that there is such a relationship between the manufacturer's representations and the circumstances of the product's nonperformance that a reasonable consumer would have believed that the product could perform safely under those circumstances.

Id. at *12. What do you imagine was sufficient to sustain the plaintiff's verdict in *McCathern* on the "representational" approach? Toyota did not explicitly represent that the vehicle would not roll over under the exact circumstances presented there—dry road conditions with the vehicle travelling at legal speed. What about generalized representations about the vehicle's maneuverability? Testimony that the vehicle,while designed for off-road use, was marketed for highway driving as in *Denny v. Ford Motor Co.*, supra Supplement in ch. 5? Awareness by the manufacturer that consumers mistakenly believed the vehicle to be safer for on-road than off-road use, when it, in fact, was less safe? What effect on application of the representational approach of a warning on the passenger's front window visor that said "the vehicle may roll over or go out of control and crash" under sharp turns?

How would the Oregon Court of Appeals treat the cigarette lighter in the *Bic* trilogy?

3. ALTERNATIVE TESTS OF DEFECT

ADD **Potter v. Chicago Pneumatic Tool Co.,** 694 A.2d 1319 (Conn. 1997), as a principal case after note 1, page 242.

Potter v. Chicago Pneumatic Tool Company

Supreme Court of Connecticut, 1997.
694 A.2d 1319.

■ KATZ, ASSOCIATE JUSTICE.

This appeal arises from a products liability action brought by the plaintiffs against the defendants, Chicago Pneumatic Tool Company (Chicago Pneumatic), Stanley Works and Dresser Industries, Inc. (Dresser). The plaintiffs claim that they were injured in the course of their employment as shipyard workers at the General Dynamics Corporation Electric Boat facility (Electric Boat) in Groton as a result of using pneumatic hand tools manufactured by the defendants. Specifically, the plaintiffs allege that the tools were defectively designed because they exposed the plaintiffs to excessive vibration, and because the defendants failed to provide adequate warnings with respect to the potential danger presented by excessive vibration.

Defendants appeal from jury verdicts in favor of plaintiffs, claiming, inter alia, that the trial court should have rendered judgment for the defendants notwithstanding the verdicts because (a) there was insufficient evidence that the tools were defective because plaintiffs had presented no evidence of a feasible alternative design, and (b) there was insufficient evidence that defendants' tools reached plaintiffs without a substantial change in condition. Defendants also claimed the trial court's instructions impermissibly shifted the burden of proof to defendants on substantial alteration or modification. Plaintiffs cross-appeal on a number of evidentiary rulings.] We agree with the defendants that the trial court's instruction with respect to the alteration or modification defense improperly shifted to the defendants the burden of disproving an essential element of the plaintiffs' case. We therefore reverse the judgment of the trial court and order a new trial.

The trial record reveals the following facts, which are undisputed for purposes of this appeal. The plaintiffs were employed at Electric Boat as "grinders," positions which required use of pneumatic hand tools to smooth welds and metal surfaces.[2] In the course of their employment, the plaintiffs used various pneumatic hand tools, including chipping and grinding tools, which were manufactured and sold by the defendants. The plaintiffs' use of the defendants' tools at Electric Boat spanned approximately twenty-five years, from the mid–1960s until 1987. The plaintiffs suffer from permanent vascular and neurological impairment of their hands, which has caused blanching of their fingers, pain, numbness, tingling, reduction of grip strength, intolerance of cold and clumsiness from restricted blood flow. As a result, the plaintiffs have been unable to continue their employment as grinders and their performance of other activities has been restricted. The plaintiffs' symptoms are consistent with a diagnosis of hand arm vibration syndrome. Expert testimony confirmed that exposure to vibration is a significant contributing factor to the development of hand arm vibration syndrome, and that a clear relationship exists between the level of vibration exposure and the risk of developing the syndrome.

In addition to these undisputed facts, the following evidence, taken in favor of the jury's verdict, was presented. Ronald Guarneri, an industrial hygienist at Electric Boat, testified that he had conducted extensive testing of tools used at the shipyard in order to identify occupational hazards. This testing revealed that a large number of the defendants' tools violated the limits for vibration exposure established by the American National Standards Institute (Institute), and exceeded the threshold limit promulgated by the American Conference of Governmental and Industrial Hygienists (Conference). Richard Alexander, a mechanical engineering professor at Texas A & M University, testified that because machinery vibration has harmful effects on machines and on people, engineers routinely research ways to reduce or to eliminate the amount of vibration that a machine produces when operated. Alexander discussed various methods available to control vibration, including isolation (the use of springs or mass to isolate vibration), dampening (adding weights to dampen vibrational effects), and balancing (adding weights to counterbalance machine imbalances that cause vibration). Alexander testified that each of these methods has been available to manufacturers for at least thirty-five years.

---

2. One expert witness explained the design and purpose of these pneumatic tools: "[T]he machines are connected to an air hose that has air pressure, and you squeeze some kind of a valve and the air pressure is re- leased into what's called an air motor, which is a turbine of sorts. The air propels the motor and rotates the grinding device and you apply the grinding wheel or attachment to the metal that you want to grind."

Alexander also stated that, in 1983, he had been engaged by another pneumatic tool manufacturer to perform testing of methods by which to reduce the level of vibration in its three horsepower vertical grinder * * * Alexander modified the design [and] as [a] result of these modifications, which were published in 1987, Alexander achieved a threefold reduction in vibration levels. [Plaintiffs also presented the testimony of Charles Suggs, a research engineer at North Carolina State University, who has been investigating machinery vibration reduction since the 1960s. Suggs had published several papers discussing his success in reducing vibration hazards in a variety of tools. Additionally, in 1988, Suggs tested the defendants' grinders and, by applying the same technique, reduced the levels of vibration by between 35 and 60 percent.]

After a six week trial, the trial court rendered judgment on jury verdicts in favor of the plaintiffs. Finding that the defendants' tools had been defectively designed so as to render them unreasonably dangerous, the jury awarded the plaintiffs compensatory damages. The jury also concluded that the manufacturers had provided inadequate warnings, [but] the plaintiffs failed to prove that adequate warnings would have prevented their injuries * * * This appeal and cross appeal followed. Additional facts will be provided as warranted.

I

We first address the defendants' argument that the trial court improperly failed to render judgment for the defendants notwithstanding the verdicts because there was insufficient evidence for the jury to have found that the tools had been defectively designed. Specifically, the defendants claim that, in order to establish a prima facie design defect case, the plaintiffs were required to prove that there was a feasible alternative design available at the time that the defendants put their tools into the stream of commerce. We disagree.

In order properly to evaluate the parties' arguments, we begin our analysis with a review of the development of strict tort liability, focusing specifically on design defect liability. [The court thoroughly reviews the evolution of strict products liability from *MacPherson* to *Escola* to the widespread adoption of section 402A. Section 402A reflects the evolution of products liability law] to hold manufacturers strictly liable for unreasonably dangerous products that cause injury to ultimate users. Nevertheless, strict tort liability does not transform manufacturers into insurers, nor does it impose absolute liability. [Citation.] As the Wisconsin Supreme Court has pointed out, "[f]rom the plaintiff's point of view the most beneficial aspect of the rule is that it relieves him of proving specific acts of negligence and protects him from the defenses of notice of breach, disclaimer, and lack of privity in the implied warranty concepts of sales and contracts." Dippel v. Sciano, 155 N.W.2d 55 (Wis. 1967). Strict tort liability merely relieves the plaintiff from proving that the manufacturer was negligent and allows the plaintiff to establish instead the defective condition of the product as the principal basis of liability. [Citations.]

Although courts have widely accepted the concept of strict tort liability, some of the specifics of strict tort liability remain in question. In particular, courts have sharply disagreed over the appropriate definition of defectiveness in design cases. As the Alaska Supreme Court has stated: "Design defects present the most perplexing problems in the field of strict products liability because there is no readily ascertainable external measure of defectiveness. While manufacturing flaws can be evaluated against the intended design of the product, no such objective standard exists in the design defect context." Caterpillar Tractor Co. v. Beck, 593 P.2d 871, 880 (Alaska 1979).

Section 402A imposes liability only for those defective products that are "unreasonably dangerous" to "the ordinary consumer who purchases it, with the ordinary knowledge common to the community as to its characteristics." Under this formulation, known as the "consumer expectation" test, a manufacturer is strictly liable for any condition not contemplated by the ultimate consumer that will be unreasonably dangerous to the consumer. [Citations.] Some courts, however, have refused to adopt the "unreasonably dangerous" definition, determining that it injects a concept of foreseeability into strict tort liability, which is inappropriate in such cases because the manufacturer's liability is not based upon negligence. See Beck, 593 P.2d at 882–83 (articulating that "unreasonably dangerous" narrows scope of recovery and unduly increases plaintiff's burden); [citation].

In Barker v. Lull Engineering Co., 573 P.2d 443 (Cal. 1978), the California Supreme Court established two alternative tests for determining design defect liability: (1) the consumer expectation analysis; and (2) a balancing test that inquires whether a product's risks outweigh its benefits. Under the latter, otherwise known as the "risk-utility," test, the manufacturer bears the burden of proving that the product's utility is not outweighed by its risks in light of various factors. Three other jurisdictions have subsequently adopted California's two-pronged test, including the burden-shifting risk-utility inquiry. See Beck, 593 P.2d at 884; Ontai v. Straub Clinic & Hospital, Inc., 659 P.2d 734 (Haw. 1983); Lamkin v. Towner, 563 N.E.2d 449 (Ill. 1990).

Other jurisdictions apply only a risk-utility test in determining whether a manufacturer is liable for a design defect. See, e.g., Armentrout v. FMC Corp., 842 P.2d 175, 183 (Colo.1992); Radiation Technology, Inc. v. Ware Construction Co., 445 So.2d 329, 331 (Fla.1983); Thibault v. Sears, Roebuck & Co., 395 A.2d 843 (N.H. 1978). To assist the jury in evaluating the product's risks and utility, these courts have set forth a list of nonexclusive factors to consider when deciding whether a product has been defectively designed.[10]

With this history in mind, we turn to the development of strict products liability law in Connecticut. In Garthwait v. Burgio, 216 A.2d 189 (Conn. 1965), this court recognized a products liability cause of action sounding in tort and became one of the first jurisdictions to adopt the rule provided in § 402A * * * This court has long held that in order to prevail in a design defect claim, "[t]he plaintiff must prove that the product is unreasonably dangerous." We have derived our definition of "unreasonably dangerous" from comment (i) to § 402A, which provides that "the article sold must be dangerous to an extent beyond that which would be contemplated by the ordinary consumer who purchases it, with the ordinary knowledge common to the community as to its characteristics." This "consumer expectation" standard is now well established in Connecticut strict products liability decisions. [Citations.] The defendants propose that it is time for this court to abandon the consumer expectation standard and adopt the requirement that the plaintiff must prove the existence of a reasonable alternative design in order to prevail on a design defect claim. We decline to accept the defendants' invitation.

In support of their position, the defendants point to the second tentative draft of the Restatement (Third) of Torts: Products Liability (1995), which provides that, as part of a plaintiff's prima facie case, the plaintiff must establish the availability of a reasonable alternative design. Specifically, § 2(b) of the Draft Restatement (Third) provides: "[A] product is defective in design when the foreseeable risks of harm posed by the product could have been reduced or avoided by the adoption of a reasonable alternative design by the seller or other distributor, or a predecessor in the commercial chain of distribution, and the omission of the alternative design renders the product not reasonably safe." The reporters to the Draft Restatement (Third) state that "[v]ery substantial authority supports the proposition that [the] plaintiff must establish a reasonable alternative design in order for a product to be adjudged defective in design." Section 2, reporters' note to comment (c).

We point out that this provision of the Draft Restatement (Third) has been a source of substantial controversy among commentators. See, e.g., Vargo, "The Emperor's New Clothes: The American Law Institute Adorns a 'New Cloth' for Section 402A Products Liability Design Defects—A Survey of the States Reveals a Different Weave," 26 U.Mem.L.Rev. 493, 501 (1996) (challenging reporters' claim that Draft Restatement (Third)'s reasonable alternative design requirement constitutes "consensus" among jurisdictions); [citations]. Contrary to the rule promulgated in the Draft Restatement (Third), our independent review of the prevailing common law

10. These factors are typically derived from an influential article by Dean John Wade. . . .

reveals that the majority of jurisdictions do not impose upon plaintiffs an absolute requirement to prove a feasible alternative design.[11]

In our view, the feasible alternative design requirement imposes an undue burden on plaintiffs that might preclude otherwise valid claims from jury consideration. Such a rule would require plaintiffs to retain an expert witness even in cases in which lay jurors can infer a design defect from circumstantial evidence. Connecticut courts, however, have consistently stated that a jury may, under appropriate circumstances, infer a defect from the evidence without the necessity of expert testimony. [Citations.]

Moreover, in some instances, a product may be in a defective condition unreasonably dangerous to the user even though no feasible alternative design is available. In such instances, the manufacturer may be strictly liable for a design defect notwithstanding the fact that there are no safer alternative designs in existence. See, e.g., O'Brien v. Muskin Corp., 463 A.2d 298 (N.J. 1983) ("other products, including some for which no alternative exists, are so dangerous and of such little use that ... a manufacturer would bear the cost of liability of harm to others"); [citations.] Accordingly, we decline to adopt the requirement that a plaintiff must prove a feasible alternative design as a sine qua non to establishing a prima facie case of design defect.

Although today we continue to adhere to our long-standing rule that a product's defectiveness is to be determined by the expectations of an ordinary consumer, we nevertheless recognize that there may be instances involving complex product designs in which an ordinary consumer may not be able to form expectations of safety. [Citation]; W. Prosser & W. Keeton on Torts, § 99, pp. 698–99 (discussing ambiguity of consumer expectation test and shortcomings in its application). In such cases, a consumer's expectations may be viewed in light of various factors that balance the utility of the product's design with the magnitude of its risks. We find persuasive the reasoning of those jurisdictions that have modified their formulation of the consumer expectation test by incorporating risk-utility factors into the ordinary consumer expectation analysis. [Citations]. Thus, the modified consumer expectation test provides the jury with the product's risks and utility and then inquires whether a reasonable consumer would consider the product unreasonably dangerous. As the Supreme Court of

---

11. Our research reveals that, of the jurisdictions that have considered the role of feasible alternative designs in design defect cases: (1) six jurisdictions affirmatively state that a plaintiff need not show a feasible alternative design in order to establish a manufacturer's liability for design defect [citations omitted]; (2) sixteen jurisdictions hold that a feasible alternative design is merely one of several factors that the jury may consider in determining whether a product design is defective [citations omitted]; (3) three jurisdictions require the defendant, not the plaintiff, to prove that the product was not defective [citations omitted]; and (4) eight jurisdictions require that the plaintiff prove a feasible alternative design in order to establish a prima facie case of design defect [citations omitted].

Washington stated in Seattle–First National Bank v. Tabert, 542 P.2d 774 (Wash. 1975), "[i]n determining the reasonable expectations of the ordinary consumer, a number of factors must be considered. The relative cost of the product, the gravity of the potential harm from the claimed defect and the cost and feasibility of eliminating or minimizing the risk may be relevant in a particular case. In other instances the nature of the product or the nature of the claimed defect may make other factors relevant to the issue." Accordingly, under this modified formulation, the consumer expectation test would establish the product's risks and utility, and the inquiry would then be whether a reasonable consumer would consider the product design unreasonably dangerous.

In our view, the relevant factors that a jury may consider include, but are not limited to, the usefulness of the product, the likelihood and severity of the danger posed by the design, the feasibility of an alternative design, the financial cost of an improved design, the ability to reduce the product's danger without impairing its usefulness or making it too expensive, and the feasibility of spreading the loss by increasing the product's price. [Citations.] The availability of a feasible alternative design is a factor that the plaintiff may, rather than must, prove in order to establish that a product's risks outweigh its utility. [Citations.]

Furthermore, we emphasize that our adoption of a risk-utility balancing component to our consumer expectation test does not signal a retreat from strict tort liability. In weighing a product's risks against its utility, the focus of the jury should be on the product itself, and not on the conduct of the manufacturer. [Citations. And while] today we adopt a modified formulation of the consumer expectation test, we emphasize that we do not require a plaintiff to present evidence relating to the product's risks and utility in every case. As the California Court of Appeals has stated: "There are certain kinds of accidents—even where fairly complex machinery is involved—[that] are so bizarre that the average juror, upon hearing the particulars, might reasonably think: 'Whatever the user may have expected from that contraption, it certainly wasn't that.' "Akers v. Kelley Co., 173 Cal.App.3d 633, 651, 219 Cal.Rptr. 513 (1985). Accordingly, the ordinary consumer expectation test is appropriate when the everyday experience of the particular product's users permits the inference that the product did not meet minimum safety expectations. See Soule v. General Motors Corp., 882 P.2d 298 (Cal. 1994).

Conversely, the jury should engage in the risk-utility balancing required by our modified consumer expectation test when the particular facts do not reasonably permit the inference that the product did not meet the safety expectations of the ordinary consumer. [Citation.] Furthermore, instructions based on the ordinary consumer expectation test would not be appropriate when, as a matter of law, there is insufficient evidence to support a jury verdict under that test. In such circumstances, the jury should be instructed solely on the modified consumer expectation test we have articulated today.

In this respect, it is the function of the trial court to determine whether an instruction based on the ordinary consumer expectation test or the modified consumer expectation test, or both, is appropriate in light of the evidence presented. In making this determination, the trial court must ascertain whether, under each test, there is sufficient evidence as a matter of law to warrant the respective instruction. [Citation.]

With these principles in mind, we now consider whether, in the present case, the trial court properly instructed the jury with respect to the definition of design defect for the purposes of strict tort liability. The trial court instructed the jury that a manufacturer may be strictly liable if the plaintiffs prove, among other elements, that the product in question was in a defective condition, unreasonably dangerous to the ultimate user. The court further instructed the jury that, in determining whether the tools were unreasonably dangerous, it may draw its conclusions based on the reasonable expectations of an ordinary user of the defendants' tools. Because there was sufficient evidence as a matter of law to support the determination that the tools were unreasonably dangerous based on the ordinary consumer expectation test, we conclude that this instruction was appropriately given to the jury.

[On appellate review, we give the evidence the most favorable reasonable construction in support of the verdict to which it is entitled. In analyzing a sufficiency of the evidence claim, the test that we employ is whether, on the basis of the evidence before the jury, a reasonable and properly motivated jury could return the verdict that it did. Whether a product is unreasonably dangerous is a question of fact to be determined by the jury, who can form their own reasonable conclusions as to the expectations of the ordinary consumer and the knowledge common in the community at large. Furthermore, the plaintiff in a strict tort action need not establish a specific defect as long as there is evidence of some unspecified dangerous condition.] The jury heard testimony that Guarneri, Electric Boat's industrial hygienist, had performed extensive testing of tools used at the shipyard, which tests revealed that a large number of the defendants' tools violated the Institute's limits for vibration exposure and exceeded the Conference's threshold limit. The jury also heard substantial testimony with respect to various methods, including isolation, dampening and balancing, available to reduce the deleterious effects of vibration caused by the defendants' tools. Moreover, there was expert testimony that exposure to vibration is a significant contributing factor to the development of hand arm vibration syndrome and that a clear relationship exists between the level of vibration exposure and the risk of developing the syndrome. Viewing the evidence in a light favorable to supporting the jury's verdicts, as we must, we conclude that the jury properly determined that the defendants' tools had been defectively designed.

[The court held that, in any event, a new trial was required because the trial court improperly instructed the jury that the defendant had the burden of proof of causation based on the substantial modification statute,

Conn. Gen. Stat. § 52–572p. Further, as to the trial court's instruction that the "state-of-the-art defense" was restricted to the plaintiffs' failure to warn claim, the court held that state-of-the-art evidence applies to strict liability design defect claims as well as to failure to warn claims, adopting the majority view. The court pointed out that "state of the art" refers to what is technologically feasible, not industry custom. A manufacturer may have an obligation to make products pursuant to a safer design even if the custom of the industry is not to use that alternative. Further, proof of compliance with state of the art does not constitute an affirmative defense to a design claim. Although state-of-the-art evidence may be dispositive on the facts of a particular case, such evidence does not constitute an affirmative defense that, if proven, would absolve the defendant from liability. The court thus characterized it as "rebuttal evidence" rather than as a defense. The court's concluding discussion of other evidentiary issues is omitted.]

4.   DEFECT-SPECIFIC TESTS

NOTE that in note 3, page 246, the reference to the Products Liability Restatement should be cross-referenced to the final version contained in this Supplement. All further references in the Casebook should be so cross-referenced.

CHAPTER 7

Types of Defect

1. Defective Manufacture

ADD at the end of note 3, page 269, the following:

The New Jersey Supreme Court adopted the Products Liability Restatement version of the malfunction theory in Myrlak v. Port Authority of New York and New Jersey, 723 A.2d 45 (N.J. 1999). *Myrlak* involved a plaintiff who had fallen backwards at work while in a chair that had been in use for five weeks. The chair was used by several employees, none of whom had misused the chair according to the evidence. The plaintiff had been seated in the chair performing his duties for about one hour and forty-five minutes when he heard a loud noise and the back of the chair cracked and gave way. As a result of the fall, plaintiff who was six feet six inches tall and weighed approximately 325 pounds, injured his lower back. No one other than the plaintiff saw the accident. Co-workers after the accident reported that the back of the chair had collapsed and appeared to be flopping back and forth. The trial court declined to give a res ipsa loquitur instruction for the plaintiff against the manufacturer of the chair but did instruct on circumstantial evidence of proof of defectiveness. The jury found that the plaintiff failed to establish a manufacturing defect.

The Appellate Division reversed and concluded that the res ipsa loquitur instruction should have been given. The Supreme Court reversed the Appellate Division, finding that res ipsa loquitur is not the appropriate doctrine to employ in strict products liability cases where proof of defectiveness is circumstantial but an inference of defectiveness is nonetheless permissible. The Court discussed the res ipsa loquitur doctrine and its opinions in *Moraca* and *Scanlon* and concluded that those cases were consistent with § 3 of the Products Liability Restatement. The Court formally adopted the so-called "indeterminate product defect test" announced in § 3, stating that "[t]he *Scanlon* rule regarding circumstantial proof of a defect in a strict products liability case was adopted recently in [§ 3 of the Products Liability Restatement]." Is the rule in *Scanlon* consistent with the rule in § 3? The *Myrlak* Court concluded that a new trial was warranted in which "plaintiff need not prove a specific defect in the chair if he can establish that the incident that harmed him is of the kind that ordinarily occurs as a result of a product defect, and that the incident was not solely the result of causes other than product defect existing at the time the chair left [the manufacturer's] control." Are the requirements of § 3 consistent with this description of the plaintiff's burden? How much negation of other likely causes of the accident is required after *Myrlak*? Under § 3?

2. DEFECTIVE DESIGN

ADD the following to note **11. Post–Accident Remedial Measures,** page 308:

Federal Rule of Evidence 407 has now been amended to read:

Fed. R. Evid. 407, Subsequent Remedial Measures:

When, after an injury or harm allegedly caused by an event, measures are taken that, if taken previously, would have made the injury or harm less likely to occur, evidence of the subsequent measures is not admissible to prove negligence, culpable conduct, a defect in a product, a defect in a product's design, or a need for a warning or instruction. This rule does not require the exclusion of evidence of subsequent measures when offered for another purpose, such as proving ownership, control, or feasibility of precautionary measures, if controverted, or impeachment.

The Advisory Committee Note to the 1997 Amendments explains the changes:

The amendment to Rule 407 makes two changes in the rule. First, the words "an injury or harm allegedly caused by" were added to clarify that the rule applies only to changes made after the occurrence that produced the damages giving rise to the action. Evidence of measures taken by the defendant prior to the "event" causing "injury or harm" do not fall within the exclusionary scope of Rule 407 even if they occurred after the manufacture or design of the product. [Citation.]

Second, Rule 407 has been amended to provide that evidence of subsequent remedial measures may not be used to prove "a defect in a product or its design, or that a warning or instruction should have accompanied a product." This amendment adopts the view of a majority of the circuits that have interpreted Rule 407 to apply to products liability actions. [Citations.]

Although this amendment adopts a uniform federal rule, it should be noted that evidence of subsequent remedial measures may be admissible pursuant to the second sentence of Rule 407. Evidence of subsequent measures that is not barred by Rule 407 may still be subject to exclusion on Rule 403 grounds when the dangers of prejudice or confusion substantially outweigh the probative value of the evidence.

ADD to the end of note **1. Trial Courts as "Gatekeepers,"** page 326, the
following:

The Court of Appeal in *Pestel* applied the *Daubert* standards to technical, skill-
based testimony based on the expert's proposed design change which had not been
tested or reviewed by others in the field. Other Courts of Appeal have disagreed
with this application of *Daubert*. In McKendall v. Crown Control Corp., 122 F.3d
803 (9th Cir. 1997), the Ninth Circuit Court of Appeals held that an expert's
mechanical engineering testimony was admissible on the expert's experience alone,
without a finding of scientific reliability because, even though the testimony was
based solely on the expert's experience, it provided technical or other specialized
knowledge that could assist the trier of fact. The Ninth Circuit specifically held that
Daubert did not apply to the evidence in question because *Daubert* only applies to
expert testimony based on scientific knowledge. *Daubert* can be found in ch. 18.

The Supreme Court resolved the split among the circuits on the applicability of
Daubert to non-scientific expert testimony in Kumho Tire Co. v. Carmichael, 119
S.Ct. 1167 (1999). The case involved a plaintiff's expert on tire failure analysis who
was prepared to testify about the defective design of the tire in question. The trial
court excluded the testimony, applying *Daubert* "flexibly" to this kind of skill-based
expert testimony. The Court of Appeals reversed, holding that *Daubert* did not apply
because it only applied to scientific expert testimony which was not in issue. The
Supreme Court reversed the Court of Appeals, and reinstated the trial court's
decision. It held that the *Daubert* "gatekeeping" obligation applies not only to
"*scientific*" testimony, but to *all* expert testimony:

> [Rule 702's] language makes no relevant distinction between 'scientific'
> knowledge and 'technical' or 'other specialized' knowledge. It makes clear
> that any such knowledge might become the subject of expert testimony. . . .
> Hence, as a matter of language, the Rule applies its reliability standard to
> all ... matters within its scope. As to the applicability of the specific
> factors identified in *Daubert* as relevant to the admissibility decision and
> the trial court's gatekeeping function, the Court observed:

> [W]e can neither rule out, nor rule in, for all cases and for all time the
> applicability of the factors mentioned in *Daubert* nor can we now do so for
> subsets of cases categorized by category of expert or by kind of evidence.
> Too much depends upon the particular circumstances of the particular case
> at issue * * * We do not believe that Rule 702 creates a schematism that
> segregates expertise by type while mapping certain kinds of questions to
> certain kinds of experts. Life and the legal cases that it generates are too
> complex to warrant so definitive a match.

The Court reiterated the importance of its 1997 decision in General Electric Co.
v Joiner, 118 S.Ct. 512 (1997), that the trial judge's admissibility decisions are to be
reversed only for an "abuse of discretion". The Courts of Appeal had split on the
standard of appellate review of exclusion of evidence, some applying a particularly
stringent standard of review. The Court in *Kumho Tire*, relying on *Joiner*, noted

that "[t]he trial court must have the same kind of latitude in deciding how to test an expert's reliability, and to decide whether or when special briefing or other proceedings are needed to investigate reliability, as it enjoys when it decides whether that expert's relevant testimony is reliable. Our opinion in *Joiner* makes clear that a court of appeals is to apply an abuse of discretion standard when it 'reviews a trial court's decision to admit or exclude expert testimony.' That standard applies as much to the trial court's decisions about how to determine reliability as to its ultimate conclusion."

For a state court opinion foreshadowing the result in *Kumho Tire*, see Gammill v. Jack Williams Chevrolet, Inc., 972 S.W.2d 713 (Tex. 1998)(state version of Rule 702 applies to all expert testimony; *Daubert* factors relevant to all admissibility inquiries).

ADD to note **3. Human Factors Experts**, on page 327, the following:

Consider plaintiff's attempt to use a human factors expert in Reiff v. Convergent Technologies, 957 F.Supp. 573 (D.N.J.1997), who was prepared to testify on the feasibility of altering the design of computer keyboards to prevent repetitive stress injuries such as carpal tunnel syndrome. Mrs. Reiff typed on a computer keyboard an average of twenty-five to thirty hours each week from 1988 to the early 1990's when she began to experience numbness and pain in her wrists and hands. She was diagnosed with bilateral carpal tunnel syndrome which required two surgeries to correct. When she returned to work, she began using a new computer keyboard (made by defendant's competitor, Microsoft) that is split into two halves with each half horizontally rotated to form an obtuse angle, arguably an ergonomically superior design. Plaintiff sued the manufacturer of her previous keyboard for design defects in (1) the excessive keying force, and (2) the conventional keyboard configuration.

Plaintiffs sought to use the testimony of an engineer and human factors expert, or ergonomist, an expert in the interaction between humans and machines, for each of the design defect claims. The expert offered testimony that the force needed to strike the keys on their edges exceeded the amount of force allowed by the ANSI standard and, thus, the design was defective. He had done studies on the force needed to strike the keys on the plaintiff's keyboard and found that the "e" key required slightly more force on its rim than allowed by the ANSI standard. Based on this research, he concluded that the keyboard was defective. The trial court concluded that "nothing in the record can explain why an almost imperceptible deviation in the force necessary to activate a single key at its rim somehow turns a safe product into a threat to its user's health and safety." Because the testimony was not relevant to proving that the design was unfit or unsafe, the trial court excluded it under the relevance prong of *Daubert*.

Plaintiff's second theory of design defect challenged the straight-edge conventional keyboard design. Plaintiff's expert argued that a split-angled design reduced musculoskeletal discomfort by easing four unnatural postures: forearm pronation, ulnar deviation, wrist extension, and upper arm abduction, thus reducing the chance for injury. The plaintiff's expert identified one article, contrary to his own published research, that concluded on the basis of anecdotal evidence that some split-angle keyboards are more comfortable than conventional keyboards to typists with prior hand and wrist pain. This led the expert to conclude that a conventional keyboard was defective in design because it increased the risk of discomfort, and thus injury, over split-angle keyboards. The trial court excluded this testimony of design defect stating: "In drawing his conclusions, [the expert] performed no scientific study; rather, he merely referenced a single journal article—at odds with his own research—which in truth stands for a proposition much more modest than that for which he cites it." The court granted defendant's motion for summary judgment on all claims (including the failure to warn claim which is discussed below) and, stated:

> Science coexists uneasily with litigation's adversary system, as the imperatives of partisan advocacy coupled with powerful economic incentives often seem to overwhelm good science. Lawyers, judges, and forensic experts sometimes engage in what literature teachers call willing suspension of disbelief. Scientific propositions that would cause even laymen to gasp in disbelief are routinely argued in courts of law. Such are the dangers of a legal system allowing partisan expert testimony.

> Imposing carpal tunnel syndrome liability based on alleged defects in keyboard design would result in a nationwide explosion of litigation at societal costs which are almost unimaginable. In a recent case sent to the jury by Judge Weinstein of the Eastern District of New York, a jury awarded damages in excess of five million dollars. [Geressy v. Digital Equip. Corp., 950 F.Supp. 519 (E.D.N.Y.1997).] Presumably *Daubert* permit[s] a trial court to be sure that this avalanche of litigation is based on something at least resembling good science. The evidence proffered in this case does not cross that threshold.

The jury verdict in *Geressy* referred to above was set aside on a number of grounds as to four of the five plaintiffs. See 980 F.Supp. 640 (E.D.N.Y. 1997), *aff'd*, 152 F.3d 919 (2d Cir.1998) (table).

---

3. DEFECTIVE MARKETING: WARNINGS & INSTRUCTIONS

ADD to notes after **Higgins v. E.I. DuPont de Nemours & Co.**, on page 358:

If the sophisticated purchaser/bulk supplier doctrine is available, such that a manufacturer's duty to warn is satisfied by warning the sophisticated purchaser, what type of warning does that obligation require? In Baker v. Monsanto Co., 962

F.Supp. 1143 (S.D.Ind.1997), plaintiffs were employees of Westinghouse whose responsibilities included repairing transformers. They claimed that during their repair work they were exposed to PCBs manufactured by Monsanto and sold to Westinghouse for use as a lubricant in the transformers. Monsanto argued that it had no duty to warn plaintiffs directly of the hazards of PCB exposure because it sold the product to a sophisticated purchaser, Westinghouse, which was fully aware of the hazards. The court, after a thorough analysis of Indiana cases, concluded that Indiana courts would adopt the "knowledgeable, sophisticated bulk purchaser" doctrine. The court also stated that the analysis is the same in both negligence and strict liability actions—a balancing of the factors identified in comment n to Restatement (Second of Torts), § 388, discussed in *Higgins*.

Plaintiffs argued that even if the sophisticated purchaser doctrine was applicable, Monsanto failed adequately to warn Westinghouse of the hazards of PCBs because Monsanto was Westinghouse's primary source of knowledge of the hazards and Monsanto did not thoroughly advise of the seriousness of the hazards. Plaintiffs contended that Monsanto's warnings to Westinghouse were "warnings with a wink" because Monsanto issued warnings saying such things as "avoid prolonged breathing of vapors," "avoid contact with eyes or prolonged contact with skin," but it undercut those warnings with unsubstantiated statements, over a thirty to forty year period, that no Monsanto worker exposed to PCBs had ever been seriously injured. In fact, Monsanto never reviewed medical files of its workers exposed to PCBs and never conducted any specific testing or evaluation of its workers for PCB-related illness. Plaintiffs maintained that this representation was a bald lie, designed to mislead Westinghouse and facilitate the continued sales of Monsanto products. The court concluded that Monsanto had adequately warned Westinghouse as a matter of law because of the extensive, independent knowledge Westinghouse, as a self-described expert on PCBs, had of the dangers of PCB exposure.

ADD to note **9. Learned Intermediary Rule—Exceptions**, page 369, the following.

Other products for which the FDA has required direct consumer warnings also fall within the exception to the learned intermediary rule. See, e.g., Edwards v. Basel Pharmaceuticals, 933 P.2d 298 (Okla. 1997) (nicotine patch must carry direct consumer warnings by statute and are thus excepted from learned intermediary rule, but compliance with the FDA's required warning does not conclusively fulfill duty to warn).

CHAPTER 8

REGULATING DEFECTIVENESS

2. THE EFFECT OF REGULATION ON PRIVATE LITIGATION

ADD to note **3. Avoiding Preemption—The Cigarette Litigation**, on page 408, the following.

Additional claims against the tobacco companies which have withstood post-*Cipollone* preemption scrutiny include Wolpin v. Philip Morris, Inc., 974 F.Supp. 1465 (S.D. Fla. 1997) (plaintiff's second-hand smoke injury claims based on duty to warn non-smokers not preempted); Philip Morris Inc. v. Harshbarger, 122 F.3d 58 (1st Cir. 1997) (Massachusetts statute requiring disclosure by tobacco companies of additives and nicotine-yield ratings, with express purpose of disclosing information to public, not preempted by federal cigarette labeling laws under *Cipollone*).

For a discussion of the survival of typical personal injury product claims after *Cipollone,* see American Tobacco Co. v. Grinnell, 951 S.W.2d 420 (Tex. 1997), in which the Texas Supreme Court concluded that design defect claims, while specifically not preempted under *Cipollone,* could not succeed as a matter of Texas law because there was no safer alternative to cigarettes, and that manufacturing defect claims based on the presence of pesticide residue in cigarettes raised fact questions precluding summary judgment.

REPLACE **Kennedy v. Collagen Corp.**, and notes 1 to 6 on pages 413–421 with **Medtronic Inc. v. Lohr,** 518 U.S. 470 (1996).

Medtronic, Inc. v. Lohr

Supreme Court of the United States, 1996.
518 U.S. 470, 116 S.Ct. 2240, 135 L.Ed.2d 700.

■ JUSTICE STEVENS announced the judgment of the Court and delivered the opinion of the Court with respect to Parts l, II, III, V, and Vll, and an opinion with respect to Parts IV and Vl, in which JUSTICE KENNEDY, JUSTICE SOUTER, and JUSTICE GINSBURG join.

Congress enacted the Medical Device Amendments of 1976, in the words of the statute's preamble, "to provide for the safety and effectiveness of medical devices intended for human use." 90 Stat. 539. The question presented is whether that statute pre-empts a state common-law negligence action against the manufacturer of an allegedly defective medical device. Specifically, we must consider whether Lora Lohr, who was injured when her pacemaker failed, may rely on Florida common law to recover damages from Medtronic, Inc., the manufacturer of the device.

I

Throughout our history the several States have exercised their police powers to protect the health and safety of their citizens. Because these are "primarily, and historically, ... matter[s] of local concern," Hillsborough County v. Automated Medical Laboratories, Inc., 471 U.S. 707, 719 (1985), the "States traditionally have had great latitude under their police powers to legislate as to the protection of the lives, limbs, health, comfort, and quiet of all persons." Metropolitan Life Ins. Co. v. Massachusetts, 471 U.S. 724, 756 (1985).

Despite the prominence of the States in matters of public health and safety, in recent decades the Federal Government has played an increasingly significant role in the protection of the health of our people. Congress' first significant enactment in the field of public health was the Food and Drug Act of 1906, a broad prohibition against the manufacture or shipment in interstate commerce of any adulterated or misbranded food or drug. [Citations.]. Partly in response to an ongoing concern about radio and newspaper advertising making false therapeutic claims for both "quack machines" and legitimate devices such as surgical instruments and orthopedic shoes, in 1938 Congress broadened the coverage of the 1906 Act to include misbranded or adulterated medical devices and cosmetics. See Federal Food, Drug, and Cosmetic Act of 1938 (FDCA), §§ 501, 502, 52 Stat. 1049–1051; [citations].

While the FDCA provided for pre-market approval of new drugs, it did not authorize any control over the introduction of new medical devices, [citations.]. As technologies advanced and medicine relied to an increasing degree on a vast array of medical equipment "[f]rom bedpans to brain-scans," including kidney dialysis units, artificial heart valves, and heart pacemakers, policymakers and the public became concerned about the increasingly severe injuries that resulted from the failure of such devices. [Citations.]

* * *

In response to the mounting consumer and regulatory concern, Congress enacted the statute at issue here: the Medical Device Amendments of 1976 (MDA or Act), 90 Stat. 539. The Act classifies medical devices in three categories based on the risk that they pose to the public. Class I devices present no unreasonable risk of illness and are subject to minimal regulation. Class II devices are potentially more harmful, need no advance approval, but manufacturers must comply with federal performance regulations. Class III devices present a potential unreasonable risk of illness or injury, or are for use in sustaining or preventing impairment of human life and health. New Class III devices may be marketed only after "reasonable assurance" of safety and effectiveness has been provided to the FDA. Establishing this "reasonable assurance" is a rigorous process known as the "premarket approval," or "PMA" process, requiring submission of detailed information regarding the safety and efficacy of their devices. Most

Class III devices on the market today have not received premarket approval because of two important exceptions to the PMA requirement. First, the statute includes a "grandfathering" provision which allows pre–1976 devices to remain on the market without FDA approval until the FDA initiates and completes the PMA, which it has not done for most grandfathered devices. Second, to prevent manufacturers of grandfathered devices from monopolizing the market and to ensure that improvements to existing devices can be rapidly introduced, devices that are "substantially equivalent" to pre-existing devices can avoid the PMA process.

["Substantially equivalent" Class III devices, as well as all new Class I and Class II devices, are subject to the requirements of § 360(k). That section imposes a limited form of review known as "premarket notification" or a "§ 510(k) process," after the number of the section in the original Act. If the FDA concludes on the basis of the § 510(k) notification that the device is "substantially equivalent" to a pre-existing device, it can be marketed without further regulatory analysis (at least until the FDA initiates the PMA process for the underlying pre–1976 device to which the new device is "substantially equivalent"). In contrast to the 1,200 hours necessary to complete a PMA review, the § 510(k) review is completed in an average of only 20 hours. As one commentator noted, "[t]he attraction of substantial equivalence to manufacturers is clear. [Section] 510(k) notification requires little information, rarely elicits a negative response from the FDA, and gets processed very quickly." Adler, The 1976 Medical Device Amendments: A Step in the Right Direction Needs Another Step in the Right Direction, 43 Food Drug Cosm. L.J. 511, 516 (1988).]

Congress anticipated that the FDA would complete the PMA process for Class III devices relatively swiftly. But because of the substantial investment of time and energy necessary for the resolution of each PMA application, the ever-increasing numbers of medical devices, and internal administrative and resource difficulties, the FDA simply could not keep up with the rigorous PMA process. As a result, the § 510(k) premarket notification process became the means by which most new medical devices—including Class III devices—were approved for the market. * * * Despite an increasing effort by the FDA to consider the safety and efficacy of substantially equivalent devices, the House reported in 1990 that 80% of new Class III devices were being introduced to the market through the § 510(k) process and without PMA review. H. R. Rep. No. 101–808, p. 14 (1990); [citations].

II

As have so many other medical device manufacturers, petitioner Medtronic took advantage of § 510(k)'s expedited process in October of 1982, when it notified FDA that it intended to market its Model 4011 pacemaker lead as a device that was "substantially equivalent" to devices already on the market. (The lead is the portion of a pacemaker that transmits the heartbeat-steadying electrical signal from the "pulse generator" to the heart itself.) On November 30,1982, the FDA found that the model was "substantially equivalent to devices introduced into interstate commerce" prior to the effective date of the Act, and advised Medtronic that it could therefore market its device subject only to the general control provisions of the Act. * * * The agency emphasized, however, that this determination should not be construed as an endorsement of the pacemaker lead's safety.

Cross-petitioner Lora Lohr is dependent on pacemaker technology for the proper functioning of her heart. In 1987 she was implanted with a Medtronic pacemaker equipped with one of the company's Model 4011 pacemaker leads. On December 30, 1990, the pacemaker failed, allegedly resulting in a "complete heart block" that required emergency surgery. According to her physician, a defect in the lead was the likely cause of the failure.

In 1993 Lohr and her husband filed this action in a Florida state court. [Their complaint alleged a breach of Medtronic's "duty to use reasonable care in the design, manufacture, assembly, and sale of the subject pacemaker", including the use of defective materials in the lead and a failure to warn or properly instruct the plaintiff or her physicians of the tendency of the pacemaker to fail, despite knowledge of other earlier failures. A strict liability count alleged that the device was in a defective condition and unreasonably dangerous to foreseeable users at the time of its sale. After removal to federal district court, Medtronic] filed a motion for summary judgment arguing that both the negligence and strict liability claims were preempted by 21 U.S.C. § 360k(a). That section, which is at the core of the dispute between the parties in this case, provides:

> § 360k. State and local requirements respecting devices. (a) General rule. Except as provided in subsection (b) of this section, no State or political subdivision of a State may establish or continue in effect with respect to a device intended for human use any requirement—(1) which is different from, or in addition to, any requirement applicable under this chapter to the device, and (2) which relates to the safety or effectiveness of the device or to any other matter included in a requirement applicable to the device under this chapter.[5]

[The District Court dismissed the complaint. The Court of Appeals reversed in part. It first decided that "common law actions are state requirements within the meaning of § 360k(a)." After concluding that the term "requirements" in § 360k(a) was unclear, it sought guidance from FDA's regulations regarding pre-emption. Those regulations provide that a state requirement is not preempted unless the FDA has established " 'specific requirements applicable to a particular device.' " The court concluded

---

5. Subsection (b) of the statute authorizes the FDA to grant exemptions to state requirements that would otherwise be preempted by subsection (a). * * * To carry out this grant of authority, the FDA has issued regulations under the statute which both construe the scope of § 360k(a) and address the instances in which the FDA will grant exemptions to its preemptive effect. See 21 CFR § 808.1 (1995).

that the Lohrs' negligence and strict liability design claims were not preempted, finding no device specific requirement regarding design, but then concluded that the negligence and strict liability failure to warn claims were preempted by FDA's general "good manufacturing practices" regulations and by the FDA labeling regulations.]

* * * Because the Courts of Appeals are divided over the extent to which state common-law claims are preempted by the MDA, we granted both [parties'] petitions.

III

As in Cipollone v. Liggett Group, Inc., 505 U.S. 504 (1992), we are presented with the task of interpreting a statutory provision that expressly preempts state law. While the preemptive language of § 360k(a) means that we need not go beyond that language to determine whether Congress intended the MDA to preempt at least some state law, we must nonetheless "identify the domain expressly preempted" by that language. Although our analysis of the scope of the pre-emption statute must begin with its text, [citation], our interpretation of that language does not occur in a contextual vacuum. Rather, that interpretation is informed by two presumptions about the nature of preemption.

First, because the States are independent sovereigns in our federal system, we have long presumed that Congress does not cavalierly preempt state-law causes of action. In all preemption cases, and particularly in those in which Congress has "legislated . . . in a field which the States have traditionally occupied," Rice v. Santa Fe Elevator Corp., 331 U.S. 218, 230 (1947), we "start with the assumption that the historic police powers of the States were not to be superseded by the Federal Act unless that was the clear and manifest purpose of Congress." Id., at 230; [citation]. Although dissenting Justices have argued that this assumption should apply only to the question whether Congress intended any preemption at all, as opposed to questions concerning the scope of its intended invalidation of state law, [citation], we used a "presumption against the preemption of state police power regulations" to support a narrow interpretation of such an express command in Cipollone. That approach is consistent with both federalism concerns and the historic primacy of state regulation of matters of health and safety.

Second, our analysis of the scope of the statute's preemption is guided by our oft-repeated comment, initially made in Retail Clerks v. Schermerhorn, 375 U.S. 96, 103 (1963), that "[t]he purpose of Congress is the ultimate touchstone" in every preemption case. See, e.g., Cipollone, 505 U.S., at 516; [citations]. As a result, any understanding of the scope of a preemption statute must rest primarily on "a fair understanding of congressional purpose." Cipollone, 505 U.S., at 530, n. 27, (opinion of STEVENS, J.). Congress' intent, of course, primarily is discerned from the language of the preemption statute and the "statutory framework" surrounding it. [Citation]. Also relevant, however, is the "structure and purpose of the statute as a whole," as revealed not only in the text, but through the reviewing court's reasoned understanding of the way in which Congress intended the statute and its surrounding regulatory scheme to affect business, consumers, and the law.

With these considerations in mind, we turn first to a consideration of petitioner Medtronic's claim that the Court of Appeals should have found the entire action preempted and then to the merits of the Lohrs' cross-petition.

IV

[Medtronic argues that the Court of Appeals erred by concluding that negligent design claims were not preempted by § 360k(a), quoted earlier. Medtronic suggests that any common-law cause of action is a "requirement" which imposes duties "different from, or in addition to" the generic federal standards that the FDA has promulgated under the MDA.] In essence, the company argues that the plain language of the statute preempts any and all common-law claims brought by an injured plaintiff against a manufacturer of medical devices.

Medtronic's argument is not only unpersuasive, it is implausible. Under Medtronic's view of the statute, Congress effectively precluded state courts from affording state consumers any protection from injuries resulting from a defective medical device. Moreover, because there is no explicit private cause of action against manufacturers contained in the MDA, and no suggestion that the Act created an implied private right of action, Congress would have barred most, if not all, relief for persons injured by defective medical devices. Medtronic's construction of § 360k would therefore have the perverse effect of granting complete immunity from design defect liability to an entire industry that, in the judgment of Congress, needed more stringent regulation in order "to provide for the safety and effectiveness of medical devices intended for human use," 90 Stat. 539 (preamble to Act). It is, to say the least, "difficult to believe that Congress would, without comment, remove all means of judicial recourse for those injured by illegal conduct," Silkwood v. Kerr–McGee Corp., 464 U.S. 238, 251 (1984), and it would take language much plainer than the text of § 360k to convince us that Congress intended that result.

Furthermore, if Congress intended to preclude all common-law causes of action, it chose a singularly odd word with which to do it. The statute would have achieved an identical result, for instance, if it had precluded any "remedy" under state law relating to medical devices. "Requirement" appears to presume that the State is imposing a specific duty upon the manufacturer, and although we have on prior occasions concluded that a statute preempting certain state "requirements" could also pre-empt common-law damages claims, see Cipollone, 505 U.S., at 521–522 (opinion of

STEVENS, J.), that statute did not sweep nearly as broadly as Medtronic would have us believe that this statute does.

The preemptive statute in *Cipollone* was targeted at a limited set of state requirements—those "based on smoking and health"—and then only at a limited subset of the possible applications of those requirements—those involving the "advertising or promotion of any cigarettes the packages of which are labeled in conformity with the provisions of" the federal statute. In that context, giving the term "requirement" its widest reasonable meaning did not have nearly the preemptive scope nor the effect on potential remedies that Medtronic's broad reading of the term would have in this case. The Court in *Cipollone* held that the petitioner in that case was able to maintain some common-law actions using theories of the case that did not run afoul of the pre-emption statute. Here, however, Medtronic's sweeping interpretation of the statute would require far greater interference with state legal remedies, producing a serious intrusion into state sovereignty while simultaneously wiping out the possibility of remedy for the Lohrs' alleged injuries.[9] Given the ambiguities in the statute and the scope of the preclusion that would occur otherwise, we cannot accept Medtronic's argument that by using the term "requirement," Congress clearly signaled its intent to deprive States of any role in protecting consumers from the dangers inherent in many medical devices.

Other differences between this statute and the one in *Cipollone* further convince us that when Congress enacted § 360k, it was primarily concerned with the problem of specific, conflicting State statutes and regulations rather than the general duties enforced by common-law actions. Unlike the statute at issue in *Cipollone*, § 360k refers to "requirements" many times throughout its text. In each instance, the word is linked with language suggesting that its focus is device-specific enactments of positive law by legislative or administrative bodies, not the application of general rules of common law by judges and juries. For instance, subsections (a)(2) and (b) of the statute also refer to "requirements"—but those "requirements" refer only to statutory and regulatory law that exists pursuant to the MDA itself, suggesting that the preempted "requirements" established or continued by States also refer primarily to positive enactments of state law. Moreover, in subsection (b) the FDA is given authority to exclude certain "requirements" from the scope of the pre-emption statute. Of the limited number of "exemptions" from preemption that the FDA has granted, none even remotely resemble common-law claims.

An examination of the basic purpose of the legislation as well as its history entirely supports our rejection of Medtronic's extreme position. The

---

9. Unlike § 360k, preemptive effect of the statute in *Cipollone* was not dependent on the issuance of any agency regulations. The territory exclusively occupied by federal law was defined in the text of the statute itself; that text specified the precise warning to smokers that Congress deemed both necessary and sufficient. In the MDA, no such specifics exist until the FDA provides them. Moreover, the statute in *Cipollone* was clearly intended to have a broader preemptive effect than its 1965 predecessor.

MDA was enacted "to provide for the safety and effectiveness of medical devices intended for human use." Medtronic asserts that the Act was also intended, however, to "protect innovations in device technology from being 'stifled by unnecessary restrictions,'" and that this interest extended to the preemption of common-law claims. While the Act certainly reflects some of these concerns, the legislative history indicates that any fears regarding regulatory burdens were related more to the risk of additional federal and state regulation rather than the danger of preexisting duties under common law. Indeed, nowhere in the materials relating to the Act's history have we discovered a reference to a fear that product liability actions would hamper the development of medical devices. To the extent that Congress was concerned about protecting the industry, that intent was manifested primarily through fewer substantive requirements under the Act, not the preemption provision; furthermore, any such concern was far outweighed by concerns about the primary issue motivating the MDA's enactment: the safety of those who use medical devices.

The legislative history also confirms our understanding that § 360(k) simply was not intended to preempt most, let alone all, general common-law duties enforced by damages actions. There is, to the best of our knowledge, nothing in the hearings, the committee reports, or the debates suggesting that any proponent of the legislation intended a sweeping pre-emption of traditional common-law remedies against manufacturers and distributors of defective devices. If Congress intended such a result, its failure even to hint at it is spectacularly odd, particularly since Members of both Houses were acutely aware of ongoing product liability litigation.[13] Along with the less-than-precise language of § 360k(a), that silence surely indicates that at least some common-law claims against medical device manufacturers may be maintained after the enactment of the MDA.

V

Medtronic asserts several specific reasons why, even if § 360k does not preempt all common-law claims, it at least preempts the Lohrs' claims in this case. In contrast, the Lohrs argue that their entire complaint should survive a reasonable evaluation of the preemptive scope of § 360k(a). [The Lohrs argue that the § 510(k) premarket notification process is not a design "requirement"; that the FDA's general manufacturing and labeling rules do not preempt state rules that merely duplicate some or all of those federal requirements; and that the State's general rules imposing common-law duties do not impose a requirement "with respect to a device" that conflicts with the FDA's general rules and are therefore not preempted.]

---

13. Furthermore, if Congress had intended the MDA to work this dramatic change in the availability of state-law remedies, one would expect some reference to that change in the extensive contemporary reviews of the legislation. We have been able to find no such reference.

Design Claim

[Medtronic suggests that the FDA's determination that Model 4011 is "substantially equivalent" to an earlier device amounts to a specific, federally enforceable design requirement that cannot be affected by state-law pressures from liability suits. This] defense exaggerates the importance of the § 510(k) process and the FDA letter to the company regarding the pacemaker's substantial equivalence to a grandfathered device. As the court below noted, "[t]he 510(k) process is focused on equivalence, not safety." As a result, "substantial equivalence determinations provide little protection to the public. These determinations simply compare a post–1976 device to a pre–1976 device to ascertain whether the later device is no more dangerous and no less effective than the earlier device." * * * [The FDA's "substantial equivalence" letter to Medtronic] only required Medtronic to comply with "general standards"—the lowest level of protection "applicable to all medical devices," and including "listing of devices, good manufacturing practices, labeling, and the misbranding and adulteration provisions of the Act" [and] explicitly warned Medtronic that the letter did "not in any way denote official FDA approval of your device." * * *

Thus, even though the FDA may well examine § 510(k) applications for Class III devices (as it examines the entire medical device industry) with a concern for the safety and effectiveness of the device, it did not "require" Medtronics' pacemaker to take any particular form for any particular reason; the agency simply allowed the pacemaker, as a device substantially equivalent to one that existed before 1976, to be marketed without running the gauntlet of the PMA process. * * * There is no suggestion in either the statutory scheme or the legislative history that the § 510(k) exemption process was intended to do anything other than maintain the status quo with respect to the marketing of existing medical devices and their substantial equivalents. * * * Given this background behind the "substantial equivalence" exemption, * * * and the presumption against preemption, the Court of Appeals properly concluded that the "substantial equivalence" provision did not preempt the Lohrs' design claims.

Identity of Requirements Claims

[The Lohrs' may allege that Medtronic has violated FDA regulations and argue that at least these claims can be maintained without being preempted by § 360k. The Court agreed, noting that § 360k does not deny the states the right to provide a traditional damages remedy for violations of common-law duties when those duties parallel federal requirements.]

The FDA regulations interpreting the scope of § 360k's preemptive effect support the Lohrs' view, and our interpretation of the preemption statute is substantially informed by those regulations. The different views expressed by the Courts of Appeals regarding the appropriate scope of federal preemption under § 360k demonstrate that the language of that section is not entirely clear. In addition, Congress has given the FDA a unique role in determining the scope of § 360k's preemptive effect. Unlike the statute construed in *Cipollone*, for instance, preemption under the MDA does not arise directly as a result of the enactment of the statute; rather, in most cases a state law will be preempted only to the extent that the FDA has promulgated a relevant federal "requirement." Because the FDA is the federal agency to which Congress has delegated its authority to implement the provisions of the Act, the agency is uniquely qualified to determine whether a particular form of state law "stands as an obstacle to the accomplishment and execution of the full purposes and objectives of Congress," Hines v. Davidowitz, 312 U.S. 52, 67 (1941), and, therefore, whether it should be preempted. For example, Congress explicitly delegated to the FDA the authority to exempt state regulations from the preemptive effect of the MDA—an authority that necessarily requires the FDA to assess the preemptive effect that the Act and its own regulations will have on state laws. FDA regulations implementing that grant of authority establish a process by which States or other individuals may request an advisory opinion from the FDA regarding whether a particular state requirement is preempted by the statute. 21 CFR § 808.5 (1995).The ambiguity in the statute—and the congressional grant of authority to the agency on the matter contained within it—provide a "sound basis" for giving substantial weight to the agency's view of the statute. See Chevron U.S.A. Inc. v. Natural Resources Defense Council, Inc., 467 U.S. 837 (1984); [citation].

The regulations promulgated by the FDA expressly support the conclusion that § 360k "does not preempt State or local requirements that are equal to, or substantially identical to, requirements imposed by or under the act." 21 CFR § 808.1(d)(2) (1995). At this early stage in the litigation, there was no reason for the Court of Appeals to preclude altogether the Lohrs' manufacturing and labeling claims to the extent that they rest on claims that Medtronic negligently failed to comply with duties "equal to, or substantially identical to, requirements imposed" under federal law.

Manufacturing and Labeling Claims

Finally, the Lohrs suggest that with respect to the manufacturing and labeling claims, the Court of Appeals should have rejected Medtronic's preemption defense in full. The Court of Appeals believed that these claims would interfere with the consistent application of general federal regulations governing the labeling and manufacture of all medical devices, and therefore concluded that the claims were preempted altogether.

The requirements identified by the Court of Appeals include labeling regulations which require manufacturers of every medical device, with a few limited exceptions, to include with the device a label containing "information for use, . . . and any relevant hazards, contraindications, side effects, and precautions." 21 CFR §§ 801.109(b) and (c) (1995). Similarly, manufacturers are required to comply with "Good Manufacturing Practices," or "GMP's," which are set forth in 32 sections and less than 10 pages in the Code of Federal Regulations.[17] In certain circumstances, the Court of Appeals recognized, the FDA will enforce these general requirements against manufacturers that violate them. [The Lohrs suggest that the general nature of these regulations simply does not preempt claims alleging that the manufacturer failed to comply with other duties under state common law. The Lohr's argue that a requirement must be specific to a particular device to be preempted.]

The Lohrs' theory is supported by the FDA regulations, which provide that state requirements are preempted "only" when the FDA has established "specific counterpart regulations or . . . other specific requirements applicable to a particular device." 21 CFR § 808.1(d) (1995). They further note that the statute is not intended to preempt "State or local requirements of general applicability where the purpose of the requirement relates either to other products in addition to devices . . . or to unfair trade practices in which the requirements are not limited to devices." § 808.1(d)(1). The regulations specifically provide, as examples of permissible general requirements, that general electrical codes and the Uniform Commercial Code warranty of fitness would not be preempted. See ibid. The regulations even go so far as to state that § 360k(a) generally "does not preempt a state or local requirement prohibiting the manufacture of adulterated or misbranded devices" unless "such a prohibition has the effect of establishing a substantive requirement for a specific device." § 808.1 (d)(6)(ii). Furthermore, under its authority to grant exemptions to the preemptive effect of § 360k(a), the FDA has never granted, nor, to the best of our knowledge, even been asked to consider granting, an exemption for a state law of general applicability; all 22 existing exemptions apply to excruciatingly specific state requirements regarding the sale of hearing aids.

Although we do not believe that this statutory and regulatory language necessarily precludes "general" federal requirements from ever preempting state requirements, or "general" state requirements from ever being preempted, it is impossible to ignore its overarching concern that preemption occur only where a particular state requirement threatens to interfere with a specific federal interest. * * * The statute and regulations * * * require a careful comparison between the allegedly preempting federal requirement and the allegedly preempted state requirement to determine whether they fall within the intended preemptive scope of the statute and regulations.[19]

---

17. Some GMPs include the duty to institute a "quality assurance program," to have an "adequate organizational structure," to ensure that personnel in contact with a device are "clean, healthy, and suitably attired" where such matters are relevant to the device's safety, and to have buildings, environmental controls, and equipment of a quality adequate to produce a safe product.

19. A plurality of this Court concluded in *Cipollone* that a similar analysis was required under the Public Health Cigarette Smoking Act of 1969. That act preempted requirements and prohibitions based on

Such a comparison mandates a conclusion that the Lohrs' common-law claims are not preempted by the federal labeling and manufacturing requirements. The generality of those requirements make this quite unlike a case in which the Federal Government has weighed the competing interests relevant to the particular requirement in question, reached an unambiguous conclusion about how those competing considerations should be resolved in a particular case or set of cases, and implemented that conclusion via a specific mandate on manufacturers or producers. Rather, the federal requirements reflect important but entirely generic concerns about device regulation generally, not the sort of concerns regarding a specific device or field of device regulation which the statute or regulations were designed to protect from potentially contradictory state requirements.

Similarly, the general state common-law requirements in this case were not specifically developed "with respect to" medical devices. Accordingly, they are not the kinds of requirements that Congress and the FDA feared would impede the ability of federal regulators to implement and enforce specific federal requirements. * * * These general obligations are no more a threat to federal requirements than would be a state-law duty to comply with local fire prevention regulations and zoning codes, or to use due care in the training and supervision of a workforce. These state requirements therefore escape preemption, not because the source of the duty is a judge-made common-law rule, but rather because their generality leaves them outside the category of requirements that § 360k envisioned to be "with respect to" specific devices such as pacemakers. As a result, none of the Lohrs' claims based on allegedly defective manufacturing or labeling are preempted by the MDA.

VI

In their cross-petition, the Lohrs present a final argument, suggesting that common-law duties are never "requirements" within the meaning of § 360k and that the statute therefore never preempts common-law actions. The Lohrs point out that our holding in *Cipollone* is not dispositive of this issue, for as Part IV, supra, suggests, there are significant textual and historical differences between the *Cipollone* statute and § 360k, and the

smoking and health "imposed under State Law with respect to the advertising or promotion" of cigarettes in packages that were labeled in conformity with the that act. 505 U.S., at 515. We held that the petitioner's fraudulent misrepresentation claims, including those based on allegedly false statements made in advertisements, were not preempted because they were "predicated not on a duty 'based on smoking and health' but rather on a more general obligation—the duty not to deceive." Id., at 528–529. The general common-law duty "not to make fraudulent state-ments" was not within the specific category of requirements or prohibitions based on smoking and health imposed under State law: with respect to the "advertising or promotion" of cigarettes that were preempted by the 1969 statute. Id., at 529. If anything, the language of the MDA's preemption statute and its counterpart regulations require an even more searching inquiry into the relationship between the federal requirement and the state requirement at issue than was true under the statute in *Cipollone*.

meaning of words must always be informed by the environment within which they are situated. We do not think that the issue is resolved by the FDA regulation suggesting that § 360k is applicable to those requirements "having the force and effect of law" that are "established by . . . court decision," 21 CFR § 808.1(b) (1995); that reference, it appears, was intended to refer to court decisions construing state statutes or regulations.

Nevertheless, we do not respond directly to this argument for two reasons. First, since none of the Lohrs' claims is preempted in this case, we need not resolve hypothetical cases that may arise in the future. Second, given the critical importance of device-specificity in our (and the FDA's) construction of § 360k, it is apparent that few, if any, common-law duties have been preempted by this statute. It will be rare indeed for a court hearing a common-law cause of action to issue a decree that has "the effect of establishing a substantive requirement for a specific device." 21 CFR § 808.1(d)(6)(ii) (1995). Until such a case arises, we see no need to determine whether the statute explicitly preempts such a claim. Even then, the issue may not need to be resolved if the claim would also be preempted under conflict preemption analysis, see Freightliner Corp. v. Myrick, 514 U.S. 280, ___ (1995).

VII

Accordingly, the judgment of the Court of Appeals is reversed insofar as it held that any of the claims were preempted and affirmed insofar as it rejected the preemption defense. The case is remanded for further proceedings. It is so ordered.

■ JUSTICE BREYER, concurring in part and concurring in the judgment.

This case raises two questions. First, do the Medical Device Amendments (MDA) to the Food, Drug, and Cosmetics Act ever preempt a state law tort action? Second, if so, does the MDA preempt the particular state-law tort claims at issue here?

I

My answer to the first question is that the MDA will sometimes preempt a state-law tort suit. I basically agree with Justice O'CONNOR's discussion of this point and with her conclusion. The statute's language, read literally, supports that conclusion. It says: "[N]o State . . . may establish . . . with respect to a device . . . any [state] requirement . . . which is different from, or in addition to, any [federal] requirement. . . . " 21 U.S.C. § 360k(a) (emphasis added). One can reasonably read the word "requirement" as including the legal requirements that grow out of the application, in particular circumstances, of a State's tort law.

* * *

II

[The second question turns on Congress' intent. Congress did not intend preemption here because f]irst, the MDA's preemption provision is highly ambiguous. That provision makes clear that federal requirements may preempt state requirements, but it says next to nothing about just when, where, or how, they may do so. The words "any [state] requirement" and "any [federal] requirement," for example, do not tell us which requirements are at issue, for every state requirement that is not identical to even one federal requirement is "different from, or in addition to" that single federal requirement. * * * Congress must have intended that courts look elsewhere for help as to just which federal requirements preempt just which state requirements, as well as just how they might do so.

Second, this Court has previously suggested that, in the absence of a clear congressional command as to preemption, courts may infer that the relevant administrative agency possesses a degree of leeway to determine which rules, regulations, or other administrative actions will have preemptive effect. [Citations.] To draw a similar inference here makes sense, and not simply because of the statutory ambiguity. The Food and Drug Administration (FDA) is fully responsible for administering the MDA. [Citation.] That responsibility means informed agency involvement and, therefore, special understanding of the likely impact of both state and federal requirements, as well as an understanding of whether (or the extent to which) state requirements may interfere with federal objectives. [Citation.] The FDA can translate these understandings into particularized preemptive intentions accompanying its various rules and regulations. * * *

Third, the FDA has promulgated a specific regulation designed to help. That regulation says: "State . . . requirements are preempted only when . . . there are . . . specific [federal] requirements applicable to a particular device . . . thereby making any existing divergent State . . . requirements applicable to the device different from, or in addition to, the specific [federal] requirements." 21 CFR § 808.1(d) (1995). The regulation does not fill all the statutory gaps, for its word "divergent" does not explain, any more than did the statute, just when different device-related federal and state requirements are closely enough related to trigger preemption analysis. But the regulation's word "specific" does narrow the universe of federal requirements that the agency intends to displace at least some state law. [The applicable FDA requirements here, even if numerous, are not "specific" in any relevant sense. The FDA does not intend these requirements to preempt the state requirements at issue here. Justice O'CONNOR's characterization of the federal standards applicable here as "comprehensive" and "extensive," is questionable, and this Court has previously said that it would "seldom infer, solely from the comprehensiveness of federal regulations, an intent to preempt in its entirety a field related to health and safety."]

It makes sense, in the absence of any indication of a contrary congressional (or agency) intent, to read the preemption statute (and the preemption regulation) in light of these basic preemption principles. The statutory terms "different from" and "in addition to" readily lend themselves to such a reading, for their language parallels preemption law's basic concerns. Without any contrary indication from the agency, one might also interpret the regulation's word "divergent" in light of these same basic preemption principles.

* * *

For these reasons, 1 concur in the Court's judgment. I also join the Court's opinion, but for Parts IV and VI. 1 do not join Part IV, which emphasizes the differences between the MDA and the preemption statute at issue in *Cipollone*, because those differences are not, in my view, relevant in this case. I do not join Part VI, because I am not convinced that future incidents of MDA preemption of common-law claims will be "few" or "rare," ante, at ___.

■ Justice O'Connor, with whom The Chief Justice, Justice Scalia, and Justice Thomas join, concurring in part and dissenting in part.

* * * As the Court points out, because Congress has expressly provided a preemption provision [in the MDA], "we need not go beyond that language to determine whether Congress intended the MDA to preempt" state law. We agree, then, on the task before us: to interpret Congress' intent by reading the statute in accordance with its terms. This, however, the Court has failed to do.

* * * I conclude that state common-law damages actions do impose "requirements" and are therefore preempted where such requirements would differ from those imposed by the FDCA. The plurality acknowledges that a common-law action might impose a "requirement," but suggests that such a preemption would be "rare indeed." To reach that determination, the opinion—without explicitly relying on Food and Drug Administration (FDA) regulations and without offering any sound basis for why deference would be warranted—imports the FDA regulations interpreting § 360k to "inform" the Court's reading. Accordingly, the principal opinion states that preemption occurs only "where a particular state requirement threatens to interfere with a specific federal interest," and for that reason, concludes that common-law claims are almost never preempted, and that the Lohrs' claims here are not preempted. This decision is bewildering and seemingly without guiding principle.

The language of § 360k demonstrates congressional intent that the MDA preempt "any requirement" by a State that is "different from, or in addition to," that applicable to the device under the FDCA. The Lohrs have raised various state common-law claims in connection with Medtronic's pacemaker lead. Analysis, therefore, must begin with the question whether state common-law actions can constitute "requirements" within the meaning of § 360k(a).

We recently addressed a similar question in *Cipollone*, where we examined the meaning of the phrase "no requirement or prohibition" under the Public Health Cigarette. Smoking Act of 1969. Cipollone v. Liggett Group, Inc., 505 U.S. 504, (1992). A majority of the Court agreed that state common-law damages actions do impose "requirements." As the plurality explained: "The phrase, '[n]o requirement or prohibition' sweeps broadly and suggests no distinction between positive enactments and common law; to the contrary, those words easily encompass obligations that take the form of common-law rules. As we noted in another context, '[state] regulation can be as effectively exerted through an award of damages as through some form of preventive relief. The obligation to pay compensation can be, indeed is designed to be, a potent method of governing conduct and controlling policy.' " San Diego Building Trades Council v. Garmon, 359 U.S. 236, 247.

That rationale is equally applicable in the present context. Whether relating to the labeling of cigarettes or the manufacture of medical devices, state common-law damages actions operate to require manufacturers to comply with common-law duties. As *Cipollone* declared, in answer to the same argument raised here that common-law actions do not impose requirements, "such an analysis is at odds both with the plain words" of the statute and "with the general understanding of common-law damages actions." Ibid. If § 360k's language is given its ordinary meaning, it clearly preempts any state common-law action that would impose a requirement different from, or in addition to, that applicable under the FDCA—just as it would pre-empt a state statute or regulation that had that effect. Justice BREYER reaches the same conclusion.

The plurality's reasons for departing from this reading are neither clear nor persuasive. It fails to refute the applicability of the reasoning of *Cipollone*. Instead, in Part IV, the plurality essentially makes the case that the statute's language, purpose, and legislative history, as well as the consequences of a different interpretation, indicate that Congress did not intend "requirement" to include state common-law claims at all. The principal opinion proceeds to disclaim this position, however, in Parts V and Vl and concludes, rather, that a state common-law action might constitute a requirement, but that such a case would be "rare indeed." The Court holds that an FDCA * * * "requirement" triggers preemption only when a conflict exists between a specific state requirement and a specific FDCA requirement applicable to the particular device.

To reach its particularized reading of the statute, the Court imports the interpretation put forth by the FDA's regulations. Justice Breyer similarly relies on the FDA regulations to arrive at an understanding of § 360(k). Apparently recognizing that *Chevron* deference is unwarranted here, the Court does not admit to deferring to these regulations, but merely permits them to "infor[m]" the Court's interpretation. It is not certain that an agency regulation determining the preemptive effect of any federal statute is entitled to deference, [citation], but one pertaining to the clear statute at issue here is surely not. "If the statute contains an express preemption clause, the task of statutory construction must in the first instance focus on the plain wording of the clause, which necessarily contains the best evidence of Congress' preemptive intent." CSX Transp., Inc. v. Easterwood, 507 U.S. 658, 664, (1993). Where the language of the statute is clear, resort to the agency's interpretation is improper. *Chevron*, 467 U.S. at 842–43. Title 21 U.S.C. § 360k(a)(1) directs the preemption of "any [state] requirement" "which is different from, or in addition to, any requirement applicable under [the FDCA] to the device." As explained above, and as Justice Breyer agrees, the term "requirement" encompasses state common-law causes of action. The Court errs when it employs an agency's narrowing construction of a statute where no such deference is warranted. The statute makes no mention of a requirement of specificity, and there is no sound basis for determining that such a restriction on "any requirement" exists.

[Justice O'Connor concludes that § 360k does not preempt the Lohrs' design claims because the "substantial equivalency" process is not a requirement on a device; that it does not preempt the claims based on violation of federal requirements; but that it does preempt the manufacturing and labeling claims.]

NOTES

1. Most pre-*Lohr* preemption cases under the Medical Device Amendments had found extensive preemption of state common law actions, based in large part on *Cipollone*'s analysis of the term "requirement." The Supreme Court remanded decisions from five of the federal circuit courts of appeals for further consideration in light of *Lohr*. Only one, Kennedy v. Collagen Corp., 67 F.3d 1453 (9th Cir.1995) (reprinted in the casebook at p. 413), was allowed to stand. *Kennedy* involved the stringent pre-market approval process under the MDA and held that the PMA process was not a device-specific requirement requiring preemption of state common law damages actions under § 360k. For a contrary conclusion post–*Lohr*, see Mitchell v. Collagen Corp., 126 F.3d 902 (7th Cir. 1997).

The remaining courts of appeals decisions remanded after *Lohr* represent cases of medical device approval under all of the different approval procedures of the MDA. One such case, Martin v. Telectronics Pacing Systems, Inc., 70 F.3d 39 (6th Cir.1995), involved a pacemaker marketed under the Investigational Device Exemption (IDE) to the MDA. The court on remand after *Lohr* continued to find all claims relating to manufacturing, design, and inadequate warning preempted, focussing on the "essential" device specific nature of the IDE requirements, which the court found to be more detailed than the pre-market notification procedures at issue in *Lohr. Martin*, 105 F.3d 1090 (6th Cir. 1997). Accord, Chambers v. Osteonics Corp., 109 F.3d 1243 (7th Cir.1997)(hip prosthesis; design and warning defect cases preempted by IDE requirements; negligent failure to comply with FDA rules not preempted, however).

2. The FDA proposed an amendment to the regulations at issue in *Medtronic* which describe the preemptive effect of regulations under the MDA. The proposed regulation, § 808.1(d)(11) and (12), stated:

> An FDA imposed requirement will preempt a State common law duty only when FDA has expressly imposed, by regulation or order, a specific substantive requirement applicable to a particular device; and the State common law, as interpreted and applied, imposes a substantive requirement applicable to the same particular device that is different from, or in addition to, FDA's counterpart requirement.

> FDA requirements that are applicable to devices in general, or that are established by means other than through regulation or order, should not result in preemption of State tort claims.

62 Fed.Reg. 65384 (Dec. 12, 1997). The FDA stated, in its summary of the proposed regulation, that it believes that, as a general matter, the MDA's general device approval processes do not preempt state common law tort claims. The Agency said it believes its review procedures insure "a significant measure of protection" against the marketing of defective medical devices, but those processes do not guarantee safety. 66 U.S.L.W. 2380 (Dec. 13, 1997). The proposed regulation was subsequently withdrawn because of concerns regarding its interplay with other regulations. 63 Fed.Reg. 39789 (July 24, 1998).

3. Both *Cipollone* and *Lohr* are plurality opinions. Are common law damages actions now "requirements" for preemption purposes after these cases? What is the effect of Justice Breyer's opinion concurring in the judgment? What is the status of implied preemption doctrine after *Lohr*?

4. Consider again the CPSC regulations at issue in *Southland Mower* and *Moe*. Analyze them under *Cipollone* and *Lohr* and evaluate whether *Moe*, at 391, is correctly decided.

CHAPTER 9

LIMITING DEFECTIVENESS: USER CHOICE

1. OBVIOUS DANGERS

ADD the following to note 1, page 427:

The Georgia Supreme Court overruled its prior adherence to the obvious danger rule in Ogletree v. Navistar International Transp. Corp., 500 S.E.2d 570 (Ga. 1998).

ADD the following to note 5 after **Laaperi v. Sears, Roebuck Co.**, on page 436:

In Reiff v. Convergent Technologies, 957 F.Supp. 573 (D.N.J.1997)(discussed above regarding proof of design defect claims), plaintiff alleged, in addition to a design defect, that the conventional computer keyboard she used at work should have had a warning of the possibility of repetitive stress injuries from use of the keyboard over time. Defendants argued that they bore no duty to warn because the keyboard contains no hidden or latent dangers. The court concluded that there is no duty to warn about the physical manipulation inherent in the use of certain objects which can in some persons and under some circumstances cause such injuries.

* * * Products whose use requires physical activity often entail a risk that such use will cause harm—harm not from the product itself but harm from the manner of a product's use. Consider the snow shovel. Each year, hundreds of people suffer heart attacks, strain their backs, and pull various muscles shoveling snow from their driveways. Since any harm posed lies not in the snow shovel but rather in its use in a particular manner, by a particular person with particular physical attributes, the law does not require that snow shovels contain warnings. For the same reasons, the law does not and ought not require that computer keyboards contain warnings relating to a keyboard's use in a particular way, by a particular person with particular physical characteristics and work habits.

Moreover, according to plaintiffs' own experts, it is one's work environment and not one's computer keyboard which truly puts a typist at risk of developing carpal tunnel syndrome. Keyboards as well as chairs, desks, monitors, lamps, document holders, and other elements of one's workstation can be arranged, configured, and designed in an unlimited number of ways. A typist's work habits, posture, typing technique, and stamina further add to this mix. Considered in this context, a computer keyboard poses no greater threat than does a chair, desk, monitor, or any other component of a work environment. Thus, requiring a keyboard to contain a warning that a particular work environment may lead to health problems makes no more sense than requiring a desk or chair or monitor to carry the same warning.

Other federal courts agree. See Howard v. Digital Equipment Corp., 1995 WL 128012 (E.D. Pa. 1995). What evidence would support a duty to warn in the case of computer keyboards or similar products which lead to injury because of the way in which they must be used? As you consider the next chapter on generic risks, or product category liability, question whether this is a claim of product category liability?

2.   GENERIC RISKS: PRODUCT CATEGORY LIABILITY

ADD to note 1, page 453, the following:

What types of products might fall into the "rare case" category in which a court should permit a jury to find that the product has such limited utility that, if it is marketed, liability will attach to injuries resulting from its use? The cases in this section suggest there are such products. *O'Brien v. Muskin* involved one such product, but *Jordan v. K–Mart* did not. Can you think of others? What about a slingshot? See Vaughn v. Nevill, 677 N.E.2d 482 (Ill. App. 1997). A b-b gun? Moss v. Crosman Corp., 136 F.3d 1169 (7th Cir. 1998).

The bullet-proof vest in *Linegar* is in a different category from the "useless" product since it has significant value. A recent case discussed the interplay between the alleged design defectiveness of a useful product of this type and the risks from its design which might support a failure to warn claim. In House v. Armour of America, 929 P.2d 340 (Utah 1996), plaintiff's decedent, a member of a S.W.A.T. team, was killed during an FBI raid while wearing defendant's armoured vest. The decedent was killed when hit by a bullet from a high caliber rifle which struck him in the armoured vest. Although his vest contained hard ceramic inserts which upgraded its stopping capabilities, the bullet struck the nonceramic inside edge of the hard armour chest panel and then penetrated through the soft-body portion of the vest, causing Lt. House's death. The plaintiff alleged a failure to warn of the risk that the vest would not protect from such a bullet and that the danger was neither open nor obvious. The court, reversing summary judgment, concluded that an issue of fact existed on whether users of the vest knew or should have known of the risk of such an injury, and thus whether there was a duty to warn, but summarily rejected the design defect claim. The court discussed the nature of the design obligation regarding obvious dangers and said:

> [W]e do not believe that [the concern that products will be designed poorly to render their defectiveness obvious] is equally applicable to products which, because of their nature and intended use, cannot be economically designed in a safe manner, such as knives. Moreover, we find persuasive the reasoning of the United States Court of Appeals for the First Circuit: "If a manufacturer had to warn consumers against every such obvious danger inherent in a product, '[t]he list of obvious practices warned against would be so long, it would fill a volume.'"*Laaperi*, 787 F.2d at 731. Accordingly, we conclude that a "manufacturer cannot be held liable for injuries which result from patent dangers, inherent in the product, completely within the cognition of a reasonable user,

and incapable of being economically alleviated." Wheeler v. John Deere Co., 935 F.2d 1090, 1104 (10th Cir.1991).

However, as noted by the court of appeals, even though a product may contain a patent danger which cannot be economically alleviated, the "product may still be unreasonably dangerous if the hazards or risks associated with its use were not such that they should have been realized by a reasonable user or consumer of the product." * * * With these principles in mind, we must determine whether the danger posed to Lt. House was open and obvious as a matter of law. We agree with defendants that Lt. House's body armor contained an open and obvious hazard which could not be economically alleviated; it did not provide complete coverage of vulnerable body parts. Thus, defendants did not have to warn Lt. House that he could still be injured or killed by ammunition striking uncovered areas. See Linegar v. Armour of America, Inc., 909 F.2d 1150, 1154 (8th Cir.1990) (holding that defendant had no duty to warn of limited nature of protection offered by bullet resistant vest). However, the bullet that killed Lt. House did not strike an exposed area. The bullet hit his body armor, which failed to contain it and thus shield Lt. House from harm. If any reasonable user of Lt. House's body armor would have believed that the vest could stop a bullet fired from a high-caliber rifle, when in reality it would not, then the product would fail to meet the reasonable expectations of its users and thus would pose an unreasonable danger requiring an adequate warning.

What kind of information will plaintiff need to support the failure to warn claim at trial? Compare Moss v. Crosman Corp., 136 F.3d 1169 (7th Cir. 1998)(no duty to warn of obvious dangers from use of b-b gun; child killed when pellet pierced eye and entered brain).

ADD to note 3, page 454, the following:

Litigation against the gun industry is not totally without success. A widely publicized plaintiff's verdict was rendered in New York against the gun industry for negligent marketing. In federal district court, a jury found several handgun manufacturers liable for negligently oversupplying gun-friendly markets, mainly in the South, aware that the excess guns flow into criminal hands via illegal markets in New York and other states with stricter anti-gun laws. The plaintiff was the victim of a careless shooting by a teenage friend who had purchased a gun out of the trunk of a car. T. Hays, *Gunmakers Found Liable for Violence*, AP, February 11, 1999. Several cities including Chicago, New York, Bridgeport, Connecticut, Miami and New Orleans have sued the gun industry alleging products liability actions as well as negligent marketing and public nuisance theories. 27 Prod. Saf. & Liab. Rptr. (BNA) at 91 (January 19, 1999). The cities allege, among other theories, that simple devices to prevent the trigger on semi-automatic weapons from firing are available. Id. at 92.

If handguns are not categorically defective, what about ammunition? The Second Circuit Court of Appeals concluded that a hollow-point bullet, designed intentionally to cause more severe injury than solid bullets, was not defective in design. In McCarthy v. Olin Corp., 119 F.3d 148 (2d Cir. 1998), the Court of Appeals concluded that the hollow-point bullets in issue, Black Talons used in the 1993 Long Island Railroad shooting which killed six people and injured nineteen, were not defective under New York law even though they were designed specifically to enhance injuries inflicted by a shooting.

Appellants ... argue that under the risk/utility test applied by new York courts, appellee should be held strictly liable because the risk of harm posed by the Black Talons outweighs the ammunition's utility. The district court properly held that the risk/utility test is inapplicable "because the risks arise from the function of the product, not any defect in the product.... There must be 'something wrong' with a product before the risk/utility analysis may be applied in determining whether the product is unreasonably dangerous." [Citation omitted.] The purpose of risk/utility analysis is to determine whether the risk of injury might have been reduced or avoided if the manufacturer had used a feasible alternative design. [Citation omitted.] However, the risk of injury to be balanced with the utility is a risk not intended as the primary function of the product. Here, the primary function of the Black Talon bullets was to kill or cause serious injury. There is no reason to search for an alternative safer design where the product's sole utility is to kill and maim. Accordingly, we hold that appellants have failed to state a cause of action under New York strict products liability law.

Id. at 155. Judge Calabresi dissented, first arguing that the question of liability should have been certified to the New York Court of Appeals. Judge Calabresi's dissent then discusses the ambiguity in New York law surrounding the test for design defectiveness after *Denny v. Ford Motor Co.*, supra, and concludes that many jurisdictions would use a risk/utility test to determine that a product is defective even though it performs as designed and intended. This is particularly the case when alternative designs exist, as in *McCarthy* where alternative bullets exist which do not "shred human flesh upon impact." Judge Calabresi quotes the Restatement of Products Liability, § 2, comments c and d, in support.

3. MISUSE

ADD to note **10. Failure to Follow Directions**, page 485, after the second paragraph, the following:

The Texas Supreme Court recently rejected comment j in a case in which the plaintiff mechanic who was attempting to mount a tire totally ignored all the conspicuous warnings given, which were not challenged as inadequate, and was seriously injured as a result of the ensuing explosion. In Uniroyal Goodrich Tire Co. v. Martinez, 977 S.W.2d 328 (Tex. 1998), the plaintiff alleged that the design of the tire was defective because an alternative was available which would make it impossible for users to mount it improperly. The jury found for the plaintiff on a defective design theory and the Supreme Court affirmed, expressly rejecting the approach described in comment j as "unfortunate" and adopting instead the approach outlined in the Products Liability Restatement § 2(b) which describes a broad range of factors to consider in determining whether an alternative design is reasonable, one of which is whether the product contains suitable warnings and instructions. Id. at 335.

CHAPTER 10

LIMITING DEFECTIVENESS: PASSAGE OF TIME

2. DISPOSAL AND DESTRUCTION

ADD to note 3, page 497, the following:

The Kentucky Supreme Court reversed the appellate opinion in *Reed v. Westinghouse Elec. Corp.* and held that disposal of the electrical transformers in issue was an unforeseeable, substantial alteration of the product so that the manufacturers of the transformers and the PCBs owed no warning obligation to the salvage workers regarding the dangers of the product, either in strict liability or negligence. Monsanto Co. v. Reed, 950 S.W.2d 811 (Ky. 1997).

3. STATE OF THE ART

ADD **Sternhagen v. Dow Company,** 935 P.2d 1139 (Mont. 1997), as a new principal case on page 543.

Sternhagen v. Dow Company

Supreme Court of Montana, 1997.
935 P.2d 1139.

■ NELSON, JUSTICE.

The United States District Court for the District of Montana has certified to this Court the following question: In a strict products liability case for injuries caused by an inherently unsafe product, is the manufacturer conclusively presumed to know the dangers inherent in his product, or is state-of-the-art evidence admissible to establish whether the manufacturer knew or through the exercise of reasonable human foresight should have known of the danger? We conclude that Montana law precludes the admission of state-of-the-art evidence in products liability cases brought under the theory of strict liability.

FACTUAL AND PROCEDURAL BACKGROUND

The United States District Court for the District of Montana found the following facts relevant to the question of law certified to this Court:

1. In her complaint filed in the United States District Court for the District of Montana, plaintiff Marlene L. Sternhagen, as the personal representative of the estate of Charles J. Sternhagen, seeks recovery for injuries and damages allegedly sustained by Charles Sternhagen as a result of his exposure to the herbicide 2,4–D during the years 1948 through 1950. Plaintiff claims that the exposure of Charles Sternhagen to 2,4–D was the cause of the cancer that resulted in his death.

2. Plaintiff seeks recovery against the defendants under the doctrine of strict liability in tort. Plaintiff claims that each of the defendants separately manufactured the 2,4–D products to which Charles Sternhagen was exposed during the years 1948 through 1950.

3. During the summer months of 1948, 1949 and 1950, Charles Sternhagen was employed by a crop spraying business in northeast Montana. Plaintiff claims that during that time, Charles Sternhagen was exposed to the herbicide, 2,4–D.

4. In 1981, Charles Sternhagen, a medical doctor specializing in radiology, was diagnosed as having a form of cancer which plaintiff claims was caused by his exposure to the herbicide 2,4–D during the years 1948 through 1950. Defendants dispute the claim that there is a causal link between the herbicide 2,4–D and the type of cancer from which Charles Sternhagen died.

5. The defendants claim neither they, nor medical science, knew or had reason to know of any alleged cancer-causing properties of the herbicide 2,4–D during the years 1948 through 1950.

DISCUSSION

Before addressing the question certified to us by the United States District Court, we will dispose of an issue injected into these proceedings by the defendants * * * [They] first argue that negligence law, not strict liability, applies to this case. Plaintiff responds that this Court should not address this issue because it goes beyond the scope of the certified question. We agree. We accepted the certified question as one involving only the doctrine of strict liability. The certified question does not ask this Court to determine whether negligence or strict liability law applies. To address this additional issue would go beyond the scope of the certified question and effectively render our decision an impermissible advisory opinion. [Citation.] * * *

The defendants next argue that if Restatement (Second) of Torts § 402A (1965), is the applicable law, then state-of-the-art evidence is admissible because Montana law recognizes the state-of-the-art defense in failure to warn claims. The defendants contend that the certified question must be read in conjunction not only with § 402A , adopted by this Court * * * but also with the comments to § 402A, including comment j. Specifically, the defendants argue that the third sentence of comment j applies, namely that "the seller is required to give warning . . . , if he has knowledge, or by the application of reasonably, developed human skill and foresight should have knowledge, of the presence of the . . . danger." The defendants assert that we have cited with approval decisions of other courts that have adopted comment j, [and have referenced certain portions of comment j so that we have, in essence, adopted portions of its language. Defendants concede that we have previously limited the extent to which we adopted comment j, but they assert that our decisions only reject that portion of comment j regarding the presumption of causation which they contend is irrelevant to the certified question before us.] Therefore, the defendants conclude that because this Court has not expressly rejected the third sentence of comment j, we recognize the state-of-the-art defense.

Furthermore, the defendants contend that in [a previous case], the plaintiff offered state-of-the-art evidence on the issue of feasibility in a design defect case. The defendants assert that if a plaintiff is allowed to offer state-of-the-art evidence to prove feasibility in a design defect case, a defendant may also offer state-of-the-art evidence to rebut feasibility as part of its defense. Therefore, the defendants argue [they] should also be allowed to offer state-of-the-art evidence to disprove the feasibility of a warning in a failure to warn case.

Plaintiff responds that the certified question must be answered based on the fundamental principles underlying strict products liability in Montana. Plaintiff asserts that when this Court * * * adopted strict liability in tort for defective products as defined in § 402A, it did so based on substantial public interest and public policy grounds which included principles of fairness and economics, maximum protection for the consumer and placement of responsibility for injury on the manufacturer. Plaintiff asserts that over the past two-plus decades, this Court has consistently returned to and relied upon these core principles. Furthermore, plaintiff contends that this Court has never adopted the state-of-the-art defense, but rather this Court has made it clear that even careful manufacturers may be strictly liable for unreasonably dangerous products which contained unforeseeable dangers. Therefore, plaintiff argues that the critical question for this Court is "whether imposition of liability for undiscovered or even undiscoverable dangers of inherently unsafe products will advance the goals and policies sought to be achieved by Montana's adoption of strict liability." In answering the certified question, plaintiff urges this Court to again return to the core principles underlying the doctrine of strict liability and thereby reject the state-of-the-art defense.

We agree with plaintiff that we have not previously adopted the state-of-the-art defense. Further, we expressly reject the state-of-the-art defense, as this defense is contrary to the doctrine of strict products liability as that body of law has developed in Montana. In reaching these conclusions, we emphasize that despite the defendants' assertion that the certified question involves a failure to warn cause of action, we note that the certified question is not so limited. Consequently, we address the certified question by addressing strict products liability law in Montana generally and without differentiating as among manufacturing defect, design defect, or failure to warn cases.

[Even after adopting § 402A, we have recognized that our adoption] "was not a wholesale adoption of the comments accompanying that provision; nor are we constrained by the comments in developing a body of products liability law." [Citation.] The defendants assert that we have either previously adopted or should now adopt the language of comment j to § 402A. However, after researching Montana law on strict products liability, we conclude that the [alleged state-of-the-art] language in comment j * * * is inconsistent with our established law concerning strict products liability and we therefore decline to adopt that language. Rather, we conclude that the imputation of knowledge doctrine, as discussed below, is more consistent with existing Montana law.

Furthermore, the defendants rely on only one part of the third sentence of comment j which, when considered in its entirety, indicates that this sentence is not applicable to the question certified to this Court. The defendants rely on the language, "the seller is required to give warning . . ., if he has knowledge, or by the application of reasonably, developed human skill and foresight should have knowledge, of the presence of the . . . danger." However, the third sentence of comment j, from which that language is extracted, states:

> Where, however, the product contains an ingredient to which a substantial number of the population are allergic, and the ingredient is one whose danger is not generally known, or if known is one which the consumer would reasonably not expect to find in the product, the seller is required to give warning against it [the ingredient to which people are allergic], if he has knowledge, or by the application of reasonable, developed human skill and foresight should have knowledge, of the presence of the ingredient [to which people are allergic] and the danger.

The certified question before us involves an alleged cancer-causing ingredient, not one to which the decedent is alleged to have been allergic. Therefore, the third sentence of comment j is not applicable to the certified question.

We adopted strict liability in torts for defective products based on important public policy considerations, to which we have consistently adhered for the past two-plus decades. "[T]he doctrine of strict liability was evolved to place liability on the party primarily responsible for the injury occurring, that is, the manufacturer of the defective product." [Citation.] We, thereafter enumerated various public policy considerations supporting adoption of the strict liability doctrine:

> 1. The manufacturer can anticipate some hazards and guard against their recurrence, which the consumer cannot do.

2.   The cost of injury may be overwhelming to the person injured while the risk of injury can be insured by the manufacturer and be distributed among the public as a cost of doing business.

3.   It is in the public interest to discourage the marketing of defective products.

4.   It is in the public interest to place responsibility for injury upon the manufacturer who was responsible for [the defective product] reaching the market.

5.   That this responsibility should also be placed upon the retailer and wholesaler of the defective product in order that they may act as the conduit through which liability may flow to reach the manufacturer, where ultimate responsibility lies.

6.   That because of the complexity of present day manufacturing processes and their secretiveness, the ability to prove negligent conduct by the injured plaintiff is almost impossible.

7.   That the consumer does not have the ability to investigate for himself the soundness of the product.

8.   That this consumer's vigilance has been lulled by advertising, marketing devices and trademarks.

[Citation.] Furthermore, we stated: "The essential rationale for imposing the doctrine of strict liability in tort is that such imposition affords the consuming public the maximum protection from dangerous defects in manufactured products by requiring the manufacturer to bear the burden of injuries and losses enhanced by such defects in its products." [Citation]

[Defendants assert that if we recognize] the imputation of knowledge doctrine, rather than the state-of-the-art defense, we will eliminate all of the elements that a plaintiff must prove to establish a strict products liability cause of action. Specifically, the defendants assert that the imputation of knowledge doctrine removes a plaintiff's burden of proving that a defect in the product caused the injury. In effect, the defendants argue that adoption of the imputation of knowledge doctrine will transform strict liability into absolute liability. We disagree.

From the time we initially adopted strict products liability, we have reassured defendants that strict liability is not absolute liability: "The adoption of the doctrine of strict liability does not relieve the plaintiff from the burden of proving his case. Vital to that proof is the necessity of proving the existence of a defect in the product and that such defect caused the injury complained of." [Citation.] We explained again ... that by imposing upon a plaintiff the burden of proving a traceable defect, causation, and damage or injury, even with a flexible rule of evidence, we assured "an appropriate limitation to a manufacturer's liability." [Citation.] This has not changed.

Under the imputation of knowledge doctrine, which is based on strict liability's focus on the product and not the manufacturer's conduct, knowledge of a product's undiscovered or undiscoverable dangers shall be imputed to the manufacturer. Our adoption of the imputation of knowledge doctrine, and concomitant rejection of the state-of-the-art defense, does not change the requirements of plaintiff's prima facie case; it only reinforces our commitment to provide the maximum protection for consumers, while still assuring "an appropriate limitation to a manufacturer's liability."

In fact, for the past two-plus decades, we have consistently adhered to the core public policy principles underlying strict products liability as set forth in [our decisions.] As stated in the certified question, state-of-the-art evidence is used to establish whether the manufacturer knew or through the exercise of reasonable human foresight should have known of the dangers inherent in his product. That is, the state-of-the-art defense raises issues of reasonableness and foreseeability—concepts fundamental to negligence law—to determine a manufacturer's liability. To recognize the state-of-the-art defense now would inject negligence principles into strict liability law and thereby sever Montana's strict products liability law from the core principles for which it was adopted—maximum protection for consumers against dangerous defects in manufactured products with the focus on the condition of the product, and not on the manufacturer's conduct or knowledge.

Contrary to the defendants' assertion, our references to comment j and our use of certain ambiguous language in previous case law does not support a conclusion that we have adopted the state-of-the-art defense * * *Rather, these cases illustrate our strict adherence to the remedial policies underlying strict liability and our recognition of the basic differences between strict liability and negligence principles. [Defendants refer to certain of our cases that have discussed the requirements for proving when a product is in a defective condition unreasonably dangerous. One of those cases refers to Phillips v. Kimwood Machine Co., 525 P.2d 1033, 1036–37 (Or. 1974). To explain the nature of the duty to warn standard we cited the Oregon Supreme Court's discussion of what differentiates strict liability from absolute liability—a test for unreasonable danger to show that something about a product makes it dangerously defective without regard to whether the manufacturer was at fault for the condition.] A dangerously defective article would be one which a reasonable person would not put into the stream of commerce if he had knowledge of its harmful character. The test, therefore, is whether the seller would be negligent if he sold the article knowing of the risk involved. Strict liability imposes what amounts to constructive knowledge of the condition of the product. *Phillips*, 525 P.2d at 1036. The Court in *Phillips* also explained that a difference exists between strict liability and negligence law because a product could be unreasonably dangerous even though the manufacturer's actions were reasonable in light of what he knew at the time he planned and sold the manufactured product. *Phillips*, 525 P.2d at 1037.

Furthermore, the Oregon Supreme Court explained that a way to determine if a product is unreasonably defective, is to assume that the manufacturer knew of the product's potential dangers and then ask whether a manufacturer with such knowledge should have done something about the danger before the product was sold. *Phillips*, 525 P.2d at 1037. When viewed in this context, it is apparent that this portion of the *Phillips* opinion to which we cited * * * does not support the state-of-the-art defense, but rather describes the imputation of knowledge doctrine.

Moreover, after citing *Phillips*, we further distinguished strict liability from negligence law and reiterated the public policy supporting strict products liability: This strict duty mandated by the theory of strict liability is warranted even though in some situations it may result in liability being imposed upon careful manufacturers. Unforeseeable product defects often cause severe physical injuries to members of the public. The manufacturer can distribute the risk from such accidents among the body of consumers, while the individual consumer must bear the financial burden alone. Placing the risk of loss on the manufacturer provides an incentive to design and produce fail-safe products which exceed reasonable standards of safety. *Phillips*, 525 P.2d at 1041. Nor can we ignore the fact that a manufacturer with research capabilities can anticipate hazards better than unsophisticated purchasers. Strict liability has its underpinnings in public policy.

[In some design defect cases, we have stated that] evidence of the technological knowledge about dangers in a design and the existence of alternative safer designs at the time of manufacture may be admitted. However, we expressly limited these opinions to cases where the alternative designs were available at the time the product at issue was manufactured. "We do not attempt to set forth an analysis which addresses all facets of strict liability under a design defect theory. We render an opinion only with regard to the [particular allegation of a feasible alternative design in issue.] We do not rule upon the fact situation where a claim of design defect is made and where no alternative design is technologically feasible. See O'Brien v. Muskin Corp., 463 A.2d 298 (N.J.1983) (holding that state-of-the-art evidence is relevant to a risk-utility analysis and admissible in a strict liability case involving defectively designed products)." [Citation. In similar cases, we have held that to determine the defectiveness of a design, only evidence concerning other designs available at the time the product at issue was manufactured would be admissible.]

We decline to extend this rule to cases where alternative designs did not exist and a product's dangers were undiscovered or undiscoverable at the time of manufacture. If we were to do so, we would inject negligence concepts into Montana's strict products liability law and eviscerate the public policy underlying strict products liability law in this State. Therefore, we hold that the rule employed in [our previous decisions] is limited to situations where alternative designs existed at the time of manufacture.

Alternatively, the argue that even if the cases * * * do not show that Montana has adopted the rule allowing state-of-the-art evidence, we should do so now based on the experience of other jurisdictions which favor the adoption of the rule. After discussing numerous cases from other jurisdictions, the defendants contend that an overwhelming majority of jurisdictions that have adopted § 402A also admit state-of-the-art evidence. Additionally, the defendants argue that the Restatement (Third) of the Law of Torts: Products Liability (Proposed Final Draft, Preliminary Version) (Oct. 18, 1996) would also allow state-of-the-art evidence. Furthermore, the defendants assert that public policy supports adoption of the state-of-the-art defense.

Despite the adoption of the state-of-the-art defense in other jurisdictions, recognition of the defense in the Restatement (Third) of the Law of Torts: Products Liability and the defendants' assertion that public policy supports adoption of the defense, we choose to continue to adhere to the clear precedent we have heretofore established which focuses on the core principles and remedial purposes underlying strict products liability. Strict liability without regard to fault is the only doctrine that fulfills the public interest goals of protecting consumers, compensating the injured and making those who profit from the market bear the risks and costs associated with the defective or dangerous products which they place in the stream of commerce. As we discussed previously, no Montana case supports the defendants' position that state-of-the-art evidence is admissible when a product's inherent dangers are undiscovered or undiscoverable.

In fact, both our case law and statutory law make it clear that even careful manufacturers may be strictly liable for unreasonably dangerous products whose dangers could not be foreseen. [Citations.] Moreover, given strict liability's focus on the product and not on the manufacturer's conduct, knowledge of any undiscovered or undiscoverable dangers should be imputed to the manufacturer. That is, while a plaintiff must still prove the three prima facie elements * * * evidence that a manufacturer knew or through the exercise of reasonable human foresight should have known of the dangers inherent in his product is irrelevant. See *Phillips*, 525 P.2d at 1036–37. Accordingly, in answer to the question certified, we conclude that, in a strict products liability case, knowledge of any undiscovered or undiscoverable dangers should be imputed to the manufacturer. Furthermore, we conclude that, in a strict products liability case, state-of-the-art evidence is not admissible to establish whether the manufacturer knew or through the exercise of reasonable human foresight should have known of the danger.

ADD to the end of note **1. Warning of the Unknowable**, page 543, the following:

The Supreme Court of Massachusetts abrogated its adherence to the *Beshada* line of reasoning in Vassallo v. Baxter Healthcare Corp., 696 N.E.2d 909 (Mass. 1998), overruling Hayes v. Ariens Co., mentioned in note 1 at page 543, which had relied on *Beshada* and was decided prior to *Feldman*. The plaintiff in *Vassallo* alleged a defective warning regarding the risks of injury from silicone gel breast implants under an implied warranty of merchantability theory. The Court noted that its decision placed Massachusetts in line with the vast majority of jurisdictions in permitting "state of the art" evidence on failure to warn claims, as well as the principles stated in the Products Liability Restatement § 2(c). Id. at 923.

5. POST-SALE DUTIES

ADD to note 1, page 559, the following:

See also, Anderson v. Nissan Motor Co., 139 F.3d 599 (8th Cir. 1998), in which the court of appeals concluded that, under Nebraska law, a forklift manufacturer was under no post-sale obligation to either retrofit or warn of dangers in the design of its forklift, made in 1982, which did not have an operator restraint system. The plaintiff lost a jury verdict on the theory that the product was defectively designed when sold in 1982; plaintiff was injured in 1990. Accord, Tabieros v. Clark Equipment Co., 944 P.2d 1279 (Hawai'i 1997).

ADD to note **6. Reform and the Restatement**, page 562, the following:

The Iowa legislature was one which had adopted statutorily a post-sale duty to warn and the Iowa Supreme Court interpreted that statute, Iowa Code § 668.12, in Lovick v. Wil–Rich, 588 N.W.2d 688 (Iowa 1999). The Court concluded, consistent with and relying on the Products Liability Restatement § 10, that post-sale failure to warn product liability claims are negligence claims just like the point-of-sale failure to warn claims explored in *Olson v. Prosoco, Inc.*, reprinted in the casebook at page 252. The Court concluded, however, that the post-sale failure to warn claim requires a more specific jury instruction than the point-of-sale failure to warn claim and, therefore, formally adopted the factors identified in § 10 of the Products Liability Restatement and required their articulation in future jury instructions regarding the reasonableness of providing a warning after the sale. Id. at 695.

6. STATUTORY REPOSE

ADD to note 2 after **Hodder v. Goodyear Tire & Rubber Co.,** on page 568:

Because of the complex nature of injury causation from toxic substance exposure, a variety of illnesses causally linked to such exposure might manifest themselves over a lengthy period of time, raising the question of whether the first known illness starts the statutory clock running on all subsequently discovered illnesses. Consider the asbestos plaintiff who has early symptoms of asbestos-related disease, but who does not know whether lung cancer, mesothelioma or some other asbestos-related injury will also ensue. If such subsequent illness occurs, is it part of the same earlier injury or a separate injury? This problem is treated in detail in the toxic substances chapter, ch. 18.

The problem was raised in Green v. American Pharmaceutical Co., 960 P.2d 912 (Wash. 1998), where plaintiff had been diagnosed in 1981 with cervical abnormalities resulting from DES ingestion by her mother. Complications in 1986 caused her to require treatment for those abnormalities and to continue to be examined for further DES-related problems. In 1992, examination revealed another DES-related abnormality. Plaintiff timely filed suit for the abnormality discovered in 1992 but did not pursue recovery for any illnesses discovered prior to that time because of the three-year statute of limitations. Defendant claimed that the 1992 injury was also time-barred because it was simply part of the same injury discovered in 1981 and which, had Ms. Green used due diligence as required, was discoverable then as well. The trial court agreed and granted summary judgment. The court of appeals reversed, stating that because the only medical testimony offered in support of the claim suggested that the plaintiff's 1992–discovered injury was separate and distinct from the abnormalities discovered in 1981, and not part of a progressive injury, the statute did not begin to run on it until 1992. The supreme court rejected the "separate and distinct injury" rule and concluded the only question, under the traditional discovery rule, was when Ms. Green should have known of the presence of her injury. The summary judgment was rejected because defendants failed to satisfy the burden of proof on that fact question. Id. at 917.

*

PART III

CAUSATION

CHAPTER 12

PROXIMATE CAUSE

1. DUTY AND FORESEEABILITY LIMITATIONS ON LIABILITY

ADD to note **5. Foreseeability—Harm vs. Use**, page 610, the following:

If fertilizer is used as a component of an explosive device, should the manufacturer be able to defend a products liability claim on the unforeseeability of such use? In Port Authority of New York and New Jersey v. Arcadian Corp., 991 F.Supp. 390 (D.N.J. 1997), the owner of the World Trade Center maintained that the manufacturers of fertilizer used to make a terrorist bomb could have used additives to make it more difficult for their products to be turned into explosives. The trial court held that the owner's allegations regarding past fertilizer explosions, "as a matter of law, simply do not permit a finding of objective foreseeability" so that the product was not defective as designed. The court also held that, even if a duty to reformulate the fertilizer to reduce the likelihood of manipulation into explosives was recognized, the terrorist's actions were superceding causes of the injuries.

ADD to the end of note **10. Foreseeability—Type of Plaintiff**, page 613, the following:

The plaintiff in *Crankshaw* was arguably a rescuer, traditionally considered a foreseeable plaintiff for purposes of defining the scope of the duty in negligence cases, though the case does not discuss that doctrine. Should that doctrine be applied to plaintiffs who come to the aid of persons injured by defective products, when the primary product liability claim is not conduct but product condition-based? See McCoy v. American Suzuki Motor Corp., 961 P.2d 952 (Wash. 1998)(motorist, struck by hit-and-run driver when he stopped to aid passengers in overturned vehicle, allowed to proceed with design defect action against manufacturer of overturned vehicle even though plaintiff was injured two hours after the accident which had prompted his attempt to rescue and after the State Police had arrived on the scene).

2.   INTERVENING CAUSES

ADD to the end of note **6. D. Employer Misconduct—Removing or Altering Guards**, the following:

(3) Effect on warning obligation. The substantial modification of a product may affect design defect liability, but what effect does such modification have on a failure to warn claim? Safety features are often removed by the employer, as in *Anderson,* and such modification often defeats a design defect claim. In such a case, should a failure to warn claim be permitted based on the allegation that had the employee been properly warned about the hazard of using the product without the safety guard he would have been more inclined to protect himself from injury? In Liriano v. Hobart Corp., 700 N.E.2d 303 (N.Y. 1998), plaintiff was injured in 1993 when his arm got stuck in a meat grinder whose safety guard had been removed after purchase by his employer in 1961. Shortly after the 1961 purchase, Hobart became aware of the removal of the safety guard by "a significant number of purchasers" and started placing warning stickers concerning removal of the safety guards on its machines in 1962. The plaintiff's design defect claim was dismissed under the substantial modification doctrine of *Robinson v. Reed–Prentice Div. of Package Machine Co.* described in note 6.D.(1) on page 627, but the New York Court of Appeals concluded that the policies behind that doctrine are not implicated in the context of a duty to warn.

> Unlike design decisions that involve the consideration of many interdependent factors, the inquiry in a duty to warn case is much more limited, focusing principally on the foreseeability of the risk and the adequacy and effectiveness of any warning. The burden of placing a warning on a product is less costly than designing a perfectly safe, tamper-resistant product. Thus, although it is virtually impossible to design a product to forestall all future risk-enhancing modifications that could occur after the sale, it is neither infeasible nor onerous, in some cases, to warn of the dangers of foreseeable modifications that pose the risk of injury. * * * We should emphasize, however that a safety device built into the integrated final product is often the most effective way to communicate that operation of the product without the device is hazardous. Thus, where the injured party was fully aware of the hazard through general knowledge, observation or common sense, or participated in the removal of the safety device whose purpose is obvious, lack of a warning about that danger may well obviate the failure to warn as a legal cause of an injury resulting from that danger." Id. at 307–08.

Does Hobart have an obligation to warn of the danger of operating the meat grinder without the safety guard? What additional facts do you need to know to answer this question?

ADD to the end of note 6, page 637, the following:

Should the manufacturer of ammonium nitrate (AN), which comes in both fertilizer grade and explosive grade, be responsible for the deaths of persons injured in a terrorist attack in which explosives were made from explosive grade AN which had been mislabeled as fertilizer grade and sold to the terrorists? Gaines–Tabb v. ICI Explosives, USA, Inc., 160 F.3d 613 (10th Cir. 1998), presented this question in the wrongful death actions of persons killed in the terrorist bombing of the Murrah Federal Building in Oklahoma City. The Court of Appeals relied on Restatement (Second) of Torts § 448 under which criminal acts of third parties may be foreseeable if (1) the situation provides a temptation to which a "recognizable percentage" of persons would yield, or (2) the temptation is created at a place where "persons of a peculiarly vicious type" are likely to be. *Held*, "due to the apparent complexity of manufacturing an AN bomb, including the difficulty of acquiring correct ingredients, mixing them properly, and triggering the resulting bomb, only a small number of persons could carry out such a crime which does not rise to a 'recognizable percentage' of the population." Id. at 621.

In the Internet age of widely available information of this type, do you agree with the Court of Appeals?

PART IV

DEFENSES AND DAMAGES

CHAPTER 14

DAMAGES

---

1. PERSONAL INJURY AND DEATH

ADD to note **7. Loss of Consortium and Companionship**, page 689, the
following:

Increasingly courts are willing to recognize loss of consortium claims for the
parent-child relationship. In Ford Motor Co. v. Miles, 967 S.W.2d 377 (Tex. 1998),
the court affirmed its 1990 holding that the parent-child relationship supports a loss
of consortium but refused to extend that holding to include the step-parent-step-
child relationship or sibling relationships. The plaintiff, rendered a quadriplegic in
an automobile accident, successfully proved defective design of the shoulder belt
restraint system. The jury awarded $30 million in compensatory and $10 million in
punitive damages against Ford.

---

2. EMOTIONAL DISTRESS

ADD to note **3. Zone of Danger,** page 701, the following:

In defining the zone of danger, consider the passengers in an automobile, one of
whom is injured as the result of an air bag deployment. Are the other passengers in
the zone of danger? In Sullivan v. Ford Motor Co.,1998 WL 60972 (S.D.N.Y. Feb. 13,
1998), the front passenger-side airbag of plaintiff's vehicle deployed following an
automobile collision. Because of the force of the collision, the driver-side and
passenger-side airbags in the vehicle instantly deployed and inflated. Plaintiff

claimed that she watched as the lid of the passenger-side airbag struck her nephew, partially decapitating and killing him. The trial judge denied defendant's summary judgment motion on plaintiff's emotional distress claim, concluding that fact issues remained in ascertaining whether the plaintiff was in the zone of danger and whether the aunt-nephew relationship was sufficient to support the claim, which required an immediate family relationship. What result under *Dillon*?

3. ECONOMIC LOSS AND PROPERTY DAMAGE

ADD to note 1. Economic Loss Rule, page 711, the following:

The New Jersey Supreme Court, whose decisions in *Santor* and *Spring Motors* have been influential in economic loss decisions, revisited the economic loss rule in Alloway v. General Marine Indus., 695 A.2d 264 (N.J. 1997). The buyer of a luxury boat that sank while docked, no personal injury or other property damage, sought to recover in strict liability for economic losses including his costs to repair that were not covered by insurance, and "the difference in value between the price paid for the boat and the market value of the boat in its defective condition." The trial court dismissed the complaint on the strength of *Spring Motors*, supra, which denied a strict liability claim for economic loss in a commercial transaction. The Appellate Division reversed relying on *Santor* which recognized that a consumer could maintain a strict liability claim for economic loss against a manufacturer in a non-commercial transaction.

The supreme court discussed at length the economic loss rule as it has developed from *Santor, Spring Motors,* and *East River*. The court noted that "the vast majority of courts across the country . . . have concluded that purchasers of personal property, whether commercial entities or consumers, should be limited to recovery under contract principles." The court concluded that the U.C.C. provides the plaintiff's sole remedy because "a tort cause of action for economic loss duplicating the one provided by the U.C.C. is superfluous and counterproductive." The court declined to overrule *Santor*, however, and did not resolve "whether tort or contract law applies to a product that poses a risk of causing personal injuries or property damage but has caused only economic loss to the product itself." The court further did not preclude a strict liability claim when the case involves unequal bargaining power, a necessary product, no alternative source for the product, or the purchaser's inability to obtain insurance for consequential damages.

ADD to note 2. Other Property, page 712, the following:

The Supreme Court recently had occasion to evaluate the meaning of "other property" in relation to the economic loss rule from *East River*. In Saratoga Fishing Co. v. J.M. Martinac & Co., 117 S.Ct. 1783 (1997), the plaintiff purchased a used tuna fishing vessel in 1974 from its initial purchaser who had added some extra equipment, an extra skiff, nets, spare parts, and communications and navigational electronics, after buying the ship from the manufacturer in 1969. The plaintiff used the ship until 1986 when an engine room fire erupted from a defective hydraulic system, original equipment installed by the manufacturer. The plaintiff sued the manufacturer for damages in tort from the loss of the extra property that the original purchaser had added to the ship. The trial court found the hydraulic system defective and awarded damages. The manufacturer appealed and argued that, under

East River, the extra equipment was part of the "product itself," the ship, and thus was not recoverable in tort. The Ninth Circuit agreed and reversed the trial court, concluding that *East River* required it to define the defective "product itself" by looking to what the plaintiff had purchased, because that is the product that the plaintiff could have asked its seller, the original purchaser, to warrant, and thus its loss could have been contractually protected.

The Supreme Court reversed, stating that the Ninth Circuit's holding "pushes *East River's* principle beyond the boundary set by the principle's rationale." The Court relied in part on "one important purpose of defective-product tort law," to encourage the manufacture of safer products. The Court reasoned, "the various tort rules that determine which foreseeable losses are recoverable aim, in part, to provide appropriate safe-product incentives. And a liability rule that diminishes liability simply because of [a subsequent resale] is a rule that, other things being equal, diminishes that basic incentive." The Court concluded that the rationale for *East River*—that the parties can contract for appropriate sharing of the risks of harm—does not support withholding liability in the context of a resale after initial use. For application of *Saratoga Fishing*, see Sea–Land Service Co. v. General Electric Co., 134 F.3d 149 (3d Cir. 1998) (every component that is an "object of the bargain" is part of the product itself).

PART V

Special Types of Defendants, Products, and Transactions

CHAPTER 15

Special Types of Defendants

2. Component Part Manufacturers and Assemblers

ADD to note **3. Assembly Process Errors**, page 762, the following:

A different kind of assembler's liability was involved in Ford Motor Co. v. Wood, 703 A.2d 1315 (Md. Ct. App. 1998). Plaintiff incurred an asbestos-related disease from exposure to asbestos-containing brake linings he installed in his job as a garage mechanic on Ford vehicles. Although Ford manufactured brake linings, plaintiff could not show that the brake linings he installed as replacement parts had been manufactured by Ford. He argued, however, that Ford, as the seller of the vehicles on which he worked, owed him a duty to warn of the dangers of installing on Ford vehicles asbestos-containing replacement brake linings manufactured by other companies. The court, noting the dearth of cases on such liability, concluded that Ford did *not* have a duty to warn of dangers of using *other* manufacturers' replacement parts, as a product's manufacturer could not be held responsible for replacement component parts that it neither manufactured nor placed into the stream of commerce.

ADD to note 5 after **Apperson v. E.I. duPont de Nemours & Co.,** on page 762:

Not all TMJ implants were made of Teflon; some were made of silicone manufactured by Dow Corning Corp. and others. After Dow Corning filed for Chapter 11 bankruptcy reorganization in 1994 largely as a result of thousands of claims alleging injury from silicone gel breast implants, plaintiffs with silicone-containing TMJ implants sued Dow Corning's parent, Dow Chemical, for its independent role in researching, testing, and developing silicone. Plaintiffs had failed to pierce the corporate veil and impose liability solely based on the vicarious responsibility stemming from the parent-subsidiary relationship. In re: Temporomandibular Joint (TMJ) Implants Prods. Liab. Litig., 113 F.3d 1484 (8th Cir.1997), involved a challenge by Dow Chemical to its direct liability. The trial court granted summary judgment and the Court of Appeals affirmed, noting that the only evidence of Dow Chemical's involvement with silicone was its performance of a number of services for Dow Corning, including limited toxicology tests on silicone compounds from 1943 to the 1970s. Plaintiffs failed to show that Dow Chemical knew that any of the silicone compounds would be contained in any TMJ implant. Consequently, the Court of Appeals concluded that on no theory of liability—negligent performance of an undertaking under § 324A of the Restatement (Second) of Torts, aiding and abetting Dow Corning's tortious conduct, fraud, or civil conspiracy—did a genuine issue of material fact exist to prevent the grant of summary judgment.

In granting summary judgment on the direct liability of Dow Chemical, the trial court relied to a great extent on the proceedings in the silicone gel breast implants litigation in the Northern District of Alabama which had granted summary judgment to Dow Chemical on virtually the identical issue. Plaintiffs in *TMJ Implants* argued on appeal that the federal court handling the breast implants cases had subsequently vacated its summary judgment order because of documents discovered after the order was entered suggesting greater Dow Chemical involvement than previously realized. The Court of Appeals refused to consider that ruling, saying that the trial court's refusal to vacate its order was not an abuse of discretion and, besides, the plaintiffs had never formally asked for additional time for discovery on the issue.

7.   SUCCESSOR CORPORATIONS

ADD as a new note 4A. on page 799, the following:

4A. Does the product line exception benefit only injured victims or can it be used by distributors and other sellers of the product to support an action of contribution or indemnity against the successor? In Mettinger v. Globe Slicing Machine Co., 709 A.2d 779 (N.J. 1998), the court concluded that the policies behind the product line exception support its use by distributors and other sellers. The court stated that the policies behind the exception, as discussed in the notes in the casebook on pages 798 to 800, would be furthered if applied to distributors and other sellers. Do you agree?

9. ALLOCATING RESPONSIBILITY AND LOSS: CONTRIBUTION AND INDEMNITY

REPLACE note 5, page 828, with the following:

5. Full Contribution. Until 1996, New York was the only state that allowed full contribution from an employer based on the employer's proportionate fault. In September 1996, the New York workers' compensation laws were reformed to impose limits on third-party claims by manufacturers against employers. Section 2 of Assembly Bill 11331 amends the workers' compensation law to provide that an employer shall not be liable for contribution unless a worker has sustained a "grave injury" defined as death, permanent and total loss of a limb, total and permanent blindness and other similarly serious injuries.

ADD to end of note 1, page 834, the following:

New York continues to refine application of its rule on partial settlements, seeking consistency with statutory objectives. In Whalen v. Kawasaki Motors Corp., 703 N.E.2d 246 (N.Y. 1998), the court of appeals concluded that when a plaintiff has been found comparatively at fault and a defendant has settled prior to trial, the settlement is deducted first from the jury's verdict, then the plaintiff's fault percentage is allocated to the remaining verdict. The court found that this approach tended to result in a more precise allocation of loss as well as an incentive to the parties to settle.

CHAPTER 16

Special Types of Products and Transactions

5. Miscellaneous "Products"

ADD to note 4, page 883, the following:

See also Rice v. Paladin Enter., Inc., 128 F.3d 233 (4th Cir. 1997)(publisher of "Hit Man" could be civilly liable under Maryland law for aiding and abetting murders; First Amendment protection for abstract advocacy did not protect instructional manual on how to commit murder).

ADD to end of note 2, p. 889, the following:

See also Monroe v. Savannah Electric & Power Co., 471 S.E.2d 854 (Ga.1996), agreeing with *Bryant* that electricity is a product but finding that the sale element of a strict liability action requires "the manufacturer to have relinquished control over the product and that the product was in a usable or marketable condition" at the time of the injury. In *Monroe*, the plaintiff was returning from a shrimping excursion and, just before docking, contacted an overhead power line of the defendants with his shrimping pole. Because at the time of the contact the electricity was still in its raw, unmarketable, unusable state, having gone through one transformer at the edge of the property but not yet "under the control of any consumer who might reasonably and foreseeably be expected to encounter it," the court concluded that no sale had taken place for purposes of strict liability and the plaintiff could not recover.

PART VI

Special Types of Litigation

CHAPTER 17

Automotive Litigation

---

1. Crashworthiness

ADD to note 1, page 915, the following:

A jury in *Tebbets* found that Ford was not negligent in its design of the 1988 Ford Escort in which Ms. Tebbetts was killed. The jury also found the car was not defective and unreasonably dangerous without an air bag. 25 Prod. Saf. & Liab. Rptr. (BNA) at 1162 (Dec. 12, 1997).

ADD to note **5. Preemption: Express or Implied?**, page 917, the following:

While *Tebbets* found no express or implied preemption, some courts (especially federal) hold that no-air-bag claims *are* impliedly preempted by FMVSS 208. The Pennsylvania Supreme Court recently so held in Cellucci v. General Motors Corp., 706 A.2d 806 (Pa. 1998), concluding that while the Act does not expressly preempt the no-air-bag claims, it does impliedly preempt them because it is not possible for auto manufacturers to comply with both the federal standard, i.e., to choose one of the three permitted restraint systems, and to also comply with state product liability law if that law results in liability for choosing one of the permissible federal options. The court stated:

> To assert that the common law does not compel manufacturers to install certain types of passive restraints disregards the reality of the situation since "an automobile manufacturer faced with the prospect of choosing the

[passive restraint options], or facing potential exposure to compensatory and punitive damages for failing to do so, has but one realistic choice." Kolbeck v. General Motors Corp., 702 F.Supp. 532, 541 (E.D.Pa.1988). Moreover, the United States Court of Appeals for the Third Circuit has stated: "That such flexibility and choice is an essential element of the regulatory framework established in Standard 208 has repeatedly been made clear in the regulatory history of this particular safety standard. See, e.g., 49 Fed.Reg. 28962, 28997 (1994) (Secretary Dole explained that the flexibility and variety built into Standard 208 was needed to "provide sufficient latitude for industry to develop the most effective [occupant restraint] systems" and to help "overcome any concerns about public acceptability by permitting some public choice"); [citations]" Pokorny v. Ford Motor Company, 902 F.2d 1116, 1124 (3d Cir.), cert. denied, 498 U.S. 853 (1990). Thus,this Court finds that to allow common law liability where, as here, the underlying claims are that either an air bag or a different passive restraint system should have been installed "frustrates the goals of the federal regulatory framework and undermines the flexibility that Congress and the Department of Transportation intended to give to automobile manufacturers in this area." Pokorny, 902 F.2d at 1123. Thus, common law tort liability will only survive the Safety Act as long as the claim does not frustrate the manufacturer's ability to comply with the regulations promulgated pursuant to the Safety Act.

* * *

The regulations promulgated under the Safety Act specifically give automobile manufacturers the option to use the three-point lap and shoulder harness safebelts, and a dashboard light and buzzer which was designed to promote the use of seat belts. Allowing a state common law standard that imposes liability on a manufacturer for choosing a federally-imposed option takes away that federally-imposed option from the manufacturer, which clearly goes against Congress' intent. Thus, common law liability which arises from the failure of a manufacturer to install air bags or other passive restraint systems is in actual conflict with the federal law and regulations which allowed the manufacturers to choose among three options.

In deciding that implied preemption applied, the Pennsylvania court relied on *Myrick*. Do you agree that *Myrick* provides support? What arguments support each position?

Most other *state* courts have found *no* implied preemption of design defective passenger restraint device claims: Munroe v. Galati, 938 P.2d 1114 (Ariz. 1997); Minton v. Honda of America Mfg., 684 N.E.2d 648 (Ohio 1997). Most *federal* courts, on the other hand, have found that such claims are impliedly preempted. See Geier v. American Honda Motor Co., 166 F.3d 1236 (D.C. Cir. 1999) (surveying preemption decisions).

CHAPTER 18

SPECIAL ISSUES IN TOXIC SUBSTANCE LITIGATION

2. JUDICIAL ADMINISTRATION

REPLACE the District Court opinion in **Castano v. American Tobacco Co.,** on page 968, with the following Court of Appeals opinion in the case.

Castano v. American Tobacco Co.

United States Court of Appeals, Fifth Circuit, 1996.
84 F.3d 734.

■ JERRY E. SMITH, JUDGE:

In what may be the largest class action ever attempted in federal court, the district court in this case embarked "on a road certainly less traveled, if ever taken at all," Castano v. American Tobacco Co., 160 F.R.D. 544, 560 (E.D.La.1995) (citing Edward C. Latham, The Poetry of Robert Frost, "The Road Not Taken" 105 (1969)), and entered a class certification order. [The trial court defined the class as "All nicotine-dependent persons in the United States * * * who have purchased and smoked cigarettes manufactured by the defendants" since 1943, and their estates and families. The trial court certified its order for interlocutory appeal.] Concluding that the district court abused its discretion in certifying the class, we reverse.

I.

A. The Class Complaint

The plaintiffs filed this class complaint against the defendant tobacco companies and the Tobacco Institute, Inc., seeking compensation solely for the injury of nicotine addiction. The gravamen of their complaint is the novel and wholly untested theory that the defendants fraudulently failed to inform consumers that nicotine is addictive and manipulated the level of nicotine in cigarettes to sustain their addictive nature. The class complaint alleges nine causes of action: fraud and deceit, negligent misrepresentation, intentional infliction of emotional distress, negligence and negligent infliction of emotional distress, violation of state consumer protection statutes, breach of express warranty, breach of implied warranty, strict product liability, and redhibition pursuant to the Louisiana Civil Code. The plaintiffs seek damages, compensatory and punitive, attorneys' fees, equitable relief, including declarations of nicotine's addictive nature and that the defendants manipulated nicotine levels with the intent to sustain addiction, an order that the defendants disgorge any profits made from the sale of cigarettes, restitution for sums paid for cigarettes, and the establishment of a medical monitoring fund. Plaintiffs conceded that addiction would have to be proven by each class member.

[Plaintiffs proposed a four-phase trial plan. In phase 1, a jury would determine common issues of "core liability." Phase 1 issues would include principally (1) issues of law and fact relating to defendants' course of conduct, fraud, and negligence liability (including duty, standard of care, misrepresentation and concealment, knowledge, intent); (2) issues of law and fact relating to defendants' alleged conspiracy and concert of action; (3) issues of fact relating to the addictive nature/dependency creating characteristics and properties of nicotine; and (4) issues of fact relating to whether defendants' wrongful conduct was intentional, reckless or negligent. In phase 2, the jury would determine compensatory damages in sample plaintiff cases. The jury then would establish a ratio of punitive damages to compensatory damages, which ratio thereafter would apply to each class member. Phase 3 would entail a complicated procedure to determine compensatory damages for individual class members "subject to verification techniques and assertion of defendants' affirmative defenses under grouping, sampling, or representative procedures to be determined by the Court." The trial plan left open how jury trials on class members' personal injury/wrongful death claims would be handled, but the trial plan discussed the possibility of bifurcation.]

B.   The Class Certification Order

Following extensive briefing, the district court granted, in part, plaintiffs' motion for class certification, concluding that the prerequisites of Fed. R. Civ. P. 23(a) had been met. The court rejected certification, under Fed. R. Civ. P. 23(b)(2), of the plaintiffs' claim for equitable relief, including the claim for medical monitoring. Appellees have not cross-appealed that portion of the order.

The court did grant the plaintiffs' motion to certify the class under Fed. R. Civ. P. 23(b)(3), organizing the class action issues into four categories: (1) core liability; (2) injury-in-fact, proximate cause, reliance and affirmative defenses; (3) compensatory damages; and (4) punitive damages. It then analyzed each category to determine whether it met the predominance and superiority requirements of rule 23(b)(3). Using its power to sever issues for certification under Fed. R. Civ. P. 23(c)(4), the court certified the class on core liability and punitive damages, and certified the class conditionally pursuant to Fed. R. Civ. P. 23(c)(1).

1.   Core Liability Issues

The court defined core liability issues as "common factual issues [of] whether defendants knew cigarette smoking was addictive, failed to inform cigarette smokers of such, and took actions to addict cigarette smokers. Common legal issues include fraud, negligence, breach of warranty (express or implied), strict liability, and violation of consumer protection statutes."

The court found that the predominance requirement of rule 23(b)(3) was satisfied for the core liability issues. Without any specific analysis regarding the multitude of issues that make up "core liability," the court found that under Jenkins v. Raymark Indus., 782 F.2d 468 (5th Cir.1986), common issues predominate because resolution of core liability issues would significantly advance the individual cases. The court did not discuss why "core liability" issues would be a significant, rather than just common, part of each individual trial, nor why the individual issues in the remaining categories did not predominate over the common "core liability" issues.

The only specific analysis on predominance analysis was on the plaintiffs' fraud claim. The court determined that it would be premature to hold that individual reliance issues predominate over common issues. Relying on Eisen v. Carlisle & Jacquelin, 417 U.S. 156 (1974), the court stated that it could not inquire into the merits of the plaintiffs' claim to determine whether reliance would be an issue in individual trials. Moreover, the court recognized the possibility that under state law, reliance can be inferred when a fraud claim is based on an omission. Accordingly, the court was convinced that it could certify the class and defer the consideration of how reliance would affect predominance.

The court also deferred substantial consideration of how variations in state law would affect predominance. Relying on two district court opinions[11], the court concluded that issues of fraud, breach of warranty, negligence, intentional tort, and strict liability do not vary so much from state to state as to cause individual issues to predominate. The court noted that any determination of how state law variations affect predominance was premature, as the court had yet to make a choice of law determination. As for the consumer protection claims, the court also deferred analysis of state law variations, because "there has been no showing that the consumer protection statutes differ so much as to make individual issues predominate."

The court also concluded that a class action is superior to other methods for adjudication of the core liability issues. Relying heavily on *Jenkins*, the court noted that having this common issue litigated in a class action was superior to repeated trials of the same evidence. Recognizing serious problems with manageability, it determined that such problems were outweighed by "the specter of thousands, if not millions, of similar

---

11. The court cited In re Asbestos Sch. Litig., 104 F.R.D. 422, 434 (E.D.Pa.1984) (discussing the similarity of negligence and strict liability in U.S. jurisdictions), aff'd in part and reversed in part sub nom. School Dist. of Lancaster v. Lake Asbestos, Ltd. (In re Sch. Asbestos Litig.) ("School Asbestos"), 789 F.2d 996, 1010 (3d Cir.1986), and In re Cordis Cardiac Pacemaker Prod. Liability Litig., No. C–3–90–374 (S.D. Ohio Dec. 23, 1992) (unpublished) (discussing similarities among negligence, strict liability, and fraud).

trials of liability proceeding in thousands of courtrooms around the nation."

2.   Injury-in-fact, Proximate Cause, Reliance, Affirmative Defenses, and Compensatory Damages

Using the same methodology as it did for the core liability issues, the district court refused to certify the issues of injury-in-fact, proximate cause, reliance, affirmative defenses, and compensatory damages, concluding that the "issues are so overwhelmingly replete with individual circumstances that they quickly outweigh predominance and superiority." Specifically, the court found that whether a person suffered emotional injury from addiction, whether his addiction was caused by the defendants' actions, whether he relied on the defendants' misrepresentations, and whether affirmative defenses unique to each class member precluded recovery were all individual issues. As to compensatory damages and the claim for medical monitoring, the court concluded that such claims were so intertwined with proximate cause and affirmative defenses that class certification would not materially advance the individual cases.

3.   Punitive Damages

In certifying punitive damages for class treatment, the court adopted the plaintiffs' trial plan for punitive damages: The class jury would develop a ratio of punitive damages to actual damages, and the court would apply that ratio in individual cases. As it did with the core liability issues, the court determined that variations in state law, including differing burdens of proof, did not preclude certification. Rather than conduct an independent review of predominance or superiority, the court relied on *Jenkins* and on Watson v. Shell Oil Co., 979 F.2d 1014 (5th Cir.1992), for support of its certification order.

II.

A district court must conduct a rigorous analysis of the rule 23 prerequisites before certifying a class. General Tel. Co. v. Falcon, 457 U.S. 147, 161 (1982); [citation]. The decision to certify is within the broad discretion of the court, but that discretion must be exercised within the framework of rule 23. Gulf Oil Co. v. Bernard, 452 U.S. 89 (1981). The party seeking certification bears the burden of proof. Horton v. Goose Creek Ind. Sch. Dist., 690 F.2d 470, 486 (5th Cir.1982); In re American Medical Sys., 75 F.3d 1069, 1086 (6th Cir.1996).

The district court erred in its analysis in two distinct ways. First, it failed to consider how variations in state law affect predominance and superiority. Second, its predominance inquiry did not include consideration of how a trial on the merits would be conducted.

Each of these defects mandates reversal. Moreover, at this time, while the tort is immature, the class complaint must be dismissed, as class certification cannot be found to be a superior method of adjudication.

A. Variations in State Law

Although rule 23(c)(1) requires that a class should be certified "as soon as practicable" and allows a court to certify a conditional class, it does not follow that the rule's requirements are lessened when the class is conditional. As a sister circuit explained:

> Conditional certification is not a means whereby the District Court can avoid deciding whether, at that time, the requirements of the Rule have been substantially met. The purpose of conditional certification is to preserve the Court's power to revoke certification in those cases wherein the magnitude or complexity of the litigation may eventually reveal problems not theretofore apparent. * * *

In re Hotel Tel. Charges, 500 F.2d 86, 90 (9th Cir.1974).

In a multi-state class action, variations in state law may swamp any common issues and defeat predominance. See Georgine v. Amchem Prods., 83 F.3d 610 (3d Cir.1996); [citation]. [A] district court must consider how variations in state law affect predominance and superiority. Walsh v. Ford Motor Co., 807 F.2d 1000 (D.C.Cir.1986). The *Walsh* court rejected the notion that a district court may defer considering variations in state law:

> Appellees see the "which law" matter as academic. They say no variations in state warranty laws relevant to this case exist. A court cannot accept such an assertion "on faith." Appellees, as class action proponents, must show that it is accurate. We have made no inquiry of our own on this score and, for the current purpose, simply note the general unstartling statement made in a leading treatise: "The Uniform Commercial Code is not uniform."

807 F.2d at 1016–17 (footnotes omitted).

A district court's duty to determine whether the plaintiff has borne its burden on class certification requires that a court consider variations in state law when a class action involves multiple jurisdictions. "In order to make the findings required to certify a class action under Rule 23(b)(3) . . . one must initially identify the substantive law issues which will control the outcome of the litigation." Alabama v. Blue Bird Body Co., 573 F.2d 309, 316 (5th Cir.1978).

A requirement that a court know which law will apply before making a predominance determination is especially important when there may be differences in state law. See In re Rhone–Poulenc Rorer, Inc. 51 F.3d 1293, 1299–1302 (7th Cir.1995); In re "Agent Orange" Prod. Liability Litig., 818 F.2d 145, 165 (2d Cir.1987). Given the plaintiffs' burden, a court cannot rely on assurances of counsel that any problems with predominance or superiority can be overcome. Windham v. American Brands, Inc., 565 F.2d 59, 70 (4th Cir.1977).

The able opinion in *School Asbestos* demonstrates what is required from a district court when variations in state law exist. There, the court affirmed class certification, despite variations in state law, because:

To meet the problem of diversity in applicable state law, class plaintiffs have undertaken an extensive analysis of the variances in products liability among the jurisdictions. That review separates the law into four categories. Even assuming additional permutations and combinations, plaintiffs have made a creditable showing, which apparently satisfied the district court, that class certification does not present insuperable obstacles. Although we have some doubt on this score, the effort may nonetheless prove successful.

789 F.2d at 1010; [citation]; *Walsh*, 807 F.2d at 1017 (holding that "nationwide class action movants must creditably demonstrate, through an 'extensive analysis' of state law variances, 'that class certification does not present insuperable obstacles' ").

A thorough review of the record demonstrates that, in this case, the district court did not properly consider how variations in state law affect predominance. The court acknowledged as much in its order granting class certification, for, in declining to make a choice of law determination, it noted that "the parties have only briefly addressed the conflict of laws issue in this matter." Similarly, the court stated that "there has been no showing that the consumer protection statutes differ so much as to make individual issues predominate."

The district court's review of state law variances can hardly be considered extensive; it conducted a cursory review of state law variations and gave short shrift to the defendants' arguments concerning variations. In response to the defendants' extensive analysis of how state law varied on fraud, products liability, affirmative defenses, negligent infliction of emotional distress, consumer protection statutes, and punitive damages[15], the court examined a sample phase 1 jury interrogatory and verdict form, a survey of medical monitoring decisions, a survey of consumer fraud class actions, and a survey of punitive damages law in the defendants' home

---

15. We find it difficult to fathom how common issues could predominate in this case when variations in state law are thoroughly considered. * * * The *Castano* class suffers from many of the difficulties [other courts have] found dispositive. The class members were exposed to nicotine through different products, for different amounts of time, and over different time periods. Each class member's knowledge about the effects of smoking differs, and each plaintiff began smoking for different reasons. Each of these factual differences impacts the application of legal rules such as causation, reliance, comparative fault, and other affirmative defenses.

Variations in state law magnify the differences. [In a fraud claim, some states require justifiable reliance on a misrepresentation while others require reasonable reliance. States impose varying standards to determine when there is a duty to disclose facts. Products liability law also differs among states, Restatement (Second) of Torts § 402A. Affirmative defenses vary widely as does the availability of comparative fault doctrine. Finally, negligent infliction of emotional distress involves wide variations.]

Despite these overwhelming individual issues, common issues might predominate. We are, however, left to speculate. The point of detailing the alleged differences is to demonstrate the inquiry the district court failed to make.

states. The court also relied on two district court opinions granting certification in multi-state class actions.

The district court's consideration of state law variations was inadequate. The surveys provided by the plaintiffs failed to discuss, in any meaningful way, how the court could deal with variations in state law. The consumer fraud survey simply quoted a few state courts that had certified state class actions. The survey of punitive damages was limited to the defendants' home states.

* * *

The court also failed to perform its duty to determine whether the class action would be manageable in light of state law variations. The court's only discussion of manageability is a citation to *Jenkins* and the claim that "while manageability of the liability issues in this case may well prove to be difficult, the Court finds that any such difficulties pale in comparison to the specter of thousands, if not millions, of similar trials of liability proceeding in thousands of courtrooms around the nation."

The problem with this approach is that it substitutes case-specific analysis with a generalized reference to *Jenkins*. The *Jenkins* court, however, was not faced with managing a novel claim involving eight causes of action, multiple jurisdictions, millions of plaintiffs, eight defendants, and over fifty years of alleged wrongful conduct. Instead, *Jenkins* involved only 893 personal injury asbestos cases, the law of only one state, and the prospect of trial occurring in only one district. Accordingly, for purposes of the instant case, *Jenkins* is largely inapposite.

In summary, whether the specter of millions of cases outweighs any manageability problems in this class is uncertain when the scope of any manageability problems is unknown. Absent considered judgment on the manageability of the class, a comparison to millions of individual trials is meaningless.

B. Predominance

The district court's second error was that it failed to consider how the plaintiffs' addiction claims would be tried, individually or on a class basis. The district court, based on Eisen v. Carlisle & Jacquelin, 417 U.S. 156 (1974), and Miller v. Mackey Int'l, 452 F.2d 424 (5th Cir.1971), believed that it could not go past the pleadings for the certification decision. The result was an incomplete and inadequate predominance inquiry.

The crux of the court's error was that it misinterpreted *Eisen* and *Miller*. Neither case suggests that a court is limited to the pleadings when deciding on certification. Both, instead, stand for the unremarkable proposition that the strength of a plaintiff's claim should not affect the certification decision. In *Eisen*, the Court held that it was improper to make a preliminary inquiry into the merits of a case, determine that the plaintiff was likely to succeed, and consequently shift the cost of providing notice to the defendant. In *Miller*, this court held that a district court could not deny certification based on its belief that the plaintiff could not prevail on the merits.

A district court certainly may look past the pleadings to determine whether the requirements of rule 23 have been met. Going beyond the pleadings is necessary, as a court must understand the claims, defenses, relevant facts, and applicable substantive law in order to make a meaningful determination of the certification issues. See Manual for Complex Litigation § 30.11 (3d ed. 1995).

The district court's predominance inquiry demonstrates why such an understanding is necessary. The premise of the court's opinion is a citation to *Jenkins* and a conclusion that class treatment of common issues would significantly advance the individual trials. Absent knowledge of how addiction-as-injury cases would actually be tried, however, it was impossible for the court to know whether the common issues would be a "significant" portion of the individual trials. The court just assumed that because the common issues would play a part in every trial, they must be significant.[18] The court's synthesis of *Jenkins* and *Eisen* would write the predominance requirement out of the rule, and any common issue would predominate if it were common to all the individual trials.[19]

18. The district court's approach to predominance stands in stark contrast to the methodology the district court used in *Jenkins*. There, the district judge had a vast amount of experience with asbestos cases. He certified the state of the art defense because it was the most significant contested issue in each case. *Jenkins*, 109 F.R.D. 269 at 279. To the contrary, however, the district court in the instant case did not, and could not, have determined that the common issues would be a significant part of each case. Unlike the judge in *Jenkins*, the district judge a quo had no experience with this type of case and did not even inquire into how a case would be tried to determine whether the defendants' conduct would be a significant portion of each case.

19. An incorrect predominance finding also implicates the court's superiority analysis: the greater the number of individual issues, the less likely superiority can be established. * * * The relationship between predominance and superiority in mass torts was recognized in the Advisory Committee's note to rule 23(b)(3), which states:

A "mass accident" resulting in injuries to numerous persons is ordinarily not appropriate for a class action because of the likelihood that significant questions, not only of damages but of liability and defenses to liability, would be present, affecting the individuals in different ways. In these circumstances an action conducted nominally as a class action would degenerate in practice into multiple lawsuits separately tried.

Fed. R. Civ. P. 23(b)(3) advisory committee's note (citation omitted) * * *

The plaintiffs assert that Professor Charles Allen Wright, a member of the Advisory Committee has now repudiated this passage in the notes. [Citation.] Professor Wright's recent statements, made as an advocate in *School Asbestos*, must be viewed with some caution. As Professor Wright has stated:

I certainly did not intend by that statement to say that a class should be certified in all mass tort cases. I merely wanted to take the sting out of the statement in the Advisory Committee Note, and even that said only that a class action is "ordinarily not appropriate" in mass-tort cases. The class action is a complex device that must be used with discernment. I think for example that Judge Jones in

The court's treatment of the fraud claim also demonstrates the error inherent in its approach. According to both the advisory committee's notes to Rule 23(b)(3) and this court's decision in Simon v. Merrill Lynch, Pierce, Fenner & Smith, Inc., 482 F.2d 880 (5th Cir.1973), a fraud class action cannot be certified when individual reliance will be an issue. The district court avoided the reach of this court's decision in *Simon* by an erroneous reading of *Eisen*; the court refused to consider whether reliance would be an issue in individual trials.

The problem with the district court's approach is that after the class trial, it might have decided that reliance must be proven in individual trials. The court then would have been faced with the difficult choice of decertifying the class after phase 1 and wasting judicial resources, or continuing with a class action that would have failed the predominance requirement of rule 23(b)(3).[21]

III.

In addition to the reasons given above, regarding the district court's procedural errors, this class must be decertified because it independently fails the superiority requirement of rule 23(b)(3). In the context of mass tort class actions, certification dramatically affects the stakes for defendants. Class certification magnifies and strengthens the number of unmeritorious claims. Aggregation of claims also makes it more likely that a defendant will be found liable and results in significantly higher damage awards. Manual for Complex Litigation § 33.26 n.1056; [citation].

In addition to skewing trial outcomes, class certification creates insurmountable pressure on defendants to settle, whereas individual trials would not. [Citation.] The risk of facing an all-or-nothing verdict presents too high a risk, even when the probability of an adverse judgment is low. [Citation.] These settlements have been referred to as judicial blackmail.

It is no surprise then, that historically, certification of mass tort litigation classes has been disfavored.[23] The traditional concern over the

---

Louisiana would be creating a Frankenstein's monster if he should allow certification of what purports to be a class action on behalf of everyone who has ever been addicted to nicotine.

Letter of Dec. 22, 1994, to N. Reid Neureiter, Williams & Connolly, Washington, D.C.

21. Severing the defendants' conduct from reliance under rule 23(c)(4) does not save the class action. A district court cannot manufacture predominance through the nimble use of subdivision (c)(4). The proper interpretation of the interaction between subdivisions (b)(3) and (c)(4) is that a cause of action, as a whole, must satisfy the predomi-

nance requirement of (b)(3) and that (c)(4) is a housekeeping rule that allows courts to sever the common issues for a class trial. [Citation omitted.] Reading rule 23(c)(4) as allowing a court to sever issues until the remaining common issue predominates over the remaining individual issues would eviscerate the predominance requirement of rule 23(b)(3); the result would be automatic certification in every case where there is a common issue, a result that could not have been intended.

23. At the time rule 23 was drafted, mass tort litigation as we now know it did not exist. [Citation.] The term had been applied to single-event accidents. Even in those rights of defendants in mass tort class actions is magnified in the instant case. Our specific concern is that a mass tort cannot be properly certified without a prior track record of trials from which the district court can draw the information necessary to make the predominance and superiority requirements required by rule 23. This is because certification of an immature tort results in a higher than normal risk that the class action may not be superior to individual adjudication.

We first address the district court's superiority analysis. The court acknowledged the extensive manageability problems with this class. Such problems include difficult choice of law determinations, subclassing of eight claims with variations in state law, Erie guesses, notice to millions of class members, further subclassing to take account of transient plaintiffs, and the difficult procedure for determining who is nicotine-dependent. Cases with far fewer manageability problems have given courts pause. [Citations.]

The district court's rationale for certification in spite of such problems i.e., that a class trial would preserve judicial resources in the millions of inevitable individual trials is based on pure speculation. Not every mass tort is asbestos, and not every mass tort will result in the same judicial crises.[24] The judicial crisis to which the district court referred is only theoretical.

What the district court failed to consider, and what no court can determine at this time, is the very real possibility that the judicial crisis may fail to materialize.[25] The plaintiffs' claims are based on a new theory of liability and the existence of new evidence. Until plaintiffs decide to file

cases, the advisory committee cautioned against certification. As modern mass tort litigation has evolved, courts have been willing to certify simple single disaster mass torts, [citation] but have been hesitant to certify more complex mass torts, [citations].

24. * * *

Where novel theories of recovery are advanced (such as addiction as injury), courts can aggressively weed out untenable theories. See, e.g., Allgood v. R.J. Reynolds Tobacco Co., 80 F.3d 168, 172 (5th Cir.1996) (rejecting failure-to-warn claim against tobacco companies based on inadequate proof of reliance and, alternatively, on "common knowledge" theory). Courts can use case management techniques to avoid discovery abuses. The parties can also turn to mediation and arbitration to settle individual or aggregated cases.

25. The plaintiffs, in seemingly inconsistent positions, argue that the lack of a judicial crisis justifies certification; they as-

sert that the reason why individual plaintiffs have not filed claims is that the tobacco industry makes individual trials far too expensive and plaintiffs are rarely successful. The fact that a party continuously loses at trial does not justify class certification, however. [Citation.] The plaintiffs' argument, if accepted, would justify class treatment whenever a defendant has better attorneys and resources at its disposal.

The plaintiffs' claim also overstates the defendants' ability to outspend plaintiffs. Assuming arguendo that the defendants pool resources and outspend plaintiffs in individual trials, there is no reason why plaintiffs still cannot prevail. The class is represented by a consortium of well-financed plaintiffs' lawyers who, over time, can develop the expertise and specialized knowledge sufficient to beat the tobacco companies at their own game. [Citation.] Courts can also overcome the defendant's alleged advantages through coordination or consolidation of cases for discovery and other pretrial matters. [Citation.]

individual claims, a court cannot, from the existence of injury, presume that all or even any plaintiffs will pursue legal remedies.[26] Nor can a court make a superiority determination based on such speculation. [Citation.]

Severe manageability problems and the lack of a judicial crisis are not the only reasons why superiority is lacking. The most compelling rationale for finding superiority in a class action—the existence of a negative value suit—is missing in this case. Accord Phillips Petroleum Co. v. Shutts, 472 U.S. 797, 809, (1985); *Rhone-Poulenc*, 51 F.3d at 1299.

As he stated in the record, plaintiffs' counsel in this case has promised to inundate the courts with individual claims if class certification is denied. Independently of the reliability of this self-serving promise, there is reason to believe that individual suits are feasible. First, individual damage claims are high, and punitive damages are available in most states. The expense of litigation does not necessarily turn this case into a negative value suit, in part because the prevailing party may recover attorneys' fees under many consumer protection statutes. [Citation.]

In a case such as this one, where each plaintiff may receive a large award, and fee shifting often is available, we find Chief Judge Posner's analysis of superiority to be persuasive:

> For this consensus or maturing of judgment the district judge proposes to substitute a single trial before a single jury.... One jury ... will hold the fate of an industry in the palm of its hand.... That kind of thing can happen in our system of civil justice.... But it need not be tolerated when the alternative exists of submitting an issue to multiple juries constituting in the aggregate a much larger and more diverse sample of decision-makers. That would not be a feasible option if the stakes to each class member were too slight to repay the cost of suit.... But this is not the case.... Each plaintiff if successful is apt to receive a judgment in the millions. With the aggregate stakes in the tens or hundreds of millions of dollars, or even in the billions, it is not a waste of judicial resources to conduct more than one trial, before more than six jurors, to determine whether a major segment of the international pharmaceutical industry is to follow the asbestos manufacturers into Chapter 11.

Rhone-Poulenc, 51 F.3d at 1300. So too here, we cannot say that it would be a waste to allow individual trials to proceed, before a district court engages in the complicated predominance and superiority analysis necessary to certify a class.

---

26. There are numerous reasons why plaintiffs with positive-value suits opt out of the tort system, including risk aversion to engaging in litigation, privacy concerns, and alternative avenues for medical treatment, such as Medicaid. [Citation.] In a case where comparative negligence is raised, plaintiffs have the best insight into their own relative fault. Ultimately, a court cannot extrapolate, from the number of potential plaintiffs, the actual number of cases that will be filed. [Citation.]

Fairness may demand that mass torts with few prior verdicts or judgments be litigated first in smaller units even single-plaintiff, single-defendant trials until general causation, typical injuries, and levels of damages become established. Thus, "mature" mass torts like asbestos or Dalkon Shield may call for procedures that are not appropriate for incipient mass tort cases, such as those involving injuries arising from new products, chemical substances, or pharmaceuticals.

The remaining rationale for superiority, judicial efficiency, is also lacking. In the context of an immature tort, any savings in judicial resources is speculative, and any imagined savings would be overwhelmed by the procedural problems that certification of a sui generis cause of action brings with it.

Even assuming arguendo that the tort system will see many more addiction-as-injury claims, a conclusion that certification will save judicial resources is premature at this stage of the litigation. Take for example the district court's plan to divide core liability from other issues such as comparative negligence and reliance. The assumption is that after a class verdict, the common issues will not be a part of follow-up trials. The court has no basis for that assumption.

It may be that comparative negligence will be raised in the individual trials, and the evidence presented at the class trial will have to be repeated. The same may be true for reliance. The net result may be a waste, not a savings, in judicial resources. Only after the courts have more experience with this type of case can a court certify issues in a way that preserves judicial resources. See *Jenkins*, 782 F.2d 468 (certifying state of the art defense because experience had demonstrated that judicial resources could by saved by certification).

Even assuming that certification at this time would result in judicial efficiencies in individual trials, certification of an immature tort brings with it unique problems that may consume more judicial resources than certification will save. These problems are not speculative; the district court faced, and ignored, many of the problems that immature torts can cause.

The primary procedural difficulty created by immature torts is the inherent difficulty a district court will have in determining whether the requirements of rule 23 have been met. We have already identified a number of defects with the district court's predominance and manageability inquires, defects that will continue to exist on remand because of the unique nature of the plaintiffs' claim.

The district court's predominance inquiry, or lack of it, squarely presents the problems associated with certification of immature torts. Determining whether the common issues are a "significant" part of each individual case has an abstract quality to it when no court in this country has ever tried an injury-as-addiction claim. As the plaintiffs admitted to the district court, "we don't have the learning curb [sic] that is necessary to say to Your Honor 'this is precisely how this case can be tried and that will not run afoul of the teachings of the 5th Circuit.' "

Yet, an accurate finding on predominance is necessary before the court can certify a class. It may turn out that the defendant's conduct, while common, is a minor part of each trial. Premature certification deprives the defendant of the opportunity to present that argument to any court and risks decertification after considerable resources have been expended.

The court's analysis of reliance also demonstrates the potential judicial inefficiencies in immature tort class actions. Individual trials will determine whether individual reliance will be an issue. Rather than guess that reliance may be inferred, a district court should base its determination that individual reliance does not predominate on the wisdom of such individual trials. The risk that a district court will make the wrong guess, that the parties will engage in years of litigation, and that the class ultimately will be decertified (because reliance predominates over common issues) prevents this class action from being a superior method of adjudication.

The complexity of the choice of law inquiry also makes individual adjudication superior to class treatment. The plaintiffs have asserted eight theories of liability from every state. Prior to certification, the district court must determine whether variations in state law defeat predominance. While the task may not be impossible, its complexity certainly makes individual trials a more attractive alternative and, ipso facto, renders class treatment not superior. [Citation.]

Through individual adjudication, the plaintiffs can winnow their claims to the strongest causes of action. The result will be an easier choice of law inquiry and a less complicated predominance inquiry. State courts can address the more novel of the plaintiffs' claims, making the federal court's *Erie* guesses less complicated. It is far more desirable to allow state courts to apply and develop their own law than to have a federal court apply "a kind of *Esperanto* [jury] instruction." *Rhone-Poulenc*, 51 F.3d at 1300; [Citation.]

The full development of trials in every state will make subclassing an easier process. The result of allowing individual trials to proceed is a more accurate determination of predominance. We have already seen the result of certifying this class without individual adjudications, and we are not alone in expressing discomfort with a district court's certification of a novel theory. See *Rhone-Poulenc*, 51 F.3d at 1300.

Another factor weighing heavily in favor of individual trials is the risk that in order to make this class action manageable, the court will be forced to bifurcate issues in violation of the Seventh Amendment. This class action is permeated with individual issues, such as proximate causation, comparative negligence, reliance, and compensatory damages. In order to manage so many individual issues, the district court proposed to empanel a class jury to adjudicate common issues. A second jury, or a number of "second" juries, will pass on the individual issues, either on a case-by-case basis or through group trials of individual plaintiffs.

The Seventh Amendment entitles parties to have fact issues decided by one jury, and prohibits a second jury from reexamining those facts and issues. Thus, Constitution allows bifurcation of issues that are so separable that the second jury will not be called upon to reconsider findings of fact by the first. * * * [The Seventh Circuit in *Rhone-Poulenc*,] described the constitutional limitation as one requiring a court to "carve at the joint" in such a way so that the same issue is not reexamined by different juries. [Citation.]

* * *

The plaintiffs' final retort is that individual trials are inadequate because time is running out for many of the plaintiffs. They point out that prior litigation against the tobacco companies has taken up to ten years to wind through the legal system. While a compelling rhetorical argument, it is ultimately inconsistent with the plaintiffs' own arguments and ignores the realities of the legal system. First, the plaintiffs' reliance on prior personal injury cases is unpersuasive, as they admit that they have new evidence and are pursuing a claim entirely different from that of past plaintiffs.

Second, the plaintiffs' claim that time is running out ignores the reality of the class action device. In a complicated case involving multiple jurisdictions, the conflict of law question itself could take decades to work its way through the courts. Once that issue has been resolved, discovery, subclassing, and ultimately the class trial would take place. Next would come the appellate process. After the class trial, the individual trials and appeals on comparative negligence and damages would have to take place. The net result could be that the class action device would lengthen, not shorten, the time it takes for the plaintiffs to reach final judgment.

IV.

The district court abused its discretion by ignoring variations in state law and how a trial on the alleged causes of action would be tried. Those errors cannot be corrected on remand because of the novelty of the plaintiffs' claims. Accordingly, class treatment is not superior to individual adjudication.

We have once before stated that "traditional ways of proceeding reflect far more than habit. They reflect the very culture of the jury trial...." In re Fibreboard Corp., 893 F.2d 706, 711 (5th Cir.1990). The collective wisdom of individual juries is necessary before this court commits the fate of an entire industry or, indeed, the fate of a class of millions, to a single jury. For the forgoing reasons, we REVERSE and REMAND with instructions that the district court dismiss the class complaint.

NOTES

Plaintiffs, as promised after the *Castano* decertification, filed at least ten state class action lawsuits against the tobacco industry alleging addiction-as-injury claims. The state class actions generally have fared poorly. A settlement class action against The Liggett Group was decertified in Walker v. Liggett Group Inc., 175 F.R.D. 226 (S.D. W. Va. 1997). More on settlement class actions will be found infra. A litigation class action certified in Pennsylvania federal court, after being removed there by the defendants, subsequently was decertified by the trial judge who had certified it. The judge concluded that even though all the plaintiffs were from Pennsylvania, common issues did not predominate because of the individual causation and damages problems. Barnes v. The American Tobacco Co., 176 F.R.D. 479 (E.D. Pa. 1997). In the first state class action to go to trial, a Florida jury found the tobacco industry liable for defrauding smokers about the health effects of smoking. S. Torry, *Cigarette Firms Lose Huge Suit*, Wash. Post, July 8, 1999, at A1.

As part of its settlement of 22 state health care reimbursement suits, Liggett agreed to help the states prove their cases against the other members of the industry by turning over potentially damaging documents. The other tobacco companies have unsuccessfully challenged dissemination of those documents, claiming privilege under joint defense agreements. The theories behind the state claims are explored in the case which follows in this Supplement.

Among Liggett's evidentiary concessions is that the nation's cigarette companies targeted teenagers. This admission was believed to support the federal government's effort to regulate nicotine as a drug, and thus to regulate, among other things, the advertising of cigarettes to children. The FDA issued its regulation of tobacco in 1996 and the tobacco companies immediately challenged FDA's jurisdiction over cigarettes. The FDA won a ruling in United States District Court that the FDA does have jurisdiction to regulate cigarettes as drug-delivery devices. See Coyne Beahm, Inc. v. U.S. Food & Drug Admin., 958 F.Supp. 1060 (M.D.N.C.1997). The Fourth Circuit Court of Appeals reversed, 153 F.3d 155 (4th Cir. 1998), and the Supreme Court granted certiorari, 119 S.Ct. 1495 (1999), to resolve the FDA's jurisdiction.

Smokers' claims other than addiction-as-injury have met with limited success. Plaintiffs won their first major jury verdict since *Cipollone* in Carter v. Brown & Williamson Tobacco Corp., 95–00934–CA (Fla. Cir. Ct., August 9, 1996). The case has been reversed on appeal based on the statute of limitations. Another Florida jury awarded $1 million to a smoker's widow including a first-ever award for $450,000 in punitive damages. Schwartz, *Jury Imposes Damages on Tobacco Firm*, Wash. Post, June 11, 1998, at A1. A class action by flight attendants in Florida settled for a $300 million contribution to fund tobacco research. Prods. Liab. Rptr. (CCH) No. 895 (October 17, 1997). Plaintiffs lost a second-hand smoke case, though, in Indiana. 26 Prod. Saf. & Liab. Rptr. (BNA) at 301 (March 29, 1998). Evidence of concealment of tobacco smoking hazards by the industry has led to very high verdicts in recent months. A California jury awarded $81 million to the family of a man who smoked for four decades; $79.5 million was for punitive damages. W. McCall, *Jury Awards Record $81 Million in Smoking Case*, AP (March 30, 1999).

As the state health care reimbursement suits proceeded toward trial, the state attorneys general and the tobacco companies reached a historic settlement in June

1997. The terms included a $368 billion fund to settle the state lawsuits and the addiction-as-injury class action suits pending nationwide. The state reimbursement suits had settled individually for significant sums: Florida settled for $11.3 billion, Mississippi for $3.6 billion, Texas for $15.3 billion, and Minnesota for $6.6 billion. After Congress failed to enact federal tobacco legislation in 1998, the states and tobacco companies agreed to a $206 billion settlement of all state claims. On the history of the tobacco litigation, see Philip J. Hilts, Smokescreen: The Truth Behind the Tobacco Industry Cover-up (1996); Stanton A. Glantz, et. al., The Cigarette Papers (1996). See generally, Symposium, Tobacco: The Growing Controversy, 24 N. Ky. L. Rev. No. 3 (1997).

ADD as a principal case **Texas v. American Tobacco Co.,** 14 F.Supp.2d 956 (E.D. Tex. 1997), after note **2. C. Public Claims**, on page 979, for a discussion of the basis of the state health care cost reimbursement actions against the tobacco industry.

Texas v. The American Tobacco Company

United States District Court, Eastern District of Texas 1997.
14 F.Supp.2d 956.

■ FOLSOM, DISTRICT JUDGE.

* * * The State of Texas (State) brought this suit seeking to recover costs incurred in providing medical care and other benefits to its citizens, including costs associated with the Medicaid program as the result of the citizens' use of cigarettes and smokeless tobacco products. Defendants are tobacco companies and public relations firms. The State's [complaint] seeks to impose liability against Defendants for their manufacturing, advertising, distributing and selling tobacco products in the United States. In response to the allegations, Defendants filed motions to dismiss the complaint contending the State's claims fail for several reasons.

* * *

ARGUMENT

Before moving for the dismissal of individual claims, Defendants put forth several arguments advocating dismissal of the action as a whole. Defendants claim the suit cannot proceed as a direct action because the State's exclusive remedy is through assignment/subrogation pursuant to Tex. Hum. Res. Code Ann. § 32.033. Defendants also contend that the State's suit, arising from personal injuries or death allegedly caused by the consumption of tobacco products, has been barred by the Texas legislature with its enactment of the Product Liability Act in 1993. Defendants further contend that the State has not suffered a direct injury, and thus cannot recover because its injury is too remote. Finally, defendants assert that the

State's direct action violates fundamental principles of due process. The Court rejects these arguments based on the following analysis.

A. SUBROGATION AS THE STATE'S EXCLUSIVE REMEDY

The State is seeking in this suit to recover payments made through its Medicaid program for health care provided to recipients for injuries allegedly caused by the consumption of tobacco products. In order to participate in the Medicaid program a state must submit for approval a plan dealing with how to provide medical assistance under the program. 42 U.S.C. § 1396. Each plan must include certain provisions that are mandated by the federal government. On of these provisions requires that a state "take all reasonable measures to ascertain the legal liability of third parties . . . to pay for care and services available under the plan." Id. at 1396a(a)(25)(A). In addition, the statute requires that if "liability is found to exist[,] . . . the State or local agency will seek reimbursement . . . to the extent of such legal liability." Id. at 1396a(a)(25)(B). Finally, Congress has required the states to "provide for mandatory assignment of rights of payment for medical support or other care owed to recipients. . . . "Id. at 1396a(a)(45). [In accordance with these provisions, Texas has enacted a "Subrogation" provision by which recipients of medical assistance assign to Texas their rights of recovery against third persons who may be responsible for personal injury to the recipient. The statute also provides for "[a] separate and distinct cause of action in favor of the state." Tex. Hum. Res. Code Ann. § 32.033(d).]

Defendants argue that the provisions of § 32.033 provide the State with its exclusive remedy to recover Medicaid expenses. They base this position on case law from the Texas Supreme Court, certain rules of statutory construction, and their reading of § 32.033. The State argues that its authority to bring this suit is rooted in the common law and that this authority has not been supplanted by § 32.033. The State also argues that the case law cited by the defendants is distinguishable, and the language of § 32.033 does not evidence an intent on the part of the Texas legislature to provide an exclusive remedy.

The court must start with the question of whether the State could maintain this action at common law in the absence of any statutory provision. In other words, if the Medicaid statute did not require the states to seek reimbursement, could a state proceed as the State of Texas has in this manner. Based on the Supreme Court's decision in Alfred L. Snapp & Son, Inc. v. Puerto Rico, 458 U.S. 592 (1982), the Court concludes that the State could bring such an action. [Snapp involved whether Puerto Rico had standing to maintain an action to enforce federal anti-discrimination in employment laws on behalf of its citizens, absent specific statutory authority. The Court concluded that "quasi-sovereign" interests acted as a basis for such authority. Quasi-sovereign interests are distinguished from a state's general sovereign interests and involve those interests a State has in the well-being of its populace, which evolve over time.] The only hard and fast rule set forth by the Court is that a State may not invoke this doctrine when it is only a nominal party asserting the interests of another. [The Court finds that the State has set forth a sufficient question that the State is not a nominal party to this suit. The State expends millions of dollars each year to provide medical care to its citizens and, if the complaint's allegations are true, the defendants have caused the economy of the State and the welfare of its people to suffer.]

Having decided that quasi-sovereign interests are at stake in this suit, the Court must next address whether the State's common law action has been supplanted by a statutory remedy that should be deemed exclusive. The crux of the Defendant's argument is that any common law action the State may have had can no longer be pursued, because the Texas legislature has provided the State with its exclusive remedy in § 32.033 of the Texas Human Resources Code. [Citation.] This principle derives from the rule of statutory construction *expressio unius est exlusio alterius*. In other words, if one thing is implied, it is implied to the exclusion of all others. [Citations.]

* * *

It is clear from [the discussed federal and Texas cases] that in order to construe these statutory provisions * * * the Court must at all times be mindful of their purpose. Upon reading [the Medicaid and Texas statutes], it is without question that their purpose is to require states such as Texas to recover money spent that can be attributed to the wrongs of third-parties in an efficient and cost effective manner. The Court is convinced that an application of *expressio unius* would frustrate this purpose.

As noted above, the Defendants would have this Court direct that the State bring individual subrogation claims pursuant to § 32.033. Although this approach may be preferred in situations where a single tortfeasor inflicts a one-time harm against a single individual who receives Medicaid benefits, the practical consequences of the Defendants' position would be to prohibit a state from ever instituting a suit that alleges a broad based harm to millions of citizens. It would be impractical, if not impossible, for the states to follow the mandates of the Medicaid statute's reimbursement provisions, because proceeding on a claim-by-claim basis would be cost prohibitive and inefficient.

* * *

To summarize, the Court concludes that the manner in which the State seeks to proceed is rooted in the common law. To prevent the State from proceeding in the present manner does not further the purpose of the Medicaid reimbursement provisions, rather it hinders it. To adopt the Defendants' position, this Court would have to determine that Congress and the Texas legislature anticipated the reimbursement issues raised by this case, considered the existence of the State's common law cause of action, and determined that a subrogation remedy would be the best way to proceed in all instances. This is too much to ask. The State's position that the presence of a statutory right normally does not extinguish nonstatutory rights is more consistent with the spirit of the reimbursement provisions of the Medicaid statute. The Texas legislature has not clearly evidenced an intent to create an exclusive remedy in § 32.033. Therefore, the Court finds that the statute does not provide the State with its exclusive remedy.

B. TEXAS PRODUCT LIABILITY ACT

Defendants contend that the State's attempt to create a direct action fails because the Texas Product Liability Act bars lawsuits arising from personal injuries or death allegedly caused by the consumption of tobacco products, Under the Act, a manufacturer or seller is not liable for a marketing or design defect claim if the product in question is a common consumer product that is inherently unsafe and the consumer knows it to be inherently unsafe. This argument rests on the premise that the State's alleged injuries are derivative of the claims of the individual smokers' claims and as such are barred by the language of the Act.

* * *

The State contends that the Act does not apply to any of its direct claims against Defendants, such as fraud and misrepresentation, because those claims are not products liability claims within the meaning of the Act as they do not arise out of personal injury, death or property damage but out of an infringement against the sovereign. [The Court has previously concluded that the State may maintain this action in its quasi-sovereign capacity to protect the physical and economic well-being of its citizenry.] The claims are not brought by the injured consumer. As such, the Court is not persuaded that this action is a "product liability action" within the meaning of the Act, and thus is not barred by the Act.

The State argues, alternatively, that even if the State's claims did arise out of the personal injury allegedly sustained by individual smokers, the "inherently unsafe" product defense does not apply when a manufacturer or seller has suppressed material information relevant to a product's safety, so that the ordinary consumer does not possess full knowledge of the product's inherent dangerousness. According to the allegations in the Second Amended Complaint, Defendants suppressed information that establishes the addictive nature of cigarettes and engaged in a conspiracy to spread disinformation about the ill effects of cigarette smoking.

To come within the purview of the Act, Defendants must establish (1) that the product is inherently unsafe and (2) that the product is known to be unsafe by the ordinary consumer who consumes the product with the ordinary knowledge common to the community. In *Joseph E. Seagram & Sons, Inc. v. McGuire*, 814 S.W.2d 385 (Tex. 1991), the Texas Supreme Court noted that encompassed within the term "common knowledge" are those facts that are so well known to the community as to be beyond dispute. The State has alleged that the public was not provided the facts, because the Defendants suppressed relevant safety information to the point that consumers could not know as a matter of common knowledge the full extent of health risks associated with smoking and the alleged addictiveness of tobacco use.

Accepting the allegations in the Plaintiff's Second Amended Complaint as true, the Court finds that while the health risks of tobacco consumption are generally known, the addictive nature of tobacco consumption is not generally known due to the concealment and misrepresentation by Defendants of its products as alleged by the State. Because the State has pled that Defendants misrepresented and concealed the addictive nature of its tobacco products, the State has taken its claim outside the purview of the Act, and the Act does not bar the State's claims. To hold otherwise would be stating beyond doubt that the State can prove no set of facts in support of its claims which would entitle it to relief in light of the Act.

* * *

C. PROXIMATE CAUSE AND DIRECT INJURY

Defendants contend that the injury allegedly suffered by the State should be considered too remote as a matter of law. Their argument is rooted in concepts of proximate cause and the related principle of "remoteness." They state that because the State's injury is dependent on individual smokers becoming sick, there are too many steps in the causal chain to allow the State to proceed. To allow this suit to go forward in this manner, it is argued, would violate traditional principles of causation. The State asserts that the presence of the individual smokers does not break the causal chain, rather it is a foreseeable consequence of the Defendants' conduct that has had a substantial part in bringing about the harm to the State.

Embodied in the concept of proximate cause is the notion that a plaintiff must assert a direct relationship between the injury it claims to have suffered and the allegedly injurious conduct. *Holmes v. Securities Investor Protection Corp.*, 503 U.S. 258, 268 (1992). It has generally been held that such a relationship cannot be established when "a plaintiff ... complain[s] of harm flowing merely from the misfortunes visited upon a third person by the defendant's act ..." *Id*. at 268–269. Such an injury is considered to be too remote.

In the *Holmes* opinion, the Supreme Court discussed three concerns that must be addressed when determining whether a plaintiff's injury is too remote. First, the less direct an injury is, the more difficult it will be to attribute damages to the conduct of the defendant as opposed to other factors. Second, allowing "indirect claims" to proceed creates a risk of multiple recoveries, because the potential plaintiffs are not parties to a particular action may someday sue in their own right. Finally, these remoteness concerns generally do not arise when those directly injured bring suit, because they can be counted on to "vindicate the law as private attorneys general." *Id.* at 269–270.

At the outset, the Court notes that the definition of "proximate cause" cited above could be satisfied by the State. In addition, a finding that the injury allegedly suffered by the State is foreseeable is also a distinct possibility. Therefore, the Court must focus its attention on the three concerns outlined in *Holmes* to decide whether the injuries asserted in this matter are too remote.

It is clear to the Court that the second and third concerns addressed in *Holmes* are not problematic in this case. With respect to multiple recovery, there can be none in this type of action. As the State points out in its brief, the State of Texas is the only party that can recover Medicaid benefits that have been paid as a result of the wrongful conduct of a third party.

Based on the nature of this cause of action, the third concern discussed in *Holmes* is also absent. As discussed in the previous section, the State brings this action based on its quasi-sovereign interests in protecting the health, welfare, and well-being of the populace of the State. This common law concept provides the State with an independent cause of action to recover the damages it has allegedly incurred. It is clear that because the State is proceeding under this theory, there can be no better party to prosecute this matter. In fact, no other party is empowered to bring this type of action.

* * *

IV. STATUTORY CLAIMS

A. RICO

Counts 1–3 of the Second Amended Complaint allege Defendants violated 18 U.S.C. § 1962(a), (b), © and (d), the Racketeer Influenced and Corrupt Organizations Act ("RICO"). Generally, the State alleges Defendants engaged in a pattern of racketeering from December 15, 1953 through the present through multiple predicate acts including, *inter alia*, wire and mail fraud, bribery, tobacco products through the mails in a manner calculated to place them in the hands of minors, intimidating witnesses in prospective legal proceedings, and obstruction of justice. [The Court is not convinced the State can make a prima facie showing of the essential elements of RICO at trial. However, taking the State's allegations of RICO violations as true, the Court will refrain from ruling on the RICO claims until after Plaintiff has completed its case in chief, at which point the Court will hear an offer of proof of Plaintiff's RICO claims outside the presence of the jury.]

B. FEDERAL AND STATE ANTITRUST CLAIMS

[The Court dismissed the State's antitrust claims because the State has not suffered the type of injury the antitrust laws were designed to prevent.]

C. DTPA CLAIMS

In Count Fourteen of the Second Amended Complaint, the State alleges Defendants violated the Texas Deceptive Trade Practices–Consumer Protection Act ("DTPA"). The State alleges that Defendant's "knowingly engaged in and continued to engage in, false, misleading or deceptive acts or practices which are declared unlawful," and that said activity began at least as early as the 1950's and continues to the present. Defendants argue that because the State is not a "consumer" within the meaning of the DTPA, it has no standing to assert a claim under the DTPA. The Court agrees.

* * *

V. COMMON LAW PLEADING DEFECTS

A. RESTITUTION/UNJUST ENRICHMENT

Defendants assert that the State's claim for recovery under theories of restitution and unjust enrichment must fail because the State did not plead that it conferred any benefit upon Defendants. The Court agrees, and grants Defendants' motion to dismiss the State's claim of restitution and unjust enrichment.

* * *

B. PUBLIC NUISANCE

The State alleges in Count Ten of the Second Amended Complaint that Defendants have intentionally interfered with the public's right to be free from unwarranted injury, disease, and sickness and have caused damage to the public health, the public safety, and the general welfare of the citizens of the State of Texas. Defendants argue that the State has not pled a proper claim for public nuisance because it has failed to plead essential allegations under Texas public nuisance law, namely that the Defendants improperly used their own property, or that the State itself has been injured in its use or employment of its property.

The Attorney General in Texas is authorized to bring suit to enjoin or abate a public nuisance. A public nuisance is defined as the use of any place for certain, specific proscribed activities such as gambling, prostitution, and the manufacture of obscene materials. "Where an action to enjoin a nuisance is brought under statutory authority, the case is limited to the provisions of the statute. The only activities which may be enjoined are those which fall within the provisions of the statute upon which the application for injunction is based." *Benton v. City of Houston*, 605 S.W.2d 679 (Tex. civ. App. 1980, no writ). Because none of the proscribed activities defined under this statutory scheme are implicated under the allegations made in the present case, the State may not maintain an action for injunctive relief pursuant to § 125.022.

Neither may the State maintain an action for damages under a public nuisance theory. The Court agrees with Defendants that the State has not pled a proper claim, because it has failed to plead essential allegations under Texas public nuisance law. Specifically, the State failed to plead that Defendants improperly used their own property, or that the State itself has been injured in its use or employment of its property. [Citations.] The overly broad definition of the elements of public nuisance urged by the State is simply not found in Texas case law and the Court is unwilling to accept the State's invitation to expand a claim for public nuisance beyond its grounding in real property. Accordingly, the Court dismisses Count Ten for public nuisance.

C. NEGLIGENT PERFORMANCE OF A VOLUNTARY UNDERTAKING

In Count Eleven, the State alleges that Defendants voluntarily assumed a duty to report honestly and completely on all research regarding cigarette smoking and health based upon their public pronouncements to do so. The State further pleads that by failing to report on such research, by publishing and publicizing fraudulent science, and failing, in general, to comply with the promises made in the "Frank Statement" and the industry's voluntary code, Defendant's breached this duty. Finally, the State alleges that Defendants knew or should have known that the State would rely on their pronouncements and that this reliance would and did in fact proximately cause injury and damages to the State.

The State's cause of action is premised on the rule that whoever voluntarily undertakes an affirmative course of action for the benefit of another has a duty to exercise reasonable care that the other's person or property will not be injured thereby. Defendants have argued that no Texas court has extended a cause of action under this section of the Restatement to create a "duty" based only on an advertisement. Moreover, Defendants contend that State's claim is deficient because even if there were a duty there was no undertaking for the benefit of the State, the State has not suffered physical harm and has made no allegation of property damage, and finally there is no allegation in the complaint that the State took any action in reliance on Defendants' statements. Because the Court finds that Defendants' first argument is valid, the Court need not address its subsequent contentions.

D. FRAUD/MISREPRESENTATION

The State alleges in Counts Twelve and Thirteen actual and constructive common law fraud as well as simple and gross negligent misrepresentations. Defendants argue that the State has failed to adequately allege that Defendants made any material representations that induced the State to act.

The elements of fraud under Texas law are (1) a material representation; (2) the representation was false; (3) when it was made the speaker knew that it was false or made it recklessly without any knowledge of the truth but as a positive assertion; (4) he made it with the intention that it should be acted upon by the party; (5) the party acted in reliance upon the representation; (6) the party thereby suffered injury. [Citation.]

In addressing this challenge to the sufficiency of the State's pleading of fraud, the Court bears in mind the Supreme Court's admonition that a complaint should not be dismissed for failure to state a claim unless it appears beyond doubt that the plaintiff can prove no set of facts in support of his claim which would entitle him to relief. Under this standard, the Court is not convinced that the State can prove no set of facts that would constitute a material representation on the part of Defendants that would entitle the State to recover. Therefore, the Court denies Defendants' Motion to Dismiss with respect to Counts Twelve and Thirteen.

IV.   CONCLUSION

The Court dismisses the State's claims for violation of the federal and state antitrust laws; the Texas deceptive trade Practices–Consumer Protection Act; restitution/unjust enrichment; public nuisance; and, negligent performance of a voluntary undertaking. Defendants' motions to dismiss in all other respects are denied.

———

REPLACE note **7. Settlement Classes**, page 983, with **Amchem Products Inc. v. Windsor**, 117 S.Ct. 2231 (1997), as a new principal case.

Amchem Products, Inc. v. Windsor

Supreme Court of the United States, 1997.
521 U.S. 591, 117 S.Ct. 2231, 138 L.Ed.2d 689.

■ JUSTICE GINSBURG delivered the opinion of the Court.

This case concerns the legitimacy under Rule 23 of the Federal Rules of Civil Procedure of a class-action certification sought to achieve global settlement of current and future asbestos-related claims. The class proposed for certification potentially encompasses hundreds of thousands, perhaps millions, of individuals tied together by this commonality: each was, or some day may be, adversely affected by past exposure to asbestos products manufactured by one or more of 20 companies. Those companies, defendants in the lower courts, are petitioners here. The United States District Court for the Eastern District of Pennsylvania certified the class for settlement only, finding that the proposed settlement was fair and that representation and notice had been adequate. That court enjoined class members from separately pursuing asbestos-related personal-injury suits in any court, federal or state, pending the issuance of a final order. The Court of Appeals for the Third Circuit vacated the District Court's orders, holding that the class certification failed to satisfy Rule 23's requirements in several critical respects. We affirm the Court of Appeals' judgment.

I

A

The settlement-class certification we confront evolved in response to an asbestos-litigation crisis. See Georgine v. Amchem Products, Inc., 83 F.3d 610, 618, and n. 2 (3d Cir. 1996) (citing commentary). A United States Judicial Conference Ad Hoc Committee on Asbestos Litigation, appointed by the Chief Justice in September 1990, described facets of the problem in a 1991 report:

> [This] is a tale of danger known in the 1930s, exposure inflicted upon millions of Americans in the 1940s and 1950s, injuries that began to take their toll in the 1960s, and a flood of lawsuits beginning in the 1970s. On the basis of past and current filing data, and because of a latency period that may last as long as 40 years for some asbestos related diseases, a continuing stream of claims can be expected. The final toll of asbestos related injuries is unknown. Predictions have been made of 200,000 asbestos disease deaths before the year 2000 and as many as 265,000 by the year 2015. "The most objectionable aspects of asbestos litigation can be briefly summarized: dockets in both federal and state courts continue to grow; long delays are routine; trials are too long; the same issues are litigated over and over; transaction costs exceed the victims' recovery by nearly two to one; exhaustion of assets threatens and distorts the process; and future claimants may lose altogether. Report of The Judicial Conference Ad Hoc Committee on Asbestos Litigation 2–3 (Mar.1991)."

Real reform, the report concluded, required federal legislation creating a national asbestos dispute-resolution scheme. [Citation.] As recommended by the Ad Hoc Committee, the Judicial Conference of the United States urged Congress to act. See Report of the Proceedings of the Judicial Conference of the United States 33 (Mar. 12, 1991). To this date, no congressional response has emerged.

In the face of legislative inaction, the federal courts—lacking authority to replace state tort systems with a national toxic tort compensation regime—endeavored to work with the procedural tools available to improve management of federal asbestos litigation. Eight federal judges, experienced in the superintendence of asbestos cases, urged the Judicial Panel on Multidistrict Litigation (MDL Panel), to consolidate in a single district all asbestos complaints then pending in federal courts. Accepting the recommendation, the MDL Panel transferred all asbestos cases then filed, but not yet on trial in federal courts to a single district, the United States District Court for the Eastern District of Pennsylvania; pursuant to the transfer order, the collected cases were consolidated for pretrial proceedings before

Judge Weiner. [Citation.] The order aggregated pending cases only; no authority resides in the MDL Panel to license for consolidated proceedings claims not yet filed.

B

After the consolidation, attorneys for plaintiffs and defendants formed separate steering committees and began settlement negotiations. Ronald L. Motley and Gene Locks—later appointed, along with Motley's law partner Joseph F. Rice, to represent the plaintiff class in this action—co-chaired the Plaintiffs' Steering Committee. Counsel for the Center for Claims Resolution (CCR), the consortium of 20 former asbestos manufacturers now before us as petitioners, participated in the Defendants' Steering Committee. Although the MDL order collected, transferred, and consolidated only cases already commenced in federal courts, settlement negotiations included efforts to find a "means of resolving ... future cases." [Citations; see also Georgine v. Amchem Products, Inc., 157 F.R.D. 246, 266 (E.D.Pa.1994) ("primary purpose of the settlement talks in the consolidated MDL litigation was to craft a national settlement that would provide an alternative resolution mechanism for asbestos claims," including claims that might be filed in the future)].

In November 1991, the Defendants' Steering Committee made an offer designed to settle all pending and future asbestos cases by providing a fund for distribution by plaintiffs' counsel among asbestos-exposed individuals. The Plaintiffs' Steering Committee rejected this offer, and negotiations fell apart. CCR, however, continued to pursue "a workable administrative system for the handling of future claims." [Citation.] To that end, CCR counsel approached the lawyers who had headed the Plaintiffs' Steering Committee in the unsuccessful negotiations, and a new round of negotiations began; that round yielded the mass settlement agreement now in controversy. At the time, the former heads of the Plaintiffs' Steering Committee represented thousands of plaintiffs with then-pending asbestos-related claims—claimants the parties to this suit call "inventory" plaintiffs. CCR indicated in these discussions that it would resist settlement of inventory cases absent "some kind of protection for the future." [Citation.]

Settlement talks thus concentrated on devising an administrative scheme for disposition of asbestos claims not yet in litigation. In these negotiations, counsel for masses of inventory plaintiffs endeavored to represent the interests of the anticipated future claimants, although those lawyers then had no attorney-client relationship with such claimants. Once negotiations seemed likely to produce an agreement purporting to bind potential plaintiffs, CCR agreed to settle, through separate agreements, the claims of plaintiffs who had already filed asbestos-related lawsuits. In one such agreement, CCR defendants promised to pay more than $200 million to gain release of the claims of numerous inventory plaintiffs. After settling the inventory claims, CCR, together with the plaintiffs' lawyers CCR had approached, launched this case, exclusively involving persons outside the MDL Panel's province—plaintiffs without already pending lawsuits.[3]

C

The class action thus instituted was not intended to be litigated. Rather, within the space of a single day, January 15, 1993, the settling parties—CCR defendants and the representatives of the plaintiff class described below—presented to the District Court a complaint, an answer, a proposed settlement agreement, and a joint motion for conditional class certification.

The complaint identified nine lead plaintiffs, designating them and members of their families as representatives of a class comprising all persons who had not filed an asbestos-related lawsuit against a CCR defendant as of the date the class action commenced, but who [had been occupationally exposed to asbestos-containing products of a CCR defendant or whose spouse or family member had been so exposed.] Untold numbers of individuals may fall within this description. [All named plaintiffs fulfilled the class definition and many alleged currently manifested physical injuries from the exposure.] The complaint delineated no subclasses; all named plaintiffs were designated as representatives of the class as a whole. [Jurisdiction was based on diversity and alleged various claims for relief including negligent and strict liability failure to warn, breach of warranty and enhanced risk and medical monitoring causes of action. Each plaintiff requested unspecified damages in excess of $100,000. The answers denied the principal allegations of the complaint and asserted various affirmative defenses.]

A stipulation of settlement accompanied the pleadings; it proposed to settle, and to preclude nearly all class members from litigating against CCR companies, all claims not filed before January 15, 1993, involving compensation for present and future asbestos-related personal injury or death. An exhaustive document exceeding 100 pages, the stipulation presents in detail an administrative mechanism and a schedule of payments to compensate class members who meet defined asbestos-exposure and medical requirements. The stipulation describes four categories of compensable disease: mesothelioma; lung cancer; certain "other cancers" (colon-rectal, laryngeal, esophageal, and stomach cancer); and "non-malignant conditions" (asbestosis and bilateral pleural thickening). * * * For each qualifying disease category, the stipulation specifies the range of damages CCR will pay to qualifying claimants. Payments under the settlement are not adjustable for inflation. Mesothelioma claimants—the most highly compensated category—are scheduled to receive between $20,000 and $200,000. [The stipulation] also establishes procedures to resolve disputes over medical diagnoses and levels of compensation [which may be obtained over the ranges in

3. It is basic to comprehension of this proceeding to notice that no transferred case is included in the settlement at issue, and no case covered by the settlement existed as a civil action at the time of the MDL Panel transfer.

limited circumstances.] But the settlement places both numerical caps and dollar limits on such claims. [The number of claims payable for each disease in a given year is also capped. Certain claims are not compensable at all even if otherwise applicable state law recognizes them. Non-compensable claims include all loss of consortium claims, "exposure-only" claimants' increased risk of cancer, fear of future injury and medical monitoring claims, and all "pleural" claims, which might be asserted by persons with asbestos-related plaques on their lungs but no accompanying physical impairment, are also excluded.] Although not entitled to present compensation, exposure-only claimants and pleural claimants may qualify for benefits when and if they develop a compensable disease and meet the relevant exposure and medical criteria. Defendants forgo defenses to liability, including statute of limitations pleas.

Class members, in the main, are bound by the settlement in perpetuity, while CCR defendants may choose to withdraw from the settlement after ten years. A small number of class members—only a few per year—may reject the settlement and pursue their claims in court. Those permitted to exercise this option, however, may not assert any punitive damages claim or any claim for increased risk of cancer. Aspects of the administration of the settlement are to be monitored by the AFL–CIO and class counsel. Class counsel are to receive attorneys' fees in an amount to be approved by the District Court.

D

[In 1993, the District Court conditionally certified an encompassing opt-out class under Federal Rule of Civil Procedure 23(b)(3). The court conducted fairness hearings at which objectors claimed, inter alia, that the settlement unfairly disadvantaged those with currently compensable conditions and that the compensation levels were intolerably low compared to awards available in litigation or paid to the inventory plaintiffs. The court found the settlement terms fair, negotiated in good faith, and the prerequisites of Rule 23 fulfilled. Vigorous objections had been raised to the adequacy of representation requirement of Rule 23(a)(4) because of purported class counsel conflicts of interests as between the different classes of claimants. The trial court disagreed and the objectors appealed. The Court of Appeals for the Third Circuit vacated the certification, holding that the requirements of Rule 23 had not been satisfied. See Georgine v. Amchem Products, Inc., 83 F.3d 610 (3d Cir. 1996)].

E

[The Court of Appeals first declined to address the serious jurisdictional challenges, of justiciability, subject-matter jurisdiction, and adequate notice, concluding that the class certification issues were dispositive. On class-action prerequisites, the Court of Appeals referred to its earlier opinion, In re General Motors Corp. Pick–Up Truck Fuel Tank Prods. Liab. Litig., 55 F.3d 768 (3d Cir. 1995), which held that although a class action may be certified for settlement purposes only, Rule 23(a)'s requirements must be satisfied as if the case were going to be litigated. While stating that the requirements of Rule 23(a) and (b)(3) must be met "without taking into account the settlement," the Court of Appeals in fact closely considered the terms of the settlement as it examined aspects of the case under Rule 23 criteria. The Court of Appeals recognized that Rule 23(a)(2)'s "commonality" requirement is superseded by the more stringent Rule 23(b)(3) "predominance" requirement and focussed its analysis there. While recognizing that the harmfulness of asbestos exposure was a common factor, the court of appeals concluded that "uncommon questions abounded," including the wide variety of asbestos-containing products to which the claimants were exposed in different ways, causing different injuries. Governing state law also varied widely on critical issues, leading the Third Circuit to conclude that uncommon issues predominated.]

[The Court of Appeals next concluded that the adequacy of representation requirement of Rule 23(a)(4) had not been met. Adverting to, but not resolving charges of attorney conflict of interests, the Third Circuit rejected the District Court's conclusion that the named class representatives would adequately advance the interests of all members simply because they were sufficiently united in their desire for a maximum recovery. The court of appeals found a wide divergence of interests between the exposure only plaintiffs and those who had already manifested injury. The Court of Appeals, therefore, also rejected the District Court's finding of typicality under Rule 23(a)(3) and superiority of the class under Rule 23(b)(3), suggesting that "a series of statewide or more narrowly defined adjudications" would be preferable. We granted certiorari, and now affirm.]

II

Objectors assert in this Court, as they did in the District Court and Court of Appeals, an array of jurisdictional barriers. [The Third Circuit declined to address these issues because they "would not exist but for the [class action] certification." The class certification issues are dispositive, and because their resolution here is logically antecedent to the existence of any Article III issues, it is appropriate to reach them first.] We therefore follow the path taken by the Court of Appeals, mindful that Rule 23's requirements must be interpreted in keeping with Article III constraints, and with the Rules Enabling Act, which instructs that rules of procedure "shall not abridge, enlarge or modify any substantive right," 28 U.S.C. § 2072(b), [citation.]

III

To place this controversy in context, we briefly describe the characteristics of class actions for which the Federal Rules provide. Rule 23, governing federal-court class actions, stems from equity practice and gained its current shape in an innovative 1966 revision. See generally Kaplan, Continuing Work of the Civil Committee: 1966 Amendments of the Federal

Rules of Civil Procedure (I), 81 Harv. L.Rev. 356, 375–400 (1967) (hereinafter Kaplan, Continuing Work). Rule 23(a) states four threshold requirements applicable to all class actions: (1) numerosity (a "class [so large] that joinder of all members is impracticable"); (2) commonality ("questions of law or fact common to the class"); (3) typicality (named parties' claims or defenses "are typical . . . of the class"); and (4) adequacy of representation (representatives "will fairly and adequately protect the interests of the class").

In addition to satisfying Rule 23(a)'s prerequisites, parties seeking class certification must show that the action is maintainable under Rule 23(b)(1), (2), or (3). [Rule 23 can be found in its entirety in the text at page 965. Eds.] In the 1966 class-action amendments, Rule 23(b)(3), the category at issue here, was "the most adventuresome" innovation. [Citation.] Rule 23(b)(3) added to the complex-litigation arsenal class actions for damages designed to secure judgments binding all class members save those who affirmatively elected to be excluded. See 7A Wright, Miller & Kane, Federal Practice and Procedure § 1777; [citation.]

Framed for situations in which "class-action treatment is not as clearly called for" as it is in Rule 23(b)(1) and (b)(2) situations, Rule 23(b)(3) permits certification where class suit "may nevertheless be convenient and desirable." Adv. Comm. Notes. To qualify for certification under Rule 23(b)(3), a class must meet two requirements beyond the Rule 23(a) prerequisites: Common questions must "predominate over any questions affecting only individual members"; and class resolution must be "superior to other available methods for the fair and efficient adjudication of the controversy." In adding "predominance" and "superiority" to the qualification-for-certification list, the Advisory Committee sought to cover cases "in which a class action would achieve economies of time, effort, and expense, and promote . . . uniformity of decision as to persons similarly situated, without sacrificing procedural fairness or bringing about other undesirable results." Sensitive to the competing tugs of individual autonomy for those who might prefer to go it alone or in a smaller unit, on the one hand, and systemic efficiency on the other, the Reporter for the 1966 amendments cautioned: "The new provision invites a close look at the case before it is accepted as a class action. . . . " Kaplan, Continuing Work at 390.

Rule 23(b)(3) includes a nonexhaustive list of factors pertinent to a court's "close look" at the predominance and superiority criteria: [see casebook p. 966.] In setting out these factors, the Advisory Committee for the 1966 reform anticipated that in each case, courts would "consider the interests of individual members of the class in controlling their own litigations and carrying them on as they see fit." Adv. Comm. Notes. They elaborated:

> The interests of individuals in conducting separate lawsuits may be so strong as to call for denial of a class action. On the other hand, these interests may be theoretic rather than practical; the

class may have a high degree of cohesion and prosecution of the action through representatives would be quite unobjectionable, or the amounts at stake for individuals may be so small that separate suits would be impracticable.

[The Third Circuit observed in the instant case that "[e]ach [personal injury] plaintiff has a significant interest in individually controlling the prosecution of [his case]." While the Rule does not exclude by its terms personal injury actions in which damages might be high, the Advisory Committee had dominantly in mind vindication of "the rights of groups of people who individually would be without effective strength to bring their opponents into court at all." The Rule also requires individual notice of the "opt out" right in (b)(3) classes. Eisen v. Carlisle and Jacquelin, 417 U.S. 156, 173–77 (1974).]

In the decades since the 1966 revision of Rule 23, class action practice has become ever more "adventuresome" as a means of coping with claims too numerous to secure their "just, speedy, and inexpensive determination" one by one. F.R.C.P. 1. The development reflects concerns about the efficient use of court resources and the conservation of funds to compensate claimants who do not line up early in a litigation queue. [Citations.] Among current applications of Rule 23(b)(3), the "settlement only" class has become a stock device. [Citations.] Although all Federal Circuits recognize the utility of Rule 23(b)(3) settlement classes, courts have divided on the extent to which a proffered settlement affects court surveillance under Rule 23's certification criteria. * * * A proposed amendment to Rule 23 would authorize settlement class certifications even though the requirements of 23(b)(3) might not otherwise be met. The Committee has not yet acted on the matter. We consider the certification at issue under the rule as it is currently framed.

IV

We granted review to decide the role settlement may play, under existing Rule 23, in determining the propriety of class certification. The Third Circuit's opinion stated that each of the requirements of Rule 23(a) and (b)(3) "must be satisfied without taking into account the settlement." That statement, petitioners urge, is incorrect.

We agree with petitioners to this limited extent: settlement is relevant to a class certification. The Third Circuit's opinion bears modification in that respect. But, as we earlier observed, the Court of Appeals in fact did not ignore the settlement; instead, that court honed in on settlement terms in explaining why it found the absentees' interests inadequately represented. The Third Circuit's close inspection of the settlement in that regard was altogether proper.

Confronted with a request for settlement-only class certification, a district court need not inquire whether the case, if tried, would present intractable management problems, for the proposal is that there be no trial. But other specifications of the rule—those designed to protect absentees by blocking unwarranted or overbroad class definitions—demand undiluted, even heightened, attention in the settlement context. Such attention is of vital importance, for a court asked to certify a settlement class will lack the opportunity, present when a case is litigated, to adjust the class, informed by the proceedings as they unfold.

And, of overriding importance, courts must be mindful that the rule as now composed sets the requirements they are bound to enforce. Federal Rules take effect after an extensive deliberative process involving many reviewers: a Rules Advisory Committee, public commenters, the Judicial Conference, this Court, the Congress. See 28 U.S.C. §§ 2073, 2074. The text of a rule thus proposed and reviewed limits judicial inventiveness. Courts are not free to amend a rule outside the process Congress ordered, a process properly tuned to the instruction that rules of procedure "shall not abridge . . . any substantive right." § 2072(b).

Rule 23(e), on settlement of class actions, reads in its entirety: "A class action shall not be dismissed or compromised without the approval of the court, and notice of the proposed dismissal or compromise shall be given to all members of the class in such manner as the court directs." This prescription was designed to function as an additional requirement, not a superseding direction, for the "class action" to which Rule 23(e) refers is one qualified for certification under Rule 23(a) and (b). [Citation.] Subdivisions (a) and (b) focus court attention on whether a proposed class has sufficient unity so that absent members can fairly be bound by decisions of class representatives. That dominant concern persists when settlement, rather than trial, is proposed.

The safeguards provided by the Rule 23(a) and (b) class-qualifying criteria, we emphasize, are not impractical impediments—checks shorn of utility—in the settlement class context. First, the standards set for the protection of absent class members serve to inhibit appraisals of the chancellor's foot kind—class certifications dependent upon the court's gestalt judgment or overarching impression of the settlement's fairness. Second, if a fairness inquiry under Rule 23(e) controlled certification, eclipsing Rule 23(a) and (b), and permitting class designation despite the impossibility of litigation, both class counsel and court would be disarmed. Class counsel confined to settlement negotiations could not use the threat of litigation to press for a better offer, [citations], and the court would face a bargain proffered for its approval without benefit of adversarial investigation, [citation].

Federal courts, in any case, lack authority to substitute for Rule 23's certification criteria a standard never adopted—that if a settlement is "fair," then certification is proper. Applying to this case criteria the rulemakers set, we conclude that the Third Circuit's appraisal is essentially correct. Although that court should have acknowledged that settlement is a factor in the calculus, a remand is not warranted on that account. The Court of Appeals' opinion amply demonstrates why—with or without a settlement on the table—the sprawling class the District Court certified does not satisfy Rule 23's requirements.

A

We address first the requirement of Rule 23(b)(3) that "[common] questions of law or fact ... predominate over any questions affecting only individual members." The District Court concluded that predominance was satisfied based on two factors: class members' shared experience of asbestos exposure and their common [desire to be compensated fairly, with little risk and cost.] The settling parties also contend that the settlement's fairness is a common question, predominating over disparate legal issues that might be pivotal in litigation but become irrelevant under the settlement.

The predominance requirement stated in Rule 23(b)(3), we hold, is not met by the factors on which the District Court relied. The benefits asbestos-exposed persons might gain from the establishment of a grand-scale compensation scheme is a matter fit for legislative consideration, but it is not pertinent to the predominance inquiry. That inquiry trains on the legal or factual questions that qualify each class member's case as a genuine controversy, questions that preexist any settlement.

The Rule 23(b)(3) predominance inquiry tests whether proposed classes are sufficiently cohesive to warrant adjudication by representation. [Citations] The inquiry appropriate under Rule 23(e), on the other hand, protects unnamed class members "from unjust or unfair settlements affecting their rights when the representatives become fainthearted before the action is adjudicated or are able to secure satisfaction of their individual claims by a compromise." [Citation.] But it is not the mission of Rule 23(e) to assure the class cohesion that legitimizes representative action in the first place. If a common interest in a fair compromise could satisfy the predominance requirement of Rule 23(b)(3), that vital prescription would be stripped of any meaning in the settlement context.

The District Court also relied upon th[e commonality of shared asbestos exposure by defendants' products.] Even if Rule 23(a)'s commonality requirement may be satisfied by that shared experience, the predominance criterion is far more demanding. [Citation.] Given the greater number of questions peculiar to the several categories of class members, and to individuals within each category, and the significance of those uncommon questions, any overarching dispute about the health consequences of asbestos exposure cannot satisfy [Rule 23(b)(3)'s predominance requirement. The disparate questions undermining class cohesion and defeating predominance include the different time, manner and amount of exposures to different products producing widely varying injuries, particularly regarding the exposure-only plaintiffs who may never contract asbestos-related disease.] Differences in state law, the Court of Appeals observed, compound these disparities. Phillips Petroleum Co. v. Shutts, 472 U.S. 797, 823 (1985).

No settlement class called to our attention is as sprawling as this one. [Citation.] Predominance is a test readily met in certain cases alleging consumer or securities fraud or violations of the antitrust laws. [Citation.] Even mass tort cases arising from a common cause or disaster may, depending upon the circumstances, satisfy the predominance requirement. The Advisory Committee for the 1966 revision of Rule 23, it is true, noted that "mass accident" cases are likely to present "significant questions, not only of damages but of liability and defenses of liability, . . . affecting the individuals in different ways." And the Committee advised that such cases are "ordinarily not appropriate" for class treatment. But the text of the rule does not categorically exclude mass tort cases from class certification, and district courts, since the late 1970s, have been certifying such cases in increasing number. [Citation.] The Committee's warning, however, continues to call for caution when individual stakes are high and disparities among class members great. As the Third Circuit's opinion makes plain, the certification in this case does not follow the counsel of caution. That certification cannot be upheld, for it rests on a conception of Rule 23(b)(3)'s predominance requirement irreconcilable with the rule's design.

B

Nor can the class approved by the District Court satisfy Rule 23(a)(4)'s requirement that the named parties "will fairly and adequately protect the interests of the class." The adequacy inquiry under Rule 23(a)(4) serves to uncover conflicts of interest between named parties and the class they seek to represent. See General Telephone Co. of Southwest v. Falcon, 457 U.S. 147, 157–158 (1982). "[A] class representative must be part of the class and 'possess the same interest and suffer the same injury' as the class members." East Tex. Motor Freight System, Inc. v. Rodriguez, 431 U.S. 395, 403 (1977).

As the Third Circuit pointed out, named parties with diverse medical conditions sought to act on behalf of a single giant class rather than on behalf of discrete subclasses. In significant respects, the interests of those within the single class are not aligned. Most saliently, for the currently injured, the critical goal is generous immediate payments. That goal tugs against the interest of exposure-only plaintiffs in ensuring an ample, inflation-protected fund for the future. [Citation. The adequacy of defendants' assets to pay the claims, despite the disparity between those claims, does not render the disparity insignificant.] Although this is not a "limited fund" case certified under Rule 23(b)(1)(B), the terms of the settlement reflect essential allocation decisions designed to confine compensation and to limit defendants' liability. For example, * * * the settlement includes no adjustment for inflation; only a few claimants per year can opt out at the back end; and loss-of-consortium claims are extinguished with no compensation.

The settling parties, in sum, achieved a global compromise with no structural assurance of fair and adequate representation for the diverse groups and individuals affected. Although the named parties alleged a range of complaints, each served generally as representative for the whole, not for a separate constituency. In an asbestos class action, the Second Circuit spoke precisely to this point: "[W]here differences among members of a class are such that subclasses must be established, we know of no authority that permits a court to approve a settlement without creating subclasses on the basis of consents by members of a unitary class, some of whom happen to be members of the distinct subgroups. . . . [T]he adversity among subgroups requires that the members of each subgroup cannot be bound to a settlement except by consents given by those who understand that their role is to represent solely the members of their respective subgroups." In re Joint E. & S. Dist. Asbestos Litig., 982 F.2d 721, 742–743 (2d Cir. 1992). The Third Circuit found no assurance here—either in the terms of the settlement or in the structure of the negotiations—that the named plaintiffs operated under a proper understanding of their representational responsibilities. That assessment, we conclude, is on the mark.

C

Impediments to the provision of adequate notice, the Third Circuit emphasized, rendered highly problematic any endeavor to tie to a settlement class persons with no perceptible asbestos-related disease at the time of the settlement. [Citation.] Many persons in the exposure-only category, the Court of Appeals stressed, may not even know of their exposure, or realize the extent of the harm they may incur. Even if they fully appreciate the significance of class notice, those without current afflictions may not have the information or foresight needed to decide, intelligently, whether to stay in or opt out.

Family members of asbestos-exposed individuals may themselves fall prey to disease or may ultimately have ripe claims for loss of consortium. Yet large numbers of people in this category—future spouses and children of asbestos victims—could not be alerted to their class membership. And current spouses and children of the occupationally exposed may know nothing of that exposure. Because we have concluded that the class in this case cannot satisfy the requirements of common issue predominance and adequacy of representation, we need not rule, definitively, on the notice given here. In accord with the Third Circuit, however, we recognize the gravity of the question whether class action notice sufficient under the Constitution and Rule 23 could ever be given to legions so unselfconscious and amorphous.

V

The argument is sensibly made that a nationwide administrative claims processing regime would provide the most secure, fair, and efficient means of compensating victims of asbestos exposure. Congress, however, has not adopted such a solution. And Rule 23, which must be interpreted with fidelity to the Rules Enabling Act and applied with the interests of absent class members in close view, cannot carry the large load CCR, class counsel, and the District Court heaped upon it. As this case exemplifies, the rulemakers' prescriptions for class actions may be endangered by "those

111

who embrace [Rule 23] too enthusiastically just as [they are by] those who approach [the rule] with distaste." [Wright, Law of Federal Courts at 508. The judgment of the Third Circuit is Affirmed.]

Justice BREYER, with whom Justice STEVENS joins, concurring in part and dissenting in part. Although I agree with the Court's basic holding that "settlement is relevant to a class certification," I find several problems in its approach that lead me to a different conclusion. First, I believe that the need for settlement in this mass tort case, with hundreds of thousands of lawsuits, is greater than the Court's opinion suggests. Second, I would give more weight than would the majority to settlement-related issues for purposes of determining whether common issues predominate. Third, I am uncertain about the Court's determination of adequacy of representation, and do not believe it appropriate for this Court to second-guess the District Court on the matter without first having the Court of Appeals consider it. Fourth, I am uncertain about the tenor of an opinion that seems to suggest the settlement is unfair. And fifth, in the absence of further review by the Court of Appeals, I cannot accept the majority's suggestions that "notice" is inadequate.

* * *

NOTES

After *Amchem Products*, another asbestos settlement class which had been on appeal to the Supreme Court was remanded for action consistent with *Amchem Products*. In In re Asbestos Litig., 90 F.3d 963 (5th Cir. 1996), the Court of Appeals had upheld the certification of a settlement class under Rule 23(b)(1)(B), the limited fund provision, against one defendant, Fibreboard. After *Amchem Products*, the Court of Appeals affirmed its holding, concluding that *Amchem Products* did not require decertification because of the difference between a Rule 23(b)(1) current and future injury plaintiffs class and a Rule 23(b)(3) future plaintiffs only class. In re Asbestos Litig., 134 F.3d 668 (5th Cir. 1998). The Supreme Court reversed sub nom. in Ortiz v. Fibreboard, 1999 WL 412604, holding that certification of a limited fund class required a showing that the fund is limited *independently* of the settlement agreement, and that proposed class members would be unconflicted and equitably treated. The Court concluded that neither showing had been made in the case.

For a discussion of the continuing viability of class actions, both litigation and settlement, post-*Amchem Products*, see Davis, Toward the Proper Role for Mass Tort Class Actions, 77 Ore. L. Rev. 101 (1998).

B. CLASS ACTION MANAGEMENT

REPLACE the United States District Court opinion in **Cimino v. Raymark Industries, Inc.**, on page 985, with the following Fifth Circuit Court of Appeals opinion in the case.

Cimino v. Raymark Industries, Inc.

United States Court of Appeals, Fifth Circuit, 1998.
151 F.3d 297.

■ GARWOOD, CIRCUIT JUDGE:

Before us are appeals and cross-appeals in personal injury and wrongful death damage suits against several manufacturers of asbestos-containing insulation products and some of their suppliers, the district court's jurisdiction being based on diversity of citizenship and the governing substantive law being that of Texas. This is the same set of cases addressed in In re Fibreboard, 893 F.2d 706 (5th Cir.1990), but the judgments now before us result from a trial plan modified following that decision. [The opinion in which the modified trial plan is more particularly set out is in the casebook at page 985.] Principally at issue on this appeal is the validity of that modified trial plan.

The district court originally consolidated the some 3,031 such cases then pending in the Beaumont Division of the Eastern District of Texas for trial of certain common issues under Fed.R.Civ.P. 42(a) and also certified a class action under Fed.R.Civ.P. 23(b)(3), the class generally consisting of the insulation and construction workers, their survivors and household members, who were plaintiffs in those pending cases. As explained in more detail below, the trial plan ultimately implemented after *Fibreboard* consisted of three phases, generally described as follows. Phase I comprised a complete jury trial of the entire individual cases of the ten class representatives and also a class-wide determination of issues of product defectiveness, warning, and punitive damages (including a multiplier as to each defendant). Phase II, which was to address exposure on a craft and job site basis, was dispensed with on the basis of a stipulation. In phase III, 160 different individual cases ("sample cases"), some from each of the five different allegedly asbestos-related diseases included in the entire group of underlying cases, were tried to two other juries to determine only each of those individual sample case plaintiffs' respective actual damages from their asbestos-related disease. Thereafter, and following a one-day bench hearing on the basis of which the district court determined that in each disease category the 160 sample cases were reliably representative of the cases involving the like disease among the remaining some 2,128 cases, the court ruled that each of these remaining 2,128 cases (the "extrapolation cases") would be assigned by the court to one of the five disease categories and each would be entitled to judgment based on an amount of actual damages equal to the average of the verdicts rendered in those of the 160 sample cases involving the same disease category. Punitive damages in each case would be essentially based on the phase I verdict.

113

By the time of the phase I trial, many of the defendants had settled and others had taken bankruptcy or otherwise been disposed of, so only five remained, namely appellant Pittsburgh Corning Corporation (Pittsburgh Corning), Carey Canada, Celotex, Fibreboard, and [Asbestos Corporation, Limited (ACL) whose case was tried to the court under the Foreign Sovereign Immunities Act, 28 U.S.C. §§ 1330(a), 1603(b).] By the time the amount of the extrapolation case judgments was to be calculated, all defendants except Pittsburgh Corning and ACL had passed out of the case.

* * * Judgment was actually entered against Pittsburgh Corning in a total of 157 cases, consisting of 9 of the class representative phase I cases, 143 of the phase III sample cases, and 5 of the extrapolation cases (1 from each of the 5 different diseases included in the class). In these 157 cases, Pittsburgh Corning has been cast in judgment for a total of approximately $69,000,000.[6] [Only Pittsburgh Corning's appeals are presented in this excerpted opinion. The issues addressed here challenge the implemented *Cimino* trial plan as a whole, particularly its asserted failure to properly try and determine individual causation and, in the five extrapolation cases, damages also, as to any plaintiffs other than the class representatives, assertedly contrary to our decision in *Fibreboard* and Texas substantive law and in derogation of Pittsburgh Corning's Seventh Amendment and Due Process rights.]

1.   Trial Plan

Initial Plan

The *Cimino* trial plan initially adopted by the district court, which we subsequently set aside in *Fibreboard*, also called for three phases. In phase I, the jury would decide which, if any, of each defendant's products were defective as marketed and unreasonably dangerous, when each defendant knew or should have known workers or their household members were at risk, whether each defendant was guilty of gross negligence in marketing its offending product and, as to each defendant so guilty, a punitive damages multiplier. In phase II, the same jury would decide the percentage of plaintiffs in the class exposed to each defendant's products, the percentage of claims barred by limitations and other defenses, and would determine a lump sum amount of actual damages for each disease category for all plaintiffs in the class. The jury in this phase would also make a full determination of liability and damages with respect to each of the eleven class representatives individually. And the jury in phase II would also hear such evidence as the parties desired to present from up to thirty other illustrative plaintiffs, fifteen chosen by the defense and fifteen by plaintiffs, as well as expert testimony regarding the total actual damages of the class, such expert testimony to be based, among other things, on questionnaires filled out by all class members and other discovery, including forty-five-minute oral depositions of class members taken by defendants. In phase III, to be non-jury, the court would distribute the awarded damages among the individual class members.

---

6. Pittsburgh Corning asserts, without dispute, that the orders for judgment in the remaining some 2,123 extrapolation cases (in which judgments have not been entered) call for judgments against Pittsburgh Corning in the approximate total amount of $1,300,000,-000 for actual damages only, excluding prejudgment interest and punitive damages.

In *Fibreboard*, we found "no impediment to the trial of Phase I," but held the balance of the plan invalid, stating:

> It infringes upon the dictates of *Erie* that we remain faithful to the law of Texas, and upon the separation of powers between the judicial and legislative branches. Texas has made its policy choices in defining the duty owed by manufacturers and suppliers of products to consumers. These choices are reflected in the requirement that a plaintiff prove both causation and damage. In Texas, it is a 'fundamental principle of traditional products liability law ... that the plaintiffs must prove that the defendant supplied the product which caused the injury.' These elements focus upon individuals, not groups. The same may be said, and with even greater confidence, of wage losses, pain and suffering, and other elements of compensation. These requirements of proof define the duty of the manufacturers.

> [The trial court's procedure focuses not on individual causation, but ultimately accepts general causation as sufficient and is, therefore,] contrary to Texas law. It is evident that these statistical estimates deal only with general causation, for 'population-based probability estimates do not speak to a probability of causation in any one case; the estimate of relative risk is a property of the studied population, not of an individual's case.' This type of procedure does not allow proof that a particular defendant's asbestos 'really' caused a particular plaintiff's disease; the only 'fact' that can be proved is that in most cases the defendant's asbestos would have been the cause. Id. at 711–712.[9]

Present Plan

Following this Court's decision in *Fibreboard*, the district court initially determined that "[t]his case will now proceed under the procedures set out in *Jenkins v. Raymark* "—i.e. phase I to be followed by a series of minitrials for all plaintiffs on their individual causation and damage issues— and set its previously adopted phase I (which we had declined to block) for trial. The court observed that its "task appears to be insurmountable," but stated that it would nonetheless "take[] its place behind the old mule and start down that long row."

Some months later, however, the court changed its mind and adopted the trial plan now before us (except that a stipulation was ultimately utilized instead of phase II), observing:

> Phase One will leave unresolved the questions of exposure, comparative causation, and damages. These remaining questions could easily be resolved by the procedure established in *Jenkins* if the numbers were manageable. The numbers are not manageable. *Jenkins* envisioned groupings of ten plaintiffs submitted to a succession of juries. If we could try one group a week, the process would take 4 1/2 years. Additional judicial power and the utilization of multiple courtrooms could shorten the time to resolve all these cases, but it would

---

9. We also stated:

Finally, it is questionable whether defendants' right to trial by jury is being faithfully honored, but we need not explore this issue. It is sufficient now to conclude that Phase II cannot go forward without changing Texas law and usurping legislative prerogatives, a step federal courts lack authority to take. Id. at 712.

115

not decrease total court time or attorney time. Transaction costs to the parties under the *Jenkins* procedure is unacceptable.

Instead of utilizing the *Jenkins* procedure, the court determined to employ new phases II and III: "asking the jury in Phase Two to make findings on exposure that are specific to job site, craft and time; and then by submitting to a jury in Phase Three individual damage cases of a statistically significant, randomly selected sample from each of the five disease categories." For purposes of phase II, twenty-two different work-sites [including refineries, shipyards, and chemical plants in several Texas and Louisiana communities] would be considered. The district court contemplated that the phase II jury (the same jury as in phase I) would [hear evidence concerning (a) the presence of the defendants' products at the worksites; (b) the presence of asbestos dust at the worksites; and (c) the nature of the various crafts at the worksites and the relationship between these crafts and the presence of asbestos dust at these facilities. The jury was to make a determination as to which crafts at the worksites were exposed to which defendants' asbestos products (if any) for a sufficient period of time to cause injury, and during which decades the exposure took place. The trial judge was to make a determination as to which plaintiffs worked for long enough to be considered members of the different worksite groups.]

In Phase III, two other juries would determine for 160 sample cases only "two damage issues," namely "(e) whether the Plaintiffs suffered from an asbestos-related injury or disease and, if so, (b) what damages the Plaintiffs incurred." The court ultimately determined, based on information from plaintiffs, that the entire class of 2,298 cases could be broken down into the 5 disease categories, and the court then randomly selected 160 sample cases, some from each disease category, as follows:

Disease	Number of Sample Cases	Number of Cases in class
Mesothelioma	15	32
Lung Cancer	25	186
Other Cancers	20	58
Asbestosis	50	1,050
Pleural Disease	50	972
Total	160	2,298

Individual judgment would be entered in each of the 160 sample cases based on the phase III verdict in that particular sample case. After phase III, the district court would assign each of the remaining 2,298 cases to one of the 5 disease categories, and in each case make an award of actual damages equal to the average of the awards in the phase III cases involving the same disease.

Phase I

The phase I trial lasted approximately eight weeks. [The jury found in answer to the first four questions when the defendants knew or should have known that their "asbestos-containing insulation products" posed a risk of asbestos-related disease. Pittsburgh Corning knew or should have known this since 1962 (when it first entered the business; it left it in 1972); the other three defendants since 1935 as to insulators and since 1955 as to other crafts; all four defendants as to household members since 1965. The jury found that, since 1962 as to Pittsburgh Corning and since 1935 as to the other defendants, the defendants' products "were defective and unreasonably dangerous as a result of not having an adequate warning." The jury found each defendant guilty of gross negligence warranting punitive damages and assigned a punitive damages multiplier of $3.00 per $1.00 of actual damages to Pittsburgh Corning, $2.00 to Celotex, and $1.50 each to Fibreboard and Carey Canada.]

Phase III

Following completion of the phase I trial (and a continuance), the district court proceeded directly into phase III, without any phase II trial. It was not until approximately seven weeks into the phase III trials that the stipulation—which ultimately replaced phase II—was entered into. It was clear from the beginning of, and throughout, the phase III trials that the two juries were not to, and did not, determine whether exposure to any of defendants' products was a cause of the sample plaintiffs' complained-of condition. In phase III the court instructed the jury that they were to assume exposure was sufficient to be a producing cause of all the disease categories. As plaintiffs admit in their brief here, in the phase III trial "the juries were told to assume that the claimants had sufficient exposure." Indeed, for the most part evidence of exposure and its likely or possible results was not allowed. Simply stated, whether there was exposure to Pittsburgh Corning's—or any other defendant's—asbestos, and, if so, whether that exposure was a cause of any of the 160 sample plaintiffs' illness, disease, or damages, was neither litigated nor determined in any of the phase III trials. * * *

Following the phase III jury verdicts (including 12 zero verdicts) in the 160 sample cases, the district court ordered remittiturs in 35 of these cases ("34 of the pulmonary and pleural cases and in one mesothelioma case"), and calculated the average actual damage award, after remittitur (and considering the zero verdicts), in each disease category to be the following: mesothelioma, $1,224,333; lung cancer, $545,200; other cancer, $917,785; asbestosis, $543, 783; pleural disease, $558,900. These were the figures to be applied to the extrapolation cases.

Phase II stipulation

We now turn to the written stipulation * * * which replaced phase II. It was executed by all the plaintiffs and by Pittsburgh Corning, Fibreboard, and Celotex * * * , and was approved "so ordered" by the district court.

Attached to the stipulation as an exhibit was a special verdict form that would consist of separate interrogatories, each with a part (a) and a part (b), one each for each of the twenty-two worksites at issue. For example, question 1(a) would ask "For Worksite No. 1, do you find that the following crafts had sufficient exposure to asbestos during the specified time periods to be a producing cause of the disease of asbestosis." The jury would answer yes or no separately as to each of over fifty listed crafts for each of four specified decades, namely 1942–52, 1952–62, 1962–72, and 1972–82. Question 1(b) would state, "For the crafts and the time periods which were answered 'yes' in question 1(a), causation is apportioned as follows." This question would be answered by stating separately for each listed craft a percentage applicable to each of the current defendants and each of the former defendants who had settled as to each of the same four decades (as to each decade the percentages were to total one hundred percent). This process would be repeated, with questions 2(a) and 2(b), 3(a) and 3(b), and so forth, separately as to each of the remaining worksites.

The stipulation provides in part that [some individuals working at the worksites during each decade from 1942 to 1982 were exposed to asbestos during the course of their employment in an amount of sufficient length and intensity to cause pulmonary asbestosis of varying degrees. Asbestos-containing products of predecessors to Celotex and Fibreboard were present during each of those decades and an asbestos-containing product of Pittsburgh Corning was present from 1962–1982. Further, "The defendants do not stipulate that any members of the various crafts at the various worksites had the same exposure to any products or that any such individuals had the same susceptibility to asbestos-related diseases in the various crafts and worksites." The stipulation provides that if the trial court were to proceed with the Phase II causation trial the jury's verdicts would assign different causation percentages to Pittsburgh Corning, Fibreboard, and Celotex for the different worksite/craft/decade combinations, nevertheless "[defendants] stipulate it shall be deemed that the Phase Two jury" assigned in all instances the following comparative causation shares: Pittsburgh Corning, ten percent; Fibreboard, ten percent; Celotex, ten percent; and Manville Personal Injury Settlement Trust, thirteen percent. The court would use these percentages to fashion judgments in the 160 phase III sample cases and in the extrapolation cases.]

Before setting out these percentages, however, the stipulation had made clear that defendants were not thereby agreeing that the trial plan— either the originally planned phase II or the contemplated extrapolation procedure—was a permissible way to adjudicate their liability and damages. * * * Defendants' reservations of their objections in this respect are * * * reflected in later passages of the stipulation. In paragraph 5 it is stated that "Defendants continue to object to these extrapolation procedures," and paragraph 8 states "Defendants reserve all rights to object to all past and future aspects of the *Cimino* trial plan and to assign as error all prior, present, and future rulings of the Court. [Defendants further confirm the limited nature of the stipulation: 'Without limitation, Defendants do not stipulate that: entry of any judgment based on actual or stipulated Phase Two findings is legally or factually sound; any Defendant in fact has legal responsibility to any individual plaintiff; any individual plaintiff was in fact exposed to injurious quantities of asbestos from the products of any Defendant; the products of any of the Defendants were in fact legal causes of injury to any individual plaintiff; or that any issue framed by the *Cimino* pleadings can be adjudicated on a jobsite or craft-wide basis.' "]

After the stipulation, the phase III trials continued for approximately five more weeks, conducted in all material respects on the same basis and in the same manner as they had been during the some seven weeks before the stipulation was entered into.

Extrapolation

The final phase was that of extrapolation. About a month after completion of the phase III trials, a one-day non-jury hearing was held in which the district court heard evidence concerning the degree to which the 160 sample cases were representative, in their respective disease categories, of the cases in the same disease category among the 2,128 extrapolation cases. Essentially the only evidence at this hearing was the testimony of three expert witnesses called by the plaintiffs [only one of whom was referred to by the trial court in its opinion dealing with extrapolation, Professor Frankewitz. He stated that he was furnished by someone in the offices of plaintiffs' counsel computerized written data reflecting, as to each of the 160 sample cases and each of the 2,128 extrapolation cases, which of the 5 disease categories the case involved, and an answer to each of 12 specific variables pertaining to the particular plaintiff—gender, race, whether living, whether ever smoked, whether was a wage earner (when not specified), age, first year of exposure, last year of exposure, total years of exposure, latency, pack years smoked, trade and predominant craft.] Professor Frankewitz testified that the sample cases in each of the five disease categories were representative of the extrapolation cases in the same disease category "in terms of the variables that I've analyzed," so that, for example, if one were to randomly select another 50 asbestosis cases from the 2,128 extrapolation cases, 99 out of 100 times (98 out of 100 in two minor respects) those 50 cases would have "the same mix of variables" as the 50 asbestosis cases which were a part of the 160 sample phase III cases. Dr. Frankewitz did not select the variables, nor did he determine what those variables were in any of the cases. * * * Similarly, he made no independent judgment as to which disease category any case fit in, but simply was furnished that conclusion by the office of plaintiffs' attorneys. And Dr. Frankewitz was even not sure just what some of the variables meant. When asked what the variable "total years of exposure" meant, he replied "As far as I'm concerned, I believe it's ... I'd be guessing. I would say it's the number of years that an individual was exposed to asbestos in a particular setting, particular situation." * * * He did not calculate "total years of exposure" and when asked who did, said "My belief would be it would be a clerk under the supervision or direction of one of the plaintiffs' attorneys." The district court concluded "that the distribution of variables between the samples and their respective subclasses is comparable."

2. Analysis

As noted, Pittsburgh Corning attacks the *Cimino* trial plan, as it did at all times below, principally on the basis that it fails to properly try and determine individual causation, and in the extrapolation cases also fails to properly try and determine individual damages, as to any plaintiffs other than the ten class representatives whose individual cases were fully tried in phase I. Pittsburgh Corning asserts in this connection, among other things, that these aspects of the trial plan are contrary to *Fibreboard*, impose liability and damages where they would not be imposed under Texas substantive law, and invade its Seventh Amendment and due process rights. Although we do not separately address the due process contention as such, we conclude that the *Cimino* trial plan is invalid in these respects, necessitating reversal of all the phase III sample case judgments as well as the five extrapolation case judgments before us.

We begin by stating some very basic propositions. These personal injury tort actions for monetary damages are "a prototypical example of an action at law, to which the Seventh Amendment applies." Wooddell v. Intern. Broth. of Elec. Workers, 502 U.S. 93 (1991). The Seventh Amendment applies notwithstanding that these are diversity cases. Simler v. Conner, 372 U.S. 221 (1963). [Citation.] But because these are diversity cases, the Rules of Decision Act, 28 U.S.C. § 1652, and Erie R. Co. v. Tompkins, 304 U.S. 64 (1938), with its seeming constitutional underpinning, mandate that the substantive law applied be that of the relevant state, here Texas. Substantive law includes not only the factual elements which must be found to impose liability and fix damages, but also the burdens of going forward with evidence and of persuasion thereon. Palmer v. Hoffman, 318 U.S. 109 (1943); [citation].

None of the foregoing is or can be altered by the utilization of Fed.R.Civ.P. 23(b)(3) or Fed.R.Civ.P. 42(a). As to the Seventh Amendment, the Court in Ross v. Bernhard, 396 U.S. 531 (1970), held that in a stockholders' derivative action seeking monetary relief—now provided for in Fed.R.Civ.P. 23.1—although the right of the stockholders to sue on behalf of the corporation was an equitable matter determinable by the court, the monetary claims of the corporation against the defendants were legal claims to which the Seventh Amendment applied. The Court observed that "The Seventh Amendment question depends on the nature of the issue to be tried rather than the character of the overall action," and "nothing turns now upon the form of the action or the procedural devices by which the parties happen to come before the court." It also noted that it was "inclined to agree with the description" of derivative suits "as one kind of 'true' class action," and that "it now seems settled in the lower federal courts that class action plaintiffs may obtain a jury trial on any legal issues they present." * * *

And, this Court has long held that the applicability of the Seventh Amendment is not altered simply because the case is Rule 23(b)(3) class action. Alabama v. Blue Bird Body Co., Inc., 573 F.2d 309, 318 (5th Cir.1978).[28]

Similarly, use of Rule 23(b)(3) or 42(a) does not alter the required elements which must be found to impose liability and fix damages (or the burden of proof thereon) or the identity of the substantive law—here that of Texas—which determines such elements. We squarely so held in *Fibreboard*. And the Rules Enabling Act, 28 U.S.C. § 2072, likewise mandates that conclusion.

Nor is deviation from these settled principles authorized because these are asbestos cases whose vast numbers swamp the courts. *Fibreboard* clearly so holds. So, also, in Jackson v. Johns–Manville Sales Corp., 750 F.2d 1314 (5th Cir.1985), a diversity asbestos case arising in Mississippi, we declined to adopt a federal common law rule for asbestos cases (or to certify to the United States Supreme Court whether to do so), stating:

... [U]nder our federal system Congress is generally the body responsible for balancing competing interests and setting national policy. There is no doubt that a desperate need exists for federal legislation in the field of asbestos litigation. Congress' silence on the matter, however, hardly authorizes the federal judiciary to assume for itself the responsibility for formulating what essentially are legislative solutions. Displacement of state law is primarily a decision for Congress, and Congress has yet to act....

When, after *Fibreboard*, the district court adopted the present trial plan, it initially justified doing so on the basis of its conclusion that "the Texas Supreme Court, if faced with the facts of this case, would apply a collective liability theory, such as the Court's plan, to an asbestos consolidated action." The court based this conclusion on a passage in Gaulding v. Celotex Corp., 772 S.W.2d 66, 71 (Tex.1989), stating "We are not to be construed as approving or disapproving alternative liability, concert of action, enterprise liability, or market share liability in an appropriate case." We are compelled to reject the district court's conclusion for each of several independently sufficient reasons. To begin with, it is contrary to *Fibreboard*, which plainly holds that under Texas substantive law causation of plaintiff's injury by defendant's product and plaintiff's resultant damages must be determined as to "individuals, not groups." *Fibreboard*'s determination of Texas law is precedent which binds this panel. [Citations.]

28. Further, Fed.R.Civ.P. 38(a) provides that: "The right of trial by jury as declared by the Seventh Amendment to the Constitution or as given by a statute of the United States shall be preserved to the parties inviolate." The original advisory committee notes reflect that: "This rule provides for the preservation of the constitutional right of trial by jury as directed in the enabling act...." See also Fed.R.Civ.P. 42(b) ("... always preserving inviolate the right of trial by jury as declared by the Seventh Amendment to the Constitution or as given by a statute of the United States").

Gaulding furnishes no basis to depart from *Fibreboard* because it was quoted and relied on therein. No Texas appellate decision or statute subsequent to *Fibreboard* casts doubt on the correctness of its reading of Texas law. In the second place, even were we not bound by *Fibreboard* we would reach the same conclusion it did, namely that under Texas personal injury products liability law causation and damages are determined respecting plaintiffs as "individuals, not groups." We know of no Texas appellate decision which in that or a similar context has even approved of in dicta, much less adopted, the theories of "alternative liability, concert of action, enterprise liability, or market share liability" which *Gaulding* states it was not "approving or disapproving." * * * We apply Texas law as it currently exits, which is correctly stated in *Fibreboard*. Finally, it is clear that this case was neither tried nor determined on any of "the collective liability theories" mentioned in *Gaulding*.

Thus, the question becomes: did the implemented trial plan include a litigated determination, consistent with the Seventh Amendment, of the Texas-law mandated issues of whether, as to each individual plaintiff, Pittsburgh Corning's product was a cause of his complained-of condition and, if so, the damages that plaintiff suffered as a result.

We turn first to the phase III plaintiffs. In these cases, the trial plan was adequately individualized and preserved Seventh Amendment rights with respect to each individual's actual damages from an asbestos-related disease. However, it was not designed or intended to, and did not, provide any trial or any determination of whether a Pittsburgh Corning product was a cause of that disease. It was strictly a damages trial as to those individual plaintiffs. The stipulation—not entered into until midway through phase III—established merely that "some" individuals working in each of the listed crafts, "during" each of the four decades 1942–1982 and at each of the twenty-two worksites, "were exposed to asbestos" with "sufficient length and intensity to cause pulmonary asbestosis of varying degrees" and that "an asbestos-containing product of Pittsburgh Corning Corporation was present during the decades 1962–1982 at the specified worksites." It was expressly not stipulated "that any members of the various crafts at the various worksites had the same exposure to any products," or "that any such individuals had the same susceptibility to asbestos-related diseases in the various crafts and worksites," or that "any individual plaintiff was in fact exposed to injurious quantities of asbestos from the products of any defendant." Phase III did not litigate or determine whether or to what extent any of the one hundred sixty individual plaintiffs was exposed to Pittsburgh Corning's—or any other defendant's— asbestos, or was exposed to asbestos at any of the twenty-two worksites, or whether any such exposure was in fact a cause of that plaintiff's illness or disease. * * *

[Pittsburgh Corning tendered evidence that workplace asbestos exposure levels were not uniform either at a site or throughout a craft or within a decade or between decades, and that most individuals employed at the

twenty-two worksites did not have sufficient exposure to cause asbestosis.]
Also so tendered was evidence indicating that exposure to asbestos below
some level would not produce asbestosis and even above that level risks
remain very low until a multiple of five or ten or twenty times the
threshold level is reached;[39] that not all those exposed to asbestos in
substantial quantities and for protracted periods of time develop asbestosis;
that asbestosis develops in "a relatively small percentage of patients with
significant asbestos exposure"; and, that although there is a dose response
relationship—the more exposure the more risk, the less, the less risk—
respecting asbestosis, nevertheless the effect of the same exposure is not
the same as between different individuals and "two similarly exposed
asbestos workers with exactly the same asbestos historical exposure can go
on to have in one case asbestosis and the other case no lung problems."
Moreover, we have held, in a Texas law diversity case, that "the appropriate test for a [plaintiff's] minimum showing of producing cause in asbestos
cases" is that stated in Lohrmann v. Pittsburgh Corning Corp., 782 F.2d
1156 (4th Cir.1986), namely the " 'frequency-regularity-proximity' test"
under which "a motion for summary judgment cannot be defeated merely
by alleging work at a shipyard in which defendants' asbestos products had
somewhere been present. Rather, there must be proof of frequent and
regular work in an area of the shipyard in proximity to some specific item
of defendants' asbestos containing product." Slaughter v. Southern Talc.
Co., 949 F.2d 167, 171 (5th Cir.1991). It is important to note that this is
merely a minimum showing; *Slaughter* makes clear that making such a
showing merely gets a plaintiff to the jury, it does not entitled him to
judgment as a matter of law. Further, it is obvious that for these purposes
a shipyard is not considered as a single, undifferentiated, and uniform
mass.

We have noted that the district court, in the order in which it initially
adopted the present plan, stated that for purposes of the then-contemplated
phase II trial it would "make a non-jury determination as to which
Plaintiffs or Plaintiffs' decedents worked for a sufficient period of time at
each worksite so as to be a proper member of that worksite's group and
which Plaintiffs were proper members of each of the crafts at these
worksites. . . . " [It is unclear whether the district court ever made these
determinations for any plaintiffs, or, if made, what criteria were used.] In
any event, it is clear not only that any such determination was made non-

---

39. Also, that lung cancer, in addition
to being caused by smoking and asbestos
exposure, can be caused by exposure to radiation, chromium, arsenic, and polynuclear aro-
matic hydrocarbons, and that exposure to
such known causes of lung cancer "are very
frequent in both shipyards and the petro-
chemical industry"; that because of the long
latency of asbestos-related lung cancer—generally 25 to 30 years, sometimes as short as
10 to 15 years—"if an individual were exposed to asbestos only a few years prior to
the diagnosis of lung cancer, that asbestos
would not be able to be incriminated" (and
"exposures occurring 15 years prior to diagnosis of lung cancer are not going to be as
important as exposures 30 or 35 years prior
to diagnosis of lung cancer in terms of being
causally related").

jury, but further that it was made without either any evidentiary (or other) hearing or any summary judgment procedure (or Fed.R.Civ.P. 50 motion). Accordingly, no such determination can serve to justify or sustain the trial plan as implemented.

With one exception, noted below, we are aware of no appellate decision approving such a group, rather than individual, determination of cause in a damage suit for personal injuries to individuals at widely different times and places. For example, in a personal injury suit by individuals living in the neighborhood of a landfill allegedly contaminated by defendant, the Sixth Circuit remarked:

> Thus, the court, as is appropriate in this type of mass tort class action litigation, divided its causation analysis into two parts. It was first established that Velsicol was responsible for the contamination and that the particular contaminants were capable of producing injuries of the types allegedly suffered by the plaintiffs. Up to this point in the proceeding, the five representative plaintiffs were acting primarily in their representative capacity to the class as a whole. This enabled the court to determine a kind of generic causation—whether the combination of the chemical contaminants and the plaintiffs' exposure to them had the capacity to cause the harm alleged. This still left the matter of individual proximate cause to be determined. Although such generic and individual causation may appear to be inextricably intertwined, the procedural device of the class action permitted the court initially to assess the defendant's potential liability for its conduct without regard to the individual components of each plaintiff's injuries. However, from this point forward, it became the responsibility of each individual plaintiff to show that his or her specific injuries or damages were proximately caused by ingestion or otherwise using the contaminated water. Sterling v. Velsicol Chemical Corp., 855 F.2d 1188, 1200 (6th Cir.1988).

See also In Re Agent Orange Product Liability Litigation, 818 F.2d 145 (2d Cir.1987)[excerpted in casebook at page 1026](in appeal from settlement in Rule 23(b)(3) class action for agent orange exposure, * * * certification proper only because of "the centrality of the military contractor defense" and that certification "would have been error" in an action by civilians for exposure during civilian affairs, noting "[t]he relevant question . . . is not whether Agent Orange has the capacity to cause harm, the generic causation issue, but whether it did cause harm and to whom. That determination is highly individualistic * * * .)" * * *

Nor do we consider that In Re Chevron U.S.A., Inc., 109 F.3d 1016 (5th Cir.1997), justifies the instant trial plan. That action involved claims by approximately 3,000 neighboring property owners for personal injury and property damage allegedly caused by contamination from Chevron's former crude oil storage waste pit. Apparently no form of class action was involved, although some cases were consolidated. The district court directed that thirty individual plaintiffs be chosen, fifteen by the plaintiffs and fifteen by the defendants, and that there be "a unitary trial on the issues of 'general liability or causation' on behalf of the remaining plaintiffs, as well as the individual causation and damage issues of the [thirty] selected plaintiffs." Apparently, the individual causation and damage issues of the remaining unselected plaintiffs would be determined subsequently in individual trials (if the unitary trial established "liability on the part of Chevron for the pollutants that, allegedly, give rise to all of the plaintiffs' claims,"). Chevron sought mandamus, contending "that the goal of the 'unitary' trial was to determine its liability, or lack thereof, in a single trial and to establish bellwether verdicts to which the remaining claims could be matched for settlement purposes." We stated that the thirty selected plaintiffs were not shown or chosen so as to be representative of the other plaintiffs, and observed that "[a] bellwether trial designed to achieve its value ascertainment function for settlement purposes or to answer troubling causation or liability issues common to the universe of claimants has as a core element representativeness. . . ." We granted mandamus prohibiting "utilization of the results obtained from the trial of the thirty (30) selected cases for any purpose affecting issues or claims of, or defenses to, the remaining untried cases." While the majority opinion (one judge specially concurred) contains language generally looking with favor on the use of bellwether verdicts when shown to be statistically representative, this language is plainly dicta, certainly insofar as it might suggest that representative bellwether verdicts could properly be used to determine individual causation and damages for other plaintiffs. * * * Finally, the majority opinion in *In Re Chevron U.S.A.* does not even cite *Fibreboard*, or the Seventh Amendment (or discuss the right to jury trial), and does not refer to the Texas substantive law elements of liability and damages in the matter before it. Clearly, *In Re Chevron U.S.A.* does not control the result here, and this panel is not bound by its dicta. * * *

In sum, as *Fibreboard* held, under Texas law causation must be determined as to "individuals, not groups." And, the Seventh Amendment gives the right to a jury trial to make that determination. There was no such trial determination made, and no jury determined, that exposure to Pittsburgh Corning's products was a cause of the asbestos disease of any of the one hundred sixty phase III plaintiffs. Nor does the stipulation determine or establish that. Accordingly, the judgments in all the one hundred forty-three phase III cases before us must be reversed and remanded.

We turn now to the extrapolation cases. As to the matter of individual causation, it is obvious that the conclusion we have reached in respect to the phase III cases applies a fortiori to the extrapolation cases. In the extrapolation cases there was no trial and no jury determination that any individual plaintiff suffered an asbestos-related disease. Indeed, in the extrapolation cases there was no trial at all—by jury or otherwise—and there was no evidence presented. So, our holding as to the phase III cases necessarily requires reversal of the judgments in the five extrapolation cases before us.

As to the matter of actual damages, the extrapolation cases are likewise fatally defective. Unlike the phase III cases, in the extrapolation cases there was neither any sort of trial determination, let alone a jury determination, nor even any evidence, of damages. The district court considered that these deficiencies were adequately compensated for by awarding each extrapolation case plaintiff who alleged an asbestos-related disease an amount of actual damages equal to the average of the awards made in the phase III cases for plaintiffs claiming the same category of disease. This plainly contravenes *Fibreboard*'s holding that under the substantive law of Texas recoverable damages are the "wage losses, pain and suffering, and other elements of compensation" suffered by each of the several particular plaintiffs as "individuals, not groups." We also observe in this connection that none of the experts at the extrapolation hearing purported to say that the damages suffered by the phase III plaintiffs in a given disease category (whether as disclosed by the phase III evidence or as found by the jury) were to any extent representative of the damages suffered by the extrapolation plaintiffs in the same disease category. The procedure also violates Pittsburgh Corning's Seventh Amendment right to have the amount of the legally recoverable damages fixed and determined by a jury. The only juries that spoke to actual damages, the phase I and III juries, received evidence only of the damages to the particular plaintiffs before them, were called on to determine only, and only determined, each of those some one hundred seventy particular plaintiffs' actual damages individually and severally (not on any kind of a group basis), and were not called on to determine, and did not determine or purport to determine, the damages of any other plaintiffs or group of plaintiffs. We have held that "inherent in the Seventh Amendment guarantee of a trial by jury is the general right of a litigant to have only one jury pass on a common issue of fact." *Blue Bird Body Co.*, 573 F.2d at 318. This requires that if separate trials are ordered, the separately tried issues must be "distinct and separable from the others." * * * These principles are fully applicable in class actions for damages. It necessarily follows from these principles that the jury's phase III findings of the actual damages of each of the individual phase III plaintiffs cannot control the determination of, or afford any basis for denial of Pittsburgh–Corning's Seventh Amendment rights to have a jury determine, the distinct and separable issues of the actual damages of each of the extrapolation plaintiffs.

We conclude that the extrapolation case judgments, as well as the phase III judgments, are fatally flawed, are contrary to the dictates of *Fibreboard*, and contravene Pittsburgh–Corning's Seventh Amendment rights. We do not act in ignorance or disregard of the asbestos crises. In Amchem Products, Inc. v. Windsor, 521 U.S. 591 (1997), the Supreme Court called attention to the report of the Judicial Conference's Ad Hoc Committee on Asbestos Litigation, stating that "Real reform, the report concluded, required federal legislation creating a national asbestos-dispute resolution scheme." The Court also observed, "The argument is sensibly made that a nationwide administrative claims processing regime would provide the most secure, fair, and efficient means of compensating victims of asbestos exposure. Congress, however, has not adopted such a solution." Nevertheless, the Court refused to stretch the law to fill the gap resulting from congressional inaction. As we said in *Fibreboard*, federal courts must remain faithful to *Erie* and must maintain "the separation of powers between the judicial and legislative branches. * * * The Judicial Branch can offer the trial of lawsuits. It has no power or competence to do more."

We accordingly reverse the judgments before us in all the one hundred forty-three phase III cases and in all the five extrapolation cases, and those one hundred forty-eight cases are remanded for further proceedings not inconsistent herewith. [The court then decided other appeal issues solely as they pertained to the nine judgments in the phase I class representative cases.]

■ REYNALDO G. GARZA, CIRCUIT JUDGE, specially concurring:

I write separately to concur in the excellent opinion in this case, but also to add some of my own comments and thoughts about these consolidated cases, which have burdened our judicial system for so many years. In particular, I wish to express my concerns raised by Pittsburgh Corning's attack on Judge Parker's ingenious but, unfortunately, legally deficient trial plan. This case is a striking example of the crisis presented by the state of asbestos litigation in our judicial system; therefore, I am also writing separately to further urge upon Congress the wisdom and necessity of a legislative solution.

Texas law simply provides no way around Pittsburgh Corning's right to a jury trial as to causation or the requirement that causation and damages be determined as to individuals and not groups. [Citation.] If Judge Parker had conducted phase II according to his plan, however, rather than replacing phase II with the phase II stipulation, the only issue before us today would be the propriety of the phase III damages determinations. Of course, the majority opinion correctly explains that these damages determinations were fatally deficient under Texas law and the Seventh Amendment as to the more than 2,000 "extrapolation" cases; however, these "extrapolated" damages determinations are valuable in and of themselves as indications of an appropriate settlement range for each of the five disease categories involved.

* * *

It appears, however, that Judge Parker's phase II plan would have been sufficient if he had implemented the plan rather than disposing of it with the phase II stipulation. Under the plan, phase II would have addressed exposure on a craft and work site basis during the relevant time periods. A jury would have made exposure findings regarding specific work sites, crafts, and time periods. The jury would have heard evidence regarding the presence of the defendants' asbestos products and asbestos dust at each work site. The jury would also have heard evidence about the nature of the different crafts at each work site and the relationship of those crafts to asbestos. Additionally, the jury would have heard evidence regarding working conditions at each work site and the relationship of those conditions to the defendants' products.

The presentation of such evidence would clearly be sufficient for a reasonable jury to conclude that the presence of the defendants' products caused injuries to individuals working in certain crafts at certain work sites during certain time periods, and how long of a time period would be sufficient to support such causation. The jury would have also heard evidence regarding the presence of the defendants' products at the relevant work sites during the relevant time periods. Based on that evidence, the jury would have apportioned responsibility among the settling and non-settling defendants. The court would then make a determination of which plaintiffs worked for sufficient periods of time at each work site and which plaintiffs were members of each craft at those work sites.

The evidence, if presented as the plan anticipated, would satisfy the plaintiffs' burden of proof, and would support a reasonable jury's determination of causation specific to craft, work site, and relevant time period. Such evidence would also support a determination of the length of time on the job required to support causation. As such, the court's task of simply plugging each plaintiff into a craft, work site, and time period would be a sufficiently individualized determination of causation for the district court to grant judgment as to the causation issue. * * *

NOTES

5A. Judge Parker, who tried *Cimino*, now sits on the Fifth Circuit Court of Appeals. Why did it take the Court of Appeals eight years to decide this case?

6.   In the trial court's opinion in *Cimino*, the defendants primarily raised due process arguments against the trial plan yet there is no mention of the due process arguments in the Court of Appeals opinion. Why?

At one point in the trial court's opinion, in the casebook at page 994, the trial court states:

> However, a due process concern remains that is very troubling to the Court. It is apparent from the effort and time required to try these 160 cases, that unless this plan or some other procedure that permits damages to be adjudicated in the aggregate is approved, these cases cannot be tried. Defendants complain about the 1% likelihood that the result would be significantly different. However, plaintiffs are facing a 100% confidence level of being denied access to the courts. The Court will leave it to the academicians and legal scholars to debate whether our notion of due process has room for balancing these competing interests.

What do you think?

3. CAUSATION

ADD to note 3, page 1019, the following:

The Texas Supreme Court reversed the plaintiff's verdict in *Havner*, concluding, in an exhaustive opinion on both the scientific and evidentiary principles, that the evidence was legally insufficient to establish causation. Merrell Dow Pharmaceutical, Inc. v. Havner, 953 S.W.2d 706 (Tex. 1997).

ADD to note 2 on page 1023–1024 after **Hopkins v. Dow Corning Corp.**, the following:

The evidence of a causal connection between silicone gel breast implants and auto-immune, connective tissue and other diseases continues to be hotly debated. Dr. Marcia Angell, executive director of the *New England Journal of Medicine*, summarized the scientific evidence on breast implants in Science on Trial: The Clash of Medical Evidence and the Law in the Breast Implant Case (1996). Dr. Angell chronicles in some detail the history of the silicone gel breast implant and describes the scientific evidence regarding implants, the misuse of that scientific evidence by the courts, and, as she describes it, the regrettable "rejection of the scientific method" by both courts and society. She concluded that based on "several good epidemiologic studies" there is no association between implants and a host of connective tissue diseases, symptoms, and abnormal lab tests. Id. at 195–96. She laments that, according to her observation, anecdotal evidence has taken the place of the scientific method in proving causation in the court system.

Courts increasingly have been dismissing breast implant claims because of the lack of scientific proof of a causal connection. A Texas jury found for the manufacturer in a breast implant case, rejecting plaintiffs' claims that silicone from ruptured implants caused a variety of medical complaints. Zolkowski v. Baxter Healthcare Corp., No. 96–7883–H (Texas Dist., 160th Judic. Dist. Sept. 19, 1996). Judge Jones of the United States District Court for the District of Oregon appointed a panel to review the scientific evidence of a causal connection between silicone breast implants and the alleged atypical connective tissue disease involved in the 70 cases before him. After the experts reported, he ruled that, under *Daubert*, the testimony failed to have scientific validity. Hall v. Baxter Healthcare Corp., 947 F.Supp. 1387 (D.Or.1996). Judge Jones deferred the effective date of his ruling pending the report of a national advisory panel appointed to evaluate the evidence in the federal multidistrict litigation in the Northern District of Alabama. The national advisory panel, under the direction of the Institute of Medicine, recently concluded that silicone does not cause the immunologic illnesses claimed, though it can cause serious side effects from its leakage including hardening and pain. Institute of Medicine, Safety of Silicone Breast Implants (1999).

On the other side of the causation debate, another study presents evidence that implants may cause unusual health problems. The study, published in the medical journal, *The Lancet*, describes a newly developed blood test for antibodies that the researchers say are produced in response to silicone. This antibody test could identify whether a woman's illness was related to her silicone implants. See Terence Monmaney, Study Claims to Link Disease, Breast Implants, L.A. Times, Feb. 15, 1997, at A1; See also Study Sees Other Risk Factors in Breast Implants, N.Y.Times, May 28, 1997, at A18 (researchers should consider lifestyle factors when studying the health risks of breast implants; women who have breast enlargements tend to drink more, have more sex partners, and get pregnant younger).

ADD to note 8. Beyond DES, A. Asbestos, page 1050, the following:

California, the originator of market share liability and the jurisdiction which claims *Summers v. Tice* alternative liability, has recently denied the application of alternative liability to an asbestos case. In Rutherford v. Owens–Illinois, Inc., 941 P.2d 1203, 1206 (Cal. 1997), the California Supreme Court denied the use of the burden-shifting principle of *Summers v. Tice* in an asbestos case, stating:

> [W]e hold that in cases of asbestos-related cancer, a jury instruction shifting the burden of proof to asbestos defendants on the element of causation is generally unnecessary and incorrect under settled statewide principles of tort law. Proof of causation in such cases will always present inherent practical difficulties, given the long latency period of asbestos-related disease, and the occupational settings that commonly exposed the worker to multiple forms and brands of asbestos products with varying degrees of toxicity. In general, however, no insuperable barriers prevent an asbestos-related cancer plaintiff from demonstrating that exposure to the defendant's asbestos products was, in reasonable medical probability, a substantial factor in causing or contributing to his risk of developing cancer. We conclude that plaintiffs are required to prove no more than this. In particular, they need *not* prove with medical exactitude that fibers from a particular defendant's asbestos-containing products were those, or among those, that actually began the cellular process of malignancy. Instruction on the limits of the plaintiff's burden of proof of causation, together with the standardized instructions defining cause-in-fact causation under the substantial factor test and the doctrine of concurrent proximate legal causation will adequately apprise the jury of the elements required to establish causation. No burden-shifting instruction is necessary on the matter of proof of causation, and in the absence of such necessity, there is no justification or basis for shifting part of the plaintiff's burden of proof to the defendant to prove that it was not a legal cause of plaintiff's asbestos-related disease or injuries.

On the uncertainty inherent in proving causation in a toxic exposure case, the court stated:

> Plaintiffs cannot be expected to prove the scientifically unknown details of carcinogenesis, or trace the unknowable path of a given asbestos fiber. But the impossibility of such proof does not dictate use of a burden shift. Instead, we can bridge this gap in the humanly knowable by holding that plaintiffs may prove causation in asbestos-related cancer cases by demonstrating the plaintiff's exposure to defendant's asbestos-containing product in reasonably medical probability was a substantial factor in contributing

to the aggregate dose of asbestos the plaintiff or decedent inhaled or ingested, and hence to the risk of developing asbestos-related cancer, without the need to demonstrate that fibers from the defendant's particular product were the ones, or among the ones, that actually produced the malignant growth.

Id. at 1219. What is the effect of the court's refinement of causation principles? Is it any different than *Summers v. Tice* alternative liability?

*

RESTATEMENT (SECOND) OF TORTS
(Approved by the ALI, 1963 and 1964)
Selected Sections*

Chapter 14
LIABILITY OF PERSONS SUPPLYING CHATTELS FOR THE USE OF OTHERS

TOPIC 1. RULES APPLICABLE TO ALL SUPPLIERS

TOPIC 1. RULES APPLICABLE TO ALL SUPPLIERS

Scope Note: This Topic states the rules which are equally applicable to all persons who in any way or for any purpose supply chattels for the use of others or permit others to use their chattels. There are other rules which impose upon the suppliers of chattels additional duties because of the purpose for which or the manner in which the chattels are supplied or because the chattel has been made by them or put out as their product. These rules are stated hereafter. The peculiar rules which determine the liability of one who supplies a chattel or permits its use for purposes in which he himself has a business interest are stated in §§ 391–393. The peculiar rules applicable to those who manufacture the chattels which they supply are stated in §§ 394–398. The rules which determine the peculiar liability of vendors of chattels manufactured by others are stated in §§ 399–402. A special rule of strict liability applicable to sellers of articles for consumption is stated in § 402 A, and a special rule as to liability for misrepresentations made by a seller of goods to the consumer is stated in § 402 B.

The peculiar rules applicable to independent contractors and repairmen are stated in §§ 403 and 404. The peculiar rules applicable to donors, lenders, and lessors of chattels are stated in §§ 405–408.

In many instances the rules stated in the Sections in this Chapter may overlap, and the plaintiff may recover under the rules stated in two or more Sections. No attempt has been made to indicate, by way of cross-reference under any one Section, the other Sections upon which recovery may possibly be based.

§ 388. Chattel Known to Be Dangerous for Intended Use

One who supplies directly or through a third person a chattel for another to use is subject to liability to those whom the supplier should expect to use the chattel with the consent of the other or to be endangered by its probable use, for physical harm caused by the use of the chattel in the manner for which and by a person for whose use it is supplied, if the supplier

(a) knows or has reason to know that the chattel is or is likely to be dangerous for the use for which it is supplied, and

(b) has no reason to believe that those for whose use the chattel is supplied will realize its dangerous condition, and

(c) fails to exercise reasonable care to inform them of its dangerous condition or of the facts which make it likely to be dangerous.

See Reporter's Notes.

Comment:

a. The words "those whom the supplier should expect to use the chattel" and the words "a person for whose use it is supplied" include not only the person to whom the chattel is turned over by the supplier, but also all those who are members of a class whom the supplier should expect to use it or occupy it or share in its use with the consent of such person, irrespective of whether the supplier has any particular person in mind. Thus, one who lends an automobile to a friend and who fails to disclose a defect of which he himself knows and which he should recognize as making it unreasonably dangerous for use, is subject to liability not only to his friend, but also to anyone whom his friend permits to drive the car or chooses to receive in it as passenger or guest, if it is understood between them that the car may be so used. So too, one entrusting a chattel to a common carrier for transportation must expect that the chattel will be handled by the carrier's employees.

In the cases thus far decided, the rule stated in this Section has been applied only in favor of those who are injured while the chattel is being used by the person to whom it is supplied, or with his consent. In all probability the rule stated would not apply in favor of a thief of the chattel, or one injured while the thief is using it. Nor would it apply, for example, in favor of a trespasser who entered an automobile and was injured by its condition. On the other hand, no reason is apparent for limiting the rule to exclude persons who are for any reason privileged to use the chattel without the consent of the person to whom it is supplied, as in the case of a police officer who commandeers an automobile to pursue a criminal, or moves it in order to avoid danger to the public safety.

b. This Section states that one who supplies a chattel for another to use for any purpose is subject to liability for physical harm caused by his failure to exercise reasonable care to give to those whom he may expect to use the chattel any information as to the character and condition of the chattel which he possesses, and which he should recognize as necessary to enable them to realize the danger of using it. A fortiori, one so supplying a chattel is subject to liability if by word or deed he leads those who are to use the chattel to believe it to be of a character or in a condition safer for use than he knows it to be or to be likely to be.

Illustration:

1. A sells to B a shotgun, knowing that B intends to give it to his son C as a birthday present. A knows, but does not tell B, that the trigger mechanism of the gun is so defective that it is likely to be discharged by a slight jolt. B gives the gun to C. While C is using the gun it is discharged, and C is injured, by reason of the defective mechanism. A is subject to liability to C.

c. Persons included as "suppliers." The rules stated in this Section and throughout this Topic apply to determine the liability of any person who for any purpose or in any manner gives possession of a chattel for another's use, or who permits another to use or occupy it while it is in his own possession or control, without disclosing his knowledge that the chattel is dangerous for the use for which it is supplied or for which it is permitted to be used. These rules, therefore, apply to sellers, lessors, donors, or lenders, irrespective of whether the chattel is made by them or by a third person. They apply to all kinds of bailors, irrespective of whether the bailment is for a reward or gratuitous, and irrespective of whether the bailment is for use, transportation, safekeeping, or repair. They also apply to one who undertakes the repair of a chattel and who delivers it back with knowledge that it is defective because of the work which he is employed to do upon it. (See § 403.)

d. One supplying a chattel to be used or dealt with by others is subject to liability under the rule stated in this Section, not only to those for whose use the chattel is supplied but also to third persons whom the supplier should expect to be endangered by its use.

e. Ambit of liability. The liability stated in this Section exists only if physical harm is caused by the use of the chattel by those for whose use the chattel is supplied, and in the manner for which it is supplied. Except possibly where there is a privilege to use the chattel, the one who supplies a chattel for another's use is not subject to liability for bodily harm caused by its use by a third person without the consent of him for whose use it is supplied. This is true although the chattel is one of a sort notoriously likely to be so used. So too, the supplier is not subject to liability for bodily harm caused by its use by a third person who uses it even with the consent of him for whom it is supplied, if the supplier has no reason to expect that such a third person may be permitted to use it.

In order that the supplier of a chattel may be subject to liability under the rule stated in this Section, not only must the person who uses the chattel be one whom the supplier should expect to use it with the consent of him to whom it is supplied, but the chattel must also be put to a use to which the supplier has reason to expect it to be put. Thus, one who lends a chattel to another to be put to a particular use for which, though defective, it is safe, is not required to give warning of the defect, although he knows of its existence and knows that it makes the chattel dangerous for other uses, unless he has reason to expect such other uses.

f. As pointed out in § 5, the phrase "subject to liability" is used to indicate that the person whose conduct is in question is liable if, but only if, there also exist the other conditions necessary to liability. The person using the chattel may disable himself from bringing an action either by his contributory negligence in voluntarily using the chattel with knowledge of its dangerous condition, or by his contributory negligence in failing to make a proper inspection which would have disclosed the defect, or in failing to use the precautions obviously necessary to the safe use of the chattel.

Comment on Clause (a):

g. The duty which the rule stated in this Section imposes upon the supplier of a chattel for another's use is to exercise reasonable care to give to those who are to use the chattel the information which the supplier possesses, and which he should realize to be necessary to make its use safe for them and those in whose vicinity it is to be used. This information enables those for whom the chattel is supplied to determine whether they shall accept and use it. Save in exceptional circumstances, as where the chattel, no matter how carefully dealt with, is incapable of any safe use, or where the person to whom it is supplied is obviously likely to misuse it, the supplier of a chattel who has given such information is entitled to assume that it will not be used for purposes for which the information given by him shows it to be unfit and, therefore, is relieved of liability for harm done by its misuse to those in the vicinity of its probable use.

A chattel may be so imperfect that it is unlikely to be safe for use for any purpose, no matter how great the care which is exercised in using it. As to the rule which determines liability in such case, see § 389.

There are many chattels which, even though perfect, are unsafe for any use or for the particular use for which they are supplied unless their properties and capabilities are known to those who use them. If such a chattel is supplied to another whom the supplier should realize to be unlikely to know its properties and capabilities, the supplier is required to exercise reasonable care to give to the other such information thereof as he himself possesses.

Illustration:

2. A is a guest in B's house. A is taken suddenly ill. B gives him a drug which B knows can only be safely used if taken in certain doses and under certain conditions. B gives the drug to A, but forgets to instruct him as to the manner in which it is to be used. A takes it in a larger dose than is proper, or fails to take the precautions which are necessary to make it safe. In consequence A's illness is increased. B is subject to liability to A.

Comment:

h. There are many articles which are so defective as to be incapable of safe use for any of the purposes for which they are normally fit or for use in the manner in which such articles are normally capable of safe use, but which are safe for limited uses or if used with particular precautions. If the appearance of such a chattel does not disclose its defective condition, the supplier is under a duty to exercise reasonable care to disclose its condition, in so far as it is known to him, to those who are to use it, or to inform them that it is fit only for these limited uses, or if used with the particular precautions.

The supplier of a defective chattel may have had peculiar experience with such chattels, and he may, therefore, be required to realize that a disclosure of the actual condition of the chattel will not be enough to inform the user of the danger of using it except for limited purposes or with particular precautions. If such is the case, it is not enough for the supplier to inform those who are to use the chattel of its actual condition. He must exercise reasonable care to apprise them of the danger of using it otherwise than for the particular purposes for which he should know it to be fit or with the particular precautions which he should realize to be necessary to make its use safe.

i. Where lot of chattels contains a few defective ones. It is not necessary in order that a supplier of a chattel for another's use be liable under the rule stated in this Section that he should know that the particular chattel is dangerous for the use for which it is supplied. It is enough that he knows of facts which make it likely that the particular chattel may be dangerous, as where he knows that it is part of a lot, some of which he has discovered to be so imperfect as to be dangerous. If so, he is required to exercise reasonable care to acquaint those for whose use the chattel is supplied of these facts, in order that they may realize the risk they will run in using the chattel and may make an intelligent choice as to the advisability of doing so.

Illustration:

3.   A sells or gives to B a can of baking powder. A knows that several, though not all, of the lot of cans of which this can is a part have exploded when opened. He does not inform B of this fact. While C, B's cook, is attempting to open the can, it explodes, causing harm to C's eyes and also the eyes of D, B's kitchen maid, who is standing nearby. A is subject to liability to C and D.

j. So too, one may put into a stock of chattels which he intends subsequently to supply for the use of others, articles which he then knows to be, or to be likely to be, dangerous for the use for which they are to be supplied. It may, however, subsequently be impossible to tell which of the chattels are of this character, and, therefore, at the time the particular article is supplied the supplier may not know that it is dangerous. He is, however, subject to liability, since he knows that it may be one of the chattels which is dangerous. This situation usually arises where the supplier is a manufacturer whose business is divided into different departments. In such a case the operative department may discover a defect in a particular chattel which the subsequent processes of manufacture may make it difficult or impossible to detect. So too, defective material may be knowingly used in the manufacture of a lot of chattels so that it is obvious that some, though not all, of these must be defective. Here again the process of manufacture may make it impossible to tell, at the time the particular chattel is supplied, which of the lot are dangerous and which safe.

Illustration:

4.   The A Manufacturing Company makes a lot of ladders out of a shipment of wood of which some is knotted. It is impossible to see the knots after the ladders have been painted. One of the ladders is sold to B. While C, B's servant, is using the ladder, it breaks because of the knots in the wood of which it is made. The A Company is subject to liability to C, although at the time the ladder was sold it appeared perfectly sound and the sales department which sold the ladder had not been informed that defective material had been used in the construction of this lot of ladders.

Comment on Clause (b):

k. *When warning of defects unnecessary.* One who supplies a chattel to others to use for any purpose is under a duty to exercise reasonable care to inform them of its dangerous character in so far as it is known to him, or of facts which to his knowledge make it likely to be dangerous, if, but only if, he has no reason to expect that those for whose use the chattel is supplied will discover its condition and realize the danger involved. It is not necessary for the supplier to inform those for whose use the chattel is supplied of a condition which a mere casual looking over will disclose, unless the circumstances under which the chattel is supplied are such as to make it likely that even so casual an inspection will not be made. However, the condition, although readily observable, may be one which only persons of special experience would realize to be dangerous. In such case, if the supplier, having such special experience, knows that the condition involves danger and has no reason to believe that those who use it will have such special experience as will enable them to perceive the danger, he is required to inform them of the risk of which he himself knows and which he has no reason to suppose that they will realize.

Comment on Clause (c):

l. The supplier's duty is to exercise reasonable care to inform those for whose use the article is supplied of dangers which are peculiarly within his knowledge. If he has done so, he is not subject to liability, even though the information never reaches those for whose use the chattel is supplied. The factors which determine whether the supplier exercises reasonable care by giving this information to third persons through whom the chattel is supplied for the use of others, are stated in Comment *n.*

m. Inspection. The fact that a chattel is supplied for the use of others does not of itself impose upon the supplier a duty to make an inspection of the chattel, no matter how cursory, in order to discover whether it is fit for the use for which it is supplied. Such a duty may be imposed because of the purpose for which the chattel is to be used by those to whom it is supplied. (See § 392.) A manufacturer of a chattel may be under a duty to inspect the materials and parts out of which it is made and to subject the finished article to such an inspection as the danger involved in an imperfect article makes reasonable. (See § 395 and Comment *e* under that Section.) Under certain conditions, stated in §§ 403, 404, and 408, an independent contractor or lessor may be under a similar duty of inspection.

n. Warnings given to third person. Chattels are often supplied for the use of others, although the chattels or the permission to use them are not given directly to those for whose use they are supplied, as when a wholesale dealer sells to a retailer goods which are obviously to be used by the persons purchasing them from him, or when a contractor furnishes the scaffoldings or other appliances which his subcontractor and the latter's servants are to use, or when an automobile is lent for the borrower to use for the conveyance of his family and friends. In all such cases the question may arise as to whether the person supplying the chattel is exercising that reasonable care, which he owes to those who are to use it, by informing the third person through whom the chattel is supplied of its actual character.

Giving to the third person through whom the chattel is supplied all the information necessary to its safe use is not in all cases sufficient to relieve the supplier from liability. It is merely a means by which this information is to be conveyed to those who are to use the chattel. The question remains whether this method gives a reasonable assurance that the information will reach those whose safety depends upon their having it. All sorts of chattels may be supplied for the use of others, through all sorts of third persons and under an infinite variety of circumstances. This being true, it is obviously impossible to state in advance any set of rules which will automatically determine in all cases whether one supplying a chattel for the use of others through a third person has satisfied his duty to those who are to use the chattel by informing the third person of the dangerous character of the chattel, or of the precautions which must be exercised in using it in order to make its use safe. There are, however, certain factors which are important in determining this question. There is necessarily some chance that information given to the third person will not be communicated by him to those who are to use the chattel. This chance varies with the circumstances existing at the time the chattel is turned over to the third person, or permission is given to him to allow others to use it. These circumstances include the known or knowable character of the third person and may also include the purpose for which the chattel is given. Modern life would be intolerable unless one were permitted to rely to a certain extent on others' doing what they normally do, particularly if it is their duty to do so. If the chattel is one which if ignorantly used contains no great chance of causing anything more than some comparatively trivial harm, it is reasonable to permit the one who supplies the chattel through a third person to rely upon the fact that the third person is an ordinary normal man to whose discredit the supplier knows nothing, as a sufficient assurance that information given to him will be passed on to those who are to use the chattel.

If, however, the third person is known to be careless or inconsiderate or if the purpose for which the chattel is to be used is to his advantage and knowledge of the true character of the chattel is likely to prevent its being used and so to deprive him of this advantage—as when goods so defective as to be unsalable are sold by a wholesaler to a retailer—the supplier of the chattel has reason to expect, or at least suspect, that the information will fail to reach those who are to use the chattel and whose safety depends upon their knowledge of its true character. In such a case, the supplier may well be required to go further than to tell such a third person of the dangerous character of the article, or, if he fails to do so, to take the risk of being subjected to liability if the information is not brought home to those whom the supplier should expect to use the chattel. In many cases the burden of doing so is slight, as when the chattel is to be used in the presence or vicinity of the person supplying it, so that he could easily give a personal warning to those who are to use the chattel. Even though the supplier has no practicable opportunity to give this information directly and in person to those who are to use the chattel or share in its use, it is not unreasonable to require him to make good any harm which is caused by his using so unreliable a method of giving the information which is obviously necessary to make the chattel safe for those who use it and those in the vicinity of its use.

Here, as in every case which involves the determination of the precautions which must be taken to satisfy the requirements of reasonable care, the magnitude of the risk involved must be compared with the burden which would be imposed by requiring them (see § 291), and the magnitude of the risk is determined not only by the chance that some harm may result but also the serious or trivial character of the harm which is likely to result (see § 293). Since the care which must be taken always increases with the danger involved, it may be reasonable to require those who supply through others chattels which if ignorantly used involve grave risk of serious harm to those who use them and those in the vicinity of their use, to take precautions to bring the information home to the users of such chattels which it would be unreasonable to demand were the chattels of a less dangerous character.

Thus, while it may be proper to permit a supplier to assume that one through whom he supplies a chattel which is only slightly dangerous will communicate the information given him to those who are to use it unless he knows that the other is careless, it may be improper to permit him to trust the conveyance of the necessary information of the actual character of a highly dangerous article to a third person of whose character he knows nothing. It may well be that he should take the risk that this information may not be communicated, unless he exercises reasonable care to ascertain the character of the third person, or unless from previous experience with him or from the excellence of his reputation the supplier has positive reason to believe that he is careful. In addition to this, if the danger involved in the ignorant use of a particular chattel is very great, it may be that the supplier does not exercise reasonable care in entrusting the communication of the necessary information even to a person whom he has good reason to believe to be careful. Many such articles can be made to carry their own message to the understanding of those who are likely to use them by the form in which they are put out, by the container in which they are supplied, or by a label or other device, indicating with a substantial sufficiency their dangerous character. Where the danger involved in the ignorant use of their true quality is great and such means of disclosure are practicable and not unduly burdensome, it may well be that the supplier should be required to adopt them. There are many statutes which require that articles which are highly dangerous if used in ignorance of their character, such as poisons, explosives, and inflammables, shall be put out in such a form as to bear on their face notice of their dangerous character, either by the additional coloring matter, the form or color of the containers, or by labels. Such statutes are customarily construed as making one who supplies such articles not so marked liable, even though he has disclosed their actual character to the person to whom he directly gives them for the use of others, and even though the statute contains no express provisions on the subject.

o. Under the rule stated in this Section one who supplies a chattel to a third person for use is subject to the liability stated in this Section if he fails to exercise reasonable care to inform those for whose use the chattel is supplied of its dangerous condition. It follows that the supplier is equally liable if he actually conceals a defect in the chattel by painting it over or by a pretense of repair, or if by express words he represents it to be safe, knowing that it is not so.

TOPIC 3. MANUFACTURER OF CHATTELS

§ 395. Negligent Manufacture of Chattel Dangerous Unless Carefully Made

A manufacturer who fails to exercise reasonable care in the manufacture of a chattel which, unless carefully made, he should recognize as involving an unreasonable risk of causing physical harm to those who use it for a purpose for which the manufacturer should expect it to be used and to those whom he should expect to be endangered by its probable use, is subject to liability for physical harm caused to them by its lawful use in a manner and for a purpose for which it is supplied.

See Reporter's Notes.

Comment:

a. History. The original common law rule was contrary to that stated in this Section. The case of Winterbottom v. Wright, 10 M. & W. 109, 152 Eng.Rep. 402 (1842), in which a seller who contracted with the buyer to keep a stagecoach in repair after the sale was held not to be liable to a passenger injured when he failed to do so, was for a long time misconstrued to mean that the original seller of a chattel could not be liable, in tort or in contract, to one other than his immediate buyer. To this rule various exceptions developed, the first of which involved the rule stated in §§ 388, 390, and 394, that a manufacturer who knew that the chattel was dangerous for its expected use and failed to disclose the danger became liable to a third person injured by the defect.

The most important of these exceptions, however, made the seller liable to a third person for negligence in the manufacture or sale of an article classified as "inherently" or "imminently" dangerous to human safety. By degrees this category was redefined to include articles "intended to preserve, destroy, or affect human life or health." For more than half a century, however, the category remained vague and imperfectly defined. It was held to include food, drugs, firearms, and explosives, but there was much rather pointless dispute in the decisions as to other articles, and as to whether, for example, such a product as chewing tobacco was to be classified as a food.

In 1916 the leading modern case of MacPherson v. Buick Motor Co., 217 N.Y. 382, 111 N.E. 1050, L.R.A. 1916F, 696, Am.Ann.Cas. 1916C, 440, 13 N.C.C.A. 1029 (1916), discarded the general rule of non-liability, by holding that "inherently dangerous" articles included any article which would be dangerous to human safety if negligently made. After the passage of more than forty years, this decision is now all but universally accepted by the American courts. Although some decisions continue to speak the language of "inherent danger," it has very largely been superseded by a recognition that what is involved is merely the ordinary duty of reasonable care imposed upon the manufacturer, as to any product which he can reasonably expect to be dangerous if he is negligent in its manufacture or sale.

b. This Section states the rule thus generally adopted. The justification for it rests upon the responsibility assumed by the manufacturer toward the consuming public, which arises, not out of contract, but out of the relation resulting from the purchase of the product by the consumer; upon the foreseeability of harm if proper care is not used; upon the representation of safety implied in the act of putting the product on the market; and upon the economic benefit derived by the manufacturer from the sale and subsequent use of the chattel.

c. *Not necessary that chattel be intended to affect, preserve, or destroy human life.* In order that the manufacturer of a chattel shall be subject to liability under the rule stated in this Section, it is not necessary that the chattel be one the use of which is intended to affect, preserve, or destroy human life. The purpose which the article, if perfect, is intended to accomplish is immaterial. The important thing is the harm which it is likely to do if it is imperfect.

d. *Not necessary that chattel be inherently dangerous.* In order that the manufacturer shall be subject to liability under the rule stated in this Section, it is not necessary that the chattel be "inherently dangerous," in the sense of involving any degree of risk of harm to those who use it even if it is properly made. It is enough that the chattel, if not carefully made, will involve such a risk of harm. It is not necessary that the risk be a great one, or that it be a risk of death or serious bodily harm. A risk of harm to property, as in the case of defective animal food, is enough. All that is necessary is that the risk be an unreasonable one, as stated in § 291. The inherent danger, or the high degree of danger, is merely a factor to be considered, as in other negligence cases, as bearing upon the extent of the precautions required.

Illustration:

1. A manufactures a mattress. Through the carelessness of one of A's employees a spring inside of the mattress is not properly tied down.

143

A sells the mattress to B, a dealer, who resells it to C. C sleeps on the mattress, and is wounded in the back by the sharp point of the spring. The wound becomes infected, and C suffers serious illness. A is subject to liability to C.

e. When inspections and tests necessary. As heretofore pointed out (§ 298, Comment *b*), the precaution necessary to comply with the standard of reasonable care varies with the danger involved. Consequently the character of harm likely to result from the failure to exercise care in manufacture affects the question as to what is reasonable care. It is reasonable to require those who make or assemble automobiles to subject the raw material, or parts, procured from even reputable manufacturers, to inspections and tests which it would be obviously unreasonable to require of a product which, although defective, is unlikely to cause more than some comparatively slight, though still substantial, harm to those who use it. A garment maker is not required to subject the finished garment to anything like so minute an inspection for the purpose of discovering whether a basting needle has not been left in a seam as is required of the maker of an automobile or of high speed machinery or of electrical devices, in which the slightest inaccuracy may involve danger of death.

f. Particulars which require care. A manufacturer is required to exercise reasonable care in manufacturing any article which, if carelessly manufactured, is likely to cause harm to those who use it in the manner for which it is manufactured. The particulars in which reasonable care is usually necessary for protection of those whose safety depends upon the character of chattels are (1) the adoption of a formula or plan which, if properly followed, will produce an article safe for the use for which it is sold, (2) the selection of material and parts to be incorporated in the finished article, (3) the fabrication of the article by every member of the operative staff no matter how high or low his position, (4) the making of such inspections and tests during the course of manufacture and after the article is completed as the manufacturer should recognize as reasonably necessary to secure the production of a safe article, and (5) the packing of the article so as to be safe for those who must be expected to unpack it.

Illustrations:

2. The A Motor Company incorporates in its car wheels manufactured by the B Wheel Company. These wheels are constructed of defective material, as an inspection made by the A Company before putting them on its car would disclose. The car is sold to C through the D Company, an independent distributor. While C is driving the car the defective wheel collapses and the car swerves and collides with that of E, causing harm to C and E, and also to F and G, who are guests in the cars of C and E respectively. The A Motor Company is subject to liability to C, E, F, and G.

g. The exercise of reasonable care in selecting raw material and parts to be incorporated in the finished article usually requires something more than a mere inspection of the material and parts. A manufacturer should have sufficient technical knowledge to select such a type of material that its use will secure a safe finished product. So too, a manufacturer who incorporates a part made by another manufacturer into his finished product should exercise reasonable care to ascertain not only the material out of which the part is made but also the plan under which it is made. He must have sufficient technical knowledge to form a reasonably accurate judgment as to whether a part made under such a plan and of such material is or is not such as to secure a safe finished product. The part is of his own selection, and it is reasonable for the users of the product to rely not only upon a careful inspection but also sufficient technical knowledge to make a careful inspection valuable in securing an article safe for use. In all of these particulars the amount of care which the manufacturer must exercise is proportionate to the extent of the risk involved in using the article if manufactured without the exercise of these precautions. Where, as in the case of an automobile or high speed machinery or high voltage electrical devices, there is danger of serious bodily harm or death unless the article is substantially perfect, it is reasonable to require the manufacturer to exercise almost meticulous precautions in all of these particulars in order to secure substantial perfection. On the other hand, it would be ridiculous to demand equal care of the manufacturer of an article which, no matter how imperfect, is unlikely to do more than some comparatively trivial harm to those who use it.

h. *Persons protected.* The words "those who use the chattel" include not only the vendee but also all persons whose right or privilege to use the article is derived from him, unless the nature of the article or the conditions of the sale make it improbable that the article will be resold by the vendee or that he will permit others to use it or to share in its use. Unless the article is made to special order for the peculiar use of a particular person, the manufacturer must realize the chance that it may be sold. This becomes a substantial certainty where the article is sold to a jobber, wholesaler, or retailer. So too, many articles are obviously made for the use of several persons or are sold under conditions which make it certain that they will be used by persons other than the purchaser. Thus the manufacturer of a seven-seated automobile which is obviously intended to carry persons other than the purchaser and his chauffeur should recognize it as likely to be used by any persons whom, as members of his family, guests, or pedestrians picked up on the road, the purchaser chooses to receive in his car. A threshing machine sold to the owner of a large farm is obviously intended for the use of his employees.

The words "those who use the chattel" include, therefore, all persons whom the vendee or his subvendee or donee permits to use the article irrespective of whether they do so as his servants, as passengers for hire or otherwise, to serve his business purposes, or as licensees permitted to use a car purely for their own benefit. They also include any person to whom the vendee sells or gives the chattel, or to whom such subvendee or donee sells or gives the chattel ad infinitum, and also all persons whom such subvendee or subdonee permits to use the chattel or to share in its use. Thus they include a person to whom an improperly prepared drug is hypodermically administered by a physician who has bought it from a drugstore which has purchased it from a wholesaler or jobber.

i. Persons endangered by use. The words "those whom he should expect to be endangered by its probable use" may likewise include a large group of persons who have no connection with the ownership or use of the chattel itself. Thus the manufacturer of an automobile, intended to be driven on the public highway, should reasonably expect that, if the automobile is dangerously defective, harm will result to any person on the highway, including pedestrians and drivers of other vehicles and their passengers and guests; and he should also expect danger to those upon land immediately abutting on the highway. Likewise the manufacturer of a cable to be used in the transmission of high voltage electric current should reasonably anticipate that if its insulation is defective its use may endanger even persons miles away from the cable itself.

j. Unforeseeable use or manner of use. The liability stated in this Section is limited to persons who are endangered and the risks which are created in the course of uses of the chattel which the manufacturer should reasonably anticipate. In the absence of special reason to expect otherwise, the maker is entitled to assume that his product will be put to a normal use, for which the product is intended or appropriate; and he is not subject to liability when it is safe for all such uses, and harm results only because it is mishandled in a way which he has no reason to expect, or is used in some unusual and unforeseeable manner. Thus a shoemaker is not liable to an obstinate lady who suffers harm because she insists on wearing a size too small for her, and the manufacturer of a bottle of cleaning fluid is not liable when the purchaser splashes it into his eye.

Illustration:

3.   A manufactures and sells to a dealer an automobile tire, which is in all respects safe for normal automobile driving. B, an automobile racer, buys the tire from the dealer and installs it on his racing car. In the course of the race the tire blows out because of the excessive speed, and B is injured. A is not liable to B.

k. Foreseeable uses and risks. The manufacturer may, however, reasonably anticipate other uses than the one for which the chattel is primarily intended. The maker of a chair, for example, may reasonably expect that some one will stand on it; and the maker of an inflammable cocktail robe may expect that it will be worn in the kitchen in close proximity to a fire. Likewise the manufacturer may know, or may be under a duty to discover, that some possible users of the product are especially susceptible to harm from it, if it contains an ingredient to which any substantial percentage of the population are allergic or otherwise sensitive, and he fails to take reasonable precautions, by giving warning or otherwise, against harm to such persons.

l. The fact that the article is leased, given, or loaned to the user rather than sold or leased does not affect the liability of the manufacturer for his negligence in making the article.

m. Manufacturer of raw material or parts of article to be assembled by third person. It is not necessary that the manufacturer should expect his product to be used in the form in which it is delivered to his immediate buyer. A manufacturer of parts to be incorporated in the product of his buyer or others is subject to liability under the rule stated in this Section, if they are so negligently made as to render the products in which they are incorporated unreasonably dangerous for use. So too, a manufacturer of raw material made and sold to be used in the fabrication of particular articles which will be dangerous for use unless the material is carefully made, is subject to liability if he fails to exercise reasonable care in its manufacture. As to the effect to be given to the fact that the defect could have been discovered before the part or material was incorporated in the finished article, see § 396.

Illustration:

4. Under the facts stated in Illustration 2, the B Wheel Company is subject to liability to C, E, F, and G.

n. The rule stated in this Section applies where the only harm which results from the manufacturer's failure to exercise reasonable care is to the manufactured chattel itself.

Illustration:

5. A manufactures and sells to a dealer an automobile, which is purchased from the dealer by B. Because of A's failure to exercise reasonable care in manufacture the car has a defective steering gear. While B is driving the steering gear gives way, and the car goes into the ditch and is damaged. B is not injured, and there is no other damage of any kind. A is subject to liability to B for the damage to the automobile.

§ 398. Chattel Made Under Dangerous Plan or Design

A manufacturer of a chattel made under a plan or design which makes it dangerous for the uses for which it is manufactured is subject to liability to others whom he should expect to use the chattel or to be endangered by its probable use for physical harm caused by his failure to exercise reasonable care in the adoption of a safe plan or design.

See Reporter's Notes.

Comment:

a. The rule stated in this Section, like that stated in § 397, is a special application of the rule stated in § 395.

b. *When dangerous plan or design known to user.* If the dangerous character of the plan or design is known to the user of the chattel, he may be in contributory fault if the risk involved in using it is unreasonably great or if he fails to take those special precautions which the known dangerous character of the chattel requires.

Illustration:

1. The A Stove Company makes a gas stove under a design which places the aperture through which it is lighted in dangerous proximity to the gas outlet. As a result of this B, a cook employed by C, who has bought one of these stoves from a dealer to whom A has sold it, while attempting to light the stove is hurt by an explosion of gas. The A Stove Company is subject to liability to B.

TOPIC 4. SELLERS OF CHATTELS MANUFACTURED BY THIRD PERSONS

§ 400. Selling as Own Product Chattel Made by Another

One who puts out as his own product a chattel manufactured by another is subject to the same liability as though he were its manufacturer.

See Reporter's Notes.

Comment:

a. The words "one who puts out a chattel" include anyone who supplies it to others for their own use or for the use of third persons, either by sale or lease or by gift or loan.

b. The rules which determine the liability of a manufacturer of a chattel are stated in §§ 394–398.

c. One who puts out as his own product chattels made by others is under a duty to exercise care, proportionate to the danger involved in the use of the chattels if improperly made, to secure the adoption of a proper formula or plan and the use of safe materials and to inspect the chattel when made. But he does not escape liability by so doing. He is liable if, because of some negligence in its fabrication or through lack of proper inspection during the process of manufacture, the article is in a dangerously defective condition which the seller could not discover after it was delivered to him.

d. The rule stated in this Section applies only where the actor puts out the chattel as his own product. The actor puts out a chattel as his own product in two types of cases. The first is where the actor appears to be the manufacturer of the chattel. The second is where the chattel appears to have been made particularly for the actor. In the first type of case the actor frequently causes the chattel to be used in reliance upon his care in making it; in the second, he frequently causes the chattel to be used in reliance upon a belief that he has required it to be made properly for him and that the actor's reputation is an assurance to the user of the quality of the product. On the other hand, where it is clear that the actor's only connection with the chattel is that of a distributor of it (for example, as a wholesale or retail seller), he does not put it out as his own product and the rule stated in this section is inapplicable. Thus, one puts out a chattel as his own product when he puts it out under his name or affixes to it his trade name or trademark. When such identification is referred to on the label as an indication of the quality or wholesomeness of the chattel, there is an added emphasis that the user can rely upon the reputation of the person so identified. The mere fact that the goods are marked with such additional words as "made for" the seller, or describe him as a distributor, particularly in the absence of a clear and distinctive designation of the real manufacturer or packer, is not sufficient to make inapplicable the rule stated in this Section. The casual reader of a label is likely to rely upon the featured name, trade name, or trademark, and overlook the qualification of the description of source. So too, the fact that the seller is known to carry on only a retail business does not prevent him from putting out as his own product a chattel which is marked in such a way as to indicate clearly it is put out as his product. However, where the real manufacturer or packer is clearly and accurately identified on the label or other markings on the goods, and it is also clearly stated that another who is also named has nothing to do with the goods except to distribute or sell them, the latter does not put out such goods as his own. That the goods are not the product of him who puts them out may also be indicated clearly in other ways.

Illustrations:

1. A puts out under his own name a floor stain which is manufactured under a secret formula by B, to whom A entrusts the selection of the formula. The stain made under this formula is inflammable, as a competent maker of such articles would have known. Of this both A and B are ignorant, and neither the advertisements nor the directions contain any warning against using it near unguarded lights. C purchases from a retail dealer a supply of this stain and while D, C's wife, is applying it to the floor of the kitchen, C strikes a match to light the gas. An explosion follows, causing harm to D and to E, a friend who is watching D stain the floor. A is subject to liability to D and E.

2. A, a wholesale distributor, sells canned corned beef labeled with A's widely known trademark and also labeled "Packed for A" and

"A, distributor". The beef was negligently packed by B and is unwholesome. C buys a can of it from D, a retail grocer, and serves it to her guest, E, who is made ill. A is liable to E.

TOPIC 5. STRICT LIABILITY

§ 402A. Special Liability of Seller of Product for Physical Harm to User or Consumer

[handwritten margin notes: ✳ See Comment (i) for "unreasonably dangerous"]

[handwritten margin notes: ✳ must have normal use]

[handwritten margin notes: ✳ Sale can be lease, donation, etc.]

(1) One who sells any product in a defective condition unreasonably dangerous to the user or consumer or to his property is subject to liability for physical harm thereby caused to the ultimate user or consumer, or to his property, if

(a) the seller is engaged in the business of selling such a product, and

(b) it is expected to and does reach the user or consumer without substantial change in the condition in which it is sold.

(2) The rule stated in Subsection (1) applies although

(a) the seller has exercised all possible care in the preparation and sale of his product, and

(b) the user or consumer has not bought the product from or entered into any contractual relation with the seller.

See Reporter's Notes.

Caveat:

The Institute expresses no opinion as to whether the rules stated in this Section may not apply

(1) to harm to persons other than users or consumers;

(2) to the seller of a product expected to be processed or otherwise substantially changed before it reaches the user or consumer; or

(3) to the seller of a component part of a product to be assembled.

Comment:

a. This Section states a special rule applicable to sellers of products. The rule is one of strict liability, making the seller subject to liability to the user or consumer even though he has exercised all possible care in the preparation and sale of the product. The Section is inserted in the Chapter dealing with the negligence liability of suppliers of chattels, for convenience of reference and comparison with other Sections dealing with negligence. The rule stated here is not exclusive, and does not preclude liability based upon the alternative ground of negligence of the seller, where such negligence can be proved.

  b. *History.* Since the early days of the common law those engaged in the business of selling food intended for human consumption have been held to a high degree of responsibility for their products. As long ago as 1266 there were enacted special criminal statutes imposing penalties upon victualers, vintners, brewers, butchers, cooks, and other persons who supplied "corrupt" food and drink. In the earlier part of this century this ancient attitude was reflected in a series of decisions in which the courts of a number of states sought to find some method of holding the seller of food liable to the ultimate consumer even though there was no showing of negligence on the part of the seller. These decisions represented a departure from, and an exception to, the general rule that a supplier of chattels was not liable to third persons in the absence of negligence or privity of contract. In the beginning, these decisions displayed considerable ingenuity in evolving more or less fictitious theories of liability to fit the case. The various devices included an agency of the intermediate dealer or another to purchase for the consumer, or to sell for the seller; a theoretical assignment of the seller's warranty to the intermediate dealer; a third party beneficiary contract; and an implied representation that the food was fit for consumption because it was placed on the market, as well as numerous others. In later years the courts have become more or less agreed upon the theory of a "warranty" from the seller to the consumer, either "running with the goods" by analogy to a covenant running with the land, or made directly to the consumer. Other decisions have indicated that the basis is merely one of strict liability in tort, which is not dependent upon either contract or negligence.

  Recent decisions, since 1950, have extended this special rule of strict liability beyond the seller of food for human consumption. The first extension was into the closely analogous cases of other products intended for intimate bodily use, where, for example, as in the case of cosmetics, the application to the body of the consumer is external rather than internal. Beginning in 1958 with a Michigan case involving cinder building blocks, a number of recent decisions have discarded any limitation to intimate association with the body, and have extended the rule of strict liability to cover the sale of any product which, if it should prove to be defective, may be expected to cause physical harm to the consumer or his property.

  c. On whatever theory, the justification for the strict liability has been said to be that the seller, by marketing his product for use and consumption, has undertaken and assumed a special responsibility toward any member of the consuming public who may be injured by it; that the public has the right to and does expect, in the case of products which it needs and for which it is forced to rely upon the seller, that reputable sellers will stand behind their goods; that public policy demands that the burden of accidental injuries caused by products intended for consumption be placed upon those who market them, and be treated as a cost of production against which liability insurance can be obtained; and that the consumer of such products is entitled to the maximum of protection at the hands of someone, and the proper persons to afford it are those who market the products.

d. The rule stated in this Section is not limited to the sale of food for human consumption, or other products for intimate bodily use, although it will obviously include them. It extends to any product sold in the condition, or substantially the same condition, in which it is expected to reach the ultimate user or consumer. Thus the rule stated applies to an automobile, a tire, an airplane, a grinding wheel, a water heater, a gas stove, a power tool, a riveting machine, a chair, and an insecticide. It applies also to products which, if they are defective, may be expected to and do cause only "physical harm" in the form of damage to the user's land or chattels, as in the case of animal food or a herbicide.

e. Normally the rule stated in this Section will be applied to articles which already have undergone some processing before sale, since there is today little in the way of consumer products which will reach the consumer without such processing. The rule is not, however, so limited, and the supplier of poisonous mushrooms which are neither cooked, canned, packaged, nor otherwise treated is subject to the liability here stated.

f. Business of selling. The rule stated in this Section applies to any person engaged in the business of selling products for use or consumption. It therefore applies to any manufacturer of such a product, to any wholesale or retail dealer or distributor, and to the operator of a restaurant. It is not necessary that the seller be engaged solely in the business of selling such products. Thus the rule applies to the owner of a motion picture theatre who sells popcorn or ice cream, either for consumption on the premises or in packages to be taken home.

The rule does not, however, apply to the occasional seller of food or other such products who is not engaged in that activity as a part of his business. Thus it does not apply to the housewife who, on one occasion, sells to her neighbor a jar of jam or a pound of sugar. Nor does it apply to the owner of an automobile who, on one occasion, sells it to his neighbor, or even sells it to a dealer in used cars, and this even though he is fully aware that the dealer plans to resell it. The basis for the rule is the ancient one of the special responsibility for the safety of the public undertaken by one who enters into the business of supplying human beings with products which may endanger the safety of their persons and property, and the forced reliance upon that undertaking on the part of those who purchase such goods. This basis is lacking in the case of the ordinary individual who makes the isolated sale, and he is not liable to a third person, or even to his buyer, in the absence of his negligence. An analogy may be found in the provision of the Uniform Sales Act, § 15, which limits the implied warranty of merchantable quality to sellers who deal in such goods; and in the similar limitation of the Uniform Commercial Code, § 2–314, to a seller who is a merchant. This Section is also not intended to apply to sales of the stock of merchants out of the usual course of business, such as execution sales, bankruptcy sales, bulk sales, and the like.

g. *Defective condition.* The rule stated in this Section applies only where the product is, at the time it leaves the seller's hands, in a condition not contemplated by the ultimate consumer, which will be unreasonably dangerous to him. The seller is not liable when he delivers the product in a safe condition, and subsequent mishandling or other causes make it harmful by the time it is consumed. The burden of proof that the product was in a defective condition at the time that it left the hands of the particular seller is upon the injured plaintiff; and unless evidence can be produced which will support the conclusion that it was then defective, the burden is not sustained.

Safe condition at the time of delivery by the seller will, however, include proper packaging, necessary sterilization, and other precautions required to permit the product to remain safe for a normal length of time when handled in a normal manner.

h. A product is not in a defective condition when it is safe for normal handling and consumption. If the injury results from abnormal handling, as where a bottled beverage is knocked against a radiator to remove the cap, or from abnormal preparation for use, as where too much salt is added to food, or from abnormal consumption, as where a child eats too much candy and is made ill, the seller is not liable. Where, however, he has reason to anticipate that danger may result from a particular use, as where a drug is sold which is safe only in limited doses, he may be required to give adequate warning of the danger (see Comment *j*), and a product sold without such warning is in a defective condition.

The defective condition may arise not only from harmful ingredients, not characteristic of the product itself either as to presence or quantity, but also from foreign objects contained in the product, from decay or deterioration before sale, or from the way in which the product is prepared or packed. No reason is apparent for distinguishing between the product itself and the container in which it is supplied; and the two are purchased by the user or consumer as an integrated whole. Where the container is itself dangerous, the product is sold in a defective condition. Thus a carbonated beverage in a bottle which is so weak, or cracked, or jagged at the edges, or bottled under such excessive pressure that it may explode or otherwise cause harm to the person who handles it, is in a defective and dangerous condition. The container cannot logically be separated from the contents when the two are sold as a unit, and the liability stated in this Section arises not only when the consumer drinks the beverage and is poisoned by it, but also when he is injured by the bottle while he is handling it preparatory to consumption.

i. *Unreasonably dangerous.* The rule stated in this Section applies only where the defective condition of the product makes it unreasonably dangerous to the user or consumer. Many products cannot possibly be made entirely safe for all consumption, and any food or drug necessarily involves some risk of harm, if only from over-consumption. Ordinary sugar is a deadly poison to diabetics, and castor oil found use under Mussolini as an instrument of torture. That is not what is meant by "unreasonably dangerous" in this Section. The article sold must be dangerous to an extent beyond that which would be contemplated by the ordinary consumer who purchases it, with the ordinary knowledge common to the community as to its characteristics. Good whiskey is not unreasonably dangerous merely because it will make some people drunk, and is especially dangerous to alcoholics; but bad whiskey, containing a dangerous amount of fusel oil, is unreasonably dangerous. Good tobacco is not unreasonably dangerous merely because the effects of smoking may be harmful; but tobacco containing something like marijuana may be unreasonably dangerous. Good butter is not unreasonably dangerous merely because, if such be the case, it deposits cholesterol in the arteries and leads to heart attacks; but bad butter, contaminated with poisonous fish oil, is unreasonably dangerous.

j. Directions or warning. In order to prevent the product from being unreasonably dangerous, the seller may be required to give directions or warning, on the container, as to its use. The seller may reasonably assume that those with common allergies, as for example to eggs or strawberries, will be aware of them, and he is not required to warn against them. Where, however, the product contains an ingredient to which a substantial number of the population are allergic, and the ingredient is one whose danger is not generally known, or if known is one which the consumer would reasonably not expect to find in the product, the seller is required to give warning against it, if he has knowledge, or by the application of reasonable, developed human skill and foresight should have knowledge, of the presence of the ingredient and the danger. Likewise in the case of poisonous drugs, or those unduly dangerous for other reasons, warning as to use may be required.

But a seller is not required to warn with respect to products, or ingredients in them, which are only dangerous, or potentially so, when consumed in excessive quantity, or over a long period of time, when the danger, or potentiality of danger, is generally known and recognized. Again the dangers of alcoholic beverages are an example, as are also those of foods containing such substances as saturated fats, which may over a period of time have a deleterious effect upon the human heart.

Where warning is given, the seller may reasonably assume that it will be read and heeded; and a product bearing such a warning, which is safe for use if it is followed, is not in defective condition, nor is it unreasonably dangerous.

k. Unavoidably unsafe products. There are some products which, in the present state of human knowledge, are quite incapable of being made safe for their intended and ordinary use. These are especially common in the field of drugs. An outstanding example is the vaccine for the Pasteur treatment of rabies, which not uncommonly leads to very serious and damaging consequences when it is injected. Since the disease itself invariably leads to a dreadful death, both the marketing and the use of the vaccine are fully justified, notwithstanding the unavoidable high degree of risk which they involve. Such a product, properly prepared, and accompanied by proper directions and warning, is not defective, nor is it *unreasonably* dangerous. The same is true of many other drugs, vaccines, and the like, many of which for this very reason cannot legally be sold except to physicians, or under the prescription of a physician. It is also true in particular of many new or experimental drugs as to which, because of lack of time and opportunity for sufficient medical experience, there can be no assurance of safety, or perhaps even of purity of ingredients, but such experience as there is justifies the marketing and use of the drug notwithstanding a medically recognizable risk. The seller of such products, again with the qualification that they are properly prepared and marketed, and proper warning is given, where the situation calls for it, is not to be held to strict liability for unfortunate consequences attending their use, merely because he has undertaken to supply the public with an apparently useful and desirable product, attended with a known but apparently reasonable risk.

l. User or consumer. In order for the rule stated in this Section to apply, it is not necessary that the ultimate user or consumer have acquired the product directly from the seller, although the rule applies equally if he does so. He may have acquired it through one or more intermediate dealers. It is not even necessary that the consumer have purchased the product at all. He may be a member of the family of the final purchaser, or his employee, or a guest at his table, or a mere donee from the purchaser. The liability stated is one in tort, and does not require any contractual relation, or privity of contract, between the plaintiff and the defendant.

"Consumers" include not only those who in fact consume the product, but also those who prepare it for consumption; and the housewife who contracts tularemia while cooking rabbits for her husband is included within the rule stated in this Section, as is also the husband who is opening a bottle of beer for his wife to drink. Consumption includes all ultimate uses for which the product is intended, and the customer in a beauty shop to whose hair a permanent wave solution is applied by the shop is a consumer. "User" includes those who are passively enjoying the benefit of the product, as in the case of passengers in automobiles or airplanes, as well as those who are utilizing it for the purpose of doing work upon it, as in the case of an employee of the ultimate buyer who is making repairs upon the automobile which he has purchased.

Illustration:

1. A manufactures and packs a can of beans, which he sells to B, a wholesaler. B sells the beans to C, a jobber, who resells it to D, a

retail grocer. E buys the can of beans from D, and gives it to F. F serves the beans at lunch to G, his guest. While eating the beans, G breaks a tooth, on a pebble of the size, shape, and color of a bean, which no reasonable inspection could possibly have discovered. There is satisfactory evidence that the pebble was in the can of beans when it was opened. Although there is no negligence on the part of A, B, C, or D, each of them is subject to liability to G. On the other hand E and F, who have not sold the beans, are not liable to G in the absence of some negligence on their part.

m.   "Warranty." The liability stated in this Section does not rest upon negligence. It is strict liability, similar in its nature to that covered by Chapters 20 and 21. The basis of liability is purely one of tort.

A number of courts, seeking a theoretical basis for the liability, have resorted to a "warranty," either running with the goods sold, by analogy to covenants running with the land, or made directly to the consumer without contract. In some instances this theory has proved to be an unfortunate one. Although warranty was in its origin a matter of tort liability, and it is generally agreed that a tort action will still lie for its breach, it has become so identified in practice with a contract of sale between the plaintiff and the defendant that the warranty theory has become something of an obstacle to the recognition of the strict liability where there is no such contract. There is nothing in this Section which would prevent any court from treating the rule stated as a matter of "warranty" to the user or consumer. But if this is done, it should be recognized and understood that the "warranty" is a very different kind of warranty from those usually found in the sale of goods, and that it is not subject to the various contract rules which have grown up to surround such sales.

The rule stated in this Section does not require any reliance on the part of the consumer upon the reputation, skill, or judgment of the seller who is to be held liable, nor any representation or undertaking on the part of that seller. The seller is strictly liable although, as is frequently the case, the consumer does not even know who he is at the time of consumption. The rule stated in this Section is not governed by the provisions of the Uniform Sales Act, or those of the Uniform Commercial Code, as to warranties; and it is not affected by limitations on the scope and content of warranties, or by limitation to "buyer" and "seller" in those statutes. Nor is the consumer required to give notice to the seller of his injury within a reasonable time after it occurs, as is provided by the Uniform Act. The consumer's cause of action does not depend upon the validity of his contract with the person from whom he acquires the product, and it is not affected by any disclaimer or other agreement, whether it be between the seller and his immediate buyer, or attached to and accompanying the product into the consumer's hands. In short, "warranty" must be given a new and different meaning if it is used in connection with this Section. It is much simpler to regard the liability here stated as merely one of strict liability in tort.

n. *Contributory negligence.* Since the liability with which this Section deals is not based upon negligence of the seller, but is strict liability, the rule applied to strict liability cases (see § 524) applies. Contributory negligence of the plaintiff is not a defense when such negligence consists merely in a failure to discover the defect in the product, or to guard against the possibility of its existence. On the other hand the form of contributory negligence which consists in voluntarily and unreasonably proceeding to encounter a known danger, and commonly passes under the name of assumption of risk, is a defense under this Section as in other cases of strict liability. If the user or consumer discovers the defect and is aware of the danger, and nevertheless proceeds unreasonably to make use of the product and is injured by it, he is barred from recovery.

Comment on Caveat:

o. *Injuries to non-users and non-consumers.* Thus far the courts, in applying the rule stated in this Section, have not gone beyond allowing recovery to users and consumers, as those terms are defined in Comment *l.* Casual bystanders, and others who may come in contact with the product, as in the case of employees of the retailer, or a passer-by injured by an exploding bottle, or a pedestrian hit by an automobile, have been denied recovery. There may be no essential reason why such plaintiffs should not be brought within the scope of the protection afforded, other than that they do not have the same reasons for expecting such protection as the consumer who buys a marketed product; but the social pressure which has been largely responsible for the development of the rule stated has been a consumers' pressure, and there is not the same demand for the protection of casual strangers. The Institute expresses neither approval nor disapproval of expansion of the rule to permit recovery by such persons.

p. *Further processing or substantial change.* Thus far the decisions applying the rule stated have not gone beyond products which are sold in the condition, or in substantially the same condition, in which they are expected to reach the hands of the ultimate user or consumer. In the absence of decisions providing a clue to the rules which are likely to develop, the Institute has refrained from taking any position as to the possible liability of the seller where the product is expected to, and does, undergo further processing or other substantial change after it leaves his hands and before it reaches those of the ultimate user or consumer.

It seems reasonably clear that the mere fact that the product is to undergo processing, or other substantial change, will not in all cases relieve the seller of liability under the rule stated in this Section. If, for example, raw coffee beans are sold to a buyer who roasts and packs them for sale to the ultimate consumer, it cannot be supposed that the seller will be relieved of all liability when the raw beans are contaminated with arsenic, or some other poison. Likewise the seller of an automobile with a defective steering gear which breaks and injures the driver, can scarcely expect to be relieved of the responsibility by reason of the fact that the car is sold to a dealer who is expected to "service" it, adjust the brakes, mount and inflate the tires, and the like, before it is ready for use. On the other hand, the manufacturer of pigiron, which is capable of a wide variety of uses, is not so likely to be held to strict liability when it turns out to be unsuitable for the child's tricycle into which it is finally made by a remote buyer. The question is essentially one of whether the responsibility for discovery and prevention of the dangerous defect is shifted to the intermediate party who is to make the changes. No doubt there will be some situations, and some defects, as to which the responsibility will be shifted, and others in which it will not. The existing decisions as yet throw no light upon the questions, and the Institute therefore expresses neither approval nor disapproval of the seller's strict liability in such a case.

q. *Component parts.* The same problem arises in cases of the sale of a component part of a product to be assembled by another, as for example a tire to be placed on a new automobile, a brake cylinder for the same purpose, or an instrument for the panel of an airplane. Again the question arises, whether the responsibility is not shifted to the assembler. It is no doubt to be expected that where there is no change in the component part itself, but it is merely incorporated into something larger, the strict liability will be found to carry through to the ultimate user or consumer. But in the absence of a sufficient number of decisions on the matter to justify a conclusion, the Institute expresses no opinion on the matter.

§ 402B. Misrepresentation by Seller of Chattels to Consumer

One engaged in the business of selling chattels who, by advertising, labels, or otherwise, makes to the public a misrepresentation of a material fact concerning the character or quality of a chattel sold by him is subject to liability for physical harm to a consumer of the chattel caused by justifiable reliance upon the misrepresentation, even though

(a) it is not made fraudulently or negligently, and

(b) the consumer has not bought the chattel from or entered into any contractual relation with the seller.

See Reporter's Notes.

Caveat:

The Institute expresses no opinion as to whether the rule stated in this Section may apply

(1) where the representation is not made to the public, but to an individual, or

(2) where physical harm is caused to one who is not a consumer of the chattel.

158

[Handwritten margin notes:]

ELEMENTS:

① S engaged in business of selling chattels (maybe also leases)

② Makes misrepresentation of a material fact
* MATERIAL if
ⓐ Reasonable person would attach importance
ⓑ Maker knows subject is very important to receiver

③ To the PUBLIC

④ Concerning character or quality of chattel sold by him

⑤ Consumer justifiably relies on misrep.

⑥ Causing PHYSICAL HARM to consumer

Comment:

a. The rule stated in this Section is one of strict liability for physical harm to the consumer, resulting from a misrepresentation of the character or quality of the chattel sold, even though the misrepresentation is an innocent one, and not made fraudulently or negligently. Although the Section deals with misrepresentation, it is inserted here in order to complete the rules dealing with the liability of suppliers of chattels for physical harm caused by the chattel. A parallel rule, as to strict liability for pecuniary loss resulting from such a misrepresentation, is stated in § 552 D.*

b. The rule stated in this Section differs from the rule of strict liability stated in § 402 A, which is a special rule applicable only to sellers of products for consumption and does not depend upon misrepresentation. The rule here stated applies to one engaged in the business of selling any type of chattel, and is limited to misrepresentations of their character or quality.

c. History. The early rule was that a seller of chattels incurred no liability for physical harm resulting from the use of the chattel to anyone other than his immediate buyer, unless there was privity of contract between them. (See § 395, Comment *a.*) Beginning with Langridge v. Levy, 2 M. & W. 519, 150 Eng.Rep. 863 (1837), an exception was developed in cases where the seller made fraudulent misrepresentations to the immediate buyer, concerning the character or quality of the chattel sold, and because of the fact misrepresented harm resulted to a third person who was using the chattel. The remedy lay in an action for deceit, and the rule which resulted is now stated in § 557 A.

Shortly after 1930, a number of the American courts began, more or less independently, to work out a further extension of liability for physical harm to the consumer of the chattel, in cases where the seller made misrepresentations to the public concerning its character or quality, and the consumer, as a member of the public, purchased the chattel in reliance upon the misrepresentation and suffered physical harm because of the fact misrepresented. In such cases the seller was held to strict liability for the misrepresentation, even though it was not made fraudulently or negligently. The leading case is Baxter v. Ford Motor Co., 168 Wash. 456, 12 P.2d 409, 88 A.L.R. 521 (1932), adhered to on rehearing, 168 Wash. 456, 15 P.2d 1118, 88 A.L.R. 521, second appeal, 179 Wash. 123, 35 P.2d 1090 (1934), in which the manufacturer of an automobile advertised to the public that the windshield glass was "shatterproof," and the purchaser was injured when a stone struck the glass and it shattered. In the beginning various theories of liability were suggested, including strict liability in deceit, and a contract

---

* Section 552D, in tentative form at the time § 402B was adopted, was ultimately re- jected by The American Law Institute.—Eds.

resulting from an offer made to the consumer to be bound by the representation, accepted by his purchase.

d. "Warranty." The theory finally adopted by most of the decisions, however, has been that of a non-contractual "express warranty" made to the consumer in the form of the representation to the public upon which he relies. The difficulties attending the use of the word "warranty" are the same as those involved under § 402 A, and Comment *m* under that Section is equally applicable here so far as it is pertinent. The liability stated in this Section is liability in tort, and not in contract; and if it is to be called one of "warranty," it is at least a different kind of warranty from that involved in the ordinary sale of goods from the immediate seller to the immediate buyer, and is subject to different rules.

e. Sellers included. The rule stated in this Section applies to any person engaged in the business of selling any type of chattel. It is not limited to sellers of food or products for intimate bodily use, as was until lately the rule stated in § 402 A. It is not limited to manufacturers of the chattel, and it includes wholesalers, retailers, and other distributors who sell it.

The rule stated applies, however, only to those who are engaged in the business of selling such chattels. It has no application to anyone who is not so engaged in business. It does not apply, for example, to a newspaper advertisement published by a private owner of a single automobile who offers it for sale.

f. Misrepresentation of character or quality. The rule stated applies to any misrepresentation of a material fact concerning the character or quality of the chattel sold which is made to the public by one so engaged in the business of selling such chattels. The fact misrepresented must be a material one, upon which the consumer may be expected to rely in making his purchase, and he must justifiably rely upon it. (See Comment *j.*) If he does so, and suffers physical harm by reason of the fact misrepresented, there is strict liability to him.

Illustration:

    1. A manufactures automobiles. He advertises in newspapers and magazines that the glass in his cars is "shatterproof." B reads this advertising, and in reliance upon it purchases from a retail dealer an automobile manufactured by A. While B is driving the car, a stone thrown up by a passing truck strikes the windshield and shatters it, injuring B. A is subject to strict liability to B.

g. Material fact. The rule stated in this Section applies only to misrepresentations of material facts concerning the character or quality of the chattel in question. It does not apply to statements of opinion, and in particular it does not apply to the kind of loose general praise of wares sold which, on the part of the seller, is considered to be "sales talk," and is commonly called "puffing"—as, for example, a statement that an automobile is the best on the market for the price. As to such general language of opinion, see § 542, and Comment *d* under that Section, which is applicable here so far as it is pertinent. In addition, the fact misrepresented must be a material one, of importance to the normal purchaser, by which the ultimate buyer may justifiably be expected to be influenced in buying the chattel.

h. "To the public." The rule stated in this Section is limited to misrepresentations which are made by the seller to the public at large, in order to induce purchase of the chattels sold, or are intended by the seller to, and do, reach the public. The form of the representation is not important. It may be made by public advertising in newspapers or television, by literature distributed to the public through dealers, by labels on the product sold, or leaflets accompanying it, or in any other manner, whether it be oral or written.

Illustrations:

2. A manufactures wire rope. He issues a manual containing statements concerning its strength, which he distributes through dealers to buyers, and to members of the public who may be expected to buy. In reliance upon the statements made in the manual, B buys a quantity of the wire rope from a dealer, and makes use of it to hoist a weight of 1,000 pounds. The strength of the rope is not as great as is represented in the manual, and as a result the rope breaks and the weight falls on B and injures him. A is subject to strict liability to B.

3. A manufactures a product for use by women at home in giving "permanent waves" to their hair. He places on the bottles labels which state that the product may safely be used in a particular manner, and will not be injurious to the hair. B reads such a label, and in reliance upon it purchases a bottle of the product from a retail dealer. She uses it as directed, and as a result her hair is destroyed. A is subject to strict liability to B.

i. Consumers. The rule stated in this Section is limited to strict liability for physical harm to consumers of the chattel. The Caveat leaves open the question whether the rule may not also apply to one who is not a consumer, but who suffers physical harm through his justifiable reliance upon the misrepresentation.

"Consumer" is to be understood in the broad sense of one who makes use of the chattel in the manner which a purchaser may be expected to use it. Thus an employee of the ultimate purchaser to whom the chattel is turned over, and who is directed to make use of it in his work, is a consumer, and so is the wife of the purchaser of an automobile who is permitted by him to drive it.

j. Justifiable reliance. The rule here stated applies only where there is justifiable reliance upon the misrepresentation of the seller, and physical harm results because of such reliance, and because of the fact which is misrepresented. It does not apply where the misrepresentation is not known, or there is indifference to it, and it does not influence the purchase or subsequent conduct. At the same time, however, the misrepresentation need not be the sole inducement to purchase, or to use the chattel, and it is sufficient that it has been a substantial factor in that inducement. (Compare § 546 and Comments.) Since the liability here is for misrepresentation, the rules as to what will constitute justifiable reliance stated in §§ 537–545 A are applicable to this Section, so far as they are pertinent.

The reliance need not necessarily be that of the consumer who is injured. It may be that of the ultimate purchaser of the chattel, who because of such reliance passes it on to the consumer who is in fact injured, but is ignorant of the misrepresentation. Thus a husband who buys an automobile in justifiable reliance upon statements concerning its brakes, and permits his wife to drive the car, supplies the element of reliance, even though the wife in fact never learns of the statements.

Illustration:

4. The same facts as in Illustration 2, except that the harm is suffered by C, an employee of B, to whom B turns over the wire rope without informing him of the representations made by A. The same result.

RESTATEMENT (THIRD) OF TORTS: PRODUCTS LIABILITY
(Approved by the ALI, 1997)
Selected Sections*

CHAPTER 1
LIABILITY OF COMMERCIAL PRODUCT SELLERS BASED ON PRODUCT DEFECTS AT TIME OF SALE

TOPIC 1
LIABILITY RULES APPLICABLE TO PRODUCTS GENERALLY

CHAPTER 3

LIABILITY OF SUCCESSORS AND APPARENT MANUFACTURERS

Chapter 1

LIABILITY OF COMMERCIAL PRODUCT SELLERS BASED ON PRODUCT DEFECTS AT TIME OF SALE

TOPIC 1. LIABILITY RULES APPLICABLE TO PRODUCTS GENERALLY

§ 1. Liability of Commercial Seller or Distributor for Harm Caused by Defective Products

One engaged in the business of selling or otherwise distributing products who sells or distributes a defective product is subject to liability for harm to persons or property caused by the defect.

Comment:

a. History. This Section states a general rule of tort liability applicable to commercial sellers and other distributors of products generally. Rules of liability applicable to special products such as prescription drugs and used products are set forth in separate Sections in Topic 2 of this Chapter.

The liability established in this Section draws on both warranty law and tort law. Historically, the focus of products liability law was on manufacturing defects. A manufacturing defect is a physical departure from a product's intended design. See § 2(a). Typically, manufacturing defects occur in only a small percentage of units in a product line. Courts early began imposing liability without fault on product sellers for harm caused by such defects, holding a seller liable for harm caused by manufacturing defects even though all possible care had been exercised by the seller in the preparation and distribution of the product. In doing so, courts relied on the concept of warranty, in connection with which fault has never been a prerequisite to liability.

The imposition of liability for manufacturing defects has a long history in the common law. As early as 1266, criminal statutes imposed liability upon victualers, vintners, brewers, butchers, cooks, and other persons who supplied contaminated food and drink. In the late 1800s, courts in many states began imposing negligence and strict warranty liability on commercial sellers of defective goods. In the early 1960s, American courts began to recognize that a commercial seller of any product having a manufacturing defect should be liable in tort for harm caused by the defect regardless of the plaintiff's ability to maintain a traditional negligence or warranty action. Liability attached even if the manufacturer's quality control in producing the defective product was reasonable. A plaintiff was not required to be in direct privity with the defendant seller to bring an action. Strict liability in tort for defectively manufactured products merges the concept of implied warranty, in which negligence is not required, with the tort concept of negligence, in which contractual privity is not required. See § 2(a).

Questions of design defects and defects based on inadequate instructions or warnings arise when the specific product unit conforms to the intended design but the intended design itself, or its sale without adequate instructions or warnings, renders the product not reasonably safe. If these forms of defect are found to exist, then every unit in the same product line is potentially defective. See § 2, Comments *d, f,* and *i.* Imposition of liability for design defects and for defects based on inadequate instructions or warnings was relatively infrequent until the late 1960s and early 1970s. A number of restrictive rules made recovery for such defects, especially design defects, difficult to obtain. As these rules eroded, courts sought to impose liability without fault for design defects and defects due to inadequate instructions or warnings under the general principles of § 402A of the Restatement, Second, of Torts. However, it soon became evident that § 402A, created to deal with liability for manufacturing defects, could not appropriately be applied to cases of design defects or defects based on inadequate instructions or warnings. A product unit that fails to meet the manufacturer's design specifications thereby fails to perform its intended function and is, almost by definition, defective. However, when the product unit meets the manufacturer's own design specifications, it is necessary to go outside those specifications to determine whether the product is defective.

Sections 2(b) and 2(c) recognize that the rule developed for manufacturing defects is inappropriate for the resolution of claims of defective design and defects based on inadequate instructions or warnings. These latter categories of cases require determinations that the product could have reasonably been made safer by a better design or instruction or warning. Sections 2(b) and 2(c) rely on a reasonableness test traditionally used in determining whether an actor has been negligent. See Restatement, Second, Torts §§ 291–293. Nevertheless, many courts insist on speaking of liability based on the standards described in §§ 2(b) and 2(c) as being "strict."

Several factors help to explain this rhetorical preference. First, in many design defect cases, if the product causes injury while being put to a reasonably foreseeable use, the seller is held to have known of the risks that foreseeably attend such use. See § 2, Comment *m*. Second, some courts have sought to limit the defense of comparative fault in certain products liability contexts. In furtherance of this objective, they have avoided characterizing the liability test as based in negligence, thereby limiting the effect of comparative or contributory fault. See § 17, Comment *d*. Third, some courts are concerned that a negligence standard might be too forgiving of a small manufacturer who might be excused for its ignorance of risk or for failing to take adequate precautions to avoid risk. Negligence, which focuses on the conduct of the defendant-manufacturer, might allow a finding that a defendant with meager resources was not negligent because it was too burdensome for such a defendant to discover risks or to design or warn against them. The concept of strict liability, which focuses on the product rather than the conduct of the manufacturer, may help make the point that a defendant is held to the expert standard of knowledge available to the relevant manufacturing community at the time the product was manufactured. Finally, the liability of nonmanufacturing sellers in the distributive chain is strict. It is no defense that they acted reasonably and did not discover a defect in the product, be it from manufacturing, design, or failure to warn. See Comment *e*.

Thus, "strict products liability" is a term of art that reflects the judgment that products liability is a discrete area of tort law which borrows from both negligence and warranty. It is not fully congruent with classical tort or contract law. Rather than perpetuating confusion spawned by existing doctrinal categories, §§ 1 and 2 define the liability for each form of defect in terms directly addressing the various kinds of defects. As long as these functional criteria are met, courts may utilize the terminology of negligence, strict liability, or the implied warranty of merchantability, or simply define liability in the terms set forth in the black letter. See § 2, Comment *n*.

b. Sale or other distribution. The rule stated in this Section applies not only to sales transactions but also to other forms of commercial product distribution that are the functional equivalent of product sales. See § 20.

c. One engaged in the business of selling or otherwise distributing. The rule stated in this Section applies only to manufacturers and other commercial sellers and distributors who are engaged in the business of selling or otherwise distributing the type of product that harmed the plaintiff. The rule does not apply to a noncommercial seller or distributor of such products. Thus, it does not apply to one who sells foodstuffs to a neighbor, nor does it apply to the private owner of an automobile who sells it to another.

It is not necessary that a commercial seller or distributor be engaged exclusively or even primarily in selling or otherwise distributing the type of product that injured the plaintiff, so long as the sale of the product is other than occasional or casual. Thus, the rule applies to a motion-picture theater's routine sales of popcorn or ice cream, either for consumption on the premises or in packages to be taken home. Similarly, a service station that does mechanical repair work on cars may also sell tires and automobile equipment as part of its regular business. Such sales are subject to the rule in this Section. However, the rule does not cover occasional sales (frequently referred to as "casual sales") outside the regular course of the seller's business. Thus, an occasional sale of surplus equipment by a business does not fall within the ambit of this rule. Whether a defendant is a commercial seller or distributor within the meaning of this Section is usually a question of law to be determined by the court.

d. Harm to persons or property. The rule stated in this Section applies only to harm to persons or property, commonly referred to as personal injury and property damage. For rules governing economic loss, see § 21.

e. Nonmanufacturing sellers or other distributors of products. The rule stated in this Section provides that all commercial sellers and distributors of products, including nonmanufacturing sellers and distributors such as wholesalers and retailers, are subject to liability for selling products that are defective. Liability attaches even when such nonmanufacturing sellers or distributors do not themselves render the products defective and regardless of whether they are in a position to prevent defects from occurring. See § 2, Comment o. Legislation has been enacted in many jurisdictions that, to some extent, immunizes nonmanufacturing sellers or distributors from strict liability. The legislation is premised on the belief that bringing nonmanufacturing sellers or distributors into products liability litigation generates wasteful legal costs. Although liability in most cases is ultimately passed on to the manufacturer who is responsible for creating the product defect, nonmanufacturing sellers or distributors must devote resources to protect their interests. In most situations, therefore, immunizing nonmanufacturers from strict liability saves those resources without jeopardizing the plaintiff's interests. To assure plaintiffs access to a responsible and solvent product seller or distributor, the statutes generally provide that the non-manufacturing seller or distributor is immunized from strict liability only if: (1) the manufacturer is subject to the jurisdiction of the court of plaintiff's domicile; and (2) the manufacturer is not, nor is likely to become, insolvent.

In connection with these statutes, two problems may need to be resolved to assure fairness to plaintiffs. First, as currently structured, the statutes typically impose upon the plaintiff the risk of insolvency of the manufacturer between the time an action is brought and the time a judgment can be enforced. If a nonmanufacturing seller or distributor is dismissed from an action at the outset when it appears that the manufacturer will be able to pay a judgment, and the manufacturer subsequently becomes insolvent and is unable to pay the judgment, the plaintiff may be left to suffer the loss uncompensated. One possible solution could be to toll the statute of limitations against nonmanufacturers so that they may be brought in if necessary. Second, a nonmanufacturing seller or distributor occasionally will be responsible for the introduction of a defect in a product even though it exercised reasonable care in handling or supervising the product in its control. In such instances, liability for a § 2(a) defect should be imposed on the nonmanufacturing seller or distributor. See § 2, Illustration 2.

§ 2. Categories of Product Defect

A product is defective when, at the time of sale or distribution, it contains a manufacturing defect, is defective in design, or is defective because of inadequate instructions or warnings. A product:

(a) contains a manufacturing defect when the product departs from its intended design even though all possible care was exercised in the preparation and marketing of the product;

(b) is defective in design when the foreseeable risks of harm posed by the product could have been reduced or avoided by the adoption of a reasonable alternative design by the seller or other distributor, or a predecessor in the commercial chain of distribution, and the omission of the alternative design renders the product not reasonably safe;

(c) is defective because of inadequate instructions or warnings when the foreseeable risks of harm posed by the product could have been reduced or avoided by the provision of reasonable instructions or warnings by the seller or other distributor, or a predecessor in the commercial chain of distribution, and the omission of the instructions or warnings renders the product not reasonably safe.

Comment:

a. Rationale. The rules set forth in this Section establish separate standards of liability for manufacturing defects, design defects, and defects based on inadequate instructions or warnings. They are generally applicable to most products. Standards of liability applicable to special product categories such as prescription drugs and used products are set forth in separate sections in Topic 2 of this Chapter.

The rule for manufacturing defects stated in Subsection (a) imposes liability whether or not the manufacturer's quality control efforts satisfy standards of reasonableness. Strict liability without fault in this context is generally believed to foster several objectives. On the premise that tort law serves the instrumental function of creating safety incentives, imposing strict liability on manufacturers for harm caused by manufacturing defects encourages greater investment in product safety than does a regime of fault-based liability under which, as a practical matter, sellers may escape their appropriate share of responsibility. Some courts and commentators also have said that strict liability discourages the consumption of defective products by causing the purchase price of products to reflect, more than would a rule of negligence, the costs of defects. And by eliminating the issue of manufacturer fault from plaintiff's case, strict liability reduces the transaction costs involved in litigating that issue.

Several important fairness concerns are also believed to support manufacturers' liability for manufacturing defects even if the plaintiff is unable to show that the manufacturer's quality control fails to meet risk-utility norms. In many cases manufacturing defects are in fact caused by manufacturer negligence but plaintiffs have difficulty proving it. Strict liability therefore performs a function similar to the concept of res ipsa loquitur, allowing deserving plaintiffs to succeed notwithstanding what would otherwise be difficult or insuperable problems of proof. Products that malfunction due to manufacturing defects disappoint reasonable expectations of product performance. Because manufacturers invest in quality control at consciously chosen levels, their knowledge that a predictable number of flawed products will enter the marketplace entails an element of deliberation about the amount of injury that will result from their activity. Finally, many believe that consumers who benefit from products without suffering harm should share, through increases in the prices charged for those products, the burden of unavoidable injury costs that result from manufacturing defects.

An often-cited rationale for holding wholesalers and retailers strictly liable for harm caused by manufacturing defects is that, as between them and innocent victims who suffer harm because of defective products, the product sellers as business entities are in a better position than are individual users and consumers to insure against such losses. In most instances, wholesalers and retailers will be able to pass liability costs up the chain of product distribution to the manufacturer. When joining the manufacturer in the tort action presents the plaintiff with procedural difficulties, local retailers can pay damages to the victims and then seek indemnity from manufacturers. Finally, holding retailers and wholesalers strictly liable creates incentives for them to deal only with reputable, financially responsible manufacturers and distributors, thereby helping to protect the interests of users and consumers. For considerations relevant to reducing nonmanufacturers' liability, see § 1, Comment *e*.

In contrast to manufacturing defects, design defects and defects based on inadequate instructions or warnings are predicated on a different concept of responsibility. In the first place, such defects cannot be determined by reference to the manufacturer's own design or marketing standards because those standards are the very ones that plaintiffs attack as unreasonable. Some sort of independent assessment of advantages and disadvantages, to which some attach the label "risk-utility balancing," is necessary. Products are not generically defective merely because they are dangerous. Many product-related accident costs can be eliminated only by excessively sacrificing product features that make products useful and desirable. Thus, the various trade-offs need to be considered in determining whether accident costs are more fairly and efficiently borne by accident victims, on the one hand, or, on the other hand, by consumers generally through the mechanism of higher product prices attributable to liability costs imposed by courts on product sellers.

Subsections (b) and (c), which impose liability for products that are defectively designed or sold without adequate warnings or instructions and are thus not reasonably safe, achieve the same general objectives as does liability predicated on negligence. The emphasis is on creating incentives for manufacturers to achieve optimal levels of safety in designing and marketing products. Society does not benefit from products that are excessively safe—for example, automobiles designed with maximum speeds of 20 miles per hour—any more than it benefits from products that are too risky. Society benefits most when the right, or optimal, amount of product safety is achieved. From a fairness perspective, requiring individual users and consumers to bear appropriate responsibility for proper product use prevents careless users and consumers from being subsidized by more careful users and consumers, when the former are paid damages out of funds to which the latter are forced to contribute through higher product prices.

In general, the rationale for imposing strict liability on manufacturers for harm caused by manufacturing defects does not apply in the context of imposing liability for defective design and defects based on inadequate instruction or warning. Consumer expectations as to proper product design or warning are typically more difficult to discern than in the case of a manufacturing defect. Moreover, the element of deliberation in setting appropriate levels of design safety is not directly analogous to the setting of levels of quality control by the manufacturer. When a manufacturer sets its quality control at a certain level, it is aware that a given number of products may leave the assembly line in a defective condition and cause injury to innocent victims who can generally do nothing to avoid injury. The implications of deliberately drawing lines with respect to product design safety are different. A reasonably designed product still carries with it elements of risk that must be protected against by the user or consumer since some risks cannot be designed out of the product at reasonable cost.

Most courts agree that, for the liability system to be fair and efficient, the balancing of risks and benefits in judging product design and marketing must be done in light of the knowledge of risks and risk-avoidance techniques reasonably attainable at the time of distribution. To hold a manufacturer liable for a risk that was not foreseeable when the product was marketed might foster increased manufacturer investment in safety. But such investment by definition would be a matter of guesswork. Furthermore, manufacturers may persuasively ask to be judged by a normative behavior standard to which it is reasonably possible for manufacturers to conform. For these reasons, Subsections (b) and (c) speak of products being defective only when risks are reasonably foreseeable.

b. *The nonexclusiveness of the definitions of defect in this Section.* When a plaintiff seeks recovery under the general rule of liability in § 1, in most instances the plaintiff must establish a prima facie case of product defect by satisfying the requirements of § 2. Section 2 is not, however, the exclusive means by which the plaintiff may establish liability in a products case based on the general rule in § 1. Some courts, for example, while recognizing that in most cases involving defective design the plaintiff must prove the availability of a reasonable alternative design, also observe that such proof is not necessary in every case involving design defects. Sections 3 and 4 and Comment *e* to § 2 provide approaches to the establishment of defective design other than that provided in § 2(b).

Section 3 provides that when circumstantial evidence supports the conclusion that a defect was a contributing cause of the harm and that the defect existed at the time of sale, it is unnecessary to identify the specific nature of the defect and meet the requisites of § 2. Section 3 frees the plaintiff from the strictures of § 2 in circumstances in which common experience teaches that an inference of defect may be warranted under the specific facts, including the failure of the product to perform its manifestly intended function. When the defect established under § 3 may involve product design, some courts recognize consumer expectations as an adequate test for defect, in apparent conflict with the reasonable alternative design requirement in § 2(b). But when the claims involve a product's failure to perform its manifestly intended function and the other requisites of § 3 are met, the apparent conflict disappears.

Section 4, dealing with violations of statutory and regulatory norms, also provides an alternate method of establishing defect. A plaintiff is not required to establish the standard for design or warning under § 2, but merely to identify a government-imposed standard.

Comment *e* provides a further qualification of the rule in § 2(b). This Restatement recognizes the possibility that product sellers may be subject to liability even absent a reasonable alternative design when the product design is manifestly unreasonable. When § 2(b) is read in conjunction with these other provisions that allow for other avenues for determining defective design, it reflects the substantial body of case law suggesting that reasonable alternative design is the predominant, yet not exclusive, method for establishing defective design.

c. Manufacturing defects. As stated in Subsection (a), a manufacturing defect is a departure from a product unit's design specifications. More distinctly than any other type of defect, manufacturing defects disappoint consumer expectations. Common examples of manufacturing defects are products that are physically flawed, damaged, or incorrectly assembled. In actions against the manufacturer, under prevailing rules concerning allocation of burdens of proof the plaintiff ordinarily bears the burden of establishing that such a defect existed in the product when it left the hands of the manufacturer.

Occasionally a defect may arise after manufacture, for example, during shipment or while in storage. Since the product, as sold to the consumer, has a defect that is a departure from the product unit's design specifications, a commercial seller or distributor down the chain of distribution is liable as if the product were defectively manufactured. As long as the plaintiff establishes that the product was defective when it left the hands of a given seller in the distributive chain, liability will attach to that seller. Such defects are referred to in this Restatement as "manufacturing defects" even when they occur after manufacture. When the manufacturer delegates some aspect of manufacture, such as final assembly or inspection, to a subsequent seller, the manufacturer may be subject to liability under rules of vicarious liability for a defect that was introduced into the product after it left the hands of the manufacturer. Although Subsection (a) calls for liability without fault, a plaintiff may seek to recover based upon allegations and proof of negligent manufacture. See Comment *n*. For the rule governing food products that contain impurities or foreign matter, see § 7. For the rule governing commercial used-product sellers' liability for harm caused by manufacturing defects, see § 8.

d. Design defects: general considerations. Whereas a manufacturing defect consists of a product unit's failure to meet the manufacturer's design specifications, a product asserted to have a defective design meets the manufacturer's design specifications but raises the question whether the specifications themselves create unreasonable risks. Answering that question requires reference to a standard outside the specifications. Subsection (b) adopts a reasonableness ("risk-utility balancing") test as the standard for judging the defectiveness of product designs. More specifically, the test is whether a reasonable alternative design would, at reasonable cost, have reduced the foreseeable risks of harm posed by the product and, if so, whether the omission of the alternative design by the seller or a predecessor in the distributive chain rendered the product not reasonably safe. (This is the primary, but not the exclusive, test for defective design. See Comment *b*.) Under prevailing rules concerning allocation of burden of proof, the plaintiff must prove that such a reasonable alternative was, or reasonably could have been, available at time of sale or distribution. See Comment *f*.

Assessment of a product design in most instances requires a comparison between an alternative design and the product design that caused the injury, undertaken from the viewpoint of a reasonable person. That approach is also used in administering the traditional reasonableness standard in negligence. See Restatement, Second, Torts § 283, Comment *c*. The policy reasons that support use of a reasonable-person perspective in connection with the general negligence standard also support its use in the products liability context.

How the defendant's design compares with other, competing designs in actual use is relevant to the issue of whether the defendant's design is defective. Defendants often seek to defend their product designs on the ground that the designs conform to the "state of the art." The term "state of the art" has been variously defined to mean that the product design conforms to industry custom, that it reflects the safest and most advanced technology developed and in commercial use, or that it reflects technology at the cutting edge of scientific knowledge. The confusion brought about by these various definitions is unfortunate. This Section states that a design is defective if the product could have been made safer by the adoption of a reasonable alternative design. If such a design could have been practically adopted at time of sale and if the omission of such a design rendered the product not reasonably safe, the plaintiff establishes defect under Subsection (b). When a defendant demonstrates that its product design was the safest in use at the time of sale, it may be difficult for the plaintiff to prove that an alternative design could have been practically adopted. The defendant is thus allowed to introduce evidence with regard to industry practice that bears on whether an alternative design was practicable. Industry practice may also be relevant to whether the omission of an alternative design rendered the product not reasonably safe. While such evidence is admissible, it is not necessarily dispositive. If the plaintiff introduces expert testimony to establish that a reasonable alternative design could practically have been adopted, a trier of fact may conclude that the product was defective notwithstanding that such a design was not adopted by any manufacturer, or even considered for commercial use, at the time of sale.

Early in the development of products liability law, courts held that a claim based on design defect could not be sustained if the dangers presented by the product were open and obvious. Subsection (b) does not recognize the obviousness of a design-related risk as precluding a finding of defectiveness. The fact that a danger is open and obvious is relevant to the issue of defectiveness, but does not necessarily preclude a plaintiff from establishing that a reasonable alternative design should have been adopted that would have reduced or prevented injury to the plaintiff.

The requirement in Subsection (b) that the plaintiff show a reasonable alternative design applies in most instances even though the plaintiff alleges that the category of product sold by the defendant is so dangerous that it should not have been marketed at all. See Comment *e*. Common and widely distributed products such as alcoholic beverages, firearms, and above-ground swimming pools may be found to be defective only upon proof of the requisite conditions in Subsection (a), (b), or (c). If such products are defectively manufactured or sold without reasonable warnings as to their danger when such warnings are appropriate, or if reasonable alternative designs could have been adopted, then liability under §§ 1 and 2 may attach. Absent proof of defect under those Sections, however, courts have not imposed liability for categories of products that are generally available and widely used and consumed, even if they pose substantial risks of harm. Instead, courts generally have concluded that legislatures and administrative agencies can, more appropriately than courts, consider the desirability of commercial distribution of some categories of widely used and consumed, but nevertheless dangerous, products.

 e. Design defects: possibility of manifestly unreasonable design. Several courts have suggested that the designs of some products are so manifestly unreasonable, in that they have low social utility and high degree of danger, that liability should attach even absent proof of a reasonable alternative design. In large part the problem is one of how the range of relevant alternative designs is described. For example, a toy gun that shoots hard rubber pellets with sufficient velocity to cause injury to children could be found to be defectively designed within the rule of Subsection (b). Toy guns unlikely to cause injury would constitute reasonable alternatives to the dangerous toy. Thus, toy guns that project ping-pong balls, soft gelatin pellets, or water might be found to be reasonable alternative designs to a toy gun that shoots hard pellets. However, if the realism of the hard-pellet gun, and thus its capacity to cause injury, is sufficiently important to those who purchase and use such products to justify the court's limiting consideration to toy guns that achieve realism by shooting hard pellets, then no reasonable alternative will, by hypothesis, be available. In that instance, the design feature that defines which alternatives are relevant—the realism of the hard-pellet gun and thus its capacity to injure—is precisely the feature on which the user places value and of which the plaintiff complains. If a court were to adopt this characterization of the product, and deem the capacity to cause injury an egregiously unacceptable quality in a toy for use by children, it could conclude that liability should attach without proof of a reasonable alternative design. The court would declare the product design to be defective and not reasonably safe because the extremely high degree of danger posed by its use or consumption so substantially outweighs its negligible social utility that no rational, reasonable person, fully aware of the relevant facts, would choose to use, or to allow children to use, the product.

    f. Design defects: factors relevant in determining whether the omission of a reasonable alternative design renders a product not reasonably safe. Subsection (b) states that a product is defective in design if the omission of a reasonable alternative design renders the product not reasonably safe. A broad range of factors may be considered in determining whether an alternative design is reasonable and whether its omission renders a product not reasonably safe. The factors include, among others, the magnitude and probability of the foreseeable risks of harm, the instructions and warnings accompanying the product, and the nature and strength of consumer expectations regarding the product, including expectations arising from product portrayal and marketing. See Comment *g*. The relative advantages and disadvantages of the product as designed and as it alternatively could have been designed may also be considered. Thus, the likely effects of the alternative design on production costs; the effects of the alternative design on product longevity, maintenance, repair, and esthetics; and the range of consumer choice among products are factors that may be taken into account. A plaintiff is not necessarily required to introduce proof on all of these factors; their relevance, and the relevance of other factors, will vary from case to case. Moreover, the factors interact with one another. For example, evidence of the magnitude and probability of foreseeable harm may be offset by evidence that the proposed alternative design would reduce the efficiency and the utility of the product. On the other hand, evidence that a proposed alternative design would increase production costs may be offset by evidence that product portrayal and marketing created substantial expectations of performance or safety, thus increasing the probability of foreseeable harm. Depending on the mix of these factors, a number of variations in the design of a given product may meet the test in Subsection (b). On the other hand, it is not a factor under Subsection (b) that the imposition of liability would have a negative effect on corporate earnings or would reduce employment in a given industry.

    When evaluating the reasonableness of a design alternative, the overall safety of the product must be considered. It is not sufficient that the alternative design would have reduced or prevented the harm suffered by the plaintiff if it would also have introduced into the product other dangers of equal or greater magnitude.

    While a plaintiff must prove that a reasonable alternative design would have reduced the foreseeable risks of harm, Subsection (b) does not require the plaintiff to produce expert testimony in every case. Cases arise in which the feasibility of a reasonable alternative design is obvious and understandable to laypersons and therefore expert testimony is unnecessary to support a finding that the product should have been designed differently and more safely. For example, when a manufacturer sells a soft stuffed toy with hard plastic buttons that are easily removable and likely to choke and suffocate a small child who foreseeably attempts to swallow them, the plaintiff should be able to reach the trier of fact with a claim that buttons on such a toy should be an integral part of the toy's fabric itself (or otherwise be unremovable by an infant) without hiring an expert to demonstrate the feasibility of an alternative safer design. Furthermore, other products already available on the market may serve the same or very similar function at lower risk and at comparable cost. Such products may serve as reasonable alternatives to the product in question.

In many cases, the plaintiff must rely on expert testimony. Subsection (b) does not, however, require the plaintiff to produce a prototype in order to make out a prima facie case. Thus, qualified expert testimony on the issue suffices, even though the expert has produced no prototype, if it reasonably supports the conclusion that a reasonable alternative design could have been practically adopted at the time of sale.

The requirements in Subsection (b) relate to what the plaintiff must prove in order to prevail at trial. This Restatement takes no position regarding the requirements of local law concerning the adequacy of pleadings or pretrial demonstrations of genuine issues of fact. It does, however, assume that the plaintiff will have the opportunity to conduct reasonable discovery so as to ascertain whether an alternative design is practical.

A test that considers such a broad range of factors in deciding whether the omission of an alternative design renders a product not reasonably safe requires a fair allocation of proof between the parties. To establish a prima facie case of defect, the plaintiff must prove the availability of a technologically feasible and practical alternative design that would have reduced or prevented the plaintiff's harm. Given inherent limitations on access to relevant data, the plaintiff is not required to establish with particularity the costs and benefits associated with adoption of the suggested alternative design.

In sum, the requirement of Subsection (b) that a product is defective in design if the foreseeable risks of harm could have been reduced by a reasonable alternative design is based on the commonsense notion that liability for harm caused by product designs should attach only when harm is reasonably preventable. For justice to be achieved, Subsection (b) should not be construed to create artificial and unreasonable barriers to recovery.

The necessity of proving a reasonable alternative design as a predicate for establishing design defect is, like any factual element in a case, addressed initially to the courts. Sufficient evidence must be presented so that reasonable persons could conclude that a reasonable alternative could have been practically adopted. Assuming that a court concludes that sufficient evidence on this issue has been presented, the issue is then for the trier of fact. This Restatement takes no position regarding the specifics of how a jury should be instructed. So long as jury instructions are generally consistent with the rule of law set forth in Subsection (b), their specific form and content are matters of local law.

g. *Consumer expectations: general considerations.* Under Subsection (b), consumer expectations do not constitute an independent standard for judging the defectiveness of product designs. Courts frequently rely, in part, on consumer expectations when discussing liability based on other theories of liability. Some courts, for example, use the term "reasonable consumer expectations" as an equivalent of "proof of a reasonable, safer design alternative," since reasonable consumers have a right to expect product designs that conform to the reasonableness standard in Subsection (b). Other courts, allowing an inference of defect to be drawn when the incident is of a kind that ordinarily would occur as a result of product defect, observe that products that fail when put to their manifestly intended use disappoint reasonable consumer expectations. See § 3. However, consumer expectations do not play a determinative role in determining defectiveness. See Comment *h.* Consumer expectations, standing alone, do not take into account whether the proposed alternative design could be implemented at reasonable cost, or whether an alternative design would provide greater overall safety. Nevertheless, consumer expectations about product performance and the dangers attendant to product use affect how risks are perceived and relate to foreseeability and frequency of the risks of harm, both of which are relevant under Subsection (b). See Comment *f.* Such expectations are often influenced by how products are portrayed and marketed and can have a significant impact on consumer behavior. Thus, although consumer expectations do not constitute an independent standard for judging the defectiveness of product designs, they may substantially influence or even be ultimately determinative on risk-utility balancing in judging whether the omission of a proposed alternative design renders the product not reasonably safe.

Subsection (b) likewise rejects conformance to consumer expectations as a defense. The mere fact that a risk presented by a product design is open and obvious, or generally known, and that the product thus satisfies expectations, does not prevent a finding that the design is defective. But the fact that a product design meets consumer expectations may substantially influence or even be ultimately determinative on risk-utility balancing in judging whether the omission of a proposed alternative design renders the product not reasonably safe. It follows that, while disappointment of consumer expectations may not serve as an independent basis for allowing recovery under Subsection (b), neither may conformance with consumer expectations serve as an independent basis for denying recovery. Such expectations may be relevant in both contexts, but in neither are they controlling.

h. *Consumer expectations: food products and used products.* With regard to two special product categories consumer expectations play a special role in determining product defect. See § 7 (food products) and § 8 (used products). On occasion it is difficult to determine whether a given food component is an inherent aspect of a product or constitutes an adulteration of the product. Whether, for example, a fish bone in commercially distributed fish chowder constitutes a manufacturing defect within the meaning of § 2(a) is best determined by focusing on reasonable consumer expectations.

Regarding commercially distributed used products, the rules set forth in § 2 are not adequate to the task of determining liability. Variations in the type and condition of used products are such that the stringent rules for imposition of liability for new products are inappropriate. On occasion the seller of a used product may market the product in a manner that would cause a reasonable person in the position of the buyer to expect the used product to present no greater risk of defect than if it were new; or a used product may be remanufactured, justifying heightened seller's responsibility. In these limited settings it is appropriate to treat the sale under rules similar to those applicable to new products. See §§ 8(b) and 8(c).

i. Inadequate instructions or warnings. Commercial product sellers must provide reasonable instructions and warnings about risks of injury posed by products. Instructions inform persons how to use and consume products safely. Warnings alert users and consumers to the existence and nature of product risks so that they can prevent harm either by appropriate conduct during use or consumption or by choosing not to use or consume. In most instances the instructions and warnings will originate with the manufacturer, but sellers down the chain of distribution must warn when doing so is feasible and reasonably necessary. In any event, sellers down the chain are liable if the instructions and warnings provided by predecessors in the chain are inadequate. See Comment *o*. Under prevailing rules concerning allocation of burdens of proof, plaintiff must prove that adequate instructions or warnings were not provided. Subsection (c) adopts a reasonableness test for judging the adequacy of product instructions and warnings. It thus parallels Subsection (b), which adopts a similar standard for judging the safety of product designs. Although the liability standard is formulated in essentially identical terms in Subsections (b) and (c), the defectiveness concept is more difficult to apply in the warnings context. In evaluating the adequacy of product warnings and instructions, courts must be sensitive to many factors. It is impossible to identify anything approaching a perfect level of detail that should be communicated in product disclosures. For example, educated or experienced product users and consumers may benefit from inclusion of more information about the full spectrum of product risks, whereas less-educated or unskilled users may benefit from more concise warnings and instructions stressing only the most crucial risks and safe-handling practices. In some contexts, products intended for special categories of users, such as children, may require more vivid and unambiguous warnings. In some cases, excessive detail may detract from the ability of typical users and consumers to focus on the important aspects of the warnings, whereas in others reasonably full disclosure will be necessary to enable informed, efficient choices by product users. Product warnings and instructions can rarely communicate all potentially relevant information, and the ability of a plaintiff to imagine a hypothetical better warning in the aftermath of an accident does not establish that the warning actually accompanying the product was inadequate. No easy guideline exists for courts to adopt in assessing the adequacy of product warnings and instructions. In making their assessments, courts must focus on various factors, such as content and comprehensibility, intensity of expression, and the characteristics of expected user groups.

Depending on the circumstances, Subsection (c) may require that instructions and warnings be given not only to purchasers, users, and consumers, but also to others who a reasonable seller should know will be in a position to reduce or avoid the risk of harm. There is no general rule as to whether one supplying a product for the use of others through an intermediary has a duty to warn the ultimate product user directly or may rely on the intermediary to relay warnings. The standard is one of reasonableness in the circumstances. Among the factors to be considered are the gravity of the risks posed by the product, the likelihood that the intermediary will convey the information to the ultimate user, and the feasibility and effectiveness of giving a warning directly to the user. Thus, when the purchaser of machinery is the owner of a workplace who provides the machinery to employees for their use, and there is reason to doubt that the employer will pass warnings on to employees, the seller is required to reach the employees directly with necessary instructions and warnings if doing so is reasonably feasible.

In addition to alerting users and consumers to the existence and nature of product risks so that they can, by appropriate conduct during use or consumption, reduce the risk of harm, warnings also may be needed to inform users and consumers of nonobvious and not generally known risks that unavoidably inhere in using or consuming the product. Such warnings allow the user or consumer to avoid the risk warned against by making an informed decision not to purchase or use the product at all and hence not to encounter the risk. In this context, warnings must be provided for inherent risks that reasonably foreseeable product users and consumers would reasonably deem material or significant in deciding whether to use or consume the product. Whether or not many persons would, when warned, nonetheless decide to use or consume the product, warnings are required to protect the interests of those reasonably foreseeable users or consumers who would, based on their own reasonable assessments of the risks and benefits, decline product use or consumption. When such warnings are necessary, their omission renders the product not reasonably safe at time of sale. Notwithstanding the defective condition of the product in the absence of adequate warnings, if a particular user or consumer would have decided to use or consume even if warned, the lack of warnings is not a legal cause of that plaintiff's harm. Judicial decisions supporting the duty to provide warnings for informed decisionmaking have arisen almost exclusively with regard to those toxic agents and pharmaceutical products with respect to which courts have recognized a distinctive need to provide risk information so that recipients of the information can decide whether they wish to purchase or utilize the product. See § 6, Comment *d*.

j. Warnings: obvious and generally known risks. In general, a product seller is not subject to liability for failing to warn or instruct regarding risks and risk-avoidance measures that should be obvious to, or generally known by, foreseeable product users. When a risk is obvious or generally known, the prospective addressee of a warning will or should already know of its existence. Warning of an obvious or generally known risk in most instances will not provide an effective additional measure of safety. Furthermore, warnings that deal with obvious or generally known risks may be ignored by users and consumers and may diminish the significance of warnings about non-obvious, not-generally-known risks. Thus, requiring warnings of obvious or generally known risks could reduce the efficacy of warnings generally. When reasonable minds may differ as to whether the risk was obvious or generally known, the issue is to be decided by the trier of fact. The obviousness of risk may bear on the issue of design defect rather than failure to warn. See Comments *d* and *g*.

k. Warnings: adverse allergic or idiosyncratic reactions. Cases of adverse allergic or idiosyncratic reactions involve a special subset of products that may be defective because of inadequate warnings. Many of these cases involve nonprescription drugs and cosmetics. However, virtually any tangible product can contain an ingredient to which some persons may be allergic. Thus, food, nonprescription drugs, toiletries, paint, solvents, building materials, clothing, and furniture have all been involved in litigation to which this Comment is relevant. Prescription drugs and medical devices are also capable of causing allergic reactions, but they are governed by § 6.

The general rule in cases involving allergic reactions is that a warning is required when the harm-causing ingredient is one to which a substantial number of persons are allergic. The degree of substantiality is not precisely quantifiable. Clearly the plaintiff in most cases must show that the allergic predisposition is not unique to the plaintiff. In determining whether the plaintiff has carried the burden in this regard, however, the court may properly consider the severity of the plaintiff's harm. The more severe the harm, the more justified is a conclusion that the number of persons at risk need not be large to be considered "substantial" so as to require a warning. Essentially, this reflects the same risk-utility balancing undertaken in warnings cases generally. But courts explicitly impose the requirement of substantiality in cases involving adverse allergic reactions.

The ingredient that causes the allergic reaction must be one whose danger or whose presence in the product is not generally known to consumers. When both the presence of an allergenic ingredient in the product and the risks presented by such ingredient are widely known, instructions and warnings about that danger are unnecessary. When the presence of the allergenic ingredient would not be anticipated by a reasonable user or consumer, warnings concerning its presence are required.

Similarly, when the presence of the ingredient is generally known to consumers, but its dangers are not, a warning of the dangers must be given.

Finally, as required in Subsection (c), warnings concerning risks of allergic reactions that are not reasonably foreseeable at the time of sale need not be provided. See Comment *m*.

l. Relationship between design and instruction or warning. Reasonable designs and instructions or warnings both play important roles in the production and distribution of reasonably safe products. In general, when a safer design can reasonably be implemented and risks can reasonably be designed out of a product, adoption of the safer design is required over a warning that leaves a significant residuum of such risks. For example, instructions and warnings may be ineffective because users of the product may not be adequately reached, may be likely to be inattentive, or may be insufficiently motivated to follow the instructions or heed the warnings. However, when an alternative design to avoid risks cannot reasonably be implemented, adequate instructions and warnings will normally be sufficient to render the product reasonably safe. Compare Comment *e*. Warnings are not, however, a substitute for the provision of a reasonably safe design.

The fact that a risk is obvious or generally known often serves the same function as a warning. See Comment *j*. However, obviousness of risk does not necessarily obviate a duty to provide a safer design. Just as warnings may be ignored, so may obvious or generally known risks be ignored, leaving a residuum of risk great enough to require adopting a safer design. See Comment *d*.

m. Reasonably foreseeable uses and risks in design and warning claims. Subsections (b) and (c) impose liability only when the product is put to uses that it is reasonable to expect a seller or distributor to foresee. Product sellers and distributors are not required to foresee and take precautions against every conceivable mode of use and abuse to which their products might be put. Increasing the costs of designing and marketing products in order to avoid the consequences of unreasonable modes of use is not required.

In cases involving a claim of design defect in a mechanical product, foreseeability of risk is rarely an issue as a practical matter. Once the plaintiff establishes that the product was put to a reasonably foreseeable use, physical risks of injury are generally known or reasonably knowable by experts in the field. It is not unfair to charge a manufacturer with knowledge of such generally known or knowable risks.

The issue of foreseeability of risk of harm is more complex in the case of products such as prescription drugs, medical devices, and toxic chemicals. Risks attendant to use and consumption of these products may, indeed, be unforeseeable at the time of sale. Unforeseeable risks arising from foreseeable product use or consumption by definition cannot specifically be warned against. Thus, in connection with a claim of inadequate design, instruction, or warning, plaintiff should bear the burden of establishing that the risk in question was known or should have been known to the relevant manufacturing community. The harms that result from unforeseeable risks—for example, in the human body's reaction to a new drug, medical device, or chemical—are not a basis of liability. Of course, a seller bears responsibility to perform reasonable testing prior to marketing a product and to discover risks and risk-avoidance measures that such testing would reveal. A seller is charged with knowledge of what reasonable testing would reveal. If testing is not undertaken, or is performed in an inadequate manner, and this failure results in a defect that causes harm, the seller is subject to liability for harm caused by such defect.

n. Relationship of definitions of defect to traditional doctrinal categories. The rules in this Section and in other provisions of this Chapter define the bases of tort liability for harm caused by product defects existing at time of sale or other distribution. The rules are stated functionally rather than in terms of traditional doctrinal categories. Claims based on product defect at time of sale or other distribution must meet the requisites set forth in Subsection (a), (b), or (c), or the other provisions in this Chapter. As long as these requisites are met, doctrinal tort categories such as negligence or strict liability may be utilized in bringing the claim.

Similarly, a product defect claim satisfying the requisites of Subsection (a), (b), or (c), or other provisions in this Chapter, may be brought under the implied warranty of merchantability provisions of the Uniform Commercial Code. It is recognized that some courts have adopted a consumer expectations definition for design and failure-to-warn defects in implied warranty cases involving harm to persons or property. This Restatement contemplates that a well-coordinated body of law governing liability for harm to persons or property arising out of the sale of defective products requires a consistent definition of defect, and that the definition properly should come from tort law, whether the claim carries a tort label or one of implied warranty of merchantability.

In connection with a claim under §§ 1 and 2 and related provisions of this Restatement, the evidence that the defendant did or did not conduct adequately reasonable research or testing before marketing the product may be admissible (but is not necessarily required) regardless of whether the claim is based on negligence, strict liability, or implied warranty of merchantability. Although a defendant is held objectively responsible for having knowledge that a reasonable seller would have had, the fact that the defendant engaged in substantial research and testing may help to support the contention that a risk was not reasonably foreseeable. Conversely, the fact that the defendant engaged in little or no research or testing may, depending on the circumstances, help to support the contention that, had reasonable research or testing been performed, the risk could have been foreseen. Moreover, as long as the requisites in Subsection (a), (b), or (c), or other provisions in this Chapter, are met, the plaintiff may in appropriate instances—for example, in connection with comparative fault or punitive damage claims—show that the defect resulted from reckless, willfully indifferent, or intentionally wrongful conduct of the defendant.

A separate and more difficult question arises as to whether a case should be submitted to a jury on multiple theories of recovery. Design and failure-to-warn claims may be combined in the same case because they rest on different factual allegations and distinct legal concepts. However, two or more factually identical defective-design claims or two or more factually identical failure-to-warn claims should not be submitted to the trier of fact in the same case under different doctrinal labels. Regardless of the doctrinal label attached to a particular claim, design and warning claims rest on a risk-utility assessment. To allow two or more factually identical risk-utility claims to go to a jury under different labels, whether "strict liability," "negligence," or "implied warranty of merchantability," would generate confusion and may well result in inconsistent verdicts.

In proceedings in which multiple theories are alleged, the Restatement leaves to local law the question of the procedural stage in a tort action at which plaintiff must decide under which theory to pursue the case.

A different approach may be appropriate for claims based on manufacturing defects, since the rule set forth in Subsection (a) does not require risk-utility assessment while a negligence claim does. That is, the two types of manufacturing defect claims are based on different factual predicates. Negligence rests on a showing of fault leading to product defect. Strict liability rests merely on a showing of product defect. When a plaintiff believes a good claim for the negligent creation of (or failure to discover) a manufacturing defect may be established, the plaintiff may assert such a claim in addition to a claim in strict liability under Subsection (a). The plaintiff in such a case should have the opportunity to prove fault and also to assert the right to recover based on strict liability. However, clearly it would be inconsistent for a trier of fact to find no manufacturing defect on a § 2(a) claim and yet return a verdict of liability because the defendant was negligent in having poor quality control. What must be shown under either theory is that the product in question did, in fact, have a manufacturing defect at time of sale that contributed to causing the plaintiff's harm.

In connection with manufacturing defects, a § 2(a) tort claim and an implied warranty of merchantability claim rest on the same factual predicate—the sale by the defendant of a product that departs from the manufacturer's specifications irrespective of anyone's fault. Thus, these two claims are duplicative and may not be pursued together in the same case.

The same analysis applies to claims against a nonmanufacturing supplier. The supplier can be held liable as the seller of a defective product under § 2(a) or can be held liable under a negligence theory for failing reasonably to inspect a product or for negligently introducing a defect into the product. Since these claims are based on different factual predicates, the plaintiff may bring actions in both strict liability and negligence. Again, of course, recovery under either theory requires a finding of defect.

The plaintiff in the nonmanufacturing-supplier case should, once again, not be free to submit a case to a jury based on both the implied warranty of merchantability and strict liability theories since they rest on the same factual base—the sale by the supplier of a defective product regardless of fault. The theories are thus duplicative and do not constitute valid separate claims that may be given to the trier of fact in the same case.

In all instances set forth above in which claims are duplicative, if one or the other theory presents an advantage to the plaintiff—in connection with the statute of limitations, for example—the plaintiff may pursue the more advantageous theory. But the trier of fact may not consider both theories on the same facts.

Plaintiffs may, consistent with the foregoing principles, join claims based on product defect existing at time of sale or other distribution and claims based on theories of recovery that do not rest on a premise of product defect at time of sale. Claims based on misrepresentation, express warranty, and implied warranty of fitness for particular purpose, in particular, are not within the scope of this Chapter and thus are unaffected by it.

Finally, negligence retains its vitality as an independent theory of recovery for a wide range of product-related, harm-causing behavior not involving defects at time of sale. This Restatement includes several such topics in later Chapters, including post-sale failure to warn (see § 10); post-sale failure to recall (see § 11); and a successor's liability for its own failure to warn (see § 13). Other topics are covered in the Restatement, Second, of Torts. Thus, for example, negligent entrustment is treated in § 390. Liability for negligent service, maintenance, or repair, or negligent overpromotion of a product, is governed by the rules set forth in §§ 291 et seq.

o. Liability of nonmanufacturing sellers for defective design and defects due to inadequate instructions or warnings. Nonmanufacturing sellers such as wholesalers and retailers often are not in a good position feasibly to adopt safer product designs or better instructions or warnings. Nevertheless, once it is determined that a reasonable alternative design or reasonable instructions or warnings could have been provided at or before the time of sale by a predecessor in the chain of distribution and would have reduced plaintiff's harm, it is no defense that a nonmanufacturing seller of such a product exercised due care. Thus, strict liability is imposed on a wholesale or retail seller who neither knew nor should have known of the relevant risks, nor was in a position to have taken action to avoid them, so long as a predecessor in the chain of distribution could have acted reasonably to avoid the risks. See Comment *a*. For exceptions to the general rule regarding the liability of a nonmanufacturer seller, see § 1, Comment *e*.

p. Misuse, modification, and alteration. Product misuse, modification, and alteration are forms of post-sale conduct by product users or others that can be relevant to the determination of the issues of defect, causation, or comparative responsibility. Whether such conduct affects one or more of the issues depends on the nature of the conduct and whether the manufacturer should have adopted a reasonable alternative design or provided a reasonable warning to protect against such conduct.

Under the rule in Subsection (b), liability for defective design attaches only if the risks of harm related to foreseeable product use could have been reduced by the adoption of a reasonable alternative design. Similarly, under the rule in Subsection (c), liability for failure to instruct or warn attaches only if the risks presented by the product could have been reduced by the adoption of reasonable instructions or warnings. Foreseeable product misuse, alteration, and modification must also be considered in deciding whether an alternative design should have been adopted. The post-sale conduct of the user may be so unreasonable, unusual, and costly to avoid that a seller has no duty to design or warn against them. When a court so concludes, the product is not defective within the meaning of Subsection (b) or (c).

A product may, however, be defective as defined in Subsection (b) or (c) due to the omission of a reasonable alternative design or the omission of an adequate warning, yet the risk that eventuates due to misuse, modification, or alteration raises questions whether the extent or scope of liability under the prevailing rules governing legal causation allow for the imposition of liability. See § 15.

Moreover, a product may be found to be defective and causally responsible for plaintiff's harm but the plaintiff may have misused, altered, or modified the product in a manner that calls for the reduction of plaintiff's recovery under the rules of comparative responsibility. Thus, an automobile may be defectively designed so as to provide inadequate protection against harm in the event of a collision, and the plaintiff's negligent modification of the automobile may have caused the collision eventuating in plaintiff's harm. See § 17.

It follows that misuse, modification, and alteration are not discrete legal issues. Rather, when relevant, they are aspects of the concepts of defect, causation, and plaintiff's fault. Jurisdictions differ on the question of who bears the burden of raising and introducing proof regarding conduct that constitutes misuse, modification, and alteration. The allocation of burdens in this regard is not addressed in this Restatement and is left to local law.

q. Causation. Under § 1, the product defect must have caused harm to the plaintiff. See §§ 17 and 18.

r. Warranty. Liability for harm caused by product defects imposed by the rules stated in this Chapter is tort liability, not liability for breach of warranty under the Uniform Commercial Code (U.C.C.). Courts may characterize claims under this Chapter as claims for breaches of the implied warranty of merchantability. But in cases involving defect-caused harm to persons or property, a well-coordinated body of law dealing with liability for such harm arising out of the sale of defective products would adopt the tort definition of product defect. See Comment *n*.

§ 3. Circumstantial Evidence Supporting Inference of Product Defect

It may be inferred that the harm sustained by the plaintiff was caused by a product defect existing at the time of sale or distribution, without proof of a specific defect, when the incident that harmed the plaintiff:

(a) was of a kind that ordinarily occurs as a result of product defect; and

(b) was not, in the particular case, solely the result of causes other than product defect existing at the time of sale or distribution.

Comment:

a. History. This Section traces its historical antecedents to the law of negligence, which has long recognized that an inference of negligence may be drawn in cases where the defendant's negligence is the best explanation for the cause of an accident, even if the plaintiff cannot explain the exact nature of the defendant's conduct. See Restatement, Second, Torts § 328D. As products liability law developed, cases arose in which an inference of product defect could be drawn from the incident in which a product caused plaintiff's harm, without proof of the specific nature of the defect. This Section sets forth the formal requisites for drawing such an inference.

b. Requirement that the harm be of a kind that ordinarily occurs as a result of product defect. The most frequent application of this Section is to cases involving manufacturing defects. When a product unit contains such a defect, and the defect affects product performance so as to cause a harmful incident, in most instances it will cause the product to malfunction in such a way that the inference of product defect is clear. From this perspective, manufacturing defects cause products to fail to perform their manifestly intended functions. Frequently, the plaintiff is able to establish specifically the nature and identity of the defect and may proceed directly under § 2(a). But when the product unit involved in the harm-causing incident is lost or destroyed in the accident, direct evidence of specific defect may not be available. Under that circumstance, this Section may offer the plaintiff the only fair opportunity to recover.

When examination of the product unit is impossible because the unit is lost or destroyed after the harm-causing incident, a somewhat different issue may be presented. Responsibility for spoliation of evidence may be relevant to the fairness of allowing the inference set forth in this Section. In any event, the issues of evidence spoliation and any sanctions that might be imposed for such conduct are beyond the scope of this Restatement Third, Torts: Products Liability.

Although the rules in this Section, for the reasons just stated, most often apply to manufacturing defects, occasionally a product design causes the product to malfunction in a manner identical to that which would ordinarily be caused by a manufacturing defect. Thus, an aircraft may inadvertently be designed in such a way that, in new condition and while flying within its intended performance parameters, the wings suddenly and unexpectedly fall off, causing harm. In theory, of course, the plaintiff in such a case would be able to show how other units in the same production line were designed, leading to a showing of a reasonable alternative design under § 2(b). As a practical matter, however, when the incident involving the aircraft is one that ordinarily occurs as a result of product defect, and evidence in the particular case establishes that the harm was not solely the result of causes other than product defect existing at time of sale, it should not be necessary for the plaintiff to incur the cost of proving whether the failure resulted from a manufacturing defect or from a defect in the design of the product. Section 3 allows the trier of fact to draw the inference that the product was defective whether due to a manufacturing defect or a design defect. Under those circumstances, the plaintiff need not specify the type of defect responsible for the product malfunction.

It is important to emphasize the difference between a general inference of defect under § 3 and claims of defect brought directly under §§ 1 and 2. Section 3 claims are limited to situations in which a product fails to perform its manifestly intended function, thus supporting the conclusion that a defect of some kind is the most probable explanation. If that is not the case, and if no other provision of Chapter 1 allows the plaintiff to establish defect independently of the requirements in § 2 (see § 4 and Comment *e* to § 2), a plaintiff is required to establish a cause of action for defect based on proof satisfying the requirements set forth in § 2. See § 2, Comment *b*.

Illustrations:

　　1.　John purchased a new electric blender. John used the blender approximately 10 times exclusively for making milkshakes. While he was making a milkshake, the blender suddenly shattered. A piece of glass struck John's eye, causing harm. The incident resulting in harm is of a kind that ordinarily occurs as a result of product defect.

　　2.　Same facts as Illustration 1, except that John accidentally dropped the blender, causing the glass to shatter. The product did not fail to function in a manner supporting an inference of defect. Whether liability can be established depends on whether the plaintiff can prove a cause of action under §§ 1 and 2.

　　3.　Mary purchased a new automobile. She drove the car 1,000 miles without incident. One day she stopped the car at a red light and leaned back to rest until the light changed. Suddenly the seat collapsed backward, causing Mary to hit the accelerator and the car to shoot out into oncoming traffic and collide with another car. Mary suffered harm in the ensuing collision. As a result of the collision, Mary's car was set afire, destroying the seat assembly. The incident resulting in the harm is of a kind that ordinarily occurs as a result of product defect. Mary need not establish whether the seat assembly contained a manufacturing defect or a design defect.

4. Same facts as in Illustration 3, except that the seat-back assembly failed when Mary, while stopped at the red light, was rearended by another automobile at 40 m.p.h. Mary cannot make out liability under this Section. The product did not fail to function in a manner supporting an inference of defect since the collapse of the seat is not the kind of incident that ordinarily occurs as a result of product defect. Liability must be established under the rules set forth in §§ 1 and 2.

5. While carefully driving a new automobile at legal speed on a well-maintained road, Driver felt something crack below where the steering column connects with the dashboard. The steering wheel spun to the right and the automobile turned sharply. Before Driver could stop, the automobile crashed into a wall and Driver suffered harm. Driver has brought an action against the manufacturer of the automobile. The automobile had been driven on short trips before the accident and had 300 miles on its odometer. Driver's qualified expert witness testifies that in her opinion the accident was caused by a defect in the steering mechanism. The expert identifies four specific manufacturing and design defects that could have caused the accident, but was unable to say, on a balance of the probabilities, which of the four defects was the cause. Under this Section it is not necessary to identify the specific defect in order to draw the inference that a product defect caused the plaintiff's harm.

c. *No requirement that plaintiff prove what aspect of the product was defective.* The inference of defect may be drawn under this Section without proof of the specific defect. Furthermore, quite apart from the question of what type of defect was involved, the plaintiff need not explain specifically what constituent part of the product failed. For example, if an inference of defect can be appropriately drawn in connection with the catastrophic failure of an airplane, the plaintiff need not establish whether the failure is attributable to fuel-tank explosion or engine malfunction.

d. *Requirement that the incident that harmed the plaintiff was not, in the particular case, solely the result of causes other than product defect existing at the time of sale.* To allow the trier of fact to conclude that a product defect caused the plaintiff's harm under this Section, the plaintiff must establish by a preponderance of the evidence that the incident was not solely the result of causal factors other than defect at time of sale. The defect need not be the only cause of the incident; if the plaintiff can prove that the most likely explanation of the harm involves the causal contribution of a product defect, the fact that there may be other concurrent causes of the harm does not preclude liability under this Section. But when the harmful incident can be attributed solely to causes other than original defect, including the conduct of others, an inference of defect under this Section cannot be drawn.

Evidence may permit the inference that a defect in the product at the time of the harm-causing incident caused the product to malfunction, but not the inference that the defect existed at the time of sale or distribution. Such factors as the age of the product, possible alteration by repairers or others, and misuse by the plaintiff or third parties may have introduced the defect that causes harm.

Illustrations:

6. While driving a new automobile at high speed one night, Driver drove off the highway and crashed into a tree. Driver suffered harm. Driver cannot remember the circumstances surrounding the accident. Driver has brought an action against ABC Company, the manufacturer of the automobile. Driver presents no evidence of a specific defect. However, Driver's qualified expert presents credible testimony that a defect in the automobile must have caused the accident. ABC's qualified expert presents credible testimony that it is equally likely that, independent of any defect, Driver lost control while speeding on the highway. If the trier of fact believes the testimony of Driver's expert, then an inference of defect may be established under this Section. If, however, ABC's expert is believed, an inference of product defect may not be drawn under this Section because Driver has failed to establish by a preponderance of the evidence that the harm did not result solely from Driver's independent loss of control at high speed.

7. Jack purchased a new ABC Electric Power Screwdriver. He inserted the bit for the appropriate screw size and turned the power button on. The bit shot out of the tool and lodged itself in Jack's arm, causing serious injury. Two weeks after purchasing the electric screwdriver, Jack believed the tool was making too much noise and brought it to the Acme Tool Repair Shop to check it out. Acme removed the mechanism that held the bit, examined it, and then reassembled it. Finding no problem, Acme returned the tool to Jack. The accident occurred the next day. On direct examination Jack's expert testifies that the accident was caused by a defect existing at time of sale. On cross-examination, however, Jack's expert admits it is equally probable that the problem with the tool was introduced by Acme. An inference that the power tool was defective at the time of sale cannot be drawn under this Section.

§ 4. Noncompliance and Compliance with Product Safety Statutes or Regulations

In connection with liability for defective design or inadequate instructions or warnings:

(a) a product's noncompliance with an applicable product safety statute or administrative regulation renders the product defective with respect to the risks sought to be reduced by the statute or regulation; and

(b) a product's compliance with an applicable product safety statute or administrative regulation is properly considered in determining whether the product is defective with respect to the risks sought to be reduced by the statute or regulation, but such compliance does not preclude as a matter of law a finding of product defect.

TOPIC 2. LIABILITY RULES APPLICABLE TO SPECIAL PRODUCTS OR PRODUCT MARKETS

§ 5. Liability of Commercial Seller or Distributor of Product Components for Harm Caused by Products Into Which Components Are Integrated

One engaged in the business of selling or otherwise distributing product components who sells or distributes a component is subject to liability for harm to persons or property caused by a product into which the component is integrated if:

(a) the component is defective in itself, as defined in this Chapter, and the defect causes the harm; or

(b)(1) the seller or distributor of the component substantially participates in the integration of the component into the design of the product; and

(2) the integration of the component causes the product to be defective, as defined in this Chapter; and

(3) the defect in the product causes the harm.

Comment:

a. Rationale. Product components include raw materials, bulk products, and other constituent products sold for integration into other products. Some components, such as raw materials, valves, or switches, have no functional capabilities unless integrated into other products. Other components, such as a truck chassis or a multi-functional machine, function on their own but still may be utilized in a variety of ways by assemblers of other products.

As a general rule, component sellers should not be liable when the component itself is not defective as defined in this Chapter. If the component is not itself defective, it would be unjust and inefficient to impose liability solely on the ground that the manufacturer of the integrated product utilizes the component in a manner that renders the integrated product defective. Imposing liability would require the component seller to scrutinize another's product which the component seller has no role in developing. This would require the component seller to develop sufficient sophistication to review the decisions of the business entity that is already charged with responsibility for the integrated product.

The refusal to impose liability on sellers of nondefective components is expressed in various ways, such as the "raw material supplier defense" or the "bulk sales/sophisticated purchaser rule." However expressed, these formulations recognize that component sellers who do not participate in the integration of the component into the design of the product should not be liable merely because the integration of the component causes the product to become dangerously defective. This Section subjects component sellers to liability when the components themselves are defective or when component providers substantially participate in the integration of components into the design of the other products.

Illustration:

> 1. ABC Chain Co. manufactures chains for a wide range of uses in industrial equipment. XYZ Mach. Co. purchases chains from ABC for use in conveyor-belt systems and informs ABC that the chains will be used for that purpose. In the design of a conveyor system by XYZ, part of the chain is exposed. The conveyor system as designed and manufactured by XYZ is defective in that it should include a safety guard under the rule stated in § 2(b). XYZ sells a conveyor system to LMN Co. LMN's employee, E, while working near the conveyor, is injured when her shirt sleeve becomes entangled in the unguarded chain in the conveyor. ABC is not subject to liability to E. The chain sold by ABC is not itself defective as defined in § 2, and ABC did not participate in the integration of its chain into the design of the XYZ conveyor. XYZ is subject to liability for harm to E as the seller of a defectively designed conveyor under the rules stated in §§ 1 and 2(b).

b. Liability when a product component is defective in itself. A commercial seller or other distributor of a product component is subject to liability for harm caused by a defect in the component. See § 19, Comment *b*. For example, if a cut-off switch is sold in defective condition due to loosely connected wiring, the seller of the switch is subject to liability for harm to persons or property caused by the improper wiring after the switch is integrated into another product. Similarly, if aluminum that departs from the aluminum manufacturer's specifications due to the presence of foreign particles is utilized in the manufacture of airplane engines, the seller of the defective aluminum is subject to liability for harm to persons or property caused by the defects in the aluminum. Both the switches in the first instance and the aluminum in the second are defective as defined in § 2(a).

The same rule applies when a component is defectively designed as defined in § 2(b). For example, if motorcycle headlights intended for rugged off-road use are so designed that they fail when the motorcycle is driven over bumpy roads, they are defective within the meaning of § 2(b). Since reasonable alternative designs are available that prevent such foreseeable failures from occurring, the headlight supplier is subject to liability for harm caused by the defectively designed headlight. Indeed, a defect may be inferable under § 3. However, a component not defective in itself as defined in § 2(b) or § 3 does not become defective merely because a purchaser decides to integrate the component into another product in a way that renders the design of the integrated product defective. See Comment *e*.

The same principles apply in determining a component seller's duty to supply reasonable instructions and warnings to the component buyer. The component seller is required to provide instructions and warnings regarding risks associated with the use of the component product. See §§ 1 and 2(c). However, when a sophisticated buyer integrates a component into another product, the component seller owes no duty to warn either the immediate buyer or ultimate consumers of dangers arising because the component is unsuited for the special purpose to which the buyer puts it. To impose a duty to warn in such a circumstance would require that component sellers monitor the development of products and systems into which their components are to be integrated. See Comment *a*. Courts have not yet confronted the question of whether, in combination, factors such as the component purchaser's lack of expertise and ignorance of the risks of integrating the component into the purchaser's product, and the component supplier's knowledge of both the relevant risks and the purchaser's ignorance thereof, give rise to a duty on the part of the component supplier to warn of risks attending integration of the component into the purchaser's product. Whether the seller of a component should be subject to liability for selling its product to one who is likely to utilize it dangerously is governed by principles of negligent entrustment. See Restatement, Second, Torts § 390.

Illustrations:

2. The same facts as Illustration 1, except that one of the chains sold by ABC to XYZ contains a manufacturing defect as defined in § 2(a). XYZ installs the defective chain in the conveyor-belt system sold by XYZ to LMN. As a result of the defect, the chain breaks, causing the conveyor belt to stop abruptly. E, LMN's employee, suffers harm when the conveyor's sudden stop causes a heavy object on the conveyor to fall on E. ABC is subject to liability to E for harm caused by the sale of the defective component. XYZ is also subject to liability to E for the sale of a defective conveyor system.

3. ABC Vinyl, Inc., sells vinyl swimming-pool liners for use in above-ground swimming pools. ABC manufactures the liners without depth markers. XYZ Pools, Inc., manufactures and sells above-ground swimming pools. XYZ installs a pool with an ABC liner at the home of Roberta. Jack, while visiting Roberta, dives into the shallow portion of

the pool that appears to him to be eight feet deep. In reality the water is only four feet deep. Jack hits his head on the bottom and suffers harm. If a court finds that the absence of the depth markers renders the design of the liner defective within the meaning of § 2(b), ABC is subject to liability to Jack. The fact that the liner is a component of the above-ground swimming pool and has been integrated into a specific swimming pool does not insulate ABC from liability for selling a component product that is defectively designed for all swimming-pool installations. XYZ is also subject to liability to Jack as the seller of a pool with a defectively designed liner.

4. ABC Foam Co. manufactures bulk foam with many different uses. XYZ Co. purchases bulk foam from ABC, then processes the foam and incorporates the processed foam in the manufacture of disposable dishware. ABC becomes aware that XYZ is using processed foam in the dishware. ABC and XYZ are both aware that there is a potential danger that processed foam may cause allergic skin reactions for some users. ABC is aware that XYZ is not warning consumers of this potential problem. ABC has no duty to warn XYZ or ultimate consumers of the dangers attendant to use of the processed foam for disposable dishware. The foam sold by ABC is not defective in itself as defined in this Chapter. A supplier of a component has no duty to warn a knowledgeable buyer of risks attendant to special application of its products when integrated into another's product. ABC did not participate in the design of the disposable dishware manufactured by XYZ, and is thus not subject to liability under Subsection (b).

c. Raw materials. Product components include raw materials. See Comment *a.* Thus, when raw materials are contaminated or otherwise defective within the meaning of § 2(a), the seller of the raw materials is subject to liability for harm caused by such defects. Regarding the seller's exposure to liability for defective design, a basic raw material such as sand, gravel, or kerosene cannot be defectively designed. Inappropriate decisions regarding the use of such materials are not attributable to the supplier of the raw materials but rather to the fabricator that puts them to improper use. The manufacturer of the integrated product has a significant comparative advantage regarding selection of materials to be used. Accordingly, raw-materials sellers are not subject to liability for harm caused by defective design of the end-product. The same considerations apply to failure-to-warn claims against sellers of raw materials. To impose a duty to warn would require the seller to develop expertise regarding a multitude of different end-products and to investigate the actual use of raw materials by manufacturers over whom the supplier has no control. Courts uniformly refuse to impose such an onerous duty to warn. For a consideration of whether special circumstances may give rise to a duty on the part of raw-material sellers to warn of risks attending integration of raw materials with other components, see Comment *b.*

Illustration:

    5. LMN Sand Co. sells sand in bulk. ABC Construction Co. purchases sand to use in mixing cement. LMN is aware that the improper mixture of its sand with other ingredients can cause cement to crack. ABC utilizes LMN's sand to form a cement supporting column in a building. As a result of improper mixture the cement column cracks and gives way during a mild earthquake and causes injury to the building's occupants. LMN is not liable to the injured occupants. The sand sold by LMN is not itself defective under §§ 1–4. LMN has no duty to warn ABC about improperly mixing sand for use in cement. LMN did not participate in ABC's design of the cement and is not subject to liability for harm caused by the sand as integrated into the cement.

    d. Incomplete products. Product components include products that can be put to different uses depending on how they are integrated into other products. For example, the chassis of a truck can be put to a variety of different uses. A truck chassis may ultimately be used with a cement mixer or a garbage compaction unit or in a flat-bed truck. Similarly, an engine for industrial machines may be adapted to a variety of different industrial uses. A seller ordinarily is not liable for failing to incorporate a safety feature that is peculiar to the specific adaptation for which another utilizes the incomplete product. A safety feature important for one adaptation may be wholly unnecessary or inappropriate for a different adaptation. The same considerations also militate against imposing a duty on the seller of the incomplete product to warn purchasers of the incomplete product, or end-users of the integrated product, of dangers arising from special adaptations of the incomplete product by others.

    e. Substantial participation in the integration of the component into the design of another product. When the component seller is substantially involved in the integration of the component into the design of the integrated product, the component seller is subject to liability when the integration results in a defective product and the defect causes harm to the plaintiff. Substantial participation can take various forms. The manufacturer or assembler of the integrated product may invite the component seller to design a component that will perform specifically as part of the integrated product or to assist in modifying the design of the integrated product to accept the seller's component. Or the component seller may play a substantial role in deciding which component best serves the requirements of the integrated product. When the component seller substantially participates in the design of the integrated product, it is fair and reasonable to hold the component seller responsible for harm caused by the defective, integrated product. A component seller who simply designs a component to its buyer's specifications, and does not substantially participate in the integration of the component into the design of the product, is not liable within the meaning of Subsection (b). Moreover, providing mechanical or technical services or advice concerning a component part does not, by itself, constitute substantial participation that would subject the component supplier to liability. One who provides a design service alone, as distinct from combining the design function with the sale of a component, generally is liable only for negligence and is not treated as a product seller. See § 19(b).

f. Integration of the component as a cause of the harm. The mere fact that the component seller substantially participates in the integration of the component into the design of a product does not subject the seller to liability unless the integration causes the product to be defective and the resulting defect causes the plaintiff's harm. The component seller is not liable for harm caused by defects in the integrated product that are unrelated to the component. For example, a manufacturer of a component valve may substantially participate in redesigning the valve so that it can be integrated into a particular kind of tank. If the tank fails due to defective steel in the body of the tank and the failure has nothing to do with the installation of the valve, the seller of the valve is not subject to liability under Subsection (b). The valve manufacturer is not liable under Subsection (b) even if it is sufficiently involved in the design of the tank so that it would be liable for harm caused by a failure of the valve as integrated into the tank. Similarly, if a raw-material supplier offers advice about processing the material and there is no evidence that the processing advice was a cause of the allegedly defective condition, the raw-material supplier should not be subject to liability.

Illustration:

6. ABC Chemical Co. sells plastic resins in bulk. XYZ Hot Water Heater Manufacturing Co. informs ABC that XYZ wishes to purchase resin for use in making its hot-water heaters and specifies resin that can withstand heat up to 212° Fahrenheit. ABC recommends that XYZ use a certain type of resin which, in ABC's testing under specified laboratory conditions, including thickness of one-quarter inch or more, was shown to be capable of withstanding temperatures in excess of 212° Fahrenheit. ABC explains these conditions to XYZ. ABC also provides XYZ with technical support and general processing advice. XYZ purchases the recommended resin from ABC and decides upon design and processing parameters, molds the resin into a plastic part, and combines the part with other materials and parts to produce hot-water heaters. XYZ tests its hot-water heaters for safety and durability and formulates instructions and warnings to accompany them. An XYZ hot-water heater subsequently fails because the plastic walls specified by its design, one-eighth inch thick, are too thin to withstand the stress imposed by its normal operating temperatures, resulting in injury to a homeowner. ABC is not liable to the homeowner. The resin sold by ABC was not in itself defective. ABC did not substantially participate in the design, manufacture or assembly of the hot-water heater.

§ 6. Liability of Commercial Seller or Distributor for Harm Caused by Defective Prescription Drugs and Medical Devices

(a) A manufacturer of a prescription drug or medical device who sells or otherwise distributes a defective drug or medical device is subject to liability for harm to persons caused by the defect. A prescription drug or medical device is one that may be legally sold or otherwise distributed only pursuant to a health-care provider's prescription.

(b) For purposes of liability under Subsection (a), a prescription drug or medical device is defective if at the time of sale or other distribution the drug or medical device:

(1) contains a manufacturing defect as defined in § 2(a); or

(2) is not reasonably safe due to defective design as defined in Subsection (c); or

(3) is not reasonably safe due to inadequate instructions or warnings as defined in Subsection (d).

(c) A prescription drug or medical device is not reasonably safe due to defective design if the foreseeable risks of harm posed by the drug or medical device are sufficiently great in relation to its foreseeable therapeutic benefits that reasonable health-care providers, knowing of such foreseeable risks and therapeutic benefits, would not prescribe the drug or medical device for any class of patients.

(d) A prescription drug or medical device is not reasonably safe due to inadequate instructions or warnings if reasonable instructions or warnings regarding foreseeable risks of harm are not provided to:

(1) prescribing and other health-care providers who are in a position to reduce the risks of harm in accordance with the instructions or warnings; or

(2) the patient when the manufacturer knows or has reason to know that health-care providers will not be in a position to reduce the risks of harm in accordance with the instructions or warnings.

(e) A retail seller or other distributor of a prescription drug or medical device is subject to liability for harm caused by the drug or device if:

(1) at the time of sale or other distribution the drug or medical device contains a manufacturing defect as defined in § 2(a); or

> **(2) at or before the time of sale or other distribution of the drug or medical device the retail seller or other distributor fails to exercise reasonable care and such failure causes harm to persons.**

Comment:

a. History. Subsections (b)(1) and (d)(1) state the traditional rules that drug and medical-device manufacturers are liable only when their products contain manufacturing defects or are sold without adequate instructions and warnings to prescribing and other health-care providers. Until recently, courts refused to impose liability based on defective designs of drugs and medical devices sold only by prescription. However, consistent with recent trends in the case law, two limited exceptions from these traditional rules are generally recognized. Subsection (d)(2) sets forth situations when a prescription-drug or medical-device manufacturer is required to warn the patient directly of risks associated with consumption or use of its product. And Subsection (c) imposes liability for a drug or medical device whose risks of harm so far outweigh its therapeutic benefits that reasonable, properly informed health-care providers would not prescribe it.

b. Rationale. The obligation of a manufacturer to warn about risks attendant to the use of drugs and medical devices that may be sold only pursuant to a health-care provider's prescription traditionally has required warnings directed to health-care providers and not to patients. The rationale supporting this "learned intermediary" rule is that only health-care professionals are in a position to understand the significance of the risks involved and to assess the relative advantages and disadvantages of a given form of prescription-based therapy. The duty then devolves on the health-care provider to supply to the patient such information as is deemed appropriate under the circumstances so that the patient can make an informed choice as to therapy. Subsection (d)(1) retains the "learned intermediary" rule. However, in certain limited therapeutic relationships the physician or other health-care provider has a much-diminished role as an evaluator or decisionmaker. In these instances it may be appropriate to impose on the manufacturer the duty to warn the patient directly. See Subsection (d)(2).

The traditional refusal by courts to impose tort liability for defective designs of prescription drugs and medical devices is based on the fact that a prescription drug or medical device entails a unique set of risks and benefits. What may be harmful to one patient may be beneficial to another. Under Subsection (c) a drug is defectively designed only when it provides no net benefit to any class of patients. Courts have concluded that as long as a drug or medical device provides net benefits to some persons under some circumstances, the drug or device manufacturer should be required to instruct and warn health-care providers of the foreseeable risks and benefits. Courts have also recognized that the regulatory system governing prescription drugs is a legitimate mechanism for setting the standards for drug design. In part, this deference reflects concerns over the possible negative effects of judicially imposed liability on the cost and availability of valuable medical technology. This deference also rests on two further assumptions: first, that prescribing health-care providers, when adequately informed by drug manufacturers, are able to assure that the right drugs and medical devices reach the right patients; and second, that governmental regulatory agencies adequately review new prescription drugs and devices, keeping unreasonably dangerous designs off the market.

Nevertheless, unqualified deference to these regulatory mechanisms is considered by a growing number of courts to be unjustified. An approved prescription drug or medical device can present significant risks without corresponding advantages. At the same time, manufacturers must have ample discretion to develop useful drugs and devices without subjecting their design decisions to the ordinary test applicable to products generally under § 2(b). Accordingly, Subsection (c) imposes a more rigorous test for defect than does § 2(b), which does not apply to prescription drugs and medical devices. The requirement for establishing defective design of a prescription drug or medical device under Subsection (c) is that the drug or device have so little merit compared with its risks that reasonable health-care providers, possessing knowledge of risks that were known or reasonably should have been known, would not have prescribed the drug or device for any class of patients. Thus, a prescription drug or medical device that has usefulness to any class of patients is not defective in design even if it is harmful to other patients. Because of the special nature of prescription drugs and medical devices, the determination of whether such products are not reasonably safe is to be made under Subsections (c) and (d) rather than under §§ 2(b) and 2(c).

The rules imposing liability on a manufacturer for inadequate warning or defective design of prescription drugs and medical devices assume that the federal regulatory standard has not preempted the imposition of tort liability under state law. When such preemption is found, liability cannot attach if the manufacturer has complied with the applicable federal standard. See § 4, Comment *e*.

The doctrine of preemption based on supremacy of federal law should be distinguished from the proposition that compliance with statutory and regulatory standards satisfies the state's requirement for product safety. Subsections (c) and (d) recognize common-law causes of action for defective drug design and for failure to provide reasonable instructions or warnings, even though the manufacturer complied with governmental standards. For the rules governing compliance with governmental standards generally, see § 4(b).

   c. Manufacturers' liability for manufacturing defects. Limitations on the liability for prescription drug and medical-device designs do not support treating drug and medical-device manufacturers differently from commercial sellers of other products with respect to manufacturing defects. Courts have traditionally subjected manufacturers of prescription products to liability for harm caused by manufacturing defects.

d. Manufacturers' liability for failure adequately to instruct or warn prescribing and other health-care providers. Failure to instruct or warn is the major basis of liability for manufacturers of prescription drugs and medical devices. When prescribing health-care providers are adequately informed of the relevant benefits and risks associated with various prescription drugs and medical devices, they can reach appropriate decisions regarding which drug or device is best for specific patients. Sometimes a warning serves to inform health-care providers of unavoidable risks that inhere in the drug or medical device. By definition, such a warning would not aid the health-care provider in reducing the risk of injury to the patient by taking precautions in how the drug is administered or the medical device is used. However, warnings of unavoidable risks allow the health-care provider, and thereby the patient, to make an informed choice whether to utilize the drug or medical device. Beyond informing prescribing health-care providers, a drug or device manufacturer may have a duty under the law of negligence to use reasonable measures to supply instructions or warnings to nonprescribing health-care providers who are in positions to act on such information so as to reduce or prevent injury to patients.

e. Direct warnings to patients. Warnings and instructions with regard to drugs or medical devices that can be sold legally only pursuant to a prescription are, under the "learned intermediary" rule, directed to health-care providers. Subsection (d)(2) recognizes that direct warnings and instructions to patients are warranted for drugs that are dispensed or administered to patients without the personal intervention or evaluation of a health-care provider. An example is the administration of a vaccine in clinics where mass inoculations are performed. In many such programs, health-care providers are not in a position to evaluate the risks attendant upon use of the drug or device or to relate them to patients. When a manufacturer supplies prescription drugs for distribution to patients in this type of unsupervised environment, if a direct warning to patients is feasible and can be effective, the law requires measures to that effect.

Although the learned intermediary rule is generally accepted and a drug manufacturer fulfills its legal obligation to warn by providing adequate warnings to the health-care provider, arguments have been advanced that in two other areas courts should consider imposing tort liability on drug manufacturers that fail to provide direct warnings to consumers. In the first, governmental regulatory agencies have mandated that patients be informed of risks attendant to the use of a drug. A noted example is the FDA requirement that birth control pills be sold to patients accompanied by a patient package insert. In the second, manufacturers have advertised a prescription drug and its indicated use in the mass media. Governmental regulations require that, when drugs are so advertised, they must be accompanied by appropriate information concerning risk so as to provide balanced advertising. The question in both instances is whether adequate warnings to the appropriate health-care provider should insulate the manufacturer from tort liability.

Those who assert the need for adequate warnings directly to consumers contend that manufacturers that communicate directly with consumers should not escape liability simply because the decision to prescribe the drug was made by the health-care provider. Proponents of the learned intermediary rule argue that, notwithstanding direct communications to the consumer, drugs cannot be dispensed unless a health-care provider makes an individualized decision that a drug is appropriate for a particular patient, and that it is for the health-care provider to decide which risks are relevant to the particular patient. The Institute leaves to developing case law whether exceptions to the learned intermediary rule in these or other situations should be recognized.

When the content of the warnings is mandated or approved by a governmental agency regulation and a court finds that compliance with such regulation federally preempts tort liability, then no liability under this Section can attach. For the rules governing compliance with governmental standards generally, see § 4(b).

f. Manufacturers' liability for defectively designed prescription drugs and medical devices. Subsection (c) reflects the judgment that, as long as a given drug or device provides net benefits for a class of patients, it should be available to them, accompanied by appropriate warnings and instructions. Learned intermediaries must generally be relied upon to see that the right drugs and devices reach the right patients. However, when a drug or device provides net benefits to no class of patients—when reasonable, informed health-care providers would not prescribe it to any class of patients—then the design of the product is defective and the manufacturer should be subject to liability for the harm caused.

A prescription drug or device manufacturer defeats a plaintiff's design claim by establishing one or more contexts in which its product would be prescribed by reasonable, informed health-care providers. That some individual providers do, in fact, prescribe defendant's product does not in itself suffice to defeat the plaintiff's claim. Evidence regarding the actual conduct of health-care providers, while relevant and admissible, is not necessarily controlling. The issue is whether, objectively viewed, reasonable providers, knowing of the foreseeable risks and benefits of the drug or medical device, would prescribe it for any class of patients. Given this very demanding objective standard, liability is likely to be imposed only under unusual circumstances. The court has the responsibility to determine when the plaintiff has introduced sufficient evidence so that reasonable persons could conclude that plaintiff has met this demanding standard.

g. Foreseeability of risks of harm in prescription drug and medical device cases. Duties concerning the design and marketing of prescription drugs and medical devices arise only with respect to risks of harm that are reasonably foreseeable at the time of sale. Imposing liability for unforeseeable risks can create inappropriate disincentives for the development of new drugs and therapeutic devices. Moreover, because actuaries cannot accurately assess unknown and unknowable risks, insuring against losses due to unknowable risks would be problematic. Drug and medical device manufacturers have the responsibility to perform reasonable testing prior to marketing a product and to discover risks and risk-avoidance measures that such testing would reveal. See § 2, Comments *a* and *m*.

h. Liability of retail seller of prescription drugs and medical devices for defective designs and defects due to inadequate instructions or warnings. The rule governing most products imposes liability on wholesalers and retailers for selling a defectively designed product, or one without adequate instructions or warnings, even though they have exercised reasonable care in marketing the product. See § 1, Comment *e*, and § 2, Comment *o*. Courts have refused to apply this general rule to nonmanufacturing retail sellers of prescription drugs and medical devices and, instead, have adopted the rule stated in Subsection (e). That rule subjects retailers to liability only if the product contains a manufacturing defect or if the retailer fails to exercise reasonable care in connection with distribution of the drug or medical device. In so limiting the liability of intermediary parties, courts have held that they should be permitted to rely on the special expertise of manufacturers, prescribing and treating health-care providers, and governmental regulatory agencies. They have also emphasized the needs of medical patients to have ready access to prescription drugs at reasonable prices.

§ 7. Liability of Commercial Seller or Distributor for Harm Caused by Defective Food Products

One engaged in the business of selling or otherwise distributing food products who sells or distributes a food product that is defective under § 2, § 3, or § 4 is subject to liability for harm to persons or property caused by the defect. Under § 2(a), a harm-causing ingredient of the food product constitutes a defect if a reasonable consumer would not expect the food product to contain that ingredient.

Comment:

a. General applicability of §§ 2, 3, and 4 to food products. Except for the special problems identified in Comment *b*, liability for harm caused by defects in commercially distributed food products are determined under the same rules generally applicable to non-food products. A food product may contain a manufacturing defect under § 2(a), as when a can of peas contains a pebble; may be defectively designed under § 2(b), as when the recipe for potato chips contains a dangerous chemical preservative; or may be sold without adequate warnings under § 2(c), as when the seller fails to inform consumers that the dye applied to the skins of oranges contains a well-known allergen. Section 3 may allow a plaintiff to reach the trier of fact when, unable to identify the specific defect, the plaintiff becomes violently ill immediately after consuming the defendant's food product and other causes are sufficiently eliminated. And § 4 may apply when a commercially distributed food product fails to conform to applicable safety statutes or administrative regulations.

b. *The special problem under § 2(a).* When a plaintiff suffers harm due to the presence in food of foreign matter clearly not intended by the product seller, such as a pebble in a can of peas or the pre-sale spoilage of a jar of mayonnaise, the claim is readily treated under § 2(a), which deals with harm caused by manufacturing defects. Food product cases, however, sometimes present unique difficulties when it is unclear whether the ingredient that caused the plaintiff's harm is an unanticipated adulteration or is an inherent aspect of the product. For example, is a one-inch chicken bone in a chicken enchilada, or a fish bone in fish chowder, a manufacturing defect or, instead, an inherent aspect of the product? The analytical problem stems from the circumstance that food products in many instances do not have specific product designs that may be used as a basis for determining whether the offending product ingredient constitutes a departure from design, and is thus a manufacturing defect. Food recipes vary over time, within the same restaurant or other commercial food-preparation facility, from facility to facility, and from locale to locale.

Faced with this indeterminacy, some courts have attempted to rely on a distinction between "foreign" and "natural" characteristics of food products to determine liability. Under that distinction, liability attaches only if the alleged adulteration is foreign rather than natural to the product. Most courts have found this approach inadequate, however. Although a one-inch chicken bone may in some sense be "natural" to a chicken enchilada, depending on the context in which consumption takes place, the bone may still be unexpected by the reasonable consumer, who will not be able to avoid injury, thus rendering the product not reasonably safe. The majority view is that, in this circumstance of uncertainty, the issue of whether a food product containing a dangerous but arguably natural component is defective under § 2(a) is to be determined by reference to reasonable consumer expectations within the relevant context of consumption. A consumer expectations test in this context relies upon culturally defined, widely shared standards that food products ought to meet. Although consumer expectations are not adequate to supply a standard for defect in other contexts, assessments of what consumers have a right to expect in various commercial food preparations are sufficiently well-formed that judges and triers of fact can sensibly resolve whether liability should be imposed using this standard.

§ 8. Liability of Commercial Seller or Distributor of Defective Used Products

One engaged in the business of selling or otherwise distributing used products who sells or distributes a defec-

tive used product is subject to liability for harm to persons or property caused by the defect if the defect:

(a) arises from the seller's failure to exercise reasonable care; or

(b) is a manufacturing defect under § 2(a) or a defect that may be inferred under § 3 and the seller's marketing of the product would cause a reasonable person in the position of the buyer to expect the used product to present no greater risk of defect than if the product were new; or

(c) is a defect under § 2 or § 3 in a used product remanufactured by the seller or a predecessor in the commercial chain of distribution of the used product; or

(d) arises from a used product's noncompliance under § 4 with a product safety statute or regulation applicable to the used product.

A used product is a product that, prior to the time of sale or other distribution referred to in this Section, is commercially sold or otherwise distributed to a buyer not in the commercial chain of distribution and used for some period of time.

Chapter 2

LIABILITY OF COMMERCIAL PRODUCT SELLERS NOT BASED ON PRODUCT DEFECTS AT TIME OF SALE

§ 9. Liability of Commercial Product Seller or Distributor for Harm Caused by Misrepresentation

[Section 9 incorporates as applicable to commercial product sellers or distributors the causes of action for fraud, negligent misrepresentation, and innocent misrepresentation available under Restatement (Second) of Torts §§ 310, 311, and 402B. Eds.]

§ 10. Liability of Commercial Product Seller or Distributor for Harm Caused by Post–Sale Failure to Warn

(a) One engaged in the business of selling or otherwise distributing products is subject to liability for harm to persons or property caused by the seller's failure to provide a warning after the time of sale or distribution of a product if a reasonable person in the seller's position would provide such a warning.

(b) A reasonable person in the seller's position would provide a warning after the time of sale if:

(1) the seller knows or reasonably should know that the product poses a substantial risk of harm to persons or property; and

(2) those to whom a warning might be provided can be identified and can reasonably be assumed to be unaware of the risk of harm; and

(3) a warning can be effectively communicated to and acted on by those to whom a warning might be provided; and

(4) the risk of harm is sufficiently great to justify the burden of providing a warning.

Comment:

a. Rationale. Judicial recognition of the seller's duty to warn of a product-related risk after the time of sale, whether or not the product is defective at the time of original sale within the meaning of other Sections of this Restatement, is relatively new. Nonetheless, a growing body of decisional and statutory law imposes such a duty. Courts recognize that warnings about risks discovered after sale are sometimes necessary to prevent significant harm to persons and property. Nevertheless, an unbounded post-sale duty to warn would impose unacceptable burdens on product sellers. The costs of identifying and communicating with product users years after sale are often daunting. Furthermore, as product designs are developed and improved over time, many risks are reduced or avoided by subsequent design changes. If every post-sale improvement in a product design were to give rise to a duty to warn users of the risks of continuing to use the existing design, the burden on product sellers would be unacceptably great.

As with all rules that raise the question whether a duty exists, courts must make the threshold decisions that, in particular cases, triers of fact could reasonably find that product sellers can practically and effectively discharge such an obligation and that the risks of harm are sufficiently great to justify what is typically a substantial post-sale undertaking. In deciding whether a claim based on breach of a post-sale duty to warn should reach the trier of fact, the court must determine whether the requirements in Subsection (b)(1) through (4) are supported by proof. The legal standard is whether a reasonable person would provide a post-sale warning. In light of the serious potential for overburdening sellers in this regard, the court should carefully examine the circumstances for and against imposing a duty to provide a post-sale warning in a particular case.

b. When a reasonable person in the seller's position would provide a warning. The standard governing the liability of the seller is objective:

whether a reasonable person in the seller's position would provide a warning. This is the standard traditionally applied in determining negligence. See Restatement, Second, Torts § 283, Comment c. In applying the reasonableness standard to members of the chain of distribution it is possible that one party's conduct may be reasonable and another's unreasonable. For example, a manufacturer may discover information under circumstances satisfying Subsection (b)(1) through (4) and thus be required to provide a post-sale warning. In contrast, a retailer is generally not in a position to know about the risk discovered by the manufacturer after sale and thus is not subject to liability because it neither knows nor should know of the risk. Once the retailer is made aware of the risk, however, whether the retailer is subject to liability for failing to issue a post-sale warning depends on whether a reasonable person in the retailer's position would warn under the criteria set forth in Subsection (b)(1) through (4).

c. *Requirement that seller or other distributor knows or should know of the product-related risk.* A duty to warn after the time of sale cannot arise unless the product seller or other distributor knows or in the exercise of reasonable care should know of the product-related risk that causes plaintiff's harm. The seller may have known or should have known of the risk at the time of sale, in which case failure to warn will cause the product to be defective under § 2(c). But even if the product is not defective at the time of sale because no reasonable seller would have known of the risk under § 2(c), knowledge of the risk may come after sale and may give rise to a duty to warn at that time.

As a practical matter, most post-sale duties to warn arise when new information is brought to the attention of the seller, after the time of sale, concerning risks accompanying the product's use or consumption. When risks are not actually brought to the attention of sellers, the burden of constantly monitoring product performance in the field is usually too burdensome to support a post-sale duty to warn. However, when reasonable grounds exist for the seller to suspect that a hitherto unknown risk exists, especially when the risk involved is great, the duty of reasonable care may require investigation. With regard to one class of products, prescription drugs and devices, courts traditionally impose a continuing duty of reasonable care to test and monitor after sale to discover product-related risks.

Illustration:

1. ABC manufactures and sells Model 1220 power drills used exclusively in heavy industry. Three years after the Model 1220 is first put on the market, ABC learns that when the drill is used continuously for more than four hours it overheats, causing it to fracture. ABC learns of the overheating problem when the Model 1220 is first used on a new metal alloy that was not previously available, and thus not in use, at the time of first distribution. The new alloy causes the drill to heat well beyond temperatures caused by any other metal for which the Model 1220 has ever been used. No reasonable person could have

foreseen the development of the new alloy when any of the drills were sold. Because the risk of overheating was not foreseeable at the time of sale of many of the Model 1220s, those units are not defective within the meaning of § 2. Whether ABC is subject to liability for failing to issue a post-sale warning regarding the risks of overheating is determined based on the factors set forth in Subsection (b)(1) through (4).

d. Requirement that the risk of harm be substantial. For a post-sale duty to arise under this Section, the risk of harm must be at least as great as the level of risk that would require a warning under § 2(c). Because post-sale warnings are invariably costly to provide, and post-sale increases in knowledge of risks are to some extent inevitable, no duty arises after the time of sale to issue warnings regarding product-related accidents that occur infrequently and are not likely to cause substantial harm. If post-sale acquisition of knowledge of adverse outcomes that are both infrequent and insubstantial were to trigger a post-sale duty to warn, sellers would face costly and potentially crushing burdens.

e. Requirement that those to whom a warning might be provided be identifiable. The problem of identifying those to whom product warnings might be provided is especially relevant in the post-sale context. When products are originally sold or distributed, most often the seller accompanies the product, together with its packaging, with whatever warnings are appropriate. When knowledge of product-related risk is available to the seller only after sale, it may be difficult for the seller to determine who, in the general population of product users and consumers, is in a position to respond to warnings effectively. In some instances, customer records may identify the population to whom warnings should be provided. Individual names and addresses are not necessarily required. Records may indicate classes of product users, or geographically limited markets. But when no such records are available, the seller's inability to identify those for whom warnings would be useful may properly prevent a post-sale duty to warn from arising. See Comment *g*.

Illustration:

2. ABC has manufactured and distributed vacuum cleaners commercially to millions of consumers over the course of many years. Only scanty and incomplete sales records have been kept by retailers, and it is practically impossible for ABC to identify who among the consuming public owns and operates its vacuums. Five years after the first commercial distribution of Model 14, ABC discovers a risk when the Model 14 is used to vacuum dust from a chemical carpet cleaner newly introduced to the market. No reasonable person in ABC's position would have foreseen the risk previously, and thus the Model 14 was not defective at time of original sale. The difficulty of ABC's identifying users of its Model 14 vacuum, together with the frequency and severity of the risk, must be weighed by the court in determining whether ABC owes a post-sale duty to warn of the newly discovered risk.

f. The reasonableness of assuming that those to whom a warning might be provided are unaware of the risk. To justify the cost of providing a post-sale warning, it must reasonably appear that those to whom a warning might be provided are unaware of the risk. See § 2, Comment *j*. Similarly, even if knowledge of the risk reasonably becomes available to the seller only after the original sale, if users and consumers are at that time generally aware of the risk a post-sale warning is not required.

g. The seller's ability to communicate the warning effectively to those who are in a position to act to prevent harm. For a post-sale duty to warn to arise, the seller must reasonably be able to communicate the warning to those identified as appropriate recipients. When original customer sales records indicate which individuals are probably using and consuming the product in question, direct communication of a warning may be feasible. When direct communication is not feasible, it may be necessary to utilize the public media to disseminate information regarding risks of substantial harm. As the group to whom warnings might be provided increases in size, costs of communicating warnings may increase and their effectiveness may decrease.

h. Requirement that those to whom a post-sale warning might be provided be able to act effectively to reduce the risk. To justify the potentially high cost of providing a post-sale warning, those to whom such warnings are provided must be in a position to reduce or prevent product-caused harm. Such recipients of warnings need not be original purchasers of the product, so long as they are able to reduce risk effectively.

i. Requirement that the risk of harm be sufficiently great to justify providing a post-sale warning. Compared with the costs of providing warnings attendant upon the original sale of a product, the costs of providing post-sale warnings are typically greater. In the post-sale context, identifying those who should receive a warning and communicating the warning to them can require large expenditures. Courts recognize these burdens and hold that a post-sale warning is required only when the risk of harm is sufficiently great to justify undertaking a post-sale warning program. Subsection (b)(4) requires that, even for a substantial risk, a seller owes a duty to warn after the time of sale only if the risk of harm is sufficiently great to justify the cost of providing a post-sale warning. The test defining unreasonable conduct is that which governs negligence generally. See Restatement, Second, Torts § 291.

j. Distinguishing post-sale failures to warn from defects existing at the time of sale. When a product is defective at the time of sale liability can be established without reference to a post-sale duty to warn. A seller who discovers after sale that its product was defective at the time of sale within the meaning of this Restatement cannot generally absolve itself of liability by issuing a post-sale warning. As long as the original defect is causally related to the harm suffered by the plaintiff, a prima facie case under this Restatement can be established notwithstanding reasonable post-sale efforts to warn. Of course, even when a product is defective at the time of sale a seller may have an independent obligation to issue a post-sale warning based on the rule stated in this Section. Thus, a plaintiff may seek recovery based on both a time-of-sale defect and a post-sale failure to warn.

Illustrations:

3. ABC manufactures and sells Model 1220 power drills used exclusively in heavy industry. ABC sells a Model 1220 drill to XYZ Industries. Six months after the sale to XYZ, ABC learns that when the Model 1220 drill is used continuously for more than four hours it overheats, causing the drill to fracture. ABC should have discovered this problem through reasonable testing before the drill was put on the market. Had ABC done so, it could have adopted a reasonable alternative design that would have avoided the problem. Model 1220 is thus defective within the meaning of § 2(b). After ABC discovers the overheating problem, it sends warning letters to all owners of the Model 1220, including XYZ, that the machine should not be used for more than four hours continuously and that after prolonged use the machine should be turned off for 30 minutes to cool. The post-sale warning states that failure to do so could cause harm. XYZ posts the warning in its plant. Several months thereafter, XYZ's employee, E, is working on the machine during a rush job and the Model 1220 is allowed to run continuously for more than four hours. The machine overheats and the drill shatters, causing harm to E. Notwithstanding ABC's post-sale efforts to warn, ABC is subject to liability for the harm to E caused by the defectively designed Model 1220 under §§ 1 and 2. Whether E's recovery should be reduced because of contributory negligence or comparative fault is governed by § 17. Whether E should be denied recovery due to the absence of proximate causation is governed by § 15.

4. Same facts as Illustration 3 except that ABC fails to issue a post-sale warning after it discovers the overheating problem. E may bring an action based on a § 2 defect and may also assert the failure of ABC to provide a post-sale warning of the overheating problem. Whether it is reasonable also to subject ABC to liability for failure to issue a post-sale warning is determined by applying the factors set forth in Subsection (b)(1) through (4).

§ 11. Liability of Commercial Product Seller or Distributor for Harm Caused by Post–Sale Failure to Recall Product

One engaged in the business of selling or otherwise distributing products is subject to liability for harm to persons or property caused by the seller's failure to recall a product after the time of sale or distribution if:

(a)(1) a governmental directive issued pursuant to a statute or administrative regulation specifically requires the seller or distributor to recall the product; or

(2) the seller or distributor, in the absence of a recall requirement under Subsection (a)(1), undertakes to recall the product; and

(b) the seller or distributor fails to act as a reasonable person in recalling the product.

Comment:

a. Rationale. Duties to recall products impose significant burdens on manufacturers. Many product lines are periodically redesigned so that they become safer over time. If every improvement in product safety were to trigger a common-law duty to recall, manufacturers would face incalculable costs every time they sought to make their product lines better and safer. Moreover, even when a product is defective within the meaning of § 2, § 3, or § 4, an involuntary duty to recall should be imposed on the seller only by a governmental directive issued pursuant to statute or regulation. Issues relating to product recalls are best evaluated by governmental agencies capable of gathering adequate data regarding the ramifications of such undertakings. The duty to recall or repair should be distinguished from a post-sale duty to warn about product hazards discovered after sale. See §§ 10 and 13.

Illustration:

1. MNO Corp. has manufactured and distributed washing machines for five years. MNO develops an improved model that includes a safety device that reduces the risk of harm to users. The washing machines sold previously conformed to the best technology available at time of sale and were not defective when sold. MNO is under no common-law obligation to recall previously-distributed machines in order to retrofit them with the new safety device.

b. Failure to recall when recall is specifically required by a governmental directive issued pursuant to statute or other governmental regulation. When a product recall is specifically required by a governmental directive issued pursuant to a statute or regulation, failure reasonably to comply with the relevant directive subjects the seller or other distributor to liability for harm caused by such failure. For the product seller or other distributor to be subject to liability under Subsection (a)(1), the directive must specifically require recall. It is not sufficient that an agency has the power to direct product recalls with regard to the product in question if the agency has failed to issue a specific recall directive, nor will it suffice that a general duty to recall is imposed by statute or regulation and the plaintiff alleges that the defendant breached that duty by failing to recall in the absence of a specific directive to do so. When a directive issued pursuant to a statute or regulation specifically requires product recall, the violation by the seller of that requirement constitutes actionable negligence. See § 4, Comment *f*.

To give rise to the duty to recall under this Section, the governmental directive must require the defendant to recall the product during the time period in which the plaintiff claims the defendant breached the duty to recall. For example, if the regulatory scheme calls for a stay of the recall directive pending appeal, no duty to recall arises under this Section until the appeal is decided in a way that makes the recall directive binding on the defendant.

Illustrations:

2. The same facts as Illustration 1, except that a federal agency directs MNO to recall the machines distributed by MNO. Thereafter, MNO unreasonably fails to notify machine owners, whom it can reasonably identify, about the recall. MNO is subject to liability for harm caused by its noncompliance with the governmental directive to recall the machines.

3. The same facts as Illustration 1, except that the agency issues no directive to MNO regarding the washing machines. A plaintiff argues that MNO owed a general tort duty under the statute to recall the washing machine, which the plaintiff claims was defectively designed as defined in § 2(b) and caused the claimant's harm. MNO is not subject to liability under Subsection (a)(1).

c. When seller or other distributor voluntarily undertakes to recall. Some courts have held that, when a seller, under no statutory or regulatory obligation to undertake a recall, volunteers to do so, the seller is subject to liability for failing to act reasonably to recall the product. The rationale for this rule lies partly in the general rule that one who undertakes a rescue, and thus induces other would-be rescuers to forbear, must act reasonably in following through. In the context of products liability, courts appear to assume that voluntary recalls are typically undertaken in the anticipation that, if the seller does not recall voluntarily, it will be directed to do so by a governmental regulator. Having presumably forestalled the regulatory recall directive, the seller should be under a common-law duty to follow through on its commitment to recall. In some instances voluntary recalls are subject to regulation by governmental agencies. Whether product sellers are subject to, or protected from, liability for harm caused by noncompliance or compliance with the terms of such regulations is governed by Restatement, Second, of Torts §§ 286–288C. See § 4, Comment *f*.

Illustration:

4. The same facts as Illustration 1, except that MNO voluntarily announces that it will recall and retrofit the washing machines it distributed earlier, and it thereafter unreasonably fails to notify own-

ers whom it can reasonably identify about the recall. MNO is subject to liability under Subsection (a)(2) for harm caused by its failure to act reasonably in undertaking to recall the machines.

d. *Distinguishing liability for post-sale failure to recall from liability for the sale or other distribution of defective products.* When a product is defective at the time of sale and the defect causes harm to persons or property, the seller is subject to liability whether or not the seller attempts to eliminate the defect by post-sale recall. The fact that one who owns or possesses a product that was defective at time of sale does not respond to a recall notice does not necessarily eliminate the causal connection between the original defect and the plaintiff's harm. See § 15. It may be foreseeable that product owners will fail to respond to recall notices. In a case involving harm caused by an original defect at the time of sale, the plaintiff's failure to act on a recall notice may be taken into account under the rules stated in § 17 governing comparative responsibility. In appropriate cases a plaintiff may seek recovery based on both a claim of original defect and a claim of post-sale failure to recall.

Illustrations:

5. XYZ Motor Co. manufactures and sells the Buster Sedan. XYZ learned that the Buster tends to oversteer dangerously. XYZ should have discovered the problem before the Buster Sedan was put on the market, when it could have adopted a reasonable alternative design. The Buster Sedan was thus defectively designed within the meaning of § 2(b). The National Highway Traffic Safety Administration directed XYZ to recall the Buster to correct the oversteering problem. Sonia Rand, who had purchased a Buster Sedan, received a recall notice. Sonia did not respond to the notice. Six months later, while driving on the highway, Sonia lost control of her car. A trier of fact could find that the oversteering in Sonia's Buster contributed to her loss of control. XYZ is subject to liability under §§ 1 and 2(b) for the injury caused by the defectively designed Buster Sedan. In her action based on the design defect, Sonia's failure to bring her car in for repair is relevant to the issue of legal causation under § 15 and the issue of comparative responsibility under § 17.

6. Same facts as Illustration 5, except that XYZ failed to undertake the recall directed by the National Highway Traffic Safety Administration. Sonia suffers injury after the time a recall notice should have been issued. XYZ is subject to liability under this Section for failure to recall. XYZ is also subject to liability under § 2(b) based on defective design. Whether XYZ is subject to liability for post-sale failure to warn is governed by the rules stated in § 10.

7. Same facts as Illustration 5, except that the National Highway Traffic Safety Administration refused, after considering the problem, to direct a recall. XYZ is subject to liability to Sonia based on a § 2(b)

design defect. XYZ is not subject to liability under this Section for failure to recall. Whether XYZ is subject to liability for post-sale failure to warn is governed by the rules stated in § 10.

e. Causal relationship between failure to recall and plaintiff's harm. For a seller to be subject to liability for post-sale failure to recall, the plaintiff must establish not only that the seller unreasonably failed to recall the product under this Section, but also that the defect that was the subject of recall was a legal cause of the plaintiff's harm. See § 15.

Chapter 3

LIABILITY OF SUCCESSORS AND APPARENT MANUFACTURERS

§ 12. Liability of Successor for Harm Caused by Defective Products Sold Commercially by Predecessor

A successor corporation or other business entity that acquires assets of a predecessor corporation or other business entity is subject to liability for harm to persons or property caused by a defective product sold or otherwise distributed commercially by the predecessor if the acquisition:

(a) is accompanied by an agreement for the successor to assume such liability; or

(b) results from a fraudulent conveyance to escape liability for the debts or liabilities of the predecessor; or

(c) constitutes a consolidation or merger with the predecessor; or

(d) results in the successor becoming a continuation of the predecessor.

Comment:

a. History. The rule that a corporation or other business entity is not, in the absence of the circumstances described in Subsections (a) through (d), subject to liability for harm caused by defective products sold by a corporation from which it purchases productive assets derives from both products liability and corporate law principles. When the alleged successor purchases the assets piecemeal with little or no further continuity of operations between the two corporations or other business entities, the nonliability of the alleged successor derives primarily from the fact that the successor is not within the basic liability rule in § 1 of this Restatement: "one ... *who sells or distributes* a defective product is subject to liability for harm ... caused by the defective product." (Emphasis added.) Thus, when one corporation commercially sells products, some of which are defective, and later transfers its productive assets to another corporation that uses those assets to manufacture products of its own, the purchaser of the assets is not liable for harm caused by a defective product sold earlier by the transferor because the transferee did not "sell or distribute" the defective product that caused the harm. When the alleged successor receives value in the form of the transferor's goodwill and continues to manufacture products of the same sort as manufactured earlier by the predecessor, and thus to some extent constitutes a continuation of the predecessor, the general rule of nonliability derives primarily from the law governing corporations, which favors the free alienability of corporate assets and limits shareholders' exposures to liability in order to facilitate the formation and investment of capital.

When the transferor goes out of business upon, or shortly after, a transfer of productive assets, the rights of plaintiffs injured by defective products sold earlier by the transferor may be adversely affected. For tort plaintiffs who have existing judgments outstanding against the predecessor at the time of transfer and dissolution, the law governing corporations and other business entities provides, within limits, legal protection. Creditors, including tort creditors, who hold existing judgments against a corporation that is in the process of transferring its assets and going out of business may satisfy those claims out of the proceeds from the transfer of assets. Moreover, if the proceeds from the transfer of assets are distributed to shareholders of the transferor corporation in violation of applicable state corporation law or fraudulent transfer law, existing creditors of the corporation may pursue the proceeds in the hands of the transferor's shareholders. These rules, in some states expressed in statutes, are designed to protect, within the limits of practicality, creditors who are identifiable at the time of the transfer of the predecessor's assets to the successor corporation and the transferor's dissolution. The same principles have been applied to the transfer of assets of proprietorships, partnerships, and other business entities.

Tort claimants who, as a result of defective products sold by a predecessor corporation, seek recovery only after transfer of assets to a successor corporation often face difficulties in attempting to bring their claims within the foregoing legal rules. Their claims typically accrue after the predecessor corporation has lawfully distributed to its shareholders the proceeds from the transfer of assets and has ceased to exist. Under these circumstances, tort claimants who were not existing creditors at the time of the transfer of assets ordinarily have no recourse against the predecessor's shareholders. Unless they can pursue their claims against the successor corporation, or can reach other funds provided by existing insurance or by a statute, their only practical remedy lies with retailers and wholesalers in the predecessor's distributive chain, who may not be available as a practical matter. Statutes and judicial precedents governing the rights of creditors after a corporate assets transfer and dissolution generally do not address this problem of post-transfer claims accrual.

Few precedents recognize tort claims against the successor corporation for harm caused by defective products sold by the predecessor unless the transaction by which productive assets are acquired meets criteria established by one of several traditional exceptions. These exceptions apply generally to creditors whose claims accrue after dissolution of the predecessor, and are not limited to products liability claimants. They fall into two basic categories: those in which some conduct of the successor, in addition to acquiring the predecessor's assets, justifies holding the successor responsible (the successor either contractually agrees to be liable or knowingly participates in a fraudulent asset transfer); and those in which the successor itself can be said to have sold or distributed the defective products because the successor constitutes the same juridical entity as the predecessor, perhaps in somewhat different form (the successor merges with, or constitutes a "mere continuation" of, the predecessor). Under this Section, a products liability claimant has a recognized claim against a successor for harm caused by defective products distributed by the predecessor in these circumstances.

A minority of jurisdictions impose liability on a successor corporation based on a broader concept of continuation of the business enterprise, even when there is no continuity of shareholders, officers, or directors. Some courts hold that the continuation of a predecessor's product line by the successor is sufficient to support imposition of successor liability for harm caused by defects in products sold before the assets transfer.

b. Rationale. Limiting the liability of successor corporations to the circumstances described in this Section is supported by fairness and efficiency considerations. An alleged successor that purchases the predecessor's productive assets piecemeal, other than as part of a going concern, cannot, by that fact alone, be said to have either manufactured or sold defective products distributed by the predecessor before the transfer of assets. In the absence of circumstances in which the successor could be said to constitute a continuation of the predecessor, or somehow to have prejudiced subsequent tort plaintiffs by its own pre-acquisition conduct, imposing liability on a business entity that did not make or distribute the defective products that caused harm could be justified only because it increases the amount of money available post-acquisition out of which to satisfy plaintiffs' claims. But that alone cannot be justification for successor liability. Thus, imposing liability on the piecemeal purchase of productive assets would, for no compelling reason, impede the free alienability of corporate assets, thereby discouraging shareholder investment of capital and increasing social costs.

Imposing liability on successor corporations constitutes acceptable public policy when the successor either agrees to be liable or is implicated in the transfer of assets in a way that, without such liability, would unfairly deprive future products liability plaintiffs of the remedies that would otherwise have been available against the predecessor. Subsections (a) through (d) describe the types of corporate asset transfers that have been determined to justify imposing liability on the successor. Subsection (a) recognizes that contractual promises by the successor to pay subsequent tort claims, for which promises the successor has presumably been compensated, should be honored. Subsection (b) provides that when a business entity makes a fraudulent transfer in which the transferee is implicated, successor liability is appropriate for the same reason that liability would be imposed in favor of other creditors. Thus, a predecessor may arrange an asset transfer at an artificially deflated price, accompanied by an agreement by the successor to compensate either the predecessor, its owners, or its managers in ways that escape easy detection; or a successor may knowingly participate in an asset transfer coupled with a liquidating dividend by the predecessor to its shareholders for the purpose of leaving tort plaintiffs without remedy. If those transfers are fraudulent under applicable state law, imposing tort liability on the transferee for having knowingly participated in such transfers is justified.

Subsections (c) and (d) deal with successors that, in a real sense, did produce and distribute the product that caused the harm, though in a somewhat different organizational form. Subsection (c) deals with the transferor corporation that merges by law or in fact into the transferee, typically with no substantial change in corporate management or ownership. Subsection (d) concerns the transfer of corporate assets in the context of a transaction involving only a change in organizational form. In both these situations, liability for harm caused by defective products distributed previously should be imposed on the business entity that emerges from the transaction. In substance, if not in form, the post-transfer entity distributed the defective products and should be held responsible for them. If mere changes in form were allowed to control substance, corporations intending to continue operations could periodically wash themselves clean of potential liability at practically zero cost, in sham transactions, and thereby unreasonably undermine incentives for producers and distributors to invest in product safety and unfairly deny tort plaintiffs adequate remedies when defective products later cause harm.

A small minority of courts have fashioned successor liability rules more advantageous to products liability claimants than the rules stated in this Section. Those minority rules, in effect, extend the "change in form only" exception just described to include circumstances in which the successor continues a product line previously distributed by the predecessor. The minority position is based on the belief that a successor who purchases productive assets should not be allowed to benefit from receiving the goodwill and reputation of the predecessor's business without the burden of responding in tort to claims for harm caused by products sold by the predecessor prior to transfer. An argument advanced to support this minority view is that holding successors liable reduces the price that predecessors receive for transferring assets, thereby helping to strengthen incentives for the managers to invest in care before the transfer of the business.

This reasoning has proven unpersuasive to a substantial majority of courts that have considered the issue. Extending successor liability beyond the exceptions set forth in Subsections (a) through (d) would, in the judgment of most courts, be unfair and socially wasteful. Post-transfer plaintiffs harmed by pre-transfer defects have a right to expect that a transfer of assets will not be allowed to prejudice financially their chances of satisfying a judgment; they have no legitimate claim that the transfer should increase those chances over what they would have been if no transfer had occurred. In the likely event that the successor is financially stronger than the predecessor, imposing a broader liability for pre-transfer product defects would unjustifiably increase the funds available to those injured by such defects compared with what would have been available to them if no transfer had taken place.

As courts have recognized, it would be difficult, and often impossible, to implement and administer a liability rule that attempted to limit post-transfer plaintiffs' rights to an aggregate amount equal to the net value of the predecessor before transfer. Tort judgments are imposed independently of one another, in various jurisdictions; no central authority exists to assure that, in the aggregate, tort judgments do not exceed a predetermined total amount. Thus, the expanded successor liability rules in a minority of states, not limited to time-of-transfer net value, replace one risk of injustice—that the assets transfer may unfairly reduce plaintiffs' recoveries in cases that do not satisfy the traditional exceptions (reflected in Subsections (a) through (d))—with another, possibly greater, injustice: that the transfer may give tort plaintiffs a windfall at the expense of companies who engage in asset transfers and, in turn, at the expense of the consuming public.

Moreover, a majority of courts have concluded that the substantial social costs of a more expansive liability rule would be incurred without actually benefiting very many tort plaintiffs. In most instances, the magnitude of future liability for products distributed pre-transfer is difficult, if not impossible, to assess. As a majority of courts have recognized, the result of imposing successor liability as a general rule would be to depress the prices for transferred assets to the point that piecemeal disposition of assets, which clearly would not subject the buyers to liability, would be a preferable alternative to sale of the assets as part of a going concern. In that event, the products liability claimant harmed by a pre-transfer product defect would still run the risk of ending up with an uncollectible judgment. The benefits to society of preserving the predecessor's assets as a going concern would be sacrificed, with no commensurate benefits to tort claimants.

And even if a more expansive successor liability rule did not invariably lead to piecemeal asset transfers, such a liability rule would depress the prices received for going-concern transfers to an extent that would threaten to undermine the objectives of the law governing corporations. One of the purposes served by the corporate structure is to provide limitation and certainty of risk to shareholders in order to encourage capital formation. Thus, the shareholders' initial risk is limited to the value of their shares of stock and they are able to withdraw from an investment by sale of the stock without incurring future potential liability. A more expansive successor liability rule might threaten shareholders' investments by significantly restraining corporate assets transfers, thereby tending to frustrate corporation law's objective of encouraging shareholder investment.

Some critics of the majority rule argue that, when the successor continues to manufacture the same products as the predecessor, often under the same trademark, consumers have legitimate expectations that the successor will stand behind the predecessor's products. Disappointing these expectations is unfair, according to the critics, quite apart from the effects of successor liability upon the formation of capital. But this argument overlooks the reality that the predecessor's products that cause harm in these cases were distributed prior to the assets transfer, when there could be no reliance by consumers on the financial viability of the successor. One cannot logically rely on post-transfer expectations regarding the successor to justify the imposition of liability on the successor for pretransfer distributions by the predecessor.

c. Nonliability in the absence of special circumstances. In the absence of the circumstances described in Subsections (a) through (d), a successor company that buys productive assets from another company is not liable for harm caused by a defective product sold or otherwise distributed by the predecessor prior to the successor's acquisition of assets. When the assets are purchased piecemeal, the alleged successor did not "sell or distribute" the product under the liability rule stated in § 1; and attempts to establish continuation of the corporate entity are recognized only under the terms set forth in this Section. The successor is liable under §§ 1–4 for harm caused by defective products it sells after acquisition. In the absence of the circumstances described in this Section, however, the successor is not liable for defective products sold by another prior to that time.

d. Agreement for successor to assume liability. When the successor agrees to assume liabilities for defective products sold by its predecessor, liability is imposed under Subsection (a) in accordance with the terms of the agreement. As a general matter, contract law governs the application of this exception. Courts have interpreted general statements that the successor agrees to assume the liabilities of the predecessor to include products liability claims even though the agreement makes no specific mention of products liability. However, assumption of products liability is not implied by the successor's assumption of specific duties with regard to product service or replacement.

e. Fraudulent transfer in order to avoid debts or liabilities. Subsection (b) incorporates by reference the relevant state law governing fraudulent conveyances and transfers. In contexts other than successor products liability, fraudulent transfers can be set aside on behalf of existing creditors of the transferor. In this context, fraudulent transfers provide a basis for holding successors liable to post-transfer tort plaintiffs. The fact that general creditors are pursuing remedies against the transferee does not prevent tort plaintiffs from pursuing remedies under Subsection (b). What constitutes a fraudulent conveyance or transfer is determined by reference to applicable state law.

f. Consolidation or merger. When statutory consolidation or merger of two corporations takes place, products liability devolves on the successor corporation under Subsection (c). A more difficult question is whether, absent statutory merger, a de facto merger has taken place. Local law governing de facto mergers is determinative. Whether a de facto merger under Subsection (c) has occurred generally depends on whether: (1) there is a continuity of management, employees, location, and assets; (2) the successor corporation acquires the assets of the predecessor with shares of its own stock so that shareholders of the transferor corporation become shareholders of the transferee corporation; (3) the predecessor corporation ceases its ordinary business operations immediately or shortly after the transfer of assets; and (4) the successor assumes those liabilities and obligations of the predecessor necessary for the uninterrupted continuation of the normal operations of the predecessor.

g. Continuation of the predecessor. The exception recognized in Subsection (d), referred to by many courts as the "mere continuation" exception, applies when there has been a formal redesignation of the predecessor corporate entity but little or no change in underlying substance. The most important indicia of continuation, in addition to the continuation of the predecessor's business activities, are common identities of officers, directors, and shareholders in the predecessor and successor corporations. A minority of jurisdictions recognize a broader exception, referred to as the "continuity of enterprise" exception, that imposes liability on the successor for continuing the business activities of the predecessor even when the corporate form of the successor is different from the predecessor. This Section does not follow that minority position.

h. Necessity for the predecessor to transfer all of its assets and go out of business. Almost all of the reported decisions applying the bases of successor liability stated in this Section involve predecessors that transfer all of their assets to successors and then dissolve or otherwise cease operations. Indeed, the predecessor's termination is the circumstance that, as a practical matter, most often gives rise to the need for a post-transfer tort plaintiff to look to the successor for recovery. The exceptions set forth in Subsections (c) and (d), merger and continuation, most frequently have significance when the predecessor has transferred all of its assets to the successor and, at least formally, has ceased to exist. But there is no reason that the exceptions set forth in Subsections (c) and (d) might not arise in connection with the transfer of a division of a large company, leaving the company in existence after the transfer. And the exceptions in Subsections (a) and (b) could arise in connection with transfers involving less than all of the predecessor's assets where the predecessor continues in existence after the transfer.

i. Relationship between the rule in this Section and the successor's independent duty to warn. This Section deals with a successor's liability for harm caused by the predecessor's defective products and is not premised on post-transfer wrongdoing by the successor itself. For the rules governing the liability of a successor for its own post-transfer failure to warn its predecessor's customers, see § 13.

§ 13. Liability of Successor for Harm Caused by Successor's Own Post–Sale Failure to Warn

(a) A successor corporation or other business entity that acquires assets of a predecessor corporation or other business entity, whether or not liable under the rule stated in § 12, is subject to liability for harm to persons or property caused by the successor's failure to warn of a risk created by a product sold or distributed by the predecessor if:

(1) the successor undertakes or agrees to provide services for maintenance or repair of the product or enters into a similar relationship with purchasers of the predecessor's products giving rise to actual or potential economic advantage to the successor, and

(2) a reasonable person in the position of the successor would provide a warning.

(b) A reasonable person in the position of the successor would provide a warning if:

(1) the successor knows or reasonably should know that the product poses a substantial risk of harm to persons or property; and

(2) those to whom a warning might be provided can be identified and can reasonably be assumed to be unaware of the risk of harm; and

(3) a warning can be effectively communicated to and acted on by those to whom a warning might be provided; and

(4) the risk of harm is sufficiently great to justify the burden of providing a warning.

Comment:

a. Rationale. Corporations that acquire assets from other corporations are liable for harm caused by defective products sold by predecessors only in limited circumstances. See § 12. This Section subjects a successor to liability for its own failure to warn after acquiring the predecessor's assets when certain conditions are satisfied and when a reasonable person in the successor's position would provide a warning. Liability under this Section is similar to liability under § 10, in which a seller is liable for harm caused by breach of a post-sale duty to warn even if the product was not defective at the time of original sale. Unlike product sellers in § 10, the successor governed by this Section did not manufacture or sell the defective product. However, by virtue of succeeding to the predecessor's interests, the successor is often in a good position to learn of problems arising from use of the predecessor's product and to prevent harm to persons or property. When the relationship between the successor and pre-transfer purchasers of the predecessor's products gives rise to actual or potential economic benefit to the successor, it is both fair and efficient to require the successor to act reasonably to prevent such harm.

   b.   *Relationship between the successor and the predecessor's customers.* Absent some additional circumstance besides having become a successor, the successor remains a pure volunteer upon whom the law usually imposes no duty to act or to warn. Many courts have recognized four elements as being significant in determining the existence of a duty to warn: (1) succession to a predecessor's service contracts; (2) coverage of the defective product under a service contract made directly with the successor; (3) actual service of the defective product by the successor; and (4) the successor's knowledge of the existence of defects and the identities of the predecessor's customers who own the defective product. However, these factors are not exhaustive and the inquiry should be whether the successor's relationships with the predecessor's customers give rise to actual or potential economic advantage.

   In most instances, in the absence of service contracts governing the predecessor's products or actual service of the defective product by the successor, it will be difficult to establish that the successor's relationships with the predecessor's customers give rise to actual or potential economic benefit to the successor. Furthermore, in the absence of service contracts, it may be difficult to establish under Subsection (b)(1) through (4) that a reasonable person in the position of the successor would provide a warning. Thus, when the successor has established no systematic relationships with the predecessor's customers through service contracts, usually the successor has no practical method of identifying those customers and communicating effectively with them. The successor who has no continuing contacts with a predecessor's customers may also be unable to discover risks that should be addressed through warnings. Similarly, when a successor has discontinued both the sale of a predecessor's product line and the provision of services to the predecessor's customers, it may not be in a position reasonably to discover risks about the discontinued line or to determine the persons to whom a warning should be addressed.

   Notwithstanding the importance of service contracts in the application of this Section, a contract is not the only method of establishing a relationship with a predecessor's customers. For example, a successor may sell or offer to sell spare parts to the predecessor's customers for machinery sold by the predecessor when the successor knows or should know the machinery is defective. Such conduct should be considered by courts in deciding whether sufficient actual or potential economic advantage has accrued to the successor to warrant the imposition of a duty to warn the predecessor's customers.

c. Factors in determining whether a reasonable successor would provide a warning. Whether a reasonable person in the successor's position would provide a warning is governed by the same requirements that determine whether a reasonable seller should provide a post-sale warning under § 10. Subsection (b)(1) through (4) are identical to the requirements set forth in Subsection (b)(1) through (4) of § 10 and are explained in the Comments to § 10.

§ 14. Selling or Distributing as One's Own a Product Manufactured by Another

One engaged in the business of selling or otherwise distributing products who sells or distributes as its own a product manufactured by another is subject to the same liability as though the seller or distributor were the product's manufacturer.

Comment:

a. History. The rule stated in this Section derives from § 400 of the Restatement, Second, of Torts, promulgated in 1965. Section 400 incorporates by reference §§ 394–398, setting forth the rules governing the liability of manufacturers of chattels. These rules establish a regime of fault-based manufacturers' liability and treat product manufacturers differently than other actors, including nonmanufacturer product sellers. After inclusion of § 402A in the Restatement, Second, imposing strict liability on all commercial sellers of defective products for harm caused by product defects, it was questionable whether § 400 remained relevant in the context of products liability. Once § 402A imposed strict liability on all product sellers it made little, if any, difference whether the seller of a defective product was a retailer or a manufacturer. Compare Comment *b*.

b. Relevance of this Section when all commercial product sellers are held to the same standards of liability under §§ 1–4. To the extent that nonmanufacturers in the chain of distribution are held to the same standards as manufacturers, the rule stated in this Section is of little practical significance. However, many jurisdictions by statute treat nonmanufacturers more leniently. See § 1, Comment *e*. To the extent that a statute specifies responsibilities, the statutory terms control. But to the extent that a statute does not, the rule in this Section states the common-law rule.

c. Representing oneself as the manufacturer or one for whom the product has been specially manufactured. When a commercial seller sells a product manufactured by another under its own trademark or logo, the seller is liable as though it were the manufacturer of the product. This rule applies even if the seller discloses that the product was produced by an identified manufacturer specifically for the seller. In this circumstance, the seller is presumed to cause the product to be used or consumed, in part at least, in reliance on the seller. The seller's reputation is an implied assurance of the quality of the product, and the seller should be estopped from denying that it stands behind that assurance.

d. Liability of trademark licensors. The rule stated in this Section does not, by its terms, apply to the owner of a trademark who licenses a manufacturer to place the licensor's trademark or logo on the manufacturer's product and distribute it as though manufactured by the licensor. In such a case, even if purchasers of the product might assume that the trademark owner was the manufacturer, the licensor does not "sell or distribute as its own a product manufactured by another." Thus, the manufacturer may be liable under §§ 1–4, but the licensor, who does not sell or otherwise distribute products, is not liable under this Section of this Restatement.

Trademark licensors are liable for harm caused by defective products distributed under the licensor's trademark or logo when they participate substantially in the design, manufacture, or distribution of the licensee's products. In these circumstances they are treated as sellers of the products bearing their trademarks.

Chapter 4

PROVISIONS OF GENERAL APPLICABILITY

TOPIC 1. CAUSATION

§ 15. General Rule Governing Causal Connection Between Product Defect and Harm

Whether a product defect caused harm to persons or property is determined by the prevailing rules and principles governing causation in tort.

Comment:

a. Requirement of causal connection between defect and harm. Sections 1, 5, 6, 7, and 8 require that the defect of which the plaintiff complains cause harm to person or property. The rules that govern causation in tort law generally are, subject to § 16, also applicable in products liability cases.

b. *Misuse, alteration, and modification.* When the plaintiff establishes product defect under the rules stated in Chapter 1, a question can arise whether the misuse, alteration, or modification of the product by the user or a third party contributed to the plaintiff's harm in such a way as to absolve the defendant from liability, in whole or in part. Such a question is to be resolved under the prevailing rules and principles governing causation or the prevailing rules and principles governing comparative responsibility, as the case may be. See § 17.

Illustrations:

1. XYZ Co. manufactures and sells automobiles. Sam purchased a new XYZ Model 300 and drove it around town for several days. Unknown to Sam, the lug nuts that hold the right front wheel to the axle were too large, allowing them to loosen and present a serious risk of eventual failure. On Sam's fifth day of ownership, a large truck rear-ended the XYZ automobile while Sam was driving it. Both Sam and the automobile suffer harm. XYZ Co. is not liable to Sam. Although the automobile was defective when Sam purchased it, and although the automobile was a cause of Sam's injuries, the defect was not a substantial factor in causing the injuries, which would have occurred even if the defect had not been present.

2. XYZ Co. manufactures and sells automobiles. Sam purchased a new XYZ Model 300 and drove it around town for several days. On one trip Sam felt the right front wheel wobbling. Upon examination Sam discovered that the five lug nuts holding the wheel to the axle were too large, causing them to loosen. Had Sam not stopped when he did, the wheel would have fallen off. Sam removed the five over-sized lug nuts, borrowed two correct-sized nuts from the right rear wheel, and reattached the right front wheel with them. Sam did nothing more about the wheels for more than a month, whereupon he loaned the automobile to a friend, saying nothing about the wheels. The friend inadvertently drove into a large pothole, causing the two nuts on the right front wheel to break. The wheel came off and both the automobile and Sam's friend suffered harm. Had five proper-sized lug nuts been on the wheel instead of just two, they would not have broken and the accident would not have occurred. XYZ Co. is not liable to Sam or Sam's friend. Although the XYZ automobile was defective when sold, and although the defect was a necessary condition to the occurrence of the accident, Sam's modification and subsequent failure to effect adequate repair were sufficiently unforeseeable that the defect was not a substantial factor in causing the friend's injury.

c. *Causation and proportional liability.* In certain cases involving generic toxic substances, the plaintiffs may be unable to identify which among a number of manufacturers produced the particular product that caused a particular plaintiff's harm. In this context, especially with respect to the drug diethylstilbestrol (DES), some courts have relieved the plaintiff of responsibility to identify the causal producer, and allow recovery instead against each producer named by the plaintiff in proportion to each defendant's market share. Other courts have refused to effect such a basic change in traditional rules of causation.

In deciding whether to adopt a rule of proportional liability, courts have considered the following factors: (1) the generic nature of the product; (2) the long latency period of the harm; (3) the inability of plaintiffs to discover which defendant's product caused plaintiff's harm, even after exhaustive discovery; (4) the clarity of the causal connection between the defective product and the harm suffered by plaintiffs; (5) the absence of other medical or environmental factors that could have caused or materially contributed to the harm; and (6) the availability of sufficient "market share" data to support a reasonable apportionment of liability. The Institute leaves to developing law the question of whether, given the appropriate factors, a rule of proportional liability should be adopted.

However, if a court does adopt some form of proportional liability, the liability of each defendant is properly limited to the individual defendant's share of the market. The rules of joint and several liability are incompatible with a market-share approach to causation. Unlike the case of concurrent tortfeasors, in which several parties contribute to a single plaintiff's entire harm, it is not established in the market-share context that all the defendants contributed to the plaintiff's injury. Instead, each defendant should pay for harm in proportion to the risk that it caused in the market at large. Joint and several liability would impose liability on each defendant for the entirety of the harm based on its presence in the market with other defendants. In the absence of some concerted conduct among the defendants, such liability is inappropriate.

§ 16. Increased Harm Due to Product Defect

(a) When a product is defective at the time of commercial sale or other distribution and the defect is a substantial factor in increasing the plaintiff's harm beyond that which would have resulted from other causes, the product seller is subject to liability for the increased harm.

(b) If proof supports a determination of the harm that would have resulted from other causes in the absence of the product defect, the product seller's liability is limited to the increased harm attributable solely to the product defect.

(c) If proof does not support a determination under Subsection (b) of the harm that would have resulted in the absence of the product defect, the product seller is liable for all of the plaintiff's harm attributable to the defect and other causes.

(d) A seller of a defective product that is held liable for part of the harm suffered by the plaintiff under Subsection (b), or all of the harm suffered by the plaintiff under Subsection (c), is jointly and severally liable or severally liable with other parties who bear legal responsibility for causing the harm, determined by applicable rules of joint and several liability.

Comment:

a. *Liability for increased harm.* This Section deals with the problem of increased harm, often referred to as the issue of "enhancement" of harm. Liability for increased harm arises most frequently in automobile crashworthiness cases, but can also arise in connection with other products. Typically, the plaintiff is involved in an automobile accident caused by conduct or circumstances other than a product defect. The plaintiff would have suffered some injury as a result of the accident even in the absence of the claimed product defect. However, the plaintiff contends that the injuries were aggravated by the vehicle's failure reasonably to protect occupants in the event of an accident.

In the early era of product design litigation, controversy arose over whether a manufacturer owed any obligation to design its product so that injuries would be reasonably minimized in the event of an accident. That controversy is now settled. Although accidents are not intended uses of products, they are generally foreseeable. A manufacturer has a duty to design and manufacture its product so as reasonably to reduce the foreseeable harm that may occur in an accident brought about by causes other than a product defect. See Comment b. Since the product seller is responsible only for the increased harm, and not for the harm that would have occurred even in the absence of the product defect, basic principles of causation limit the damages to those resulting from the increased harm caused by the defect. The plaintiff must establish that the defect was a substantial factor in increasing the harm beyond that which would have resulted from other causes. Once the plaintiff establishes such increased harm, Subsection (b) or (c) applies. If proof supports a determination of what harm would have occurred without a defect, then liability is limited to the increased harm. If proof does not support such a determination, then the product seller is liable for all of the plaintiff's harm from both the defect and other causes.

Illustrations:

1. Bob negligently lost control of his car and collided with Ann's car, causing Ann to suffer harm from being thrown against her car's steering wheel. Ann was driving a car manufactured by XYZ Motor Co. In addition to suing Bob for his negligence, Ann sues XYZ. Expert testimony establishes that a reasonable alternative design of the steering mechanism was available that would have cushioned the impact

between Ann and the steering column and that its omission rendered the car not reasonably safe. Further expert testimony describes the extent to which the omission of the alternative design increased the harm. Defendant XYZ is liable for harm that the trier of fact concludes the plaintiff suffered beyond the harm that would have been suffered had the car been equipped with the reasonable alternative design.

2. While Arthur was driving a snowmobile manufactured by ABC Co., the snowmobile hit a snow-covered rock. On impact, Arthur fell off the snowmobile and his face struck a brake bracket on the side of the snowmobile. Two sharp metal protrusions on the bracket caused serious facial injury. Competent testimony establishes that the brake bracket could have been covered by a safety guard that would have prevented such serious injury and that omission of the guard rendered the product not reasonably safe. Competent testimony also indicates the extent to which absence of the guard increased Arthur's harm. ABC is subject to liability for the harm that the trier of fact finds would have been prevented by a safety guard.

b. Establishing defect in increased-harm cases. To establish liability for increased harm, the plaintiff must prove that a product defect caused the harm under the rules stated in §§ 1–4. When the plaintiff alleges that a manufacturing defect caused increased harm, the plaintiff must establish a defect as set forth in § 2(a). When the plaintiff alleges that a design defect or a defect due to inadequate instructions or warnings caused increased harm, the plaintiff must establish that a reasonable alternative design could have been adopted, or that reasonable instructions or warnings could have been provided, as set forth in §§ 2(b) and 2(c).

In connection with a design defect claim in the context of increased harm, the plaintiff must establish that a reasonable alternative design would have reduced the plaintiff's harm. The factors enumerated in § 2, Comment *f,* for determining the reasonableness of an alternative design and the reasonable safety of the product are fully applicable to establishing defect in an increased-harm case. Furthermore, the alternative to the product design must increase the overall safety of the product. It is not sufficient that the alternative design would have reduced or prevented the harm the plaintiff suffered if the alternative would introduce into the product other dangers of equal or greater magnitude.

Proof of defect does not, of itself, establish a case of increased harm. The plaintiff must also establish that the defect was a substantial factor in increasing the plaintiff's harm beyond the harm that would have occurred from other causes. Subsection (c) provides that, when proof does not support a determination of increased harm, the product seller is liable for all harm suffered by the victim. However, the rule stated in Subsection (c) does not take effect until the plaintiff establishes under Subsection (a), by competent testimony, that the plaintiff's harm was increased as a result of the product defect.

Illustrations:

3. George was a passenger in a van manufactured by the XYZ Motor Co. The van was driven by a co-worker, Alice, who was proceeding non-negligently along a highway at 50 mph. To avoid a dog that unexpectedly ran across the highway, Alice swerved and lost control of the van, which struck an abutment. The force and angle of the collision caused the van to fly in the air and travel 75 feet before coming to rest upside down. During or after the initial collision, the roof panel separated from the van. George was thrown through the roof area and landed 50 feet from the van. Competent testimony by George's expert establishes that the welds meant to hold the roof to the body of the van were defective and did not meet the XYZ design standards. George's expert evidence also supports a determination that, had the roof been properly welded, it would not have come off as a result of the collision, that George would have remained in the van, and that the harm he suffered as a result of being thrown from the van was more serious than it would have been if the roof had kept George inside the van. Expert testimony also supports a determination of the extent to which George would have been harmed if he had stayed in the van, and thus the extent to which George's harm was increased by the failure of the roof to remain attached to the van. XYZ is liable for George's harm above that which the trier of fact determines George would have suffered in the absence of the defective welds.

4. Alice was operating a tractor manufactured by XYZ Farm Equipment. The tractor was designed for use on hills and sharp inclines. The tractor struck a large rock protruding from the ground, causing the tractor to roll over down a slope. Alice was thrown from the tractor and pinned beneath it. Alice's expert testifies that, had the tractor been designed with a rollover protection system, Alice would not have been thrown from the tractor and that the omission of the rollover protection system rendered the product not reasonably safe. This testimony supports a finding of defective design. Expert testimony also describes the extent to which Alice's harm was increased by the omission of the rollover protection system. Defendant XYZ is subject to liability for Alice's harm beyond that which the trier of fact finds she would have suffered had the tractor been equipped with the rollover protection system.

5. Richard suffered harm as a result of an automobile accident that occurred when he lost control of his car on a rain-soaked highway. The car slid off the highway and collided sideways with a steel pole. As a result of the force of the collision, the pole ripped through the body of the car and crushed Richard between the front seat and the area of the roof just above the windshield. Richard brings suit against the XYZ Motor Co., the manufacturer of the car, alleging that the car was defective in design in that it did not have a continuous steel frame extending through the door panels. Richard's experts assert that, had

the vehicle been so designed, it would have bounced off the pole, preventing penetration by the pole into the passenger space. XYZ's experts assert that a continuous steel frame would also reduce front-to-back deformation of the body of the vehicle in a head-on crash. Deformation is desirable in head-on crashes because it absorbs the impact of the crash and decreases risk of harm to the occupants of the vehicle. Richard's experts admit on cross-examination that, for head-on automobile accidents, the alternative design offered by Richard would decrease safety. Even if the design alternative offered by Richard would have reduced his harm, if the trier of fact finds that Richard's proposed alternative would have decreased the overall safety of the vehicle, it should return a verdict for XYZ.

c. *Determination of what harm would have resulted in the absence of the product defect.* The task of determining what harm would have resulted had the product not been defective under Subsection (b) is often difficult. Outright guesswork is not permitted, but neither should anything approaching certainty be required. When an expert offers a rational explanation derived from a causal analysis, the testimony should, subject to the normal discretion of the trial court, be admitted for consideration by the trier of fact.

d. *Extent of liability for increased harm when proof does not support determination of what harm would have resulted in the absence of the product defect.* Subsection (c) provides that when the plaintiff has proved defect-caused increased harm, the product seller is subject to liability for all harm suffered by the plaintiff if proof does not support a determination of what harm would have resulted if the product had not been defective. The defendant, a wrongdoer who in fact has caused harm to the plaintiff, should not escape liability because the nature of the harm makes such a determination impossible. Compare § 433B(2) of the Restatement, Second, of Torts.

Illustration:

6. The same facts as Illustration 3, in that George proves that the defect was a substantial factor in increasing the harm beyond that which he would have suffered if the roof had kept him inside the van, but George is unable to quantify the extent of the increased harm. Neither party introduces proof that supports the apportionment of liability. XYZ is liable for all of George's harm.

e. *Joint and several liability for increased harm.* When the plaintiff proves defect-caused increased harm, and the seller of the defective product is held liable for part of the harm suffered by the plaintiff under Subsection (b) or all of the harm suffered by the plaintiff under Subsection (c), liability of the seller and other tortfeasors is joint and several. In a case under Subsection (b), the manufacturer is jointly and severally liable only for the increased harm; in a case under Subsection (c), for the entire harm. Joint and several liability is imposed because there is no practical method of apportioning responsibility that would reflect the separate causal contributions of those tortfeasors who caused the increased harm. The general rules governing joint and several liability determine the liability of the parties to the injured plaintiff. In those jurisdictions that retain the common-law rule, all parties bear full responsibility for the entirety of the harm. In many jurisdictions, the common-law rules of joint and several liability have undergone significant legislative modification limiting liability to the percentage of fault allocated to each party.

Illustrations:

   7.   Same facts as Illustration 6, except that Alice's negligent driving caused her to lose control of her van. The XYZ Motor Co. is liable under Subsection (c) for all of George's harm. The case is governed by the law of State A, which follows the common-law rule of joint and several liability. George may recover all of his damages from either Alice or XYZ.

   8.   Same facts as Illustration 7. The XYZ Motor Co. is liable under Subsection (c) for all of George's harm. The case is governed by the law of State B, whose statute limits the liability of joint tortfeasors to the percentage of responsibility allocated to each party. The trier of fact allocates 40 percent of the responsibility to Alice and 60 percent of the responsibility to XYZ. XYZ's liability is limited to 60 percent of the total damages.

   9.   Same facts as Illustration 7. The XYZ Motor Co. is liable under Subsection (c) for all of George's harm. The case is governed by the law of State C, whose statute retains the common-law rule of joint and several liability for economic loss but limits the liability of joint tortfeasors for noneconomic loss to the percentage of responsibility allocated to each party. The trier of fact has allocated 40 percent of the responsibility to Alice and 60 percent to XYZ. George may recover all of his economic loss damages from either Alice or XYZ. His recovery from XYZ for noneconomic damages is limited to 60 percent.

   f.   Plaintiff's fault in cases of increased harm. Section 17 sets forth the general rules governing plaintiff's fault in products liability litigation. It provides that plaintiff's fault is relevant in apportioning liability between the plaintiff and the product seller. The seriousness of the plaintiff's fault and the nature of the product defect are relevant in apportioning the appropriate percentages of responsibility between the plaintiff and the product seller. See § 17, Comment *d*. Accordingly, the contributory fault of the plaintiff in causing an accident that results in defect-related increased harm is relevant in apportioning responsibility between or among the parties, according to applicable apportionment law. In apportioning responsibility in such cases, it may be important that requiring a product to be designed reasonably to prevent increased harm aims to protect persons in circumstances in which they are unable to protect themselves.

TOPIC 2. AFFIRMATIVE DEFENSES

§ 17. Apportionment of Responsibility Between or Among Plaintiff, Sellers and Distributors of Defective Products, and Others

(a) A plaintiff's recovery of damages for harm caused by a product defect may be reduced if the conduct of the plaintiff combines with the product defect to cause the harm and the plaintiff's conduct fails to conform to generally applicable rules establishing appropriate standards of care.

(b) The manner and extent of the reduction under Subsection (a) and the apportionment of plaintiff's recovery among multiple defendants are governed by generally applicable rules apportioning responsibility.

Comment:

a. History. The rule stated in this Section recognizes that the fault of the plaintiff is relevant in assessing liability for product-caused harm. Section 402A of the Restatement, Second, of Torts, recognizing strict liability for harm caused by defective products, was adopted in 1964 when the overwhelming majority rule treated contributory negligence as a total bar to recovery. Understandably, the Institute was reluctant to bar a plaintiff's products liability claim in tort based on conduct that was not egregious. Thus, § 402A, Comment *n*, altered the general tort defenses by narrowing the applicability of contributory negligence and emphasizing assumption of risk as the primary defense. Since then, comparative fault has swept the country. Only a tiny minority of states retain contributory fault as a total bar.

A strong majority of jurisdictions apply the comparative responsibility doctrine to products liability actions. Courts today do not limit the relevance of plaintiff's fault as did the Restatement, Second, of Torts to conduct characterized as voluntary assumption of the risk. See Comment *d*.

Certain forms of consumer behavior—product misuse and product alteration or modification—have been the subject of much confusion and misunderstanding. Early decisions treated product misuse, alteration, and modification, whether by the plaintiff or a third party, as a total bar to recovery against a product seller. Today misuse, alteration, and modification relate to one of three issues in a products liability action. In some cases, misuse, alteration, and modification are important in determining whether the product is defective. In others, they are relevant to the issue of legal cause. Finally, when the plaintiff misuses, alters, or modifies the product, such conduct may constitute contributory fault and reduce the plaintiff's recovery under the rules of comparative responsibility. See Comment *c*.

b.   *Conduct of the plaintiff*. The applicable rules of apportionment of responsibility vary among jurisdictions. Some states have adopted "pure" comparative fault, which allocates responsibility to each actor purely in proportion to the actor's percentage of total fault. Others follow some variant of "modified" comparative fault, in which actors' responsibilities are adjusted according to predetermined thresholds of responsibility. For example, in many modified jurisdictions the plaintiff is totally barred if found more than 50 percent at fault. The apportionment of responsibility principles as they have developed in each jurisdiction should be applied to products liability cases. With respect to whether special exceptions should be made in products liability cases for certain categories of plaintiff conduct, see Comment *d*.

c.   *Misuse, alteration, and modification*. Product misuse, alteration, and modification, whether by a third party or the plaintiff, are not discrete doctrines within products liability law. Instead such conduct is relevant to the determination of the issues of defect, causation, and comparative responsibility. See § 2, Comment *p*.

Jurisdictions differ on the question of who bears the burden of proof regarding conduct that constitutes misuse, modification, and alteration. The allocation of burdens in this regard is not addressed in this Restatement and is left to local law.

d.   *Particular forms or categories of plaintiff's conduct*. Some courts accord different treatment to special categories of plaintiff conduct. For example, some decisions hold that when the plaintiff's negligence is the failure to discover a product defect, reduction of damages on the basis of apportionment of responsibility is improper, reasoning that a consumer has a right to expect a defect-free product and should not be burdened with a duty to inspect for defects. Other decisions hold that apportionment of responsibility is improper when the product lacked a safety feature that would protect against the risk that resulted in the injury in question, reasoning that the defendant's responsibility should not be diminished when the plaintiff engages in the very conduct that the product design should have prevented. On the other hand, some decisions hold that a plaintiff's assumption of the risk is a complete defense to a products liability action, not merely a basis for apportionment of responsibility. Product misuse, alteration, and modification have been treated by some courts as an absolute bar to recovery and by others as a form of plaintiff fault that should be compared with that of other parties to reduce recovery. The majority position is that all forms of plaintiff's failure to conform to applicable standards of care are to be considered for the purpose of apportioning responsibility between the plaintiff and the product seller or distributor.

Before the court will allow any apportionment of responsibility, the defendant must introduce sufficient evidence to support a finding of fault on the part of the plaintiff. Thus, for example, when the defendant claims that the plaintiff failed to discover a defect, there must be evidence that the plaintiff's conduct in failing to discover a defect did, in fact, fail to meet a standard of reasonable care. In general, a plaintiff has no reason to expect that a new product contains a defect and would have little reason to be on guard to discover it. Or when a plaintiff is injured due to inattention to a danger that should have been eliminated by a safety feature, there must be evidence supporting the conclusion that the plaintiff's momentary inattention or inadvertence in a workplace setting constitutes failure to exercise reasonable care. In the absence of such evidence courts refuse to submit the plaintiff's conduct to the trier of fact for apportionment based on the principles of comparative responsibility. When evidence of plaintiff fault is established, how much responsibility to attribute to a plaintiff will vary with the circumstances. The seriousness of the plaintiff's fault and the nature of the product defect are relevant in apportioning the appropriate percentages of responsibility between the plaintiff and the product seller.

§ 18. Disclaimers, Limitations, Waivers, and Other Contractual Exculpations as Defenses to Products Liability Claims for Harm to Persons

Disclaimers and limitations of remedies by product sellers or other distributors, waivers by product purchasers, and other similar contractual exculpations, oral or written, do not bar or reduce otherwise valid products liability claims against sellers or other distributors of new products for harm to persons.

Comment:

a. Effects of contract defenses on products liability tort claims for harm to persons. A commercial seller or other distributor of a new product is not permitted to avoid liability for harm to persons through limiting terms in a contract governing the sale of a product. It is presumed that the ordinary product user or consumer lacks sufficient information and bargaining power to execute a fair contractual limitation of rights to recover. For a limited exception to this general rule, see Comment *d.* The rule in this Section applies only to "sellers or other distributors of new products." For rules governing commercial sellers of used products, including whether they may rely on disclaimers, waivers, and other contractual defenses, see § 8. Nothing in this Section is intended to constrain parties within the commercial chain of distribution from contracting inter se for indemnity agreements or save-harmless clauses.

b. Distinguishing disclaimers from warnings. This Section invalidates disclaimers and contractual exculpations of liability by sellers of new products when they are interjected to bar or limit claims by plaintiffs for harm to persons. Disclaimers should be distinguished from warnings. Warnings convey information to the buyer about avoiding risk in using the product. In some cases warnings inform the consumer of risks that cannot be avoided. Both types of warnings provide consumers with valuable information concerning the risks attendant to using the product. A product sold with reasonable instructions or warnings may be nondefective. See § 2, Comments *i, j, k,* and *l.* Disclaimers attempt contractually to avoid liability for defective products. For the reasons set forth in Comment *a,* courts refuse to enforce disclaimers that purport to deny recovery for harm to persons caused by new products that were defective at the time of sale.

c. *Effects of disclaimers on claims for harm to property or for economic loss.* For the effect of disclaimers on tort claims for defect-caused harm to property or for economic loss, see § 21, Comment *f.*

d. *Waiver of rights in contractual settings in which product purchasers possess both adequate knowledge and sufficient economic power.* The rule in this Section applies to cases in which commercial product sellers attempt unfairly to disclaim or otherwise limit their liability to the majority of users and consumers who are presumed to lack information and bargaining power adequate to protect their interests. This Section does not address whether consumers, especially when represented by informed and economically powerful consumer groups or intermediaries, with full information and sufficient bargaining power, may contract with product sellers to accept curtailment of liability in exchange for concomitant benefits, or whether such consumers might be allowed to agree to substitute alternative dispute resolution mechanisms in place of traditional adjudication. When such contracts are accompanied by alternative nontort remedies that serve as an adequate quid pro quo for reducing or eliminating rights to recover in tort, arguments may support giving effect to such agreements. Such contractual arrangements raise policy questions different from those raised by this Section and require careful consideration by the courts.

TOPIC 3. DEFINITIONS

§ 19. Definition of "Product"

For purposes of this Restatement:

(a) A product is tangible personal property distributed commercially for use or consumption. Other items, such as real property and electricity, are products when the context of their distribution and use is sufficiently analogous to the distribution and use of tangible personal property that it is appropriate to apply the rules stated in this Restatement.

(b) Services, even when provided commercially, are not products.

(c) Human blood and human tissue, even when provided commercially, are not subject to the rules of this Restatement.

Comment:

a. History. The question of whether something distributed in commerce is a product for purposes of tort liability is important in this Restatement, but relatively less so than it was in the period from the early 1960s to the early 1980s. Before 1960, American courts had not yet recognized strict liability in tort for harm caused by defective products, particularly if there was no privity of contract between plaintiff and defendant. Thus, prior to that time, plaintiffs claiming in tort against product sellers were required to prove causal negligence; if they could prove negligence they could usually recover in tort whether or not a product was involved. Once the era of strict products liability in tort arrived in the early 1960s, liability turned primarily on whether what the defendant distributed was, or was not, a product. Most of the focus during this period was on liability for harm caused by manufacturing defects, in connection with which strict liability had a distinctive character. See § 2(a).

By the early 1980s, the emphasis of products liability litigation had shifted from manufacturing defects to defective designs and defects due to inadequate instructions and warnings. Thereafter, design and warning cases came to dominate. Given that design and warning cases turn on essentially risk-utility evaluations, see § 2, Comment *d,* the practical importance of whether something is, or is not, a product has diminished somewhat. Nevertheless, that issue remains important in the modern era to the extent that the concept of strict liability retains functional meaning. See § 1, Comment *a.* Statutes enacted to reform products liability law, many of which impose nontraditional conditions and limitations on product-related liability, tend to enhance the importance of classifying something as a product.

Apart from statutes that define "product" for purposes of determining products liability, in every instance it is for the court to determine as a matter of law whether something is, or is not, a product.

b. Tangible personal property: in general. For purposes of this Restatement, most but not necessarily all products are tangible personal property. In certain situations, however, intangible personal property (see Comment *d*) and real property (see Comment *e*) may be products. Component parts are products, whether sold or distributed separately or assembled with other component parts. An assemblage of component parts is also, itself, a product. Raw materials are products, whether manufactured, such as sheet metal; processed, such as lumber; or gathered and sold or distributed in raw condition, such as unwashed gravel and farm produce. For treatment of the special problems presented when plaintiffs join sellers of component parts and raw materials in actions against those who subsequently combined those materials to create defective products, see § 10.

Courts are divided regarding whether living animals, such as pets or livestock, should be considered to be products for the purpose of determining a commercial seller's liability in tort. Frequently, as when diseased livestock are sold and subsequently must be destroyed, the claim to recover for their value involves a claim for harm to the product itself and thus represents a claim for pure economic loss not permitted by this Restatement. See § 21. But when a living animal is sold commercially in a diseased condition and causes harm to other property or to persons, the animal constitutes a product for purposes of this Restatement.

c. Tangible personal property: human blood and human tissue. Although human blood and human tissue meet the formal requisites of Subsection (a), they are specifically excluded from the coverage of this Restatement. Almost all the litigation regarding such products has dealt with contamination of human blood and blood-related products by the hepatitis virus or the HIV virus. Absent a special rule dealing with human blood and tissue, such contamination presumably would be subject to the rules of §§ 1 and 2(a). Those Sections impose strict liability when a product departs from its intended design even though all possible care was exercised in the preparation and marketing of the product. However, legislation in almost all jurisdictions limits the liability of sellers of human blood and human tissue to the failure to exercise reasonable care, often by providing that human blood and human tissue are not "products" or that their provision is a "service." Where legislation has not addressed the problem, courts have concluded that strict liability is inappropriate for harm caused by such product contamination.

What constitutes reasonable care for those engaged in providing professional services is defined in § 299A of the Restatement, Second, of Torts.

d. Intangible personal property. Two basic types of intangible personal property are involved. The first consists of information in media such as books, maps, and navigational charts. Plaintiffs allege that the information delivered was false and misleading, causing harm when actors relied on it. They seek to recover against publishers in strict liability in tort based on product defect, rather than on negligence or some form of misrepresentation. Although a tangible medium such as a book, itself clearly a product, delivers the information, the plaintiff's grievance in such cases is with the information, not with the tangible medium. Most courts, expressing concern that imposing strict liability for the dissemination of false and defective information would significantly impinge on free speech have, appropriately, refused to impose strict products liability in these cases. One area in which some courts have imposed strict products liability involves false information contained in maps and navigational charts. In that context the falsity of the factual information is unambiguous and more akin to a classic product defect. However, the better view is that false information in such documents constitutes a misrepresentation that the user may properly rely upon.

The second major category of intangible, harm-causing products involves the transmission of intangible forces such as electricity and X rays. With respect to transmission of electricity, a majority of courts have held that electricity becomes a product only when it passes through the customer's meter and enters the customer's premises. Until then, the system of high-voltage transmission provides, not a product, but a service; before passing the meter and entering the plaintiff's premises, so it is said, the electricity has not entered the stream of commerce. Some courts employ this analysis to conclude that, while electricity is a "product" prior to delivery, it has not yet been "sold or otherwise distributed." Whether or not these rationales are cogent, the distinction drawn between pre-and post-delivery is reasonable. Plaintiffs in the post-delivery cases typically complain of unexpected drops or surges in voltage, resulting in personal injury or property damage. Those claims seem better governed by principles of strict liability for physical deviations from intended design. Plaintiffs in the pre-delivery, high-voltage cases complain of the inherent dangers that unavoidably accompany the transmission of high-voltage electricity. Courts have refused to impose strict liability on electric utilities for high voltage-related accidents either on a strict products liability basis or under the abnormally dangerous activities doctrine set out in § 520 of the Restatement, Second, of Torts. This Restatement does not alter that approach.

The cases involving harm caused by X-rays and radiation treatments rest not on assertions that the X-rays themselves were defective, but rather on assertions that they were improperly administered by medical technicians. Courts have refused to impose liability in the absence of a showing by plaintiff either that the X-rays or other forms of radiation treatment were defective or that the medical technicians acted negligently. These cases may also reflect courts' traditional refusal to impose strict liability on providers of medical care.

e. Real property. Traditionally, courts have been reluctant to impose products liability on sellers of improved real property in that such property does not constitute goods or personalty. A housing contractor, building and selling one house at a time, does not fit the pattern of a mass producer of manufactured products, nor is such a builder perceived to be more capable than are purchasers of controlling or insuring against risks presented by weather conditions or earth movements. More recently, courts have treated sellers of improved real property as product sellers in a number of contexts. When a building contractor sells a building that contains a variety of appliances or other manufactured equipment, the builder, together with the equipment manufacturer and other distributors, are held as product sellers with respect to such equipment notwithstanding the fact that the built-in equipment may have become, for other legal purposes, attachments to and thus part of the underlying real property. Moreover, the builder may be treated as a product seller even with respect to the building itself when the building has been prefabricated—and thus manufactured—and later assembled on-or off-site. Finally, courts impose strict liability for defects in construction when dwellings are built, even if on-site, on a major scale, as in a large housing project.

f. The distinction between services and products. Services, even when provided commercially, are not products for purposes of this Restatement. Thus, apart from the sale of a product incidental to the service, one who agrees for a monetary fee to mow the lawn of another is the provider of a service even if the provider is a large firm engaged commercially in lawn care. Moreover, it is irrelevant that the service provided relates directly to products commercially distributed. For example, one who contracts to inspect, repair, and maintain machinery owned and operated by another is the provider of a product-related service rather than the provider of a product. If a product repairer replaces a worn-out component part with a new part, the replacement constitutes a sale of the part; but the repair itself constitutes a service. For consideration of commercial transactions combining elements of both sale and service, see § 20(c).

§ 20. Definition of "One Who Sells or Otherwise Distributes"

For purposes of this Restatement:

(a) One sells a product when, in a commercial context, one transfers ownership thereto either for use or consumption or for resale leading to ultimate use or consumption. Commercial product sellers include, but are not limited to, manufacturers, wholesalers, and retailers.

(b) One otherwise distributes a product when, in a commercial transaction other than a sale, one provides the product to another either for use or consumption or as a preliminary step leading to ultimate use or consumption. Commercial nonsale product distributors include, but are not limited to, lessors, bailors, and those who provide products to others as a means of promoting either the use or consumption of such products or some other commercial activity.

(c) One also sells or otherwise distributes a product when, in a commercial transaction, one provides a combination of products and services and either the transaction taken as a whole, or the product component thereof, satisfies the criteria in Subsection (a) or (b).

Comment:

a. History. Until the mid–1960s, the only transactions that gave rise to what today is known as "products liability" were commercial product sales, as defined in Subsection (a). In large part this limitation reflects the origins of liability without fault in the law of warranty, which has traditionally focused on sales transactions. During the formative years in the development of strict products liability, courts extended liability to some nonsale transactions, but always by assimilating such transactions to sales. Section 402A of the Restatement, Second, of Torts, approved in 1964, limited itself to "one who *sells* a product in a defective condition...."(Emphasis added). After the promulgation of § 402A, courts began to extend strict liability for harm caused by product defects to some nonsale commercial transactions involving the distribution of products. Rather than stretching to call these transactions "sales," courts simply declared that the same policy objectives that supported strict liability in the sales context supported strict liability in other contexts. The first significant extension involved commercial product lessors. Although title does not pass in lease transactions, courts have reasoned that the same policy objectives that are served by holding commercial product sellers strictly liable also apply to commercial product lessors. Over time, courts have extended strict products liability to a wide range of nonsale, nonlease transactions.

   b. Product sales and giveaways. Sales occur at all levels in the distributive chain including manufacturer sellers, wholesale sellers, and retail sellers. Food served in a restaurant is sold to the customer, as are products given away free of separate charge in the context of a commercial sales promotion. Thus, businesses are liable for defects in free samples or defects in products given away for other promotional purposes. Even if the final transaction through which a defective product reaches the plaintiff is not a commercial sales transaction, with the result that products liability is not imposed on the final transferor—as when one buys a soft drink at a store and then gives it to a friend—a plaintiff may recover in tort for resulting harm against all commercial sellers who sold the product in a defective condition.

   c. Commercial product leases. A commercial lessor of new and like-new products is generally subject to the rules governing new product sellers. When an individual rents a new or an almost-new used product on a short-term basis, with the lessee having no opportunity to inspect the product or adequately to assess its condition, and the product unit is drawn from a pool of rental units that includes new and almost-new used units with no attempt by the leasing agent to distinguish among units on the basis of age and condition, the lessor is subject to liability as if it were the retail seller of a new product. When the rental units are in obviously used condition, liability of the lessor depends on the rules stated in § 8.

   d. Sales-service combinations. When the same person provides both products and services in a commercial transaction, whether a product has been sold may be difficult to determine. When the product and service components are kept separate by the parties to the transaction, as when a lawn-care firm bills separately for fertilizer applied to a customer's lawn or when a machinery repairer replaces a component part and bills separately for it, the firm will be held to be the seller of the product. This is especially true when the parties to the transaction explicitly characterize the property aspect as a sale.

When the parties do not clearly separate the product and service components, courts differ in their treatment of these so-called "sale-service hybrid transactions." These transactions tend to fall into two categories. In the first, the product component is consumed in the course of providing the service, as when a hair dye is used in treating a customer's hair in a salon. Even when the service provider does not charge the customer separately for the dye, the transaction ordinarily is treated as a sale of the material that is consumed in providing the service. When the product component in the sale-service transaction is not consumed or permanently transferred to the customer—as when defective scissors are used in the hair salon—the transaction ordinarily is treated as one not involving a sale of the product to the customer. But while the salon is not a seller, all commercial sellers in the chain of distribution of the scissors, from the manufacturer through the retailer who sold them to the salon, are clearly sellers of the scissors and are subject to liability to the salon customer under the rules of this Restatement. It should be noted that, in a strong majority of jurisdictions, hospitals are held not to be sellers of products they supply in connection with the provision of medical care, regardless of the circumstances.

e.   Other means of commercial distribution: finance leases. A finance lessor, as distinct from a commercial lessor under Comment *c*, is not subject to the rule of this Section in the absence of active participation in the underlying commercial product distribution.

f.   Other means of commercial distribution: product bailments. Bailments typically involve short-term transfers of possession. Several categories of cases are fairly clear. When the defendant is in the business of selling the same type of product as is the subject of the bailment, the seller/bailor is subject to strict liability for harm caused by defects. Thus, an automobile dealer who allows a prospective customer to test-drive a demonstrator will be treated the same as a seller of the demonstrator car. Even when sale of a product is not contemplated, the commercial bailor is subject to strict liability if a charge is imposed as a condition of the bailment. Thus, a laundromat is subject to strict liability for a defective clothes dryer, and a roller rink that rents skates is treated similarly. When products are made available as a convenience to customers who are on the defendant's premises primarily for different, although related purposes, and no separate charge is made, strict liability is not imposed. Thus, bowling alleys that supply bowling balls for customer use and markets that supply shopping carts are not subject to strict products liability for harm caused by defects in those items. Similarly, doctors who use medical devices while treating patients are not considered distributors of those products.

g.   Other means of commercial distribution: product distribution facilitators. Persons assisting or providing services to product distributors, while indirectly facilitating the commercial distribution of products, are not subject to liability under the rules of this Restatement. Thus, commercial firms engaged in advertising products are outside the rules of this Restatement, as are firms engaged exclusively in the financing of product sale or lease transactions. Sales personnel and commercial auctioneers are also outside the rules of this Restatement.

§ 21. Definition of "Harm to Persons or Property": Recovery for Economic Loss

For purposes of this Restatement, harm to persons or property includes economic loss if caused by harm to:

(a) the plaintiff's person; or

(b) the person of another when harm to the other interferes with an interest of the plaintiff protected by tort law; or

(c) the plaintiff's property other than the defective product itself.

Comment:

a. Rationale. This Section limits the kinds of harm for which recovery is available under this Restatement. Two major constraints on tort recovery give content to this Section. First, products liability law lies at the boundary between tort and contract. Some categories of loss, including those often referred to as "pure economic loss," are more appropriately assigned to contract law and the remedies set forth in Articles 2 and 2A of the Uniform Commercial Code. When the Code governs a claim, its provisions regarding such issues as statutes of limitation, privity, notice of claim, and disclaimer ordinarily govern the litigation. Second, some forms of economic loss have traditionally been excluded from the realm of tort law even when the plaintiff has no contractual remedy for a claim.

b. Economic loss resulting from harm to plaintiff's person. Loss of earnings and reductions in earning capacity are common forms of economic loss resulting from harm to the plaintiff's person and are included in Subsection (a). Other forms of economic loss resulting from harm to the plaintiff's person are recoverable if they are within the general principles of legal cause. See Restatement, Second, Torts §§ 430–461.

c. When harm to another interferes with an interest of the plaintiff protected by tort law. When tort law recognizes the right of a plaintiff to recover for economic loss arising from harm to another's person, that right is included within the rules of this Restatement Third, Torts: Products Liability. Thus, for example, actions under local common law and statutes for loss of consortium or wrongful death on behalf of next of kin, although not direct harms to the plaintiff's person, are included in Subsection (b). Other examples of such rights may be recognized under local law, but the categories included in Subsection (b) have traditionally been limited in number.

d. *Harm to the defective product itself.* When a product defect results in harm to the product itself, the law governing commercial transactions sets forth a comprehensive scheme governing the rights of the buyer and seller. Harm to the product itself takes two forms. A product defect may render the product ineffective so that repair or replacement is necessary. Such a defect may also result in consequential loss to the buyer. For example, a machine that becomes inoperative may cause the assembly line in which it is being used to break down and may lead to a wide range of consequential economic losses to the business that owns the machine. These losses are not recoverable in tort under the rules of this Restatement. A somewhat more difficult question is presented when the defect in the product renders it unreasonably dangerous, but the product does not cause harm to persons or property. In these situations the danger either (1) never eventuates in harm because the product defect is discovered before it causes harm, or (2) eventuates in harm to the product itself but not in harm to persons or other property. A plausible argument can be made that products that are dangerous, rather than merely ineffectual, should be governed by the rules governing products liability law. However, a majority of courts have concluded that the remedies provided under the Uniform Commercial Code—repair and replacement costs and, in appropriate circumstances, consequential economic loss—are sufficient. Thus, the rules of this Restatement do not apply in such situations.

A second category of economic loss excluded from the coverage of this Restatement includes losses suffered by a plaintiff but not as a direct result of harm to the plaintiff's person or property. For example, a defective product may destroy a commercial business establishment, whose employees patronize a particular restaurant, resulting in economic loss to the restaurant. The loss suffered by the restaurant generally is not recoverable in tort and in any event is not cognizable under products liability law.

e. *Harm to the plaintiff's property other than the defective product itself.* A defective product that causes harm to property other than the defective product itself is governed by the rules of this Restatement. What constitutes harm to other property rather than harm to the product itself may be difficult to determine. A product that nondangerously fails to function due to a product defect has clearly caused harm only to itself. A product that fails to function and causes harm to surrounding property has clearly caused harm to other property. However, when a component part of a machine or a system destroys the rest of the machine or system, the characterization process becomes more difficult. When the product or system is deemed to be an integrated whole, courts treat such damage as harm to the product itself. When so characterized, the damage is excluded from the coverage of this Restatement. A contrary holding would require a finding of property damage in virtually every case in which a product harms itself and would prevent contractual rules from serving their legitimate function in governing commercial transactions.

The characterization of a claim as harm to other property may trigger liability not only for the harm to physical property but also for incidental economic loss. The extent to which incidental economic loss is recoverable in tort is governed by general principles of legal cause. See Restatement, Second, Torts §§ 430–461.

One category of claims stands apart. In the case of asbestos contamination in buildings, most courts have taken the position that the contamination constitutes harm to the building as other property. The serious health threat caused by asbestos contamination has led the courts to this conclusion. Thus, actions seeking recovery for the costs of asbestos removal have been held to be within the purview of products liability law rather than commercial law.

f. Harm to other property: disclaimers and limitations of remedies. Although recovery for harm to property other than the defective product itself is governed by this Restatement, the Institute leaves to developing case law the questions of whether and under what circumstances contracting parties may disclaim or limit remedies for harm to other property. Of course, such contractual limitations would be effective only between the parties themselves. When a defective product causes harm to property owned by third persons, the contractual arrangements between the contracting parties should not shield the seller from liability to the third party. However, contractual limitations on tort liability for harm to property, when fairly bargained for, may provide an effective way for the contracting parties efficiently to allocate risks of such harm between themselves.

UNIFORM COMMERCIAL CODE
Selected Sections*

UNIFORM COMMERCIAL CODE
*Table of Jurisdictions Wherein Code Has Been Adopted**

Jurisdiction	Laws	Effective Date	Statutory Citation
Alabama	1965, Act No. 549	1–1–1967	Code 1975, §§ 7–1–101 to 7–11–108
Alaska	1962, c. 114	1–1–1963	AS §§ 45.01 to 45.09, 45.12, 45.14
Arizona	1967, c. 3	1–1–1968	A.R.S. §§ 47–1101 to 47–11107
Arkansas	1961, Act No. 185	1–1–1962	Code 1987, §§ 4–1–101 to 4–10–104
California	Stats.1963, c. 819	1–1–1965	West's Ann.Cal.Com.Code, §§ 1101 to 15104
Colorado	1965, c. 330	7–1–1966	C.R.S. §§ 4–1–101 to 4–11–102
Connecticut	1959, No. 133	10–1–1961	C.G.S.A. §§ 42a–1–101 to 42a–10–109
Delaware	1966, c. 349	7–1–1967	6 Del.C. §§ 1–101 to 11–109
Dist. of Columbia	P.L. 88–243	1–1–1965	D.C.Code 1981, §§ 28:1–101 to 28:11–108
Florida	1965, c. 65–254	1–1–1967	West's F.S.A. §§ 670.101 to 670.507; 671.101 to 680.532
Georgia	1962, Act 713	1–1–1964	O.C.G.A. §§ 11–1–101 to 11–11–104
Hawaii	1965, No. 208	1–1–1967	HRS §§ 490:1–101 to 490:11–108
Idaho	1967, c. 161	1–1–1968	I.C. §§ 28–1–101 to 28–10–104; 28–12–101 to 28–12–532
Illinois	1961, p. 2101	7–2–1962	S.H.A. 810 ILCS 5/1–101 to 5/12–102
Indiana	1963, c. 317	7–1–1964	West's A.I.C. 26–1–1–101 to 26–1–10–104
Iowa	1965, (61 G.A.) c. 413	7–4–1966	I.C.A. §§ 554.1101 to 554.13532
Kansas	1965, c. 564	1–1–1966	K.S.A. 84–1–101 to 84–10–102
Kentucky	1958, c. 77	7–1–1960	KRS 355.1–101 to 355.11–108
Louisiana	1974, No. 92	1–1–1975	LSA–R.S. 10:1–101 to 10:5–117
Maine	1963, c. 362	12–31–1964	11 M.R.S.A. §§ 1–101 to 10–108
Maryland	1963, c. 538	2–1–1964	Code, Commercial Law, §§ 1–101 to 10–112
Massachusetts	1957, c. 765	10–1–1958	M.G.L.A. c. 106, §§ 1–101 to 9–507
Michigan	1962, P.A. 174	1–1–1964	M.C.L.A. §§ 440.1101 to 440.11102
Minnesota	1965, c. 811	7–1–1966	M.S.A. §§ 336.1–101 to 336.11–108
Mississippi	1966, c. 316	3–31–1968	Code 1972, §§ 75–1–101 to 75–11–108
Missouri	1963, p. 503	7–1–1965	V.A.M.S. §§ 400.1–101 to 400.11–107
Montana	1963, c. 264	1–2–1965	MCA 30–1–101 to 30–9–511
Nebraska	1963, c. 544	9–2–1965	Neb.U.C.C. §§ 1–101 to 10–104
Nevada	1965, c. 353	3–1–1967	N.R.S. 104.1101 to 104.9507; 104A.010 to 104A.2531

* For the versions of the UCC adopted in each state, see Uniform Commercial Code (U.L.A.) at 1–2 (1989 and Supp.1996). Eds.

Jurisdiction	Laws	Effective Date	Statutory Citation
New Hampshire	1959, c. 247	7–1–1961	RSA 382–A:1–101 to 382–A:9–507
New Jersey	1961, c. 120	1–1–1963	N.J.S.A. 12A:1–101 to 12A:11–108
New Mexico	1961, c. 96	1–1–1962	NMSA 1978, §§ 55–1–101 to 55–12–108
New York	1962, c. 553	9–27–1964	McKinney's Uniform Commercial Code, §§ 1–101 to 13–105
North Carolina	1965, c. 700	7–1–1967	G.S. §§ 25–1–101 to 25–11–108
North Dakota	1965, c. 296	7–1–1966	NDCC 41–01–02 to 41–09–53
Ohio	1961, p. 13	7–1–1962	R.C. §§ 1301.01 to 1310.78
Oklahoma	1961, p. 70	1–1–1963	12A Okl.St.Ann. §§ 1–101 to 11–107
Oregon	1961, c. 726	9–1–1963	ORS 71.1010 to 79.6010
Pennsylvania	1953, P.L. 3	7–1–1954	13 Pa.C.S.A. §§ 1101 to 9507
Rhode Island	1960, c. 147	1–2–1962	Gen.Laws 1956, §§ 6A–1–101 to 6A–9–507
South Carolina	1966, c. 1065	1–1–1968	Code 1976, §§ 36–1–101 to 36–11–108
South Dakota	1966, c. 150	7–1–1967	SDCL 57A–1–101 to 57A–11–108
Tennessee	1963, c. 81	7–1–1964	West's Tenn.Code §§ 47–1–101 to 47–9–607
Texas	1965, c. 721	7–1–1966	V.T.C.A., Bus. & C. §§ 1.101 to 11.108
Utah	1965, c. 154	1–1–1966	U.C.A.1953, 70A–1–101 to 70A–11–108
Vermont	1966, No. 29	1–1–1967	9A V.S.A. §§ 1–101 to 9–607
Virgin Islands	1965, No. 1299	7–1–1965	11A V.I.C. §§ 1–101 to 9–507
Virginia	1964, c. 219	1–1–1966	Code 1950, §§ 8.1–101 to 8.11–108
Washington	1965, Ex.Sess., c. 157	7–1–1967	West's RCWA 62A.1–101 to 62A.11–109
West Virginia	1963, c. 193	7–1–1964	Code, 46–1–101 to 46–11–108
Wisconsin	1963, c. 158	7–1–1965	W.S.A. 401.101 to 411.901
Wyoming	1961, c. 219	1–2–1962	W.S.1977, §§ 34.1–1–101 to 34.1–10–104

ARTICLE 1

GENERAL PROVISIONS

PART 1

SHORT TITLE, CONSTRUCTION, APPLICATION AND SUBJECT MATTER OF THE ACT

§ 1–101. Short Title

This Act shall be known and may be cited as Uniform Commercial Code.

* * *

§ 1–102. Purposes; Rules of Construction; Variation by Agreement

(1) This Act shall be liberally construed and applied to promote its underlying purposes and policies.

(2) Underlying purposes and policies of this Act are

(a) to simplify, clarify and modernize the law governing commercial transactions;

(b) to permit the continued expansion of commercial practices through custom, usage and agreement of the parties;

(c) to make uniform the law among the various jurisdictions.

(3) The effect of provisions of this Act may be varied by agreement, except as otherwise provided in this Act and except that the obligations of good faith, diligence, reasonableness and care prescribed by this Act may not be disclaimed by agreement but the parties may by agreement determine the standards by which the performance of such obligations is to be measured if such standards are not manifestly unreasonable.

(4) The presence in certain provisions of this Act of the words "unless otherwise agreed" or words of similar import does not imply that the effect of other provisions may not be varied by agreement under subsection (3).

(5) In this Act unless the context otherwise requires

(a) words in the singular number include the plural, and in the plural include the singular;

(b) words of the masculine gender include the feminine and the neuter, and when the sense so indicates words of the neuter gender may refer to any gender.

* * *

§ 1–103. Supplementary General Principles of Law Applicable

Unless displaced by the particular provisions of this Act, the principles of law and equity, including the law merchant and the law relative to capacity to contract, principal and agent, estoppel, fraud, misrepresentation, duress, coercion, mistake, bankruptcy, or other validating or invalidating cause shall supplement its provisions.

* * *

§ 1–104. Construction Against Implicit Repeal

This Act being a general act intended as a unified coverage of its subject matter, no part of it shall be deemed to be impliedly repealed by subsequent legislation if such construction can reasonably be avoided.

* * *

§ 1–105. Territorial Application of the Act; Parties' Power to Choose Applicable Law

(1) Except as provided hereafter in this section, when a transaction bears a reasonable relation to this state and also to another state or nation

the parties may agree that the law either of this state or of such other state or nation shall govern their rights and duties. Failing such agreement this Act applies to transactions bearing an appropriate relation to this state.

* * *

Official Comment

Prior Uniform Statutory Provision: None.

Purposes:

1. Subsection (1) states affirmatively the right of the parties to a multi-state transaction or a transaction involving foreign trade to choose their own law. That right is subject to the firm rules stated in the five sections listed in subsection (2), and is limited to jurisdictions to which the transaction bears a "reasonable relation." In general, the test of "reasonable relation" is similar to that laid down by the Supreme Court in Seeman v. Philadelphia Warehouse Co., 274 U.S. 403, 47 S.Ct. 626, 71 L.Ed. 1123 (1927). Ordinarily the law chosen must be that of a jurisdiction where a significant enough portion of the making or performance of the contract is to occur or occurs. But an agreement as to choice of law may sometimes take effect as a shorthand expression of the intent of the parties as to matters governed by their agreement, even though the transaction has no significant contact with the jurisdiction chosen.

2. Where there is no agreement as to the governing law, the Act is applicable to any transaction having an "appropriate" relation to any state which enacts it. Of course, the Act applies to any transaction which takes place in its entirety in a state which has enacted the Act. But the mere fact that suit is brought in a state does not make it appropriate to apply the substantive law of that state. Cases where a relation to the enacting state is not "appropriate" include, for example, those where the parties have clearly contracted on the basis of some other law, as where the law of the place of contracting and the law of the place of contemplated performance are the same and are contrary to the law under the Code.

3. Where a transaction has significant contacts with a state which has enacted the Act and also with other jurisdictions, the question what relation is "appropriate" is left to judicial decision. In deciding that question, the court is not strictly bound by precedents established in other contexts. Thus a conflict-of-laws decision refusing to apply a purely local statute or rule of law to a particular multi-state transaction may not be valid precedent for refusal to apply the Code in an analogous situation. Application of the Code in such circumstances may be justified by its comprehensiveness, by the policy of uniformity, and by the fact that it is in large part a reformulation and restatement of the law merchant and of the understanding of a business community which transcends state and even national boundaries. Compare Global Commerce Corp. v. Clark–Babbitt Industries, Inc., 239 F.2d 716, 719 (2d Cir.1956). In particular, where a transaction is governed in large part by the Code, application of another law to some detail of performance because of an accident of geography may violate the commercial understanding of the parties.

4. The Act does not attempt to prescribe choice-of-law rules for states which do not enact it, but this section does not prevent application of the Act in a court of such a state. Common-law choice of law often rests on policies of giving effect to agreements and of uniformity of result regardless of where suit is brought. To the extent that such

policies prevail, the relevant considerations are similar in such a court to those outlined above.

* * *

§ 1–106. Remedies to Be Liberally Administered

(1) The remedies provided by this Act shall be liberally administered to the end that the aggrieved party may be put in as good a position as if the other party had fully performed but neither consequential or special nor penal damages may be had except as specifically provided in this Act or by other rule of law.

(2) Any right or obligation declared by this Act is enforceable by action unless the provision declaring it specifies a different and limited effect.

Official Comment

Prior Uniform Statutory Provision: Subsection (1)—none; Subsection (2)—Section 72, Uniform Sales Act.

Changes: Reworded.

Purposes of Changes and New Matter: Subsection (1) is intended to effect three things:

1. First, to negate the unduly narrow or technical interpretation of some remedial provisions of prior legislation by providing that the remedies in this Act are to be liberally administered to the end stated in the section. Second, to make it clear that compensatory damages are limited to compensation. They do not include consequential or special damages, or penal damages; and the Act elsewhere makes it clear that damages must be minimized. Cf. Sections 1–203, 2–706(1), and 2–712(2). The third purpose of subsection (1) is to reject any doctrine that damages must be calcula-ble with mathematical accuracy. Compensatory damages are often at best approximate: they have to be proved with whatever definiteness and accuracy the facts permit, but no more. Cf. Section 2–204(3).

2. Under subsection (2) any right or obligation described in this Act is enforceable by court action, even though no remedy may be expressly provided, unless a particular provision specifies a different and limited effect. Whether specific performance or other equitable relief is available is determined not by this section but by specific provisions and by supplementary principles. Cf. Sections 1–103, 2–716.

3. "Consequential" or "special" damages and "penal" damages are not defined in terms in the Code, but are used in the sense given them by the leading cases on the subject.

§ 1–107. Waiver or Renunciation of Claim or Right After Breach

Any claim or right arising out of an alleged breach can be discharged in whole or in part without consideration by a written waiver or renunciation signed and delivered by the aggrieved party.

Official Comment

Prior Uniform Statutory Provision: Compare Section 1, Uniform Written Obligations Act; Sections 119(3), 120(2) and 122, Uniform Negotiable Instruments Law.

Purposes:

This section makes consideration unnecessary to the effective renunciation or waiver of rights or claims arising out of an alleged breach of a commercial contract where such renunciation is in writing and signed and delivered by the aggrieved party. Its provisions, however, must be read in conjunction with the section imposing an obligation of good faith. (Section 1–203). There may, of course, also be an oral renunciation or waiver sustained by consideration but subject to Statute of Frauds provisions and to the section of Article 2 on Sales dealing with the modification of signed writings (Section 2–209). As is made express in the latter section this Act fully recognizes the effectiveness of waiver and estoppel.

* * *

PART 2
GENERAL DEFINITIONS AND PRINCIPLES OF INTERPRETATION

§ 1–201. General Definitions

Subject to additional definitions contained in the subsequent Articles of this Act which are applicable to specific Articles or Parts thereof, and unless the context otherwise requires, in this Act:

(1) "Action" in the sense of a judicial proceeding includes recoupment, counterclaim, set-off, suit in equity and any other proceedings in which rights are determined.

(2) "Aggrieved party" means a party entitled to resort to a remedy.

(3) "Agreement" means the bargain of the parties in fact as found in their language or by implication from other circumstances including course of dealing or usage of trade or course of performance as provided in this Act (Sections 1–205 and 2–208). Whether an agreement has legal consequences is determined by the provisions of this Act, if applicable; otherwise by the law of contracts (Section 1–103). (Compare "Contract".)

* * *

(10) "Conspicuous": A term or clause is conspicuous when it is so written that a reasonable person against whom it is to operate ought to have noticed it. A printed heading in capitals (as: NON-NEGOTIABLE BILL OF LADING) is conspicuous. Language in the body of a form is "conspicuous" if it is in larger or other contrasting type or color. But in a telegram any stated term is "conspicuous". Whether a term or clause is "conspicuous" or not is for decision by the court.

(11) "Contract" means the total legal obligation which results from the parties' agreement as affected by this Act and any other applicable rules of law. (Compare "Agreement".)

* * *

(13) "Defendant" includes a person in the position of defendant in a cross-action or counterclaim.

* * *

(16) "Fault" means wrongful act, omission or breach.

* * *

(19) "Good faith" means honesty in fact in the conduct or transaction concerned.

* * *

(25) A person has "notice" of a fact when

(a) he has actual knowledge of it; or

(b) he has received a notice or notification of it; or

(c) from all the facts and circumstances known to him at the time in question he has reason to know that it exists.

A person "knows" or has "knowledge" of a fact when he has actual knowledge of it. "Discover" or "learn" or a word or phrase of similar import refers to knowledge rather than to reason to know. The time and circumstances under which a notice or notification may cease to be effective are not determined by this Act.

(26) A person "notifies" or "gives" a notice or notification to another by taking such steps as may be reasonably required to inform the other in ordinary course whether or not such other actually comes to know of it. A person "receives" a notice or notification when

(a) it comes to his attention; or

(b) it is duly delivered at the place of business through which the contract was made or at any other place held out by him as the place for receipt of such communications.

(27) Notice, knowledge or a notice or notification received by an organization is effective for a particular transaction from the time when it is brought to the attention of the individual conducting that transaction, and in any event from the time when it would have been brought to his attention if the organization had exercised due diligence. An organization exercises due diligence if it maintains reasonable routines for communicating significant information to the person conducting the transaction and there is reasonable compliance with the routines. Due diligence does not require an individual acting for the organization to communicate information unless such communication is part of his regular duties or unless he has reason to know of the transaction and that the transaction would be materially affected by the information.

(28) "Organization" includes a corporation, government or governmental subdivision or agency, business trust, estate, trust, partnership or

association, two or more persons having a joint or common interest, or any other legal or commercial entity.

(29) "Party", as distinct from "third party", means a person who has engaged in a transaction or made an agreement within this Act.

(30) "Person" includes an individual or an organization (See Section 1–102).

(31) "Presumption" or "presumed" means that the trier of fact must find the existence of the fact presumed unless and until evidence is introduced which would support a finding of its non-existence.

(32) "Purchase" includes taking by sale, discount, negotiation, mortgage, pledge, lien, issue or re-issue, gift or any other voluntary transaction creating an interest in property.

(33) "Purchaser" means a person who takes by purchase.

(34) "Remedy" means any remedial right to which an aggrieved party is entitled with or without resort to a tribunal.

(35) "Representative" includes an agent, an officer of a corporation or association, and a trustee, executor or administrator of an estate, or any other person empowered to act for another.

(36) "Rights" includes remedies.

* * *

Official Comment

* * *

10. "Conspicuous". New. This is intended to indicate some of the methods of making a term attention-calling. But the test is whether attention can reasonably be expected to be called to it.

* * *

19. "Good faith". See Section 76(2), Uniform Sales Act; Section 58(2), Uniform Warehouse Receipts Act; Section 53(2), Uniform Bills of Lading Act; Section 22(2), Uniform Stock Transfer Act. "Good faith", whenever it is used in the Code, means at least what is here stated. In certain Articles, by specific provision, additional requirements are made applicable. See, e.g., Secs. 2–103(1)(b), 7–404. To illustrate, in the Article on Sales, Section 2–103, good faith is expressly defined as including in the case of a merchant observance of reasonable commercial standards of fair dealing in the trade, so that throughout that Article wherever a merchant appears in the case an inquiry into his observance of such standards is necessary to determine his good faith.

* * *

25. "Notice". New. Compare N.I.L. Sec. 56. Under the definition a person has notice when he has received a notification of the fact in question. But by the last sentence the act leaves open the time and circumstances under which notice or notification may cease to be effective. Therefore such cases as Graham v. White–Phillips Co., 296 U.S. 27, 56 S.Ct. 21, 80 L.Ed. 20 (1935), are not overruled.

26. "Notifies". New. This is the word used when the essential fact is the proper dispatch of the notice, not its receipt. Compare "Send". When the essential fact is the other party's receipt of

the notice, that is stated. The second sentence states when a notification is received.

27. New. This makes clear that reason to know, knowledge, or a notification, although "received" for instance by a clerk in Department A of an organization, is effective for a transaction conducted in Department B only from the time when it was or should have been communicated to the individual conducting that transaction.

28. "Organization". This is the definition of every type of entity or association, excluding an individual, acting as such. Definitions of "person" were included in Section 191, Uniform Negotiable Instruments Law; Section 76, Uniform Sales Act; Section 58, Uniform Warehouse Receipts Act; Section 53, Uniform Bills of Lading Act; Section 22, Uniform Stock Transfer Act; Section 1, Uniform Trust Receipts Act. The definition of "organization" given here includes a number of entities or associations not specifically mentioned in prior definition of "person", namely, government, governmental subdivision or agency, business trust, trust and estate.

* * *

§ 1-203. Obligation of Good Faith

Every contract or duty within this Act imposes an obligation of good faith in its performance or enforcement.

Official Comment

Prior Uniform Statutory Provision:
None.

Purposes:

This section sets forth a basic principle running throughout this Act. The principle involved is that in commercial transactions good faith is required in the performance and enforcement of all agreements or duties. * * *

It is to be noted that under the Sales Article definition of good faith (Section 2-103), contracts made by a merchant have incorporated in them the explicit standard not only of honesty in fact (Section 1-201), but also of observance by the merchant of reasonable commercial standards of fair dealing in the trade.

* * *

§ 1-204. Time; Reasonable Time; "Seasonably"

(1) Whenever this Act requires any action to be taken within a reasonable time, any time which is not manifestly unreasonable may be fixed by agreement.

(2) What is a reasonable time for taking any action depends on the nature, purpose and circumstances of such action.

(3) An action is taken "seasonably" when it is taken at or within the time agreed or if no time is agreed at or within a reasonable time.

Official Comment

Prior Uniform Statutory Provision:
None.

Purposes:

1. Subsection (1) recognizes that nothing is stronger evidence of a reasonable time than the fixing of such time by a fair agreement between the parties.

However, provision is made for disregarding a clause which whether by inadvertence or overreaching fixes a time so unreasonable that it amounts to eliminating all remedy under the contract. The parties are not required to fix the most reasonable time but may fix any time which is not obviously unfair as judged by the time of contracting.

2. Under the section, the agreement which fixes the time need not be part of the main agreement, but may occur separately. Notice also that under the definition of "agreement" (Section 1-201) the circumstances of the transaction, including course of dealing or usages of trade or course of performance may be material. On the question what is a reasonable time these matters will often be important.

* * *

§ 1-205. Course of Dealing and Usage of Trade

(1) A course of dealing is a sequence of previous conduct between the parties to a particular transaction which is fairly to be regarded as establishing a common basis of understanding for interpreting their expressions and other conduct.

(2) A usage of trade is any practice or method of dealing having such regularity of observance in a place, vocation or trade as to justify an expectation that it will be observed with respect to the transaction in question. The existence and scope of such a usage are to be proved as facts. If it is established that such a usage is embodied in a written trade code or similar writing the interpretation of the writing is for the court.

(3) A course of dealing between parties and any usage of trade in the vocation or trade in which they are engaged or of which they are or should be aware give particular meaning to and supplement or qualify terms of an agreement.

(4) The express terms of an agreement and an applicable course of dealing or usage of trade shall be construed wherever reasonable as consistent with each other; but when such construction is unreasonable express terms control both course of dealing and usage of trade and course of dealing controls usage of trade.

(5) An applicable usage of trade in the place where any part of performance is to occur shall be used in interpreting the agreement as to that part of the performance.

(6) Evidence of a relevant usage of trade offered by one party is not admissible unless and until he has given the other party such notice as the court finds sufficient to prevent unfair surprise to the latter.

Official Comment

Prior Uniform Statutory Provision: No such general provision but see Sections 9(1), 15(5), 18(2), and 71, Uniform Sales Act.

Purposes: This section makes it clear that:

1. This Act rejects both the "lay-dictionary" and the "conveyancer's" reading of a commercial agreement. Instead the meaning of the agreement of

the parties is to be determined by the language used by them and by their action, read and interpreted in the light of commercial practices and other surrounding circumstances. The measure and background for interpretation are set by the commercial context, which may explain and supplement even the language of a formal or final writing.

2.   Course of dealing under subsection (1) is restricted, literally, to a sequence of conduct between the parties previous to the agreement. However, the provisions of the Act on course of performance make it clear that a sequence of conduct after or under the agreement may have equivalent meaning. (Section 2-208.)

3.   "Course of dealing" may enter the agreement either by explicit provisions of the agreement or by tacit recognition.

4.   This Act deals with "usage of trade" as a factor in reaching the commercial meaning of the agreement which the parties have made. The language used is to be interpreted as meaning what it may fairly be expected to mean to parties involved in the particular commercial transaction in a given locality or in a given vocation or trade. By adopting in this context the term "usage of trade" this Act expresses its intent to reject those cases which see evidence of "custom" as representing an effort to displace or negate "established rules of law." A distinction is to be drawn between mandatory rules of law such as the Statute of Frauds provisions of Article 2 on Sales whose very office is to control and restrict the actions of the parties, and which cannot be abrogated by agreement, or by a usage of trade, and those rules of law (such as those in Part 3 of Article 2 on Sales) which fill in points which the parties have not considered and in fact agreed upon. The latter rules hold "unless otherwise agreed" but yield to the contrary agreement of the parties. Part of the agreement of the parties to which such rules yield is to be sought for in the usages of trade which furnish the background and give particular meaning to the language used, and are the framework of common understanding controlling any general rules of law which hold only when there is no such understanding.

5.   A usage of trade under subsection (2) must have the "regularity of observance" specified. The ancient English tests for "custom" are abandoned in this connection. Therefore, it is not required that a usage of trade be "ancient or immemorial," "universal" or the like. Under the requirement of subsection (2) full recognition is thus available for new usages and for usages currently observed by the great majority of decent dealers, even though dissidents ready to cut corners do not agree. There is room also for proper recognition of usage agreed upon by merchants in trade codes.

6.   The policy of this Act controlling explicit unconscionable contracts and clauses (Sections 1-203, 2-302) applies to implicit clauses which rest on usage of trade and carries forward the policy underlying the ancient requirement that a custom or usage must be "reasonable." However, the emphasis is shifted. The very fact of commercial acceptance makes out a prima facie case that the usage is reasonable, and the burden is no longer on the usage to establish itself as being reasonable. But the anciently established policing of usage by the courts is continued to the extent necessary to cope with the situation arising if an unconscionable or dishonest practice should become standard.

7.   Subsection (3), giving the prescribed effect to usages of which the parties "are or should be aware", reinforces the provision of subsection (2) requiring not universality but only the described "regularity of observance" of the practice or method. This subsection

also reinforces the point of subsection (2) that such usages may be either general to trade or particular to a special branch of trade.

8. Although the terms in which this Act defines "agreement" include the elements of course of dealing and usage of trade, the fact that express reference is made in some sections to those elements is not to be construed as carrying a contrary intent or implication elsewhere. Compare Section 1–102(4).

9. In cases of a well established line of usage varying from the general rules of this Act where the precise amount of the variation has not been worked out into a single standard, the party relying on the usage is entitled, in any event, to the minimum variation demonstrated. The whole is not to be disregarded because no particular line of detail has been established. In case a dominant pattern has been fairly evidenced, the party relying on the usage is entitled under this section to go to the trier of fact on the question of whether such dominant pattern has been incorporated into the agreement.

10. Subsection (6) is intended to insure that this Act's liberal recognition of the needs of commerce in regard to usage of trade shall not be made into an instrument of abuse.

* * *

ARTICLE 2

SALES

PART 1

SHORT TITLE, GENERAL CONSTRUCTION AND SUBJECT MATTER

§ 2–101. Short Title

This Article shall be known and may be cited as Uniform Commercial Code—Sales.

Official Comment

This Article is a complete revision and modernization of the Uniform Sales Act which was promulgated by the National Conference of Commissioners on Uniform State Laws in 1906 and has been adopted in 34 states and Alaska, the District of Columbia and Hawaii.

The coverage of the present Article is much more extensive than that of the old Sales Act and extends to the various bodies of case law which have been developed both outside of and under the latter.

The arrangement of the present Article is in terms of contract for sale and the various steps of its performance. The legal consequences are stated as following directly from the contract and action taken under it without resorting to the idea of when property or title passed or was to pass as being the determining factor. The purpose is to avoid making practical issues between practical men turn upon the location of an intangible something, the passing of which no man can prove by evidence and to substitute for such abstractions proof of words and actions of a tangible character.

* * *

§ 2-103. Definitions and Index of Definitions

(1) In this Article unless the context otherwise requires

(a) "Buyer" means a person who buys or contracts to buy goods.

(b) "Good faith" in the case of a merchant means honesty in fact and the observance of reasonable commercial standards of fair dealing in the trade.

(c) "Receipt" of goods means taking physical possession of them.

(d) "Seller" means a person who sells or contracts to sell goods.

* * *

§ 2-104. Definitions: "Merchant"; "Between Merchants"; "Financing Agency"

(1) "Merchant" means a person who deals in goods of the kind or otherwise by his occupation holds himself out as having knowledge or skill peculiar to the practices or goods involved in the transaction or to whom such knowledge or skill may be attributed by his employment of an agent or broker or other intermediary who by his occupation holds himself out as having such knowledge or skill.

* * *

(3) "Between merchants" means in any transaction with respect to which both parties are chargeable with the knowledge or skill of merchants.

Official Comment

Prior Uniform Statutory Provision: None. But see Sections 15(2), (5), 16(c), 45(2) and 71, Uniform Sales Act, and Sections 35 and 37, Uniform Bills of Lading Act for examples of the policy expressly provided for in this Article.

Purposes:

1. This Article assumes that transactions between professionals in a given field require special and clear rules which may not apply to a casual or inexperienced seller or buyer. It thus adopts a policy of expressly stating rules applicable "between merchants" and "as against a merchant", wherever they are needed instead of making them depend upon the circumstances of each case as in the statutes cited above. This section lays the foundation of this policy by defining those who are to be regarded as professionals or "merchants" and by stating when a transaction is deemed to be "between merchants".

2. The term "merchant" as defined here roots in the "law merchant" concept of a professional in business. The professional status under the definition may be based upon specialized knowledge as to the goods, specialized knowledge as to business practices, or specialized knowledge as to both and which kind of specialized knowledge may be sufficient to establish the merchant status is indicated by the nature of the provisions.

The special provisions as to merchants appear only in this Article and they are of three kinds. Sections 2-201(2), 2-205, 2-207 and 2-209 dealing with the statute of frauds, firm offers, confirmatory memoranda and modification rest on normal business practices which are or ought to be typical of and familiar to any person in business. For purposes of these sections almost every person in business would, therefore, be deemed to be a "merchant" under the language "who ... by his occupation holds himself out as having knowledge or skill peculiar to the practices ... involved in the transaction ..." since the practices involved in the transaction are non-specialized business practices such as answering mail. In this type of provision, banks or even universities, for example, well may be "merchants." But even these sections only apply to a merchant in his mercantile capacity; a lawyer or bank president buying fishing tackle for his own use is not a merchant.

On the other hand, in Section 2–314 on the warranty of merchantability, such warranty is implied only "if the seller is a merchant with respect to goods of that kind." Obviously this qualification restricts the implied warranty to a much smaller group than everyone who is engaged in business and requires a professional status as to particular kinds of goods. The exception in Section 2–402(2) for retention of possession by a merchant-seller falls in the same class;

as does Section 2–403(2) on entrusting of possession to a merchant "who deals in goods of that kind".

A third group of sections includes 2–103(1)(b), which provides that in the case of a merchant "good faith" includes observance of reasonable commercial standards of fair dealing in the trade; 2–327(1)(c), 2–603 and 2–605, dealing with responsibilities of merchant buyers to follow seller's instructions, etc.; 2–509 on risk of loss, and 2–609 on adequate assurance of performance. This group of sections applies to persons who are merchants under either the "practices" or the "goods" aspect of the definition of merchant.

3. The "or to whom such knowledge or skill may be attributed by his employment of an agent or broker ..." clause of the definition of merchant means that even persons such as universities, for example, can come within the definition of merchant if they have regular purchasing departments or business personnel who are familiar with business practices and who are equipped to take any action required.

* * *

§ 2–105. Definitions: Transferability; "Goods"; "Future" Goods; "Lot"; "Commercial Unit"

(1) "Goods" means all things (including specially manufactured goods) which are movable at the time of identification to the contract for sale other than the money in which the price is to be paid, investment securities (Article 8) and things in action. "Goods" also includes the unborn young of animals and growing crops and other identified things attached to realty as described in the section on goods to be severed from realty (Section 2–107).

* * *

Official Comment

Prior Uniform Statutory Provision: Subsections (1), (2), (3) and (4)—Sections 5, 6 and 76, Uniform Sales Act; Subsections (5) and (6)—none.

Changes: Rewritten.

Purposes of Changes and New Matter:

1. Subsection (1) on "goods": The phraseology of the prior uniform statutory provision has been changed so that:

The definition of goods is based on the concept of movability and the term "chattels personal" is not used. It is not intended to deal with things which are not fairly identifiable as movables before the contract is performed.

Growing crops are included within the definition of goods since they are frequently intended for sale. The concept of "industrial" growing crops has been abandoned, for under modern practices fruit, perennial hay, nursery stock and the like must be brought within the scope of this Article. The young of animals are also included expressly in this definition since they, too, are frequently intended for sale and may be contracted for before birth. The period of gestation of domestic animals is such that the provisions of the section on identification can apply as in the case of crops to be planted. The reason of this definition also leads to the inclusion of a wool crop or the like as "goods" subject to identification under this Article.

The exclusion of "money in which the price is to be paid" from the definition of goods does not mean that foreign currency which is included in the definition of money may not be the subject matter of a sales transaction. Goods is intended to cover the sale of money when money is being treated as a commodity but not to include it when money is the medium of payment.

As to contracts to sell timber, minerals, or structures to be removed from the land Section 2–107(1)(Goods to be severed from Realty: recording) controls.

The use of the word "fixtures" is avoided in view of the diversity of definitions of that term. This Article in including within its scope "things attached to realty" adds the further test that they must be capable of severance without material harm thereto. As between the parties any identified things which fall within that definition become "goods" upon the making of the contract for sale.

* * *

§ 2–106. Definitions: "Contract"; "Agreement"; "Contract for Sale"; "Sale"; "Present Sale"; "Conforming" to Contract; "Termination"; "Cancellation"

(1) In this Article unless the context otherwise requires "contract" and "agreement" are limited to those relating to the present or future sale of goods. "Contract for sale" includes both a present sale of goods and a contract to sell goods at a future time. A "sale" consists in the passing of title from the seller to the buyer for a price (Section 2–401). A "present sale" means a sale which is accomplished by the making of the contract.

(2) Goods or conduct including any part of a performance are "conforming" or conform to the contract when they are in accordance with the obligations under the contract.

(3) "Termination" occurs when either party pursuant to a power created by agreement or law puts an end to the contract otherwise than for its breach. On "termination" all obligations which are still executory on both sides are discharged but any right based on prior breach or performance survives.

(4) "Cancellation" occurs when either party puts an end to the contract for breach by the other and its effect is the same as that of

"termination" except that the cancelling party also retains any remedy for breach of the whole contract or any unperformed balance.

Official Comment

Prior Uniform Statutory Provision: Subsection (1)—Section 1(1) and (2), Uniform Sales Act; Subsection (2)—none, but subsection generally continues policy of Sections 11, 44 and 69, Uniform Sales Act; Subsections (3) and (4)—none.

Changes: Completely rewritten.

Purposes of Changes and New Matter:

1. Subsection (1): "Contract for sale" is used as a general concept throughout this Article, but the rights of the parties do not vary according to whether the transaction is a present sale or a contract to sell unless the Article expressly so provides.

2. Subsection (2): It is in general intended to continue the policy of requiring exact performance by the seller of his obligations as a condition to his right to require acceptance. However, the seller is in part safeguarded against surprise as a result of sudden technicality on the buyer's part by the provisions of Section 2–508 on seller's cure of improper tender or delivery. Moreover usage of trade frequently permits commercial leeways in performance and the language of the agreement itself must be read in the light of such custom or usage and also, prior course of dealing, and in a long term contract, the course of performance.

3. Subsections (3) and (4): These subsections are intended to make clear the distinction carried forward throughout this Article between termination and cancellation.

* * *

PART 2
FORM, FORMATION AND READJUSTMENT OF CONTRACT

§ 2–201. Formal Requirements; Statute of Frauds

(1) Except as otherwise provided in this section a contract for the sale of goods for the price of $500 or more is not enforceable by way of action or defense unless there is some writing sufficient to indicate that a contract for sale has been made between the parties and signed by the party against whom enforcement is sought or by his authorized agent or broker. A writing is not insufficient because it omits or incorrectly states a term agreed upon but the contract is not enforceable under this paragraph beyond the quantity of goods shown in such writing.

(2) Between merchants if within a reasonable time a writing in confirmation of the contract and sufficient against the sender is received and the party receiving it has reason to know its contents, it satisfies the requirements of subsection (1) against such party unless written notice of objection to its contents is given within 10 days after it is received.

(3) A contract which does not satisfy the requirements of subsection (1) but which is valid in other respects is enforceable

    (a) if the goods are to be specially manufactured for the buyer and are not suitable for sale to others in the ordinary course of the seller's business and the seller, before notice of repudiation is received and under circumstances which reasonably indicate that the goods are for the buyer, has made either a substantial beginning of their manufacture or commitments for their procurement; or

(b) if the party against whom enforcement is sought admits in his pleading, testimony or otherwise in court that a contract for sale was made, but the contract is not enforceable under this provision beyond the quantity of goods admitted; or

(c) with respect to goods for which payment has been made and accepted or which have been received and accepted (Sec. 2–606).

Official Comment

Prior Uniform Statutory Provision: Section 4, Uniform Sales Act (which was based on Section 17 of the Statute of 29 Charles II).

Changes: Completely rephrased; restricted to sale of goods. See also Sections 1–206, 8–319 and 9–203.

Purposes of Changes: The changed phraseology of this section is intended to make it clear that:

1. The required writing need not contain all the material terms of the contract and such material terms as are stated need not be precisely stated. All that is required is that the writing afford a basis for believing that the offered oral evidence rests on a real transaction. It may be written in lead pencil on a scratch pad. It need not indicate which party is the buyer and which the seller. The only term which must appear is the quantity term which need not be accurately stated but recovery is limited to the amount stated. The price, time and place of payment or delivery, the general quality of the goods, or any particular warranties may all be omitted.

Special emphasis must be placed on the permissibility of omitting the price term in view of the insistence of some courts on the express inclusion of this term even where the parties have contracted on the basis of a published price list. In many valid contracts for sale the parties do not mention the price in express terms, the buyer being bound to pay and the seller to accept a reasonable price which the trier of the fact may well be trusted to determine. Again, frequently the price is not mentioned since the parties have based their agreement on a price list or catalogue known to both of them and this list serves as an efficient safeguard against perjury. Finally, "market" prices and valuations that are current in the vicinity constitute a similar check. Thus if the price is not stated in the memorandum it can normally be supplied without danger of fraud. Of course if the "price" consists of goods rather than money the quantity of goods must be stated.

Only three definite and invariable requirements as to the memorandum are made by this subsection. First, it must evidence a contract for the sale of goods; second, it must be "signed", a word which includes any authentication which identifies the party to be charged; and third, it must specify a quantity.

2. "Partial performance" as a substitute for the required memorandum can validate the contract only for the goods which have been accepted or for which payment has been made and accepted.

Receipt and acceptance either of goods or of the price constitutes an unambiguous overt admission by both parties that a contract actually exists. If the court can make a just apportionment, therefore, the agreed price of any goods actually delivered can be recovered without a writing or, if the price has been paid, the seller can be forced to deliver an apportionable part of the goods. The overt actions of the parties make admissible evidence of the other terms of the contract necessary to a just apportionment. This is true even though the actions of the parties are not in themselves inconsistent with a different transaction such as a consignment for resale or a mere loan of money.

Part performance by the buyer requires the delivery of something by him that is accepted by the seller as such performance. Thus, part payment may be made by money or check, accepted by the seller. If the agreed price consists of goods or services, then they must also have been delivered and accepted.

3. Between merchants, failure to answer a written confirmation of a contract within ten days of receipt is tantamount to a writing under subsection (2) and is sufficient against both parties under subsection (1). The only effect, however, is to take away from the party who fails to answer the defense of the Statute of Frauds; the burden of persuading the trier of fact that a contract was in fact made orally prior to the written confirmation is unaffected. Compare the effect of a failure to reply under Section 2-207.

4. Failure to satisfy the requirements of this section does not render the contract void for all purposes, but merely prevents it from being judicially enforced in favor of a party to the contract. For example, a buyer who takes possession of goods as provided in an oral contract which the seller has not meanwhile repudiated, is not a trespasser. Nor would the Statute of Frauds provisions of this section be a defense to a third person who wrongfully induces a party to refuse to perform an oral contract, even though the injured party cannot maintain an action for damages against the party so refusing to perform.

5. The requirement of "signing" is discussed in the comment to Section 1-201.

6. It is not necessary that the writing be delivered to anybody. It need not be signed or authenticated by both parties but it is, of course, not sufficient against one who has not signed it. Prior to a dispute no one can determine which party's signing of the memorandum may be necessary but from the time of contracting each party should be aware that to him it is signing by the other which is important.

7. If the making of a contract is admitted in court, either in a written pleading, by stipulation or by oral statement before the court, no additional writing is necessary for protection against fraud. Under this section it is no longer possible to admit the contract in court and still treat the Statute as a defense. However, the contract is not thus conclusively established. The admission so made by a party is itself evidential against him of the truth of the facts so admitted and of nothing more; as against the other party, it is not evidential at all.

* * *

§ 2-202. Final Written Expression: Parol or Extrinsic Evidence

Terms with respect to which the confirmatory memoranda of the parties agree or which are otherwise set forth in a writing intended by the parties as a final expression of their agreement with respect to such terms as are included therein may not be contradicted by evidence of any prior agreement or of a contemporaneous oral agreement but may be explained or supplemented

*[handwritten margin note: * ADD'TL terms only to explain or supplement NOT TO CONTRADICT]*

*[handwritten note: * If merger clause, can use only COP, COD, UT]*

(a) by course of dealing or usage of trade (Section 1–205) or by course of performance (Section 2–208); and

(b) by evidence of consistent additional terms unless the court finds the writing to have been intended also as a complete and exclusive statement of the terms of the agreement.

Official Comment

Prior Uniform Statutory Provision: None.

Purposes:

1. This section definitely rejects:

(a) Any assumption that because a writing has been worked out which is final on some matters, it is to be taken as including all the matters agreed upon;

(b) The premise that the language used has the meaning attributable to such language by rules of construction existing in the law rather than the meaning which arises out of the commercial context in which it was used; and

(c) The requirement that a condition precedent to the admissibility of the type of evidence specified in paragraph (a) is an original determination by the court that the language used is ambiguous.

2. Paragraph (a) makes admissible evidence of course of dealing, usage of trade and course of performance to explain or supplement the terms of any writing stating the agreement of the parties in order that the true understanding of the parties as to the agreement may be reached. Such writings are to be read on the assumption that the course of prior dealings between the parties and the usages of trade were taken for granted when the document was phrased. Unless carefully negated they have become an element of the meaning of the words used. Similarly, the course of actual performance by the parties is considered the best indication of what they intended the writing to mean.

3. Under paragraph (b) consistent additional terms, not reduced to writing, may be proved unless the court finds that the writing was intended by both parties as a complete and exclusive statement of all the terms. If the additional terms are such that, if agreed upon, they would certainly have been included in the document in the view of the court, then evidence of their alleged making must be kept from the trier of fact.

* * *

§ 2–204. Formation in General

(1) A contract for sale of goods may be made in any manner sufficient to show agreement, including conduct by both parties which recognizes the existence of such a contract.

(2) An agreement sufficient to constitute a contract for sale may be found even though the moment of its making is undetermined.

(3) Even though one or more terms are left open a contract for sale does not fail for indefiniteness if the parties have intended to make a contract and there is a reasonably certain basis for giving an appropriate remedy.

* * *

§ 2–206. Offer and Acceptance in Formation of Contract

(1) Unless otherwise unambiguously indicated by the language or circumstances

    (a) an offer to make a contract shall be construed as inviting acceptance in any manner and by any medium reasonable in the circumstances;

    (b) an order or other offer to buy goods for prompt or current shipment shall be construed as inviting acceptance either by a prompt promise to ship or by the prompt or current shipment of conforming or non-conforming goods, but such a shipment of non-conforming goods does not constitute an acceptance if the seller seasonably notifies the buyer that the shipment is offered only as an accommodation to the buyer.

(2) Where the beginning of a requested performance is a reasonable mode of acceptance an offeror who is not notified of acceptance within a reasonable time may treat the offer as having lapsed before acceptance.

* * *

§ 2–207. Additional Terms in Acceptance or Confirmation

(1) A definite and seasonable expression of acceptance or a written confirmation which is sent within a reasonable time operates as an acceptance even though it states terms additional to or different from those offered or agreed upon, unless acceptance is expressly made conditional on assent to the additional or different terms.

(2) The additional terms are to be construed as proposals for addition to the contract. Between merchants such terms become part of the contract unless:

    (a) the offer expressly limits acceptance to the terms of the offer;

    (b) they materially alter it; or

    (c) notification of objection to them has already been given or is given within a reasonable time after notice of them is received.

(3) Conduct by both parties which recognizes the existence of a contract is sufficient to establish a contract for sale although the writings of the parties do not otherwise establish a contract. In such case the terms of the particular contract consist of those terms on which the writings of the parties agree, together with any supplementary terms incorporated under any other provisions of this Act.

* * *

§ 2–208. Course of Performance or Practical Construction

(1) Where the contract for sale involves repeated occasions for performance by either party with knowledge of the nature of the performance

and opportunity for objection to it by the other, any course of performance accepted or acquiesced in without objection shall be relevant to determine the meaning of the agreement.

(2) The express terms of the agreement and any such course of performance, as well as any course of dealing and usage of trade, shall be construed whenever reasonable as consistent with each other; but when such construction is unreasonable, express terms shall control course of performance and course of performance shall control both course of dealing and usage of trade (Section 1–205).

(3) Subject to the provisions of the next section on modification and waiver, such course of performance shall be relevant to show a waiver or modification of any term inconsistent with such course of performance.

Official Comment

Prior Uniform Statutory Provision: No such general provision but concept of this section recognized by terms such as "course of dealing", "the circumstances of the case," "the conduct of the parties," etc., in Uniform Sales Act.

Purposes:

1. The parties themselves know best what they have meant by their words of agreement and their action under that agreement is the best indication of what that meaning was. This section thus rounds out the set of factors which determines the meaning of the "agreement" and therefore also of the "unless otherwise agreed" qualification to various provisions of this Article.

2. Under this section a course of performance is always relevant to determine the meaning of the agreement. Express mention of course of performance elsewhere in this Article carries no contrary implication when there is a failure to refer to it in other sections.

3. Where it is difficult to determine whether a particular act merely sheds light on the meaning of the agreement or represents a waiver of a term of the agreement, the preference is in favor of "waiver" whenever such construction, plus the application of the provisions on the reinstatement of rights waived (see Section 2–209), is needed to preserve the flexible character of commercial contracts and to prevent surprise or other hardship.

4. A single occasion of conduct does not fall within the language of this section but other sections such as the ones on silence after acceptance and failure to specify particular defects can affect the parties' rights on a single occasion (see Sections 2–605 and 2–607).

* * *

§ 2–209. Modification, Rescission and Waiver

(1) An agreement modifying a contract within this Article needs no consideration to be binding.

(2) A signed agreement which excludes modification or rescission except by a signed writing cannot be otherwise modified or rescinded, but except as between merchants such a requirement on a form supplied by the merchant must be separately signed by the other party.

(3) The requirements of the statute of frauds section of this Article (Section 2–201) must be satisfied if the contract as modified is within its provisions.

(4) Although an attempt at modification or rescission does not satisfy the requirements of subsection (2) or (3) it can operate as a waiver.

(5) A party who has made a waiver affecting an executory portion of the contract may retract the waiver by reasonable notification received by the other party that strict performance will be required of any term waived, unless the retraction would be unjust in view of a material change of position in reliance on the waiver.

Official Comment

Prior Uniform Statutory Provision: Subsection (1)—Compare Section 1, Uniform Written Obligations Act; Subsections (2) to (5)—none.

Purposes of Changes and New Matter:

1. This section seeks to protect and make effective all necessary and desirable modifications of sales contracts without regard to the technicalities which at present hamper such adjustments.

2. Subsection (1) provides that an agreement modifying a sales contract needs no consideration to be binding.

However, modifications made thereunder must meet the test of good faith imposed by this Act. The effective use of bad faith to escape performance on the original contract terms is barred, and the extortion of a "modification" without legitimate commercial reason is ineffective as a violation of the duty of good faith. Nor can a mere technical consideration support a modification made in bad faith.

The test of "good faith" between merchants or as against merchants includes "observance of reasonable commercial standards of fair dealing in the trade" (Section 2–103), and may in some situations require an objectively demonstrable reason for seeking a modification. But such matters as a market shift which makes performance come to involve a loss may provide such a reason even though there is no such unforeseen difficulty as would make out a legal ex-

cuse from performance under Sections 2–615 and 2–616.

3. Subsections (2) and (3) are intended to protect against false allegations of oral modifications. "Modification or rescission" includes abandonment or other change by mutual consent, contrary to the decision in Green v. Doniger, 300 N.Y. 238, 90 N.E.2d 56 (1949); it does not include unilateral "termination" or "cancellation" as defined in Section 2–106.

The Statute of Frauds provisions of this Article are expressly applied to modifications by subsection (3). Under those provisions the "delivery and acceptance" test is limited to the goods which have been accepted, that is, to the past. "Modification" for the future cannot therefore be conjured up by oral testimony if the price involved is $500.00 or more since such modification must be shown at least by an authenticated memo. And since a memo is limited in its effect to the quantity of goods set forth in it there is safeguard against oral evidence.

Subsection (2) permits the parties in effect to make their own Statute of Frauds as regards any future modification of the contract by giving effect to a clause in a signed agreement which expressly requires any modification to be by signed writing. But note that if a consumer is to be held to such a clause on a form supplied by a merchant it must be separately signed.

4. Subsection (4) is intended, despite the provisions of subsections (2) and (3), to prevent contractual provi-

sions excluding modification except by a signed writing from limiting in other respects the legal effect of the parties' actual later conduct. The effect of such conduct as a waiver is further regulated in subsection (5).

* * *

PART 3
GENERAL OBLIGATION AND CONSTRUCTION OF CONTRACT

§ 2–301. General Obligations of Parties

The obligation of the seller is to transfer and deliver and that of the buyer is to accept and pay in accordance with the contract.

Official Comment

Prior Uniform Statutory Provision: Sections 11 and 41, Uniform Sales Act.

Changes: Rewritten.

Purposes of Changes: This section uses the term "obligation" in contrast to the term "duty" in order to provide for the "condition" aspects of delivery and payment insofar as they are not modified by other sections of this Article such as those on cure of tender. It thus replaces not only the general provisions of the Uniform Sales Act on the parties' duties, but also the general provisions of that Act on the effect of conditions. In order to determine what is "in accordance with the contract" under this Article usage of trade, course of dealing and performance, and the general background of circumstances must be given due consideration in conjunction with the lay meaning of the words used to define the scope of the conditions and duties.

* * *

§ 2–302. Unconscionable Contract or Clause

(1) If the court as a matter of law finds the contract or any clause of the contract to have been unconscionable at the time it was made the court may refuse to enforce the contract, or it may enforce the remainder of the contract without the unconscionable clause, or it may so limit the application of any unconscionable clause as to avoid any unconscionable result.

(2) When it is claimed or appears to the court that the contract or any clause thereof may be unconscionable the parties shall be afforded a reasonable opportunity to present evidence as to its commercial setting, purpose and effect to aid the court in making the determination.

Official Comment

Prior Uniform Statutory Provision: None.

Purposes:

1. This section is intended to make it possible for the courts to police explicitly against the contracts or clauses which they find to be unconscionable. In the past such policing has been ac- complished by adverse construction of language, by manipulation of the rules of offer and acceptance or by determina- tions that the clause is contrary to pub- lic policy or to the dominant purpose of the contract. This section is intended to allow the court to pass directly on the unconscionability of the contract or par- ticular clause therein and to make a conclusion of law as to its unconsciona-

bility. The basic test is whether, in the light of the general commercial background and the commercial needs of the particular trade or case, the clauses involved are so one-sided as to be unconscionable under the circumstances existing at the time of the making of the contract. Subsection (2) makes it clear that it is proper for the court to hear evidence upon these questions. The principle is one of the prevention of oppression and unfair surprise (Cf. Campbell Soup Co. v. Wentz, 172 F.2d 80 (3d Cir.1948)) and not of disturbance of allocation of risks because of superior bargaining power. The underlying basis of this section is illustrated by the results in cases such as the following:

Kansas City Wholesale Grocery Co. v. Weber Packing Corporation, 93 Utah 414, 73 P.2d 1272 (1937), where a clause limiting time for complaints was held inapplicable to latent defects in a shipment of catsup which could be discovered only by microscopic analysis; Hardy v. General Motors Acceptance Corporation, 38 Ga.App. 463, 144 S.E. 327 (1928), holding that a disclaimer of warranty clause applied only to express warranties, thus letting in a fair implied warranty; Andrews Bros. v. Singer & Co. (1934 CA) 1 K.B. 17, holding that where a car with substantial mileage was delivered instead of a "new" car, a disclaimer of warranties, including those "implied," left unaffected an "express obligation" on the description, even though the Sale of Goods Act called such an implied warranty; New Prague Flouring Mill Co. v. Spears, 194 Iowa 417, 189 N.W. 815 (1922), holding that a clause permitting the seller, upon the buyer's failure to supply shipping instructions, to cancel, ship, or allow delivery date to be indefinitely postponed 30 days at a time by the inaction, does not indefinitely postpone the date of measuring damages for the buyer's breach, to the seller's advantage; and Kansas Flour Mills Co. v. Dirks, 100 Kan. 376, 164 P.

273 (1917), where under a similar clause in a rising market the court permitted the buyer to measure his damages for non-delivery at the end of only one 30 day postponement; Green v. Arcos, Ltd. (1931 CA) 47 T.L.R. 336, where a blanket clause prohibiting rejection of shipments by the buyer was restricted to apply to shipments where discrepancies represented merely mercantile variations; Meyer v. Packard Cleveland Motor Co., 106 Ohio St. 328, 140 N.E. 118 (1922), in which the court held that a "waiver" of all agreements not specified did not preclude implied warranty of fitness of a rebuilt dump truck for ordinary use as a dump truck; F.C. Austin Co. v. J.H. Tillman Co., 104 Or. 541, 209 P. 131 (1922), where a clause limiting the buyer's remedy to return was held to be applicable only if the seller had delivered a machine needed for a construction job which reasonably met the contract description; Bekkevold v. Potts, 173 Minn. 87, 216 N.W. 790, 59 A.L.R. 1164 (1927), refusing to allow warranty of fitness for purpose imposed by law to be negated by clause excluding all warranties "made" by the seller; Robert A. Munroe & Co. v. Meyer (1930) 2 K.B. 312, holding that the warranty of description overrides a clause reading "with all faults and defects" where adulterated meat not up to the contract description was delivered.

2. Under this section the court, in its discretion, may refuse to enforce the contract as a whole if it is permeated by the unconscionability, or it may strike any single clause or group of clauses which are so tainted or which are contrary to the essential purpose of the agreement, or it may simply limit unconscionable clauses so as to avoid unconscionable results.

3. The present section is addressed to the court, and the decision is to be made by it. The commercial evidence referred to in subsection (2) is for the court's consideration, not the jury's.

Only the agreement which results from the court's action on these matters is to be submitted to the general triers of the facts.

* * *

§ 2-303.   Allocation or Division of Risks

Where this Article allocates a risk or a burden as between the parties "unless otherwise agreed", the agreement may not only shift the allocation but may also divide the risk or burden.

Official Comment

Prior Uniform Statutory Provision: None.

Purposes:

1. This section is intended to make it clear that the parties may modify or allocate "unless otherwise agreed" risks or burdens imposed by this Article as they desire, always subject, of course, to the provisions on unconscionability.

Compare Section 1-102(4).

2. The risk or burden may be divided by the express terms of the agreement or by the attending circumstances, since under the definition of "agreement" in this Act the circumstances surrounding the transaction as well as the express language used by the parties enter into the meaning and substance of the agreement.

* * *

§ 2-313.   Express Warranties by Affirmation, Promise, Description, Sample

[handwritten margin note: 3 Schools of thought on RELIANCE (ELEMENT #3 BELOW)
① TRADITIONAL (OH): TT has pleading/proof burden
② ORTHODOX PRESUMPTION (UCC)
③ NO RELIANCE REQ'MENT]

(1) Express warranties by the seller are created as follows:

(a) Any affirmation of fact or promise made by the seller to the buyer which relates to the goods and becomes part of the basis of the bargain creates an express warranty that the goods shall conform to the affirmation or promise.

(b) Any description of the goods which is made part of the basis of the bargain creates an express warranty that the goods shall conform to the description.

(c) Any sample or model which is made part of the basis of the bargain creates an express warranty that the whole of the goods shall conform to the sample or model.

(2) It is not necessary to the creation of an express warranty that the seller use formal words such as "warrant" or "guarantee" or that he have a specific intention to make a warranty, but an affirmation merely of the value of the goods or a statement purporting to be merely the seller's opinion or commendation of the goods does not create a warranty.

[handwritten note:
ELEMENTS of 2-313 CLAIM:
① SALE of GOODS ② S MAKES AFFIRMATIONS of FACT
③ AFFIRMATIONS BECOME PART of BASIS of BARGAIN
④ GOODS FAIL TO CONFORM, which is ⑤ ACTUAL and PROXIMATE CAUSE of
⑥ COMPENSIBLE DAMAGES — AND —
⑦ B GIVES TIMELY NOTICE of BREACH]

Official Comment

Prior Uniform Statutory Provision: Sections 12, 14 and 16, Uniform Sales Act.

Changes: Rewritten.

Purposes of Changes: To consolidate and systematize basic principles with the result that:

1. "Express" warranties rest on "dickered" aspects of the individual bargain, and go so clearly to the essence of that bargain that words of disclaimer in a form are repugnant to the basic dickered terms. "Implied" warranties rest so clearly on a common factual situation or set of conditions that no particular language or action is necessary to evidence them and they will arise in such a situation unless unmistakably negated.

This section reverts to the older case law insofar as the warranties of description and sample are designated "express" rather than "implied".

2. Although this section is limited in its scope and direct purpose to warranties made by the seller to the buyer as part of a contract for sale, the warranty sections of this Article are not designed in any way to disturb those lines of case law growth which have recognized that warranties need not be confined either to sales contracts or to the direct parties to such a contract. They may arise in other appropriate circumstances such as in the case of bailments for hire, whether such bailment is itself the main contract or is merely a supplying of containers under a contract for the sale of their contents. The provisions of Section 2–318 on third party beneficiaries expressly recognize this case law development within one particular area. Beyond that, the matter is left to the case law with the intention that the policies of this Act may offer useful guidance in dealing with further cases as they arise.

3. The present section deals with affirmations of fact by the seller, descriptions of the goods or exhibitions of samples, exactly as any other part of a negotiation which ends in a contract is dealt with. No specific intention to make a warranty is necessary if any of these factors is made part of the basis of the bargain. In actual practice affirmations of fact made by the seller about the goods during a bargain are regarded as part of the description of those goods; hence no particular reliance on such statements need be shown in order to weave them into the fabric of the agreement. Rather, any fact which is to take such affirmations, once made, out of the agreement requires clear affirmative proof. The issue normally is one of fact.

4. In view of the principle that the whole purpose of the law of warranty is to determine what it is that the seller has in essence agreed to sell, the policy is adopted of those cases which refuse except in unusual circumstances to recognize a material deletion of the seller's obligation. Thus, a contract is normally a contract for a sale of something describable and described. A clause generally disclaiming "all warranties, express or implied" cannot reduce the seller's obligation with respect to such description and therefore cannot be given literal effect under Section 2–316.

This is not intended to mean that the parties, if they consciously desire, cannot make their own bargain as they wish. But in determining what they have agreed upon good faith is a factor and consideration should be given to the fact that the probability is small that a real price is intended to be exchanged for a pseudo-obligation.

5. Paragraph (1)(b) makes specific some of the principles set forth above when a description of the goods is given by the seller.

A description need not be by words. Technical specifications, blueprints and

EXPRESS WARRANTIES travel to subseq. buyers _only_ if Seller appointed as "agent" by manufacturer or adopts M'er W's by posting them.

the like can afford more exact description than mere language and if made part of the basis of the bargain goods must conform with them. Past deliveries may set the description of quality, either expressly or impliedly by course of dealing. Of course, all descriptions by merchants must be read against the applicable trade usages with the general rules as to merchantability resolving any doubts.

6. The basic situation as to statements affecting the true essence of the bargain is no different when a sample or model is involved in the transaction. This section includes both a "sample" actually drawn from the bulk of goods which is the subject matter of the sale, and a "model" which is offered for inspection when the subject matter is not at hand and which has not been drawn from the bulk of the goods.

Although the underlying principles are unchanged, the facts are often ambiguous when something is shown as illustrative, rather than as a straight sample. In general, the presumption is that any sample or model just as any affirmation of fact is intended to become a basis of the bargain. But there is no escape from the question of fact. When the seller exhibits a sample purporting to be drawn from an existing bulk, good faith of course requires that the sample be fairly drawn. But in mercantile experience the mere exhibition of a "sample" does not of itself show whether it is merely intended to "suggest" or to "be" the character of the subject-matter of the contract. The question is whether the seller has so acted with reference to the sample as to make him responsible that the whole shall have at least the values shown by it. The circumstances aid in answering this question. If the

sample has been drawn from an existing bulk, it must be regarded as describing values of the goods contracted for unless it is accompanied by an unmistakable denial of such responsibility. If, on the other hand, a model of merchandise not on hand is offered, the mercantile presumption that it has become a literal description of the subject matter is not so strong, and particularly so if modification on the buyer's initiative impairs any feature of the model.

7. The precise time when words of description or affirmation are made or samples are shown is not material. The sole question is whether the language or samples or models are fairly to be regarded as part of the contract. If language is used after the closing of the deal (as when the buyer when taking delivery asks and receives an additional assurance), the warranty becomes a modification, and need not be supported by consideration if it is otherwise reasonable and in order (Section 2–209).

8. Concerning affirmations of value or a seller's opinion or commendation under subsection (2), the basic question remains the same: What statements of the seller have in the circumstances and in objective judgment become part of the basis of the bargain? As indicated above, all of the statements of the seller do so unless good reason is shown to the contrary. The provisions of subsection (2) are included, however, since common experience discloses that some statements or predictions cannot fairly be viewed as entering into the bargain. Even as to false statements of value, however, the possibility is left open that a remedy may be provided by the law relating to fraud or misrepresentation.

* * *

§ 2–314. Implied Warranty: Merchantability; Usage of Trade

(1) Unless excluded or modified (Section 2–316), a warranty that the goods shall be merchantable is implied in a contract for their sale if the

274

[handwritten:] ELEMENTS of 2–314 CLAIM
① SALE of GOODS   ② BY A MERCHANT (see 2–104(1))
③ AT TIME of SALE, GOODS NOT MERCHANTABLE
* MERCHANTABLE = "Reasonably fit for intended purposes and pass w/o objection in the trade"

seller is a merchant with respect to goods of that kind. Under this section the serving for value of food or drink to be consumed either on the premises or elsewhere is a sale.

(2) Goods to be merchantable must be at least such as

(a) pass without objection in the trade under the contract description; and

(b) in the case of fungible goods, are of fair average quality within the description; and

(c) are fit for the ordinary purposes for which such goods are used; and

(d) run, within the variations permitted by the agreement, of even kind, quality and quantity within each unit and among all units involved; and

(e) are adequately contained, packaged, and labeled as the agreement may require; and

(f) conform to the promises or affirmations of fact made on the container or label if any.

(3) Unless excluded or modified (Section 2–316) other implied warranties may arise from course of dealing or usage of trade.

Official Comment

Prior Uniform Statutory Provision: Section 15(2), Uniform Sales Act.

Changes: Completely rewritten.

Purposes of Changes: This section, drawn in view of the steadily developing case law on the subject, is intended to make it clear that:

1. The seller's obligation applies to present sales as well as to contracts to sell subject to the effects of any examination of specific goods. (Subsection (2) of Section 2–316). Also, the warranty of merchantability applies to sales for use as well as to sales for resale.

2. The question when the warranty is imposed turns basically on the meaning of the terms of the agreement as recognized in the trade. Goods delivered under an agreement made by a merchant in a given line of trade must be of a quality comparable to that generally acceptable in that line of trade under the description or other designation of the goods used in the agreement. The responsibility imposed rests on any mer-

chant-seller, and the absence of the words "grower or manufacturer or not" which appeared in Section 15(2) of the Uniform Sales Act does not restrict the applicability of this section.

3. A specific designation of goods by the buyer does not exclude the seller's obligation that they be fit for the general purposes appropriate to such goods. A contract for the sale of second-hand goods, however, involves only such obligation as is appropriate to such goods for that is their contract description. A person making an isolated sale of goods is not a "merchant" within the meaning of the full scope of this section and, thus, no warranty of merchantability would apply. His knowledge of any defects not apparent on inspection would, however, without need for express agreement and in keeping with the underlying reason of the present section and the provisions on good faith, impose an obligation that known material but hidden defects be fully disclosed.

4. Although a seller may not be a "merchant" as to the goods in question,

④ Failure to conform is ACTUAL + PROX. CAUSE of

⑤ Compensable damages

  * Direct Economic Loss, Incidental, and Consequential

⑥ -AND- B gives timely notice of breach

if he states generally that they are "guaranteed" the provisions of this section may furnish a guide to the content of the resulting express warranty. This has particular significance in the case of second-hand sales, and has further significance in limiting the effect of fine-print disclaimer clauses where their effect would be inconsistent with large-print assertions of "guarantee".

5. The second sentence of subsection (1) covers the warranty with respect to food and drink. Serving food or drink for value is a sale, whether to be consumed on the premises or elsewhere. Cases to the contrary are rejected. The principal warranty is that stated in subsections (1) and (2)(c) of this section.

6. Subsection (2) does not purport to exhaust the meaning of "merchantable" nor to negate any of its attributes not specifically mentioned in the text of the statute, but arising by usage of trade or through case law. The language used is "must be at least such as . . . ," and the intention is to leave open other possible attributes of merchantability.

7. Paragraphs (a) and (b) of subsection (2) are to be read together. Both refer, as indicated above, to the standards of that line of the trade which fits the transaction and the seller's business. "Fair average" is a term directly appropriate to agricultural bulk products and means goods centering around the middle belt of quality, not the least or the worst that can be understood in the particular trade by the designation, but such as can pass "without objection." Of course a fair percentage of the least is permissible but the goods are not "fair average" if they are all of the least or worst quality possible under the description. In cases of doubt as to what quality is intended, the price at which a merchant closes a contract is an excellent index of the nature and scope of his obligation under the present section.

8. Fitness for the ordinary purposes for which goods of the type are used is a fundamental concept of the present section and is covered in paragraph (c). As stated above, merchantability is also a part of the obligation owing to the purchaser for use. Correspondingly, protection, under this aspect of the warranty, of the person buying for resale to the ultimate consumer is equally necessary, and merchantable goods must therefore be "honestly" resalable in the normal course of business because they are what they purport to be.

9. Paragraph (d) on evenness of kind, quality and quantity follows case law. But precautionary language has been added as a reminder of the frequent usages of trade which permit substantial variations both with and without an allowance or an obligation to replace the varying units.

10. Paragraph (e) applies only where the nature of the goods and of the transaction require a certain type of container, package or label. Paragraph (f) applies, on the other hand, wherever there is a label or container on which representations are made, even though the original contract, either by express terms or usage of trade, may not have required either the labelling or the representation. This follows from the general obligation of good faith which requires that a buyer should not be placed in the position of reselling or using goods delivered under false representations appearing on the package or container. No problem of extra consideration arises in this connection since, under this Article, an obligation is imposed by the original contract not to deliver mislabeled articles, and the obligation is imposed where mercantile good faith so requires and without reference to the doctrine of consideration.

11. Exclusion or modification of the warranty of merchantability, or of any part of it, is dealt with in the sec-

tion to which the text of the present section makes explicit precautionary references. That section must be read with particular reference to its subsection (4) on limitation of remedies. The warranty of merchantability, wherever it is normal, is so commonly taken for granted that its exclusion from the contract is a matter threatening surprise and therefore requiring special precaution.

12. Subsection (3) is to make explicit that usage of trade and course of dealing can create warranties and that they are implied rather than express warranties and thus subject to exclusion or modification under Section 2–316. A typical instance would be the obligation to provide pedigree papers to evidence conformity of the animal to the contract in the case of a pedigreed dog or blooded bull.

13. In an action based on breach of warranty, it is of course necessary to show not only the existence of the warranty but the fact that the warranty was broken and that the breach of the warranty was the proximate cause of the loss sustained. In such an action an affirmative showing by the seller that the loss resulted from some action or event following his own delivery of the goods can operate as a defense. Equally, evidence indicating that the seller exercised care in the manufacture, processing or selection of the goods is relevant to the issue of whether the warranty was in fact broken. Action by the buyer following an examination of the goods which ought to have indicated the defect complained of can be shown as matter bearing on whether the breach itself was the cause of the injury.

* * *

§ 2–315. Implied Warranty: Fitness for Particular Purpose

Where the seller at the time of contracting has reason to know any particular purpose for which the goods are required and that the buyer is relying on the seller's skill or judgment to select or furnish suitable goods, there is unless excluded or modified under the next section an implied warranty that the goods shall be fit for such purpose.

* NON-MERCHANTS MAY BE SUBJECT TO 2-315 W

Official Comment

Prior Uniform Statutory Provision: Section 15(1), (4), (5), Uniform Sales Act.

Changes: Rewritten.

Purposes of Changes:

1. Whether or not this warranty arises in any individual case is basically a question of fact to be determined by the circumstances of the contracting. Under this section the buyer need not bring home to the seller actual knowledge of the particular purpose for which the goods are intended or of his reliance on the seller's skill and judgment, if the circumstances are such that the seller has reason to realize the purpose intended or that the reliance exists. The buyer, of course, must actually be relying on the seller.

2. A "particular purpose" differs from the ordinary purpose for which the goods are used in that it envisages a specific use by the buyer which is peculiar to the nature of his business whereas the ordinary purposes for which goods are used are those envisaged in the concept of merchantability and go to uses which are customarily made of the goods in question. For example, shoes are generally used for the purpose of walking upon ordinary ground, but a seller may know that a particular pair was selected to be used for climbing mountains.

A contract may of course include both a warranty of merchantability and one of fitness for a particular purpose.

The provisions of this Article on the cumulation and conflict of express and implied warranties must be considered on the question of inconsistency between or among warranties. In such a case any question of fact as to which warranty was intended by the parties to apply must be resolved in favor of the warranty of fitness for particular purpose as against all other warranties except where the buyer has taken upon himself the responsibility of furnishing the technical specifications.

3. In connection with the warranty of fitness for a particular purpose the provisions of this Article on the allocation or division of risks are particularly applicable in any transaction in which the purpose for which the goods are to be used combines requirements both as to the quality of the goods themselves and compliance with certain laws or regulations. How the risks are divided is a question of fact to be determined, where not expressly contained in the agreement, from the circumstances of contracting, usage of trade, course of performance and the like, matters which may constitute the "otherwise agreement" of the parties by which they may divide the risk or burden.

4. The absence from this section of the language used in the Uniform Sales Act in referring to the seller, "whether he be the grower or manufacturer or not," is not intended to impose any requirement that the seller be a grower or manufacturer. Although normally the warranty will arise only where the seller is a merchant with the appropriate "skill or judgment," it can arise as to non-merchants where this is justified by the particular circumstances.

5. The elimination of the "patent or other trade name" exception constitutes the major extension of the warranty of fitness which has been made by the cases and continued in this Article. Under the present section the existence of a patent or other trade name and the designation of the article by that name, or indeed in any other definite manner, is only one of the facts to be considered on the question of whether the buyer actually relied on the seller, but it is not of itself decisive of the issue. If the buyer himself is insisting on a particular brand he is not relying on the seller's skill and judgment and so no warranty results. But the mere fact that the article purchased has a particular patent or trade name is not sufficient to indicate nonreliance if the article has been recommended by the seller as adequate for the buyer's purposes.

6. The specific reference forward in the present section to the following section on exclusion or modification of warranties is to call attention to the possibility of eliminating the warranty in any given case. However it must be noted that under the following section the warranty of fitness for a particular purpose must be excluded or modified by a conspicuous writing.

* * *

§ 2–316.   Exclusion or Modification of Warranties

(1) Words or conduct relevant to the creation of an express warranty and words or conduct tending to negate or limit warranty shall be construed wherever reasonable as consistent with each other; but subject to the provisions of this Article on parol or extrinsic evidence (Section 2–202) negation or limitation is inoperative to the extent that such construction is unreasonable.

* USE PLUS/MINUS WORDS

(2) Subject to subsection (3), to exclude or modify the implied warranty of merchantability or any part of it the language must mention merchantability and in case of a writing must be conspicuous, and to exclude or modify any implied warranty of fitness the exclusion must be by a writing and conspicuous. Language to exclude all implied warranties of fitness is sufficient if it states, for example, that "There are no warranties which extend beyond the description on the face hereof."

(3) Notwithstanding subsection (2)

(a) unless the circumstances indicate otherwise, all implied warranties are excluded by expressions like "as is," "with all faults" or other language which in common understanding calls the buyer's attention to the exclusion of warranties and makes plain that there is no implied warranty; and

(b) when the buyer before entering into the contract has examined the goods or the sample or model as fully as he desired or has refused to examine the goods there is no implied warranty with regard to defects which an examination ought in the circumstances to have revealed to him; and

(c) an implied warranty can also be excluded or modified by course of dealing or course of performance or usage of trade.

(4) Remedies for breach of warranty can be limited in accordance with the provisions of this Article on liquidation or limitation of damages and on contractual modification of remedy (Sections 2–718 and 2–719).

Official Comment

Prior Uniform Statutory Provision: None. See sections 15 and 71, Uniform Sales Act.

Purposes:

1. This section is designed principally to deal with those frequent clauses in sales contracts which seek to exclude "all warranties, express or implied." It seeks to protect a buyer from unexpected and unbargained language of disclaimer by denying effect to such language when inconsistent with language of express warranty and permitting the exclusion of implied warranties only by conspicuous language or other circumstances which protect the buyer from surprise.

2. The seller is protected under this Article against false allegations of oral warranties by its provisions on parol and extrinsic evidence and against unauthorized representations by the customary "lack of authority" clauses. This Article treats the limitation or avoidance of consequential damages as a matter of limiting remedies for breach, separate from the matter of creation of liability under a warranty. If no warranty exists, there is of course no problem of limiting remedies for breach of warranty. Under subsection (4) the question of limitation of remedy is governed by the sections referred to rather than by this section.

3. Disclaimer of the implied warranty of merchantability is permitted under subsection (2), but with the safeguard that such disclaimers must mention merchantability and in case of a writing must be conspicuous.

4. Unlike the implied warranty of merchantability, implied warranties of

To DISCLAIM:

2-314 : Must say "merchantability" and be conspicuous

2-315 : Must be in writing and be conspicuous

See 1-201(10) for definition of conspicuous

fitness for a particular purpose may be excluded by general language, but only if it is in writing and conspicuous.

5. Subsection (2) presupposes that the implied warranty in question exists unless excluded or modified. Whether or not language of disclaimer satisfies the requirements of this section, such language may be relevant under other sections to the question whether the warranty was ever in fact created. Thus, unless the provisions of this Article on parol and extrinsic evidence prevent, oral language of disclaimer may raise issues of fact as to whether reliance by the buyer occurred and whether the seller had "reason to know" under the section on implied warranty of fitness for a particular purpose.

6. The exceptions to the general rule set forth in paragraphs (a), (b) and (c) of subsection (3) are common factual situations in which the circumstances surrounding the transaction are in themselves sufficient to call the buyer's attention to the fact that no implied warranties are made or that a certain implied warranty is being excluded.

7. Paragraph (a) of subsection (3) deals with general terms such as "as is," "as they stand," "with all faults," and the like. Such terms in ordinary commercial usage are understood to mean that the buyer takes the entire risk as to the quality of the goods involved. The terms covered by paragraph (a) are in fact merely a particularization of paragraph (c) which provides for exclusion or modification of implied warranties by usage of trade.

8. Under paragraph (b) of subsection (3) warranties may be excluded or modified by the circumstances where the buyer examines the goods or a sample or model of them before entering into the contract. "Examination" as used in this paragraph is not synonymous with inspection before acceptance or at any other time after the contract

[handwritten margin note: User conduct in breach of W claim]

has been made. It goes rather to the nature of the responsibility assumed by the seller at the time of the making of the contract. Of course if the buyer discovers the defect and uses the goods anyway, or if he unreasonably fails to examine the goods before he uses them, resulting injuries may be found to result from his own action rather than proximately from a breach of warranty. See Sections 2—314 and 2—715 and comments thereto.

In order to bring the transaction within the scope of "refused to examine" in paragraph (b), it is not sufficient that the goods are available for inspection. There must in addition be a demand by the seller that the buyer examine the goods fully. The seller by the demand puts the buyer on notice that he is assuming the risk of defects which the examination ought to reveal. The language "refused to examine" in this paragraph is intended to make clear the necessity for such demand.

Application of the doctrine of "caveat emptor" in all cases where the buyer examines the goods regardless of statements made by the seller is, however, rejected by this Article. Thus, if the offer of examination is accompanied by words as to their merchantability or specific attributes and the buyer indicates clearly that he is relying on those words rather than on his examination, they give rise to an "express" warranty. In such cases the question is one of fact as to whether a warranty of merchantability has been expressly incorporated in the agreement. Disclaimer of such an express warranty is governed by subsection (1) of the present section.

The particular buyer's skill and the normal method of examining goods in the circumstances determine what defects are excluded by the examination. A failure to notice defects which are obvious cannot excuse the buyer. However, an examination under circumstances which do not permit chemical or other testing of the goods would not exclude defects which could be ascertained only by such testing. Nor can latent defects be excluded by a simple examination. A professional buyer examining a product in his field will be held to have assumed the risk as to all defects which a professional in the field ought to observe, while a nonprofessional buyer will be held to have assumed the risk only for such defects as a layman might be expected to observe.

9. The situation in which the buyer gives precise and complete specifications to the seller is not explicitly covered in this section, but this is a frequent circumstance by which the implied warranties may be excluded. The warranty of fitness for a particular purpose would not normally arise since in such a situation there is usually no reliance on the seller by the buyer. The warranty of merchantability in such a transaction, however, must be considered in connection with the next section on the cumulation and conflict of warranties. Under paragraph (c) of that section in case of such an inconsistency the implied warranty of merchantability is displaced by the express warranty that the goods will comply with the specifications. Thus, where the buyer gives detailed specifications as to the goods, neither of the implied warranties as to quality will normally apply to the transaction unless consistent with the specifications.

* * *

§ 2-317. Cumulation and Conflict of Warranties Express or Implied

Warranties whether express or implied shall be construed as consistent with each other and as cumulative, but if such construction is unreasonable the intention of the parties shall determine which warranty is dominant. In ascertaining that intention the following rules apply:

(a) Exact or technical specifications displace an inconsistent sample or model or general language of description.

(b) A sample from an existing bulk displaces inconsistent general language of description.

(c) Express warranties displace inconsistent implied warranties other than an implied warranty of fitness for a particular purpose.

Official Comment

Prior Uniform Statutory Provision: On cumulation of warranties see Sections 14, 15, and 16, Uniform Sales Act.

Changes: Completely rewritten into one section.

Purposes of Changes:

1. The present section rests on the basic policy of this Article that no warranty is created except by some conduct (either affirmative action or failure to disclose) on the part of the seller. Therefore, all warranties are made cumulative unless this construction of the contract is impossible or unreasonable.

This Article thus follows the general policy of the Uniform Sales Act except that in case of the sale of an article by its patent or trade name the elimination of the warranty of fitness depends solely on whether the buyer has relied on the seller's skill and judgment; the use of the patent or trade name is but one factor in making this determination.

2. The rules of this section are designed to aid in determining the inten-

281

tion of the parties as to which of inconsistent warranties which have arisen from the circumstances of their transaction shall prevail. These rules of intention are to be applied only where factors making for an equitable estoppel of the seller do not exist and where he has in perfect good faith made warranties which later turn out to be inconsistent. To the extent that the seller has led the buyer to believe that all of the warranties can be performed, he is estopped from setting up any essential inconsistency as a defense.

3. The rules in subsections (a), (b) and (c) are designed to ascertain the intention of the parties by reference to the factor which probably claimed the attention of the parties in the first instance. These rules are not absolute but may be changed by evidence showing that the conditions which existed at the time of contracting make the construction called for by the section inconsistent or unreasonable.

* * *

§ 2–318. Third Party Beneficiaries of Warranties Express or Implied

Note: *If this Act is introduced in the Congress of the United States this section should be omitted. (States to select one alternative.)*

Alternative A

A seller's warranty whether express or implied extends to any natural person who is in the family or household of his buyer or who is a guest in his home if it is reasonable to expect that such person may use, consume or be affected by the goods and who is injured in person by breach of the warranty. A seller may not exclude or limit the operation of this section.

Alternative B

A seller's warranty whether express or implied extends to any natural person who may reasonably be expected to use, consume or be affected by the goods and who is injured in person by breach of the warranty. A seller may not exclude or limit the operation of this section.

Alternative C

A seller's warranty whether express or implied extends to any person who may reasonably be expected to use, consume or be affected by the goods and who is injured by breach of the warranty. A seller may not exclude or limit the operation of this section with respect to injury to the person of an individual to whom the warranty extends. As amended 1966.

Official Comment

Purposes:

1. The last sentence of this section does not mean that a seller is precluded from excluding or disclaiming a warranty which might otherwise arise in connection with the sale provided such exclusion or modification is permitted by Section 2–316. Nor does that sentence preclude the seller from limiting the remedies of his own buyer and of any beneficiaries, in any manner provided in Sections 2–718 or 2–719. To the extent that the contract of sale contains provisions under which warranties are ex-

cluded or modified, or remedies for breach are limited, such provisions are equally operative against beneficiaries of warranties under this section. What this last sentence forbids is exclusion of liability by the seller to the persons to whom the warranties which he has made to his buyer would extend under this section.

2. The purpose of this section is to give certain beneficiaries the benefit of the same warranty which the buyer received in the contract of sale, thereby freeing any such beneficiaries from any technical rules as to "privity." It seeks to accomplish this purpose without any derogation of any right or remedy resting on negligence. It rests primarily upon the merchant-seller's warranty under this Article that the goods sold are merchantable and fit for the ordinary purposes for which such goods are used rather than the warranty of fitness for a particular purpose. Implicit in the section is that any beneficiary of a warran-

ty may bring a direct action for breach of warranty against the seller whose warranty extends to him [As amended in 1966].

3. The first alternative expressly includes as beneficiaries within its provisions the family, household and guests of the purchaser. Beyond this, the section in this form is neutral and is not intended to enlarge or restrict the developing case law on whether the seller's warranties, given to his buyer who resells, extend to other persons in the distributive chain. The second alternative is designed for states where the case law has already developed further and for those that desire to expand the class of beneficiaries. The third alternative goes further, following the trend of modern decisions as indicated by Restatement of Torts 2d § 402 A (Tentative Draft No. 10, 1965) in extending the rule beyond injuries to the person [As amended in 1966].

* * *

PART 5
PERFORMANCE

* * *

§ 2–503. Manner of Seller's Tender of Delivery

(1) Tender of delivery requires that the seller put and hold conforming goods at the buyer's disposition and give the buyer any notification reasonably necessary to enable him to take delivery. The manner, time and place for tender are determined by the agreement and this Article, and in particular

    (a) tender must be at a reasonable hour, and if it is of goods they must be kept available for the period reasonably necessary to enable the buyer to take possession; but

    (b) unless otherwise agreed the buyer must furnish facilities reasonably suited to the receipt of the goods.

(2) Where the case is within the next section respecting shipment tender requires that the seller comply with its provisions.

(3) Where the seller is required to deliver at a particular destination tender requires that he comply with subsection (1) and also in any

appropriate case tender documents as described in subsections (4) and (5) of this section.

(4) Where goods are in the possession of a bailee and are to be delivered without being moved

(a) tender requires that the seller either tender a negotiable document of title covering such goods or procure acknowledgment by the bailee of the buyer's right to possession of the goods; but

(b) tender to the buyer of a non-negotiable document of title or of a written direction to the bailee to deliver is sufficient tender unless the buyer seasonably objects, and receipt by the bailee of notification of the buyer's rights fixes those rights as against the bailee and all third persons; but risk of loss of the goods and of any failure by the bailee to honor the non-negotiable document of title or to obey the direction remains on the seller until the buyer has had a reasonable time to present the document or direction, and a refusal by the bailee to honor the document or to obey the direction defeats the tender.

(5) Where the contract requires the seller to deliver documents

(a) he must tender all such documents in correct form, except as provided in this Article with respect to bills of lading in a set (subsection (2) of Section 2–323); and

(b) tender through customary banking channels is sufficient and dishonor of a draft accompanying the documents constitutes non-acceptance or rejection.

* * *

§ 2–507. Effect of Seller's Tender; Delivery on Condition

(1) Tender of delivery is a condition to the buyer's duty to accept the goods and, unless otherwise agreed, to his duty to pay for them. Tender entitles the seller to acceptance of the goods and to payment according to the contract.

(2) Where payment is due and demanded on the delivery to the buyer of goods or documents of title, his right as against the seller to retain or dispose of them is conditional upon his making the payment due.

* * *

§ 2–508. Cure by Seller of Improper Tender or Delivery; Replacement

(1) Where any tender or delivery by the seller is rejected because non-conforming and the time for performance has not yet expired, the seller may seasonably notify the buyer of his intention to cure and may then within the contract time make a conforming delivery.

(2) Where the buyer rejects a non-conforming tender which the seller had reasonable grounds to believe would be acceptable with or without money allowance the seller may if he seasonably notifies the buyer have a further reasonable time to substitute a conforming tender.

Official Comment

Prior Uniform Statutory Provision: None.

Purposes:

1. Subsection (1) permits a seller who has made a non-conforming tender in any case to make a conforming delivery within the contract time upon seasonable notification to the buyer. It applies even where the seller has taken back the non-conforming goods and refunded the purchase price. He may still make a good tender within the contract period. The closer, however, it is to the contract date, the greater is the necessity for extreme promptness on the seller's part in notifying of his intention to cure, if such notification is to be "seasonable" under this subsection.

The rule of this subsection, moreover, is qualified by its underlying reasons. Thus if, after contracting for June delivery, a buyer later makes known to the seller his need for shipment early in the month and the seller ships accordingly, the "contract time" has been cut down by the supervening modification and the time for cure of tender must be referred to this modified time term.

2. Subsection (2) seeks to avoid injustice to the seller by reason of a surprise rejection by the buyer. However, the seller is not protected unless he had "reasonable grounds to believe" that the tender would be acceptable. Such reasonable grounds can lie in prior course of dealing, course of performance or usage of trade as well as in the particular circumstances surrounding the making of the contract. The seller is charged with commercial knowledge of any factors in a particular sales situation which require him to comply strictly with his obligations under the contract as, for example, strict conformity of documents in an overseas shipment or the sale of precision parts or chemicals for use in manufacture. Further, if the buyer gives notice either implicitly, as by a prior course of dealing involving rigorous inspections, or expressly, as by the deliberate inclusion of a "no replacement" clause in the contract, the seller is to be held to rigid compliance. If the clause appears in a "form" contract evidence that it is out of line with trade usage or the prior course of dealing and was not called to the seller's attention may be sufficient to show that the seller had reasonable grounds to believe that the tender would be acceptable.

3. The words "a further reasonable time to substitute a conforming tender" are intended as words of limitation to protect the buyer. What is a "reasonable time" depends upon the attending circumstances. Compare Section 2–511 on the comparable case of a seller's surprise demand for legal tender.

4. Existing trade usages permitting variations without rejection but with price allowance enter into the agreement itself as contractual limitations of remedy and are not covered by this section.

* * *

§ 2–515. Preserving Evidence of Goods in Dispute

In furtherance of the adjustment of any claim or dispute

(a) either party on reasonable notification to the other and for the purpose of ascertaining the facts and preserving evidence has the right to inspect, test and sample the goods including such of them as may be in the possession or control of the other; and

(b) the parties may agree to a third party inspection or survey to determine the conformity or condition of the goods and may agree that the findings shall be binding upon them in any subsequent litigation or adjustment.

Official Comment

Prior Uniform Statutory Provision: None.

Purposes:

1. To meet certain serious problems which arise when there is a dispute as to the quality of the goods and thereby perhaps to aid the parties in reaching a settlement, and to further the use of devices which will promote certainty as to the condition of the goods, or at least aid in preserving evidence of their condition.

2. Under paragraph (a), to afford either party an opportunity for preserving evidence, whether or not agreement has been reached, and thereby to reduce uncertainty in any litigation and, in turn perhaps, to promote agreement.

Paragraph (a) does not conflict with the provisions on the seller's right to resell rejected goods or the buyer's similar right. Apparent conflict between these provisions which will be suggested in certain circumstances is to be resolved by requiring prompt action by the parties. Nor does paragraph (a) impair the effect of a term for payment before inspection. Short of such defects as amount to fraud or substantial failure of consideration, non-conformity is neither an excuse nor a defense to an action for non-acceptance of documents. Normally, therefore, until the buyer has made payment, inspected and rejected the goods, there is no occasion or use for the rights under paragraph (a).

3. Under paragraph (b), to provide for third party inspection upon the agreement of the parties, thereby opening the door to amicable adjustments based upon the findings of such third parties.

The use of the phrase "conformity or condition" makes it clear that the parties' agreement may range from a complete settlement of all aspects of the dispute by a third party to the use of a third party merely to determine and record the condition of the goods so that they can be resold or used to reduce the stake in controversy. "Conformity", at one end of the scale of possible issues, includes the whole question of interpretation of the agreement and its legal effect, the state of the goods in regard to quality and condition, whether any defects are due to factors which operate at the risk of the buyer, and the degree of non-conformity where that may be material. "Condition", at the other end of the scale, includes nothing but the degree of damage or deterioration which the goods show. Paragraph (b) is intended to reach any point in the gamut which the parties may agree upon.

The principle of the section on reservation of rights reinforces this paragraph in simplifying such adjustments as the parties wish to make in partial settlement while reserving their rights as to any further points. Paragraph (b) also suggests the use of arbitration, where desired, of any points left open, but nothing in this section is intended to repeal or amend any statute governing arbitration. Where any question arises as to the extent of the parties' agreement under the paragraph, the presumption should be that it was meant to extend only to the relation between the contract description and the goods as delivered, since that is what a craftsman in the trade would normally be expected to report upon. Finally, a written and authenticated report of inspection or tests by a third party, whether or not sampling has been practicable, is entitled to be admitted as evidence under this Act, for it is a third party document.

* * *

PART 6

BREACH, REPUDIATION AND EXCUSE

§ 2–601. Buyer's Rights on Improper Delivery

Subject to the provisions of this Article on breach in installment contracts (Section 2–612) and unless otherwise agreed under the sections on contractual limitations of remedy (Sections 2–718 and 2–719), if the goods or the tender of delivery fail in any respect to conform to the contract, the buyer may

(a) reject the whole; or

(b) accept the whole; or

(c) accept any commercial unit or units and reject the rest.

Official Comment

Prior Uniform Statutory Provision: No one general equivalent provision but numerous provisions, dealing with situations of non-conformity where buyer may accept or reject, including Sections 11, 44 and 69(1), Uniform Sales Act.

Changes: Partial acceptance in good faith is recognized and the buyer's remedies on the contract for breach of warranty and the like, where the buyer has returned the goods after transfer of title, are no longer barred.

Purposes of Changes: To make it clear that:

1. A buyer accepting a nonconforming tender is not penalized by the loss of any remedy otherwise open to him. This policy extends to cover and regulate the acceptance of a part of any lot improperly tendered in any case where the price can reasonably be apportioned. Partial acceptance is permitted whether the part of the goods accepted conforms or not. The only limitation on partial acceptance is that good faith and commercial reasonable-ness must be used to avoid undue impairment of the value of the remaining portion of the goods. This is the reason for the insistence on the "commercial unit" in paragraph (c). In this respect, the test is not only what unit has been the basis of contract, but whether the partial acceptance produces so materially adverse an effect on the remainder as to constitute bad faith.

2. Acceptance made with the knowledge of the other party is final. An original refusal to accept may be withdrawn by a later acceptance if the seller has indicated that he is holding the tender open. However, if the buyer attempts to accept, either in whole or in part, after his original rejection has caused the seller to arrange for other disposition of the goods, the buyer must answer for any ensuing damage since the next section provides that any exercise of ownership after rejection is wrongful as against the seller. Further, he is liable even though the seller may choose to treat his action as acceptance rather than conversion, since the damage flows from the misleading notice.

Such arrangements for resale or other disposition of the goods by the seller must be viewed as within the normal contemplation of a buyer who has given notice of rejection. However, the buyer's attempts in good faith to dispose of defective goods where the seller has failed to give instructions within a reasonable time are not to be regarded as an acceptance.

* * *

§ 2–602. Manner and Effect of Rightful Rejection

(1) Rejection of goods must be within a reasonable time after their delivery or tender. It is ineffective unless the buyer seasonably notifies the seller.

(2) Subject to the provisions of the two following sections on rejected goods (Sections 2–603 and 2–604),

(a) after rejection any exercise of ownership by the buyer with respect to any commercial unit is wrongful as against the seller; and

(b) if the buyer has before rejection taken physical possession of goods in which he does not have a security interest under the provisions of this Article (subsection (3) of Section 2–711), he is under a duty after rejection to hold them with reasonable care at the seller's disposition for a time sufficient to permit the seller to remove them; but

(c) the buyer has no further obligations with regard to goods rightfully rejected.

(3) The seller's rights with respect to goods wrongfully rejected are governed by the provisions of this Article on Seller's remedies in general (Section 2–703).

Official Comment

Prior Uniform Statutory Provision: Section 50, Uniform Sales Act.

Changes: Rewritten.

Purposes of Changes: To make it clear that:

1. A tender or delivery of goods made pursuant to a contract of sale, even though wholly non-conforming, requires affirmative action by the buyer to avoid acceptance. Under subsection (1), therefore, the buyer is given a reasonable time to notify the seller of his rejection, but without such seasonable notification his rejection is ineffective. The sections of this Article dealing with inspection of goods must be read in connection with the buyer's reasonable time for action under this subsection. Contract provisions limiting the time for rejection fall within the rule of the section on "Time" and are effective if the time set gives the buyer a reasonable time for discovery of defects. What constitutes a due "notifying" of rejection by the buyer to the seller is defined in Section 1–201.

2. Subsection (2) lays down the normal duties of the buyer upon rejection, which flow from the relationship of the parties. Beyond his duty to hold the goods with reasonable care for the buyer's [seller's] disposition, this section continues the policy of prior uniform legislation in generally relieving the buyer from any duties with respect to them, except when the circumstances impose the limited obligation of salvage upon him under the next section.

3. The present section applies only to rightful rejection by the buyer. If the seller has made a tender which in all respects conforms to the contract, the buyer has a positive duty to accept and his failure to do so constitutes a "wrongful rejection" which gives the seller immediate remedies for breach. Subsection (3) is included here to em-phasize the sharp distinction between the rejection of an improper tender and the non-acceptance which is a breach by the buyer.

4. The provisions of this section are to be appropriately limited or modified when a negotiation is in process.

* * *

§ 2–605. Waiver of Buyer's Objections by Failure to Particularize

(1) The buyer's failure to state in connection with rejection a particular defect which is ascertainable by reasonable inspection precludes him from relying on the unstated defect to justify rejection or to establish breach

(a) where the seller could have cured it if stated seasonably; or

(b) between merchants when the seller has after rejection made a request in writing for a full and final written statement of all defects on which the buyer proposes to rely.

(2) Payment against documents made without reservation of rights precludes recovery of the payment for defects apparent on the face of the documents.

* * *

§ 2–606. What Constitutes Acceptance of Goods

(1) Acceptance of goods occurs when the buyer

(a) after a reasonable opportunity to inspect the goods signifies to the seller that the goods are conforming or that he will take or retain them in spite of their nonconformity; or

(b) fails to make an effective rejection (subsection (1) of Section 2–602), but such acceptance does not occur until the buyer has had a reasonable opportunity to inspect them; or

(c) does any act inconsistent with the seller's ownership; but if such act is wrongful as against the seller it is an acceptance only if ratified by him.

(2) Acceptance of a part of any commercial unit is acceptance of that entire unit.

Official Comment

Prior Uniform Statutory Provision: Section 48, Uniform Sales Act.

Changes: Rewritten, the qualification in paragraph (c) and subsection (2) being new; otherwise the general policy of the prior legislation is continued.

Purposes of Changes and New Matter: To make it clear that:

1. Under this Article "acceptance" as applied to goods means that the buyer, pursuant to the contract, takes particular goods which have been appropriated to the contract as his own, whether or not he is obligated to do so, and whether he does so by words, action, or silence when it is time to speak. If the goods conform to the contract, acceptance amounts only to the performance by the buyer of one part of his legal obligations.

2. Under this Article acceptance of goods is always acceptance of identified goods which have been appropriated to the contract or are appropriated by the contract. There is no provision for "acceptance of title" apart from acceptance in general, since acceptance of title is not material under this Article to the detailed rights and duties of the parties. (See Section 2–401). The refinements of the older law between acceptance of goods and of title become unnecessary in view of the provisions of the sections on effect and revocation of acceptance, on effects of identification and on risk of loss, and those sections which free the seller's and buyer's remedies from the complications and confusions caused by the question of whether title has or has not passed to the buyer before breach.

3. Under paragraph (a), payment made after tender is always one circumstance tending to signify acceptance of the goods but in itself it can never be more than one circumstance and is not conclusive. Also, a conditional communication of acceptance always remains subject to its expressed conditions.

4. Under paragraph (c), any action taken by the buyer, which is inconsistent with his claim that he has rejected the goods, constitutes an acceptance. However, the provisions of paragraph (c) are subject to the sections dealing with rejection by the buyer which permit the buyer to take certain actions with respect to the goods pursuant to his options and duties imposed by those sections, without effecting an acceptance of the goods. The second clause of paragraph (c) modifies some of the prior case law and makes it clear that "acceptance" in law based on the wrongful act of the acceptor is acceptance only as against the wrongdoer and then only at the option of the party wronged.

In the same manner in which a buyer can bind himself, despite his insistence that he is rejecting or has rejected the goods, by an act inconsistent with the seller's ownership under paragraph (c), he can obligate himself by a communication of acceptance despite a prior rejection under paragraph (a). However, the sections on buyer's rights on improper delivery and on the effect of rightful rejection, make it clear that after he once rejects a tender, paragraph (a) does not operate in favor of the buyer unless the seller has re-tendered the goods or has taken affirmative action indicating that he is holding the tender open. See also Comment 2 to Section 2–601.

5. Subsection (2) supplements the policy of the section on buyer's rights on improper delivery, recognizing the validity of a partial acceptance but insisting that the buyer exercise this right only as to whole commercial units.

* * *

§ 2–607. Effect of Acceptance; Notice of Breach; Burden of Establishing Breach After Acceptance; Notice of Claim or Litigation to Person Answerable Over

(1) The buyer must pay at the contract rate for any goods accepted.

(2) Acceptance of goods by the buyer precludes rejection of the goods accepted and if made with knowledge of a non-conformity cannot be revoked because of it unless the acceptance was on the reasonable assumption that the non-conformity would be seasonably cured but acceptance does not of itself impair any other remedy provided by this Article for non-conformity.

(3) Where a tender has been accepted

(a) the buyer must within a reasonable time after he discovers or should have discovered any breach notify the seller of breach or be barred from any remedy; and

(b) if the claim is one for infringement or the like (subsection (3) of Section 2–312) and the buyer is sued as a result of such a breach he must so notify the seller within a reasonable time after he receives notice of the litigation or be barred from any remedy over for liability established by the litigation.

(4) The burden is on the buyer to establish any breach with respect to the goods accepted.

(5) Where the buyer is sued for breach of a warranty or other obligation for which his seller is answerable over

(a) he may give his seller written notice of the litigation. If the notice states that the seller may come in and defend and that if the seller does not do so he will be bound in any action against him by his buyer by any determination of fact common to the two litigations, then unless the seller after seasonable receipt of the notice does come in and defend he is so bound.

(b) if the claim is one for infringement or the like (subsection (3) of Section 2–312) the original seller may demand in writing that his buyer turn over to him control of the litigation including settlement or else be barred from any remedy over and if he also agrees to bear all expense and to satisfy any adverse judgment, then unless the buyer after seasonable receipt of the demand does turn over control the buyer is so barred.

(6) The provisions of subsections (3), (4) and (5) apply to any obligation of a buyer to hold the seller harmless against infringement or the like (subsection (3) of Section 2–312).

Official Comment

Prior Uniform Statutory Provision: Subsection (1)—Section 41, Uniform Sales Act; Subsections (2) and (3)—Sections 49 and 69, Uniform Sales Act.

Changes: Rewritten.

Purposes of Changes: To continue the prior basic policies with respect to acceptance of goods while making a number of minor though material changes in the interest of simplicity and commercial convenience so that:

1. Under subsection (1), once the buyer accepts a tender the seller acquires a right to its price on the contract terms. In cases of partial acceptance, the

price of any part accepted is, if possible, to be reasonably apportioned, using the type of apportionment familiar to the courts in quantum valebat cases, to be determined in terms of "the contract rate," which is the rate determined from the bargain in fact (the agreement) after the rules and policies of this Article have been brought to bear.

2. Under subsection (2) acceptance of goods precludes their subsequent rejection. Any return of the goods thereafter must be by way of revocation of acceptance under the next section. Revocation is unavailable for a non-conformity known to the buyer at the time of acceptance, except where the buyer has accepted on the reasonable assumption that the non-conformity would be seasonably cured.

3. All other remedies of the buyer remain unimpaired under subsection (2). This is intended to include the buyer's full rights with respect to future installments despite his acceptance of any earlier non-conforming installment.

4. The time of notification is to be determined by applying commercial standards to a merchant buyer. "A reasonable time" for notification from a retail consumer is to be judged by different standards so that in his case it will be extended, for the rule of requiring notification is designed to defeat commercial bad faith, not to deprive a good faith consumer of his remedy.

The content of the notification need merely be sufficient to let the seller know that the transaction is still troublesome and must be watched. There is no reason to require that the notification which saves the buyer's rights under this section must include a clear statement of all the objections that will be relied on by the buyer, as under the section covering statements of defects upon rejection (Section 2–605). Nor is there reason for requiring the notification to be a claim for damages or of any

threatened litigation or other resort to a remedy. The notification which saves the buyer's rights under this Article need only be such as informs the seller that the transaction is claimed to involve a breach, and thus opens the way for normal settlement through negotiation.

5. Under this Article various beneficiaries are given rights for injuries sustained by them because of the seller's breach of warranty. Such a beneficiary does not fall within the reason of the present section in regard to discovery of defects and the giving of notice within a reasonable time after acceptance, since he has nothing to do with acceptance. However, the reason of this section does extend to requiring the beneficiary to notify the seller that an injury has occurred. What is said above, with regard to the extended time for reasonable notification from the lay consumer after the injury is also applicable here; but even a beneficiary can be properly held to the use of good faith in notifying, once he has had time to become aware of the legal situation.

6. Subsection (4) unambiguously places the burden of proof to establish breach on the buyer after acceptance. However, this rule becomes one purely of procedure when the tender accepted was non-conforming and the buyer has given the seller notice of breach under subsection (3). For subsection (2) makes it clear that acceptance leaves unimpaired the buyer's right to be made whole, and that right can be exercised by the buyer not only by way of cross-claim for damages, but also by way of recoupment in diminution or extinction of the price.

7. Subsections (3)(b) and (5)(b) give a warrantor against infringement an opportunity to defend or compromise third-party claims or be relieved of his liability. Subsection (5)(a) codifies for all warranties the practice of voucher to

defend. Compare Section 3–803. Subsection (6) makes these provisions applicable to the buyer's liability for infringement under Section 2–312.

8. All of the provisions of the present section are subject to any explicit reservation of rights.

* * *

§ 2–608. Revocation of Acceptance in Whole or in Part

(1) The buyer may revoke his acceptance of a lot or commercial unit whose non-conformity substantially impairs its value to him if he has accepted it

    (a) on the reasonable assumption that its non-conformity would be cured and it has not been seasonably cured; or

    (b) without discovery of such non-conformity if his acceptance was reasonably induced either by the difficulty of discovery before acceptance or by the seller's assurances.

(2) Revocation of acceptance must occur within a reasonable time after the buyer discovers or should have discovered the ground for it and before any substantial change in condition of the goods which is not caused by their own defects. It is not effective until the buyer notifies the seller of it.

(3) A buyer who so revokes has the same rights and duties with regard to the goods involved as if he had rejected them.

Official Comment

Prior Uniform Statutory Provision: Section 69(1)(d), (3), (4) and (5), Uniform Sales Act.

Changes: Rewritten.

Purposes of Changes: To make it clear that:

1. Although the prior basic policy is continued, the buyer is no longer required to elect between revocation of acceptance and recovery of damages for breach. Both are now available to him. The non-alternative character of the two remedies is stressed by the terms used in the present section. The section no longer speaks of "rescission," a term capable of ambiguous application either to transfer of title to the goods or to the contract of sale and susceptible also of confusion with cancellation for cause of an executed or executory portion of the contract. The remedy under this section is instead referred to simply as "revocation of acceptance" of goods tendered under a contract for sale and involves no suggestion of "election" of any sort.

2. Revocation of acceptance is possible only where the non-conformity substantially impairs the value of the goods to the buyer. For this purpose the test is not what the seller had reason to know at the time of contracting; the question is whether the non-conformity is such as will in fact cause a substantial impairment of value to the buyer though the seller had no advance knowledge as to the buyer's particular circumstances.

3. "Assurances" by the seller under paragraph (b) of subsection (1) can rest as well in the circumstances or in the contract as in explicit language used at the time of delivery. The reason for recognizing such assurances is that they induce the buyer to delay discovery. These are the only assurances involved in paragraph (b). Explicit assurances may be made either in good faith or bad faith. In either case any remedy accord-

ed by this Article is available to the buyer under the section on remedies for fraud.

4. Subsection (2) requires notification of revocation of acceptance within a reasonable time after discovery of the grounds for such revocation. Since this remedy will be generally resorted to only after attempts at adjustment have failed, the reasonable time period should extend in most cases beyond the time in which notification of breach must be given, beyond the time for discovery of non-conformity after acceptance and beyond the time for rejection after tender. The parties may by their agreement limit the time for notification under this section, but the same sanctions and considerations apply to such agreements as are discussed in the comment on manner and effect of rightful rejection.

5. The content of the notice under subsection (2) is to be determined in this case as in others by considerations of good faith, prevention of surprise, and reasonable adjustment. More will generally be necessary than the mere notification of breach required under the preceding section. On the other hand the requirements of the section on waiver of buyer's objections do not apply here. The fact that quick notification of trouble is desirable affords good ground for being slow to bind a buyer by his first statement. Following the general policy of this Article, the requirements of the content of notification are less stringent in the case of a non-merchant buyer.

6. Under subsection (2) the prior policy is continued of seeking substantial justice in regard to the condition of goods restored to the seller. Thus the buyer may not revoke his acceptance if the goods have materially deteriorated except by reason of their own defects. Worthless goods, however, need not be offered back and minor defects in the articles reoffered are to be disregarded.

7. The policy of the section allowing partial acceptance is carried over into the present section and the buyer may revoke his acceptance, in appropriate cases, as to the entire lot or any commercial unit thereof.

* * *

PART 7
REMEDIES

* * *

§ 2–711. Buyer's Remedies in General; Buyer's Security Interest in Rejected Goods

(1) Where the seller fails to make delivery or repudiates or the buyer rightfully rejects or justifiably revokes acceptance then with respect to any goods involved, and with respect to the whole if the breach goes to the whole contract (Section 2–612), the buyer may cancel and whether or not he has done so may in addition to recovering so much of the price as has been paid

(a) "cover" and have damages under the next section as to all the goods affected whether or not they have been identified to the contract; or

(b) recover damages for non-delivery as provided in this Article (Section 2–713).

(2) Where the seller fails to deliver or repudiates the buyer may also

(a) if the goods have been identified recover them as provided in this Article (Section 2–502); or

(b) in a proper case obtain specific performance or replevy the goods as provided in this Article (Section 2–716).

(3) On rightful rejection or justifiable revocation of acceptance a buyer has a security interest in goods in his possession or control for any payments made on their price and any expenses reasonably incurred in their inspection, receipt, transportation, care and custody and may hold such goods and resell them in like manner as an aggrieved seller (Section 2–706).

Official Comment

Prior Uniform Statutory Provision: No comparable index section; Subsection (3)—Section 69(5), Uniform Sales Act.

Changes: The prior uniform statutory provision is generally continued and expanded in Subsection (3).

Purposes of Changes and New Matter:

1. To index in this section the buyer's remedies, subsection (1) covering those remedies permitting the recovery of money damages, and subsection (2) covering those which permit reaching the goods themselves. The remedies listed here are those available to a buyer who has not accepted the goods or who has justifiably revoked his acceptance. The remedies available to a buyer with regard to goods finally accepted appear in the section dealing with breach in regard to accepted goods. The buyer's right to proceed as to all goods when the breach is as to only some of the goods is determined by the section on breach in installment contracts and by the section on partial acceptance.

Despite the seller's breach, proper retender of delivery under the section on cure of improper tender or replacement can effectively preclude the buyer's remedies under this section, except for any delay involved.

2. To make it clear in subsection (3) that the buyer may hold and resell rejected goods if he has paid a part of the price or incurred expenses of the type specified. "Paid" as used here includes acceptance of a draft or other time negotiable instrument or the signing of a negotiable note. His freedom of resale is coextensive with that of a seller under this Article except that the buyer may not keep any profit resulting from the resale and is limited to retaining only the amount of the price paid and the costs involved in the inspection and handling of the goods. The buyer's security interest in the goods is intended to be limited to the items listed in subsection (3), and the buyer is not permitted to retain such funds as he might believe adequate for his damages. The buyer's right to cover, or to have damages for non-delivery, is not impaired by his exercise of his right of resale.

3. It should also be noted that this Act requires its remedies to be liberally administered and provides that any right or obligation which it declares is enforceable by action unless a different effect is specifically prescribed (Section 1–106).

* * *

§ 2–714. Buyer's Damages for Breach in Regard to Accepted Goods

(1) Where the buyer has accepted goods and given notification (subsection (3) of Section 2–607) he may recover as damages for any nonconformity of tender the loss resulting in the ordinary course of events from the seller's breach as determined in any manner which is reasonable.

(2) The measure of damages for breach of warranty is the difference at the time and place of acceptance between the value of the goods accepted and the value they would have had if they had been as warranted, unless special circumstances show proximate damages of a different amount.

(3) In a proper case any incidental and consequential damages under the next section may also be recovered.

Official Comment

Prior Uniform Statutory Provision: Section 69(6) and (7), Uniform Sales Act.

Changes: Rewritten.

Purposes of Changes:

1. This section deals with the remedies available to the buyer after the goods have been accepted and the time for revocation of acceptance has gone by. In general this section adopts the rule of the prior uniform statutory provision for measuring damages where there has been a breach of warranty as to goods accepted, but goes further to lay down an explicit provision as to the time and place for determining the loss.

The section on deduction of damages from price provides an additional remedy for a buyer who still owes part of the purchase price, and frequently the two remedies will be available concurrently. The buyer's failure to notify of his claim under the section on effects of acceptance, however, operates to bar his remedies under either that section or the present section.

2. The "non-conformity" referred to in subsection (1) includes not only breaches of warranties but also any failure of the seller to perform according to his obligations under the contract. In the case of such non-conformity, the buyer is permitted to recover for his loss "in any manner which is reasonable."

3. Subsection (2) describes the usual, standard and reasonable method of ascertaining damages in the case of breach of warranty but it is not intended as an exclusive measure. It departs from the measure of damages for non-delivery in utilizing the place of acceptance rather than the place of tender. In some cases the two may coincide, as where the buyer signifies his acceptance upon the tender. If, however, the non-conformity is such as would justify revocation of acceptance, the time and place of acceptance under this section is determined as of the buyer's decision not to revoke.

4. The incidental and consequential damages referred to in subsection (3), which will usually accompany an action brought under this section, are discussed in detail in the comment on the next section.

* * *

§ 2–715. Buyer's Incidental and Consequential Damages

(1) Incidental damages resulting from the seller's breach include expenses reasonably incurred in inspection, receipt, transportation and care

and custody of goods rightfully rejected, any commercially reasonable charges, expenses or commissions in connection with effecting cover and any other reasonable expense incident to the delay or other breach.

(2) Consequential damages resulting from the seller's breach include

(a) any loss resulting from general or particular requirements and needs of which the seller at the time of contracting had reason to know and which could not reasonably be prevented by cover or otherwise; and

(b) injury to person or property proximately resulting from any breach of warranty.

Official Comment

Prior Uniform Statutory Provisions: Subsection (2)(b)—Sections 69(7) and 70, Uniform Sales Act.

Changes: Rewritten.

Purposes of Changes and New Matter:

1. Subsection (1) is intended to provide reimbursement for the buyer who incurs reasonable expenses in connection with the handling of rightfully rejected goods or goods whose acceptance may be justifiably revoked, or in connection with effecting cover where the breach of the contract lies in non-conformity or non-delivery of the goods. The incidental damages listed are not intended to be exhaustive but are merely illustrative of the typical kinds of incidental damage.

2. Subsection (2) operates to allow the buyer, in an appropriate case, any consequential damages which are the result of the seller's breach. The "tacit agreement" test for the recovery of consequential damages is rejected. Although the older rule at common law which made the seller liable for all consequential damages of which he had "reason to know" in advance is followed, the liberality of that rule is modified by refusing to permit recovery unless the buyer could not reasonably have prevented the loss by cover or otherwise. Subparagraph (2) carries forward the provisions of the prior uniform statutory provision

as to consequential damages resulting from breach of warranty, but modifies the rule by requiring first that the buyer attempt to minimize his damages in good faith, either by cover or otherwise.

3. In the absence of excuse under the section on merchant's excuse by failure of presupposed conditions, the seller is liable for consequential damages in all cases where he had reason to know of the buyer's general or particular requirements at the time of contracting. It is not necessary that there be a conscious acceptance of an insurer's liability on the seller's part, nor is his obligation for consequential damages limited to cases in which he fails to use due effort in good faith.

Particular needs of the buyer must generally be made known to the seller while general needs must rarely be made known to charge the seller with knowledge.

Any seller who does not wish to take the risk of consequential damages has available the section on contractual limitation of remedy.

4. The burden of proving the extent of loss incurred by way of consequential damage is on the buyer, but the section on liberal administration of remedies rejects any doctrine of certainty which requires almost mathematical precision in the proof of loss. Loss may be determined in any manner which is reasonable under the circumstances.

*USER
Conduct in
breach of W
claim
AS TO PROX CAUSE*

5. Subsection (2)(b) states the usual rule as to breach of warranty, allowing recovery for injuries "proximately" resulting from the breach. Where the injury involved follows the use of goods without discovery of the defect causing the damage, the question of "proximate" cause turns on whether it was reasonable for the buyer to use the goods without such inspection as would have revealed the defects. If it was not reasonable for him to do so, or if he did in fact discover the defect prior to his use, the injury would not proximately result from the breach of warranty.

6. In the case of sale of wares to one in the business of reselling them, resale is one of the requirements of which the seller has reason to know within the meaning of subsection (2)(a).

* * *

§ 2–716. Buyer's Right to Specific Performance or Replevin

(1) Specific performance may be decreed where the goods are unique or in other proper circumstances.

(2) The decree for specific performance may include such terms and conditions as to payment of the price, damages, or other relief as the court may deem just.

(3) The buyer has a right of replevin for goods identified to the contract if after reasonable effort he is unable to effect cover for such goods or the circumstances reasonably indicate that such effort will be unavailing or if the goods have been shipped under reservation and satisfaction of the security interest in them has been made or tendered.

Official Comment

Prior Uniform Statutory Provision: Section 68, Uniform Sales Act.

Changes: Rephrased.

Purposes of Changes: To make it clear that:

1. The present section continues in general prior policy as to specific performance and injunction against breach. However, without intending to impair in any way the exercise of the court's sound discretion in the matter, this Article seeks to further a more liberal attitude than some courts have shown in connection with the specific performance of contracts of sale.

2. In view of this Article's emphasis on the commercial feasibility of replacement, a new concept of what are "unique" goods is introduced under this section. Specific performance is no longer limited to goods which are already specific or ascertained at the time of contracting. The test of uniqueness under this section must be made in terms of the total situation which characterizes the contract. Output and requirements contracts involving a particular or peculiarly available source or market present today the typical commercial specific performance situation, as contrasted with contracts for the sale of heirlooms or priceless works of art which were usually involved in the older cases. However, uniqueness is not the sole basis of the remedy under this section for the relief may also be granted "in other proper circumstances" and inability to cover is strong evidence of "other proper circumstances".

3. The legal remedy of replevin is given the buyer in cases in which cover is reasonably unavailable and goods have been identified to the contract. This is in addition to the buyer's right to recover identified goods on the seller's insolvency (Section 2–502).

4. This section is intended to give the buyer rights to the goods comparable to the seller's rights to the price.

5. If a negotiable document of title is outstanding, the buyer's right of re-

plevin relates of course to the document not directly to the goods. See Article 7, especially Section 7–602.

* * *

§ 2–717. Deduction of Damages From the Price

The buyer on notifying the seller of his intention to do so may deduct all or any part of the damages resulting from any breach of the contract from any part of the price still due under the same contract.

Official Comment

Prior Uniform Statutory Provision: See Section 69(1)(a), Uniform Sales Act.

Purposes:

1. This section permits the buyer to deduct from the price damages resulting from any breach by the seller and does not limit the relief to cases of breach of warranty as did the prior uniform statutory provision. To bring this provision into application the breach involved must be of the same contract under which the price in question is claimed to have been earned.

2. The buyer, however, must give notice of his intention to withhold all or part of the price if he wishes to avoid a default within the meaning of the section on insecurity and right to assurances. In conformity with the general policies of this Article, no formality of notice is required and any language which reasonably indicates the buyer's reason for holding up his payment is sufficient.

* * *

§ 2–718. Liquidation or Limitation of Damages; Deposits

(1) Damages for breach by either party may be liquidated in the agreement but only at an amount which is reasonable in the light of the anticipated or actual harm caused by the breach, the difficulties of proof of loss, and the inconvenience or nonfeasibility of otherwise obtaining an adequate remedy. A term fixing unreasonably large liquidated damages is void as a penalty.

(2) Where the seller justifiably withholds delivery of goods because of the buyer's breach, the buyer is entitled to restitution of any amount by which the sum of his payments exceeds

(a) the amount to which the seller is entitled by virtue of terms liquidating the seller's damages in accordance with subsection (1), or

(b) in the absence of such terms, twenty per cent of the value of the total performance for which the buyer is obligated under the contract or $500, whichever is smaller.

(3) The buyer's right to restitution under subsection (2) is subject to offset to the extent that the seller establishes

(a) a right to recover damages under the provisions of this Article other than subsection (1), and

(b) the amount or value of any benefits received by the buyer directly or indirectly by reason of the contract.

(4) Where a seller has received payment in goods their reasonable value or the proceeds of their resale shall be treated as payments for the purposes of subsection (2); but if the seller has notice of the buyer's breach before reselling goods received in part performance, his resale is subject to the conditions laid down in this Article on resale by an aggrieved seller (Section 2—706).

Official Comment

Prior Uniform Statutory Provision: None.

Purposes:

1. Under subsection (1) liquidated damage clauses are allowed where the amount involved is reasonable in the light of the circumstances of the case. The subsection sets forth explicitly the elements to be considered in determining the reasonableness of a liquidated damage clause. A term fixing unreasonably large liquidated damages is expressly made void as a penalty. An unreasonably small amount would be subject to similar criticism and might be stricken under the section on unconscionable contracts or clauses.

2. Subsection (2) refuses to recognize a forfeiture unless the amount of the payment so forfeited represents a reasonable liquidation of damages as determined under subsection (1). A special exception is made in the case of small amounts (20% of the price or $500, whichever is smaller) deposited as security. No distinction is made between cases in which the payment is to be applied on the price and those in which it is intended as security for performance. Subsection (2) is applicable to any deposit or down or part payment. In the case of a deposit or turn in of goods resold before the breach, the amount actually received on the resale is to be viewed as the deposit rather than the amount allowed the buyer for the trade in. However, if the seller knows of the breach prior to the resale of the goods turned in, he must make reasonable efforts to realize their true value, and this is assured by requiring him to comply with the conditions laid down in the section on resale by an aggrieved seller.

* * *

§ 2–719. Contractual Modification or Limitation of Remedy

(1) Subject to the provisions of subsections (2) and (3) of this section and of the preceding section on liquidation and limitation of damages,

(a) the agreement may provide for remedies in addition to or in substitution for those provided in this Article and may limit or alter the measure of damages recoverable under this Article, as by limiting the buyer's remedies to return of the goods and repayment of the price or to repair and replacement of non-conforming goods or parts; and

(b) resort to a remedy as provided is optional unless the remedy is expressly agreed to be exclusive, in which case it is the sole remedy.

(2) Where circumstances cause an exclusive or limited remedy to fail of its essential purpose, remedy may be had as provided in this Act.

(3) Consequential damages may be limited or excluded unless the limitation or exclusion is unconscionable. Limitation of consequential damages for injury to the person in the case of consumer goods is prima facie unconscionable but limitation of damages where the loss is commercial is not.

What is PRIMA FACIE unconscionable?

Official Comment

Prior Uniform Statutory Provision: None.

Purposes:

1. Under this section parties are left free to shape their remedies to their particular requirements and reasonable agreements limiting or modifying remedies are to be given effect.

However, it is of the very essence of a sales contract that at least minimum adequate remedies be available. If the parties intend to conclude a contract for sale within this Article they must accept the legal consequence that there be at least a fair quantum of remedy for breach of the obligations or duties outlined in the contract. Thus any clause purporting to modify or limit the remedial provisions of this Article in an unconscionable manner is subject to deletion and in that event the remedies made available by this Article are applicable as if the stricken clause had never existed. Similarly, under subsection (2), where an apparently fair and reasonable clause because of circumstances fails in its purpose or operates to deprive either party of the substantial value of the bargain, it must give way to the general remedy provisions of this Article.

2. Subsection (1)(b) creates a presumption that clauses prescribing remedies are cumulative rather than exclusive. If the parties intend the term to describe the sole remedy under the contract, this must be clearly expressed.

3. Subsection (3) recognizes the validity of clauses limiting or excluding consequential damages but makes it clear that they may not operate in an unconscionable manner. Actually such terms are merely an allocation of unknown or undeterminable risks. The seller in all cases is free to disclaim warranties in the manner provided in Section 2–316.

* * *

§ 2–720. Effect of "Cancellation" or "Rescission" on Claims for Antecedent Breach

Unless the contrary intention clearly appears, expressions of "cancellation" or "rescission" of the contract or the like shall not be construed as a renunciation or discharge of any claim in damages for an antecedent breach.

Official Comment

Prior Uniform Statutory Provision: None.

Purpose: This section is designed to safeguard a person holding a right of action from any unintentional loss of rights by the ill-advised use of such terms as "cancellation", "rescission", or the like. Once a party's rights have accrued they are not to be lightly impaired by concessions made in business decency and without intention to forego them. Therefore, unless the cancellation of a contract expressly declares that it is "without reservation of rights", or the like, it cannot be considered to be a renunciation under this section.

* * *

301

§ 2-721.　Remedies for Fraud

Remedies for material misrepresentation or fraud include all remedies available under this Article for non-fraudulent breach. Neither rescission or a claim for rescission of the contract for sale nor rejection or return of the goods shall bar or be deemed inconsistent with a claim for damages or other remedy.

Official Comment

Prior Uniform Statutory Provision: None.

Purposes: To correct the situation by which remedies for fraud have been more circumscribed than the more modern and mercantile remedies for breach of warranty. Thus the remedies for fraud are extended by this section to coincide in scope with those for non-fraudulent breach. This section thus makes it clear that neither rescission of the contract for fraud nor rejection of the goods bars other remedies unless the circumstances of the case make the remedies incompatible.

* * *

§ 2-725.　Statute of Limitations in Contracts for Sale

(1) An action for breach of any contract for sale must be commenced within four years after the cause of action has accrued. By the original agreement the parties may reduce the period of limitation to not less than one year but may not extend it.

(2) A cause of action accrues when the breach occurs, regardless of the aggrieved party's lack of knowledge of the breach. A breach of warranty occurs when tender of delivery is made, except that where a warranty explicitly extends to future performance of the goods and discovery of the breach must await the time of such performance the cause of action accrues when the breach is or should have been discovered.

[handwritten margin notes:]
① W can't be tested until circumstance in future arises
② Lifetime Warranty
③ "6 years or 60k miles"

(3) Where an action commenced within the time limited by subsection (1) is so terminated as to leave available a remedy by another action for the same breach such other action may be commenced after the expiration of the time limited and within six months after the termination of the first action unless the termination resulted from voluntary discontinuance or from dismissal for failure or neglect to prosecute.

(4) This section does not alter the law on tolling of the statute of limitations nor does it apply to causes of action which have accrued before this Act becomes effective.

Official Comment

Prior Uniform Statutory Provision: None.

Purposes: To introduce a uniform statute of limitations for sales contracts, thus eliminating the jurisdictional variations and providing needed relief for concerns doing business on a nationwide scale whose contracts have heretofore been governed by several different periods of limitation depending upon the state in which the transaction occurred. This Article takes sales contracts out of the general laws limiting the time for commencing contractual actions and se-

[handwritten note:] NOTE: SoL for injury is 2 years in OH

lects a four year period as the most appropriate to modern business practice. This is within the normal commercial record keeping period.

Subsection (1) permits the parties to reduce the period of limitation. The minimum period is set at one year. The parties may not, however, extend the statutory period.

Subsection (2), providing that the cause of action accrues when the breach occurs, states an exception where the warranty extends to future performance.

Subsection (3) states the saving provision included in many state statutes and permits an additional short period for bringing new actions, where suits begun within the four year period have been terminated so as to leave a remedy still available for the same breach.

Subsection (4) makes it clear that this Article does not purport to alter or modify in any respect the law on tolling of the statute of limitations as it now prevails in the various jurisdictions.

* * *

PRODUCTS LIABILITY STATUTES
Selected States

————

ARIZONA REVISED STATUTES ANNOTATED

(1978, 1989 (§ 12–701), and 1995)

§ 12–551. Product liability. A product liability action as defined in § 12–681 shall be commenced and prosecuted within the period prescribed in § 12–542, except that no product liability action may be commenced and prosecuted if the cause of action accrues more than twelve years after the product was first sold for use or consumption, unless the cause of action is based upon the negligence of the manufacturer or seller or a breach of an express warranty provided by the manufacturer or seller.

§ 12–681. Definitions. In this article, unless the context otherwise requires:

1. "Manufacturer" means a person or entity who designs, assembles, fabricates, produces, constructs or otherwise prepares a product or component part of a product prior to its sale to a user or consumer, including a seller owned in whole or significant part by the manufacturer or a seller, owning the manufacturer in whole or significant part.

2. "Product" means the individual product or any component part of such product which is the subject of a product liability action.

3. "Product liability action" means any action brought against a manufacturer or seller of a product for damages for bodily injury, death or property damage caused by or resulting from the manufacture, construction, design, formula, installation, preparation, assembly, testing, packaging, labeling, sale, use or consumption of any product, the failure to warn or protect against a danger or hazard in the use or misuse of the product or the failure to provide proper instructions for the use or consumption of any product.

4. "Product safety analysis or review" means any investigation, inquiry, review, evaluation or other means by which a person or entity seeks to determine, calculate, predict, estimate, evaluate or report the safety or health effects of the use of any of its products, systems, services or processes. Product safety analysis or review includes an analysis or review by a component manufacturer of the safety and health effects of component parts in end products. A product safety analysis or review may be conducted by employees of the person or entity or by consultants engaged specifically to perform the analysis or review.

5. "Reasonable remedial measures" means actions taken as a result of a product safety analysis or review and intended to improve the safety of products, systems, services or processes or to lessen the likelihood of a safety-related accident. These actions include:

(a) Modifications to the product, system, service or process.

(b) Changes in quality assurance procedures or policies.

(c) Modifications made to the design or method of manufacturing, to manufacturing equipment or to the testing of the product, system, service or process.

(d) Changes or additions to training programs or safety education programs.

(e) Personnel or human resources measures related to the product, system, service or process.

(f) The use or modification of warnings, notices or changes to owner manuals and related materials.

(g) The recall of products.

6. "Reasonably foreseeable alteration, modification, use or consumption" means an alteration, modification, use or consumption of the product which would be expected of an ordinary and prudent purchaser, user or consumer and which an ordinary and prudent manufacturer should have anticipated.

7. "Seller" means a person or entity, including a wholesaler, distributor, retailer or lessor, engaged in the business of leasing any product or selling any product for resale, use or consumption.

8. "State of the art" means the technical, mechanical and scientific knowledge of manufacturing, designing, testing or labeling the same or similar products which was in existence and reasonably feasible for use at the time of manufacture.

§ 12–682. Limitation. The previously existing common law of products liability is modified only to the extent specifically stated in this article and § 12–551.

§ 12–683. Affirmative defenses. In any product liability action, a defendant shall not be liable if the defendant proves that any of the following apply:

1. The defect in the product is alleged to result from inadequate design or fabrication, and if the plans or designs for the product or the methods and techniques of manufacturing, inspecting, testing and labeling the product conformed with the state of the art at the time the product was first sold by the defendant.

2. The proximate cause of the incident giving rise to the action was an alteration or modification of the product which was not reasonably

foreseeable, made by a person other than the defendant and subsequent to the time the product was first sold by the defendant.

3.   The proximate cause of the incident giving rise to the action was a use or consumption of the product which was for a purpose, in a manner or in an activity other than that which was reasonably foreseeable or was contrary to any express and adequate instructions or warnings appearing on or attached to the product or on its original container or wrapping, if the injured person knew or with the exercise of reasonable and diligent care should have known of such instructions or warnings.

§ 12–684. Indemnification—Tender of defense—Execution. A. In any product liability action where the manufacturer refuses to accept a tender of defense from the seller, the manufacturer shall indemnify the seller for any judgment rendered against the seller and shall also reimburse the seller for reasonable attorneys' fees and costs incurred by the seller in defending such action, unless either paragraph 1 or 2 applies:

1.   The seller had knowledge of the defect in the product.

2.   The seller altered, modified or installed the product, and such alteration, modification or installation was a substantial cause of the incident giving rise to the action, was not authorized or requested by the manufacturer and was not performed in compliance with the directions or specifications of the manufacturer.

B.   If a judgment is rendered in favor of the plaintiff and a seller is granted indemnity against a manufacturer, the plaintiff shall first attempt to satisfy the judgment by levying execution upon the manufacturer in this state or in the state where the manufacturer's principal place of business is located and by making demand upon any liability insurance carrier of the manufacturer whose identity is known to plaintiff before attempting to collect the judgment from the seller or the seller's liability insurance carrier. The return of a writ of execution partially or wholly unsatisfied or the failure of the manufacturer's insurance carrier to pay the judgment upon demand shall be deemed full compliance with the plaintiff's obligation to attempt to collect from the manufacturer.

C.   In any product liability action the manufacturer of the product shall be indemnified by the seller of the product for any judgment rendered against the manufacturer and shall also reimburse the manufacturer for reasonable attorneys' fees and costs incurred in defending such action, if the seller provided the plans or specifications for the manufacturer or preparation of the product and such plans or specifications were a substantial cause of the product's alleged defect and if the product was manufactured in compliance with and according to the plans or specifications of the seller. If a judgment is rendered in favor of the plaintiff and a manufacturer is granted indemnity against a seller, the plaintiff shall first attempt to satisfy the judgment by levying execution upon the seller in this state or in the state where the seller's principal place of business is located and by making demand upon any liability insurance carrier of the seller whose identity is known to plaintiff before attempting to collect the judgment from the manufacturer or manufacturer's liability insurance carrier. The return of a writ of execution partially or wholly unsatisfied or the failure of the seller's insurance carrier to pay the judgment upon demand shall be deemed full compliance with the plaintiff's obligation to attempt to collect from the seller. The provisions of this subsection shall not apply if the manufacturer had knowledge or with the exercise of reasonable and diligent care should have had knowledge of the defect in the product.

§ 12-685. Contents of complaint—Amount of recovery. In any product liability action no dollar amount or figure shall be included in the complaint. The complaint shall pray for such damages as are reasonable in the premises. The complaint shall include a statement reciting that the jurisdictional amount established for filing the action is satisfied.

§ 12-686. Inadmissible evidence—State of the art—Modification. In any product liability action, the following shall not be admissible as direct evidence of a defect:

1. Evidence of advancements or changes in the state of the art subsequent to the time the product was first sold by the defendant.

2. Evidence of any change made in the design or methods of manufacturing or testing the product or any similar product subsequent to the time the product was first sold by the defendant.

§ 12-687. Reasonable remedial measures; cause of action; punitive damages. If a person or entity conducts a product safety analysis or review and, as a result, takes reasonable remedial measures, the following shall apply to a product liability action brought against the person or entity:

1. The plaintiff may not use the product safety analysis or review or the reasonable remedial measures to prove negligence, that the product was defective or unreasonably dangerous, or other culpable conduct in a product liability action. However, the plaintiff may use the product safety analysis or review or reasonable remedial measures for other purposes, such as proving feasibility of precautionary measures, impeachment or to controvert any position taken by a defendant in litigation which is inconsistent with the contents of the product safety analysis or review or reasonable remedial measures.

2. This subsection does not prevent a plaintiff in a product liability action from proving negligence, that the product was defective or unreasonably dangerous, or other culpable conduct by other independent evidence or sources, even if such evidence or sources are mentioned or included in the product safety analysis or review or reasonable remedial measures.

3. The plaintiff may not use the product safety analysis or review or the reasonable remedial measures to prove conduct that would subject the person or entity that caused the product safety analysis or review to be performed to punitive or exemplary damages, unless the plaintiff estab-

lishes that the analysis or review, or the reasonable remedial measures, were undertaken in bad faith or solely for the purpose of affecting the litigation instituted by the plaintiff.

4.   The existence and contents of a product safety analysis or review and any resulting reasonable remedial measures are discoverable and subject to disclosure in a product liability action unless otherwise privileged. However, a portion of a product safety analysis or review may be designated and maintained as confidential and protected from public disclosure pursuant to applicable rules of civil procedures if the portion involves trade secrets as defined in section 44–401, proprietary material or competitively sensitive information. Any dispute as to confidentiality shall be determined by a court following an in camera review of the portion of the analysis or review in question.

§ 12–701. Drugs—Exemplary or punitive damages—Definition.
A. The manufacturer or seller of a drug is not liable for exemplary or punitive damages if the drug alleged to cause the harm either:

1.   was manufactured and labeled in relevant and material respects in accordance with the terms of an approval or license issued by the federal Food and Drug Administration under the Food, Drug and Cosmetic Act (21 United States Code Section 301, et seq.) or the Public Health Service Act (42 United States Code Section 201, et seq.) or

2.   is generally recognized as safe and effective pursuant to conditions established by the federal food and drug administration and applicable regulations, including packaging and labeling regulations.

B.   Subsection A does not apply if the plaintiff proves, by clear and convincing evidence, that the defendant, either before or after making the drug available for public use, knowingly, in violation of applicable federal food and drug administration regulations, withheld from or misrepresented to the administration information known to be material and relevant to the harm which the plaintiff allegedly suffered.

C.   In this section, "drug" means the same as provided in Section 201(g)(1) of the federal food, drug and cosmetic act (21 United States Code Section 321(g)(1)).

CALIFORNIA HEALTH & SAFETY CODE

(1983, concerning firearms and ammunition liability)

§ **1714.4.** (a) In a product liability action, no firearm or ammunition shall be deemed defective in design on the basis that the benefits of the product do not outweigh the risk of injury posed by its potential to cause serious injury, damage, or death when discharged.

(b) For purposes of this section:

(1) The potential of a firearm or ammunition to cause serious injury, damage, or death when discharged does not make the product defective in design.

(2) Injuries or damages resulting from the discharge of a firearm or ammunition are not proximately caused by its potential to cause serious injury, damage, or death, but are proximately caused by the actual discharge of the product.

(c) This section shall not affect a products liability cause of action based upon the improper selection of design alternatives.

(d) This section is declaratory of existing law.

(1987, 1997, 1998 concerning certain inherent dangers)

§ **1714.45.** (a) In a products liability action, a manufacturer or seller shall not be liable if:

(1) The product is inherently unsafe and the product is known to be unsafe by the ordinary consumer who consumes the product with the ordinary knowledge common to the community; and

(2) The product is a common consumer product intended for personal consumption, such as sugar, castor oil, alcohol, and butter, as identified in comment *i* to Section 402A of the *Restatement (Second) of Torts*.

(b) This section does not exempt the manufacture or sale of tobacco products by tobacco manufacturers and their successors in interest from product liability actions, but does exempt the sale or distribution of tobacco products by any other person, including, but not limited to, retailers or distributors.

(c) For purposes of this section, the term "product liability action" means any action for injury or death caused by a product, except that the term does not include an action based on a manufacturing defect or breach of an express warranty.

(d) This section is intended to be declarative of and does not alter or amend existing California law, including *Cronin v. J.B.E. Olson Corp.,* (1972) 8 Cal.3d 121, and shall apply to all product liability actions pending on, or commenced after, January 1, 1988.

(e) This section does not apply to, and never applied to, an action brought by a public entity to recover the value of benefits provided to individuals injured by a tobacco-related illness caused by the tortious conduct of a tobacco company or its successor in interest, including, but not limited to, an action brought pursuant to Section 14124.71 of the Welfare and Institutions Code. In such an action brought by a public entity, the fact that the injured individual's claim against the defendant may be barred by a prior version of this section shall not be a defense. This subdivision does not constitute a change in, but is declaratory of, existing law relating to tobacco products.

(f) It is the intention of the Legislature in enacting the amendments to subdivisions (a) and (b) of this section adopted at the 1997–98 Regular Session to declare that there exists no statutory bar to tobacco-related personal injury, wrongful death, or other tort claims against tobacco manufacturers and their successors in interest by California smokers or others who have suffered or incurred injuries, damages, or costs arising from the promotion, marketing, sale, or consumption of tobacco products. It is also the intention of the Legislature to clarify that such claims which were or are brought shall be determined on their merits, without the imposition of any claim of statutory bar or categorical defense.

(g) This section shall not be construed to grant immunity to a tobacco industry research organization.

CONNECTICUT GENERAL STATUTES
(1982-90)

§ 52-572h. Negligence actions—Doctrines applicable. (a) For purposes of this section: (1) "economic damages" means compensation determined by the trier of fact for pecuniary losses including, but not limited to, the cost of reasonable and necessary medical care, rehabilitative services, custodial care and loss of earnings or earning capacity excluding any noneconomic damages; (2) "noneconomic damages" means compensation determined by the trier of fact for all nonpecuniary losses including, but not limited to, physical pain and suffering and mental or emotional pain and suffering; (3) "recoverable economic damages" means the economic damages reduced by any applicable findings including, but not limited to, set-offs, credits, comparative negligence, additur and remittitur, and any reduction provided by section 52-225a, as amended by section 4 of this Act; (4) "recoverable noneconomic damages" means the noneconomic damages reduced by any applicable findings including but not limited to set-offs, credits, comparative negligence, additur and remittitur.

(b) In causes of action based on negligence, contributory negligence shall not bar recovery in an action by any person or his legal representative to recover damages resulting from personal injury, wrongful death or damage to property if the negligence was not greater than the combined negligence of the person or persons against whom recovery is sought including settled or released persons under subsection (n) of this section. The economic or noneconomic damages allowed shall be diminished in the proportion of the percentage of negligence attributable to the person recovering which percentage shall be determined pursuant to subsection (f) of this section.

(c) In a negligence action to recover damages resulting from personal injury, wrongful death or damage to property occurring on or after October 1, 1987, if the damages are determined to be proximately caused by the negligence of more than one party, each party against whom recovery is allowed shall be liable to the claimant only for his proportionate share of the recoverable economic damages and the recoverable noneconomic damages except as provided in subsection (g) of this section.

(d) The proportionate share of damages for which each party is liable is calculated by multiplying the recoverable economic damages and the recoverable noneconomic damages by a fraction in which the numerator is the party's percentage of negligence, which percentage shall be determined pursuant to subsection (f) of this section, and the denominator is the total of the percentages of negligence, which percentages shall be determined pursuant to subsection (f) of this section, to be attributable to all parties whose negligent actions were a proximate cause of the injury, death or damage to property including settled or released parties under subsection (n) of this section. Any percentage of negligence attributable to the claimant shall not be included in the denominator of the fraction.

(e) In any action to which this section is applicable, the instructions to the jury given by the court shall include an explanation of the effect on awards and liabilities of the percentage of negligence found by the jury to be attributable to each party.

(f) The jury or, if there is no jury, the court shall specify: (1) The amount of economic damages; (2) the amount of noneconomic damages; (3) any findings of fact necessary for the court to specify recoverable economic damages and recoverable noneconomic damages; (4) the percentage of negligence that proximately caused the injury, death or damage to property in relation to one hundred per cent, that is attributable to each party whose negligent actions were a proximate cause of the injury, death or damage to property including settled or released persons under subsection (n) of this section; and (5) the percentage of such negligence attributable to the claimant.

(g)(1) Upon motion by the claimant to open the judgment filed, after good faith efforts by the claimant to collect from a liable defendant, not later than one year after judgment becomes final through lapse of time or through exhaustion of appeal, whichever occurs later, the court shall determine whether all or part of a defendant's proportionate share of the recoverable economic damages and recoverable noneconomic damages is uncollectible from that party, and shall reallocate such uncollectible amount among the other defendants in accordance with the provisions of this subsection. (2) The court shall order that the portion of such uncollectible amount which represents recoverable noneconomic damages be reallocated among the other defendants according to their percentages of negligence, provided that the court shall not reallocate to any such defendant an amount greater than that defendant's percentage of negligence multiplied by such uncollectible amount. (3) The court shall order that the portion of such uncollectible amount which represents recoverable economic damages be reallocated among the other defendants. The court shall reallocate to any such other defendant an amount equal to such uncollectible amount of recoverable economic damages multiplied by a fraction in which the numerator is such defendant's percentage of negligence and the denominator is the total of the percentages of negligence of all defendants, excluding any defendant whose liability is being reallocated. (4) The defendant whose liability is reallocated is nonetheless subject to contribution pursuant to subsection (h) of this section and to any continuing liability to the claimant on the judgment.

(h)(1) A right of contribution exists in parties who, pursuant to subsection (g) of this section are required to pay more than their proportionate share of such judgment. The total recovery by a party seeking contribution shall be limited to the amount paid by such party in excess of such party's proportionate share of such judgment.

(2) An action for contribution shall be brought within two years after the party seeking contribution has made the final payment in excess of his proportionate share of the claim.

(i) This section shall not limit or impair any right of subrogation arising from any other relationship.

(j) This section shall not impair any right to indemnity under existing law. Where one tortfeasor is entitled to indemnity from another, the right of the indemnitee is for indemnity and not contribution, and the indemnitor is not entitled to contribution from the indemnitee for any portion of his indemnity obligation.

(k) This section shall not apply to breaches of trust or of other fiduciary obligation.

(l) The legal doctrines of last clear chance and assumption of risk in actions to which this section is applicable are abolished.

(m) The family car doctrine shall not be applied to impute contributory or comparative negligence pursuant to this section to the owner of any motor vehicle or motor boat.

(n) A release, settlement or similar agreement entered into by a claimant and a person discharges that person from all liability for contribution, but it does not discharge any other persons liable upon the same claim unless it so provides. However, the total award of damages is reduced by the amount of the released person's percentage of negligence determined in accordance with subsection (f) of this section.

§ 52–572l. Strict tort liability, contributory negligence and comparative negligence not bar to recovery. In causes of action based on strict tort liability, contributory negligence or comparative negligence shall not be a bar to recovery. The provisions of this section shall apply to all actions pending on or brought after June 7, 1977, claiming strict tort liability notwithstanding the date on which the cause of action accrued. Nothing in this section shall be construed as barring the defense of misuse of the product or the defense of knowingly using the product in a defective condition in an action based on strict tort liability.

§ 52–572m. Product liability actions—Definitions. As used in this section and sections 52–240a, 52–572n to 52–572r, inclusive, and 52–577a, as amended by sections 243 to 245, inclusive, and 247 of this act:

(a) "Product seller" means any person or entity, including a manufacturer, wholesaler, distributor or retailer who is engaged in the business of selling such products whether the sale is for resale or for use or consumption. The term "product seller" also includes lessors or bailors of products who are engaged in the business of leasing or bailment of products.

(b) "Product liability claim" includes all claims or actions brought for personal injury, death or property damage caused by the manufacture, construction, design, formula, preparation, assembly, installation, testing, warnings, instructions, marketing, packaging or labeling of any product. "Product liability claim" shall include, but is not limited to, all actions based on the following theories: strict liability in tort; negligence; breach of or failure to discharge a duty to warn or instruct, whether negligent or innocent; misrepresentation or nondisclosure, whether negligent or innocent.

(c) "Claimant" means a person asserting a product liability claim for damages incurred by the claimant or one for whom the claimant is acting in a representative capacity.

(d) "Harm" includes damage to property, including the product itself, and personal injuries including wrongful death. As between commercial parties, "harm" does not include commercial loss.

(e) "Manufacturer" includes product sellers who design, assemble, fabricate, construct, process, package or otherwise prepare a product or component part of a product prior to its sale to a user or consumer. It includes a product seller or entity not otherwise a manufacturer that holds itself out as a manufacturer.

§ 52–572n. Product liability claims. (a) A product liability claim as provided in sections 52–240a, 52–240b, 52–572m to 52–572r, inclusive, and 52–577a may be asserted and shall be in lieu of all other claims against product sellers, including actions of negligence, strict liability and warranty, for harm caused by a product.

(b) A claim may be asserted successfully under said sections notwithstanding the claimant did not buy the product from or enter into any contractual relationship with the product seller.

(c) As between commercial parties, commercial loss caused by a product is not harm and may not be recovered by a commercial claimant in a product liability claim. An action for commercial loss caused by a product may be brought only under, and shall be governed by, title 42a, the Uniform Commercial Code.

§ 52–572o. Comparative responsibility—Award of damages—Action for contribution. (a) In any claim under sections 52–240a, 52–240b, 52–572m to 52–572r, inclusive, or 52–577a, the comparative responsibility of, or attributed to, the claimant, shall not bar recovery but shall diminish the award of compensatory damages proportionately, according to the measure of responsibility attributed to the claimant.

(b) In any claim involving comparative responsibility, the court may instruct the jury to give answers to special interrogatories, or if there is no jury, the court may make its own findings, indicating (1) the amount of damages each claimant would receive if comparative responsibility were disregarded, and (2) the percentage of responsibility allocated to each party, including the claimant, as compared with the combined responsibility of all parties to the action. For this purpose, the court may decide that it is appropriate to treat two or more persons as a single party.

(c) In determining the percentage of responsibility, the trier of fact shall consider, on a comparative basis, both the nature and quality of the conduct of the party.

(d) The court shall determine the award for each claimant according to these findings and shall enter judgment against parties liable on the basis of the common law joint and several liability of joint tortfeasors. The judgment shall also specify the proportionate amount of damages allocated against each party liable, according to the percentage of responsibility established for such party.

(e) If a judgment has been rendered, any action for contribution must be brought within one year after the judgment becomes final. If no judgment has been rendered, the person bringing the action for contribution either must have (1) discharged by payment the common liability within the period of the statute of limitations applicable to the right of action of the claimant against him and commenced the action for contribution within one year after payment, or (2) agreed while action was pending to discharge the common liability and, within one year after the agreement, have paid the liability and brought an action for contribution.

§ 52–572p. Limitation of liability of product seller. (a) A product seller shall not be liable for harm that would not have occurred but for the fact that his product was altered or modified by a third party unless: (1) The alteration or modification was in accordance with the instructions or specifications of the product seller; (2) the alteration or modification was made with the consent of the product seller; or (3) the alteration or modification was the result of conduct that reasonably should have been anticipated by the product seller.

(b) For the purposes of this section, alteration or modification includes changes in the design, formula, function or use of the product from that originally designed, tested or intended by the product seller.

§ 52–572q. Liability of product seller—Adequate warnings or instructions. (a) A product seller may be subject to liability for harm caused to a claimant who proves by a fair preponderance of the evidence that the product was defective in that adequate warnings or instructions were not provided.

(b) In determining whether instructions or warnings were required and, if required, whether they were adequate the trier of fact may consider: (1) The likelihood that the product would cause the harm suffered by the claimant; (2) the ability of the product seller to anticipate at the time of manufacture that the expected product user would be aware of the product risk, and the nature of the potential harm; and (3) the technological feasibility and cost of warnings and instructions.

(c) In claims based on this section, the claimant shall prove by a fair preponderance of the evidence that if adequate warnings or instructions had been provided, the claimant would not have suffered the harm.

(d) A product seller may not be considered to have provided adequate warnings or instructions unless they were devised to communicate with the person best able to take or recommend precautions against the potential harm.

(1995; concerning apportionment of liability)

§ 52–102(b) (a) A defendant in any civil action to which section 52–572h of the general statutes applies may serve a writ, summons and complaint upon a person not a party to the action who is or may be liable pursuant to said section for a proportionate share of the plaintiff's damages in which case the demand for relief shall seek an apportionment of liability. Any such writ, summons and complaint, hereinafter called the apportionment complaint, shall be served within one hundred twenty days of the return date specified in the plaintiff's original complaint. The defendant filing an apportionment complaint shall serve a copy of such apportionment complaint on all parties to the original action in accordance with the rules of practice of the superior court on or before the return date specified in the apportionment complaint. The person upon whom the apportionment complaint is served, hereinafter called the apportionment defendant, shall be a party for all purposes, including all purposes under section 52–572h of the general statutes.

(b) The apportionment complaint shall be equivalent in all respects to an original writ, summons and complaint, except that it shall include the docket number assigned to the original action and no new entry fee shall be imposed. The apportionment defendant shall have available to him all remedies available to an original defendant including the right to assert defenses, set-offs or counterclaims against any party. If the apportionment complaint is served within the time period specified in subsection (a) of this section, no statute of limitation or repose shall be a defense or bar to such claim for apportionment, except that, if the action against the defendant who instituted the apportionment complaint pursuant to subsection (a) of this section is subject to such a defense or bar, the apportionment defendant may plead such a defense or bar to any claim brought by the plaintiff directly against the apportionment defendant pursuant to subsection (d) of this section.

(c) No person who is immune from liability shall be made an apportionment defendant nor shall such person's liability be considered for apportionment purposes pursuant to section 52–572h of the general statutes. If a defendant claims that the negligence of any person, who was not made a party to the action, was a proximate cause of the plaintiff's injuries or damage and the plaintiff has previously settled or released the plaintiff's claims against such person, then a defendant may cause such person's liability to be apportioned by filing a notice specifically identifying such person by name and last known address and the fact that the plaintiff's claims against such person have been settled or released. Such notice shall also set forth the factual basis of the defendant's claim that the negligence of such person was a proximate cause of the plaintiff's injuries or damages.

No such notice shall be required if such person with whom the plaintiff settled or whom the plaintiff released was previously a party to the action.

(d) Notwithstanding any applicable statute of limitation or repose, the plaintiff may, within sixty days of the return date of the apportionment complaint served pursuant to subsection (a) of this section, assert any claim against the apportionment defendant arising out of the transaction or occurrence that is the subject matter of the original complaint.

(e) When a counterclaim is asserted against a plaintiff, he may cause a person not a party to the action to be brought in as an apportionment defendant under circumstances which under this section would entitle a defendant to do so.

(f) This section shall be the exclusive means by which a defendant may add a person who is or may be liable pursuant to section 52–572h of the general statutes for a proportionate share of the plaintiff's damages as a party to the action.

(g) In no event shall any proportionate share of negligence determined pursuant to subsection (f) of section 52–572h of the general statutes attributable to an apportionment defendant against whom the plaintiff did not assert a claim be reallocated under subsection (g) of said section. Such proportionate share of negligence shall, however, be included in or added to the combined negligence of the person or persons against whom the plaintiff seeks recovery, including persons with whom the plaintiff settled or whom the plaintiff released under subsection (n) of section 52–572h of the general statutes, when comparing any negligence of the plaintiff to other parties and persons under subsection (b) of said section.

(1979)

§ 52–240a. **Award of attorney's fees in product liability action.** If the court determines that the claim or defense is frivolous, the court may award reasonable attorney's fees to the prevailing party in a products liability action.

§ 52–240b. **Punitive damages in product liability actions.** Punitive damages may be awarded if the claimant proves that the harm suffered was the result of the product seller's reckless disregard for the safety of product users, consumers or others who were injured by the product. If the trier of fact determines that punitive damages should be awarded, the court shall determine that amount of damages not to exceed an amount equal to twice the damages awarded to the plaintiff.

(1991, concerning AIDS vaccine)

§ 19a–591. **Definitions.** As used in sections 19a–591 to 19a–591c, inclusive:

(1) "AIDS vaccine" means a vaccine which has been developed by a manufacturer, is being tested and administered at a research institution for

purposes of determining whether it provides immunity to acquired immune deficiency syndrome or is of therapeutic benefit to persons or fetuses infected with the acquired immune deficiency syndrome virus, and for which an investigational new drug application is on file with the federal Food and Drug Administration and is in effect.

(2) "Manufacturer" means any person who is domiciled or has his principal place of business in this state and has developed an AIDS vaccine.

(3) "Research institution" means a hospital which is accredited by the Joint Commission on the Accreditation of Healthcare Organizations, or a recognized medical school which operates, or is affiliated with, or is operated by an accredited hospital.

(4) "Research subject" means a person who is administered an AIDS vaccine, or a fetus of a person administered an AIDS vaccine, or a child born to a person administered an AIDS vaccine.

(5) "Researcher" means a person employed by or affiliated with a manufacturer or a research institution, who participates in the development or testing or administration of an AIDS vaccine, or who is involved in the diagnosis and treatment of a research subject.

§ 19–591a. Administration of AIDS vaccine. A manufacturer, research institution or researcher shall, prior to the administration of an AIDS vaccine to a person, provide a written explanation of the immunity provisions of section 19a–591b to such person and obtain such person's informed consent. A parent or legal guardian of a child may give informed consent for such child. A copy of the informed consent shall be maintained with such person's medical records.

§ 19–591b. Immunity from liability for civil damages for personal injury to research subject. Exceptions. A manufacturer, research institution or researcher shall not be liable to a research subject for civil damages for personal injury resulting from the administration of any AIDS vaccine to such research subject, unless such injury was caused by the gross negligence or reckless, wilful or wanton misconduct of such manufacturer, research institution or researcher or such manufacturer, research institution or researcher has failed to comply with the provisions of section 19–591a. The immunity provided by this section shall not apply to a manufacturer, research institution or researcher who intentionally provided false information in connection with an investigational new drug application.

§ 19–591c. Research subjects. No person shall be denied the opportunity to be a research subject because of the inability to pay for medical treatment.

DISTRICT OF COLUMBIA CODE ANNOTATED

ILLEGAL FIREARM SALE AND DISTRIBUTION STRICT LIABILITY ACT OF 1992

§ 6–2381. Definitions. For the purposes of this act, the term:

(1) "Dealer" means:

(A) Any person engaged in the business of selling firearms at wholesale or retail;

(B) Any person engaged in the business of repairing firearms or of making or fitting special barrels, stocks, or trigger mechanisms to firearms; or

(C) Any person who is a pawnbroker who takes or receives by way of pledge or pawn, any firearm as security for the payment or repayment of money.

(2) "Engaged in the business" means:

(A) A person who devotes time, attention, and labor to dealing in firearms as a regular course of trade or business with the principal objective of livelihood and profit through the repetitive purchase and resale of firearms. The term "engaged in business" shall not include a person who makes occasional sales, exchanges, or purchases of firearms for the enhancement of a personal collection or for a hobby, or who sells all or part of this personal collection of firearms; or

(B) A person who devotes time, attention, and labor to importing firearms as a regular course of trade or business with the principal objective of livelihood and profit through the sale or distribution of the firearms imported.

(3) "Firearm" shall have the same meaning as in paragraph 9 of section 101 of the Firearms Control Regulations Act of 1975, effective September 24, 1976 (D.C.Law 1–85; D.C.Code § 6–2302(9)).

(4) "Illegal sale" means:

(A) Failure to establish proof of the purchaser's residence in a jurisdiction where the purchase of the weapon is legal or ignoring proof of the purchaser's residence in the District of Columbia;

(B) Failure to comply with District of Columbia registration and waiting requirements prior to delivery of the firearm to the purchaser when proof of District of Columbia residence is provided;

(C) Failure to maintain full, complete, and accurate records of firearm sales as required by local, state, and federal law; or

(D) Knowingly and willfully maintaining false records with the intent to misrepresent the name and address of persons purchasing firearms, or the type of firearm sold to those persons.

(5) "Importer" means any person engaged in the business of importing or bringing firearms or ammunition into the United States for purposes of sale or distribution.

(6) "Law enforcement agency" means a federal, state, or local law enforcement agency, state militia, or an agency of the United States government.

(7) "Law enforcement officer" means any employee or agent of a law enforcement agency who is authorized to use a firearm in the course of employment.

(8) "Manufacturer" means any person in business to manufacture or assemble a firearm or ammunition for sale or distribution.

(9) "Pawnbroker" means any person whose business or occupation includes the taking or receiving, by way of pledge or pawn, of any firearm as security for the payment or repayment of money.

§ 6–2382. Liability. (a) Any manufacturer, importer, or dealer of a firearm who can be shown by a preponderance of the evidence to have knowingly and willfully engaged in the illegal sale of a firearm shall be held strictly liable in tort, without regard to fault and without regard to either: (1) an intent to interfere with a legally protected interest, or (2) a breach of duty to exercise reasonable care, for all direct and consequential damages that arise from bodily injury or death if the bodily injury or death proximately results from the discharge of the firearm in the District of Columbia, regardless of whether or not the person operating the firearm is the original, illegal purchaser.

(b) Any individual who can be shown by a preponderance of the evidence to have knowingly and willfully engaged in the illegal sale, loan, lease, or rental of a firearm for money or anything of value shall be held strictly liable in tort, without regard to fault and without regard to either: (1) an intent to interfere with a legally protected interest, or (2) a breach of duty to exercise reasonable care, for all direct and consequential damages that arise from bodily injury or death if the bodily injury or death proximately results from the discharge of the firearm in the District of Columbia regardless of whether or not the person operating the firearm is the original, illegal purchaser.

(c) Nothing in this act shall relieve from liability any person who commits a crime, is negligent, or who might otherwise be liable for acts committed with the firearm.

§ 6–2383. Exemptions. (a) No firearm originally distributed to a law enforcement agency or a law enforcement officer shall provide the basis for liability under this act.

(b) No action may be brought pursuant to this act by a person who can be shown by a preponderance of the evidence to have committed a self-inflicted injury or by a person injured by a firearm while committing a crime, attempting to commit a crime, engaged in criminal activity, or engaged in a delinquent act.

(c) No action may be brought pursuant to this act by a person who can be shown by a preponderance of the evidence to be engaged in the sale or distribution of illegal narcotics.

(d) No action may be brought pursuant to this act by a person who either: (1) assumed the risk of the injury that occurred, or (2) negligently contributed to the injury that occurred.

§ 6–2384. Firearms Bounty Fund. (a) There is established a fund to be known as the Firearms Bounty Fund ("Fund") to be administered by the Metropolitan Police Department. The Fund shall be operated as a proprietary fund and shall consist of monies appropriated to the Fund, federal grants to the Fund, or private monies donated to the Fund.

(b) Disbursements from the Fund shall be used exclusively for the payment of cash rewards to persons who provide District of Columbia law enforcement agencies with tips that lead to the adjudication or conviction of:

(1) A person or entity engaged in the illegal sale, rental, lease, or loan of a firearm in exchange for money or other thing of value; or

(2) A person who has committed a crime with a firearm.

(c) The amount of each cash reward shall be determined at the discretion of the Chief of the Metropolitan Police Department and the cash reward may range up to $100,000 per tip.

(d) The Chief of the Metropolitan Police Department shall report annually to the Mayor and Council all income and expenditures of the Fund.

(e) The Mayor, by a proposed notice to the Council, may terminate the Fund if the Mayor determines that the Fund is no longer necessary to pay cash rewards.

(f) If monies exist in the Fund at the time of its termination, the monies shall be deposited in the General Fund of the District of Columbia.

(g) The proposed notice to terminate the fund shall be submitted to the Council for a 45–day period of review, excluding Saturdays, Sundays, legal holidays, and days of Council recess. If the Council does not approve or disapprove by resolution within the 45–day review period, the proposed notice to terminate the Fund shall be deemed approved.

ASSAULT WEAPON MANUFACTURING STRICT LIABILITY ACT OF 1990 and 1994

§ 6–2391. Definitions. For the purposes of this act, the term:

(1) "Assault weapon" includes:

(A) The following weapons:

(i) Norinco, Mitchell, and Poly Technologies Avtomat Kalashnikovs (all models);

(ii) Action Arms Israeli Military Industries UZI and Galil;

(iii) Beretta AR–70 (SC–70);

(iv) Colt AR–15 and CAR–15;

(v) Fabrique Nationale FN/FAL, FN/LAR, and FNC;

(vi) MAC 10 and MAC 11;

(vii) Steyr AUG;

(viii) INTRATEC TEC–9; and

(ix) Street Sweeper and Striker 12.

(2) "Handgun" means a firearm with a barrel less than 12 inches in length at the time of manufacture.

(3) "Dealer" and "importer" shall have the same meaning as in section 902 of the Gun Control Act of 1968, approved June 19, 1968 (82 Stat. 226; 18 U.S.C. 921).

(4) "Machine gun" shall have the same meaning as in section 101 of the Firearms Control Regulations Act of 1975, effective September 24, 1976 (D.C.Law 1–85; D.C.Code, sec. 6–2302(10)).

(5) "Manufacturer" means any person in business to manufacture or assemble a firearm or ammunition for sale or distribution.

(6) "Law enforcement agency" means a federal, state, or local law enforcement agency, state militia, or an agency of the United States government.

(7) "Law enforcement officer" means any officer or agent of an agency defined in paragraph (6) of this section who is authorized to use a handgun or machine gun in the course of his or her work.

§ 6–2392. Liability. Any manufacturer, importer, or dealer of an assault weapon or machine gun shall be held strictly liable in tort, without regard to fault or proof of defect, for all direct and consequential damages that arise from bodily injury or death if the bodily injury or death proximately results from the discharge of the assault weapon or machine gun in the District of Columbia.

§ 6–2393. Exemptions. (a) No assault weapon originally distributed to a law enforcement agency or a law enforcement officer shall provide the basis for liability under this act.

(b) No action may be brought pursuant to this act by a person injured by an assault weapon while committing a crime.

(c) This section shall not operate to limit in scope any cause of action, other than that provided by this act, available to a person injured by an assault weapon.

(d) Any defense that is available in a strict liability action shall be available as a defense under this act.

(e) Recovery shall not be allowed under this act for a self-inflicted injury that results from a reckless, wanton, or willful discharge of an assault weapon.

Idaho Code
(1980 and (§ 6–1410) 1986)

§ 6–1401. Scope. The previous existing applicable law of this state on product liability is modified only to the extent set forth in this act.

§ 6–1402. Definitions. (1) "Product seller" means any person or entity that is engaged in the business of selling products, whether the sale is for resale, or for use or consumption. The term includes a manufacturer, wholesaler, distributor, or retailer of the relevant product. The term also includes a party who is in the business of leasing or bailing such products. The term "product seller" does not include:

(a) A provider of professional services who utilizes or sells products within the legally authorized scope of its professional practice. A nonprofessional provider of services is not included unless the sale or use of a product is the principal part of the transaction, and the essence of the relationship between the seller and purchaser is not the furnishing of judgment, skill, or services;

(b) A commercial seller of used products who resells a product after use by a consumer or other product user, provided the used product is in essentially the same condition as when it was acquired for resale; and

(c) A finance lessor who is not otherwise a product seller. A "finance lessor" is one who acts in a financial capacity, who is not a manufacturer, wholesaler, distributor, or retailer, and who leases a product without having a reasonable opportunity to inspect and discover defects in the product, under a lease arrangement in which the selection, possession, maintenance, and operation of the product are controlled by a person other than the lessor.

(2) "Manufacturer" includes a product seller who designs, produces, makes, fabricates, constructs, or remanufactures the relevant product or component part of a product before its sale to a user or consumer. It includes a product seller or entity not otherwise a manufacturer that holds itself out as a manufacturer. A product seller acting primarily as a wholesaler, distributor, or retailer of a product may be a "manufacturer" but only to the extent that it designs, produces, makes, fabricates, constructs, or remanufactures the product before its sale.

(3) "Product" means any object possessing intrinsic value, capable of delivery either as an assembled whole or as a component part or parts, and produced for introduction into trade or commerce. Human tissue and organs, including human blood and its components, are excluded from this term. The "relevant product" under this chapter is that product, or its component part or parts, which gave rise to the product liability claim.

(4) "Claimant" means a person or entity asserting a product liability claim, including a wrongful death action, and, if the claim is asserted through or on behalf of an estate, the term includes claimant's decedent. "Claimant" includes any person or entity that suffers harm.

(5) "Reasonably anticipated conduct" means the conduct which would be expected of an ordinary reasonably prudent person who is likely to use the product in the same or similar circumstances.

§ 6-1403. Length of time product sellers are subject to liability.

(1) Useful safe life.

(a) Except as provided in subsection (1)(b) hereof, a product seller shall not be subject to liability to a claimant for harm under this chapter if the product seller proves by a preponderance of the evidence that the harm was caused after the product's "useful safe life" had expired.

"Useful safe life" begins at the time of delivery of the product and extends for the time during which the product would normally be likely to perform or be stored in a safe manner. For the purposes of this chapter, "time of delivery" means the time of delivery of a product to its first purchaser or lessee who was not engaged in the business of either selling such products or using them as component parts of another product to be sold.

(b) A product seller may be subject to liability for harm caused by a product used beyond its useful safe life to the extent that the product seller has expressly warranted the product for a longer period.

(2) Statute of repose.

(a) Generally. In claims that involve harm caused more than ten (10) years after time of delivery, a presumption arises that the harm was caused after the useful safe life had expired. This presumption may only be rebutted by clear and convincing evidence.

(b) Limitations on statute of repose.

1. If a product seller expressly warrants that its product can be utilized safely for a period longer than ten (10) years, the period of repose, after which the presumption created in subsection (2)(a) hereof arises, shall be extended according to that warranty or promise.

2. The ten (10) year period of repose established in subsection (2)(a) hereof does not apply if the product seller intentionally misrepresents facts about its product, or fraudulently conceals information about it, and that conduct was a substantial cause of the claimant's harm.

3. Nothing contained in subsection (2) of this section shall affect the right of any person found liable under this chapter to seek and obtain contribution or indemnity from any other person who is responsible for harm under this chapter.

4. The ten (10) year period of repose established in subsection (2)(a) hereof shall not apply if the harm was caused by prolonged exposure to a defective product, or if the injury-causing aspect of the product that existed at the time of delivery was not discoverable by an ordinary reasonably prudent person until more than ten (10) years after the time of delivery, or

if the harm, caused within ten (10) years after the time of delivery, did not manifest itself until after that time.

(3) Statute of limitation. No claim under this chapter may be brought more than two (2) years from the time the cause of action accrued as defined in section 5–219, Idaho Code.

§ 6–1404. Comparative responsibility.

Comparative responsibility shall not bar recovery in an action by any person or his legal representative to recover damages for product liability resulting in death or injury to person or property, if such responsibility was not as great as the responsibility of the person against whom recovery is sought, but any damages allowed shall be diminished in the proportion to the amount of responsibility attributable to the person recovering.

§ 6–1405. Conduct affecting comparative responsibility.

(1) Failure to discover a defective condition.

(a) Claimant's failure to inspect. A claimant is not required to have inspected the product for a defective condition. Failure to have done so does not render the claimant responsible for the harm caused or reduce the claimant's damages.

(b) Claimant's failure to observe an obvious defective condition. When the product seller proves by a preponderance of the evidence that the claimant, while using the product, was injured by a defective condition that would have been obvious to an ordinary reasonably prudent person, the claimant's damages shall be subject to reduction.

(c) A nonclaimant's failure to inspect for defects or to observe an obvious defective condition. A nonclaimant's failure to inspect for a defective condition or to observe a defective condition that would have been obvious to an ordinary reasonably prudent person, shall not reduce claimant's damages.

(2) Use of a product with a known defective condition.

(a) By a claimant. When the product seller proves, by a preponderance of the evidence, that the claimant knew about the product's defective condition, and voluntarily used the product or voluntarily assumed the risk of harm from the product, the claimant's damages shall be subject to reduction to the extent that the claimant did not act as an ordinary reasonably prudent person under the circumstances.

(b) By a nonclaimant product user. If the product seller proves by a preponderance of the evidence that a product user, other than the claimant, knew about a product's defective condition, but voluntarily and unreasonably used or stored the product and thereby proximately caused claimant's harm, the claimant's damages shall be subject to apportionment.

(3) Misuse of a product.

(a) "Misuse" occurs when the product user does not act in a manner that would be expected of an ordinary reasonably prudent person who is likely to use the product in the same or similar circumstances.

(b) When the product seller proves, by a preponderance of the evidence, that product misuse by a claimant, or by a party other than the claimant or the product seller has proximately caused the claimant's harm, the claimant's damages shall be subject to reduction or apportionment to the extent that the misuse was a proximate cause of the harm.

(4) Alteration or modification of a product.

(a) "Alteration or modification" occurs when a person or entity other than the product seller changes the design, construction, or formula of the product, or changes or removes warnings or instructions that accompanied or were displayed on the product. "Alteration or modification" of a product includes the failure to observe routine care and maintenance, but does not include ordinary wear and tear.

(b) When the product seller proves, by a preponderance of the evidence, that an alteration or modification of the product by the claimant, or by a party other than the claimant or the product seller has proximately caused the claimant's harm, the claimant's damages shall be subject to reduction or apportionment to the extent that the alteration or modification was a proximate cause of the harm.

This subsection shall not be applicable if:

1. The alteration or modification was in accord with the product seller's instructions or specifications;

2. The alteration or modification was made with the express or implied consent of the product seller; or

3. The alteration or modification was reasonably anticipated conduct, and the product was defective because of the product seller's failure to provide adequate warnings or instructions with respect to the alteration or modification.

§ 6–1406. Relevance of industry custom, safety or performance standards, and technological feasibility. (1) Evidence of changes in (a) a product's design, (b) warnings or instructions concerning the product, (c) technological feasibility, (d) "state of the art," or (e) the custom of the product seller's industry or business, occurring after the product was manufactured and delivered to its first purchaser or lessee who was not engaged in the business of either selling such products or using them as component parts of another product to be sold, is not admissible for the purpose of proving that the product was defective in design or that a warning or instruction should have accompanied the product at the time of manufacture. The provisions of this section shall not relieve the product seller of any duty to warn of known defects discovered after the product was designed and manufactured.

(2) If the court finds outside the presence of a jury that the probative value of such evidence substantially outweighs its prejudicial effect and that there is no other proof available, this evidence may be admitted for other relevant purposes, including but not limited to proving ownership or control, or impeachment.

(3) For purposes of this section, "custom" refers to the practices followed by an ordinary product seller in the product seller's industry or business.

(4) For purposes of this section, "technological feasibility" means the technological, mechanical and scientific knowledge relating to product safety that was reasonably feasible for use, in light of economic practicality, at the time of manufacture.

§ 6–1407. **Individual rights and responsibilities of product sellers other than manufacturers.** (1) In the absence of express warranties to the contrary, product sellers other than manufacturers shall not be subject to liability in circumstances where they do not have a reasonable opportunity to inspect the product in a manner which would or should, in the exercise of reasonable care, reveal the existence of the defective condition which is in issue; or where the product seller acquires the product in a sealed package or container and sells the product in the same sealed package or container. The liability limitation of this subsection shall not apply if:

(a) The product seller had knowledge or reason to know of the defect in the product;

(b) The product seller altered, modified, or installed the product, and such alteration, modification or installation was a substantial proximate cause of the incident giving rise to the action, was not authorized or requested by the manufacturer and was not performed in compliance with the directions or specifications of the manufacturer;

(c) The product seller provided the plans or specifications for the manufacturer or preparation of the product and such plans or specifications were a substantial cause of the product's alleged defect;

(d) The product seller is a wholly-owned subsidiary of the manufacturer, the manufacturer is a wholly-owned subsidiary of the product seller;

(e) The product seller sold the product after the expiration date placed on the product or its package by the manufacturer.

(2) In an action where the liability limitation of subsection (1) applies, any manufacturer who refuses to accept a tender of defense from the product seller, shall indemnify the product seller for reasonable attorney's fees and costs incurred by the product seller in defending such action.

(3) In any product liability action, the manufacturer of the product shall be indemnified by the product seller of the product for any judgment

rendered against the manufacturer and shall also be reimbursed for reasonable attorney's fees and costs incurred in defending such action:

(a) If the product seller provided the plans or specifications for the manufacture or preparation of the product;

(b) If such plans or specifications were a substantial cause of the product's alleged defect; and

(c) If the product was manufactured in compliance with and according to the plans or specifications of the seller.

The provisions of this subsection shall not apply if the manufacturer had knowledge or with the exercise of reasonable and diligent care should have had knowledge of the defect in the product.

(4) A product seller, other than a manufacturer, is also subject to the liability of manufacturer if:

(a) The manufacturer is not subject to service of process under the laws of the claimant's domicile; or

(b) The manufacturer has been judicially declared insolvent in that the manufacturer is unable to pay its debts as they become due in the ordinary course of business; or

(c) The court outside the presence of a jury determines that it is highly probable that the claimant would be unable to enforce a judgment against the product manufacturer.

§ 6-1408. Contents of complaint—Amount of recovery. In any product liability action no dollar amount or figure shall be included in the complaint. The complaint shall pray for such damages as are reasonable in the premises. The complaint shall include a statement reciting that the jurisdictional amount established for filing the action is satisfied.

§ 6-1409. Short title. This act shall be known and may be cited as the "Idaho Product Liability Reform Act."

§ 6-1410. Products liability—Defectiveness of firearms or ammunition. (1) In a products liability action, no firearm or ammunition shall be deemed defective in design on the basis that the benefits of the product do not outweigh the risk of injury posed by its potential to cause serious injury, damage, or death when discharged.

(2) For purposes of this section:

(a) The potential of a firearm or ammunition to cause serious injury, damage, or death when discharged does not make the product defective in design;

(b) Injuries or damages resulting from the discharge of a firearm or ammunition are not proximately caused by its potential to cause serious injury, damage, or death, but are proximately caused by the actual discharge of the product;

(3) The provisions of this section shall not affect a products liability cause of action based upon the improper selection of design alternatives.

ILLINOIS REVISED STATUTES
(1991 and 1995)*

§ 5/2–621. Product liability actions. (a) In any product liability action based on any theory or doctrine commenced or maintained against a defendant or defendants other than the manufacturer, that party shall upon answering or otherwise pleading file an affidavit certifying the correct identity of the manufacturer of the product allegedly causing injury, death or damage. The commencement of a product liability action based in whole or in part on the doctrine of strict liability in tort against said defendant or said defendants shall toll the applicable statute of limitation and statute of repose relative to said defendant or defendants for purposes of asserting a strict liability in tort cause of action.

(b) Once the plaintiff has filed a complaint against the manufacturer or manufacturers, and the manufacturer or manufacturers have or are required to have answered or otherwise pleaded, the court shall order the dismissal of a product liability action based on any theory or doctrine against the certifying defendant or defendants, provided the certifying defendant or defendants are not within the categories set forth in subsection (c) of this Section. Due diligence shall be exercised by the certifying defendant or defendants in providing the plaintiff with the correct identity of the manufacturer or manufacturers, and due diligence shall be exercised by the plaintiff in filing a law suit and obtaining jurisdiction over the manufacturer or manufacturers.

The plaintiff may at any time subsequent to the dismissal move to vacate the order of dismissal and reinstate the certifying defendant or defendants, provided plaintiff can show one or more of the following:

(1) That the applicable period of statute of limitation or statute of repose bars the assertion of a cause of action against the manufacturer or manufacturers of the product allegedly causing the injury, death or damage; or

(2) That the identity of the manufacturer given to the plaintiff by the certifying defendant or defendants was incorrect. Once the correct identity of the manufacturer has been given by the certifying defendant or defendants the court shall again dismiss the certifying defendant or defendants; or

(3) That the manufacturer no longer exists, cannot be subject to the jurisdiction of the courts of this state, or, despite due diligence, the manufacturer is not amenable to service of process; or

---

* The Illinois Civil Justice Reform Act of 1995 has been struck down as unconstitutional by the Illinois Supreme Court in Best v. Taylor Machine Works, 689 N.E.2d 1057 (Ill. 1997). The Court struck several provisions, including § 5/2–1115.1, under the Illinois constitution, and struck the entire statute on grounds of non–severability, including the products liability presumptions and statute of repose. The Illinois legislature remains free to re-enact these severed provisions.

(4) That the manufacturer is unable to satisfy any judgment as determined by the court; or

(5) That the court determines that the manufacturer would be unable to satisfy a reasonable settlement or other agreement with plaintiff.

(c). A court shall not enter a dismissal order relative to any certifying defendant or defendants other than the manufacturer even though full compliance with subsection (a) of this Section has been made where the plaintiff can show one or more of the following:

(1) That the defendant has exercised some significant control over the design or manufacture of the product, or has provided instructions or warnings to the manufacturer relative to the alleged defect in the product which caused the injury, death or damage; or

(2) That the defendant had actual knowledge of the defect in the product which caused the injury, death or damage; or

(3) That the defendant created the defect in the product which caused the injury, death or damage.

(d) Nothing contained in this Section shall be construed to grant a cause of action on any legal theory or doctrine, or to affect the right of any person to seek and obtain indemnity or contribution.

(e) This section applies to all causes of action accruing on or after September 24, 1979.

§ 5/2–623. Certificate of merit; product liability. (a) In a product liability action, as defined in Section 5/2–2101, in which the plaintiff seeks damages for harm, the plaintiff's attorney or the plaintiff, if the plaintiff is proceeding pro se, shall file an affidavit, attached to the original and all copies of the complaint, declaring one of the following:

(1) That the affiant has consulted and reviewed the facts of the case with a qualified expert, as defined in subsection (c), who has completed a written report, after examination of the product or a review of literature pertaining to the product, in accordance with the following requirements:

(A) In an action based on strict liability in tort or implied warranty, the report must:

(i) identify specific defects in the product that have a potential for harm beyond that which would be objectively contemplated by the ordinary user of the product; and

(ii) contain a determination that the product was unreasonably dangerous and in a defective condition when it left the control of the manufacturer.

(b) When the defective condition referred to in the written report required under paragraph (1) of subsection (a) is based on a design defect, the affiant shall further state that the qualified expert, as defined in subsection (c), has identified in the written report required under subsection (a) either: (i) a feasible alternative design that existed at the time the product left the manufacturer's control; or (ii) an applicable government or industry standard to which the product did not conform.

(c) A qualified expert, for the purposes of subsections (a) and (b), is someone who possesses scientific, technical, or other specialized knowledge regarding the product at issue or similar products and who is qualified to prepare the report required by subsections (a) and (b).

(d) A copy of the written report required by subsections (a) and (b) shall be attached to the original and all copies of the complaint. The report shall include the name and address of the expert.

(e) The failure to file an affidavit required by subsections (a) and (b) shall be grounds for dismissal under Section 5/2–619.

(f) Any related allegations concerning healing art malpractice must include an affidavit under Section 5/2–622.

(Part 11. Trial. 1996)

§ 5/2–1115.05. Limitations on recovery of punitive damages in cases other than healing art or legal malpractice cases. (a) In all cases on account of bodily injury, or physical damage to property based on negligence, or product liability based on any theory or doctrine, other than those cases described in Section 2–1115, punitive damages may be awarded only if actual damages are awarded. The amount of punitive damages that may be awarded for a claim in any civil action subject to this Section shall not exceed 3 times the amount awarded to the claimant for the economic damages on which such claim is based.

(b) To recover punitive damages in cases described in subsection (a), a plaintiff must show by clear and convincing evidence that the defendant's conduct was with evil motive or with a reckless and outrageous indifference to a highly unreasonable risk of harm and with a conscious indifference to the rights and safety of others. "Clear and convincing evidence" means that measure or degree of proof that will produce in the mind of the trier of fact a high degree of certainty as to the truth of the allegations sought to be established. This evidence requires a greater degree of persuasion than is necessary to meet the preponderance of the evidence standard.

(c) In any action including a claim for punitive damages, a defendant may request that the issues relating to punitive damages be tried separately from the other issues in the action. If such a request is made, the trier of fact shall first hear evidence relevant to, and render a verdict upon, the defendant's liability for compensatory damages and the amount thereof. If the trier of fact makes an award of actual damages, the same trier of fact shall immediately hear any additional evidence relevant to, and render a verdict upon, the defendant's liability for punitive damages and the amount thereof. If no award of actual damages is made, the claim for punitive damages shall be dismissed. If the defendant requests a separate proceeding concerning liability for punitive damages pursuant to this Section, and the proceeding is held, evidence relevant only to the claim of punitive damages shall be inadmissible in any proceeding to determine whether compensatory damages are to be awarded.

(d) The limitations of subsection (a) shall not apply in a case in which a plaintiff seeks damages against an individual on account of death, bodily injury, or physical damage to property based on any theory or doctrine due to an incident or occurrence for which the individual has been charged and convicted of a criminal act for which a period of incarceration is or may be a part of the sentence.

(e) Nothing in this Section shall be construed to create a right to recover punitive damages.

(f) This amendatory Act of 1995 applies to causes of action accruing on or after its effective date.

§ 5/2–1115.1. Limitations on recovery of non-economic damages.

[In December 1997, the $500,000 cap on non-economic damages was found unconstitutional by the Supreme Court of Illinois in *Best v. Taylor Machine Works*, 689 N.E.2d 1057 (Ill. 1997).]

§ 5/2–1115.2. Economic and non-economic loss. In all actions on account of bodily injury, death, physical damage to property based on negligence, or a product liability action as defined in Section 2–2101, the following terms have the following meanings:

(a) "Economic loss" or "economic damages" means all damages which are tangible, such as damages for past and future medical expenses, loss of income or earnings and other property loss.

(b) "Non-economic loss" or "non-economic damages" means damages which are intangible, including but not limited to damages for pain and suffering, disability, disfigurement, loss of consortium, and loss of society.

(c) "Compensatory damages" or "actual damages" are the sum of economic and non-economic damages.

This amendatory Act of 1995 applies to causes of action filed on or after its effective date.

(Part 21. Product Liability. 1996)

§ 5/2–2101. Definitions. For purposes of this Part, the terms listed have the following meanings:

"Clear and convincing evidence" means that measure or degree of proof that will produce in the mind of the trier of fact a high degree of certainty as to the truth of the allegations sought to be established. This evidence requires a greater degree of persuasion than is necessary to meet the preponderance of the evidence standard.

"Harm" means (i) damage to property other than the product itself; (ii) personal physical injury, illness, or death; (iii) mental anguish or emotional harm to the extent recognized by applicable law; (iv) any loss of consortium or services; or (v) other loss deriving from any type of harm described in item (i), (ii), (iii), or (iv).

"Manufacturer" means (i) any person who is engaged in a business to design or formulate and to produce, create, make, or construct any product or component part of a product; (ii) a product seller with respect to all component parts of a product or a component part of a product that is created or affected when, before placing the product in the stream of commerce, the product seller designs or formulates and produces, creates, makes, or constructs an aspect of a product or a component part of a product made by another; or (iii) any product seller not described in (ii) that holds itself out as a manufacturer to the user of the product.

"Product liability action" means a civil action brought on any theory against a manufacturer or product seller for harm caused by a product.

"Product seller" means a person who, in the course of a business conducted for that purpose, sells, distributes, leases, installs, prepares, blends, packages, labels, markets, repairs, maintains, or otherwise is involved in placing a product in the stream of commerce.

§ 5/2–2103. Federal and State Standards; presumption. In a product liability action, a product or product component shall be presumed to be reasonably safe if the aspect of the product or product component that allegedly caused the harm was specified or required, or if the aspect is specifically exempted for particular applications or users, by a federal or State statute or regulation promulgated by an agency of the federal or State government responsible for the safety or use of the product before the product was distributed into the stream of commerce.

§ 5/2–2104. No practical and feasible alternative design; presumption. If the design of a product or product component is in issue in a product liability action, the design shall be presumed to be reasonably safe unless, at the time the product left the control of the manufacturer, a practical and technically feasible alternative design was available that would have prevented the harm without significantly impairing the usefulness, desirability, or marketability of the product. An alternative design is practical and feasible if the technical, medical, or scientific knowledge relating to safety of the product left the control of the manufacturer, available and developed for commercial use and acceptable in the marketplace.

§ 5/2–2105. Changes in design or warning; inadmissibility. When measures are taken which, if taken previously, would have made an event less likely to occur, evidence of the subsequent measures is not admissible to prove a defect in a product, negligence, or culpable conduct in connection with the event. In a product liability action brought under any theory or doctrine, if the feasibility of a design change or change in warnings is not controverted, then a subsequent design change or change in warnings shall not be admissible into evidence. This rule does not require the exclusion of evidence of subsequent measures when offered for another purpose such as proving ownership, control, or impeachment.

§ 5/2–2106. Provision of written warnings to users of product; nonliability. (a) The warning, instructing, or labeling of a product or specific product component shall be deemed to be adequate if pamphlets, booklets, labels, or other written warnings were provided that gave adequate notice to reasonably anticipated users or knowledgeable intermediaries of the material risks of injury, death, or property damage connected with the reasonably anticipated use of the product and instructions as to the reasonably anticipated uses, applications, or limitations of the product anticipated by the defendant.

(b) In the defense of a product liability action, warnings, instructions or labeling shall be deemed to be adequate if the warnings, instructions or labels furnished with the product were in conformity with the generally recognized standards in the industry at the time the product was distributed into the stream of commerce.

(c) Notwithstanding subsections (a) and (b), a defendant shall not be liable for failure to warn of material risks that were obvious to a reasonably prudent product user and material risks that were a matter of common knowledge to persons in the same position as or similar positions to that of the plaintiff in a product liability action.

(d) In any product liability action brought against a manufacturer or product seller for harm allegedly caused by a failure to provide adequate warnings or instructions, a defendant manufacturer or product seller shall not be liable if, at the time the product left the control of the manufacturer, the knowledge of the danger that caused the harm was not reasonably available or obtainable in light of existing scientific, technical, or medical information.

§ 5/2–2106.5. Inherent characteristics of products; nonliability. In a product liability action, a manufacturer or product seller shall not be liable for harm allegedly caused by a product if the alleged harm was caused by an inherent characteristic of the product which is a generic aspect of the product that cannot be eliminated without substantially compromising the product's usefulness or desirability and which is recognized by the ordinary person with the ordinary knowledge common to the community.

§ 5/2–2107. Punitive damages. In a product liability action, punitive damages shall not be awarded against a manufacturer or product seller if the conduct of the defendant manufacturer, seller, or reseller that allegedly caused the harm was approved by or was in compliance with standards set forth in an applicable federal or State statute or in a regulation or other administrative action promulgated by an agency of the federal or State government responsible for the safety or use of the product, which statute or regulation was in effect at the time of the manufacturer's or product seller's alleged misconduct, unless the plaintiff proves by clear and convincing evidence that the manufacturer or product seller intentionally withheld from or misrepresented to Congress, the State legislature, or the relevant federal or State agency material information relative to the safety or use of the product that would or could have resulted in a changed decision relative to the law, standard, or other administrative action.

§ 5/13–213. Product liability; statute of repose. (a) As used in this Section, the term:

(1) "alteration, modification or change" or "altered, modified, or changed" means an alteration, modification or change that was made in the original makeup characteristics, function or design of a product or in the original recommendations, instructions and warnings given with respect to a product including the failure properly to maintain and care for a product.

(2) "product" means any tangible object or goods distributed in commerce, including any service provided in connection with the product. Where the term "product unit" is used, it refers to a single item or unit of a product.

(3) "product liability action" means any action based on any theory or doctrine brought against the seller of a product on account of personal injury, (including illness, disease, disability and death) or property, economic or other damage allegedly caused by or resulting from the manufacture, construction, preparation, assembly, installation, testing, makeup, characteristics, functions, design, formula, plan, recommendation, specification, prescription, advertising, sale, marketing, packaging, labeling, repair, maintenance or disposal of, or warning or instruction regarding any product. This definition excludes actions brought by State or federal regulatory agencies pursuant to statute.

(4) "seller" means one who, in the course of a business conducted for the purpose, sells, distributes, leases, assembles, installs, produces, manufactures, fabricates, prepares, constructs, packages, labels, markets, repairs, maintains, or otherwise is involved in placing a product in the stream of commerce.

(b) Subject to the provisions of subsections (c) and (d) no product liability action based on any theory or doctrine shall be commenced except within the applicable limitations period and, in any event, within 12 years from the date of first sale, lease or delivery of possession by a seller or 10 years from the date of first sale, lease or delivery of possession to its initial user, consumer, or other non-seller, whichever period expires earlier, of any product unit that is claimed to have injured or damaged the plaintiff, unless the defendant expressly has warranted or promised the product for a longer period and the action is brought within that period.

(c) No product liability action based on any theory or doctrine to recover for injury or damage claimed to have resulted from an alteration, modification or change of the product unit subsequent to the date of first sale, lease or delivery of possession of the product unit to its initial user, consumer or other non-seller shall be limited or barred by subsection (b) hereof if:

(1) the action is brought against a seller making, authorizing, or furnishing materials for the accomplishment of such alteration, modification or change (or against a seller furnishing specifications or instructions for the accomplishment of such alteration, modification or change when the injury is claimed to have resulted from failure to provide adequate specifications or instructions), and

(2) the action commenced within the applicable limitation period and, in any event, within 10 years from the date such alteration, modification or change was made, unless defendant expressly has warranted or promised the product for a longer period and the action is brought within that period, and

(3) when the injury or damage is claimed to have resulted from an alteration, modification or change of a product unit, there is proof that such alteration, modification or change had the effect of introducing into the use of the product unit, by reason of defective materials or workmanship, a hazard not existing prior to such alteration, modification or change.

(d) Notwithstanding the provisions of subsection (b) and paragraph (2) of subsection (c) if the injury complained of occurs within any of the periods provided by subsection (b) and paragraph (2) of subsection (c), the plaintiff may bring an action within 2 years after the date on which the claimant knew, or through the use of reasonable diligence should have known, of the existence of the personal injury, death or property damage, but in no event shall such action be brought more than 8 years after the date on which such personal injury, death or property damage occurred. In any such case, if the person entitled to bring the action was, at the time the personal injury, death or property damage occurred, under the age of 18 years, or under a legal disability, then the period of limitations does not begin to run until the person attains the age of 18 years, or the disability is removed.

(e) Replacement of a component part of a product unit with a substitute part having the same formula or design as the original part shall not be deemed a sale, lease or delivery of possession or an alteration, modification or change for the purpose of permitting commencement of a product liability action based on any theory or doctrine to recovery for injury or damage claimed to have resulted from the formula or design of such product unit or of the substitute part when such action would otherwise be barred according to the provisions of subsection (b) of this Section.

(f) Nothing in this Section shall be construed to create a cause of action or to affect the right of any person to seek and obtain indemnity or contribution.

(g) The provisions of this Section 13–213 of this Act apply to any cause of action accruing on or after January 1, 1979, involving any product which was in or entered the stream of commerce prior to, on, or after January 1, 1979.

INDIANA CODE ANNOTATED

(1998)

Ind. Code § 34–20 is added as a new Article to read as follows [effective July 1, 1998]:

ARTICLE 20. CAUSES OF ACTION: PRODUCTS LIABILITY

Chapter 1. General Provisions. § 1. This article governs all actions that are:

(1) brought by a user or consumer;

(2) against a manufacturer or seller; and

(3) for physical harm caused by a product;

regardless of the substantive legal theory or theories upon which the action is brought.

§ 2. This article shall not be construed to limit any other action from being brought against a seller of a product.

§ 3. If a provision of this article or its application to a person or circumstance is held invalid, the invalidity does not affect other provisions or applications, and to this end the provisions of this article are severable.

§ 4. This article does not apply to a cause of action that accrues before June 1, 1978.

Chapter 2. Product Liability Actions. § 1. Except as provided in section 3 of this chapter, a person who sells, leases, or otherwise puts into the stream of commerce any product in a defective condition unreasonably dangerous to any user or consumer or to the user's or consumer's property is subject to liability for physical harm caused by that product to the user or consumer or to the user's or consumer's property if:

(1) that user or consumer is in the class of persons that the seller should reasonably foresee as being subject to the harm caused by the defective condition;

(2) the seller is engaged in the business of selling the product; and

(3) the product is expected to and does reach the user or consumer without substantial alteration in the condition in which the product is sold by the person sought to be held liable under this article.

§ 2. The rule stated in section 1 of this chapter applies although:

(1) the seller has exercised all reasonable care in the manufacture and preparation of the product; and

(2) the user or consumer has not bought the product from or entered into any contractual relation with the seller.

However, in an action based on an alleged design defect in the product or based on an alleged failure to provide adequate warnings or instructions regarding the use of the product, the party making the claim must establish that the manufacturer or seller failed to exercise reasonable care under the circumstances in designing the product or in providing the warnings or instructions.

§ 3.   A product liability action based on the doctrine of strict liability in tort may not be commenced or maintained against a seller of a product that is alleged to contain or possess a defective condition unreasonably dangerous to the user or consumer unless the seller is a manufacturer of the product or of the part of the product alleged to be defective.

§ 4.   If a court is unable to hold jurisdiction over a particular manufacturer of a product or part of a product alleged to be defective, then that manufacturer's principal distributor or seller over whom a court may hold jurisdiction shall be considered, for the purposes of this chapter, the manufacturer of the product.

Chapter 3. Statute of Limitations. § 1. (a) This section applies to all persons regardless of minority or legal disability. Notwithstanding IC 34–11–6–1, this section applies in any product liability action in which the theory of liability is negligence or strict liability in tort.

(b) Except as provided in section 2 of this chapter, a product liability action must be commenced:

(1) within two (2) years after the cause of action accrues; or

(2) within ten (10) years after the delivery of the product to the initial user or consumer.

However, if the cause of action accrues at least eight (8) years but less than ten (10) years after that initial delivery, the action may be commenced at any time within two (2) years after the cause of action accrues.

§ 2.   (a) A product liability action that is based on:

(1) property damage resulting from asbestos; or

(2) personal injury, disability, disease, or death resulting from exposure to asbestos;

must be commenced within two (2) years after the cause of action accrues. The subsequent development of an additional asbestos related disease or injury is a new injury and is a separate cause of action.

(b) A product liability action for personal injury, disability, disease, or death resulting from exposure to asbestos accrues on the date when the injured person knows that the person has an asbestos related disease or injury.

(c) A product liability action for property damage accrues on the date when the injured person knows that the property damage has resulted from asbestos.

(d) This section applies only to product liability actions against:

(1) persons who mined and sold commercial asbestos; and

(2) funds that have, as a result of bankruptcy proceedings or to avoid bankruptcy proceedings, been created for the payment of asbestos related disease claims or asbestos related property damage claims.

(e) For the purposes of IC 1–1–1–8, if any part of this section is held invalid, the entire section is void.

(f) Except for the cause of action expressly recognized in this section, this section does not otherwise modify the limitation of action or repose period contained in section 1 of this chapter.

Chapter 4. Defective Products. § 1. A product is in a defective condition under this article if, at the time it is conveyed by the seller to another party, it is in a condition:

(1) not contemplated by reasonable persons among those considered expected users or consumers of the product; and

(2) that will be unreasonably dangerous to the expected user or consumer when used in reasonably expectable ways of handling or consumption.

§ 2. A product is defective under this article if the seller fails to:

(1) properly package or label the product to give reasonable warnings of danger about the product; or

(2) give reasonably complete instructions on proper use of the product; when the seller, by exercising reasonable diligence, could have made such warnings or instructions available to the user or consumer.

§ 3. A product is not defective under this article if it is safe for reasonably expectable handling and consumption. If an injury results from handling, preparation for use, or consumption that is not reasonably expectable, the seller is not liable under this article.

§ 4. A product is not defective under this article if the product is incapable of being made safe for its reasonably expectable use, when manufactured, sold, handled, and packaged properly.

Chapter 5. Rebuttable Presumption that Product Is Not Defective. § 1. In a product liability action, there is a rebuttable presumption that the product that caused the physical harm was not defective and that the manufacturer or seller of the product was not negligent if, before the sale by the manufacturer, the product:

(1) was in conformity with the generally recognized state of the art applicable to the safety of the product at the time the product was designed, manufactured, packaged, and labeled; or

(2) complied with applicable codes, standards, regulations, or specifications established, adopted, promulgated, or approved by the United States or by Indiana, or by an agency of the United States or Indiana.

Chapter 6. Defenses. § 1. The defenses in this chapter are defenses to an action brought under this article (or IC 33–1–1.5 before its repeal).

§ **2.**   The burden of proof of any defense raised in an action under this article (or IC 33–1–1.5 before its repeal) is on the party raising the defense.

§ **3.**   It is a defense to an action under this article (or IC 33–1–1.5 before its repeal) that the user or consumer bringing the action:

(1) knew of the defect;

(2) was aware of the danger in the product; and

(3) nevertheless proceeded to make use of the product and was injured.

§ **4.**   It is a defense to an action under this article (or IC 33–1–1.5 before its repeal) that a cause of the physical harm is a misuse of the product by the claimant or any other person not reasonably expected by the seller at the time the seller sold or otherwise conveyed the product to another party.

§ **5.**   It is a defense to an action under this article (or IC 33–1–1.5 before its repeal) that a cause of the physical harm is a modification or alteration of the product made by any person after the product's delivery to the initial user or consumer if the modification or alteration is the proximate cause of physical harm where the modification or alteration is not reasonably expectable to the seller.

Chapter 7. Assessing Liability With Multiple Defendants. § 1. In a product liability action where liability is assessed against more than one (1) defendant, a defendant is not liable for more than the amount of fault, as determined under IC 34–20–8, directly attributable to that defendant. A defendant in a product liability action may not be held jointly liable for damages attributable to the fault of another defendant.

Chapter 8. Assessing Percentage of Fault. § 1. (a) In a product liability action, the fault of the person suffering the physical harm, as well as the fault of all others who caused or contributed to cause the harm, shall be compared by the trier of fact in accordance with IC 34–57–2–7, IC 34–57–2–8, or IC 34–57–2–9.

(b) In assessing percentage of fault, the jury shall consider the fault of all persons who contributed to the physical harm, regardless of whether the person was or could have been named as a party, as long as the nonparty was alleged to have caused or contributed to cause the physical harm.

Chapter 9. Indemnity. § 1. This article does not affect the right of any person who is found liable to seek and obtain indemnity from any other person whose actual fault caused a product to be defective.

KANSAS STATUTES ANNOTATED
(1981–92)

§ 60–3301. Short title. The act shall be known and may be cited as the "Kansas product liability act."

§ 60–3302. Definitions. (a) "Product seller" means any person or entity that is engaged in the business of selling products, whether the sale is for resale, or for use or consumption. The term includes a manufacturer, wholesaler, distributor or retailer of the relevant product, but does not include a health care provider, as defined in subsection (f) of K.S.A. 40–3401 and amendments thereto, who utilizes a product in the course of rendering professional services.

(b) "Manufacturer" includes a product seller who designs, produces, makes, fabricates, constructs, or remanufactures the relevant product or component part of a product before its sale to a user or consumer. It includes a product seller or entity not otherwise a manufacturer that holds itself out as a manufacturer, or that is owned in whole or in part by the manufacturer.

(c) "Product liability claim" includes any claim or action brought for harm caused by the manufacture, production, making, construction, fabrication, design, formula, preparation, assembly, installation, testing, warnings, instructions, marketing, packaging, storage or labeling of the relevant product. It includes, but is not limited to, any action based on strict liability in tort, negligence, breach of express or implied warranty, breach of, or failure to discharge a duty to warn or instruct, whether negligent or innocent, misrepresentation, concealment or nondisclosure, whether negligent or innocent, or under any other substantive legal theory.

(d) "Harm" includes: 1. damage to property; 2. personal physical injuries, illness and death; 3. mental anguish or emotional harm attendant to such personal physical injuries, illness or death. The term "harm" does not include direct or consequential economic loss.

§ 60–3303. Useful safe life, ten-year period of repose, evidence; latent disease exception; reviving certain causes of action. (a)(1) Except as provided in paragraph 2 of this subsection, a product seller shall not be subject to liability in a product liability claim if the product seller proves by a preponderance of the evidence that the harm was caused after the product's "useful safe life" had expired. "Useful safe life" begins at the time of delivery of the product and extends for the time during which the product would normally be likely to perform or be stored in a safe manner. For the purposes of this section, "time of delivery" means the time of delivery of a product to its first purchaser or lessee who was not engaged in the business of either selling such products or using them as component parts of another product to be sold.

Examples of evidence that is especially probative in determining whether a product's useful safe life had expired include:

(A) The amount of wear and tear to which the product had been subject;

(B) the effect of deterioration from natural causes, and from climate and other conditions under which the product was used or stored;

(C) the normal practices of the user, similar users and the product seller with respect to the circumstances, frequency and purposes of the product's use, and with respect to repairs, renewals and replacements;

(D) any representations, instructions or warnings made by the product seller concerning proper maintenance, storage and use of the product or the expected useful safe life of the product; and

(E) any modification or alteration of the product by a user or third party.

(2) A product seller may be subject to liability for harm caused by a product used beyond its useful safe life to the extent that the product seller has expressly warranted the product for a longer period.

(b)(1) In claims that involve harm caused more than 10 years after time of delivery, a presumption arises that the harm was caused after the useful safe life had expired. This presumption may only be rebutted by clear and convincing evidence.

(2)(A) If a product seller expressly warrants that its product can be utilized safely for a period longer than 10 years, the period of repose, after which the presumption created in paragraph 1. of this subsection arises, shall be extended according to that warranty or promise.

(B) The ten-year period of repose established in paragraph 1. of this subsection does not apply if the product seller intentionally misrepresents facts about its product, or fraudulently conceals information about it, and that conduct was a substantial cause of the claimant's harm.

(C) Nothing contained in this subsection shall affect the right of any person liable under a product liability claim to seek and obtain indemnity from any other person who is responsible for the harm which gave rise to the product liability claim.

(D) The ten-year period of repose established in paragraph 1. of this subsection shall not apply if the harm was caused by prolonged exposure to a defective product, or if the injury-causing aspect of the product that existed at the time of delivery was not discoverable by a reasonably prudent person until more than 10 years after the time of delivery, or if the harm caused within 10 years after the time of delivery did not manifest itself until after that time.

(c) Except as provided in subsections (d) and (e), nothing contained in subsections (a) and (b) above shall modify the application of K.S.A. 60–513, and amendments thereto.

(d)(1) In a product liability claim against the product seller, the ten-year limitation, as defined in K.S.A. 60–513, and amendments thereto, shall not apply to the time to discover a disease which is latent caused by exposure to a harmful material, in which event the action shall be deemed to have accrued when the disease and such disease's cause have been made known to the person or at the point the person should have been aware of the disease and such disease's cause.

(2) The term "harmful material" means silicone gel breast implants, which were implanted prior to July 1, 1992; any chemical substances commonly known as asbestos, dioxins, or polychlorinated biphenyls, whether alone or as part of any product, or any substance which is determined to present an unreasonable risk of injury to health or the environment by the United States Environmental Protection Agency pursuant to the Federal Toxic Substances Control Act, 15 U.S.C. § 2601 et seq., or the state of Kansas, and because of such risk is regulated by the state or the Environmental Protection Agency.

(e) Upon the effective date of this act through July 1, 1991, the provisions of this subsection shall revive such causes of action for latent diseases caused by exposure to a harmful material for: (1) Any person whose cause of action had accrued, as defined in subsection (d) on or after March 3, 1987; or (2) any person who had an action pending in any court on March 3, 1989, and because of the judicial interpretation of the ten-year limitation contained in subsection (b) of K.S.A. 60–513, and amendments thereto, as applied to latent disease caused by exposure to a harmful material the: (A) action was dismissed; (B) dismissal of the action was affirmed; or (C) action was subject to dismissal. The intent of this subsection is to revive causes of action for latent diseases caused by exposure to a harmful material which were barred by interpretation of K.S.A. 60–513, and amendments thereto, in effect prior to this enactment.

§ 60–3304. Legislative regulatory standards or administrative regulatory safety standards or mandatory government contract specifications—Defenses. (a) When the injury-causing aspect of the product was, at the time of manufacture, in compliance with legislative regulatory standards or administrative regulatory safety standards relating to design or performance, the product shall be deemed not defective by reason of design or performance, or, if the standard addressed warnings or instructions, the product shall be deemed not defective by reason of warnings or instructions, unless the claimant proves by a preponderance of the evidence that a reasonably prudent product seller could and would have taken additional precautions.

(b) When the injury-causing aspect of the product was not, at the time of manufacture, in compliance with legislative regulatory standards or administrative regulatory safety standards relating to design, performance, warnings or instructions, the product shall be deemed defective unless the product seller proves by a preponderance of the evidence that its failure to comply was a reasonably prudent course of conduct under the circumstances.

(c) When the injury-causing aspect of the product was, at the time of manufacture, in compliance with a mandatory government contract specification relating to design, this shall be an absolute defense and the product shall be deemed not defective for that reason, or, if the specification related to warnings or instructions, then the product shall be deemed not defective for that reason.

(d) When the injury-causing aspect of the product was not, at the time of manufacture, in compliance with a mandatory government contract specification relating to design, the product shall be deemed defective for that reason, or if the specification related to warnings or instructions, the product shall be deemed defective for that reason.

§ 60–3305. Manufacturer's or seller's duty to warn or protect against danger, when. In any product liability claim any duty on the part of the manufacturer or seller of the product to warn or protect against a danger or hazard which could or did arise in the use or misuse of such product, and any duty to have properly instructed in the use of such product shall not extend: (a) To warnings, protecting against or instructing with regard to those safeguards, precautions and actions which a reasonable user or consumer of the product, with the training, experience, education and any special knowledge the user or consumer did, should or was required to possess, could and should have taken for such user or consumer or others, under all the facts and circumstances;

(b) to situations where the safeguards, precautions and actions would or should have been taken by a reasonable user or consumer of the product similarly situated exercising reasonable care, caution and procedure; or

(c) to warnings, protecting against or instructing with regard to dangers, hazards or risks which are patent, open or obvious and which should have been realized by a reasonable user or consumer of the product.

§ 60–3306. Seller not subject to liability. A product seller shall not be subject to liability in a product liability claim arising from an alleged defect in a product, if the product seller establishes that: (a) Such seller had no knowledge of the defect;

(b) such seller in the performance of any duties the seller performed, or was required to perform, could not have discovered the defect while exercising reasonable care;

(c) the seller was not a manufacturer of the defective product or product component;

(d) the manufacturer of the defective product or product component is subject to service of process either under the laws of the state of Kansas or the domicile of the person making the product liability claim; and

(e) any judgment against the manufacturer obtained by the person making the product liability claim would be reasonably certain of being satisfied.

§ 60–3307. Inadmissible evidence. (a) In a product liability claim, the following evidence shall not be admissible for any purpose:

(1) Evidence of any advancements or changes in technical or other knowledge or techniques, in design theory or philosophy, in manufacturing or testing knowledge, techniques or processes in labeling, warning of risks or hazards, instructions for the use of such product, if such advancements or changes have been made, learned or placed into common use subsequent to the time the product in issue was designed, formulated, tested, manufactured or sold by the manufacturer; and

(2) evidence of any changes made in the designing, planning, formulating, testing, preparing, manufacturing, packaging, warnings, labeling or instructing for use of, or with regard to, the product in issue, or any similar product, which changes were made subsequent to the time the product in issue was designed, formulated, tested, manufactured or sold by the manufacturer.

(b) This section does not require the exclusion of evidence of a subsequent measure if offered to impeach a witness for the manufacturer or seller of a product who has expressly denied the feasibility of such a measure.

KENTUCKY STATUTES ANNOTATED

(1979)

§ 411.300. Definitions. (1) As used in KRS 411.310 to 411.340, a "product liability action" shall include any action brought for or on account of personal injury, death or property damage caused by or resulting from the manufacture, construction, design, formulation, development of standards, preparation, processing, assembly, testing, listing, certifying, warning, instructing, marketing, advertising, packaging or labeling of any product.

(2) As used in KRS 411.310 to 411.340, a "plaintiff" shall mean a person asserting a claim and, if said claim is asserted on behalf of an estate, "plaintiff" shall include plaintiff's decedent.

§ 411.310. Presumptions in product liability actions. (1) In any product liability action, it shall be presumed, until rebutted by a preponderance of the evidence to the contrary, that the subject product was not defective if the injury, death or property damage occurred either more than five (5) years after the date of sale to the first consumer or more than eight (8) years after the date of manufacture.

(2) In any product liability action, it shall be presumed, until rebutted by a preponderance of the evidence to the contrary, that the product was not defective if the design, methods of manufacture, and testing conformed to the generally recognized and prevailing standards or the state of the art in existence at the time the design was prepared, and the product was manufactured.

§ 411.320. Circumstances under which defendant is liable. (1) In any product liability action, a manufacturer shall be liable only for the personal injury, death or property damage that would have occurred if the product had been used in its original, unaltered and unmodified condition. For the purpose of this section, product alteration or modification shall include failure to observe routine care and maintenance, but shall not include ordinary wear and tear. This section shall apply to alterations or modifications made by any person or entity, except those made in accordance with specifications or instructions furnished by the manufacturer.

(2) In any product liability action, if the plaintiff performed an unauthorized alteration or an unauthorized modification, and such alteration or modification was a substantial cause of the occurrence that caused injury or damage to the plaintiff, the defendant shall not be liable whether or not said defendant was at fault or the product was defective.

(3) In any product liability action, if the plaintiff failed to exercise ordinary care in the circumstances in his use of the product, and such failure was a substantial cause of the occurrence that caused injury or damage to the plaintiff, the defendant shall not be liable whether or not said defendant was at fault or the product was defective.

§ 411.340. When wholesaler, distributor, or retailer to be held liable. In any product liability action, if the manufacturer is identified and subject to the jurisdiction of the court, a wholesaler, distributor, or retailer who distributes or sells a product, upon his showing by a preponderance of the evidence that said product was sold by him in its original manufactured condition or package, or in the same condition such product was in when received by said wholesaler, distributor or retailer, shall not be liable to the plaintiff for damages arising solely from the distribution or sale of such product, unless such wholesaler, distributor or retailer, breached an express warranty or knew or should have known at the time of distribution or sale of such product that the product was in a defective condition, unreasonably dangerous to the user or consumer.

LOUISIANA REVISED STATUTES ANNOTATED

(1988)

§ 2800.51. Short title. This Chapter shall be known and may be cited as the "Louisiana Products Liability Act."

§ 2800.52. Scope of this chapter. This Chapter establishes the exclusive theories of liability for manufacturers for damage caused by their products. A claimant may not recover from a manufacturer for damage caused by a product on the basis of any theory of liability that is not set forth in this Chapter. Conduct or circumstances that result in liability under this Chapter are "fault" within the meaning of Civil Code Article 2315. This Chapter does not apply to the rights of an employee or his personal representatives, dependents or relations against a manufacturer who is the employee's employer or against any principal or any officer, director, stockholder, partner or employee of such manufacturer or principal as limited by R.S. 23:1032, or to the rights of a claimant against the following, unless they assume the status of a manufacturer as defined in R.S. 9:2800.53(1):

(1) Providers of professional services, even if the service results in a product.

(2) Providers of nonprofessional services where the essence of the service is the furnishing of judgment or skill, even if the service results in a product.

(3) Producers of natural fruits and other raw products in their natural state that are derived from animals, fowl, aquatic life or invertebrates, including but not limited to milk, eggs, honey and wool.

(4) Farmers and other producers of agricultural plants in their natural state.

(5) Ranchers and other producers of animals, fowl, aquatic life or invertebrates in their natural state.

(6) Harvesters and other producers of fish, crawfish, oysters, crabs, mollusks or other aquatic animals in their natural state.

§ 2800.53. Definitions. The following terms have the following meanings for the purpose of this Chapter:

(1) "Manufacturer" means a person or entity who is in the business of manufacturing a product for placement into trade or commerce. "Manufacturing a product" means producing, making, fabricating, constructing, designing, remanufacturing, reconditioning or refurbishing a product. "Manufacturer" also means:

(a) A person or entity who labels a product as his own or who otherwise holds himself out to be the manufacturer of the product.

(b) A seller of a product who exercises control over or influences a characteristic of the design, construction or quality of the product that causes damage.

(c) A manufacturer of a product who incorporates into the product a component or part manufactured by another manufacturer.

(d) A seller of a product of an alien manufacturer if the seller is in the business of importing or distributing the product for resale and the seller is the alter ego of the alien manufacturer. The court shall take into consideration the following in determining whether the seller is the alien manufacturer's alter ego: whether the seller is affiliated with the alien manufacturer by way of common ownership or control; whether the seller assumes or administers product warranty obligations of the alien manufacturer; whether the seller prepares or modifies the product for distribution; or any other relevant evidence. A "product of an alien manufacturer" is a product that is manufactured outside the United States by a manufacturer who is a citizen of another country or who is organized under the laws of another country.

(2) "Seller" means a person or entity who is not a manufacturer and who is in the business of conveying title to or possession of a product to another person or entity in exchange for anything of value.

(3) "Product" means a corporeal movable that is manufactured for placement into trade or commerce, including a product that forms a component part of or that is subsequently incorporated into another product or an immovable. "Product" does not mean human blood, blood components, human organs, human tissue or approved animal tissue to the extent such are governed by R.S. 9:2797.

(4) "Claimant" means a person or entity who asserts a claim under this Chapter against the manufacturer of a product or his insurer for damage caused by the product.

(5) "Damage" means all damage caused by a product, including survival and wrongful death damages, for which Civil Code Articles 2315, 2315.1 and 2315.2 allow recovery. "Damage" includes damage to the product itself and economic loss arising from a deficiency in or loss of use of the product only to the extent that Section 3 of Chapter 6 of Title VII of Book III of the Civil Code, entitled "Of the Vices of the Thing Sold," does not allow recovery for such damage or economic loss. Attorneys' fees are not recoverable under this Chapter.

(6) "Express warranty" means a representation, statement of alleged fact or promise about a product or its nature, material or workmanship that represents, affirms or promises that the product or its nature, material or workmanship possesses specified characteristics or qualities or will meet a specified level of performance. "Express warranty" does not mean a general opinion about or general praise of a product. A sample or model of a product is an express warranty.

(7) "Reasonably anticipated use" means a use or handling of a product that the product's manufacturer should reasonably expect of an ordinary person in the same or similar circumstances.

(8) "Reasonably anticipated alteration or modification" means a change in a product that the product's manufacturer should reasonably expect to be made by an ordinary person in the same or similar circumstances, and also means a change arising from ordinary wear and tear. "Reasonably anticipated alteration or modification" does not mean the following:

(a) Alteration, modification or removal of an otherwise adequate warning provided about a product.

(b) The failure of a person or entity, other than the manufacturer of a product, reasonably to provide to the product user or handler an adequate warning that the manufacturer provided about the product, when the manufacturer has satisfied his obligation to use reasonable care to provide the adequate warning by providing it to such person or entity rather than to the product user or handler.

(c) Changes to or in a product or its operation because the product does not receive reasonable care and maintenance.

(9) "Adequate warning" means a warning or instruction that would lead an ordinary reasonable user or handler of a product to contemplate the danger in using or handling the product and either to decline to use or handle the product or, if possible, to use or handle the product in such a manner as to avoid the damage for which the claim is made.

§ 2800.54. Manufacturer responsibility and burden of proof.

A. The manufacturer of a product shall be liable to a claimant for damage proximately caused by a characteristic of the product that renders the product unreasonably dangerous when such damage arose from a reasonably anticipated use of the product by the claimant or another person or entity.

B.   A product is unreasonably dangerous if and only if:

(1) The product is unreasonably dangerous in construction or composition as provided in R.S. 9:2800.55;

(2) The product is unreasonably dangerous in design as provided in R.S. 9:2800.56;

(3) The product is unreasonably dangerous because an adequate warning about the product has not been provided as provided in R.S. 9:2800.57; or

(4) The product is unreasonably dangerous because it does not conform to an express warranty of the manufacturer about the product as provided in R.S. 9:2800.58.

C.   The characteristic of the product that renders it unreasonably dangerous under R.S. 9:2800.55 must exist at the time the product left the control of its manufacturer. The characteristic of the product that renders it unreasonably dangerous under R.S. 9:2800.56 or 9:2800.57 must exist at the time the product left the control of its manufacturer or result from a reasonably anticipated alteration or modification of the product.

D.   The claimant has the burden of proving the elements of Subsections A, B and C of this Section.

§ 2800.55.   **Unreasonably dangerous in construction or composition.** A product is unreasonably dangerous in construction or composition if, at the time the product left its manufacturer's control, the product deviated in a material way from the manufacturer's specifications or performance standards for the product or from otherwise identical products manufactured by the same manufacturer.

§ 2800.56.   **Unreasonably dangerous in design.** A product is unreasonably dangerous in design if, at the time the product left its manufacturer's control:

(1)   There existed an alternative design for the product that was capable of preventing the claimant's damage; and

(2)   The likelihood that the product's design would cause the claimant's damage and the gravity of that damage outweighed the burden on the manufacturer of adopting such alternative design and the adverse effect, if any, of such alternative design on the utility of the product. An adequate warning about a product shall be considered in evaluating the likelihood of damage when the manufacturer has used reasonable care to provide the adequate warning to users and handlers of the product.

§ 2800.57.   **Unreasonably dangerous because of inadequate warning.** A. A product is unreasonably dangerous because an adequate warning about the product has not been provided if, at the time the product left its manufacturer's control, the product possessed a characteristic that may cause damage and the manufacturer failed to use reasonable care to provide an adequate warning of such characteristic and its danger to users and handlers of the product.

B.   A manufacturer is not required to provide an adequate warning about his product when:

(1)   The product is not dangerous to an extent beyond that which would be contemplated by the ordinary user or handler of the product, with the ordinary knowledge common to the community as to the product's characteristics; or

(2)   The user or handler of the product already knows or reasonably should be expected to know of the characteristic of the product that may cause damage and the danger of such characteristic.

C.   A manufacturer of a product who, after the product has left his control, acquires knowledge of a characteristic of the product that may cause damage and the danger of such characteristic, or who would have acquired such knowledge had he acted as a reasonably prudent manufacturer, is liable for damage caused by his subsequent failure to use reasonable care to provide an adequate warning of such characteristic and its danger to users and handlers of the product.

§ 2800.58. Unreasonably dangerous because of nonconformity to express warranty. A product is unreasonably dangerous when it does not conform to an express warranty made at any time by the manufacturer about the product if the express warranty has induced the claimant or another person or entity to use the product and the claimant's damage was proximately caused because the express warranty was untrue.

§ 2800.59. Manufacturer knowledge, design feasibility and burden of proof. A. Notwithstanding R.S. 9:2800.56, a manufacturer of a product shall not be liable for damage proximately caused by a characteristic of the product's design if the manufacturer proves that, at the time the product left his control:

(1) He did not know and, in light of then-existing reasonably available scientific and technological knowledge, could not have known of the design characteristic that caused the damage or the danger of such characteristic; or

(2) He did not know and, in light of then-existing reasonably available scientific and technological knowledge, could not have known of the alternative design identified by the claimant under R.S. 9:2800.56(1); or

(3) The alternative design identified by the claimant under R.S. 9:2800.56(1) was not feasible, in light of then-existing reasonably available scientific and technological knowledge or then-existing economic practicality.

B. Notwithstanding R.S. 9:2800.57(A) or (B), a manufacturer of a product shall not be liable for damage proximately caused by a characteristic of the product if the manufacturer proves that, at the time the product left his control, he did not know and, in light of then-existing reasonably available scientific and technological knowledge, could not have known of the characteristic that caused the damage or the danger of such characteristic.

§ **600.2945.** As used in this section and sections 1629, 2945 to 2949a, and 5805:

(a) "Alteration" means a material change in a product after the product leaves the control of the manufacturer or seller. Alteration includes a change in the product's design, packaging, or labeling; a change to or removal of a safety feature, warning, or instruction; deterioration or damage caused by failure to observe routine care and maintenance or failure to observe an installation, preparation, or storage procedure; or a change resulting from repair, renovation, reconditioning, recycling, or reclamation of the product.

(b) "Drug" means that term as defined in section 201 of the federal food, drug, and cosmetic act, chapter 675, 52.1040, 21 U.S.C. 321. However, drug does not include a medical appliance or device.

(c) "Economic loss" means objectively verifiable pecuniary damages arising from medical expenses or medical care, rehabilitation services, custodial care, loss of wages, loss of future earnings, burial costs, loss of use of property, costs of repair or replacement of property, costs of obtaining substitute domestic services, loss of employment, or other objectively verifiable monetary losses.

(d) "Gross negligence" means conduct so reckless as to demonstrate a substantial lack of concern for whether injury results.

(e) "Misuse" means use of a product in a materially different manner than the product's intended use. Misuse includes uses inconsistent with the specifications and standards applicable to the product, uses contrary to a warning or instruction provided by the manufacturer, seller, or another person possessing knowledge or training regarding the use or maintenance of the product, and uses other than those for which the product would be considered suitable by a reasonably prudent person in the same or similar circumstances.

(f) "Noneconomic loss" means any type of pain, suffering, inconvenience, physical impairment, mental anguish, emotional distress, loss of society and companionship, loss of consortium injury to reputation, humiliation, or other nonpecuniary damages.

(g) "Product" includes any and all component parts to a product.

(h) "Product liability action" means an action based on a legal or equitable, theory of liability brought for the death of a person or for injury to a person or damage to property caused by or resulting from the production of a product.

(i) "Production" means manufacture, construction, design, formulation, development of standards, preparation, processing, assembly, inspection, testing, listing, certifying, warning, instructing, marketing, selling, advertising, packaging, or labeling.

(j) "Sophisticated user" means a person or entity that, by virtue of training, experience, a profession, or legal obligations, is or is generally expected to be knowledgeable about a product's properties, including a potential hazard or adverse effect. An employee who does not have actual knowledge of the product's potential hazard or adverse effect that caused the injury is not a sophisticated user.

§ 600.2946. Products Liability action; admissible evidence. (1) It shall be admissible as evidence in a product liability action that the production of the product was in accordance with the generally recognized and prevailing nongovernmental standards in existence at the time the specific unit of the product was sold or delivered by the defendant to the initial purchaser or user.

(2) In a product liability action brought against a manufacturer or seller for harm allegedly caused by a production defect, the manufacturer or seller is not liable unless the plaintiff establishes that the product was not reasonably safe at the time the specific unit of the product left the control of the manufacturer or seller and that, according to generally accepted production practices at the time the specific unit of the product left the control of the manufacturer or seller, a practical and technically feasible alternative production practice was available that would have prevented the harm without significantly impairing the usefulness or desirability of the product to users and without creating equal or greater risk of harm to others. An alternative production practice is practical and feasible only if the technical, medical, or scientific knowledge relating to production of the product, at the time the specific unit of the product left the control of the manufacturer or seller, was developed, available and capable of use in the production of the product and was economically feasible for use by the manufacturer. Technical, medical, or scientific knowledge is not economically feasible for use by the manufacturer if use of that knowledge in production of the product would significantly compromise the product's usefulness or desirability.

(3) With regard to the production of a product that is the subject of a product liability action, evidence of a philosophy, theory, knowledge, technique, or procedure that is learned, placed in use, or discontinued after the event resulting in the death of the person or injury to the person or property, which if learned, placed in use, or discontinued before the event would have made the event less likely to occur, is admissible only for the purpose of providing the feasibility of precautions, if controverted, or for impeachment.

(4) In a product liability action brought against a manufacturer or seller for harm allegedly caused by a product, there is a rebuttable presumption that the manufacturer or seller is not liable if; at the time the specific unit of the product was sold or delivered to the initial purchaser or

user, the aspect of the product that allegedly caused the harm was in compliance with standards relevant to the event causing the death or injury set forth in a federal or state statute or was approved by, or was in compliance with regulations or standards relevant to the event causing the death or injury promulgated by, a federal or state agency responsible for reviewing the safety of the product. Noncompliance with a standard relevant to the event causing the death or injury set forth in a federal or state statute or lack of approval by, or noncompliance with regulations or standards relevant to the event causing the death or injury promulgated by, a federal or state agency does not raise a presumption of negligence on the part of a manufacturer or seller. Evidence of compliance or noncompliance with a regulation or standard not relevant to the event causing the death or injury is not admissible.

(5) In a product liability action against a manufacturer or seller, a product that is a drug is not defective or unreasonably dangerous, and the manufacturer or seller is not liable, if the drug was approved for safety and efficacy by the United States Food and Drug Administration, and the drug and its labeling were in compliance with the United States food and drug administration's approval at the time the drug left the control of the manufacturer or seller. However, this subsection does not apply to a drug that is sold in the United States after the effective date of an order of the United States food and drug administration to remove the drug from the market or to withdraw its approval. This subsection does not apply if the defendant at any time before the event that allegedly caused the injury does any of the following: (a) Intentionally withholds from or misrepresents to the United States Food and Drug Administration information concerning the drug that is required to be submitted under the federal food, drug, and cosmetic act, chapter 675, 52 Stat. 1040, 21 U.S.C. 301 to 321, 331 to 343–2, 344 to 346a, 347, 348 to 353, 355 to 360, 360b to 376, and 378 to 395, and the drug would not have been approved, or the United States food and drug administration would have withdrawn approval for the drug if the information were accurately submitted.

(b) Makes an illegal payment to an official or employee of the United States Food and Drug Administration for the purpose of securing or maintaining approval of the drug.

§ 600.2946a. Determination of damages; limitation. (1) In an action for product liability, the total amount of damages for noneconomic loss shall not exceed $280,000.00, unless the defect in the product caused either the person's death or permanent loss of a vital bodily function, in which case the total amount of damages for noneconomic loss shall not exceed $500,000.00. On the effective date of the amendatory act that added this section, the state treasurer shall adjust the limitations set forth in this subsection so that the limitations are equal to the limitations provided in section 1483. After that date, the state treasurer shall adjust the limitations set forth in this subsection at the end of each calendar year so that they continue to be equal to the limitations provided in section 1483.

(2) In awarding damages in a product liability action, the trier of fact shall itemize damages into economic and noneconomic losses. Neither the court nor counsel for a party shall inform the jury of the limitations under subsection (1). The court shall adjust an award of noneconomic loss to conform to the limitations under subsection (1).

(3) The limitation on damages under subsection (1) for death or permanent loss of a vital bodily function does not apply to a defendant if the trier of fact determines by a preponderance of the evidence that the death or loss was the result of the defendant's gross negligence, or if the court finds that the matters stated in section 2949a are true.

(4) If damages for economic loss cannot readily be ascertained by the trier of fact, then the trier fact shall calculate damages for economic loss based on an amount that is equal to the state average median family income as reported in the immediately preceding federal decennial census and adjusted by the state treasurer in the same manner as provided in subsection (1).

§ 600.2947. Product liability action; liability of manufacturer or seller. (1) A manufacturer or seller is not liable in a product liability action for harm caused by an alteration of the product unless the alteration was reasonably foreseeable. Whether there was an alteration of a product and whether an alteration was reasonably foreseeable are legal issues to be resolved by the court.

(2) A manufacturer or seller is not liable in a product liability action for harm caused by misuse of a product unless the misuse was reasonably foreseeable. Whether there was misuse of a product and whether misuse was reasonably foreseeable are legal issues to be resolved by the court.

(3) A manufacturer or seller is not liable in a product liability action if the purchaser or user of the product was aware that use of the product created an unreasonable risk of personal injury and voluntarily exposed himself or herself to that risk and the risk that he or she exposed himself or herself to was the proximate cause of the injury. This subsection does not relieve a manufacturer or seller from a duty to use reasonable care in a product's production.

(4) Except to the extent a state or federal statute or regulation requires a manufacturer to warn, a manufacturer or seller is not liable in a product liability action for failure to provide an adequate warning if the product is provided for use by a sophisticated user.

(5) A manufacturer or seller is not liable in a product liability action if the alleged harm was caused by an inherent characteristic of the product that cannot be eliminated without substantially compromising the product's usefulness or desirability, and that is recognized by a person with the ordinary knowledge common to the community.

(6) In a product liability action, a seller other than a manufacturer is not liable for harm allegedly caused by the product unless either of the following is true:

(a) The seller failed to exercise reasonable care, including breach of any implied warranty, with respect to the product and that failure was a proximate cause of the person's injuries.

(b) The seller made an express warranty as to the product, the product failed to conform to the warranty, and the failure to conform to the warranty was a proximate cause of the person's harm.

§ 600.2948. Death or Injury; warning as evidence. (1) Evidence is admissible in a product liability action that, before the death of the person or injury to the person or damage to property, pamphlets, booklets, labels, or other written warnings were provided that gave notice to foreseeable users of the material risk of injury, death, or damage connected with the foreseeable use of the product or provided instructions as to the foreseeable uses, applications, or limitations of the product that the defendant knew or should have known.

(2) A defendant is not liable for failure to warn of a material risk that is or should be obvious to a reasonably prudent product user or a material risk that is or should be a matter of common knowledge to persons in the same or similar position as the person upon whose injury or death the claim is based in a product liability action.

(3) In a product liability action brought against a manufacturer or seller for harm allegedly caused by a failure to provide adequate warnings or instructions, a manufacturer or seller is not liable unless the plaintiff proves that the manufacturer knew or should have known about the risk of harm based on the scientific, technical, or medical information reasonably available at the time the specific unit of the product left the control of the manufacturer.

(4) This section does not limit a manufacturer's or seller's duty to use reasonable care in relation to a product after the product has left the manufacturer's or seller's control.

§ 600.2949a. Knowledge of Defective Product. In a product liability action, if the court determines that at the time of manufacture or distribution the defendant had actual knowledge that the product was defective and that there was a substantial likelihood that the defect would cause the injury that is the basis of the action, and the defendant willfully disregarded that knowledge in the manufacture or distribution of the product, then sections 2946(4), 2946a, 2947(1) to (4), and 2948(2) do not apply.

GENERAL LAWS OF MISSISSIPPI
(1993)

The purpose of [this Act] is to clearly state the rules which apply to Mississippi products liability actions and to cases seeking punitive damages. The bill as amended:

- Codifies the common-sense rule that a manufacturer should not be liable unless a product contains a defect and the defect caused the claimant's harm.

- Provides that liability should not be imposed for harm caused by products that are inherently risky (e.g., guns and knives) if the risk is recognized by the ordinary consumer and cannot be eliminated without substantially reducing the product's usefulness.

- Recognizes that a company should not be required to warn of dangers that were not known or knowable when the product was manufactured.

- Does not allow recovery of damages if the danger posed by a product is open or obvious or if the injured person knew of the danger and voluntarily chose to expose himself to the danger.

- Provides that liability should not be imposed in a design-defect case unless there was a feasible alternative design that would have prevented the alleged harm.

- Requires a manufacturer who is found liable to indemnify the product seller for litigation costs, reasonable expenses, attorneys' fees and any damages awarded against a seller who had no control over the manufacture or design of the product.

- Requires punitive damages awards to be supported by clear and convincing evidence that the defendant acted with actual malice, actual fraud or with willful, wanton, or reckless disregard for the safety of others.

- Requires the question of liability for compensatory damages to be decided by the jury before the punitive damages issue is addressed.

- Prohibits punitive damages in the absence of a compensatory damage award.

- Provides several factors for the jury to consider when determining the amount of punitive damages and requires the amount to be rationally related to the harm caused.

- Protects innocent retailers and wholesalers from liability for punitive damages if the seller had no control over the manufacture or design of the product.

§ 11–1–63. Product Liability actions; conditions for liability; what constitutes defective product. In any action for damages caused by a product except for commercial damage to the product itself:

(a) The manufacturer or seller of the product shall not be liable if the claimant does not prove by the preponderance of the evidence that at the time the product left the control of the manufacturer or seller:

(i)1. The product was defective because it deviated in a material way from the manufacturer's specifications or from otherwise identical units manufactured to the same manufacturing specifications, or

2. The product was defective because it failed to contain adequate warnings or instructions, or

3. The product was designed in a defective manner, or

4. The product breached an express warranty or failed to conform to other express factual representations upon which the claimant justifiably relied in electing to use the product; and

(ii) The defective condition rendered the product unreasonably dangerous to the user or consumer; and

(iii) The defective and unreasonably dangerous condition of the product proximately caused the damages for which recovery is sought.

(b) A product is not defective in design or formulation if the harm for which the claimant seeks to recover compensatory damages was caused by an inherent characteristic of the product which is a generic aspect of the product that cannot be eliminated without substantially compromising the product's usefulness or desirability and which is recognized by the ordinary person with the ordinary knowledge common to the community.

(c)(i) In any action alleging that a product is defective because it failed to contain adequate warnings or instructions pursuant to paragraph (a)(i)2 of this section, the manufacturer or seller shall not be liable if the claimant does not prove by the preponderance of the evidence that at the time the product left the control of the manufacturer or seller, the manufacturer or seller knew or in light of reasonably available knowledge should have known about the danger that caused the damage for which recovery is sought and that the ordinary user or consumer would not realize its dangerous condition.

(ii) An adequate product warning or instruction is one that a reasonably prudent person in the same or similar circumstances would have provided with respect to the danger and that communicates sufficient information on the dangers and safe use of the product, taking into account the characteristics of, and the ordinary knowledge common to an ordinary consumer who purchases the product; or in the case of a prescription drug, medical device or other product that is intended to be used only under the supervision of a physician or other licensed professional person, taking into account the characteristics of, and the ordinary knowledge common to, a physician or other licensed professional who prescribes the drug, device or other product.

(d) In any action alleging that a product is defective pursuant to paragraph (a) of this section, the manufacturer or seller shall not be liable if the claimant (i) had knowledge of a condition of the product that was inconsistent with his safety; (ii) appreciated the danger in the condition; and (iii) deliberately and voluntarily chose to expose himself to the danger in such a manner to register assent on the continuance of the dangerous condition.

(e) In any action alleging that a product is defective pursuant to paragraph (a)(i)2 of this section, the manufacturer or seller shall not be liable if the danger posed by the product is known or is open and obvious to the user or consumer of the product, or should have been known or open and obvious to the user or consumer of the product, taking into account the characteristics of, and the ordinary knowledge common to, the persons who ordinarily use or consume the product.

(f) In any action alleging that a product is defective because of its design pursuant to paragraph (a)(i)3 of this section, the manufacturer or product seller shall not be liable if the claimant does not prove by the preponderance of the evidence that at the time the product left the control of the manufacturer or seller:

(i) The manufacturer or seller knew, or in light of reasonably available knowledge or in the exercise of reasonable care should have known, about the danger that caused the damage for which recovery is sought; and

(ii) The product failed to function as expected and there existed a feasible design alternative that would have to a reasonable probability prevented the harm. A feasible design alternative is a design that would have to a reasonable probability prevented the harm without impairing the utility, usefulness, practicality or desirability of the product to users or consumers.

(g)(i) The manufacturer of a product who is found liable for a defective product pursuant to Section 1(a) shall indemnify a product seller for the costs of litigation, any reasonable expenses, reasonable attorney's fees and any damages awarded by the trier of fact unless the seller exercised substantial control over that aspect of the design, testing, manufacture, packaging or labeling of the product that caused the harm for which recovery of damages is sought; the seller altered or modified the product, and the alteration or modification was a substantial factor in causing the harm for which recovery of damages is sought; the seller had actual knowledge of the defective condition of the product at the time he supplied same; or the seller made an express factual representation about the aspect of the product which caused the harm for which recovery of damages is sought.

(ii) Subparagraph (i) shall not apply unless the seller has given prompt notice of the suit to the manufacturer within thirty (30) days of the filing of the complaint against the seller.

(h) Nothing in this section shall be construed to eliminate any common law defense to an action for damages caused by a product.

§ 11–1–65. Punitive Damages. (1) In any action in which punitive damages are sought:

(a) Punitive damages may not be awarded if the claimant does not prove by clear and convincing evidence that the defendant against whom punitive damages are sought acted with actual malice, gross negligence which evidences a willful, wanton or reckless disregard for the safety of others, or committed actual fraud.

(b) In any action in which the claimant seeks an award of punitive damages, the trier of fact shall first determine whether compensatory damages are to be awarded and in what amount, before addressing any issues related to punitive damages.

(c) If, but only if, an award of compensatory damages has been made against a party, the court shall promptly commence an evidentiary hearing before the same trier of fact to determine whether punitive damages may be considered.

(d) The court shall determine whether the issue of punitive damages may be submitted to the trier of fact; and, if so, the trier of fact shall determine whether to award punitive damages and in what amount.

(e) In all cases involving an award of punitive damages, the fact finder, in determining the amount of punitive damages, shall consider, to the extent relevant, the following: the defendant's financial condition and net worth; the nature and reprehensibility of the defendant's wrongdoing, for example, the impact of the defendant's conduct on the plaintiff, or the relationship of the defendant to the plaintiff; the defendant's awareness of the amount of harm being caused and the defendant's motivation in causing such harm; the duration of the defendant's misconduct and whether the defendant attempted to conceal such misconduct; and any other circumstances shown by the evidence that bear on determining a proper amount of punitive damages. The trier of fact shall be instructed that the primary purpose of punitive damages is to punish the wrongdoer and deter similar misconduct in the future by the defendant and others while the purpose of compensatory damages is to make the plaintiff whole.

(f)(i) Before entering judgment for an award of punitive damages the trial court shall ascertain that the award is reasonable in its amount and rationally related to the purpose to punish what occurred giving rise to the award and to deter its repetition by the defendant and others.

(ii) In determining whether the award is excessive, the court shall take into consideration the following factors:

1. Whether there is a reasonable relationship between the punitive damage award and the harm likely to result from the defendant's conduct as well as the harm that actually occurred;

2. The degree of reprehensibility of the defendant's conduct, the duration of that conduct, the defendant's awareness, any concealment, and the existence and frequency of similar past conduct;

3. The financial condition and net worth of the defendant; and

4. In mitigation, the imposition of criminal sanctions on the defendant for its conduct and the existence of other civil awards against the defendant for the same conduct.

(g) The seller of a product other than the manufacturer shall not be liable for punitive damages unless the seller exercised substantial control over that aspect of the design, testing, manufacture, packaging or labeling of the product that caused the harm for which recovery of damages is sought; the seller altered or modified the product, and the alteration or modification was a substantial factor in causing the harm for which recovery of damages is sought; the seller had actual knowledge of the defective condition of the product at the time he supplied same; or the seller made an express factual representation about the aspect of the product which caused the harm for which recovery of damages is sought.

(2) The provisions of Section 11–1–65 shall not apply to:

(a) Contracts;

(b) Libel and slander; or

(c) Causes of action for persons and property arising out of asbestos.

Missouri Revised Statutes
(1987)

§ **537.760.** As used in sections 33 to 36 of this act, the term "products liability claim" means a claim or portion of a claim in which the plaintiff seeks relief in the form of damages on a theory that the defendant is strictly liable for such damages because:

(1) The defendant, wherever situated in the chain of commerce, transferred a product in the course of his business; and

(2) The product was used in a manner reasonably anticipated; and

(3) Either or both of the following:

(a) The product was then in a defective condition unreasonably dangerous when put to a reasonably anticipated use, and the plaintiff was damaged as a direct result of such defective condition as existed when the product was sold; or

(b) The product was then unreasonably dangerous when put to a reasonably anticipated use without knowledge of its characteristics, and the plaintiff was damaged as a direct result of the product being sold without an adequate warning.

§ **537.762.** 1. A defendant whose liability is based solely on his status as a seller in the stream of commerce may be dismissed from a products liability claim as provided in this section.

2. This section shall apply to any products liability claim in which another defendant, including the manufacturer, is properly before the court and from whom total recovery may be had for plaintiff's claim.

3. A defendant may move for dismissal under this section within the time for filing an answer or other responsive pleading unless permitted by the court at a later time for good cause shown. The motion shall be accompanied by an affidavit which shall be made under oath and shall state that the defendant is aware of no facts or circumstances upon which a verdict might be reached against him, other than his status as a seller in the stream of commerce.

4. The parties shall have sixty days in which to conduct discovery on the issues raised in the motion and affidavit. The court for good cause shown, may extend the time for discovery, and may enter a protective order pursuant to the rules of civil procedure regarding the scope of discovery on other issues.

5. Any party may move for a hearing on a motion to dismiss under this section. If the requirements of subsections 2 and 3 of this section are met, and no party comes forward at such a hearing with evidence of facts which would render the defendant seeking dismissal under this section liable on some basis other than his status as a seller in the stream of commerce, the court shall dismiss without prejudice the claim as to that defendant.

6. No order of dismissal under this section shall operate to divest a court of venue or jurisdiction otherwise proper at the time the action was commenced. A defendant dismissed pursuant to this section shall be considered to remain a party to such action only for such purposes.

7. An order of dismissal under this section shall be interlocutory until final disposition of plaintiff's claim by settlement or judgment and may be set aside for good cause shown at anytime prior to such disposition.

§ 537.764. 1. As used in this section, "state of the art" means that the dangerous nature of the product was not known and could not reasonably be discovered at the time the product was placed into the stream of commerce.

2. The state of the art shall be a complete defense and relevant evidence only in an action based upon strict liability for failure to warn of the dangerous condition of a product. This defense shall be pleaded as an affirmative defense and the party asserting it shall have the burden of proof.

3. Nothing in this section shall be construed as limiting the rights of an injured party to maintain an action for negligence whenever such a cause of action would otherwise exist.

4. This section shall not be construed to permit or prohibit evidence of feasibility in products liability claims.

§ 537.765. 1. Contributory fault, as a complete bar to plaintiff's recovery in a products liability claim, is abolished. The doctrine of pure comparative fault shall apply to products liability claims as provided in this section.

2. Defendant may plead and prove the fault of the plaintiff as an affirmative defense. Any fault chargeable to the plaintiff shall diminish proportionately the amount awarded as compensatory damages but shall not bar recovery.

3. For purposes of this section, "fault" is limited to:

(1) The failure to use the product as reasonably anticipated by the manufacturer;

(2) Use of the product for a purpose not intended by the manufacturer;

(3) Use of the product with knowledge of a danger involved in such use with reasonable appreciation of the consequences and the voluntary and unreasonable exposure to said danger;

(4) Unreasonable failure to appreciate the danger involved in use of the product or the consequences thereof and the unreasonable exposure to said danger;

(5) The failure to undertake the precautions a reasonably careful user of the product would take to protect himself against dangers which he would reasonably appreciate under the same or similar circumstances; or

(6) The failure to mitigate damages.

NEW JERSEY REVISED STATUTES
(1987 and 1995)

§ 2A:58c–1. a. Legislative findings; definitions. a. The Legislature finds that there is an urgent need for remedial legislation to establish clear rules with respect to certain matters relating to actions for damages for harm caused by products, including certain principles under which liability is imposed and the standards and procedures for the award of punitive damages. This act is not intended to codify all issues relating to product liability, but only to deal with matters that require clarification. The Legislature further finds that such sponsors' or committee statements that may be adopted or included in the legislative history of this act shall be consulted in the interpretation and construction of this act.

b. As used in this Act:

(1) "Claimant" means any person who brings a product liability action, and if such an action is brought through or on behalf of an estate, the term includes the person's decedent, or if an action is brought through or on behalf of a minor, the term includes the person's parent or guardian.

(2) "Harm" means (a) physical damage to property, other than to the product itself; (b) personal physical illness, injury or death; (c) pain and suffering, mental anguish or emotional harm; and (d) any loss of consortium or services or other loss deriving from any type of harm described in subparagraphs (a) through (c) of this paragraph.

(3) "Product liability action" means any claim or action brought by a claimant for harm caused by a product, irrespective of the theory underlying the claim, except actions for harm caused by breach of an express warranty.

(4) "Environmental tort action" means a civil action seeking damages for harm where the cause of the harm is exposure to toxic chemicals or substances, but does not mean actions involving drugs or products intended for personal consumption or use.

§ 2A:58c–2. Liability of manufacturer or seller in product liability action. A manufacturer or seller of a product shall be liable in a product liability action only if the claimant proves by a preponderance of the evidence that the product causing the harm was not reasonably fit, suitable or safe for its intended purpose because it: a. deviated from the design specifications, formulae, or performance standards of the manufacturer or from otherwise identical units manufactured to the same manufacturing specifications or formulae, or b. failed to contain adequate warnings or instructions, or c. was designed in a defective manner.

§ 2A:58c–3. Exemptions from liability. a. In any product liability action against a manufacturer or seller for harm allegedly caused by a product that was designed in a defective manner, the manufacturer or seller shall not be liable if:

(1) At the time the product left the control of the manufacturer, there was not a practical and technically feasible alternative design that would have prevented the harm without substantially impairing the reasonably anticipated or intended function of the product; or

(2) The characteristics of the product are known to the ordinary consumer or user, and the harm was caused by an unsafe aspect of the product that is an inherent characteristic of the product and that would be recognized by the ordinary person who uses or consumes the product with the ordinary knowledge common to the class of persons for whom the product is intended, except that this paragraph shall not apply to industrial machinery or other equipment used in the workplace and it is not intended to apply to dangers posed by products such as machinery or equipment that can feasibly be eliminated without impairing the usefulness of the product; or

(3) The harm was caused by an unavoidably unsafe aspect of the product and the product was accompanied by an adequate warning or instruction as defined in section 4 of this act.

b.   The provisions of paragraph (1) of subsection a. of this section shall not apply if the court, on the basis of clear and convincing evidence, makes all of the following determinations:

(1) The product is egregiously unsafe or ultra-hazardous;

(2) The ordinary user or consumer of the product cannot reasonably be expected to have knowledge of the product's risks, or the product poses a risk of serious injury to persons other than the user or consumer; and

(3) The product has little or no usefulness.

c.   No provision of subsection a. of this section is intended to establish any rule, or alter any existing rule, with respect to the burden of proof.

§ 2A:58c–4. No liability if warning provided. In any product liability action the manufacturer or seller shall not be liable for harm caused by a failure to warn if the product contains an adequate warning or instruction or, in the case of dangers a manufacturer or seller discovers or reasonably should discover after the product leaves its control, if the manufacturer or seller provides an adequate warning or instruction. An adequate product warning or instruction is one that a reasonably prudent person in the same or similar circumstances would have provided with respect to the danger and that communicates adequate information on the dangers and safe use of the product, taking into account the characteristics of, and the ordinary knowledge common to, the persons by whom the product is intended to be used, or in the case of prescription drugs, taking into account the characteristics of, and the ordinary knowledge common to, the prescribing physician. If the warning or instruction given in connection with a drug or device or food or food additive has been approved or prescribed by the federal Food and Drug Administration under the "Federal Food, Drug, and Cosmetic Act," 52 Stat. 1040, 21 U.S.C. § 301 et seq. or the "Public Health Service Act," 58 Stat. 682, 42 U.S.C. § 201 et seq., a rebuttable presumption shall arise that the warning or instruction is adequate. For purposes of this section, the terms "drug", "device", "food", and "food additive" have the meanings defined in the "Federal Food, Drug, and Cosmetic Act."

§ 2A:58c–5. Punitive damages under food and drug product liability; limitation. Punitive damages shall not be awarded if a drug or device or food or food additive which caused the claimant's harm was subject to premarket approval or licensure by the federal Food and Drug Administration under the "Federal Food, Drug, and Cosmetic Act," 52 Stat. 1040, 21 U.S.C. § 301 et seq. or the "Public Health Service Act," 58 Stat. 682, 42 U.S.C. § 201 et seq. and was approved or licensed; or is generally recognized as safe and effective pursuant to conditions established by the federal Food and Drug Administration and applicable regulations, including packaging and labeling regulations. However, where the product manufacturer knowingly withheld or misrepresented information required to be submitted under the agency's regulations, which information was material and relevant to the harm in question, punitive damages may be awarded. For purposes of this subsection, the terms "drug", "device", "food", and "food additive" have the meanings defined in the "Federal Food, Drug, and Cosmetic Act."

§ 2A:58c–6. Environmental tort action—Inapplicability of Act. The provisions of this act shall not apply to any environmental tort action.

§ 2A:58c–7. Burden of proof rules unaltered. Except as otherwise expressly provided in this act, no provision of this act is intended to establish any rule, or alter any existing rule, with respect to the burden of proof in a product liability action.

§ 2A:58c–8. Definitions relative to actions against product seller. (1) As used in this act:

"Manufacturer" means (1) any person who designs, formulates, produces, creates, makes, packages, labels or constructs any product or component of a product; (2) a product seller with respect to a given product to the extent the product seller designs, formulates, produces, creates, makes, packages, labels or constructs the product before its sale; (3) any product seller not described in paragraph (2) which holds itself out as a manufacturer to the user of the product; or (4) a United States domestic sales subsidiary of a foreign manufacturer if the foreign manufacturer has a controlling interest in the domestic sales subsidiary.

"Product liability action" means any claim or action brought by a claimant for harm caused by a product, irrespective of the theory underlying the claim, except actions for harm caused by breach of an express warranty.

"Product seller" means any person who, in the course of a business conducted for that purpose: sells; distributes; leases; installs; prepares or assembles a manufacturer's product according to the manufacturer's plan, intention, design, specifications or formulations; blends; packages; labels; markets; repairs; maintains or otherwise is involved in placing a product in the line if commerce. The term "product seller" does not include:

(1) A seller of real property; or

(2) A provider of professional services in any case in which the sale or use of a product is incidental to the transaction and the essence of the transaction is the furnishing of judgment, skill or services; or

(3) Any person who acts in only a financial capacity with respect to the sale of a product.

§ 2A:58c–9. Affidavit by seller identifying manufacturer; product seller liability. a. In any product liability action against a product seller where the manufacturer has not been named a defendant, the product seller may file an affidavit certifying the correct identity of the manufacturer of the product which allegedly caused the injury, death or damage.

b. Upon filing the affidavit pursuant to subsection a. of this section, the product seller shall be relieved of all strict liability claims, subject to the provisions set forth in subsection d. Of this section. Due diligence shall be exercised in providing the plaintiff with the correct identity of the manufacturer or manufacturers.

c. The product seller shall be subject to strict liability if:

(1) The identity of the manufacturer given to the plaintiff by the product seller was incorrect. Once the correct identity of the manufacturer has been provided, the product seller shall again be relieved of all strict liability claims, subject to subsection d. of this section; or

(2) The manufacturer has no known agents, facility, or other presence within the United States; or

(3) The manufacturer has no attachable assets or has been adjudicated bankrupt and a judgment is not otherwise recoverable from the assets of the bankruptcy estate.

d. A product seller shall be liable if:

(1) The product seller has exercised some significant control over the design, manufacture, packaging or labeling of the product relative to the alleged defect in the product which caused the injury, death or damage; or

(2) The product seller knew or should have known of the defect in the product which caused the injury, death or damage or the plaintiff can affirmatively demonstrate that the product seller was in possession of facts from which a reasonable person would conclude that the product seller had or should have had knowledge of the alleged defect in the product which caused the injury, death or damage; or

(3) The product seller created the defect in the product which caused the injury, death or damage.

e.   The commencement of a product liability action based in whole or in part on the doctrine of strict liability against a product seller shall toll the applicable statute of limitations with respect to manufacturers who have been identified pursuant to the provisions of subsection a of this section.

2.   This act shall take effect immediately and shall apply to causes of action which occur on or after the effective date of this act.

§ 2A:58c–10. Definitions relative to health care providers. As used in this act:

"Health care provider" or "provider" means a provider of health care services and includes, but is not limited to, health care professionals, hospitals, nursing homes and other health care facilities.

"Health care service" means a service or product sold by a health care provider and includes, but is not limited to, hospital, medical, surgical, dental, hearing and vision services or products.

"Medical device" or "device" means a "device" as defined in subsection (h) of section 201 of the "Federal Food, Drug and Cosmetic Act," 52 Stat. 1040, (21 U.S.C. § 321).

§ 2A:58c–11. Liability of health care providers for medical devices. In any product liability action against a health care provider for harm allegedly caused by a medical device that was manufactured or designed in a defective manner, or for harm caused by a failure to warn of a danger related to the use of a medical device, the provider shall not be liable unless:

(1) the provider has exercised some significant control over the design, manufacture, packaging or labeling of the medical device relative to the alleged defect in the device which caused the injury, death or damage; or

(2) the provider knew or should have known of the defect in the medical device which caused the injury, death or damage, or the plaintiff can affirmatively demonstrate that the provider was in possession of facts from which a reasonable person would conclude that the provider had or should have had knowledge of the alleged defect in the medical device which caused the injury, death or damage; or

(3) the provider created the defect in the medical device which caused the injury, death or damage.

NORTH CAROLINA GENERAL STATUTES
(1979, 1987 and 1995)

§ 99B–1. Definitions. When used in this Chapter, unless the context otherwise requires:

(1) "Claimant" means a person or other entity asserting a claim and, if said claim is asserted on behalf of an estate, an incompetent or a minor, "claimant" includes plaintiff's decedent, guardian, or guardian ad litem.

(2) "Manufacturer" means a person or entity who designs, assembles, fabricates, produces, constructs or otherwise prepares a product or component part of a product prior to its sale to a user or consumer, including a seller owned in whole or significant part by the manufacturer or a seller owning the manufacturer in whole or significant part.

(3) "Product liability action" includes any action brought for or on account of personal injury, death or property damage caused by or resulting from the manufacture, construction, design, formulation, development of standards, preparation, processing, assembly, testing, listing, certifying, warning, instructing, marketing, selling, advertising, packaging, or labeling of any product.

(4) "Seller" includes a retailer, wholesaler, or distributor, and means any individual or entity engaged in the business of selling a product, whether such sale is for resale or for use or consumption. "Seller" also includes a lessor or bailor engaged in the business of leasing or bailment of a product.

§ 99B–1.1. Strict liability. There shall be no strict liability in tort in product liability actions.

§ 99B–1.2. Breach of warranty. Nothing in this act shall preclude a product liability action that otherwise exists against a manufacturer or seller for breach of warranty. The defenses provided for in this Chapter shall apply to claims for breach of warranty unless expressly excluded under this Chapter.

§ 99B–2. Seller's opportunity to inspect; privity requirements for warranty claims. (a) No product liability action, except an action for breach of express warranty, shall be commenced or maintained against any seller when the product was acquired and sold by the seller in a sealed container or when the product was acquired and sold by the seller under circumstances in which the seller was afforded no reasonable opportunity to inspect the product in such a manner that would have or should have, in the exercise of reasonable care, revealed the existence of the condition complained of, unless the seller damaged or mishandled the product while in his possession; provided, that the provisions of this section shall not apply if the manufacturer of the product is not subject to the jurisdiction of the courts of this State or if such manufacturer has been judicially declared insolvent.

(b) A claimant who is a buyer, as defined in the Uniform Commercial Code, of the product involved, or who is a member or a guest of a member of the family of the buyer, a guest of the buyer, or an employee of the buyer may bring a product liability action directly against the manufacturer of the product involved for breach of implied warranty; and the lack of privity of contract shall not be grounds for the dismissal of such action.

§ 99B–3. Alteration or modification of product. (a) No manufacturer or seller of a product shall be held liable in any product liability action where a proximate cause of the personal injury, death, or damage to property was either an alteration or modification of the product by a party other than the manufacturer or seller, which alteration or modification occurred after the product left the control of such manufacturer or such seller unless:

(1) The alteration or modification was in accordance with the instructions or specifications of such manufacturer or such seller; or

(2) The alteration or modification was made with the express consent of such manufacturer or such seller.

(b) For the purposes of this section, alteration or modification includes changes in the design, formula, function, or use of the product from that originally designed, tested, or intended by the manufacturer. It includes failure to observe routine care and maintenance, but does not include ordinary wear and tear.

§ 99B–4. Knowledge or reasonable care. No manufacturer or seller shall be held liable in any product liability action if:

(1) The use of the product giving rise to the product liability action was contrary to any express and adequate instructions or warnings delivered with, appearing on, or attached to the product or on its original container or wrapping, if the user knew or with the exercise of reasonable and diligent care should have known of such instructions or warnings; or

(2) The user knew of or discovered a defect or dangerous condition of the product that was inconsistent with the safe use of the product, and then unreasonably and voluntarily exposed himself or herself to the danger, and was injured by or caused injury with that product; or

(3) The claimant failed to exercise reasonable care under the circumstances in the use of the product, and such failure was a proximate cause of the occurrence that caused the injury or damage complained of.

§ 99B–5. Claims based on inadequate warning or instruction. (a) No manufacturer or seller of a product shall be held liable in any product liability action for a claim based upon inadequate warning or instruction unless the claimant proves that the manufacturer or seller acted unreasonably in failing to provide such warning or instruction, that the failure to provide adequate warning or instruction was a proximate cause of the harm for which damages are sought, and also proves one of the following:

(1) At the time the product left the control of the manufacturer or seller, the product, without an adequate warning or instruction, created an unreasonably dangerous condition that the manufacturer or seller knew, or in the exercise of ordinary care should have known, posed a substantial risk of harm to a reasonably foreseeable claimant.

(2) After the product left the control of the manufacturer or seller, the manufacturer or seller became aware of or in the exercise of ordinary care should have known that the product posed a substantial risk of harm to a reasonably foreseeable user or consumer and failed to take reasonable steps to give adequate warning or instruction or to take other reasonable action under the circumstances.

(b) Notwithstanding subsection (a) of this section, no manufacturer or seller of a product shall be held liable in any product liability action for failing to warn about an open and obvious risk or a risk that is a matter of common knowledge.

(c) Notwithstanding subsection (a) of this section, no manufacturer or seller of a prescription drug shall be liable in a products liability action for failing to provide a warning or instruction directly to a consumer if an adequate warning or instruction has been provided to the physician or other legally authorized person who prescribes or dispenses that prescription drug for the claimant unless the United States Food and Drug Administration requires such direct consumer warning or instruction to accompany the product.

§ 99B–6. Claims based on inadequate design or formulation. (a) No manufacturer of a product shall be held liable in any product liability action for the inadequate design or formulation of the product unless the claimant proves that at the time of its manufacture the manufacturer acted unreasonably in designing or formulating the product, that this conduct was a proximate cause of the harm for which damages are sought, and also proves one of the following:

(1) At the time the product left the control of the manufacturer, the manufacturer unreasonably failed to adopt a safer, practical, feasible, and otherwise reasonable alternative design or formulation that could then have been reasonably adopted and that would have prevented or substantially reduced the risk of harm without substantially impairing the usefulness, practicality, or desirability of the product.

(2) At the time the product left the control of the manufacturer, the design or formulation of the product was so unreasonable that a reasonable person, aware of the relevant facts, would not use or consume a product of this design.

(b) In determining whether the manufacturer acted unreasonably under subsection (a) of this section, the factors to be considered shall include, but are not limited to, the following:

(1) The nature and magnitude of the risks of harm associated with the design or formulation in light of the intended and reasonably foreseeable uses, modifications, or alterations of the product.

(2) The likely awareness of product users, whether based on warnings, general knowledge, or otherwise, of those risks of harm.

(3) The extent to which the design or formulation conformed to any applicable government standard that was in effect when the product left the control of its manufacturer.

(4) The extent to which the labeling for a prescription or nonprescription drug approved by the United States Food and Drug Administration conformed to any applicable government or private standard that was in effect when the product left the control of its manufacturer.

(5) The utility of the product, including the performance, safety, and other advantages associated with that design or formulation.

(6) The technical, economic, and practical feasibility of using an alternative design or formulation at the time of manufacture.

(7) The nature and magnitude of any foreseeable risks associated with the alternative design or formulation.

(c) No manufacturer of a product shall be held liable in any product liability action for a claim under this section to the extent that it is based upon an inherent characteristic of the product that cannot be eliminated without substantially compromising the product's usefulness or desirability and that is recognized by the ordinary person with the ordinary knowledge common to the community.

(d) No manufacturer of a prescription drug shall be liable in a product liability action on account of some aspect of the prescription drug that is unavoidably unsafe, if an adequate warning and instruction has been provided pursuant to G.S. 99B–5(c). As used in this subsection, "unavoidably unsafe" means that, in the state of technical, scientific, and medical knowledge generally prevailing at the time the product left the control of its manufacturer, an aspect of that product that caused the claimant's harm was not reasonably capable of being made safe.

(e) Nothing in this section precludes an action against a manufacturer in accordance with the provisions of G.S. 99B–5.

§ **99B–7 through 99B–9.** Reserved for future codification purposes.

§ **99B–10. Immunity for donated food.** (a) Notwithstanding the provisions of Article 12 of Chapter 106 of the General Statutes, or any other provision of law, any person, including but not limited to a seller, farmer, processor, distributor, wholesaler, or retailer of food, who donates an item of food for use or distribution by a nonprofit organization or nonprofit corporation shall not be liable for civil damages or criminal penalties resulting from the nature, age, condition, or packaging of the donated food, unless an injury is caused by the gross negligence, reckless-ness, or intentional misconduct of the donor.

(b) Notwithstanding any other provision of law, any nonprofit organi-zation or nonprofit corporation that uses or distributes food that has been donated to it for such use or distribution shall not be liable for civil damages or criminal penalties resulting from the nature, age, condition, or packaging of the donated food, unless an injury is caused by the gross negligence, recklessness, or intentional misconduct of the organization or corporation.

§ 99B–11. Claims based on defective design of firearms.

(a) In a products liability action involving firearms or ammunition, whether a firearm or ammunition shell is defective in design shall not be based on a comparison or weighing of the benefits of the product against the risk of injury, damage, or death posed by its potential to cause that injury, damage, or death when discharged.

(b) In a products liability action brought against a firearm or ammuni-tion manufacturer, importer, distributor, or retailer that alleges a design defect, the burden is on the plaintiff to prove, in addition to any other elements required to be proved:

(1) That the actual design of the firearm or ammunition was defective, causing it not to function in a manner reasonably expected by an ordinary consumer of firearms or ammunition; and

(2) That any defective design was the proximate cause of the injury, damage, or death.

ELEMENTS
① Civil Action
② vs. Manufacturer
   (sometimes supplier)
③ of a PRODUCT
④ Manuf/Supplier
   makes a representation
⑤ Product is DEFECTIVE
⑥ at the Time product
   leaves Manuf/Supp
   control
⑦ Failure to Conform
   is ACTUAL + PROX,
   CAUSE of
⑧ HARM

OHIO REVISED CODE ANNOTATED
(1987 and 1997)

§ 2305.10. Product liability, bodily injury or injury to personal property.

(A) Except as provided in division (C) of this section, an action based on a product liability claim and an action for bodily injury or injuring personal property shall be brought within two years after the cause of action accrues. Except as provided in divisions (B)(1) to (4) of this section, a cause of action accrues under this division when the injury or loss to person or property occurs.

(B)(1) For purposes of division (A) of this section, a cause of action for bodily injury that is not described in division (B)(2), (3), or (4) of this section and that is caused by exposure to hazardous or toxic chemicals, ethical drugs, or ethical medical devices accrues upon the date on which the plaintiff is informed by competent medical authority that the plaintiff has an injury that is related to the exposure, or upon the date on which by the exercise of reasonable diligence the plaintiff should have known that the plaintiff has an injury that is related to the exposure, whichever date occurs first.

(2) For purposes of division (A) of this section, a cause of action for bodily injury caused by exposure to asbestos or to chromium in any of its chemical forms accrues upon the date on which the plaintiff is informed by competent medical authority that the plaintiff has an injury that is related to the exposure, or upon the date on which by the exercise of reasonable diligence the plaintiff should have known that the plaintiff has an injury that is related to the exposure, whichever date occurs first.

(3) For purposes of division (A) of this section, a cause of action for bodily injury incurred by a veteran through exposure to chemical defoliants or herbicides or other causative agents, including agent orange, accrues upon the date on which the plaintiff is informed by competent medical authority that the plaintiff has an injury that is related to the exposure.

(4) For purposes of division (A) of this section, a cause of action for bodily injury caused by exposure to diethylstilbestrol or other nonsteroidal synthetic estrogens, including exposure before birth, accrues upon the date on which the plaintiff is informed by competent medical authority that the plaintiff has an injury that is related to the exposure, or upon the date on which by the exercise of reasonable diligence the plaintiff should have known that the plaintiff has an injury that is related to the exposure, whichever date occurs first.

(C)(1) Except as otherwise provided in divisions (C)(2), (3), (4), (5), and (6) of this section, no cause of action based on a product liability claim shall accrue against the manufacturer or supplier of a product later than fifteen

years from the date that the product was delivered to its first purchaser or first lessee who was not engaged in a business in which the product was used as a component in the production, construction, creation, assembly, or rebuilding of another product.

(2) Division (C)(1) of this section does not apply if the manufacturer or supplier of a product engaged in fraud in regard to information about the product and the fraud contributed to the harm that is alleged in a product liability claim.

(3) Division (C)(1) of this section does not bar an action based on a product liability claim against a manufacturer or supplier of a product who made an express, written warranty as to the safety of the product that was for a period longer than fifteen years and that has not expired in accordance with the terms of that warranty.

(4) If the cause of action relative to a product liability claim accrues during the fifteen-year period described in division (C)(1) of this section but less than two years prior to the expiration of that period, an action based on the product liability claim may be commenced within two years after the cause of action accrues.

(5) If a cause of action relative to a product liability claim accrues during the fifteen-year period described in division (C)(1) of this section and the claimant cannot commence an action during that period due to a disability described in section 2305.16 of the Revised Code, an action based on the product liability claim may be commenced within two years after the disability is removed.

(6)(a) Division (C)(1) of this section does not bar an action based on a product liability claim against a manufacturer or supplier of a product if all of the following apply:

(i) The action is for bodily injury.

(ii) The product involved is a substance described in division (B) of this section.

(iii) The bodily injury results from exposure to the product during the fifteen-year period described in division (C)(1) of this section.

(b) If division (C)(6)(a) of this section applies, the cause of action shall accrue upon the date on which the claimant is informed by competent medical authority that the bodily injury was related to the exposure to the product, or upon the date on which by the exercise of reasonable diligence the claimant should have known that the bodily injury was related to the exposure to the product, whichever date occurs first. The action based on the product liability claim shall be commenced within two years after the cause of action accrues and shall not be commenced more than two years after the cause of action accrues.

(D) This section does not create a new cause of action or substantive legal right against any person involving a product liability claim.

(E) As used in this section:

(1) "Agent orange," "causative agent," and "veteran" have the same meanings as in section 5903.21 of the Revised Code.

(2) "Ethical drug," "ethical medical device," "manufacturer," "product," and "supplier" have the same meanings as in section 2307.71 of the Revised Code.

(3) "Harm" means injury, death, or loss to person or property.

(4) "Product liability claim" means a claim that seeks to recover compensatory damages from a manufacturer or supplier for harm that allegedly arose from the design, formulation, production, construction, creation, assembly, rebuilding, testing, or marketing of a product, from a warning, instruction, or lack of warning or instruction associated with a product, or from a failure of a product to conform to a relevant representation or warranty.

(F) This section shall be considered to be purely remedial in operation and shall be applied in a remedial manner in any civil action commenced on or after the effective date of this section, in which this section is relevant, regardless of when the cause of action accrued and notwithstanding any other section of the Revised Code or prior rule of law of this state, but shall not be construed to apply to any civil action pending prior to the effective date of this section.

§ **2307.71 Definitions.** As used in sections 2307.71 to 2307.801 of the Revised Code:

(A) "Claimant" means either of the following:

(1) A person who asserts a product liability claim or on whose behalf a product liability claim is asserted;

(2) If a product liability claim is asserted on behalf of the surviving spouse, children, parents, or other next of kin of a decedent or on behalf of the estate of a decedent, whether as a claim in an action for wrongful death under Chapter 2125. of the Revised Code or as a survivorship claim, whichever of the following is appropriate:

(a) The decedent, if the reference is to the person who allegedly sustained harm or economic loss for which, or in connection with which, compensatory damages or punitive or exemplary damages are sought to be recovered;

(b) The personal representative of the decedent or the estate of the decedent, if the reference is to the person who is asserting or has asserted the product liability claim.

(B) "Economic loss" means direct, incidental, or consequential pecuniary loss, including, but not limited to, damage to the product involved and nonphysical damage to property other than that product. Harm is not "economic loss."

(C) "Environment" means navigable waters, surface water, ground water, drinking water supplies, land surface, subsurface strata, and air.

(D) "Ethical drug" means a prescription drug that is prescribed or dispensed by a physician or any other person who is legally authorized to prescribe or dispense a prescription drug.

(E) "Ethical medical device" means a medical device that is prescribed, dispensed, or implanted by a physician or any other person who is legally authorized to prescribe, dispense, or implant a medical device and that is regulated under the "Federal Food, Drug, and Cosmetic Act," 52 Stat. 1040, 21 U.S.C. 301–392, as amended.

(F) "Foreseeable risk" means a risk of harm that satisfies both of the following:

(1) It is associated with an intended or reasonably foreseeable use, modification, or alteration of a product.

(2) It is a risk that the manufacturer of the product should recognize while exercising both of the following:

(a) The attention, perception, memory, knowledge, and intelligence that a reasonable manufacturer should possess;

(b) Any superior attention, perception, memory, knowledge, or intelligence that the manufacturer possesses.

(G) "Harm" means death, physical injury to person, serious emotional distress, or physical damage to property other than the product involved. Economic loss is not "harm."

(H) "Hazardous or toxic substances" include, but are not limited to, hazardous waste as defined in section 3734.01 of the Revised Code, hazardous waste as specified in the rules of the director of environmental protection pursuant to division (A) of section 3734.12 of the Revised Code, hazardous substances as defined in section 3716.01 of the Revised Code, and hazardous substances, pollutants, and contaminants as defined in or by regulations adopted pursuant to the "Comprehensive Environmental Response, Compensation, and Liability Act of 1980," 94 Stat. 2767, 42 U.S.C. 9601, as amended.

(I) "Manufacturer" means a person engaged in a business to design, formulate, produce, create, make, construct, assemble, or rebuild a product or a component of a product.

(J) "Person" has the same meaning as in division (C) of section 1.59 of the Revised Code and also includes governmental entities.

(K) "Physician" means a person who is licensed to practice medicine and surgery or osteopathic medicine and surgery by the state medical board or a person who otherwise is authorized to practice medicine and surgery or osteopathic medicine and surgery in this state.

(L)(1) "Product" means, subject to division (L)(2) of this section, any object, substance, mixture, or raw material that constitutes tangible personal property and that satisfies all of the following:

(a) It is capable of delivery itself, or as an assembled whole in a mixed or combined state, or as a component or ingredient.

(b) It is produced, manufactured, or supplied for introduction into trade or commerce.

(c) It is intended for sale or lease to persons for commercial or personal use.

(2) "Product" does not include human tissue, blood, or organs.

(M) "Product liability claim" means a claim that is asserted in a civil action and that seeks to recover compensatory damages from a manufacturer or supplier for death, physical injury to person, emotional distress, or physical damage to property other than the product involved, that allegedly arose from any of the following:

(1) The design, formulation, production, construction, creation, assembly, rebuilding, testing, or marketing of that product;

(2) Any warning or instruction, or lack of warning or instruction, associated with that product;

(3) Any failure of that product to conform to any relevant representation or warranty.

(N) "Recall notification" means a written communication that is issued by a manufacturer or supplier voluntarily or pursuant to federal law or a section of the Revised Code, that applies to a particular product, that is addressed to the purchaser or lessee of the product, and that advises the purchaser or lessee to return the product to its manufacturer or a supplier of the product for repairs to or replacement of the product.

(O) "Representation" means an express representation of a material fact concerning the character, quality, or safety of a product.

(P)(1) "Supplier" means, subject to division (P)(2) of this section, either of the following:

(a) A person that, in the course of a business conducted for the purpose, sells, distributes, leases, prepares, blends, packages, labels, or otherwise participates in the placing of a product in the stream of commerce;

(b) A person that, in the course of a business conducted for the purpose, installs, repairs, or maintains any aspect of a product that allegedly causes harm.

(2) "Supplier" does not include any of the following:

(a) A manufacturer;

(b) A seller of real property;

(c) A provider of professional services who, incidental to a professional transaction the essence of which is the furnishing of judgment, skill, or services, sells or uses a product;

*Supplier subject to S/L only:
① Supp. makes a representation and product fails to conform
② Manuf. is insolvent or outside reach of court

380

(d) Any person who acts only in a financial capacity with respect to the sale of a product, or who leases a product under a lease arrangement in which the selection, possession, maintenance, and operation of the product are controlled by a person other than the lessor.

(Q) "Trier of fact" means the jury or, in a nonjury action, the court.

(R) "Unavoidably unsafe" means that, in the state of technical, scientific, and medical knowledge at the time a product left the control of its manufacturer, an aspect of that product was incapable of being made safe.

§ 2307.72. Damages recoverable on product liability claim; environmental damage. (A) Any recovery of compensatory damages based on a product liability claim is subject to sections 2307.71 to 2307.801 of the Revised Code.

(B) Any recovery of punitive or exemplary damages in connection with a product liability claim is subject to sections 2307.71 to 2307.801 of the Revised Code.

(C) Any recovery of compensatory damages for economic loss based on a claim that is asserted in a civil action, other than a product liability claim, is not subject to sections 2307.71 to 2307.801 of the Revised Code but may occur under the common law of this state or other applicable sections of the Revised Code.

(D)(1) Except as provided in division (C) of section 2307.73 and sections 2307.791 [2307.79.1] and 2307.792 [2307.79.2] of the Revised Code, sections 2307.71 to 2307.801 [2307.80.1] of the Revised Code do not supersede, modify, or otherwise affect any statute, regulation, or rule of this state or of the United States, or the common law of this state or of the United States, that relates to liability in compensatory damages or punitive or exemplary damages for injury, death, or loss to person or property, or to relief in the form of the abatement of a nuisance, civil penalties, cleanup costs, cost recovery, an injunction or temporary restraining order, or restitution, that arises, in whole or in part, from contamination or pollution of the environment or a threat of contamination or pollution of the environment, including contamination or pollution or a threat of contamination or pollution from hazardous or toxic substances.

(2) Consistent with the Rules of Civil Procedure, in the same civil action against the same defendant or different defendants, a claimant may assert both of the following:

(a) A product liability claim, including a claim for the recovery of punitive or exemplary damages in connection with a product liability claim;

(b) A claim for the recovery of compensatory damages or punitive or exemplary damages for injury, death, or loss to person or property, or for relief in the form of the abatement of a nuisance, civil penalties, cleanup costs, cost recovery, an injunction or temporary restraining order, or restitution, that arises, in whole or in part, from contamination or pollution of the environment or a threat of contamination or pollution of the environment, including contamination or pollution or a threat of contamination or pollution from hazardous or toxic substances.

§ 2307.73. When manufacturer is liable for compensatory damages; successor corporation liability; evidence of subsequent measures. (A) A manufacturer is subject to liability for compensatory damages based on a product liability claim only if the claimant establishes, by a preponderance of the evidence, all of the following:

(1) Subject to division (B) of this section, the product was defective in manufacture or construction as described in section 2307.74 of the Revised Code, was defective in design or formulation as described in section 2307.75 of the Revised Code, was defective due to inadequate warning or instruction as described in section 2307.76 of the Revised Code, or was defective because it did not conform to a representation made by the manufacturer as described in section 2307.77 of the Revised Code.

(2) Subject to sections 2307.80, 2315.20, and 2323.59 of the Revised Code, a defective aspect of the product as described in division (A)(1) of this section was a proximate cause of harm for which the claimant seeks to recover compensatory damages.

(3) The manufacturer designed, formulated, produced, created, made, constructed, assembled, or rebuilt the product.

(B) If a claimant is unable because a product was destroyed to establish by direct evidence that the product was defective or if a claimant otherwise is unable to establish by direct evidence that a product was defective, it shall be sufficient for the claimant to present, consistent with the Rules of Evidence, circumstantial or other competent evidence that establishes, by a preponderance of the evidence, that the product was defective in any one of the four respects specified in division (A)(1) of this section.

(C) A manufacturer shall not be held liable for compensatory damages based on a product liability claim that asserts successor corporation liability in the sale of assets context, unless one of the following factual situations applies:

(1) A corporation that purchases the assets of a manufacturer expressly or impliedly assumes liability for harm caused by a product of the selling manufacturer.

(2) The sale of the assets of a manufacturer to a purchasing corporation amounts to a de facto merger or consolidation of the selling manufacturer and the purchasing corporation.

(3) The corporation that purchases the assets of a corporate manufacturer is a mere continuation of that corporate manufacturer.

(4) The sale of the assets of a manufacturer is for the primary purpose of avoiding liability through reliance on this section.

(D) In a civil action based on a product liability claim, evidence of measures that are taken after an event and that, if taken prior to the event, would have made the event less likely to occur is not admissible. Evidence of subsequent measures of that nature is admissible when offered for another purpose, including, but not limited to, impeachment or proving ownership or control, if controverted.

(E) This section shall be considered to be purely remedial in operation and shall be applied in a remedial manner in any civil action commenced on or after the effective date of this section, in which this section is relevant, regardless of when the cause of action accrued and notwithstanding any other section of the Revised Code or prior rule of law of this state, but shall not be construed to apply to any civil action pending prior to the effective date of this section.

§ 2307.74. When product is defective in manufacture or construction. A product is defective in manufacture or construction if, when it left the control of its manufacturer, it deviated in a material way from the design specifications, formula, or performance standards of the manufacturer, or from otherwise identical units manufactured to the same design specifications, formula, or performance standards. A product may be defective in manufacture or construction as described in this section even though its manufacturer exercised all possible care in its manufacture or construction.

§ 2307.75. When product is defective in design or formulation. (A) Subject to divisions (D), (E), and (F) of this section, a product is defective in design or formulation if, at the time it left the control of its manufacturer, the foreseeable risks associated with its design or formulation as determined pursuant to division (B) of this section exceeded the benefits associated with that design or formulation as determined pursuant to division (C) of this section.

(B) The foreseeable risks associated with the design or formulation of a product shall be determined by considering factors including, but not limited to, the following:

(1) The nature and magnitude of the risks of harm associated with that design or formulation in light of the intended and reasonably foreseeable uses, modifications, or alterations of the product;

(2) The likely awareness of product users, whether based on warnings, general knowledge, or otherwise, of those risks of harm;

(3) The likelihood that that design or formulation would cause harm in light of the intended and reasonably foreseeable uses, modifications, or alterations of the product;

(4) The extent to which that design or formulation conformed to any applicable public or private product standard that was in effect when the product left the control of its manufacturer.

(C) The benefits associated with the design or formulation of a product shall be determined by considering factors including, but not limited to, the following:

(1) The intended or actual utility of the product, including any performance or safety advantages associated with that design or formulation;

(2) The technical and economic feasibility, when the product left the control of its manufacturer, of using an alternative design or formulation;

(3) The nature and magnitude of any foreseeable risks associated with an alternative design or formulation.

(D) An ethical drug or ethical medical device is not defective in design or formulation because some aspect of it is unavoidably unsafe, if the manufacturer of the ethical drug or ethical medical device provides adequate warning and instruction under section 2307.76 of the Revised Code concerning that unavoidably unsafe aspect.

(E) A product is not defective in design or formulation if the harm for which the claimant seeks to recover compensatory damages was caused by an inherent characteristic of the product which is a generic aspect of the product that cannot be eliminated without substantially compromising the product's usefulness or desirability and which is recognized by the ordinary person with the ordinary knowledge common to the community.

(F) A product is not defective in design or formulation if, at the time the product left the control of its manufacturer, a practical and technically feasible alternative design or formulation was not available that would have prevented the harm for which the claimant seeks to recover compensatory damages without substantially impairing the usefulness or intended purpose of the product, unless the manufacturer acted unreasonably in introducing the product into trade or commerce.

§ 2307.76. **When product is defective due to inadequate warning or instruction.** (A) Subject to divisions (B) and (C) of this section, a product is defective due to inadequate warning or instruction if either of the following applies:

(1) it is defective due to inadequate warning or instruction at the time of marketing if, when it left the control of its manufacturer, both of the following applied:

(a) the manufacturer knew or, in the exercise of reasonable care, should have known about a risk that is associated with the product and that allegedly caused harm for which the claimant seeks to recover compensatory damages;

(b) the manufacturer failed to provide the warning or instruction that a manufacturer exercising reasonable care would have provided concerning that risk, in light of the likelihood that the product would cause harm of the type for which the claimant seeks to recover compensatory damages and in light of the likely seriousness of that harm.

(2) It is defective due to inadequate post-marketing warning or instruction if, at a relevant time after it left the control of its manufacturer, both of the following applied:

(a) the manufacturer knew or, in the exercise of reasonable care, should have known about a risk that is associated with the product and that allegedly caused harm for which the claimant seeks to recover compensatory damages;

(b) the manufacturer failed to provide the post-marketing warning or instruction that a manufacturer exercising reasonable care would have provided concerning that risk, in light of the likelihood that the product would cause harm of the type for which the claimant seeks to recover compensatory damages and in light of the likely seriousness of that harm.

(B) A product is not defective due to lack of warning or instruction or inadequate warning or instruction as a result of the failure of its manufacturer to warn or instruct about an open and obvious risk or a risk that is a matter of common knowledge.

(C) An ethical drug is not defective due to inadequate warning or instruction if its manufacturer provides otherwise adequate warning and instruction to the physician or other legally authorized person who prescribes or dispenses that ethical drug for a claimant in question and if the federal Food and Drug Administration has not provided that warning or instruction relative to that ethical drug is to be given directly to the ultimate user of it.

§ 2307.77. Conformance to representation. A product is defective if it did not conform, when it left the control of its manufacturer, to a representation made by that manufacturer. A product may be defective because it did not conform to a representation even though its manufacturer did not act fraudulently, recklessly, or negligently in making the representation.

§ 2307.78. Liability of supplier. (A) Subject to division (B) of this section and subject to sections 2307.80, 2315.20, and 2323.59 of the Revised Code, a supplier is subject to liability for compensatory damages based on a product liability claim only if the claimant establishes, by a preponderance of the evidence, that either of the following applies:

(1) The supplier was negligent, and, the negligence was a proximate cause of harm for which the claimant seeks to recover compensatory damages.

(2) The product did not conform, when it left the control of the supplier, to a representation made by the supplier, and the representation and the failure to conform to it were a proximate cause of harm for which the claimant seeks to recover compensatory damages. A supplier is subject to liability for the representation and the failure to conform to it even though the supplier did not act fraudulently, recklessly, or negligently in making the representation.

(B) A supplier of a product is subject to liability for compensatory damages based on a product liability claim under sections 2307.71 to 2307.77 of the Revised Code, as if it were the manufacturer of that product, if the manufacturer of that product is or would be subject to liability for compensatory damages based on a product liability claim under sections 2307.71 to 2307.77 of the Revised Code and any of the following applies:

(1) The manufacturer of that product is not subject to judicial process in this state.

(2) The claimant will be unable to enforce a judgment against the manufacturer of that product due to actual or asserted insolvency of the manufacturer.

(3) The supplier owns or, when it supplied that product, owned, in whole or in part, the manufacturer of that product.

(4) The supplier is owned or, when it supplied that product, was owned, in whole or in part, by the manufacturer of that product.

(5) The supplier created or furnished a manufacturer with the design or formulation that was used to produce, create, make, construct, assemble, or rebuild that product or a component of that product.

(6) The supplier altered, modified, or failed to maintain that product after it came into the possession of, and before it left the possession of, the supplier, and the alteration, modification, or failure to maintain that product rendered it defective.

(7) The supplier marketed that product under its own label or trade name.

(8) The supplier failed to respond timely and reasonably to a written request by or on behalf of the claimant to disclose to the claimant the name and address of the manufacturer of that product.

§ 2307.79. Compensatory damages for economic loss. (A) If a claimant is entitled to recover compensatory damages for harm from a manufacturer in accordance with section 2307.73 of the Revised Code or from a supplier in accordance with division (B) of section 2307.78 of the Revised Code, the claimant may recover from the manufacturer or supplier in question, in that action, compensatory damages for any economic loss that proximately resulted from the defective aspect of the product in question.

"Piggyback"

(B) If a claimant is entitled to recover compensatory damages for harm from a supplier in accordance with division (A) of section 2307.78 of the Revised Code, the claimant may recover from the supplier in question, in that action, compensatory damages for any economic loss that proximately resulted from the negligence of that supplier or from the representation made by that supplier and the failure of the product in question to conform to that representation.

* NO PRE-EMPTION *

§ 2307.791. Industrywide, enterprise or alternative liability.

A manufacturer shall not be held liable for damages based on a product liability claim that asserts any of the following theories:

(A) Industrywide or enterprise liability, including, but not limited to, any claim that seeks to impose liability on an entire industry or enterprise, on any members of an entire industry or enterprise, or on any trade association of an entire industry or enterprise that alleges both of the following:

(1) Joint awareness of product risks;

(2) Joint development of product safety standards or delegation of safety functions to an industry trade association or another entity;

(B) Alternative liability, except when all possible tortfeasors are named and subject to the jurisdiction of the court.

§ 2307.792. Claim of injury from exposure to hazardous or toxic substance.
If a plaintiff alleges injury from exposure to hazardous or toxic substances as a result of the tortious acts of one or more defendants, in order to maintain a cause of action against any of those defendants based on that injury, the plaintiff must prove that the conduct of that particular defendant was a substantial factor in causing the injury on which the cause of action is based.

A plaintiff who alleges injury from exposure to hazardous or toxic substances has the burden of proving that the plaintiff was exposed to a hazardous or toxic substance that was manufactured, supplied, installed, or used by the defendant and that the hazardous or toxic substance was a substantial factor in causing the plaintiff's injury. In determining whether a hazardous or toxic substance was a substantial factor in causing the plaintiff's injury, the trier of fact shall consider, without limitation, all of the following:

(A) The manner in which the plaintiff was exposed to the hazardous or toxic substance;

(B) The proximity of the hazardous or toxic substance to the plaintiff when exposure occurred;

(C) The frequency and length of exposure;

(D) Any factors that mitigated or enhanced exposure.

§ 2307.80. Evidence of recall notification.
(A) If the product involved in a product liability claim was the subject of a recall notification issued before the cause of action accrued upon the basis of which the product liability claim is asserted and if the defective aspect of the product described in the recall notification is the defective aspect of the product that the claimant alleges was a proximate cause of harm for which the claimant seeks to recover compensatory damages under sections 2307.71 to 2307.80 of the Revised Code or punitive or exemplary damages under section 2307.801 [2307.80.1] of the Revised Code from a manufacturer or

supplier of the product, evidence of the recall notification is admissible in that civil action as follows:

(1) The manufacturer or supplier that issued the recall notification may submit the following types of evidence:

(a) Evidence pertaining to the manner in which the recall notification was issued to the purchaser or lessee of the product;

(b) Evidence pertaining to the manner in which the recall notification described the defective aspect of the product and the other terms and conditions of the recall notification;

(c) Evidence that the purchaser or lessee of the product failed to comply with the terms and conditions of the recall notification and had a reasonable time to so comply prior to the occurrence of the harm that the claimant alleges was proximately caused by the defective aspect of the product described in the recall notification;

(d) Evidence that, if the purchaser or lessee of the product had complied with the terms and conditions of the recall notification, the harm that the claimant alleges was proximately caused by the defective aspect of the product described in the recall notification likely would not have occurred.

(2) If a manufacturer or supplier submits evidence as described in division (A)(1) of this section, the claimant may present either of the following types of evidence:

(a) Evidence that the purchaser or lessee of the product never received the recall notification allegedly issued by the manufacturer or supplier;

(b) Evidence establishing justification for noncompliance with the terms and conditions of the recall notification prior to the occurrence of the harm that the claimant alleges was proximately caused by the defective aspect of the product described in the recall notification.

(B) If a manufacturer or supplier submits evidence as described in division (A)(1) of this section in connection with a product liability claim, the trier of fact shall consider that evidence and any evidence presented by the claimant as described in division (A)(2) of this section in making its determination on the product liability claim. After weighing the evidence of the manufacturer or supplier against the evidence of the claimant, if the trier of fact finds that the evidence of the manufacturer or supplier outweighs the evidence of the claimant, the trier of fact may consider the manufacturer's or supplier's evidence as follows:

(1) If the claimant and the purchaser or lessee of the product involved are the same person, the trier of fact may consider the noncompliance with the terms and conditions of the recall notification to constitute an implied assumption of the risk for purposes of section 2315.20 of the Revised Code.

(2) If the claimant and the purchaser or lessee of the product involved are not the same person, the trier of fact may consider the purchaser's or

lessee's noncompliance with the terms and conditions of the recall notification to be a superseding or intervening cause of the harm that the claimant alleges was proximately caused by the defective aspect of the product described in the recall notification.

(3) For purposes of determining liability for punitive or exemplary damages under section 2307.801 [2307.80.1] of the Revised Code, the trier of fact may consider the fact that the manufacturer or supplier issued the recall notification as evidence of an absence of misconduct that manifested a flagrant disregard of the safety of persons who might be harmed by the product involved.

(C) Regardless of whether a purchaser or lessee of a product involved in a product liability claim complied with the terms and conditions of a recall notification, if the claimant alleges that the product was defective in manufacture or construction as described in section 2307.74 of the Revised Code and submits evidence that the harm for which the claimant seeks to recover compensatory damages was proximately caused by the defective aspect of the product described in the recall notification, the fact of the issuance of the recall notification may be introduced into evidence for the purpose of creating an inference that the defective aspect of the product described in the recall notification existed at the time that the product left the control of its manufacturer.

(D) Except as otherwise provided in division (C) of this section, in a civil action based on a product liability claim, recall notifications shall not be presented to or considered by the trier of fact for any purpose other than the following purposes:

(1) To prove ownership or control of the product;

(2) Impeachment;

(3) Those specifically set forth in this section.

§ 2307.801. Punitive or exemplary damages. (A) Subject to divisions (C) and (D) of this section, punitive or exemplary damages may be awarded against a manufacturer or supplier in connection with a product liability claim only if the claimant establishes, by clear and convincing evidence, that harm for which the claimant is entitled to recover compensatory damages in accordance with sections 2307.71 to 2307.801 [2307.80.1] of the Revised Code was the result of misconduct of the manufacturer or supplier that manifested a flagrant disregard of the safety of persons who might be harmed by the product involved. The fact by itself that a product is defective does not establish a flagrant disregard of the safety of persons who might be harmed by that product.

(B) Whether the trier of fact is a jury or the court, if the trier of fact determines that a manufacturer or supplier is liable for punitive or exemplary damages in connection with a product liability claim, the trier of fact shall determine the amount of those damages after considering all relevant factors, including, but not limited to, the following:

(1) The likelihood that serious harm would arise from the misconduct of the manufacturer or supplier;

(2) The degree of the awareness of the manufacturer or supplier of that likelihood;

(3) The duration of the misconduct and any concealment of it by the manufacturer or supplier;

(4) The attitude and conduct of the manufacturer or supplier upon the discovery of the misconduct and whether the misconduct has terminated;

(5) The financial condition of the manufacturer or supplier.

(C)(1) Except as provided in division (C)(2) of this section, if a claimant alleges in a product liability claim that a drug or device caused harm to the claimant, the manufacturer of the drug or device shall not be liable for punitive or exemplary damages in connection with that product liability claim if the drug or device that allegedly caused the harm satisfies either of the following:

(a) It was manufactured and labeled in relevant and material respects in accordance with the terms of an approval or license issued by the federal food and drug administration under the "Federal Food, Drug, and Cosmetic Act," 52 Stat. 1040 (1938), 21 U.S.C. 301–392, as amended, or the "Public Health Service Act," 58 Stat. 682 (1944), 42 U.S.C. 201–300cc–15, as amended.

(b) It was an over-the-counter drug marketed pursuant to federal regulations, was generally recognized as safe and effective and as not being misbranded pursuant to the applicable federal regulations, and satisfied in relevant and material respects each of the conditions contained in the applicable federal regulations and each of the conditions contained in an applicable monograph.

(2) Division (C)(1) of this section does not apply if the claimant establishes, by a preponderance of the evidence, that the manufacturer fraudulently and in violation of applicable regulations of the food and drug administration withheld from the food and drug administration information known to be material and relevant to the harm that the claimant allegedly suffered or misrepresented to the food and drug administration information of that type.

(3) For purposes of divisions (C) and (D) of this section:

(a) "Drug" has the same meaning as in the "Federal Food, Drug, and Cosmetic Act," 52 Stat. 1040, 1041 (1938), 21 U.S.C. 321(g)(1), as amended.

(b) "Federal regulations" means regulations of the food and drug administration that are adopted pursuant to the "Federal Food, Drug, and Cosmetic Act," 52 Stat. 1040 (1938), 21 U.S.C. 301–392, as amended, and that are set forth in Parts 300, 400, 600, 800, and 1000 of Chapter I of Title 21 of the Code of Federal Regulations, 21 C.F.R. 300, 400, 600, 800, and 1000, as amended.

(c) "Device" has the same meaning as in the "Federal Food, Drug, and Cosmetic Act," 52 Stat. 1040, 1041 (1938), 21 U.S.C. 321(h), as amended.

(D) If a claimant alleges in a product liability claim that a product other than a drug or device caused harm to the claimant, the manufacturer or supplier of the product shall not be liable for punitive or exemplary damages in connection with the claim if the manufacturer or supplier fully complied with all applicable government standards relative to the product's manufacture or construction, the product's design or formulation, adequate warnings or instructions, and representations when the product left the control of the manufacturer or supplier.

(E) The bifurcated trial provisions of division (B) of section 2315.21 of the Revised Code, the ceiling on recoverable punitive or exemplary damages specified in division (D)(1) of that section, and the provisions of division (D)(3) of that section apply to awards of punitive or exemplary damages under this section.

§ 2315.20. Assumption of risk, contributory negligence or other contributory tortious conduct in product liability claims.

(A) As used in this section:

(1) "Claimant," "harm," and "product liability claim" have the same meanings as in section 2307.71 of the Revised Code.

(2) "Conduct" means actions or omissions.

(3) "Economic loss" and "noneconomic loss" have the same meanings as in section 2323.54 of the Revised Code.

(4) "Other contributory tortious conduct" or "other tortious conduct" means tortious conduct that contributes to the injury, death, or loss to person or property for which the plaintiff or the person for whom the plaintiff is legal representative is seeking relief but does not include conduct constituting express assumption of the risk or implied assumption of the risk.

(B)(1) Express or implied assumption of the risk may be asserted as an affirmative defense to a product liability claim.

(2) If express or implied assumption of the risk is asserted as an affirmative defense to a product liability claim and if it is determined that the claimant expressly or impliedly assumed a risk and that the express or implied assumption of the risk was a direct and proximate cause of harm for which the claimant seeks to recover damages, the express or implied assumption of the risk is a complete bar to the recovery of those damages.

(C) Contributory negligence or other contributory tortious conduct may be asserted as an affirmative defense to a product liability claim. Contributory negligence or other contributory tortious conduct of a plaintiff or of a person for whom the plaintiff is the legal representative does not bar the plaintiff from recovering damages that have directly and proximately resulted from the tortious conduct of one or more other persons, if the contributory negligence or other contributory tortious conduct of the plaintiff or of the person for whom the plaintiff is legal representative was no greater than the combined tortious conduct of all other persons from whom the plaintiff seeks recovery and of all other persons from whom the plaintiff does not seek recovery, including, but not limited to, persons who have entered into a settlement agreement with the plaintiff, persons whom the plaintiff has dismissed from the action without prejudice, and persons whom the plaintiff has dismissed from the action with prejudice, whether or not a person was or could have been a party to the action. However, the compensatory damages recoverable by the plaintiff shall be diminished by an amount that is proportionately equal to the percentage of negligence or other tortious conduct of the plaintiff or of the person for whom the plaintiff is legal representative, which percentage is determined pursuant to division (D) of this section. This section does not apply to actions described in section 4113.03 of the Revised Code.

(D) If contributory negligence or other contributory tortious conduct is asserted and established as an affirmative defense to a product liability claim, the court in a nonjury action shall make findings of fact, and the jury in a jury action shall return a general verdict accompanied by answers to interrogatories, that shall specify the following:

(1) The total amount of the compensatory damages that would have been recoverable on that product liability claim but for the negligence or other tortious conduct of the plaintiff or the person for whom the plaintiff is legal representative;

(2) The portion of the compensatory damages specified under division (D)(1) of this section that represents economic loss;

(3) The portion of the compensatory damages specified under division (D)(1) of this section that represents noneconomic loss;

(4) The percentage of negligence or other tortious conduct determined pursuant to division (C) of section 2307.31 of the Revised Code.

(E) After the court makes its findings of fact or after the jury returns its general verdict accompanied by answers to interrogatories as described in division (D) of this section, the court shall diminish the total amount of the compensatory damages that would have been recoverable by an amount that is proportionately equal to the percentage of negligence or other tortious conduct that is attributable to the plaintiff or the person for whom the plaintiff is legal representative, which percentage was determined pursuant to division (D) of this section. If the percentage of the negligence or other tortious conduct that is attributable to the plaintiff or the person for whom the plaintiff is legal representative is greater than the total of the percentages of the tortious conduct that are attributable to all parties from whom the plaintiff seeks recovery and to all persons from whom the plaintiff does not seek recovery, including, but not limited to, persons who have entered into a settlement agreement with the plaintiff, persons whom the plaintiff has dismissed from the action without prejudice, and persons whom the plaintiff has dismissed from the action with prejudice, whether or not a person was or could have been a party to the action, which percentages were determined pursuant to division (D) of this section, the court shall enter judgment in favor of those parties.

(F) If contributory negligence or other contributory tortious conduct is asserted as an affirmative defense to a product liability claim, if it is determined that the plaintiff or the person for whom the plaintiff is legal representative was contributorily negligent or engaged in other contributory tortious conduct and that the contributory negligence or other contributory tortious conduct was a direct and proximate cause of the injury, death, or loss to person or property involved, and if the plaintiff is entitled to recover compensatory damages pursuant to this section from more than one party, after it makes findings of fact or after the jury returns its general verdict

accompanied by answers to interrogatories as described in division (D) of this section, the court shall enter a judgment that is in favor of the plaintiff and that imposes liability pursuant to division (B) of section 2307.31 of the Revised Code.

(G) This section shall be considered to be purely remedial in operation and shall be applied in a remedial manner in any civil action commenced on or after the effective date of this section, in which this section is relevant, regardless of when the cause of action accrued and notwithstanding any other section of the Revised Code or prior rule of law of this state, but shall not be construed to apply to any civil action pending prior to the effective date of this section.

§ 2315.21. Recovery of punitive or exemplary damages in tort actions. (A) As used in this section:

(1) "Economic loss" has the same meaning as in section 2323.54 of the Revised Code.

(2) "Employer" includes, but is not limited to, a parent, subsidiary, affiliate, division, or department of the employer. If the employer is an individual, the individual shall be considered an employer under this section only if the subject of the tort action is related to the individual's capacity as an employer.

(3) "Large employer" means an employer who employs more than twenty-five persons on a full-time permanent basis.

(4) "Tort action" means a civil action for damages for injury, death, or loss to person or property. "Tort action" includes a product liability claim but does not include a civil action for damages for a breach of contract or another agreement between persons.

(5) "Trier of fact" means the jury or, in a nonjury action, the court.

(B)(1) In a tort action in which a plaintiff makes a claim for compensatory damages and a claim for punitive or exemplary damages, upon the motion of any party, the trial of the tort action shall be bifurcated as follows:

(a) The initial stage of the trial shall relate only to the presentation of evidence, and a determination by the trier of fact, with respect to whether the plaintiff is entitled to recover compensatory damages for the injury or loss to person or property from the defendant. During this stage, no party to the tort action shall present, and the court shall not permit a party to present, evidence that relates solely to the issue of whether the plaintiff is entitled to recover punitive or exemplary damages for the injury or loss to person or property from the defendant.

(b) If the trier of fact determines in the initial stage of the trial that the plaintiff is entitled to recover compensatory damages for the injury or loss to person or property from the defendant, evidence may be presented in the second stage of the trial, and a determination by the trier of fact shall be made, with respect to whether the plaintiff additionally is entitled to recover punitive or exemplary damages for the injury or loss to person or property from the defendant.

(2) In a tort action that is tried to a jury and in which a plaintiff makes a claim for both compensatory damages and punitive or exemplary damages, the court shall instruct the jury to return, and the jury shall return, a general verdict and, if that verdict is in favor of the plaintiff, answers to an interrogatory that specifies the total compensatory damages recoverable by the plaintiff from each defendant.

(3) In a tort action that is tried to a court and in which a plaintiff makes a claim for both compensatory damages and punitive or exemplary damages, the court shall make its determination whether the plaintiff is entitled to recover compensatory damages for the injury or loss to person or property from the defendant and, if that determination is in favor of the plaintiff, shall make findings of fact that specify the total compensatory damages recoverable by the plaintiff from the defendant.

(C) Subject to division (E) of this section, punitive or exemplary damages are not recoverable from a defendant in a tort action unless both of the following apply:

(1) The actions or omissions of that defendant demonstrate malice, aggravated or egregious fraud, or insult, or that defendant as principal or master authorized, participated in, or ratified actions or omissions of an agent or servant that so demonstrate.

(2) The trier of fact has returned a verdict or has made a determination pursuant to division (B)(2) or (3) of this section of the total compensatory damages recoverable by the plaintiff from that defendant.

(D)(1) In a tort action, the trier of fact shall determine the liability of a defendant for punitive or exemplary damages and the amount of those damages to be awarded.

(a) Except as otherwise provided in division (D)(3)(b) of this section, the court shall not enter judgment for punitive or exemplary damages in excess of the lesser of three times the amount of the compensatory damages awarded to the plaintiff from that defendant or one hundred thousand dollars, as determined pursuant to division (B)(2) or (3) of this section.

(b) If the defendant is a large employer, except as otherwise provided in division (D)(3)(b) of this section, the court shall not enter judgment for punitive or exemplary damages in excess of the greater of three times the amount of the compensatory damages awarded to the plaintiff from that defendant or two hundred fifty thousand dollars, as determined pursuant to division (B)(2) or (3) of this section.

(c) When determining the amount of an award of punitive or exemplary damages, the trier of fact shall consider both of the following:

(i) The ability of the defendant to pay the award of punitive or exemplary damages based on the defendant's assets, income, and net worth;

(ii) Whether the amount of punitive or exemplary damages is sufficient to deter future tortious conduct.

(2) In a tort action, the burden of proof shall be upon the plaintiff to establish, by clear and convincing evidence, that the plaintiff is entitled to recover punitive or exemplary damages from the defendant.

(3)(a) In any tort action, except as provided in division (D)(3)(b) of this section, punitive or exemplary damages shall not be awarded against any defendant if that defendant files with the court a certified judgment, judgment entries, or other evidence showing that punitive or exemplary damages have already been awarded and have been collected, in any state or federal court, against that defendant based on the same act or course of conduct that is alleged to have caused the injury or loss to person or property for which the plaintiff seeks compensatory damages and that the aggregate of those previous punitive or exemplary damage awards exceeds one hundred thousand dollars or, if the defendant is a large employer, two hundred fifty thousand dollars.

(b) Notwithstanding division (D)(3)(a) of this section, punitive or exemplary damages may be awarded against a defendant in either of the following types of tort actions:

(i) In subsequent tort actions involving the same act or course of conduct for which punitive or exemplary damages have already been awarded, if the court determines by clear and convincing evidence that the plaintiff will offer new and substantial evidence of previously undiscovered, additional behavior as described in division (C) of this section on the part of that defendant, other than the injury or loss for which the plaintiff seeks compensatory damages. In that case, the court shall make specific findings of fact in the record to support its conclusion. The court shall reduce the amount of any punitive or exemplary damages otherwise awardable pursuant to this section by the sum of the punitive or exemplary damages awards previously rendered against that defendant in any state or federal court. The court shall not inform the jury about the court's determination and action under division (D)(3)(b)(i) of this section.

(ii) In subsequent tort actions involving the same act or course of conduct for which punitive or exemplary damages have already been awarded, if the court determines by clear and convincing evidence that the total amount of prior punitive or exemplary damages awards was totally insufficient to punish that defendant's behavior as described in division (C) of this section and to deter that defendant and others from similar behavior in the future. In that case, the court shall make specific findings of fact in the record to support its conclusion. The court shall reduce the amount of any punitive or exemplary damages otherwise awardable pursuant to this section by the sum of the punitive or exemplary damages awards previously rendered against that defendant in any state or federal court. The court shall not inform the jury about the court's determination and action under division (D)(3)(b)(ii) of this section.

(c) For purposes of product liability claims subject to sections 2307.71 to 2307.801 [2307.80.1] of the Revised Code, substantially the same defects in manufacture or construction, substantially the same defects in design or formulation, or substantially the same defects due to inadequate warnings or instructions, with respect to substantially similar units of a product shall be considered the same act or course of conduct for purposes of division (D)(3) of this section.

(E) This section does not apply to tort actions against the state in the court of claims, including, but not limited to, tort actions against a state university or college that are subject to division (B)(1) of section 3345.40 of the Revised Code, to tort actions against political subdivisions of this state that are commenced under or are subject to Chapter 2744. of the Revised Code, or to the extent that another section of the Revised Code expressly provides any of the following:

(1) Punitive or exemplary damages are recoverable from a defendant in a tort action on a basis other than that the actions or omissions of that defendant demonstrate malice, aggravated or egregious fraud, or insult, or on a basis other than that the defendant as principal or master authorized, participated in, or ratified actions or omissions of an agent or servant that so demonstrate.

(2) Punitive or exemplary damages are recoverable from a defendant in a tort action irrespective of whether the plaintiff has been determined by the trier of fact to be entitled to recover compensatory damages for the injury or loss to person or property from a defendant.

(3) The burden of proof upon a plaintiff to recover punitive or exemplary damages from a defendant in a tort action is one other than clear and convincing evidence.

(4) Punitive or exemplary damages are not recoverable from a defendant in a tort action.

(5) Punitive or exemplary damages recoverable from a defendant may exceed an amount described in division (D)(1) or (3) of this section, may be in another specified amount, or are not subject to any limitation on amount.

(F) If the trier of fact is a jury, the court shall not instruct the jury with respect to the limits on punitive or exemplary damages pursuant to division (D) of this section, and neither counsel for any party nor a witness shall inform the jury or potential jurors of those limits.

(G) Except for divisions (C) and (D)(1) and (2) of this section, this section shall be considered to be purely remedial in its operation and shall be applied in a remedial manner in any civil action in which this section is relevant, whether the civil action is pending in court or commenced on or after the effective date of this section, regardless of when the cause of action accrued and notwithstanding any other provision of statute or prior rule of law of this state.

Divisions (C) and (D)(2) of this section shall be considered to be purely remedial in operation and shall be applied in a remedial manner in any civil action commenced on or after the effective date of this section, in which this section is relevant, regardless of when the cause of action accrued and notwithstanding any other section of the Revised Code or prior rule of law of this state, but shall not be construed to apply to any civil action pending prior to the effective date of this section.

§ 2323.54. **Limits on recovery for noneconomic loss in tort actions.** (A) As used in this section:

(1) "Economic loss" means any of the following types of pecuniary harm:

(a) All wages, salaries, or other compensation lost as a result of an injury, death, or loss to person or property that is a subject of a tort action, including wages, salaries, or other compensation lost as of the date of a judgment and future expected lost earnings;

(b) All expenditures for medical care or treatment, rehabilitation services, or other care, treatment, services, products, or accommodations incurred as a result of an injury, death, or loss to person that is a subject of a tort action, including expenditures for those purposes that were incurred as of the date of a judgment and expenditures for those purposes that, in the determination of the trier of fact, will be incurred in the future because of the injury, whether paid by the injured person or by another person on behalf of the injured person;

(c) All expenditures of a person whose property was injured or destroyed or of another person on behalf of the person whose property was injured or destroyed in order to repair or replace the property;

(d) Any other expenditures incurred as a result of an injury, death, or loss to person or property that is a subject of a tort action, except expenditures of the injured person, the person whose property was injured or destroyed, or another person on behalf of the injured person or the person whose property was injured or destroyed in relation to the actual preparation or presentation of the claim involved.

(2) "Noneconomic loss" means nonpecuniary harm that results from an injury, death, or loss to person that is a subject of a tort action, including, but not limited to, pain and suffering, loss of society, consortium, companionship, care, assistance, attention, protection, advice, guidance, counsel, instruction, training, or education, mental anguish, and any other intangible loss.

(3) "Tort action" means a civil action for damages for injury, death, or loss to person or property. "Tort action" includes a product liability claim but does not include a civil action for damages for a breach of contract or another agreement between persons.

(4) "Trier of fact" means the jury or, in a nonjury action, the court.

(B)(1) Except as otherwise provided in division (B)(2) of this section, the amount of compensatory damages that represents damages for noneconomic loss that is recoverable in a tort action shall not exceed the greater of two hundred fifty thousand dollars or an amount that is equal to three times the plaintiff's economic loss, as determined by the trier of fact, to a maximum of five hundred thousand dollars.

(2) The amount recoverable for noneconomic losses may exceed the amount described in division (B)(1) of this section but shall not exceed the greater of one million dollars or thirty-five thousand dollars times the number of years remaining in the plaintiff's expected life if the noneconomic losses of the plaintiff are for either of the following:

(a) Permanent and substantial physical deformity, loss of use of a limb, or loss of a bodily organ system;

(b) Permanent physical functional injury that permanently prevents the injured person from being able to independently care for herself or himself and perform life sustaining activities.

(C) If a trial is conducted in a tort action and a plaintiff prevails with respect to any claim for relief, the court in a nonjury trial shall make findings of fact, and the jury in a jury trial shall return a general verdict accompanied by answers to interrogatories, that shall specify all of the following:

(1) The total compensatory damages recoverable by the plaintiff, subject to possible adjustment under division (D) of this section;

(2) The portion of the total compensatory damages that represents damages for economic loss;

(3) The portion of the total compensatory damages that represents damages for noneconomic loss and that is subject to possible adjustment under division (D) of this section.

(D) After the trier of fact in a tort action complies with division (C) of this section, the court shall enter a judgment in favor of the plaintiff for compensatory damages for economic loss in the amount determined pursuant to division (C)(2) of this section and a judgment in favor of the plaintiff for compensatory damages for noneconomic loss in whichever of the following amounts applies:

(1) The amount determined pursuant to division (C)(3) of this section if that amount is equal to or less than the applicable maximum amount recoverable for noneconomic loss as provided in division (B) of this section;

(2) The maximum amount recoverable for noneconomic loss as provided in division (B) of this section if the amount determined pursuant to division (C)(3) of this section is greater than the applicable maximum amount recoverable for noneconomic loss as provided in division (B) of this section.

(E) Nothing in this section shall be construed to create a new right or cause of action for noneconomic loss or damages.

(F) This section does not affect an award of court costs to a plaintiff pursuant to Civil Rule 54 or an award of reasonable attorney's fees to a plaintiff when authorized by a section of the Revised Code or the Rules of Civil Procedure.

(G) This section does not apply as follows:

(1) In tort actions against the state in the court of claims, including, but not limited to, tort actions in which a state university or college is a defendant and to which division (B)(3) of section 3345.40 of the Revised Code applies;

(2) In tort actions against political subdivisions of this state that are commenced under or are subject to Chapter 2744. of the Revised Code. Division (C) of section 2744.05 of the Revised Code applies to recoverable damages in those tort actions.

(H) If the trier of fact is a jury, the court shall not instruct the jury with respect to the limit on compensatory damages for noneconomic loss described in divisions (B) and (D) of this section, and neither counsel for any party nor a witness shall inform the jury or potential jurors of that limit.

Oregon Revised Statutes
(1977, 1979, 1989, and 1995)

§ 30.900. "Product liability civil action" defined. As used in ORS 30.900 to 30.920 "product liability civil action" means a civil action brought against a manufacturer, distributor, seller or lessor of a product for damages for personal injury, death or property damage arising out of:

(1) Any design, inspection, testing, manufacturing or other defect in a product;

(2) Any failure to warn regarding a product; or

(3) Any failure to properly instruct in the use of a product.

§ 30.905. Time limitation for commencement of action. (1) Notwithstanding ORS 12.115 or 12.140 and except as provided in subsection (2) of this section and ORS 30.907, a product liability civil action shall be commenced not later than eight years after the date on which the product was first purchased for use or consumption.

(2) Except as provided in ORS 30.907, a product liability civil action shall be commenced not later than two years after the date on which the death, injury or damage complained of occurs.

Note: Section 7, chapter 259, Oregon Laws 1993, provides:

Sec. 7. (1) Sections 2, 4 and 5 of this Act (12.276 and 30.908) and the amendments to ORS 30.905 by section of this Act apply to all causes of action whether arising before, on or after the effective date of the Act (July 6, 1993), and except as provided in subsection 2 of this section shall act to revive any cause of action barred by the operation of . . . ORS 30.905 (1991 Edition).

(2) Sections 2, 4 and 5 of this Act and the amendments to ORS 30.905 by section of this Act shall not operate to revive any cause of action that has been settled, compromised or adjudicated except that any cause of action based on death, injury or damage resulting from a breast implant containing silicone, silica or silicon as a component that was dismissed or adjudged based on the operation of . . . ORS 30.905 (1991 Edition) within one year before the effective date of this Act shall be revived. Notwithstanding any other provision of law, a cause of action revived under the provisions of this subsection must be brought within one year after the effective date of this Act. [1993 c. 259 § 7].

§ 30.907. Action for damages from asbestos related disease; limitations. A product liability civil action for damages resulting from asbestos related disease shall be commenced not later than two years after the date on which the plaintiff first discovered, or in the exercise of reasonable care should have discovered, the disease and the cause thereof.

§ 30.908. Action arising out of injury from breast implants; limitations. (1) Notwithstanding ORS 30.020, a product liability civil action for death, injury or damage resulting from breast implants containing silicone, silica or silicon as a component must be commenced not later than two years after the date on which the plaintiff first discovered, or in the exercise of reasonable care should have discovered:

(a) The death or specific injury, disease or damage for which the plaintiff seeks recovery;

(b) The tortious nature of the act or omission of the defendant that gives rise to a claim for relief against the defendant; and

(c) All other elements required to establish plaintiff's claim for relief.

(2) A product liability civil action for death, injury or damage resulting from breast implants containing silicone, silica or silicon as a component is not subject to ORS 30.905 or any other statute of repose in Oregon Revised Statutes.

(3) For the purposes of subsection (1) of this section, an action for wrongful death must be commenced not later than two years after the earliest date that the discoveries required by subsection (1) of this section are made by any of the following persons:

(a) The decedent;

(b) The personal representative for the decedent; or

(c) Any person for whose benefit the action could be brought.

(4) Subsections (1) to (4) of this section do not apply to a person that supplied component parts or raw materials to manufacturers of breast implants containing silicone, silica or silicon as a component, and the person shall remain subject to the limitations on actions imposed by ORS 30.020 and 30.905, if:

(a) The person did not manufacture breast implants containing silicone, silica or silicon as a component at any time; and

(b) The person was not owned by and did not own a business that manufactured breast implants containing silicone, silica or silicon as a component at any time.

(5) A physician licensed pursuant to ORS chapter 677 is not a manufacturer, distributor, seller or lessor of a breast implant for the purposes of ORS 30.900 to 30.920 if the implant is provided by the physician to a patient as part of a medical implant procedure.

(6) A health care facility licensed under ORS chapter 442 is not a manufacturer, distributor, seller or lessor of a breast implant for the purposes of ORS 30.900 to 30.920 if the implant is provided by the facility to a patient as part of a medical implant procedure.

§ 30.910. **Product disputably presumed not unreasonably dangerous.** It is a disputable presumption in a products liability civil action that a product as manufactured and sold or leased is not unreasonably dangerous for its intended use.

§ 30.915. Defenses. It shall be a defense to a product liability civil action that an alteration or modification of a product occurred under the following circumstances:

(1) The alteration or modification was made without the consent of or was made not in accordance with the instructions or specifications of the manufacturer, distributor, seller or lessor;

(2) The alteration or modification was a substantial contributing factor to the personal injury, death or property damage; and

(3) If the alteration or modification was reasonably foreseeable, the manufacturer, distributor, seller or lessor gave adequate warning.

§ 30.920. When seller or lessor of product liable—Effect of liability rule. (1) One who sells or leases any product in a defective condition unreasonably dangerous to the user or consumer or to his property is subject to liability for physical harm or damage to property caused by that condition, if:

(a) The seller or lessor is engaged in the business of selling or leasing such a product; and

(b) The product is expected to and does reach the user or consumer without substantial change in the condition in which it is sold or leased.

(2) The rule stated in subsection (1) of this section shall apply, even though:

(a) The seller or lessor has exercised all possible care in the preparation and sale or lease of the product; and

(b) The user, consumer or injured party has not purchased or leased the product from or entered into any contractual relations with the seller or lessor.

(3) It is the intent of the Legislative Assembly that the rule stated in subsections (1) and (2) of this section shall be construed in accordance with the *Restatement (Second) of Torts* § 402A, Comments *a* to *m* (1965). All references in these comments to sale, sell, selling or seller shall be construed to include lease, leases, leasing or lessor.

(4) Nothing in this section shall be construed to limit the rights and liabilities of sellers and lessors under principles of common law negligence or under ORS chapter 72.

§ 30.925. Punitive damages. (1) In a product liability civil action, punitive damages shall not be recoverable except as provided in ORS 18.537.

(2) Punitive damages, if any, shall be determined and awarded based upon the following criteria:

(a) The likelihood at the time that serious harm would arise from the defendant's misconduct;

(b) The degree of the defendant's awareness of that likelihood;

(c) The profitability of the defendant's misconduct;

(d) The duration of the misconduct and any concealment of it;

(e) The attitude and conduct of the defendant upon discovery of the misconduct;

(f) The financial condition of the defendant; and

(g) The total deterrent effect of other punishment imposed upon the defendant as a result of the misconduct, including, but not limited to, punitive damage awards to persons in situations similar to the claimant's and the severity of criminal penalties to which the defendant has been or may be subjected.

Note: Section 5, chapter 688, Oregon Laws 1995, provides:

Sec. 5. Sections 2 and 3 of this Act [18.537 and 18.535], the amendments to ORS 18.540 and 30.925 by sections 1 and 4 of this Act, and the repeal of ORS 41.315 by section 6 of this Act, apply only to actions commenced on or after the effective date of this Act [September 9, 1995].

§ 30.927. When manufacturer of drug not liable for punitive damages; exceptions. (1) Where a drug allegedly caused the plaintiff harm, the manufacturer of the drug shall not be liable for punitive damages if the drug product alleged to have caused the harm:

(a) Was manufactured and labeled in relevant and material respects in accordance with the terms of an approval or license issued by the Federal Food and Drug Administration under the Federal Food, Drug and Cosmetic Act or the Public Health Service Act; or

(b) Is generally recognized as safe and effective pursuant to conditions established by the Federal Food and Drug Administration and applicable regulations, including packaging and labeling regulations.

(2) Subsection (1) of this section does not apply if the plaintiff proves, in accordance with the standard of proof set forth in ORS 30.925 (1), that the defendant, either before or after making the drug available for public use, knowingly in violation of applicable Federal Food and Drug Administration regulations withheld from or misrepresented to the agency or prescribing physician information known to be material and relevant to the harm which the plaintiff allegedly suffered.

(3) Nothing contained in this section bars an award of punitive damages where a manufacturer of a drug intentionally fails to conduct a recall required by a valid order of a federal or state agency authorized by statute to require such a recall.

(4) For the purposes of this section, the term "drug" has the meaning given to the term in section 1201 (g)(1) of the Federal Food, Drug and Cosmetic Act, 21 U.S.C. 321 (g)(1).

§ 18.537. Standards for award of punitive damages; required review of award by court; additional reduction of award for reme-

dial measures. (1) Punitive damages are not recoverable in a civil action unless it is proven by clear and convincing evidence that the party against whom punitive damages are sought has acted with malice or has shown a reckless and outrageous indifference to a highly unreasonable risk of harm and has acted with a conscious indifference to the health, safety and welfare of others.

(2) If an award of punitive damages is made by a jury, the court shall review the award to determine whether the award is within the range of damages that a rational juror would be entitled to award based on the record as a whole, viewing the statutory and common-law factors that allow an award of punitive damages for the specific type of claim at issue in the proceeding.

(3) In addition to any reduction that may be made under subsection (2) of this section, upon the motion of a defendant the court may reduce the amount of any judgment requiring the payment of punitive damages entered against the defendant if the defendant establishes that the defendant has taken remedial measures that are reasonable under the circumstances to prevent reoccurrence of the conduct that gave rise to the claim for punitive damages. In reducing awards of punitive damages under the provisions of this subsection, the court shall consider the amount of any previous judgment for punitive damages entered against the same defendant for the same conduct giving rise to a claim for punitive damages.

SOUTH CAROLINA CODE ANNOTATED

(1974)

§ 15–73–10. Liability of seller for defective product. (1) One who sells any product in a defective condition unreasonably dangerous to the user or consumer or to his property is subject to liability for physical harm caused to the ultimate user or consumer, or to his property, if

a. The seller is engaged in the business of selling such a product, and

b. It is expected to and does reach the user or consumer without substantial change in the condition in which it is sold.

2. The rule stated in subsection (1) shall apply although

a. The seller has exercised all possible care in the preparation and sale of his product, and

b. The user or consumer has not brought the product from or entered into any contractual relation with the seller.

§ 15–73–20. Situation in which recovery shall be barred. If the user or consumer discovers the defect and is aware of the danger, and nevertheless proceeds unreasonably to make use of the product and is injured by it, he is barred from recovery.

§ 15–73–30. Intent of chapter. Comments to § 402A of the Restatement of Torts, 2d, are incorporated herein by reference thereto as the legislative intent of this chapter.

Texas Statutes Annotated

(1993)

§ 82.001. **Definitions.** In this chapter:

(1) "Claimant" means a party seeking relief, including a plaintiff, counterclaimant, or cross-claimant.

(2) "Products liability action" means any action against a manufacturer or seller for recovery of damages arising out of personal injury, death, or property damage allegedly caused by a defective product whether the action is based in strict tort liability, strict products liability, negligence, misrepresentation, breach of express or implied warranty, or any other theory or combination of theories.

(3) "Seller" means a person who is engaged in the business of distributing or otherwise placing, for any commercial purpose, in the stream of commerce for use or consumption a product or any component part thereof.

(4) "Manufacturer" means a person who is a designer, formulator, constructor, rebuilder, fabricator, producer, compounder, processor, or assembler of any product or any component part thereof and who places the product or any component part thereof in the stream of commerce.

§ 82.002. **Manufacturer's Duty to Indemnify.** (a) A manufacturer shall indemnify and hold harmless a seller against loss arising out of a products liability action, except for any loss caused by the seller's negligence, intentional misconduct, or other act or omission, such as negligently modifying or altering the product, for which the seller is independently liable.

(b) For purposes of this section, "loss" includes court costs and other reasonable expenses, reasonable attorney fees, and any reasonable damages.

(c) Damages awarded by the trier of fact shall, on final judgment, be deemed reasonable for purposes of this section.

(d) For purposes of this section, a wholesale distributor or retail seller who completely or partially assembles a product in accordance with the manufacturer's instructions shall be considered a seller.

(e) The duty to indemnify under this section:

(1) applies without regard to the manner in which the action is concluded; and

(2) is in addition to any duty to indemnify established by law, contract, or otherwise.

(f) A seller eligible for indemnification under this section shall give reasonable notice to the manufacturer of a product claimed in a petition or complaint to be defective, unless the manufacturer has been served as a party or otherwise has actual notice of the action.

(g) A seller is entitled to recover from the manufacturer court costs and other reasonable expenses, reasonable attorney fees, and any reasonable damages incurred by the seller to enforce the seller's right to indemnification under this section.

[§ 82.003 omitted by legislature.]

§ 82.004. Inherently Unsafe Products. (a) In a products liability action, a manufacturer or seller shall not be liable if:

(1) the product is inherently unsafe and the product is known to be unsafe by the ordinary consumer who consumes the product with the ordinary knowledge common to the community; and

(2) the product is a common consumer product intended for personal consumption, such as sugar, castor oil, alcohol, tobacco, and butter, as identified in Comment i to Section 402A of the Restatement (Second) of Torts.

(b) For purposes of this section, the term "products liability action" does not include an action based on manufacturing defect or breach of an express warranty.

§ 82.005 Design Defects. (a) In a products liability action in which a claimant alleges a design defect, the burden is on the claimant to prove by a preponderance of the evidence that:

(1) there was a safer alternative design; and

(2) the defect was a producing cause of the personal injury, property damage, or death for which the claimant seeks recovery.

(b) In this section, "safer alternative design" means a product design other than the one actually used that in reasonable probability:

(1) would have prevented or significantly reduced the risk of the claimant's personal injury, property damage, or death without substantially impairing the product's utility; and

(2) was economically and technologically feasible at the time the product left the control of the manufacturer or seller by the application of existing or reasonably achievable scientific knowledge.

(c) This section does not supersede or modify any statute, regulation, or other law of this state or of the United States that relates to liability for, or to relief in the form of, abatement of nuisance, civil penalties, cleanup costs, cost recovery, an injunction, or restitution that arises from contamination or pollution of the environment.

(d) This section does not apply to:

(1) a cause of action based on a toxic or environmental tort as defined by Sections 33.013(c)(2) and (3); or

(2) a drug or device, as those terms are defined in the federal Food, Drug, and Cosmetic Act (21 U.S.C. Section 321).

(e) This section is not declarative, by implication or otherwise, of the common law with respect to any product and shall not be construed to restrict the courts of this state in developing the common law with respect to any product which is not subject to this section.

§ 82.006. Firearms and Ammunition. (a) In a products liability action brought against a manufacturer or seller of a firearm or ammunition that alleges a design defect in the firearm or ammunition, the burden is on the claimant to prove, in addition to any other elements that the claimant must prove, that:

(1) the actual design of the firearm or ammunition was defective, causing the firearm or ammunition not to function in a manner reasonably expected by an ordinary consumer of firearms or ammunition; and

(2) the defective design was a producing cause of the personal injury, property damage, or death.

(b) The claimant may not prove the existence of the defective design by a comparison or weighing of the benefits of the firearm or ammunition against the risk of personal injury, property damage, or death posed by its potential to cause such injury, damage, or death when discharged.

§ 16.012. Products Liability: Manufacturing Equipment. (a) In this section:

(1) "Claimant," "products liability action," "seller," and "manufacturer" have the meanings assigned by Section 82.001.

(2) "Manufacturing equipment" means equipment and machinery used in the manufacturing, processing, or fabrication of tangible personal property but does not include agricultural equipment or machinery.

(b) Except as provided by Subsection (c), a claimant must commence a products liability action against a manufacturer or seller of manufacturing equipment before the end of 15 years after the date of the sale of the equipment by the defendant.

(c) If a manufacturer or seller expressly represents that the manufacturing equipment has a useful safe life of longer than 15 years, a claimant must commence a products liability action against that manufacturer or seller of the equipment before the end of the number of years represented after the date of the sale of the equipment by that seller.

(d) This section does not reduce a limitations period that applies to a products liability action involving manufacturing equipment that accrues before the end of the limitations period under this section.

(e) This section does not extend the limitations period within which a products liability action involving manufacturing equipment may be commenced under any other law.

(f) This section applies only to the sale and not to the lease of manufacturing equipment.

WASHINGTON REVISED CODE ANNOTATED
(1981–91)

§ **7.72.010. Definitions.** For the purposes of this chapter, unless the context clearly indicates to the contrary:

(1) Product seller. "Product seller" means any person or entity that is engaged in the business of selling products, whether the sale is for resale, or for use or consumption. The term includes a manufacturer, wholesaler, distributor, or retailer of the relevant product. The term also includes a party who is in the business of leasing or bailing such products. The term "product seller" does not include:

(a) A seller of real property, unless that person is engaged in the mass production and sale of standardized dwellings or is otherwise a product seller;

(b) A provider of professional services who utilizes or sells products within the legally authorized scope of the professional practice of the provider;

(c) A commercial seller of used products who resells a product after use by a consumer or other product user: Provided, That when it is resold, the used product is in essentially the same condition as when it was acquired for resale;

(d) A finance lessor who is not otherwise a product seller. A "finance lessor" is one who acts in a financial capacity, who is not a manufacturer, wholesaler, distributor, or retailer, and who leases a product without having a reasonable opportunity to inspect and discover defects in the product, under a lease arrangement in which the selection, possession, maintenance, and operation of the product are controlled by a person other than the lessor; and

(e) A licensed pharmacist who dispenses a prescription product in the form manufactured by a commercial manufacturer pursuant to a prescription issued by a licensed prescribing practitioner if the claim against the pharmacist is based upon strict liability in tort or the implied warranty provisions under the uniform commercial code, Title 62A RCW, and if the pharmacist complies with recordkeeping requirements pursuant to chapters 18.64, 69.41, and 69.50 RCW, and related administrative rules as provided in RCW 7.72.040. Nothing in this subsection (1)(e) affects a pharmacist's liability under RCW 7.72.040(1).

(2) Manufacturer. "Manufacturer" includes a product seller who designs, produces, makes, fabricates, constructs, or remanufactures the relevant product or component part of a product before its sale to a user or consumer. The term also includes a product seller or entity not otherwise a manufacturer that holds itself out as a manufacturer.

A product seller acting primarily as a wholesaler, distributor, or retailer of a product may be a "manufacturer" but only to the extent that it designs, produces, makes, fabricates, constructs, or remanufactures the product for its sale. A product seller who performs minor assembly of a product in accordance with the instructions of the manufacturer shall not be deemed a manufacturer. A product seller that did not participate in the design of a product and that constructed the product in accordance with the design specifications of the claimant or another product seller shall not be deemed a manufacturer for the purposes of RCW 7.72.030(1)(a).

(3) Product. "Product" means any object possessing intrinsic value, capable of delivery either as an assembled whole or as a component part or parts, and produced for introduction into trade or commerce. Human tissue and organs, including human blood and its components, are excluded from this term.

The "relevant product" under this chapter is that product or its component part or parts, which gave rise to the product liability claim.

(4) Product liability claim. "Product liability claim" includes any claim or action brought for harm caused by the manufacture, production, making, construction, fabrication, design, formula, preparation, assembly, installation, testing, warnings, instructions, marketing, packaging, storage or labeling of the relevant product. It includes, but is not limited to, any claim or action previously based on: Strict liability in tort; negligence; breach of express or implied warranty; breach of, or failure to, discharge a duty to warn or instruct, whether negligent or innocent; misrepresentation, concealment, or nondisclosure, whether negligent or innocent; or other claim or action previously based on any other substantive legal theory except fraud, intentionally caused harm or a claim or action under the consumer protection act, chapter 19.86 RCW.

(5) Claimant. "Claimant" means a person or entity asserting a product liability claim, including a wrongful death action, and, if the claim is asserted through or on behalf of an estate, the term includes claimant's decedent. "Claimant" includes any person or entity that suffers harm. A claim may be asserted under this chapter even though the claimant did not buy the product from, or enter into any contractual relationship with, the product seller.

(6) Harm. "Harm" includes any damages recognized by the courts of this state: Provided, That the term "harm" does not include direct or consequential economic loss under Title 62A RCW [Uniform Commercial Code].

§ 7.72.020. Scope. (1) The previous existing applicable law of this state on product liability is modified only to the extent set forth in this chapter.

(2) Nothing in [this] chapter shall prevent the recovery of direct or consequential economic loss under Title 62A RCW [Uniform Commercial Code].

§ 7.72.030. Liability of manufacturers. (1) A product manufacturer is subject to liability to a claimant if the claimant's harm was proximately caused by the negligence of the manufacturer in that the product was not reasonably safe as designed or not reasonably safe because adequate warnings or instructions were not provided.

(a) A product is not reasonably safe as designed, if, at the time of manufacture, the likelihood that the product would cause the claimant's harm or similar harms, and the seriousness of those harms, outweighed the burden on the manufacturer to design a product that would have prevented those harms and the adverse effect that an alternative design that was practical and feasible would have on the usefulness of the product: Provided, That a firearm or ammunition shall not be deemed defective in design on the basis that the benefits of the product do not outweigh the risk of injury posed by its potential to cause serious injury, damage, or death when discharged.

(b) A product that is not reasonably safe because adequate warnings or instructions were not provided with the product, if, at the time of manufacture, the likelihood that the product would cause the claimant's harm or similar harms, and the seriousness of those harms, rendered the warnings or instructions of the manufacturer inadequate and the manufacturer could have provided the warnings or instructions which the claimant alleges would have been adequate.

(c) A product is not reasonably safe because adequate warnings or instructions were not provided after the product was manufactured where a manufacturer learned or where a reasonably prudent manufacturer should have learned about a danger connected with the product after it was manufactured. In such a case, the manufacturer is under a duty to act with regard to issuing warnings or instructions concerning the danger in the manner that a reasonably prudent manufacturer would act in the same or similar circumstances. This duty is satisfied if the manufacturer exercises reasonable care to inform product users.

(2) A product manufacturer is subject to strict liability to a claimant if the claimant's harm was proximately caused by the fact that the product was not reasonably safe in construction or not reasonably safe because it did not conform to the manufacturer's express warranty or to the implied warranties under Title 62A RCW [Uniform Commercial Code].

(a) A product is not reasonably safe in construction if, when the product left the control of the manufacturer, the product deviated in some material way from the design specifications or performance standards of the manufacturer, or deviated in some material way from otherwise identical units of the same product line.

(b) A product does not conform to the express warranty of the manufacturer if it is made part of the basis of the bargain and relates to a material fact or facts concerning the product and the express warranty proved to be untrue.

(c) Whether or not a product conforms to an implied warranty created under Title 62A RCW [Uniform Commercial Code] shall be determined under that title.

(3) In determining whether a product was not reasonably safe under this section, the trier of fact shall consider whether the product was unsafe to an extent beyond that which would be contemplated by the ordinary consumer.

§ 7.72.040. Liability of product sellers other than manufacturers. (1) Except as provided in subsection (2) of this section, a product seller other than a manufacturer is liable to the claimant only if the claimant's harm was proximately caused by:

(a) The negligence of such product seller; or

(b) Breach of an express warranty made by such product seller; or

(c) The intentional misrepresentation of facts about the product by such product seller or the intentional concealment of information about the product by such product seller.

(2) A product seller, other than a manufacturer, shall have the liability of a manufacturer to the claimant if:

(a) No solvent manufacturer who would be liable to the claimant is subject to service of process under the laws of the claimant's domicile or the state of Washington; or

(b) The court determines that it is highly probable that the claimant would be unable to enforce a judgment against any manufacturer; or

(c) The product seller is a controlled subsidiary of a manufacturer, or the manufacturer is a controlled subsidiary of the product seller; or

(d) The product seller provided the plans or specifications for the manufacture or preparation of the product and such plans or specifications were a proximate cause of the defect in the product; or

(e) The product was marketed under a trade name or brand name of the product seller.

(3) Subsection (2) of this section does not apply to a pharmacist who dispenses a prescription product in the form manufactured by a commercial manufacturer pursuant to a prescription issued by a licensed practitioner if the pharmacist complies with recordkeeping requirements pursuant to chapters 18.64, 69.41, and 69.50 RCW, and related administrative rules.

§ 7.72.050. Relevance of industry custom, technological feasibility, and nongovernmental, legislative or administrative regulatory standards. (1) Evidence of custom in the product seller's industry, technological feasibility or that the product was or was not, in compliance with nongovernmental standards or with legislative regulatory standards or administrative regulatory standards, whether relating to design, construction or performance of the product or to warnings or instructions as to its use may be considered by the trier of fact.

(2) When the injury-causing aspect of the product was, at the time of manufacture, in compliance with a specific mandatory government contract specification relating to design or warnings, this compliance shall be an absolute defense. When the injury-causing aspect of the product was not, at the time of manufacture, in compliance with a specific mandatory government specification relating to design or warnings, the product shall be deemed not reasonably safe under RCW 7.72.030(1).

§ 7.72.060. **Length of time product sellers are subject to liability.** (1) *Useful safe life.* (a) Except as provided in subsection (1)(b) hereof, a product seller shall not be subject to liability to a claimant for harm under this chapter if the product seller proves by a preponderance of the evidence that the harm was caused after the product's "useful safe life" had expired.

"Useful safe life" begins at the time of delivery of the product and extends for the time during which the product would normally be likely to perform or be stored in a safe manner. For the purposes of this chapter, "time of delivery" means the time of delivery of a product to its first purchaser or lessee who was not engaged in the business of either selling such products or using them as component parts of another product to be sold. In the case of a product which has been remanufactured by a manufacturer, "time of delivery" means the time of delivery of the remanufactured product to its first purchaser or lessee who was not engaged in the business of either selling such products or using them as component parts of another product to be sold.

(b) A product seller may be subject to liability for harm caused by a product used beyond its useful safe life, if:

(i) The product seller has warranted that the product may be utilized safely for such longer period; or

(ii) The product seller intentionally misrepresents facts about its product, or intentionally conceals information about it, and that conduct was a proximate cause of the claimant's harm; or

(iii) The harm was caused by exposure to a defective product, which exposure first occurred within the useful safe life of the product, even though the harm did not manifest itself until after the useful safe life had expired.

(2) *Presumption regarding useful safe life.* If the harm was caused more than twelve years after the time of delivery, a presumption arises that the harm was caused after the useful safe life had expired. This presumption may only be rebutted by a preponderance of the evidence.

(3) *Statute of limitation.* Subject to the applicable provisions of chapter 4.16 RCW pertaining to the tolling and extension of any statute of limitation, no claim under this chapter may be brought more than three years from the time the claimant discovered or in the exercise of due diligence should have discovered the harm and its cause.

CONSUMER PRODUCT SAFETY ACT*
Selected Sections

* 15 U.S.C.A. § 2051–82; Act of October 27, 1972, Pub.L. 92–573, 86 Stat. 1207–33; as amended by Consumer Product Safety Improvement Act of 1990, Pub.L. 101–608, 104 Stat. 3110; Consumer Product Safety Amendments of 1981, Pub.L. 97–35, 95 Stat. 724, Emergency Interim Consumer Product Safety Standard Act of 1978, Pub.L. 95–319, 92 Stat. 386, and Consumer Product Safety Commission Improvements Act of 1976, Pub.L. 94–284, 90 Stat. 503.

§ 2051. Congressional findings and declaration of purpose

(a) The Congress finds that—

(1) an unacceptable number of consumer products which present unreasonable risks of injury are distributed in commerce;

(2) complexities of consumer products and the diverse nature and abilities of consumers using them frequently result in an inability of users to anticipate risks and to safeguard themselves adequately;

(3) the public should be protected against unreasonable risks of injury associated with consumer products;

(4) control by State and local governments of unreasonable risks of injury associated with consumer products is inadequate and may be burdensome to manufacturers;

(5) existing Federal authority to protect consumers from exposure to consumer products presenting unreasonable risks of injury is inadequate; and

(6) regulation of consumer products the distribution or use of which affects interstate or foreign commerce is necessary to carry out this chapter.

(b) The purposes of this chapter are—

(1) to protect the public against unreasonable risks of injury associated with consumer products;

(2) to assist consumers in evaluating the comparative safety of consumer products;

(3) to develop uniform safety standards for consumer products and to minimize conflicting State and local regulations; and

(4) to promote research and investigation into the causes and prevention of product-related deaths, illnesses, and injuries.

Pub.L. 92–573, § 2, Oct. 27, 1972, 86 Stat. 1207.

§ 2052. Definitions

(a) For purposes of this chapter:

(1) The term "consumer product" means any article, or component part thereof, produced or distributed (i) for sale to a consumer for use in or around a permanent or temporary household or residence, a school, in recreation, or otherwise, or (ii) for the personal use, consumption or enjoyment of a consumer in or around a permanent or temporary household or residence, a school, in recreation, or otherwise; but such term does not include—

(A) any article which is not customarily produced or distributed for sale to, or use or consumption by, or enjoyment of, a consumer,

(B) tobacco and tobacco products,

(C) motor vehicles or motor vehicle equipment (as defined by sections 102(3) and (4) of the National Traffic and Motor Vehicle Safety Act of 1966),

(D) pesticides (as defined by the Federal Insecticide, Fungicide, and Rodenticide Act),

(E) any article which, if sold by the manufacturer, producer, or importer, would be subject to the tax imposed by section 4181 of the Internal Revenue Code of 1954 (determined without regard to any exemptions from such tax provided by section 4182 or 4221, or any other provision of such Code), or any component of any such article,

(F) aircraft, aircraft engines, propellers, or appliances (as defined in section 101 of the Federal Aviation Act of 1958),

(G) boats which could be subjected to safety regulation under the Federal Boat Safety Act of 1971; vessels, and appurtenances to vessels (other than such boats), which could be subjected to safety regulation under title 52 of the Revised Statutes or other marine safety statutes administered by the department in which the Coast Guard is operating; and equipment (including associated equipment, as defined in section 3(8) of the Federal Boat Safety Act of 1971) to the extent that a risk of injury associated with the use of such equipment on boats or vessels could be eliminated or reduced by actions taken under any statute referred to in this subparagraph,

(H) drugs, devices, or cosmetics (as such terms are defined in sections 201(g), (h), and (i) of the Federal Food, Drug, and Cosmetic Act), or

(I) food. The term "food", as used in this subparagraph means all "food", as defined in section 201(f) of the Federal Food, Drug, and Cosmetic Act, including poultry and poultry products (as defined in sections 4(e) and (f) of the Poultry Products Inspection Act), meat, meat food products (as defined in section 1(j) of the Federal Meat Inspection Act), and eggs and egg products (as defined in section 4 of the Egg Products Inspection Act).

Such term includes any mechanical device which carries or conveys passengers along, around, or over a fixed or restricted route or course or within a defined area for the purpose of giving its passengers amusement, which is customarily controlled or directed by an individual who is employed for that purpose and who is not a consumer with respect to such device, and which is not permanently fixed to a site. Such term does not include such a device which is permanently fixed to a site. Except for the regulation under this chapter or the Federal Hazardous Substances Act of fireworks devices or any substance intended for use as a component of any such device, the Commission shall have no authority under the functions transferred pursuant to section 2079 of this title to regulate any product or article described in subparagraph (E) of this paragraph or described, without regard to quantity, in section 845(a)(5) of Title 18. See sections 2079(d) and 2080 of this title, for other limitations on Commission's authority to regulate certain consumer products.

(2) The term "consumer product safety rule" means a consumer products safety standard described in section 2056(a) of this title, or a rule under this chapter declaring a consumer product a banned hazardous product.

(3) The term "risk of injury" means a risk of death, personal injury, or serious or frequent illness.

(4) The term "manufacturer" means any person who manufactures or imports a consumer product.

(5) The term "distributor" means a person to whom a consumer product is delivered or sold for purposes of distribution in commerce, except that such term does not include a manufacturer or retailer of such product.

(6) The term "retailer" means a person to whom a consumer product is delivered or sold for purposes of sale or distribution by such person to a consumer.

(7)(A) The term "private labeler" means an owner of a brand or trademark on the label of a consumer product which bears a private label.

(B) A consumer product bears a private label if (i) the product (or its container) is labeled with the brand or trademark of a person other than a manufacturer of the product, (ii) the person with whose brand or trademark the product (or container) is labeled has authorized or caused the product to be so labeled, and (iii) the brand or trademark of a manufacturer of such product does not appear on such label.

(8) The term "manufactured" means to manufacture, produce, or assemble.

(9) The term "Commission" means the Consumer Product Safety Commission, established by section 2053 of this title.

(10) The term "State" means a State, the District of Columbia, the Commonwealth of Puerto Rico, the Virgin Islands, Guam, Wake Island, Midway Island, Kingman Reef, Johnston Island, the Canal Zone, American Samoa, or the Trust Territory of the Pacific Islands.

(11) The terms "to distribute in commerce" and "distribution in commerce" mean to sell in commerce, to introduce or deliver for introduction into commerce, or to hold for sale or distribution after introduction into commerce.

(12) The term "commerce" means trade, traffic, commerce, or transportation—

(A) between a place in a State and any place outside thereof, or

(B) which affects trade, traffic, commerce, or transportation described in subparagraph (A).

(13) The terms "import" and "importation" include reimporting a consumer product manufactured or processed, in whole or in part, in the United States.

(14) The term "United States", when used in the geographic sense, means all of the States (as defined in paragraph (10)).

(b) A common carrier, contract carrier, or freight forwarder shall not, for purposes of this chapter, be deemed to be a manufacturer, distributor, or retailer of a consumer product solely by reason of receiving or transporting a consumer product in the ordinary course of its business as such a carrier or forwarder.

As amended Pub.L. 94–284, § 3(b), (d), May 11, 1976, 90 Stat. 503; Pub.L. 97–35, Title XII, § 1213, Aug. 13, 1981, 95 Stat. 724.

§ 2053. Consumer Product Safety Commission

(a) Establishment; Chairman

(a) An independent regulatory commission is hereby established, to be known as the Consumer Product Safety Commission, consisting of five Commissioners who shall be appointed by the President, by and with the advice and consent of the Senate. In making such appointments, the President shall consider individuals who, by reason of their background and expertise in areas related to consumer products and protection of the public from risks to safety, are qualified to serve as members of the Commission. The Chairman shall be appointed by the President, by and with the advice and consent of the Senate, from among the members of the Commission. An individual may be appointed as a member of the Commission and as Chairman at the same time. Any member of the Commission may be removed by the President for neglect of duty or malfeasance in office but for no other cause.

(b) Term; vacancies

(b)(1) Except as provided in paragraph (2), (A) the Commissioners first appointed under this section shall be appointed for terms ending three, four, five, six, and seven years, respectively, after October 27, 1972, the term of each to be designated by the President at the time of nomination; and (B) each of their successors shall be appointed for a term of seven years from the date of the expiration of the term for which his predecessor was appointed.

(2) Any Commissioner appointed to fill a vacancy occurring prior to the expiration of the term for which his predecessor was appointed shall be appointed only for the remainder of such term. A Commissioner may continue to serve after the expiration of his term until his successor has taken office, except that he may not so continue to serve more than one year after the date on which his term would otherwise expire under this subsection.

(c) Restrictions on Commissioners' outside activities

(c) Not more than three of the Commissioners shall be affiliated with the same political party. No individual (1) in the employ of, or holding any official relation to, any person engaged in selling or manufacturing consumer products, or (2) owning stock or bonds of substantial value in a person so engaged, or (3) who is in any other manner pecuniarily interested in such a person, or in a substantial supplier of such a person, shall hold the office of Commissioner. A Commissioner may not engage in any other business, vocation, or employment.

(d) Quorum; seal; Vice Chairman

(d) No vacancy in the Commission shall impair the right of the remaining Commissioners to exercise all the powers of the Commission, but three members of the Commission shall constitute a quorum for the transaction of business, except that if there are only three members serving on the Commission because of vacancies in the Commission, two members of the Commission shall constitute a quorum for the transaction of business, and if there are only two members serving on the Commission because of vacancies in the Commission, two members shall constitute a quorum for the six month period beginning on the date of the vacancy which caused the number on the Commission to decline to two. The Commission shall have an official seal of which judicial notice shall be taken. The Commission shall annually elect a Vice Chairman to act in the absence or disability of the Chairman or in case of a vacancy in the office of the Chairman.

(e) Offices

(e) The Commission shall maintain a principal office and such field offices as it deems necessary and may meet and exercise any of its powers at any other place.

(f) Functions of Chairman

(f)(1) The Chairman of the Commission shall be the principal executive officer of the Commission, and he shall exercise all of the executive and administrative functions of the Commission, including functions of the Commission with respect to (A) the appointment and supervision of personnel employed under the Commission (other than personnel employed regularly and full time in the immediate offices of commissioners other than the Chairman), (B) the distribution of business among personnel appointed and supervised by the Chairman and among administrative units of the Commission, and (C) the use and expenditure of funds.

(2) In carrying out any of his functions under the provisions of this subsection the Chairman shall be governed by general policies of the Commission and by such regulatory decisions, findings, and determinations as the Commission may by law be authorized to make.

(3) Requests or estimates for regular, supplemental, or deficiency appropriations on behalf of the Commission may not be submitted by the Chairman without the prior approval of the Commission.

(g) Executive Director; officers and employees

(g)(1)(A) The Chairman, subject to the approval of the Commission, shall appoint as officers of the Commission an Executive Director, a General Counsel, an Associate Executive Director for Engineering Sciences, an Associate Executive Director for Epidemiology, an Associate Director for Compliance and Administrative Litigation, an Associate Executive Director for Health Sciences, an Associate Executive Director for Economic Analysis, an Associate Executive Director for Administration, an Associate Executive Director for Field Operations, a Director for Office of Program, Management and Budget, and a Director for Office of Information and Public Affairs. Any other individual appointed to a position designated as an Associate Executive Director shall be appointed by the Chairman subject to the removal of the Commission. The Chairman may only appoint an attorney to the position of Associate Executive Director of Compliance and Administrative Litigation except the position of Acting Associate Executive Director of Compliance and Administrative Litigation.

(B)(i) No individual may be appointed to such a position on an acting basis for a period longer than 90 days unless such appointment is approved by the Commission.

(ii) The Chairman, with the approval of the Commission, may remove any individual serving in a position appointed under subparagraph (A).

(C) Subparagraph (A) shall not be construed to prohibit appropriate reorganizations or changes in classifications.

(2) The Chairman, subject to subsection (f)(2), of this section, may employ such other officers and employees (including attorneys) as are necessary in the execution of the Commission's functions. No regular officer or employee of the Commission who was at any time during the 12 months preceding the termination of his employment with the Commission compensated at a rate in excess of the annual rate of basic pay in effect for grade GS–14 of the General Schedule, shall accept employment or compensation from any manufacturer subject to this chapter, for a period of 12 months after terminating employment with the Commission.

(3) In addition to the number of positions authorized by section 5108(a) of Title 5, the Chairman, subject to the approval of the Commission, and subject to the standards and procedures prescribed by chapter 51 of Title 5, may place a total of twelve positions in grades GS–16, GS–17, and GS–18.

(4) The appointment of any officer (other than a Commissioner) or employee of the Commission shall not be subject, directly or indirectly, to review or approval by any officer or entity within the Executive Office of the President.

(h) Civil action against the United States

(h) Subsections (a) and (h) of section 2680 of Title 28 do not prohibit the bringing of a civil action on a claim against the United States which—

(1) is based upon—

(A) misrepresentation or deceit on the part of the Commission or any employee thereof, or

(B) any exercise or performance, or failure to exercise or perform, a discretionary function on the part of the Commission or any employee thereof, which exercise, performance, or failure was grossly negligent; and

(2) is not made with respect to any agency action (as defined in section 551(13) of Title 5).

In the case of a civil action on a claim based upon the exercise or performance of, or failure to exercise or perform, a discretionary function, no judgment may be entered against the United States unless the court in which such action was brought determines (based upon consideration of all the relevant circumstances, including the statutory responsibility of the Commission and the public interest in encouraging rather than inhibiting the exercise of discretion) that such exercise, performance, or failure to exercise or perform was unreasonable.

(i) Agenda; establishment and comments

At least 30 days before the beginning of each fiscal year, the Commission shall establish an agenda for Commission action under the Acts under its jurisdiction and, to the extent feasible, shall establish priorities for such actions. Before establishing such agenda and priorities, the Commission shall conduct a public hearing on the agenda and priorities and shall provide reasonable opportunity for the submission of comments.

As amended Pub.L. 94–284, §§ 4, 5(a), May 11, 1976, 90 Stat. 504; Pub.L. 95–631, § 2, Nov. 10, 1978, 92 Stat. 3742; Pub.L. 96–373, Oct. 3, 1980, 94 Stat. 1366; Pub.L. 101–608, Title I §§ 102–104, 105(a), Nov. 16, 1990, 104 Stat. 3110, 3111.

§ 2054. Product safety information and research

(a) Injury Information Clearinghouse; duties

(a) The Commission shall—

(1) maintain an Injury Information Clearinghouse to collect, investigate, analyze, and disseminate injury data, and information, relating to the causes and prevention of death, injury, and illness associated with consumer products;

(2) conduct such continuing studies and investigations of deaths, injuries, diseases, other health impairments, and economic losses resulting from accidents involving consumer products as it deems necessary;

(3) following publication of an advance notice of proposed rulemaking or a notice of proposed rulemaking for a product safety rule under any rulemaking authority administered by the Commission, assist public and private organizations or groups of manufacturers, administratively and technically, in the development of safety standards addressing the risk of injury identified in such notice; and

(4) to the extent practicable and appropriate (taking into account the resources and priorities of the Commission), assist public and private organizations or groups of manufacturers, administratively and

technically, in the development of product safety standards and test methods.

(b) Research, investigation and testing of consumer products

(b) The Commission may—

(1) conduct research, studies, and investigations on the safety of consumer products and on improving the safety of such products;

(2) test consumer products and develop product safety test methods and testing devices; and

(3) offer training in product safety investigation and test methods.

(c) Grants and contracts for conduct of functions

(c) In carrying out its functions under this section, the Commission may make grants or enter into contracts for the conduct of such functions with any person (including a governmental entity).

(d) Availability to public of information

(d) Whenever the Federal contribution for any information, research, or development activity authorized by this chapter is more than minimal, the Commission shall include in any contract, grant, or other arrangement for such activity, provisions effective to insure that the rights to all information, uses, processes, patents, and other developments resulting from that activity will be made available to the public without charge on a nonexclusive basis. Nothing in this subsection shall be construed to deprive any person of any right which he may have had, prior to entering into any arrangement referred to in this subsection, to any patent, patent application, or invention.

As amended Pub.L. 97–35, Title XII, § 1209(a), (b), Aug. 13, 1981, 95 Stat. 720.

§ 2055. Public disclosure of information

(a) Disclosure requirements for manufacturers or private labelers; procedures applicable

(a)(1) Nothing contained in this Act shall be construed to require the release of any information described by subsection (b) of section 552 of Title 5 or which is otherwise protected by law from disclosure to the public.

(2) All information reported to or otherwise obtained by the Commission or its representative under this Act which information contains or relates to a trade secret or other matter referred to in section 1905 of Title 18 or subject to section 552(b)(4) of Title 5 shall be considered confidential and shall not be disclosed.

(3) The Commission shall, prior to the disclosure of any information which will permit the public to ascertain readily the identity of a manufacturer or private labeler of a consumer product, offer such manufacturer or private labeler an opportunity to mark such information as confidential and therefore barred from disclosure under paragraph (2).

(4) All information that a manufacturer or private labeler has marked to be confidential and barred from disclosure under paragraph (2), either at the time of submission or pursuant to paragraph (3), shall not be disclosed, except in accordance with the procedures established in paragraphs (5) and (6).

(5) If the Commission determines that a document marked as confidential by a manufacturer or private labeler to be barred from disclosure under paragraph (2) may be disclosed because it is not confidential information as provided in paragraph (2), the Commission shall notify such person in writing that the Commission intends to disclose such document at a date not less than 10 days after the date of receipt of notification.

(6) Any person receiving such notification may, if he believes such disclosure is barred by paragraph (2), before the date set for release of the document, bring an action in the district court of the United States in the district in which the complainant resides, or has his principal place of business, or in which the documents are located, or in the United States District Court for the District of Columbia to restrain disclosure of the document. Any person receiving such notification may file with the appropriate district court or court of appeals of the United States, as appropriate, an application for a stay of disclosure. The documents shall not be disclosed until the court has ruled on the application for a stay.

(7) Nothing in this Act shall authorize the withholding of information by the Commission or any officer or employee under its control from the duly authorized committees or subcommittees of the Congress, and the provisions of paragraphs (2) through (6) shall not apply to such disclosures, except that the Commission shall immediately notify the manufacturer or private labeler of any such request for information designated as confidential by the manufacturer or private labeler.

(8) The provisions of paragraphs (2) through (6) shall not prohibit the disclosure of information to other officers or employees, or other representatives of the Commission (including contractors) concerned with carrying out this chapter or when relevant to any administrative proceeding under this chapter or in judicial proceedings to which the Commission is a party. Any disclosure of relevant information—

(A) in Commission administrative proceedings or in judicial proceedings to which the Commission is a party, or

(B) to representatives of the Commission (including contractors),

shall be governed by the rules of the Commission (including in camera review rules for confidential material) for such proceedings or for disclosures to such representatives or by court rules or orders, except that the rules of the Commission shall not be amended in a manner inconsistent with the purposes of this section.

(b) Additional disclosure requirements for manufacturers or private labelers; procedures applicable

(b)(1) Except as provided by paragraph (4) of this subsection, not less than 30 days prior to its public disclosure of any information obtained under this Act, or to be disclosed to the public in connection therewith (unless the Commission finds that the public health and safety requires a lesser period of notice and publishes such a finding in the Federal Register), the Commission shall, to the extent practicable, notify and provide a summary of the information to, each manufacturer or private labeler of any consumer product to which such information pertains, if the manner in which such consumer product is to be designated or described in such information will permit the public to ascertain readily the identity of such manufacturer or private labeler, and shall provide such manufacturer or private labeler with a reasonable opportunity to submit comments to the Commission in regard to such information. The Commission shall take reasonable steps to assure, prior to its public disclosure thereof, that information from which the identity of such manufacturer or private labeler may be readily ascertained is accurate, and that such disclosure is fair in the circumstances and reasonably related to effectuating the purposes of this Act. In disclosing any information under this subsection, the Commission may, and upon the request of the manufacturer or private labeler shall, include with the disclosure any comments or other information or a summary thereof submitted by such manufacturer or private labeler to the extent permitted by and subject to the requirements of this section.

(2) If the Commission determines that a document claimed to be inaccurate by a manufacturer or private labeler under paragraph (1) should be disclosed because the Commission believes it has complied with paragraph (1), the Commission shall notify the manufacturer or private labeler that the Commission intends to disclose such document at a date not less than 10 days after the date of the receipt of notification. The Commission may provide a lesser period of notice of intent to disclose if the Commission finds that the public health and safety requires a lesser period of notice and publishes such finding in the Federal Register.

(3) Prior to the date set for release of the document, the manufacturer or private labeler receiving the notice described in paragraph (2) may bring an action in the district court of the United States in the district in which the complainant resides, or has his principal place of business, or in which the documents are located or in the United States District Court for the District of Columbia to enjoin disclosure of the document. The district

court may enjoin such disclosure if the Commission has failed to take the reasonable steps prescribed in paragraph (1).

(4) Paragraphs (1) through (3) of this subsection shall not apply to the public disclosure of (A) information about any consumer product with respect to which product the Commission has filed an action under section 2061 of this title (relating to imminently hazardous products), or which the Commission has reasonable cause to believe is in violation of section 2068 of this title (relating to prohibited acts); or (B) information in the course of or concerning a rulemaking proceeding (which shall commence upon the publication of an advance notice of proposed rulemaking or a notice of proposed rulemaking), an adjudicatory proceeding (which shall commence upon the issuance of a complaint) or other administrative or judicial proceeding under this Act.

(5) In addition to the requirements of paragraph (1), the Commission shall not disclose to the public information submitted pursuant to section 2064(b) of this title respecting a consumer product unless—

(A) the Commission has issued a complaint under section 2064(c) or (d) of this title alleging that such product presents a substantial product hazard;

(B) in lieu of proceeding against such product under section 2064(c) or (d) of this title, the Commission has accepted in writing a remedial settlement agreement dealing with such product; or

(C) the person who submitted the information under section 2064(b) of this title agrees to its public disclosure.

The provisions of this paragraph shall not apply to the public disclosure of information with respect to a consumer product which is the subject of an action brought under section 2061 of this title, or which the Commission has reasonable cause to believe is in violation of section 2068(a) of this title, or information in the course of or concerning a judicial proceeding.

(6) Where the Commission initiates the public disclosure of information that reflects on the safety of a consumer product or class of consumer products, whether or not such information would enable the public to ascertain readily the identity of a manufacturer or private labeler, the Commission shall establish procedures designed to ensure that such information is accurate and not misleading.

(7) If the Commission finds that, in the administration of this Act, it has made public disclosure of inaccurate or misleading information which reflects adversely upon the safety of any consumer product or class of consumer products, or the practices of any manufacturer, private labeler, distributor, or retailer of consumer products, it shall, in a manner equivalent to that in which such disclosure was made, take reasonable steps to publish a retraction of such inaccurate or misleading information.

(8) If, after the commencement of a rulemaking or the initiation of an adjudicatory proceeding, the Commission decides to terminate the proceed-

ing before taking final action, the Commission shall, in a manner equivalent to that in which such commencement or initiation was publicized, take reasonable steps to make known the decision to terminate.

(c) Communications with manufacturers

(c) The Commission shall communicate to each manufacturer of a consumer product, insofar as may be practicable, information as to any significant risk of injury associated with such product.

(d) Definition; coverage

(d)(1) For purposes of this section, the term "Act" means the Consumer Product Safety Act, the Flammable Fabrics Act, the Poison Prevention Packaging Act, and the Federal Hazardous Substances Act.

(2) The provisions of this section shall apply whenever information is to be disclosed by the Commission, any member of the Commission, or any employee, agent, or representative of the Commission in an official capacity. Commission shall include in any contract, grant, or other arrangement for such activity, provisions effective to insure that the rights to all information, uses, processes, patents, and other developments resulting from that activity will be made available to the public without charge on a nonexclusive basis. Nothing in this subsection shall be construed to deprive any person of any right which he may have had, prior to entering into any arrangement referred to in this subsection, to any patent, patent application, or invention.

(e) Disclosure of information

(e)(1) Notwithstanding the provisions of section 552 of Title 5, subsection (a)(7) of this section, or of any other law, except as provided in paragraphs (2), (3), and (4), no member of the Commission, no officer or employee of the Commission, and no officer or employee of the Department of Justice may—

(A) publicly disclose information furnished under subsection (c)(1) or (c)(2)(A) of section 2084 of this title;

(B) use such information for any purpose other than to carry out the Commission's responsibilities; or

(C) permit anyone (other than the members, officers and employees of the Commission or officers or employees of the Department of Justice who require such information for an action filed on behalf of the Commission) to examine such information.

(2) Any report furnished under subsection (c)(1) or (c)(2)(A) of section 2084 of this title shall be immune from legal process and shall not be subject to subpoena or other discovery in any civil action in a State or

Federal court or in any administrative proceeding, except in an action against such manufacturer under section 2069, 2070 or 2071 of this title for failure to furnish information required by section 2084 of this title.

(3) The Commission may, upon written request, furnish to any manufacturer or to the authorized agent of such manufacturer authenticated copies of reports furnished by or on behalf of such manufacturer in accordance with section 2084 of this title, upon payment of the actual or estimated cost of searching the records and furnishing the copies.

(4) Upon written request of the Chairman or Ranking Minority Member of the Committee on Commerce, Science and Transportation of the Senate or the Committee on Energy and Commerce of the House of Representatives or any subcommittee of such committee, the Commission shall provide to the Chairman or Ranking Minority Member any information furnished to the Commission under section 2084 of this title for purposes that are related to the jurisdiction of such committee or subcommittee.

(5) Any officer or employee of the Commission or other officer or employee of the Federal Government who receives information provided under section 2084 of this title, who willfully violates the requirements of this subsection shall be subject to dismissal or other appropriate disciplinary action consistent with procedures and requirements established by the Office of Personnel Management.

As amended Pub.L. 97–35, Title XII, § 1204(a), (b), Aug. 13, 1981, 95 Stat. 713, Pub.L. 97–414, § 9(j)(1), Jan. 4, 1983, 96 Stat. 2064; Pub.L. 101–608, Title I, § 106, 112(c), Nov. 16, 1990, 104 Stat. 3111, 3116.

§ 2056.   Consumer product safety standards

(a) Types of requirements

(a) The Commission may promulgate consumer product safety standards in accordance with the provisions of section 2058 of this title. A consumer product safety standard shall consist of one or more of any of the following types of requirements:

(1) Requirements expressed in terms of performance requirements.

(2) Requirements that a consumer product be marked with or accompanied by clear and adequate warnings or instructions, or requirements respecting the form of warnings or instructions.

Any requirement of such a standard shall be reasonably necessary to prevent or reduce an unreasonable risk of injury associated with such product.

(b) Reliance of Commission upon voluntary standards

(b)(1) The Commission shall rely upon voluntary consumer product safety standards rather than promulgate a consumer product safety standard prescribing requirements described in subsection (a) of this section whenever compliance with such voluntary standards would eliminate or adequately reduce the risk of injury addressed and it is likely that there will be substantial compliance with such voluntary standards.

(2) The Commission shall devise procedures to monitor compliance with any voluntary standards—

(A) upon which the Commission has relied under paragraph (1);

(B) which were developed with the participation of the Commission; or

(C) whose development the Commission has monitored.

(c) Contribution of Commission to development cost

(c) If any person participates with the Commission in the development of a consumer product safety standard, the Commission may agree to contribute to the person's cost with respect to such participation, in any case in which the Commission determines that such contribution is likely to result in a more satisfactory standard than would be developed without such contribution, and that the person is financially responsible. Regulations of the Commission shall set forth the items of cost in which it may participate, and shall exclude any contribution to the acquisition of land or buildings. Payments under agreements entered into under this subsection may be made without regard to section 3324(a) and (b) of Title 31.

As amended Pub.L. 94–284, §§ 6–8(a), May 11, 1976, 90 Stat. 505, 506; Pub.L. 95–631, §§ 3, 4(a)-(c), 5, Nov. 10, 1978, 92 Stat. 3742–3744; Pub.L. 97–35, Title XII, § 1202, Aug. 13, 1981, 95 Stat. 703, 97–258, § 4(b), Sept. 13, 1982, 96 Stat. 1067; Pub.L. 101–608, Title I, § 107(a), Nov. 16, 1990, 104 Stat. 3111.

§ 2057. Banned hazardous products

Whenever the Commission finds that—

(1) a consumer product is being, or will be, distributed in commerce and such consumer product presents an unreasonable risk of injury; and

(2) no feasible consumer product safety standard under this chapter would adequately protect the public from the unreasonable risk of injury associated with such product,

the Commission may, in accordance with section 2058 of this title, promulgate a rule declaring such product a banned hazardous product.

As amended Pub.L. 97–35, Title XII, § 1203(c), Aug. 13, 1981, 95 Stat. 713.

§ 2058. Procedure for consumer product safety rules

(a) Commencement of proceeding; publication of prescribed notice of proposed rulemaking; transmittal of notice

(a) A proceeding for the development of a consumer product safety rule shall be commenced by the publication in the Federal Register of an advance notice of proposed rulemaking which shall—

(1) identify the product and the nature of the risk of injury associated with the product;

(2) include a summary of each of the regulatory alternatives under consideration by the Commission (including voluntary consumer product safety standards);

(3) include information with respect to any existing standard known to the Commission which may be relevant to the proceedings, together with a summary of the reasons why the Commission believes preliminarily that such standard does not eliminate or adequately reduce the risk of injury identified in paragraph (1);

(4) invite interested persons to submit to the Commission, within such period as the Commission shall specify in the notice (which period shall not be less than 30 days or more than 60 days after the date of publication of the notice), comments with respect to the risk of injury identified by the Commission, the regulatory alternatives being considered, and other possible alternatives for addressing the risk;

(5) invite any person (other than the Commission) to submit to the Commission, within such period as the Commission shall specify in the notice (which period shall not be less than 30 days after the date of publication of the notice), an existing standard or a portion of a standard as a proposed consumer product safety standard; and

(6) invite any person (other than the Commission) to submit to the Commission, within such period as the Commission shall specify in the notice (which period shall not be less than 30 days after the date of publication of the notice), a statement of intention to modify or develop a voluntary consumer product safety standard to address the risk of injury identified in paragraph (1) together with a description of a plan to modify or develop the standard.

The Commission shall transmit such notice within 10 calendar days to the Committee on Commerce, Science, and Transportation of the Senate and the Committee on Energy and Commerce of the House of Representatives.

(b) Voluntary standard; publication as proposed rule; notice of reliance of Commission on standard

(b)(1) If the Commission determines that any standard submitted to it in response to an invitation in a notice published under subsection (a)(5) of this section if promulgated (in whole, in part, or in combination with any other standard submitted to the Commission or any part of such a standard) as a consumer product safety standard, would eliminate or adequately reduce the risk of injury identified in the notice under subsection (a)(1), of this section, the Commission may publish such standard, in whole, in part, or in such combination and with nonmaterial modifications, as a proposed consumer product safety rule.

(2) If the Commission determines that—

(A) compliance with any standard submitted to it in response to an invitation in a notice published under subsection (a)(6) of this section is likely to result in the elimination or adequate reduction of the risk of injury identified in the notice, and

(B) it is likely that there will be substantial compliance with such standard,

the Commission shall terminate any proceeding to promulgate a consumer product safety rule respecting such risk of injury and shall publish in the Federal Register a notice which includes the determination of the Commission and which notifies the public that the Commission will rely on the voluntary standard to eliminate or reduce the risk of injury, except that the Commission shall terminate any such proceeding and rely on a voluntary standard only if such voluntary standard is in existence. For purposes of this section, a voluntary standard shall be considered to be in existence when it is finally approved by the organization or other person which developed such standard, irrespective of the effective date of the standard. Before relying on any voluntary consumer product safety standard, the Commission shall afford interested persons (including manufacturers, consumers and consumer organizations) a reasonable opportunity to submit written comments regarding such standard. The Commission shall consider such comments in making any determination regarding reliance on the involved voluntary standard under this subsection.

(c) Publication of proposed rule; preliminary regulatory analysis; contents; transmittal of notice

(c) No consumer product safety rule may be proposed by the Commission unless, not less than 60 days after publication of the notice required in subsection (a) of this section, the Commission publishes in the Federal Register the text of the proposed rule, including any alternatives, which the Commission proposes to promulgate, together with a preliminary regulatory analysis containing—

(1) a preliminary description of the potential benefits and potential costs of the proposed rule, including any benefits or costs that

cannot be quantified in monetary terms, and an identification of those likely to receive the benefits and bear the costs;

(2) a discussion of the reasons any standard or portion of a standard submitted to the Commission under subsection (a)(5) of this section was not published by the Commission as the proposed rule or part of the proposed rule;

(3) a discussion of the reasons for the Commission's preliminary determination that efforts proposed under subsection (a)(6) of this section and assisted by the Commission as required by section 2054(a)(3) of this title would not, within a reasonable period of time, be likely to result in the development of a voluntary consumer product safety standard that would eliminate or adequately reduce the risk of injury addressed by the proposed rule; and

(4) a description of any reasonable alternatives to the proposed rule, together with a summary description of their potential costs and benefits, and a brief explanation of why such alternatives should not be published as a proposed rule.

The Commission shall transmit such notice within 10 calendar days to the Committee on Commerce, Science, and Transportation of the Senate and the Committee on Energy and Commerce of the House of Representatives. Any proposed consumer product safety rule shall be issued within twelve months after the date of publication of an advance notice of proposed rulemaking under subsection (a) of this section relating to the product involved, unless the Commission determines that such proposed rule is not in the public interest. The Commission may extend the twelve-month period for good cause. If the Commission extends such period, it shall immediately transmit notice of such an extension to the Committee on Commerce, Science, and Transportation of the Senate and the Committee on Energy and Commerce of the House of Representatives. Such notice shall include an explanation for the reasons for such extension, together with an estimate of the date by which the Commission anticipates such rulemaking will be completed. The Commission shall publish notice of such an extension and the information submitted to the Congress in the Federal Register.

(d) Promulgation of rule; time

(d)(1) Within 60 days after the publication under subsection (c) of this section of a proposed consumer product safety rule respecting a risk of injury associated with a consumer product, the Commission shall—

(A) promulgate a consumer product safety rule respecting the risk of injury associated with such product, if it makes the findings required under subsection (f) of this section, or

(B) withdraw the applicable notice of proposed rulemaking if it determines that such rule is not (i) reasonably necessary to eliminate or reduce an unreasonable risk of injury associated with the product, or (ii) in the public interest;

except that the Commission may extend such 60–day period for good cause shown (if it publishes its reasons therefor in the Federal Register).

(2) Consumer product safety rules shall be promulgated in accordance with section 553 of Title 5 except that the Commission shall give interested persons an opportunity for the oral presentation of data, views, or arguments, in addition to an opportunity to make written submissions. A transcript shall be kept of any oral presentation.

(e) Expression of risk of injury; consideration of available product data; needs of elderly and handicapped

(e) A consumer product safety rule shall express in the rule itself the risk of injury which the standard is designed to eliminate or reduce. In promulgating such a rule the Commission shall consider relevant available product data including the results of research, development, testing, and investigation activities conducted generally and pursuant to this chapter. In the promulgation of such a rule the Commission shall also consider and take into account the special needs of elderly and handicapped persons to determine the extent to which such persons may be adversely affected by such rule.

(f) Findings; final regulatory analysis; judicial review of rule

(f)(1) Prior to promulgating a consumer product safety rule, the Commission shall consider, and shall make appropriate findings for inclusion in such rule with respect to—

(A) the degree and nature of the risk of injury the rule is designed to eliminate or reduce;

(B) the approximate number of consumer products, or types or classes thereof, subject to such rule;

(C) the need of the public for the consumer products subject to such rule, and the probable effect of such rule upon the utility, cost, or availability of such products to meet such need; and

(D) any means of achieving the objective of the order while minimizing adverse effects on competition or disruption or dislocation of manufacturing and other commercial practices consistent with the public health and safety.

(2) The Commission shall not promulgate a consumer product safety rule unless it has prepared, on the basis of the findings of the Commission under paragraph (1) and on other information before the Commission, a final regulatory analysis of the rule containing the following information:

(A) A description of the potential benefits and potential costs of the rule, including costs and benefits that cannot be quantified in monetary terms, and the identification of those likely to receive the benefits and bear the costs.

(B) A description of any alternatives to the final rule which were considered by the Commission, together with a summary description of their potential benefits and costs and a brief explanation of the reasons why these alternatives were not chosen.

(C) A summary of any significant issues raised by the comments submitted during the public comment period in response to the preliminary regulatory analysis, and a summary of the assessment by the Commission of such issues.

The Commission shall publish its final regulatory analysis with the rule.

(3) The Commission shall not promulgate a consumer product safety rule unless it finds (and includes such finding in the rule)—

(A) that the rule (including its effective date) is reasonably necessary to eliminate or reduce an unreasonable risk of injury associated with such product;

(B) that the promulgation of the rule is in the public interest;

(C) in the case of a rule declaring the product a banned hazardous product, that no feasible consumer product safety standard under this chapter would adequately protect the public from the unreasonable risk of injury associated with such product;

(D) in the case of a rule which relates to a risk of injury with respect to which persons who would be subject to such rule have adopted and implemented a voluntary consumer product safety standard, that—

(i) compliance with such voluntary consumer product safety standard is not likely to result in the elimination or adequate reduction of such risk of injury; or

(ii) it is unlikely that there will be substantial compliance with such voluntary consumer product safety standard;

(E) that the benefits expected from the rule bear a reasonable relationship to its costs; and

(F) that the rule imposes the least burdensome requirement which prevents or adequately reduces the risk of injury for which the rule is being promulgated.

(4)(A) Any preliminary or final regulatory analysis prepared under subsection (c) or (f)(2) of this section shall not be subject to independent judicial review, except that when an action for judicial review of a rule is instituted, the contents of any such regulatory analysis shall constitute part of the whole rulemaking record of agency action in connection with such review.

(B) The provisions of subparagraph (A) shall not be construed to alter the substantive or procedural standards otherwise applicable to judicial review of any action by the Commission.

(g) Effective date of rule or standard; stockpiling of product

(g)(1) Each consumer product safety rule shall specify the date such rule is to take effect not exceeding 180 days from the date promulgated, unless the Commission finds, for good cause shown, that a later effective date is in the public interest and publishes its reasons for such finding. The effective date of a consumer product safety standard under this chapter shall be set at a date at least 30 days after the date of promulgation unless the Commission for good cause shown determines that an earlier effective date is in the public interest. In no case may the effective date be set at a date which is earlier than the date of promulgation. A consumer product safety standard shall be applicable only to consumer products manufactured after the effective date.

(2) The Commission may by rule prohibit a manufacturer of a consumer product from stockpiling any product to which a consumer product safety rule applies, so as to prevent such manufacturer from circumventing the purpose of such consumer product safety rule. For purposes of this paragraph, the term "stockpiling" means manufacturing or importing a product between the date of promulgation of such consumer product safety rule and its effective date at a rate which is significantly greater (as determined under the rule under this paragraph) than the rate at which such product was produced or imported during a base period (prescribed in the rule under this paragraph) ending before the date of promulgation of the consumer product safety rule.

(h) Amendment or revocation of rule

(h) The Commission may by rule amend or revoke any consumer product safety rule. Such amendment or revocation shall specify the date on which it is to take effect which shall not exceed 180 days from the date the amendment or revocation is published unless the Commission finds for good cause shown that a later effective date is in the public interest and publishes its reasons for such finding. Where an amendment involves a material change in a consumer product safety rule, sections 2056 and 2057 of this title, and subsections (a) through (g) of this section shall apply. In order to revoke a consumer product safety rule, the Commission shall publish a proposal to revoke such rule in the Federal Register, and allow oral and written presentations in accordance with subsection (d)(2) of this section. It may revoke such rule only if it determines that the rule is not reasonably necessary to eliminate or reduce an unreasonable risk of injury associated with the product. Section 2060 of this title shall apply to any amendment of a consumer product safety rule which involves a material change and to any revocation of a consumer product safety rule, in the same manner and to the same extent as such section applies to the Commission's action in promulgating such a rule.

(i) Petition to initiate rulemaking

(i) The Commission shall grant, in whole or in part, or deny any petition under section 553(e) of Title 5, requesting the Commission to initiate a rulemaking, within a reasonable time after the date on which such petition is field. The Commission shall state the reasons for granting or denying such petition. The Commission may not deny any such petition on the basis of a voluntary standard unless the voluntary standard is in existence at the time of the denial of the petition, the Commission has determined that the voluntary standard is likely to result in the elimination or adequate reduction of the risk of injury identified with the petition, and it is likely that there will be substantial compliance with the standard.

As amended Pub.L. 94–284, § 9, May 11, 1976, 90 Stat. 506; Pub.L. 95–631, § 4(d), Nov. 10, 1978, 92 Stat. 3744; Pub.L. 97–35, Title XII, § 1203(a), Aug. 13, 1981, 95 Stat. 704; Pub.L. 101–608, Title I, § 108(a), 109, 110(a), Nov. 16, 1990, 104 Stat. 3112, 3113.

§ 2060. Judicial review of consumer product safety rules

(a) Petition by persons adversely affected, consumers, or consumer organizations

(a) Not later than 60 days after a consumer product safety rule is promulgated by the Commission, any person adversely affected by such rule, or any consumer or consumer organization, may file a petition with the United States court of appeals for the District of Columbia or for the circuit in which such person, consumer, or organization resides or has his principal place of business for judicial review of such rule. Copies of the petition shall be forthwith transmitted by the clerk of the court to the Commission or other officer designated by it for that purpose and to the Attorney General. The record of the proceedings on which the Commission based its rule shall be filed in the court as provided for in section 2112 of Title 28. For purposes of this section, the term "record" means such consumer product safety rule; any notice or proposal published pursuant to section 2056, 2057, or 2058 of this title; the transcript required by section 2058(d)(2) of this title of any oral presentation; any written submission of interested parties; and any other information which the Commission considers relevant to such rule.

(b) Additional data, views, or arguments

(b) If the petitioner applies to the court for leave to adduce additional data, views, or arguments and shows to the satisfaction of the court that such additional data, views, or arguments are material and that there were reasonable grounds for the petitioner's failure to adduce such data, views, or arguments in the proceeding before the Commission, the court may order the Commission to provide additional opportunity for the oral presentation of data, views, or arguments and for written submissions. The Commission may modify its findings, or make new findings by reason of the additional data, views, or arguments so taken and shall file such modified or new findings, and its recommendation, if any, for the modification or setting aside of its original rule, with the return of such additional data, views, or arguments.

(c) Jurisdiction; costs and attorneys' fees; substantial evidence to support administrative findings

(c) Upon the filing of the petition under subsection (a) of this section the court shall have jurisdiction to review the consumer product safety rule in accordance with chapter 7 of Title 5, and to grant appropriate relief, including interim relief, as provided in such chapter. A court may in the interest of justice include in such relief an award of the costs of suit, including reasonable attorneys' fees (determined in accordance with subsection (f) of this section) and reasonable expert witnesses' fees. Attorneys' fees may be awarded against the United States (or any agency or official of the United States) without regard to section 2412 of Title 28 or any other provision of law. The consumer product safety rule shall not be affirmed unless the Commission's findings under sections 2058(f)(1) and 2058(f)(3) of this title are supported by substantial evidence on the record taken as a whole.

(d) Supreme Court review

(d) The judgment of the court affirming or setting aside, in whole or in part, any consumer product safety rule shall be final, subject to review by the Supreme Court of the United States upon certiorari or certification, as provided in section 1254 of Title 28.

(e) Availability of other remedies

(e) The remedies provided for in this section shall be in addition to and not in lieu of any other remedies provided by law.

(f) Computation of reasonable fee for attorney

(f) For purposes of this section and sections 2072(a) and 2073 of this title, a reasonable attorney's fee is a fee (1) which is based upon (A) the actual time expended by an attorney in providing advice and other legal services in connection with representing a person in an action brought under this section, and (B) such reasonable expenses as may be incurred by the attorney in the provision of such services, and (2) which is computed at the rate prevailing for the provision of similar services with respect to actions brought in the court which is awarding such fee.

As amended Pub.L. 94–284, §§ 10(b), 11(a), May 11, 1976, 90 Stat. 507; Pub.L. 97–35, Title XII, § 1211(h)(1)–(3)(A), Aug. 13, 1981, 95 Stat. 723; Pub.L. 97–414, § 9(j)(2), Jan. 4, 1983, 96 Stat. 2064.

§ 2061. Imminent hazards

(a) Filing of action

(a) The Commission may file in a United States district court an action (1) against an imminently hazardous consumer product for seizure of such product under subsection (b)(2) of this section, or (2) against any person who is a manufacturer, distributor, or retailer of such product, or (3) against both. Such an action may be filed notwithstanding the existence of a consumer product safety rule applicable to such product, or the pendency of any administrative or judicial proceedings under any other provision of this chapter. As used in this section, and hereinafter in this chapter, the term "imminently hazardous consumer product" means a consumer product which presents imminent and unreasonable risk of death, serious illness, or severe personal injury.

(b) Relief; product condemnation and seizure

(b)(1) The district court in which such action is filed shall have jurisdiction to declare such product an imminently hazardous consumer product, and (in the case of an action under subsection (a)(2) of this section) to grant (as ancillary to such declaration or in lieu thereof) such temporary or permanent relief as may be necessary to protect the public from such risk. Such relief may include a mandatory order requiring the notification of such risk to purchasers of such product known to the defendant, public notice, the recall, the repair or the replacement of, or refund for, such product.

(2) In the case of an action under subsection (a)(1) of this section, the consumer product may be proceeded against by process of libel for the seizure and condemnation of such product in any United States district court within the jurisdiction of which such consumer product is found. Proceedings and cases instituted under the authority of the preceding sentence shall conform as nearly as possible to proceedings in rem in admiralty.

(c) Consumer product safety rule

(c) Where appropriate, concurrently with the filing of such action or as soon thereafter as may be practicable, the Commission shall initiate a proceeding to promulgate a consumer product safety rule applicable to the consumer product with respect to which such action is filed.

(d) Jurisdiction and venue; process; subpoena

(d)(1) An action under subsection (a)(2) of this section may be brought in the United States district court for the District of Columbia or in any judicial district in which any of the defendants is found, is an inhabitant or transacts business; and process in such an action may be served on a defendant in any other district in which such defendant resides or may be found. Subpenas requiring attendance of witnesses in such an action may run into any other district. In determining the judicial district in which an action may be brought under this section in instances in which such action may be brought in more than one judicial district, the Commission shall take into account the convenience of the parties.

(2) Whenever proceedings under this section involving substantially similar consumer products are pending in courts in two or more judicial districts, they shall be consolidated for trial by order of any such court upon application reasonably made by any party in interest, upon notice to all other parties in interest.

(e) Employment of attorneys by Commission

(e) Notwithstanding any other provision of law, in any action under this section, the Commission may direct attorneys employed by it to appear and represent it.

(g) Consideration of cost of compliance

(g) Nothing in this section shall be construed to require the Commission, in determining whether to bring an action against a consumer product or a person under this section, to prepare a comparison of the costs that would be incurred in complying with the relief that may be ordered in such action with the benefits to the public from such relief. [Note: this subsection was added at the end, notwithstanding the fact that no subsection (f) has been enacted.]

As amended Pub.L. 97–35, Title XII, § 1205(a)(2), Aug. 13, 1981, 95 Stat. 716; Pub.L. 101–608, Title I, § 111(a)(1), Nov. 16, 1990, 104 Stat. 3114.

§ 2063. Product certification and labeling

(a)(1) Every manufacturer of a product which is subject to a consumer product safety standard under this chapter and which is distributed in commerce (and the private labeler of such product if it bears a private label) shall issue a certificate which shall certify that such product conforms to all applicable consumer product safety standards, and shall specify any standard which is applicable. Such certificate shall accompany the product or shall otherwise be furnished to any distributor or retailer to whom the product is delivered. Any certificate under this subsection shall be based on a test of each product or upon a reasonable testing program; shall state the name of the manufacturer or private labeler issuing the certificate; and shall include the date and place of manufacture.

(2) In the case of a consumer product for which there is more than one manufacturer or more than one private labeler, the Commission may by rule designate one or more of such manufacturers or one or more of such private labelers (as the case may be) as the persons who shall issue the certificate required by paragraph (1) of this subsection, and may exempt all other manufacturers of such product or all other private labelers of the product (as the case may be) from the requirement under paragraph (1) to issue a certificate with respect to such product.

(b) The Commission may by rule prescribe reasonable testing programs for consumer products which are subject to consumer product safety standards under this chapter and for which a certificate is required under subsection (a) of this section. Any test or testing program on the basis of which a certificate is issued under subsection (a) of this section may, at the option of the person required to certify the product, be conducted by an independent third party qualified to perform such tests or testing programs.

(c) The Commission may by rule require the use and prescribe the form and content of labels which contain the following information (or that portion of it specified in the rule)—

(1) The date and place of manufacture of any consumer product.

(2) A suitable identification of the manufacturer of the consumer product, unless the product bears a private label in which case it shall identify the private labeler and shall also contain a code mark which will permit the seller of such product to identify the manufacturer thereof to the purchaser upon his request.

(3) In the case of a consumer product subject to a consumer product safety rule, a certification that the product meets all applicable consumer product safety standards and a specification of the standards which are applicable.

Such labels, where practicable, may be required by the Commission to be permanently marked on or affixed to any such consumer product. The Commission may, in appropriate cases, permit information required under paragraphs (1) and (2) of this subsection to be coded.

Pub.L. 92–573, § 14, Oct. 27, 1972, 86 Stat. 1220.

§ 2064.   Substantial product hazards

(a) Definition

(a) For purposes of this section, the term "substantial product hazard" means—

(1) a failure to comply with an applicable consumer product safety rule which creates a substantial risk of injury to the public, or

(2) a product defect which (because of the pattern of defect, the number of defective products distributed in commerce, the severity of the risk, or otherwise) creates a substantial risk of injury to the public.

(b) Noncompliance with applicable consumer product safety rules; product defects; notice to Commission by manufacturer, distributor, or retailer

Every manufacturer of a consumer product distributed in commerce, and every distributor and retailer of such product, who obtains information which reasonably supports the conclusion that such product—

(1) fails to comply with an applicable consumer product safety rule or with a voluntary consumer product safety standard upon which the Commission has relied under section 2058 of this title;

(2) contains a defect which could create a substantial product hazard described in subsection (a)(2) of this section; or

(3) creates an unreasonable risk of serious injury or death, shall immediately inform the Commission of such failure to comply, of such defect, or of such risk, unless such manufacturer, distributor, or retailer has actual knowledge that the Commission has been adequately informed of such defect, failure to comply, or such risk.

(c) Public notice of defect or failure to comply; mail notice

(c) If the Commission determines (after affording interested persons, including consumers and consumer organizations, an opportunity for a hearing in accordance with subsection (f) of this section) that a product distributed in commerce presents a substantial product hazard and that notification is required in order to adequately protect the public from such substantial product hazard, the Commission may order the manufacturer or any distributor or retailer of the product to take any one or more of the following actions:

(1) To give public notice of the defect or failure to comply.

(2) To mail notice to each person who is a manufacturer, distributor, or retailer of such product.

(3) To mail notice to every person to whom the person required to give notice knows such product was delivered or sold.

Any such order shall specify the form and content of any notice required to be given under such order.

(d) Repair; replacement; refunds; action plan

(d) If the Commission determines (after affording interested parties, including consumers and consumer organizations, an opportunity for a hearing in accordance with subsection (f) of this section) that a product distributed in commerce presents a substantial product hazard and that action under this subsection is in the public interest, it may order the manufacturer or any distributor or retailer of such product to take whichever of the following actions the person to whom the order is directed elects:

(1) To bring such product into conformity with the requirements of the applicable consumer product safety rule or to repair the defect in such product.

(2) To replace such product with a like or equivalent product which complies with the applicable consumer product safety rule or which does not contain the defect.

(3) To refund the purchase price of such product (less a reasonable allowance for use, if such product has been in the possession of a consumer for one year or more (A) at the time of public notice under subsection (c) of this section, or (B) at the time the consumer receives actual notice of the defect or noncompliance, whichever first occurs).

An order under this subsection may also require the person to whom it applies to submit a plan, satisfactory to the Commission, for taking action under whichever of the preceding paragraphs of this subsection under which such person has elected to act. The Commission shall specify in the order the persons to whom refunds must be made if the person to whom the order is directed elects to take the action described in paragraph (3). If an order under this subsection is directed to more than one person, the Commission shall specify which person has the election under this subsection. An order under this subsection may prohibit the person to whom it applies from manufacturing for sale, offering for sale, distributing in commerce, or importing into the customs territory of the United States (as defined in general note 2 to the Harmonized Tariff Schedule of the United States), or from doing any combination of such actions, the product with respect to which the order was issued.

(e) Reimbursement

(e)(1) No charge shall be made to any person (other than a manufacturer, distributor, or retailer) who avails himself of any remedy provided under an order issued under subsection (d) of this section, and the person subject to the order shall reimburse each person (other than a manufacturer, distributor, or retailer) who is entitled to such a remedy for any reasonable and foreseeable expenses incurred by such person in availing himself of such remedy.

(2) An order issued under subsection (c) or (d) of this section with respect to a product may require any person who is a manufacturer, distributor, or retailer of the product to reimburse any other person who is a manufacturer, distributor, or retailer of such product for such other

person's expenses in connection with carrying out the order, if the Commission determines such reimbursement to be in the public interest.

(f) Hearing

(f) An order under subsection (c) or (d) of this section may be issued only after an opportunity for a hearing in accordance with section 554 of Title 5, except that, if the Commission determines that any person who wishes to participate in such hearing is a part of a class of participants who share an identity of interest, the Commission may limit such person's participation in such hearing to participation through a single representative designated by such class (or by the Commission if such class fails to designate such a representative). Any settlement offer which is submitted to the presiding officer at a hearing under this subsection shall be transmitted by the officer to the Commission for its consideration unless the settlement offer is clearly frivolous or duplicative of offers previously made.

(g) Preliminary injunction

(g)(1) If the Commission has initiated a proceeding under this section for the issuance of an order under subsection (d) of this section with respect to a product which the Commission has reason to believe presents a substantial product hazard, the Commission (without regard to section 2076(b)(7) of this title) or the Attorney General may, in accordance with section 2061(d)(1) of this title, apply to a district court of the United States for the issuance of a preliminary injunction to restrain the distribution in commerce of such product pending the completion of such proceeding. If such a preliminary injunction has been issued, the Commission (or Attorney General if the preliminary injunction was issued upon an application of the Attorney General) may apply to the issuing court for extensions of such preliminary injunction.

(2) Any preliminary injunction, and any extension of a preliminary injunction, issued under this subsection with respect to a product shall be in effect for such period as the issuing court prescribes not to exceed a period which extends beyond the thirtieth day from the date of the issuance of the preliminary injunction (or, in the case of a preliminary injunction which has been extended, the date of its extension) or the date of the completion or termination of the proceeding under this section respecting such product, whichever date occurs first.

(3) The amount in controversy requirement of section 1331 of Title 28, does not apply with respect to the jurisdiction of a district court of the United States to issue or exend[1] a preliminary injunction under this subsection.

1. So in original. Probably should read "extend".

(h) Consideration of cost of notification

(h) Nothing in this section shall be construed to require the Commission, in determining that a product distributed in commerce presents a substantial product hazard and that notification or other action under this section should be taken, to prepare a comparison of the costs that would be incurred in providing notification or taking other action under this section with the benefits from such notification or action.

Pub.L. 92–573, § 15, Oct. 27, 1972, 86 Stat. 1221; Pub.L. 94–284, § 12(a), May 11, 1976, 90 Stat. 508; Pub.L. 97–35, Title XII, § 1211(h)(4), Aug. 13, 1981, 95 Stat. 723, as amended Pub.L. 97–414, § 9(j)(3), Jan. 4, 1983, 96 Stat. 2064; Pub.L. 97–35, Title XII, § 1211(h)(4), as amended Pub.L. 97–414, § 9(m), Jan. 4, 1983, 96 Stat. 2065; Pub.L. 100–418, Title I, § 1214(d), Aug. 23, 1988, 102 Stat. 1156; Pub.L. 101–608, Title I, §§ 111(a)(2), 112(a), 113, Nov. 16, 1990, 104 Stat. 3114, 3115, 3117.

§ 2065. Inspection and recordkeeping

(a) For purposes of implementing this chapter, or rules or orders prescribed under this chapter, officers or employees duly designated by the Commission, upon presenting appropriate credentials and a written notice from the Commission to the owner, operator, or agent in charge, are authorized—

(1) to enter, at reasonable times, (A) any factory, warehouse, or establishment in which consumer products are manufactured or held, in connection with distribution in commerce, or (B) any conveyance being used to transport consumer products in connection with distribution in commerce; and

(2) to inspect, at reasonable times and in a reasonable manner such conveyance or those areas of such factory, warehouse, or establishment where such products are manufactured, held, or transported and which may relate to the safety of such products. Each such inspection shall be commenced and completed with reasonable promptness.

(b) Every person who is a manufacturer, private labeler, or distributor of a consumer product shall establish and maintain such records, make such reports, and provide such information as the Commission may, by rule, reasonably require for the purposes of implementing this chapter, or to determine compliance with rules or orders prescribed under this chapter. Upon request of an officer or employee duly designated by the Commission, every such manufacturer, private labeler, or distributor shall permit the inspection of appropriate books, records, and papers relevant to determining whether such manufacturer, private labeler, or distributor has acted or is acting in compliance with this chapter and rules under this chapter.

Pub.L. 92–573, § 16, Oct. 27, 1972, 86 Stat. 1222.

§ 2066. Imported products

(a) Refusal of admission

(a) Any consumer product offered for importation into the customs territory of the United States (as defined in general note 2 to the Harmonized Tariff Schedule of the United States) shall be refused admission into such customs territory if such product—

(1) fails to comply with an applicable consumer product safety rule;

(2) is not accompanied by a certificate required by section 2063 of this title, or is not labeled in accordance with regulations under section 2063(c) of this title;

(3) is or has been determined to be an imminently hazardous consumer product in a proceeding brought under section 2061 of this title;

(4) has a product defect which constitutes a substantial product hazard (within the meaning of section 2064(a)(2) of this title); or

(5) is a product which was manufactured by a person who the Commission has informed the Secretary of the Treasury is in violation of subsection (g) of this section.

(b) Samples

(b) The Secretary of the Treasury shall obtain without charge and deliver to the Commission, upon the latter's request, a reasonable number of samples of consumer products being offered for import. Except for those owners or consignees who are or have been afforded an opportunity for a hearing in a proceeding under section 2061 of this title with respect to an imminently hazardous product, the owner or consignee of the product shall be afforded an opportunity by the Commission for a hearing in accordance with section 554 of Title 5 with respect to the importation of such products into the customs territory of the United States. If it appears from examination of such samples or otherwise that a product must be refused admission under the terms of subsection (a) of this section, such product shall be refused admission, unless subsection (c) of this section applies and is complied with.

(c) Modification

(c) If it appears to the Commission that any consumer product which may be refused admission pursuant to subsection (a) of this section can be so modified that it need not (under the terms of paragraphs (1) through (4) of subsection (a) of this section) be refused admission, the Commission may defer final determination as to the admission of such product and, in accordance with such regulations as the Commission and the Secretary of the Treasury shall jointly agree to, permit such product to be delivered from customs custody under bond for the purpose of permitting the owner or consignee an opportunity to so modify such product.

(d) Supervision of modifications

(d) All actions taken by an owner or consignee to modify such product under subsection (c) of this section shall be subject to the supervision of an officer or employee of the Commission and of the Department of the Treasury. If it appears to the Commission that the product cannot be so modified or that the owner or consignee is not proceeding satisfactorily to modify such product, it shall be refused admission into the customs territory of the United States, and the Commission may direct the Secretary to demand redelivery of the product into customs custody, and to seize the product in accordance with section 2071(b) of this title if it is not so redelivered.

(e) Product destruction

(e) Products refused admission into the customs territory of the United States under this section must be exported, except that upon application, the Secretary of the Treasury may permit the destruction of the product in lieu of exportation. If the owner or consignee does not export the product within a reasonable time, the Department of the Treasury may destroy the product.

(f) Payment of expenses occasioned by refusal of admission

(f) All expenses (including travel, per diem or subsistence, and salaries of officers or employees of the United States) in connection with the destruction provided for in this section (the amount of such expenses to be determined in accordance with regulations of the Secretary of the Treasury) and all expenses in connection with the storage, cartage, or labor with respect to any consumer product refused admission under this section, shall be paid by the owner or consignee and, in default of such payment, shall constitute a lien against any future importations made by such owner or consignee.

(g) Importation conditioned upon manufacturer's compliance

(g) The Commission may, by rule, condition the importation of a consumer product on the manufacturer's compliance with the inspection and recordkeeping requirements of this chapter and the Commission's rules with respect to such requirements.

(h) Product surveillance program

(h)(1) The Commission shall establish and maintain a permanent product surveillance program, in cooperation with other appropriate Federal agencies, for the purpose of carrying out the Commission's responsibilities under this chapter and the other Acts administered by the Commission and preventing the entry of unsafe consumer products into the commerce of the United States.

(2) The Commission may provide to the agencies with which it is cooperating under paragraph (1) such information, data, violator lists, test results, and other support, guidance and documents as may be necessary or helpful for such agencies to cooperate with the Commission to carry out the product surveillance program under paragraph (1).

(3) The Commission shall periodically report to the Congress the results of the surveillance program under paragraph (1).

Pub.L. 92–573, § 17, Oct. 27, 1972, 86 Stat. 1223; as amended Pub.L. 100–418, Title I, § 1214(d), Aug. 23, 1988, 103 Stat. 1156; Pub.L. 101–608, Title I, § 114, Nov. 16, 1990, 104 Stat. 3118.

§ 2067. Exemption of exports

(a) Risk of injury to consumers within United States

(a) This chapter shall not apply to any consumer product if (1) it can be shown that such product is manufactured, sold, or held for sale for export from the United States (or that such product was imported for export), unless (A) such consumer product is in fact distributed in commerce for use in the United States, or (B) the Commission determines that exportation of such product presents an unreasonable risk of injury to consumers within the United States, and (2) such consumer product when distributed in commerce, or any container in which it is enclosed when so distributed, bears a stamp or label stating that such consumer product is intended for export; except that this chapter shall apply to any consumer product manufactured for sale, offered for sale, or sold for shipment to any installation of the United States located outside of the United States.

(b) Statement of exportation: filing period, information; notification of foreign country; petition for minimum filing period: good cause

(b) Not less than thirty days before any person exports to a foreign country any product—

> (1) which is not in conformity with an applicable consumer product safety standard in effect under this chapter, or

> (2) which is declared to be a banned hazardous substance by a rule promulgated under section 2058 of this title,

such person shall file a statement with the Commission notifying the Commission of such exportation, and the Commission, upon receipt of such statement, shall promptly notify the government of such country of such exportation and the basis for such safety standard or rule. Any statement filed with the Commission under the preceding sentence shall specify the anticipated date of shipment of such product, the country and port of destination of such product, and the quantity of such product that will be exported, and shall contain such other information as the Commission may by regulation require. Upon petition filed with the Commission by any person required to file a statement under this subsection respecting an exportation, the Commission may, for good cause shown, exempt such person from the requirement of this subsection that such a statement be filed no less than thirty days before the date of the exportation, except that in no case shall the Commission permit such a statement to be filed later than the tenth day before such date.

As amended Pub.L. 95–631, § 6(a), Nov. 10, 1978, 92 Stat. 3745.

§ 2068. Prohibited acts

(a) It shall be unlawful for any person to——

(1) manufacture for sale, offer for sale, distribute in commerce, or import into the United States any consumer product which is not in conformity with an applicable consumer product safety standard under this chapter;

(2) manufacture for sale, offer for sale, distribute in commerce, or import into the United States any consumer product which has been declared a banned hazardous product by a rule under this chapter;

(3) fail or refuse to permit access to or copying of records, or fail or refuse to establish or maintain records, or fail or refuse to make reports or provide information, or fail or refuse to permit entry or inspection, as required under this chapter or rule thereunder;

(4) fail to furnish information required by section 2064(b) of this title;

(5) fail to comply with an order issued under section 2064(c) or (d) of this title (relating to notification, to repair, replacement, and refund, and to prohibited acts);

(6) fail to furnish a certificate required by section 2063 of this title or issue a false certificate if such person in the exercise of due care has reason to know that such certificate is false or misleading in any material respect; or to fail to comply with any rule under section 2063(c) of this title (relating to labeling);

(7) fail to comply with any rule under section 2058(g)(2) of this title (relating to stockpiling); or

(8) fail to comply with any rule under section 2076(e) of this title (relating to provision of performance and technical data); and

(9) fail to comply with any rule or requirement under section 2082 of this title (relating to labeling and testing of cellulose insulation).

(10) fail to file a statement with the Commission pursuant to section 2067(b) of this title.

(11) fail to furnish information required by section 2084 of this title.

(b) Paragraphs (1) and (2) of subsection (a) of this section shall not apply to any person (1) who holds a certificate issued in accordance with section 2063(a) of this title to the effect that such consumer product conforms to all applicable consumer product safety rules, unless such person knows that such consumer product does not conform, or (2) who relies in good faith on the representation of the manufacturer or a distributor of such product that the product is not subject to an applicable product safety rule.

As amended Pub.L. 97–414, § 9(j)(4), Jan. 4, 1983, 96 Stat. 2064; Pub.L. 101–608, Title I, § 112(d), Nov. 16, 1990, 104 Stat. 3117.

§ 2069. Civil penalties

(a) Amount of penalty

(a)(1) Any person who knowingly violates section 2068 of this title shall be subject to a civil penalty not to exceed $5,000 for each such violation. Subject to paragraph (2), a violation of section 2068(a)(1), (2), (4), (5), (6), (7), (8), (9), (10), or (11) of this title shall constitute a separate offense with respect to each consumer product involved, except that the maximum civil penalty shall not exceed $1,250,000 for any related series of violations. A violation of section 2068(a)(3) of this title shall constitute a separate violation with respect to each failure or refusal to allow or perform an act required thereby; and, if such violation is a continuing one, each day of such violation shall constitute a separate offense, except that the maximum civil penalty shall not exceed $1,250,000 for any related series of violations.

(2) The second sentence of paragraph (1) of this subsection shall not apply to violations of paragraph (1) or (2) of section 2068(a) of this title—

(A) if the person who violated such paragraphs is not the manufacturer or private labeler or a distributor of the products involved, and

(B) if such person did not have either (i) actual knowledge that his distribution or sale of the product violated such paragraphs or (ii) notice from the Commission that such distribution or sale would be a violation of such paragraphs.

(3)(A) The maximum penalty amounts authorized in paragraph (1) shall be adjusted for inflation as provided in this paragraph.

(B) Not later than December 1, 1994, and December 1 of each fifth calendar year thereafter, the Commission shall prescribe and publish in the Federal Register a schedule of maximum authorized penalties that shall apply for violations that occur after January 1 of the year immediately following such publication.

(C) The schedule of maximum authorized penalties shall be prescribed by increasing each of the amounts referred to in paragraph (1) by the cost-of-living adjustment for the preceding five years. Any increase determined under the preceding sentence shall be rounded to—

(i) in the case of penalties greater than $1,000 but less than or equal to $10,000, the nearest multiple of $1,000;

(ii) in the case of penalties greater than $10,000 but less than or equal to $100,000, the nearest multiple of $5,000;

(iii) in the case of penalties greater than $100,000, but less than or equal to $200,000, the nearest multiple of $10,000; and

(iv) in the case of penalties greater than $200,000, the nearest multiple of $25,000.

(D) For purposes of this subsection:

(i) The term "Consumer Price Index" means the Consumer Price Index for all urban consumers published by the Department of Labor.

(ii) The term "cost-of-living adjustment for the preceding five years" means the percentage by which—

(I) the Consumer Price Index for the month of June of the calendar year preceding the adjustment; exceeds

(II) the Consumer Price Index for the month of June preceding the date on which the maximum authorized penalty was last adjusted.

(b) Relevant factors in assessment of penalty

(b) In determining the amount of any penalty to be sought upon commencing an action seeking to assess a penalty for a violation of section 2068(a) of this title, the Commission shall consider the nature of the product defect, the severity of the risk of injury, the occurrence or absence of injury, the number of defective products distributed, and the appropriateness of such penalty in relation to the size of the business of the person charged.

(c) Compromise of penalty; deductions from penalty

(c) Any civil penalty under this section may be compromised by the Commission. In determining the amount of such penalty or whether it should be remitted or mitigated and in what amount, the Commission shall consider the appropriateness of such penalty to the size of the business of the person charged, the nature of the product defect, the severity of the risk of injury, the occurrence or absence of injury, and the number of defective products distributed. The amount of such penalty when finally determined, or the amount agreed on compromise, may be deducted from any sums owing by the United States to the person charged.

(d) "Knowingly" defined

(d) As used in the first sentence of subsection (a)(1) of this section, the term "knowingly" means (1) the having of actual knowledge, or (2) the presumed having of knowledge deemed to be possessed by a reasonable man who acts in the circumstances, including knowledge obtainable upon the exercise of due care to ascertain the truth of representations.

As amended Pub.L. 94–284, § 13(b), May 11, 1976, 90 Stat. 509; Pub.L. 95–631, § 6(c), Nov. 10, 1978, 92 Stat. 3745; Pub.L. 97–35, Title XII, § 1211(c), Aug. 13, 1981, 95 Stat. 721; As amended Pub.L. 101–608, Title I, §§ 112(e), 115(a), Nov. 16, 1990, 104 Stat. 3117, 3118.

§ 2070. Criminal penalties

(a) Any person who knowingly and willfully violates section 2068 of this title after having received notice of noncompliance from the Commission shall be fined not more than $50,000 or be imprisoned not more than one year, or both.

(b) Any individual director, officer, or agent of a corporation who knowingly and willfully authorizes, orders, or performs any of the acts or practices constituting in whole or in part a violation of section 2068 of this title, and who has knowledge of notice of noncompliance received by the corporation from the Commission, shall be subject to penalties under this section without regard to any penalties to which that corporation may be subject under subsection (a) of this section.

Pub.L. 92–573, § 21, Oct. 27, 1972, 86 Stat. 1225.

§ 2071. Injunctive enforcement and seizure

(a) The United States district courts shall have jurisdiction to take the following action:

(1) Restrain any violation of section 2068 of this title.

(2) Restrain any person from manufacturing for sale, offering for sale, distributing in commerce, or importing into the United States a product in violation of an order in effect under section 2064(d) of this title.

(3) Restrain any person from distributing in commerce a product which does not comply with a consumer product safety rule.

Such actions may be brought by the Commission (without regard to section 2076(b)(7)(A) of this title) or by the Attorney General in any United States district court for a district wherein any act, omission, or transaction constituting the violation occurred, or in such court for the district wherein the defendant is found or transacts business. In any action under this section process may be served on a defendant in any other district in which the defendant resides or may be found.

(b) Any consumer product—

(1) which fails to conform with an applicable consumer product safety rule, or

(2) the manufacture for sale, offering for sale, distribution in commerce, or the importation into the United States of which has been prohibited by an order in effect under section 2064(d) of this title, when introduced into or while in commerce or while held for sale after shipment in commerce shall be liable to be proceeded against on libel of information and condemned in any district court of the United States within the jurisdiction of which such consumer product is found. Proceedings in cases instituted under the authority of this subsection shall conform as nearly as possible to proceedings in rem in admiralty. Whenever such proceedings involving substantially similar consumer products are pending in courts of two or more judicial districts they shall be consolidated for trial by order of any such court upon application reasonably made by any party in interest upon notice to all other parties in interest.

As amended Pub.L. 94–284, §§ 11(b), 12(c), May 11, 1976, 90 Stat. 507, 508.

§ 2072. Suits for damages

(a) Persons injured; costs; amount in controversy

(a) Any person who shall sustain injury by reason of any knowing (including willful) violation of a consumer product safety rule, or any other rule or order issued by the Commission may sue any person who knowingly (including willfully) violated any such rule or order in any district court of the United States in the district in which the defendant resides or is found or has an agent, shall recover damages sustained, and may, if the court determines it to be in the interest of justice, recover the costs of suit, including reasonable attorneys' fees (determined in accordance with section 2060(f) of this title) and reasonable expert witnesses' fees: Provided, That the matter in controversy exceeds the sum or value of $10,000, exclusive of interest and costs, unless such action is brought against the United States, any agency thereof, or any officer or employee thereof in his official capacity.

(b) Denial and imposition of costs

(b) Except when express provision is made in a statute of the United States, in any case in which the plaintiff is finally adjudged to be entitled to recover less than the sum or value of $10,000, computed without regard to any setoff or counterclaim to which the defendant may be adjudged to be entitled, and exclusive of interests and costs, the district court may deny costs to the plaintiff and, in addition, may impose costs on the plaintiff.

(c) Remedies available

(c) The remedies provided for in this section shall be in addition to and not in lieu of any other remedies provided by common law or under Federal or State law.

As amended Pub.L. 94–284, § 10(c), May 11, 1976, 90 Stat. 507; Pub.L. 96–486, § 3, Dec. 1, 1980, 94 Stat. 2369; Pub.L. 97–35, Title XII, § 1211(h)(3)(B), Aug. 13, 1981, 95 Stat. 723.

§ 2073. Private enforcement

Any interested person (including any individual or nonprofit, business, or other entity) may bring an action in any United States district court for the district in which the defendant is found or transacts business to enforce a consumer product safety rule or an order under section 2064 of this title, and to obtain appropriate injunctive relief. Not less than thirty days prior to the commencement of such action, such interested person shall give notice by registered mail to the Commission, to the Attorney General, and to the person against whom such action is directed. Such notice shall state the nature of the alleged violation of any such standard or order, the relief to be requested, and the court in which the action will be brought. No separate suit shall be brought under this section if at the time the suit is brought the same alleged violation is the subject of a pending civil or criminal action by the United States under this chapter. In any action under this section the court may in the interest of justice award the costs of suit, including reasonable attorneys' fees (determined in accordance with section 2060(f) of this title) and reasonable expert witnesses' fees.

As amended Pub.L. 94–284, § 10(d), May 11, 1976, 90 Stat. 507; Pub.L. 97–35, Title XII, § 1211(a), (h)(3)(C), Aug. 13, 1981, 95 Stat. 721, 723.

§ 2074. Private remedies

(a) Liability at common law or under State statute not relieved by compliance

(a) Compliance with consumer product safety rules or other rules or orders under this chapter shall not relieve any person from liability at common law or under State statutory law to any other person.

(b) Evidence of Commission's inaction inadmissible in actions relating to consumer products

(b) The failure of the Commission to take any action or commence a proceeding with respect to the safety of a consumer product shall not be admissible in evidence in litigation at common law or under State statutory law relating to such consumer product.

(c) Public information

(c) Subject to sections 2055(a)(2) and 2055(b) of this title but notwithstanding section 2055(a)(1) of this title, (1) any accident or investigation report made under this chapter by an officer or employee of the Commission shall be made available to the public in a manner which will not identify any injured person or any person treating him, without the consent of the person so identified, and (2) all reports on research projects, demonstration projects, and other related activities shall be public information.

Pub.L. 92–573, § 25, Oct. 27, 1972, 86 Stat. 1227.

§ 2075. State standards

(a) State compliance to Federal standards

(a) Whenever a consumer product safety standard under this chapter is in effect and applies to a risk of injury associated with a consumer product, no State or political subdivision of a State shall have any authority either to establish or to continue in effect any provision of a safety standard or regulation which prescribes any requirements as to the performance, composition, contents, design, finish, construction, packaging, or labeling of such product which are designed to deal with the same risk of injury associated with such consumer product, unless such requirements are identical to the requirements of the Federal standard.

(b) Consumer product safety requirements which impose performance standards more stringent than Federal standards

(b) Subsection (a) of this section does not prevent the Federal Government or the government of any State or political subdivision of a State from establishing or continuing in effect a safety requirement applicable to a consumer product for its own use which requirement is designed to protect against a risk of injury associated with the product and which is not identical to the consumer product safety standard applicable to the product under this chapter if the Federal, State, or political subdivision requirement provides a higher degree of protection from such risk of injury than the standard applicable under this chapter.

(c) Exemptions

(c) Upon application of a State or political subdivision of a State, the Commission may by rule, after notice and opportunity for oral presentation of views, exempt from the provisions of subsection (a) of this section (under such conditions as it may impose in the rule) any proposed safety standard or regulation which is described in such application and which is designed to protect against a risk of injury associated with a consumer product subject to a consumer product safety standard under this chapter if the State or political subdivision standard or regulation—

(1) provides a significantly higher degree of protection from such risk of injury than the consumer product safety standard under this chapter, and

(2) does not unduly burden interstate commerce.

In determining the burden, if any, of a State or political subdivision standard or regulation on interstate commerce, the Commission shall consider and make appropriate (as determined by the Commission in its discretion) findings on the technological and economic feasibility of complying with such standard or regulation, the cost of complying with such standard or regulation, the geographic distribution of the consumer product to which the standard or regulation would apply, the probability of other States or political subdivisions applying for an exemption under this subsection for a similar standard or regulation, and the need for a national, uniform standard under this chapter for such consumer product.

As amended Pub.L. 94–284, § 17(d), May 11, 1976, 90 Stat. 514.

§ 2076. Additional functions of Consumer Product Safety Commission

(a) Authority to conduct hearings or other inquiries

(a) The Commission may, by one or more of its members or by such agents or agency as it may designate, conduct any hearing or other inquiry necessary or appropriate to its functions anywhere in the United States. A Commissioner who participates in such a hearing or other inquiry shall not be disqualified solely by reason of such participation from subsequently participating in a decision of the Commission in the same matter. The Commission shall publish notice of any proposed hearing in the Federal Register and shall afford a reasonable opportunity for interested persons to present relevant testimony and data.

(b) Commission powers; orders

(b) The commission shall also have the power—

(1) to require, by special or general orders, any person to submit in writing such reports and answers to questions as the Commission

may prescribe to carry out a specific regulatory or enforcement function of the Commission; and such submission shall be made within such reasonable period and under oath or otherwise as the Commission may determine;

(2) to administer oaths;

(3) to require by subpena the attendance and testimony of witnesses and the production of all documentary evidence relating to the execution of its duties;

(4) in any proceeding or investigation to order testimony to be taken by deposition before any person who is designated by the Commission and has the power to administer oaths and, in such instances, to compel testimony and the production of evidence in the same manner as authorized under paragraph (3) of this subsection;

(5) to pay witnesses the same fees and mileage as are paid in like circumstances in the courts of the United States;

(6) to accept gifts and voluntary and uncompensated services, notwithstanding the provisions of section 1342 of Title 31;

(7) to—

(A) initiate, prosecute, defend, or appeal (other than to the Supreme Court of the United States), through its own legal representative and in the name of the Commission, any civil action if the Commission makes a written request to the Attorney General for representation in such civil action and the Attorney General does not within the 45–day period beginning on the date such request was made notify the Commission in writing that the Attorney General will represent the Commission in such civil action, and

(B) initiate, prosecute, or appeal, through its own legal representative, with the concurrence of the Attorney General or through the Attorney General, any criminal action,

for the purpose of enforcing the laws subject to its jurisdiction;

(8) to lease buildings or parts of buildings in the District of Columbia, without regard to the Act of March 3, 1877 (section 34 of Title 40), for the use of the Commission; and

(9) to delegate any of its functions or powers, other than the power to issue subpenas under paragraph (3), to any officer or employee of the Commission.

An order issued under paragraph (1) shall contain a complete statement of the reason the Commission requires the report or answers specified in the order to carry out a specific regulatory or enforcement function of the Commission. Such an order shall be designed to place the least burden on the person subject to the order as is practicable taking into account the purpose for which the order was issued.

(c) Noncompliance with subpoena or Commission order; contempt

(c) Any United States district court within the jurisdiction of which any inquiry is carried on, may, upon petition by the Commission (subject to subsection (b)(7) of this section) or by the Attorney General, in case of refusal to obey a subpena or order of the Commission issued under subsection (b) of this section, issue an order requiring compliance therewith; and any failure to obey the order of the court may be punished by the court as a contempt thereof.

(d) Disclosure of information

(d) No person shall be subject to civil liability to any person (other than the Commission or the United States) for disclosing information at the request of the Commission.

(e) Performance and technical data

(e) The Commission may by rule require any manufacturer of consumer products to provide to the Commission such performance and technical data related to performance and safety as may be required to carry out the purposes of this chapter, and to give such notification of such performance and technical data at the time of original purchase to prospective purchasers and to the first purchaser of such product for purposes other than resale, as it determines necessary to carry out the purposes of this chapter.

(f) Purchase of consumer products by Commission

(f) For purposes of carrying out this chapter, the Commission may purchase any consumer product and it may require any manufacturer, distributor, or retailer of a consumer product to sell the product to the Commission at manufacturer's, distributor's, or retailer's cost.

(g) Contract authority

(g) The Commission is authorized to enter into contracts with governmental entities, private organizations, or individuals for the conduct of activities authorized by this chapter.

(h) Research, development, and testing facilities

(h) The Commission may plan, construct, and operate a facility or facilities suitable for research, development, and testing of consumer products in order to carry out this chapter.

(i) Recordkeeping; audit

(i)(1) Each recipient of assistance under this chapter pursuant to grants or contracts entered into under other than competitive bidding procedures shall keep such records as the Commission by rule shall prescribe, including records which fully disclose the amount and disposition by such recipient of the proceeds of such assistance, the total cost of the project undertaken in connection with which such assistance is given or used, and the amount of that portion of the cost of the project or undertaking supplied by other sources, and such other records as will facilitate an effective audit.

(2) The Commission and the Comptroller General of the United States, or their duly authorized representatives, shall have access for the purpose of audit and examination to any books, documents, papers, and records of the recipients that are pertinent to the grants or contracts entered into under this chapter under other than competitive bidding procedures.

(j) Report to President and Congress

(j) The Commission shall prepare and submit to the President and the Congress at the beginning of each regular session of Congress a comprehensive report on the administration of this chapter for the preceding fiscal year. Such report shall include—

(1) a thorough appraisal, including statistical analyses, estimates, and long-term projections, of the incidence of injury and effects to the population resulting from consumer products, with a breakdown, insofar as practicable, among the various sources of such injury;

(2) a list of consumer product safety rules prescribed or in effect during such year;

(3) an evaluation of the degree of observance of consumer product safety rules, including a list of enforcement actions, court decisions, and compromises of alleged violations, by location and company name;

(4) a summary of outstanding problems confronting the administration of this chapter in order of priority;

(5) an analysis and evaluation of public and private consumer product safety research activities;

(6) a list, with a brief statement of the issues, of completed or pending judicial actions under this chapter;

(7) the extent to which technical information was disseminated to the scientific and commercial communities and consumer information was made available to the public;

(8) the extent of cooperation between Commission officials and representatives of industry and other interested parties in the imple-

mentation of this chapter, including a log or summary of meetings held between Commission officials and representatives of industry and other interested parties;

(9) an appraisal of significant actions of State and local governments relating to the responsibilities of the Commission;

(10) with respect to voluntary consumer product safety standards for which the Commission has participated in the development through monitoring or offering of assistance and with respect to voluntary consumer product safety standards relating to risks of injury that are the subject of regulatory action by the Commission, a description of—

(A) the number of such standards adopted;

(B) the nature and number of the products which are the subject of such standards;

(C) the effectiveness of such standards in reducing potential harm from consumer products;

(D) the degree to which staff members of the Commission participate in the development of such standards;

(E) the amount of resources of the Commission devoted to encouraging development of such standards; and

(F) such other information as the Commission determines appropriate or necessary to inform the Congress on the current status of the voluntary consumer product safety standard program; and

(11) such recommendations for additional legislation as the Commission deems necessary to carry out the purposes of this chapter.

(k) Budget estimates and requests; legislative recommendations; testimony; comments on legislation

(k)(1) Whenever the Commission submits any budget estimate or request to the President or the Office of Management and Budget, it shall concurrently transmit a copy of that estimate or request to the Congress.

(2) Whenever the Commission submits any legislative recommendations, or testimony, or comments on legislation to the President or the Office of Management and Budget, it shall concurrently transmit a copy thereof to the Congress. No officer or agency of the United States shall have any authority to require the Commission to submit its legislative recommendations, or testimony, or comments on legislation, to any officer or agency of the United States for approval, comments, or review, prior to the submission of such recommendations, testimony, or comments to the Congress.

Pub.L. 94–273, § 31, Apr. 21, 1976, 90 Stat. 380; Pub.L. 94–284, §§ 8(b), 11(c), (d), 14, May 11, 1976, 90 Stat. 506–509; Pub.L. 95–631, § 11, Nov.

10, 1978, 92 Stat. 3748; Pub.L. 97–35, Title XII, §§ 1207(b), 1208, 1209(c), 1211(d), Aug. 13, 1981, 95 Stat. 718, 720, 721, Pub.L. 97–258, § 4(b), Sept. 13, 1982, 96 Stat. 1067.

§ 2076a.   Report on civil penalties

(1) Beginning 1 year after Nov. 16, 1990, and every year thereafter, the Consumer Product Safety Commission shall submit to the Committee on Commerce, Science, and Transportation of the Senate and the Committee on Energy and Commerce of the House of Representatives the information specified in paragraph (2) of this subsection. Such information may be included in the annual report to the Congress submitted by the Commission.

(2) The Commission shall submit information with respect to the imposition of civil penalties under the statutes which it administers. The information shall included the number of civil penalties imposed, an identification of the violations that led to the imposition of such penalties, and the amount of revenue recovered from the imposition of such penalties.

Pub.L. 101–608, Title I, § 115(d), Nov. 16, 1990, 104 Stat. 3121.

§ 2077.   Chronic Hazard Advisory Panels

(a) Appointment; purposes

(a) The Commission shall appoint Chronic Hazard Advisory Panels (hereinafter referred to as the Panel or Panels) to advise the Commission in accordance with the provisions of section 2080(b) of this title respecting the chronic hazards of cancer, birth defects, and gene mutations associated with consumer products.

(b) Composition; membership

(b) Each Panel shall consist of 7 members appointed by the Commission from a list of nominees who shall be nominated by the President of the National Academy of Sciences from scientists—

(1) who are not officers or employees of the United States, (other than employees of the National Institutes of Health, the National Toxicology Program, or the National Center for Toxicological Research) and who do not receive compensation from or have any substantial financial interest in any manufacturer, distributor, or retailer of a consumer product; and

(2) who have demonstrated the ability to critically assess chronic hazards and risks to human health presented by the exposure of humans to toxic substances or as demonstrated by the exposure of animals to such substances.

The President of the National Academy of Sciences shall nominate for each Panel a number of individuals equal to three times the number of members to be appointed to the Panel.

(c) Chairman and Vice Chairman; election; term

(c) The Chairman and Vice Chairman of the Panel shall be elected from among the members and shall serve for the duration of the Panel.

(d) Majority vote

(d) Decisions of the Panel shall be made by a majority of the Panel.

(e) Administrative support services

(e) The Commission shall provide each Panel with such administrative support services as it may require to carry out its duties under section 2080 of this title.

(f) Compensation

(f) A member of a Panel appointed under subsection (a) of this section shall be paid at a rate not to exceed the daily equivalent of the annual rate of basic pay in effect for grade GS–18 of the General Schedule for each day (including travel time) during which the member is engaged in the actual performance of the duties of the Panel.

(g) Requests for and disclosures of information

(g) Each Panel shall request information and disclose information to the public, as provided in subsection (h) of this section, only through the Commission.

(h) Information from other Federal departments and agencies

(h)(1) Notwithstanding any statutory restriction on the authority of agencies and departments of the Federal Government to share information, such agencies and departments shall provide the Panel with such information and data as each Panel, through the Commission, may request to carry out its duties under section 2080 of this title. Each Panel may request information, through the Commission, from States, industry and other private sources as it may require to carry out its responsibilities.

(2) Section 2055 of this title shall apply to the disclosure of information by the Panel but shall not apply to the disclosure of information to the Panel.

Pub.L. 92–573, § 28, as added Pub.L. 97–35, Title XII, § 1206(a), Aug. 13, 1981, 95 Stat. 716; as amended Pub.L. 101–608, Title I § 116, Nov. 16, 1990, 104 Stat. 3121.

§ 2078. Cooperation with States and other Federal agencies

(a) The Commission shall establish a program to promote Federal–State cooperation for the purposes of carrying out this chapter. In implementing such program the Commission may——

(1) accept from any State or local authorities engaged in activities relating to health, safety, or consumer protection assistance in such functions as injury data collection, investigation, and educational programs, as well as other assistance in the administration and enforcement of this chapter which such States or localities may be able and willing to provide and, if so agreed, may pay in advance or otherwise for the reasonable cost of such assistance, and

(2) commission any qualified officer or employee of any State or local agency as an officer of the Commission for the purpose of conducting examinations, investigations, and inspections.

(b) In determining whether such proposed State and local programs are appropriate in implementing the purposes of this chapter, the Commission shall give favorable consideration to programs which establish separate State and local agencies to consolidate functions relating to product safety and other consumer protection activities.

(c) The Commission may obtain from any Federal department or agency such statistics, data, program reports, and other materials as it may deem necessary to carry out its functions under this chapter. Each such department or agency may cooperate with the Commission and, to the extent permitted by law, furnish such materials to it. The Commission and the heads of other departments and agencies engaged in administering programs related to product safety shall, to the maximum extent practicable, cooperate and consult in order to insure fully coordinated efforts.

(d) The Commission shall, to the maximum extent practicable, utilize the resources and facilities of the National Institute of Standards and Technology, on a reimbursable basis, to perform research and analyses related to risks of injury associated with consumer products (including fire and flammability risks), to develop test methods, to conduct studies and investigations, and to provide technical advice and assistance in connection with the functions of the Commission.

(e) The Commission may provide to another Federal agency or a State or local agency or authority engaged in activities relating to health, safety, or consumer protection, copies of any accident or investigation report made under this chapter by any officer, employee or agent of the Commission only if (1) information which under section 2055(a)(2) of this title is to be considered confidential and is not included in any copy of such report which is provided under this subsection; and (2) each Federal agency and State and local agency and authority which is to receive under this subsection a copy of such report provided assurances satisfactory to the Commission that the identity of any injured person will not, without the consent of the person identified, be included in—

(A) any copy of such report, or

(B) any information contained in any such report,

which the agency or authority makes available to any member of the public. No Federal agency or State or local agency or authority may disclose to the public any information contained in a report received by the agency or authority under this subsection unless with respect to such information the Commission has complied with the applicable requirements of section 2055(b) of this title.

Pub.L. 92–573, § 29, Oct. 27, 1972, 86 Stat. 1230; Pub.L. 94–284, § 15, May 11, 1976, 90 Stat. 510; as amended Pub.L. 100–418, Title V, § 5115(c), Aug. 23, 1988, 102 Stat. 1433.

§ 2079. Transfers of functions

(a) Hazardous substances and poisons

(a) The functions of the Secretary of Health, Education, and Welfare under the Federal Hazardous Substances Act and the Poison Prevention Packaging Act of 1970 are transferred to the Commission. The functions of the Secretary of Health, Education, and Welfare under the Federal Food, Drug, and Cosmetic Act (15 U.S.C. 301 et seq.[2]), to the extent such functions relate to the administration and enforcement of the Poison Prevention Packaging Act of 1970, are transferred to the Commission.

(b) Flammable fabrics

(b) The functions of the Secretary of Health, Education, and Welfare, the Secretary of Commerce, and the Federal Trade Commission under the Flammable Fabrics Act are transferred to the Commission. The functions of the Federal Trade Commission under the Federal Trade Commission Act, to the extent such functions relate to the administration and enforcement of the Flammable Fabrics Act, are transferred to the Commission.

(c) Household refrigerators

(c) The functions of the Secretary of Commerce and the Federal Trade Commission under the Act of August 2, 1956, are transferred to the Commission.

(d) Regulation by Commission of consumer products in accordance with other provisions of law

2. So in original. Probably should be "21 U.S.C. 301 et seq.".

(d) A risk of injury which is associated with a consumer product and which could be eliminated or reduced to a sufficient extent by action under the Federal Hazardous Substances Act, the Poison Prevention Packaging Act of 1970, or the Flammable Fabrics Act may be regulated under this chapter only if the Commission by rule finds that it is in the public interest to regulate such risk of injury under this chapter. Such a rule shall identify the risk of injury proposed to be regulated under this chapter and shall be promulgated in accordance with section 553 of Title 5; except that the period to be provided by the Commission pursuant to subsection (c) of such section for the submission of data, views, and arguments respecting the rule shall not exceed thirty days from the date of publication pursuant to subsection (b) of such section of a notice respecting the rule.

(e) Transfer of personnel, property, records, etc.; continued application of orders, rules, etc.

(e)(1)(A) All personnel, property, records, obligations, and commitments, which are used primarily with respect to any function transferred under the provisions of subsections (a), (b) and (c) of this section shall be transferred to the Commission, except those associated with fire and flammability research in the National Institute of Standards and Technology. The transfer of personnel pursuant to this paragraph shall be without reduction in classification or compensation for one year after such transfer, except that the Chairman of the Commission shall have full authority to assign personnel during such one-year period in order to efficiently carry out functions transferred to the Commission under this section.

(B) Any commissioned officer of the Public Health Service who upon the day before the effective date of this section, is serving as such officer primarily in the performance of functions transferred by this chapter to the Commission, may, if such officer so elects, acquire competitive status and be transferred to a competitive position in the Commission subject to subparagraph (A) of this paragraph, under the terms prescribed in paragraphs (3) through (8)(A) of section 15(b) of the Clean Air Amendments of 1970.

(2) All orders, determinations, rules, regulations, permits, contracts, certificates, licenses, and privileges (A) which have been issued, made, granted, or allowed to become effective in the exercise of functions which are transferred under this section by any department or agency, any functions of which are transferred by this section, and (B) which are in effect at the time this section takes effect, shall continue in effect according to their terms until modified, terminated, superseded, set aside, or repealed by the Commission, by any court of competent jurisdiction, or by operation of law.

(3) The provisions of this section shall not affect any proceedings pending at the time this section takes effect before any department or

agency, functions of which are transferred by this section; except that such proceedings, to the extent that they relate to functions so transferred, shall be continued before the Commission. Orders shall be issued in such proceedings, appeals shall be taken therefrom, and payments shall be made pursuant to such orders, as if this section had not been enacted; and orders issued in any such proceedings shall continue in effect until modified, terminated, superseded, or repealed by the Commission, by a court of competent jurisdiction, or by operation of law.

(4) The provisions of this section shall not affect suits commenced prior to the date this section takes effect and in all such suits proceedings shall be had, appeals taken, and judgments rendered, in the same manner and effect as if this section had not been enacted; except that if before the date on which this section takes effect, any department or agency (or officer thereof in his official capacity) is a party to a suit involving functions transferred to the Commission, then such suit shall be continued by the Commission. No cause of action, and no suit, action, or other proceeding, by or against any department or agency (or officer thereof in his official capacity) functions of which are transferred by this section, shall abate by reason of the enactment of this section. Causes of actions, suits, actions, or other proceedings may be asserted by or against the United States or the Commission as may be appropriate and, in any litigation pending when this section takes effect, the court may at any time, on its own motion or that of any party, enter an order which will give effect of the provisions of this paragraph.

(f) Definition of "function"

(f) For purposes of this section, (1) the term "function" includes power and duty, and (2) the transfer of a function, under any provision of law, of an agency or the head of a department shall also be a transfer of all functions under such law which are exercised by any office or officer of such agency or department.

As amended Pub.L. 94–284, §§ 3(f), 16, May 11, 1976, 90 Stat. 504, 510; as amended Pub.L. 100–418, Title V, § 5115(c), Aug. 23, 1988, 102 Stat. 1433.

§ 2080. Limitations on Jurisdiction of Consumer Product Safety Commission

(a) Authority to regulate

(a) The Commission shall have no authority under this chapter to regulate any risk of injury associated with a consumer product if such risk could be eliminated or reduced to a sufficient extent by actions taken under the Occupational Safety and Health Act of 1970; the Atomic Energy Act of 1954; or the Clean Air Act. The Commission shall have no authority under this chapter to regulate any risk of injury associated with electronic product radiation emitted from an electronic product (as such terms are defined by sections 355(1) and (2) of the Public Health Service Act) if such risk of injury may be subjected to regulation under subpart 3 of part F of title III of the Public Health Service Act.

(b) Certain notices of proposed rulemaking; duties of Chronic Hazard Advisory Panel

(1) The Commission may not issue—

(A) an advance notice of proposed rulemaking for a consumer product safety rule,

(B) a notice of proposed rulemaking for a rule under section 2076(e) of this title, or

(C) an advance notice of proposed rulemaking for regulations under section 1261(q)(1) of this title,

relating to a risk of cancer, birth defects, or gene mutations from a consumer product unless a Chronic Hazard Advisory Panel, established under section 2077 of this title, has, in accordance with paragraph (2), submitted a report to the Commission with respect to whether a substance contained in such product is a carcinogen, mutagen, or teratogen.

(2)(A) Before the Commission issues an advance notice of proposed rulemaking for—

(i) a consumer product safety rule,

(ii) a rule under section 2076(e) of this title, or

(iii) a regulation under section 1261(q)(1) of this title,

relating to a risk of cancer, birth defects, or gene mutations from a consumer product, the Commission shall request the Panel to review the scientific data and other relevant information relating to such risk to determine if any substance in the product is a carcinogen, mutagen, or a teratogen and to report its determination to the Commission.

(B) When the Commission appoints a Panel, the Panel shall convene within 30 days after the date the final appointment is made to the Panel. The Panel shall report its determination to the Commission not later than 120 days after the date the Panel is convened or, if the Panel requests additional time, within a time period specified by the Commission. If the determination reported to the Commission states that a substance in a product is a carcinogen, mutagen, or a teratogen, the Panel shall include in its report an estimate, if such an estimate is feasible, of the probable harm to human health that will result from exposure to the substance.

(C) A Panel appointed under section 2077 of this title shall terminate when it has submitted its report unless the Commission extends the existence of the Panel.

(D) The Federal Advisory Committee Act shall not apply with respect to any Panel established under this section.

(c) Panel report; incorporation into advance notice and final rule

(c) Each Panel's report shall contain a complete statement of the basis for the Panel's determination. The Commission shall consider the report of the Panel and incorporate such report into the advance notice of proposed rulemaking and final rule.

Pub.L. 97–35, Title XII, § 1206(b), Aug. 13, 1981, 95 Stat. 717, Pub.L. 97–414, § 9(j)(5), Jan. 4, 1983, 96 Stat. 2064.

§ **2081.** Authorization of appropriations

(a) There are authorized to be appropriated for the purposes of carrying out the provisions of this chapter (other than the provisions of section 2076(h) of this title which authorize the planning and construction of research, development, and testing facilities) and for the purpose of carrying out the functions, powers, and duties transferred to the Commission under section 2079 of this title, not to exceed—

  (1) $42,000,000 for fiscal year 1991, and

  (2) $45,000,000 for fiscal year 1992.

For payment of accumulated and accrued leave under section 5551 of Title 5 severance pay under section 5595 under such title, and any other expense related to a reduction in force in the Commission, there are authorized to be appropriated such sums as may be necessary.

(b)(1) There are authorized to be appropriated such sums as may be necessary for the planning and construction of research, development and testing facilities described in section 2076(h) of this title; except that no appropriation shall be made for any such planning or construction involving an expenditure in excess of $100,000 if such planning or construction has not been approved by resolutions adopted in substantially the same form by the Committee on Energy and Commerce of the House of Representatives, and by the Committee on Commerce, Science, and Transportation of the Senate. For the purpose of securing consideration of such approval the Commission shall transmit to Congress a prospectus of the proposed facility including (but not limited to)—

  (A) a brief description of the facility to be planned or constructed;

  (B) the location of the facility, and an estimate of the maximum cost of the facility;

  (C) a statement of those agencies, private and public, which will use such facility, together with the contribution to be made by each such agency toward the cost of such facility; and

  (D) a statement of justification of the need for such facility.

(2) The estimated maximum cost of any facility approved under this subsection as set forth in the prospectus may be increased by the amount equal to the percentage increase, if any, as determined by the Commission, in construction costs, from the date of the transmittal of such prospectus to Congress, but in no event shall the increase authorized by this paragraph exceed 10 per centum of such estimated maximum cost.

(c) No funds appropriated under subsection (a) of this section may be used to pay any claim described in section 2053(h) of this title whether pursuant to a judgment of a court or under any award, compromise, or settlement of such claim made under section 2672 of Title 28, or under any other provision of law.

As amended Pub.L. 94–284, §§ 2, 5(b), May 11, 1976, 90 Stat. 503, 505; S.Res. 4, Feb. 4, 1977; Pub.L. 95–631, § 1, Nov. 10, 1978, 92 Stat. 3742; H.Res. 459, Mar. 25, 1980; Pub.L. 97–35, Title XII, § 1214, Aug. 13, 1981, 95 Stat. 724; as amended Pub.L. 101–608, § 117, Nov. 16, 1990, 104 Stat. 3121; Pub.L. 103–437, § 5(c)(1), Nov. 2, 1994, 108 Stat. 4582.

§ 2082. Interim cellulose insulation safety standard

(a) Applicability of specification of General Services Administration; authority and effect of interim standard; modifications; criteria; labeling requirements

(a)(1) Subject to the provisions of paragraph (2), on and after the last day of the 60–day period beginning on the effective date of this section, the requirements for flame resistance and corrosiveness set forth in the General Services Administration's specification for cellulose insulation, HH–I–515C (as such specification was in effect on February 1, 1978), shall be deemed to be an interim consumer product safety standard which shall have all the authority and effect of any other consumer product safety standard promulgated by the Commission under this chapter. During the 45–day period beginning on the effective date of this section, the Commission may make, and shall publish in the Federal Register, such technical, nonsubstantive changes in such requirements as it deems appropriate to make such requirements suitable for promulgation as a consumer product safety standard. At the end of the 60–day period specified in the first sentence of this paragraph, the Commission shall publish in the Federal Register such interim consumer product safety standard, as altered by the Commission under this paragraph.

(2) The interim consumer product safety standard established in paragraph (1) shall provide that any cellulose insulation which is produced or distributed for sale or use as a consumer product shall have a flame spread rating of 0 to 25, as such rating is set forth in the General Services Administration's specification for cellulose insulation, HH–I–515C.

(3) During the period for which the interim consumer product safety standard established in subsection (a) of this section is in effect, in addition

470

to complying with any labeling requirement established by the Commission under this chapter, each manufacturer or private labeler of cellulose insulation shall include the following statement on any container of such cellulose insulation: "ATTENTION: This material meets the applicable minimum Federal flammability standard. This standard is based upon laboratory tests only, which do not represent actual conditions which may occur in the home". Such statement shall be located in a conspicuous place on such container and shall appear in conspicuous and legible type in contrast by typography, layout, and color with other printed matter on such container.

(b) Scope of judicial review

(b) Judicial review of the interim consumer product safety standard established in subsection (a) of this section, as such standard is in effect on and after the last day of the 60–day period specified in such subsection, shall be limited solely to the issue of whether any changes made by the Commission under paragraph (1) are technical, nonsubstantive changes. For purposes of such review, any change made by the Commission under paragraph (1) which requires that any test to determine the flame spread rating of cellulose insulation shall include a correction for variations in test results caused by equipment used in the test shall be considered a technical, nonsubstantive change.

(c) Enforcement; violations; promulgation of final standard; procedures applicable to promulgation; revision of interim standard; procedures applicable to revision

(c)(1)(A) Any interim consumer product safety standard established pursuant to this section shall be enforced in the same manner as any other consumer product safety standard until such time as there is in effect a final consumer product safety standard promulgated by the Commission, as provided in subparagraph (B), or until such time as it is revoked by the Commission under section 2058(e) of this title. A violation of the interim consumer product safety standard shall be deemed to be a violation of a consumer product safety standard promulgated by the Commission under section 2058 of this title.

(B) If the Commission determines that the interim consumer product safety standard does not adequately protect the public from the unreasonable risk of injury associated with flammable or corrosive cellulose insulation, it shall promulgate a final consumer product safety standard to protect against such risk. Such final standard shall be promulgated pursuant to section 553 of Title 5, except that the Commission shall give interested persons an opportunity for the oral presentation of data, views, or arguments, in addition to an opportunity to make written submissions. A transcript shall be kept of any oral presentation. The provisions of section 2058(b), (c), and (d) of this title shall apply to any proceeding to promulgate such final standard. In any judicial review of such final standard under section 2060 of this title, the court shall not require any demonstration that each particular finding made by the Commission under section 2058(c) of this title is supported by substantial evidence. The court shall affirm the action of the Commission unless the court determines that such action is not supported by substantial evidence on the record taken as a whole.

(2)(A) Until there is in effect such a final consumer product safety standard, the Commission shall incorporate into the interim consumer product safety standard, in accordance with the provisions of this paragraph, each revision superseding the requirements for flame resistance and corrosiveness referred to in subsection (a) of this section and promulgated by the General Services Administration.

(B) At least 45 days before any revision superseding such requirements is to become effective, the Administrator of the General Services Administration shall notify the Commission of such revision. In the case of any such revision which becomes effective during the period beginning on February 1, 1978, and ending on the effective date of this section, such notice from the Administrator of the General Services Administration shall be deemed to have been made on the effective date of this section.

(C)(i) No later than 45 days after receiving any notice under subparagraph (B), the Commission shall publish the revision, including such changes in the revision as it considers appropriate to make the revision suitable for promulgation as an amendment to the interim consumer product safety standard, in the Federal Register as a proposed amendment to the interim consumer product safety standard.

(ii) The Commission may extend the 45–day period specified in clause (i) for an additional period of not more than 150 days if the Commission determines that such extension is necessary to study the technical and scientific basis for the revision involved, or to study the safety and economic consequences of such revision.

(D)(i) Additional extensions of the 45–day period specified in subparagraph (C)(i) may be taken by the Commission if—

(I) the Commission makes the determination required in subparagraph (C)(ii) with respect to each such extension; and

(II) in the case of further extensions proposed by the Commission after an initial extension under this clause, such further extensions have not been disapproved under clause (iv).

(ii) Any extension made by the Commission under this subparagraph shall be for a period of not more than 45 days.

(iii) Prior notice of each extension made by the Commission under this subparagraph, together with a statement of the reasons for such extension and an estimate of the length of time required by the Commission to complete its action upon the revision involved, shall be published in the

Federal Register and shall be submitted to the Committee on Commerce, Science, and Transportation of the Senate and the Committee on Interstate and Foreign Commerce of the House of Representatives.

(iv) In any case in which the Commission takes an initial 45-day extension under clause (i), the Commission may not take any further extensions under clause (i) if each committee referred to in clause (iii) disapproves by committee resolution any such further extensions before the end of the 15-day period following notice of such initial extension made by the Commission in accordance with clause (iii).

(E) The Commission shall give interested persons an opportunity to comment upon any proposed amendment to the interim consumer product safety standard during the 30-day period following any publication by the Commission under subparagraph (C).

(F) No later than 90 days after the end of the period specified in subparagraph (E), the Commission shall promulgate the amendment to the interim consumer product safety standard unless the Commission determines, after consultation with the Secretary of Energy, that—

(i) such amendment is not necessary for the protection of consumers from the unreasonable risk of injury associated with flammable or corrosive cellulose insulation; or

(ii) implementation of such amendment will create an undue burden upon persons who are subject to the interim consumer product safety standard.

(G) The provisions of section 2060 of this title shall not apply to any judicial review of any amendment to the interim product safety standard promulgated under this paragraph.

(d) Reporting requirements of other Federal departments, agencies, etc. of violations

(d) Any Federal department, agency, or instrumentality, or any Federal independent regulatory agency, which obtains information which reasonably indicates that cellulose insulation is being manufactured or distributed in violation of this chapter shall immediately inform the Commission of such information.

(e) Reporting requirements of Commission to Congressional committees; contents, time of submission, etc.

(e)(1) The Commission, no later than 45 days after the effective date of this section, shall submit a report to the Committee on Commerce, Science, and Transportation of the Senate and to the Committee on Interstate and Foreign Commerce of the House of Representatives which shall contain a detailed statement of the manner in which the Commission intends to carry out the enforcement of this section.

(2)(A) The Commission, no later than 6 months after the date upon which the report required in paragraph (1) is due (and no later than the end of each 6–month period thereafter), shall submit a report to each committee referred to in paragraph (1) which shall describe the enforcement activities of the Commission with respect to this section during the most recent 6–month period.

(B) The first report which the Commission submits under subparagraph (A) shall include the results of tests of cellulose insulation manufactured by at least 25 manufacturers which the Commission shall conduct to determine whether such cellulose insulation complies with the interim consumer product safety standard. The second such report shall include the results of such tests with respect to 50 manufacturers who were not included in testing conducted by the Commission for inclusion in the first report.

(f) Compliance with certification requirements; implementation; waiver; rules and regulations

(f)(1) The Commission shall have the authority to require that any person required to comply with the certification requirements of section 2063 of this title with respect to the manufacture of cellulose insulation shall provide for the performance of any test or testing program required for such certification through the use of an independent third party qualified to perform such test or testing program. The Commission may impose such requirement whether or not the Commission has established a testing program for cellulose insulation under section 2063(b) of this title.

(2) The Commission, upon petition by a manufacturer, may waive the requirements of paragraph (1) with respect to such manufacturer if the Commission determines that the use of an independent third party is not necessary in order for such manufacturer to comply with the certification requirements of section 2063 of this title.

(3) The Commission may prescribe such rules as it considers necessary to carry out the provisions of this subsection.

(g) Authorization of appropriations

(g) There are authorized to be appropriated, for each of the fiscal years 1978, 1979, 1980, and 1981, such sums as may be necessary to carry out the provisions of this section.

Pub.L. 92–573, § 35, as added Pub.L. 95–319, § 3(a), July 11, 1978, 92 Stat. 386; H.Res. 549, Mar. 25, 1980; as amended Pub.L. 104–437, § 5(c)(2), Nov. 2, 1994, 108 Stat. 4582.

§ 2083. Congressional veto of consumer product safety rules

Unconstitutionality of Legislative Veto Provisions

The provisions of former section 1254(c)(2) of Title 8, Aliens and Nationality, which authorized a House of Congress, by resolution, to invali-

date an action of the Executive Branch, were declared unconstitutional in Immigration and Naturalization Service v. Chadha, 1983, 462 U.S. 919, 103 S.Ct. 2764, 77 L.Ed.2d 317. See similar provisions in this section.

(a) Transmission to Congress

(a) The Commission shall transmit to the Secretary of the Senate and the Clerk of the House of Representatives a copy of any consumer product safety rule promulgated by the Commission under section 2058 of this title.

(b) Disapproval by concurrent resolution

(b) Any rule specified in subsection (a) of this section shall not take effect if—

(1) within the 90 calendar days of continuous session of the Congress which occur after the date of the promulgation of such rule, both Houses of the Congress adopt a concurrent resolution, the matter after the resolving clause of which is as follows (with the blank spaces appropriately filled): "That the Congress disapproves the consumer product safety rule which was promulgated by the Consumer Product Safety Commission with respect to _____ and which was transmitted to the Congress on _____ and disapproves the rule for the following reasons: _____."; or

(2) within the 60 calendar days of continuous session of the Congress which occur after the date of the promulgation of such rule, one House of the Congress adopts such concurrent resolution and transmits such resolution to the other House and such resolution is not disapproved by such other House within the 30 calendar days of continuous session of the Congress which occur after the date of such transmittal.

(c) Presumptions from Congressional action or inaction

(c) Congressional inaction on, or rejection of, a concurrent resolution of disapproval under this section shall not be construed as an expression of approval of the rule involved, and shall not be construed to create any presumption of validity with respect to such rule.

(d) Continuous session of Congress

(d) For purposes of this section—

(1) continuity of session is broken only by an adjournment of the Congress sine die; and

(2) the days on which either House is not in session because of an adjournment of more than 3 days to a day certain are excluded in the computation of the periods of continuous session of the Congress specified in subsection (b) of this section.

Pub.L. 92–573, § 36, as added Pub.L. 97–35, Title XII, § 1207(a), Aug. 13, 1981, 95 Stat. 718.

§ 2084. Information reporting

(a) Notification of settlements or judgments

(a) If a particular model of a consumer product is the subject of at least 3 civil actions that have been filed in Federal or State court for death or grievous bodily injury which in each of the 24–month periods defined in subsection (b) of this section result in either a final settlement involving the manufacturer or a court judgment in favor of the plaintiff, the manufacturer of said product shall, in accordance with subsection (c) of this section, report to the Commission each such civil action within 30 days after the final settlement or court judgment in the third of such civil actions, and, within 30 days after any subsequent settlement or judgment in that 24–month period, any other such action.

(b) Calculation of the 24 month period

(b) The 24–month periods referred to in subsection (a) of this section are in the 24–month period commencing on January 1, 1991, and subsequent 24–month periods beginning January 1 of the calendar year that is two years following the beginning of the previous 24–month period.

(c) Information required to be reported

(c)(1) The information required by subsection (a) of this section to be reported to the Commission with respect to each civil action described in subsection (a) of this section, shall include and in addition to any voluntary information provided under paragraph (2) shall be limited to the following:

(A) The name and address of the manufacturer.

(B) The model and model number or designation of the consumer product subject to the civil action.

(C) A statement as to whether the civil action alleged death or grievous bodily injury, and in the case of an allegation of grievous bodily injury, a statement of the category of such injury.

(D) A statement as to whether the civil action resulted in a final settlement or a judgment in favor of the plaintiff.

(E) in the case of a judgment in favor of the plaintiff, the name of the civil action, the number assigned the civil action, and the court in which the civil action was filed.

(2) A manufacturer furnishing the report required by paragraph (1) may include (A) a statement as to whether any judgment in favor of the plaintiff is under appeal or is expected to be appealed or (B) any other

information which the manufacturer chooses to provide. A manufacturer reporting to the Commission under subsection (a) of this section need not admit or may specifically deny that the information it submits reasonably supports the conclusion that its consumer product caused a death or grievous bodily injury.

(3) No statement of the amount paid by the manufacturer in a final settlement shall bee required as part of the report furnished under subsection (a) of this section, nor shall such a statement of settlement amount be required under any other section of this chapter.

(d) Report not deemed an admission of liability

The reporting of a civil action described in subsection (a) of this section by a manufacturer shall not constitute an admission of—

(1) an unreasonable risk of injury,

(2) a defect in the consumer product which was the subject of this action,

(3) a substantial product hazard,

(4) an imminent hazard, or

(5) any other admission of liability under any statute or under any common law.

(e) Definitions

For purposes of this section:

(1) A grievous bodily injury includes any of the following categories of injury: mutilation, amputation, dismemberment, disfigurement, loss of important bodily functions, debilitating internal disorder, severe burn, severe electric shock, and injuries likely to require extended hospitalization.

(2) For purposes of this section, a particular model of a consumer product is one that is distinctive in functional design, construction, warnings or instructions related to safety, function, user population, or other characteristics which could affect the product's safety related performance.

Pub.L. 92–573, § 37, as added Pub.L. 101–608, § 112(b), Nov. 16, 1990, 104 Stat. 3115.

MAGNUSON–MOSS WARRANTY ACT*

Enacted as Title I of "Magnuson–Moss Warranty— Federal Trade Commission Improvement Act"

* Act of January 4, 1975, Public Law 93–637, 88 Stat. 2183–93; 15 U.S.C.A. §§ 2301– 12.

Code of Federal Regulations

Rules, Regulations, Statements and Interpretations under the Magnuson–Moss Warranty Act, see 16 CFR 701.1 et seq.

§ 2301. Definitions

For the purposes of this chapter:

(1) The term "consumer product" means any tangible personal property which is distributed in commerce and which is normally used for personal, family, or household purposes (including any such property intended to be attached to or installed in any real property without regard to whether it is so attached or installed).

(2) The term "Commission" means the Federal Trade Commission.

(3) The term "consumer" means a buyer (other than for purposes of resale) of any consumer product, any person to whom such product is transferred during the duration of an implied or written warranty (or service contract) applicable to the product, and any other person who is entitled by the terms of such warranty (or service contract) or under applicable State law to enforce against the warrantor (or service contractor) the obligations of the (warranty or service contract).

(4) The term "supplier" means any person engaged in the business of making a consumer product directly or indirectly available to consumers.

(5) The term "warrantor" means any supplier or other person who gives or offers to give a written warranty or who is or may be obligated under an implied warranty.

(6) The term "written warranty" means—

(A) any written affirmation of fact or written promise made in connection with the sale of a consumer product by a supplier to a buyer which relates to the nature of the material or workmanship and affirms or promises that such material or workmanship is defect free or will meet a specified level of performance over a specified period of time, or

(B) any undertaking in writing in connection with the sale by a supplier of a consumer product to refund, repair, replace, or take other remedial action with respect to such product in the event that such product fails to meet the specifications set forth in the undertaking.

which written affirmation, promise, or undertaking becomes part of the basis of the bargain between a supplier and a buyer for purposes other than resale of such product.

(7) The term "implied warranty" means an implied warranty arising under State law (as modified by sections 2308 and 2304(a) of this title) in connection with the sale by a supplier of a consumer product.

(8) The term "service contract" means a contract in writing to perform, over a fixed period of time or for a specified duration, services relating to the maintenance or repair (or both) of a consumer product.

(9) The term "reasonable and necessary maintenance" consists of those operations (A) which the consumer reasonably can be expected to perform or have performed and (B) which are necessary to keep any consumer product performing its intended function and operating at a reasonable level of performance.

(10) The term "remedy" means whichever of the following actions the warrantor elects:

(A) repair,

(B) replacement, or

(C) refund;

except that the warrantor may not elect refund unless (i) the warrantor is unable to provide replacement and repair is not commercially practicable or cannot be timely made, or (ii) the consumer is willing to accept such refund.

(11) The term "replacement" means furnishing a new consumer product which is identical or reasonably equivalent to the warranted consumer product.

(12) The term "refund" means refunding the actual purchase price (less reasonable depreciation based on actual use where permitted by rules of the Commission).

(13) The term "distributed in commerce" means sold in commerce, introduced or delivered for introduction into commerce, or held for sale or distribution after introduction into commerce.

(14) The term "commerce" means trade, traffic, commerce, or transportation—

(A) between a place in a State and any place outside thereof, or

(B) which affects trade, traffic, commerce, or transportation described in subparagraph (A).

(15) The term "State" means a State, the District of Columbia, the Commonwealth of Puerto Rico, the Virgin Islands, Guam, the Canal Zone, or American Samoa. The term "State law" includes a law of the United States applicable only to the District of Columbia or only to a territory or possession of the United States; and the term "Federal law" excludes any State law.

Pub.L. 93–637, Title I, § 101, Jan. 4, 1975, 88 Stat. 2183.

§ 2302. Rules governing contents of warranties

(a) Full and conspicuous disclosure of terms and conditions; additional requirements for contents

(a) In order to improve the adequacy of information available to consumers, prevent deception, and improve competition in the marketing of consumer products any warrantor warranting a consumer product to a consumer by means of a written warranty shall, to the extent required by rules of the Commission, fully and conspicuously disclose in simple and readily understood language the terms and conditions of such warranty. Such rules may require inclusion in the written warranty of any of the following items among others:

(1) The clear identification of the names and addresses of the warrantors.

(2) The identity of the party or parties to whom the warranty is extended.

(3) The products or parts covered.

(4) A statement of what the warrantor will do in the event of a defect, malfunction, or failure to conform with such written warranty—at whose expense—and for what period of time.

(5) A statement of what the consumer must do and expenses he must bear.

(6) Exceptions and exclusions from the terms of the warranty.

(7) The step-by-step procedure which the consumer should take in order to obtain performance of any obligation under the warranty, including the identification of any person or class of persons authorized to perform the obligation set forth in the warranty.

(8) Information respecting the availability of any informal dispute settlement procedure offered by the warrantor and a recital, where the warranty so provides, that the purchaser may be required to resort to such procedure before pursuing any legal remedies in the courts.

(9) A brief, general description of the legal remedies available to the consumer.

(10) The time at which the warrantor will perform any obligations under the warranty.

(11) The period of time within which, after notice of a defect, malfunction, or failure to conform with the warranty, the warrantor will perform any obligations under the warranty.

(12) The characteristics or properties of the products, or parts thereof, that are not covered by the warranty.

(13) The elements of the warranty in words or phrases which would not mislead a reasonable, average consumer as to the nature or scope of the warranty.

(b) Availability of terms to consumer; manner and form for presentation and display of information; duration; extension of period for written warranty or service contract

(b)(1)(A) The Commission shall prescribe rules requiring that the terms of any written warranty on a consumer product be made available to the consumer (or prospective consumer) prior to the sale of the product to him.

(B) The Commission may prescribe rules for determining the manner and form in which information with respect to any written warranty of a consumer product shall be clearly and conspicuously presented or displayed so as not to mislead the reasonable, average consumer, when such information is contained in advertising, labeling, point-of-sale material, or other representations in writing.

(2) Nothing in this chapter (other than paragraph (3) of this subsection) shall be deemed to authorize the Commission to prescribe the duration of written warranties given or to require that a consumer product or any of its components be warranted.

(3) The Commission may prescribe rules for extending the period of time a written warranty or service contract is in effect to correspond with any period of time in excess of a reasonable period (not less than 10 days) during which the consumer is deprived of the use of such consumer product by reason of failure of the product to conform with the written warranty or by reason of the failure of the warrantor (or service contractor) to carry out such warranty (or service contract) within the period specified in the warranty (or service contract).

(c) Prohibition on conditions for written or implied warranty; waiver by Commission

(c) No warrantor of a consumer product may condition his written or implied warranty of such product on the consumer's using, in connection with such product, any article or service (other than article or service provided without charge under the terms of the warranty) which is identified by brand, trade, or corporate name; except that the prohibition of this subsection may be waived by the Commission if—

(1) the warrantor satisfies the Commission that the warranted product will function properly only if the article or service so identified is used in connection with the warranted product, and

(2) the Commission finds that such a waiver is in the public interest.

The Commission shall identify in the Federal Register, and permit public comment on, all applications for waiver of the prohibition of this subsection, and shall publish in the Federal Register its disposition of any such application, including the reasons therefor.

(d) Incorporation by reference of detailed substantive warranty provisions

(d) The Commission may by rule devise detailed substantive warranty provisions which warrantors may incorporate by reference in their warranties.

(e) Applicability to consumer products costing more than $5.00

(e) The provisions of this section apply only to warranties which pertain to consumer products actually costing the consumer more than $5.

Pub.L. 93–637, Title I, § 102, Jan. 4, 1975, 88 Stat. 2185.

§ 2303. Designation of written warranties

(a) Full (statement of duration) or limited warranty

(a) Any warrantor warranting a consumer product by means of a written warranty shall clearly and conspicuously designate such warranty in the following manner, unless exempted from doing so by the Commission pursuant to subsection (c) of this section:

(1) If the written warranty meets the Federal minimum standards for warranty set forth in section 2304 of this title, then it shall be conspicuously designated a "full (statement of duration) warranty".

(2) If the written warranty does not meet the Federal minimum standards for warranty set forth in section 2304 of this title, then it shall be conspicuously designated a "limited warranty".

(b) Applicability of requirements, standards, etc., to representations or statements of customer satisfaction

(b) This section and sections 2302 and 2304 of this title shall not apply to statements or representations which are similar to expressions of general policy concerning customer satisfaction and which are not subject to any specific limitations.

(c) Exemptions by Commission

(c) In addition to exercising the authority pertaining to disclosure granted in section 2302 of this title, the Commission may by rule determine when a written warranty does not have to be designated either "full (statement of duration)" or "limited" in accordance with this section.

(d) Applicability to consumer products costing more than $10.00 and not designated as full warranties

(d) The provisions of subsections (a) and (c) of this section apply only to warranties which pertain to consumer products actually costing the consumer more than $10 and which are not designated "full (statement of duration) warranties".

Pub.L. 93–637, Title I, § 103, Jan. 4, 1975, 88 Stat. 2187.

§ 2304.　Federal minimum standards for warranties

(a) Remedies under written warranty; duration of implied warranty; exclusion or limitation on consequential damages for breach of written or implied warranty; election of refund or replacement

(a) In order for a warrantor warranting a consumer product by means of a written warranty to meet the Federal minimum standards for warranty—

(1) such warrantor must as a minimum remedy such consumer product within a reasonable time and without charge, in the case of a defect, malfunction, or failure to conform with such written warranty;

(2) notwithstanding section 2308(b) of this title, such warrantor may not impose any limitation on the duration of any implied warranty on the product;

(3) such warrantor may not exclude or limit consequential damages for breach of any written or implied warranty on such product, unless such exclusion or limitation conspicuously appears on the face of the warranty; and

(4) if the product (or a component part thereof) contains a defect or malfunction after a reasonable number of attempts by the warrantor to remedy defects or malfunctions in such product, such warrantor must permit the consumer to elect either a refund for, or replacement without charge of, such product or part (as the case may be). The Commission may by rule specify for purposes of this paragraph, what constitutes a reasonable number of attempts to remedy particular kinds of defects or malfunctions under different circumstances. If the

warrantor replaces a component part of a consumer product, such replacement shall include installing the part in the product without charge.

(b) Duties and conditions imposed on consumer by warrantor

(b)(1) In fulfilling the duties under subsection (a) of this section respecting a written warranty, the warrantor shall not impose any duty other than notification upon any consumer as a condition of securing remedy of any consumer product which malfunctions, is defective, or does not conform to the written warranty, unless the warrantor has demonstrated in a rulemaking proceeding, or can demonstrate in an administrative or judicial enforcement proceeding (including private enforcement), or in an informal dispute settlement proceeding, that such a duty is reasonable.

(2) Notwithstanding paragraph (1), a warrantor may require, as a condition to replacement of, or refund for, any consumer product under subsection (a) of this section, that such consumer product shall be made available to the warrantor free and clear of liens and other encumbrances, except as otherwise provided by rule or order of the Commission in cases in which such a requirement would not be practicable.

(3) The Commission may, by rule define in detail the duties set forth in subsection (a) of this section and the applicability of such duties to warrantors of different categories of consumer products with "full (statement of duration)" warranties.

(4) The duties under subsection (a) of this section extend from the warrantor to each person who is a consumer with respect to the consumer product.

(c) Waiver of standards

(c) The performance of the duties under subsection (a) of this section shall not be required of the warrantor if he can show that the defect, malfunction, or failure of any warranted consumer product to conform with a written warranty, was caused by damage (not resulting from defect or malfunction) while in the possession of the consumer, or unreasonable use (including failure to provide reasonable and necessary maintenance).

(d) Remedy without charge

(d) For purposes of this section and of section 2302(c) of this title, the term "without charge" means that the warrantor may not assess the consumer for any costs the warrantor or his representatives incur in connection with the required remedy of a warranted consumer product. An obligation under subsection (a)(1)(A) of this section to remedy without charge does not necessarily require the warrantor to compensate the consumer for incidental expenses; however, if any incidental expenses are incurred because the remedy is not made within a reasonable time or because the warrantor imposed an unreasonable duty upon the consumer as a condition of securing remedy, then the consumer shall be entitled to recover reasonable incidental expenses which are so incurred in any action against the warrantor.

(e) Incorporation of standards to products designated with full warranty for purposes of judicial actions

(e) If a supplier designates a warranty applicable to a consumer product as a "full (statement of duration)" warranty, then the warranty on such product shall, for purposes of any action under section 2310(d) of this title or under any State law, be deemed to incorporate at least the minimum requirements of this section and rules prescribed under this section.

Pub.L. 93–637, Title I, § 104, Jan. 4, 1975, 88 Stat. 2187.

§ 2305. Full and limited warranting of a consumer product

Nothing in this chapter shall prohibit the selling of a consumer product which has both full and limited warranties if such warranties are clearly and conspicuously differentiated.

Pub.L. 93–637, Title I, § 105, Jan. 4, 1975, 88 Stat. 2188.

§ 2306. Service contracts; rules for full, clear and conspicuous disclosure of terms and conditions; addition to or in lieu of written warranty

(a) The Commission may prescribe by rule the manner and form in which the terms and conditions of service contracts shall be fully, clearly, and conspicuously disclosed.

(b) Nothing in this chapter shall be construed to prevent a supplier or warrantor from entering into a service contract with the consumer in addition to or in lieu of a written warranty if such contract fully, clearly, and conspicuously discloses its terms and conditions in simple and readily understood language.

Pub.L. 93–637, Title I, § 106, Jan. 4, 1975, 88 Stat. 2188.

§ 2307. Designation of representatives by warrantor to perform duties under written or implied warranty

Nothing in this chapter shall be construed to prevent any warrantor from designating representatives to perform duties under the written or implied warranty: *Provided,* That such warrantor shall make reasonable arrangements for compensation of such designated representatives, but no such designation shall relieve the warrantor of his direct responsibilities to the consumer or make the representative a cowarrantor.

Pub.L. 93–637, Title I, § 107, Jan. 4, 1975, 88 Stat. 2189.

§ 2308. Implied warranties

(a) Restrictions on disclaimers or modifications

(a) No supplier may disclaim or modify (except as provided in subsection (b) of this section) any implied warranty to a consumer with respect to such consumer product if (1) such supplier makes any written warranty to the consumer with respect to such consumer product, or (2) at the time of sale, or within 90 days thereafter, such supplier enters into a service contract with the consumer which applies to such consumer product.

(b) Limitation on duration

(b) For purposes of this chapter (other than section 2304(a)(2) of this title), implied warranties may be limited in duration to the duration of a written warranty of reasonable duration, if such limitation is conscionable and is set forth in clear and unmistakable language and prominently displayed on the face of the warranty.

(c) Effectiveness of disclaimers, modifications, or limitations

(c) A disclaimer, modification, or limitation made in violation of this section shall be ineffective for purposes of this chapter and State law. Pub.L. 93–637, Title I, § 108, Jan. 4, 1975, 88 Stat. 2189.

§ 2309. Procedures applicable to promulgation of rules by Commission; rulemaking proceeding for warranty and warranty practices involved in sale of used motor vehicles

(a) Any rule prescribed under this chapter shall be prescribed in accordance with section 553 of Title 5; except that the Commission shall give interested persons an opportunity for oral presentations of data, views, and arguments, in addition to written submissions. A transcript shall be kept of any oral presentation. Any such rule shall be subject to judicial review under section 57a(e) of this title in the same manner as rules prescribed under section 57a(a)(1)(B) of this title, except that section 57a(e)(3)(B) of this title shall not apply.

(b) The Commission shall initiate within one year after January 4, 1975, a rulemaking proceeding dealing with warranties and warranty practices in connection with the sale of used motor vehicles; and, to the extent necessary to supplement the protections offered the consumer by this chapter, shall prescribe rules dealing with such warranties and practices. In prescribing rules under this subsection, the Commission may exercise any authority it may have under this chapter, or other law, and in addition it may require disclosure that a used motor vehicle is sold without any warranty and specify the form and content of such disclosure.

Pub.L. 93–637, Title I, § 109, Jan. 4, 1975, 88 Stat. 2189.

§ 2310.   Remedies in consumer disputes

(a) Informal dispute settlement procedures; establishment; rules setting forth minimum requirements; effect of compliance by warrantor; review of informal procedures or implementation by Commission; application to existing informal procedures

(a)(1) Congress hereby declares it to be its policy to encourage warrantors to establish procedures whereby consumer disputes are fairly and expeditiously settled through informal dispute settlement mechanisms.

(2) The Commission shall prescribe rules setting forth minimum requirements for any informal dispute settlement procedure which is incorporated into the terms of a written warranty to which any provision of this chapter applies. Such rules shall provide for participation in such procedure by independent or governmental entities.

(3) One or more warrantors may establish an informal dispute settlement procedure which meets the requirements of the Commission's rules under paragraph (2). If—

(A) a warrantor establishes such a procedure,

(B) such procedure, and its implementation, meets the requirements of such rules, and

(C) he incorporates in a written warranty a requirement that the consumer resort to such procedure before pursuing any legal remedy under this section respecting such warranty,

then (i) the consumer may not commence a civil action (other than a class action) under subsection (d) of this section unless he initially resorts to such procedure; and (ii) a class of consumers may not proceed in a class action under subsection (d) of this section except to the extent the court determines necessary to establish the representative capacity of the named plaintiffs, unless the named plaintiffs (upon notifying the defendant that they are named plaintiffs in a class action with respect to a warranty obligation) initially resort to such procedure. In the case of such a class action which is brought in a district court of the United States, the representative capacity of the named plaintiffs shall be established in the application of rule 23 of the Federal Rules of Civil Procedure. In any civil action arising out of a warranty obligation and relating to a matter considered in such a procedure, any decision in such procedure shall be admissible in evidence.

(4) The Commission on its own initiative may, or upon written complaint filed by any interested person shall, review the bona fide operation of any dispute settlement procedure resort to which is stated in a written warranty to be a prerequisite to pursuing a legal remedy under this section. If the Commission finds that such procedure or its implementation fails to

comply with the requirements of the rules under paragraph (2), the Commission may take appropriate remedial action under any authority it may have under this chapter or any other provision of law.

(5) Until rules under paragraph (2) take effect, this subsection shall not affect the validity of any informal dispute settlement procedure respecting consumer warranties, but in any action under subsection (d) of this section, the court may invalidate any such procedure if it finds that such procedure is unfair.

(b) Prohibited acts

(b) It shall be a violation of section 45(a)(1) of this title for any person to fail to comply with any requirement imposed on such person by this chapter (or a rule thereunder) or to violate any prohibition contained in this chapter (or a rule thereunder).

(c) Injunction proceedings by Attorney General or Commission for deceptive warranty, noncompliance with requirements, or violating prohibitions; procedures; definitions

(c)(1) The district courts of the United States shall have jurisdiction of any action brought by the Attorney General (in his capacity as such), or by the Commission by any of its attorneys designated by it for such purpose, to restrain (A) any warrantor from making a deceptive warranty with respect to a consumer product, or (B) any person from failing to comply with any requirement imposed on such person by or pursuant to this chapter or from violating any prohibition contained in this chapter. Upon proper showing that, weighing the equities and considering the Commission's or Attorney General's likelihood of ultimate success, such action would be in the public interest and after notice to the defendant, a temporary restraining order or preliminary injunction may be granted without bond. In the case of an action brought by the Commission, if a complaint under section 45 of Title 15 is not filed within such period (not exceeding 10 days) as may be specified by the court after the issuance of the temporary restraining order or preliminary injunction, the order or injunction shall be dissolved by the court and be of no further force and effect. Any suit shall be brought in the district in which such person resides or transacts business. Whenever it appears to the court that the ends of justice require that other persons should be parties in the action, the court may cause them to be summoned whether or not they reside in the district in which the court is held, and to that end process may be served in any district.

(2) For the purposes of this subsection, the term "deceptive warranty" means (A) a written warranty which (i) contains an affirmation, promise, deception, or representation which is either false or fraudulent, or which, in light of all the circumstances, would mislead a reasonable individual exercising due care; or (ii) fails to contain information which is necessary in

light of all of the circumstances, to make the warranty not misleading to a reasonable individual exercising due care; or (B) a written warranty created by the use of such terms as "guaranty" or "warranty", if the terms and conditions of such warranty so limit its scope and application as to deceive a reasonable individual.

(d) Civil action by consumer for damages, etc.; jurisdiction; recovery of costs and expenses; cognizable claims

(d)(1) Subject to subsections (a)(3) and (e) of this section, a consumer who is damaged by the failure of a supplier, warrantor, or service contractor to comply with any obligation under this chapter, or under a written warranty, implied warranty, or service contract, may bring suit for damages and other legal and equitable relief—

(A) in any court of competent jurisdiction in any State or the District of Columbia; or

(B) in an appropriate district court of the United States, subject to paragraph (3) of this subsection.

(2) If a consumer finally prevails in any action brought under paragraph (1) of this subsection, he may be allowed by the court to recover as part of the judgment a sum equal to the aggregate amount of cost and expenses (including attorneys' fees based on actual time expended) determined by the court to have been reasonably incurred by the plaintiff for or in connection with the commencement and prosecution of such action, unless the court in its discretion shall determine that such an award of attorneys' fees would be inappropriate.

(3) No claim shall be cognizable in a suit brought under paragraph (1)(B) of this subsection—

(A) if the amount in controversy of any individual claim is less than the sum or value of $25;

(B) if the amount in controversy is less than the sum or value of $50,000 (exclusive of interests and costs) computed on the basis of all claims to be determined in this suit; or

(C) if the action is brought as a class action, and the number of named plaintiffs is less than one hundred.

(e) Class actions; conditions; procedures applicable

(e) No action (other than a class action or an action respecting a warranty to which subsection (a)(3) of this section applies) may be brought under subsection (d) of this section for failure to comply with any obligation under any written or implied warranty or service contract, and a class of consumers may not proceed in a class action under such subsection with respect to such a failure except to the extent the court determines necessary to establish the representative capacity of the named plaintiffs, unless the person obligated under the warranty or service contract is afforded a reasonable opportunity to cure such failure to comply. In the case of such a class action (other than a class action respecting a warranty to which subsection (a)(3) of this section applies) brought under subsection (d) of this section for breach of any written or implied warranty or service contract, such reasonable opportunity will be afforded by the named plaintiffs and they shall at that time notify the defendant that they are acting on behalf of the class. In the case of such a class action which is brought in a district court of the United States, the representative capacity of the named plaintiffs shall be established in the application of rule 23 of the Federal Rules of Civil Procedure.

(f) Warrantors subject to enforcement of remedies

(f) For purposes of this section, only the warrantor actually making a written affirmation of fact, promise, or undertaking shall be deemed to have created a written warranty, and any rights arising thereunder may be enforced under this section only against such warrantor and no other person.

Pub.L. 93–637, Title I, § 110, Jan. 4, 1975, 88 Stat. 2189.

§ 2311. Applicability of provisions to other Federal or State laws and requirements

(a)(1) Nothing contained in this chapter shall be construed to repeal, invalidate, or supersede the Federal Trade Commission Act or any statute defined therein as an Antitrust Act.

(2) Nothing in this chapter shall be construed to repeal, invalidate, or supersede the Federal Seed Act and nothing in this chapter shall apply to seed for planting.

(b)(1) Nothing in this chapter shall invalidate or restrict any right or remedy of any consumer under State law or any other Federal law.

(2) Nothing in this chapter (other than sections 2304(a)(2) and (4) and 2308 of this title) shall (A) affect the liability of, or impose liability on, any person for personal injury, or (B) supersede any provision of State law regarding consequential damages for injury to the person or other injury.

(c)(1) Except as provided in subsection (b) of this section and in paragraph (2) of this subsection, a State requirement—

    (A) which relates to labeling or disclosure with respect to written warranties or performance thereunder;

    (B) which is within the scope of an applicable requirement of sections 2302, 2303, and 2304 of this title (and rules implementing such sections), and

    (C) which is not identical to a requirement of section 2302, 2303, or 2304 of this title (or a rule thereunder), shall not be applicable to written warranties complying with such sections (or rules thereunder).

(2) If, upon application of an appropriate State agency, the Commission determines (pursuant to rules issued in accordance with section 2309 of this title) that any requirement of such State covering any transaction to which this chapter applies (A) affords protection to consumers greater than the requirements of this chapter and (B) does not unduly burden interstate commerce, then such State requirement shall be applicable (notwithstanding the provisions of paragraph (1) of this subsection) to the extent specified in such determination for so long as the State administers and enforces effectively any such greater requirement.

(d) This chapter (other than section 2302(c) of this title) shall be inapplicable to any written warranty the making or content of which is otherwise governed by Federal law. If only a portion of a written warranty is so governed by Federal law, the remaining portion shall be subject to this chapter.

Pub.L. 93–637, Title I, § 111, Jan. 4, 1975, 88 Stat. 2192.

§ 2312.　Effective dates; time for promulgation of rules by Commission

(a) Except as provided in subsection (b) of this section, this chapter shall take effect 6 months after January 4, 1975, but shall not apply to consumer products manufactured prior to such date.

(b) Section 2302(a) of this title shall take effect 6 months after the final publication of rules respecting such section; except that the Commission, for good cause shown, may postpone the applicability of such sections until one year after such final publication in order to permit any designated classes of suppliers to bring their written warranties into compliance with rules promulgated pursuant to this chapter.

(c) The Commission shall promulgate rules for initial implementation of this chapter as soon as possible after January 4, 1975, but in no event later than one year after such date.

Pub.L. 93–637, Title I, § 112, Jan. 4, 1975, 88 Stat. 2192.

MODEL UNIFORM PRODUCT LIABILITY ACT*

* 44 Fed.Reg. 62,714 (1979).

Introduction

The Department of Commerce publishes herein its "Model Uniform Product Liability Act." It is offered for voluntary use by the states.

This Model Law will help to assure that persons injured by unreasonably unsafe products receive reasonable compensation for their injuries. It should also help to stabilize product liability insurance rates.

The Model Law, if enacted by the states, would introduce uniformity and stability into the law of product liability. This, in turn, would help stabilize product liability insurance rates. Uniformity and stability in this area are needed because product liability insurance rates are set on a countrywide basis. Thus, product liability law differs from medical malpractice, automobile, and other standard lines of liability.

The current system of having individual state courts develop product liability law on a case-by-case basis is not consistent with commercial necessity. Product sellers and insurers need uniformity in product liability law so they will know the rules by which they are to be judged. At the same time, product users are entitled to the assurance that their rights will be protected and will not be restricted by "reform" legislation formulated in a crisis atmosphere. Thus, the Model Law meets the needs of product users, sellers, and insurers.

Background of the Act

The Department of Commerce chaired an 18-month interagency study on the topic of product liability and published its final report[1] on November 1, 1977.

The genesis of the "Uniform Product Liability Act" can be traced directly to the Task Force study. The Task Force found that uncertainties in the tort-litigation system were a principal cause of the product liability problem. The "Task Force Report" noted that a few courts had come

> very close to holding that the tort-litigation system should provide a recovery for persons who merely proved that they were injured by a product [and that] while these cases appear to be relatively few in number, insurers have regarded them as quite important in their pricing practices.[2]

The "Task Force Report" called for improvement in insurer rate-making practices but indicated that even if this were done, "the specter of these cases could still serve as an arguable justification for increasing premiums."[3] Decisions supporting this view continue to appear.

On the basis of the "Task Force Report," representatives from the Office of Management and Budget and the Domestic Policy Staff of the White House asked Commerce to

---

1. The "Final Report (cited as the "Task Force Report") of the Federal Interagency Task Force on Product Liability" (cited as the "Task Force").

2. "Task Force Report" at p. I–27.

3. *Id.*

prepare an options paper regarding what action, if any, the Federal Government should take to address the product liability problem. That paper was published in the **Federal Register** on April 6, 1978. 43 FR 14612 (1978).[4]

One of Commerce's recommendations was that a uniform product liability law be prepared. The overwhelming majority of public comment received in response to the "Options Paper" supported this recommendation.[5]

On July 20, 1978, the Administration announced its program to address the product liability problem. Included in that program as the principal long-range measure was the drafting of a model uniform product liability law.

On January 12, 1979, Commerce's "Draft Uniform Product Liability Law" was published in the **Federal Register** for public comment.[6] The written commentary received by Commerce regarding the Draft Law totals approximately 1500 pages, representing 240 separate communications.[7] The Department also made a special effort to bring the Draft Law to the attention of consumers. Working with its Director of Consumer Affairs and the

Office of the Special Assistant to the President for Consumer Affairs, Commerce conducted consumer forums in Washington, D.C., Detroit, Los Angeles, and Atlanta.

In addition to meeting with consumer groups, the drafters of this Act met with representatives of product seller and insurer groups which expressed an interest in the proposal. The Draft Law was also reviewed at hearings before the Subcommittee on Oversight and Minority Enterprises of the House Committee on Small Business, and before the Subcommittee on Consumer Protection and Finance of the House Committee on Interstate and Foreign Commerce.

The final version of the "Uniform Product Liability Act" has benefited substantially from its review by, and input from, the various groups affected by the product liability problem.

Other Sources of the Act

Apart from the public comment, this Act is based on the work products of the Interagency Task Force on Product Liability, including its "Final Report," its "Legal Study," its "Industry Study," and its "Insurance Study."[8] Also, a thorough

---

4. Public comment on the "Options Paper" was later published in the **Federal Register** on September 11, 1978. 43 FR 40438 (1978).

5. 43 FR 40443.

6. 44 FR 2996.

7. On file, Law Library, U.S. Department of Commerce.

8. The Task Force's reports are available from the National Technical Information Service, Springfield, Virginia 22161 (Attention: Sales Desk). Reference should be made

to the appropriate accession number, and a check made payable to NTIS in the proper amount should be enclosed:

Final Report—PB 273–220, $20.00 (1 vol.)(1977).

Selected Papers—PB 278–625, $17.50 (1 vol.)(1978).

Legal Study—PB 263–601, $31.25 (7 vol.)(1977)(The Research Group, Inc.).

Legal Study:

Executive Summary—PB 265–450, $6.00 (first of 7 vol.)(1977).

review was conducted of all major case law and law review literature that had been published since the time of the Task Force's "Legal Study."

As will be apparent from the Act's section-by-section analysis, attention was given to:

(1) The findings of the extensive "Product Liability Closed Claims Survey" conducted by the Insurance Services Office in 1976–77;

(2) All product liability legislation enacted at the state level, plus major proposals introduced in state legislatures in the past two years;

(3) Congressional hearings on product liability and the Report of the House Subcommittee on Capital, Investment and Business Opportunities of the Committee on Small Business. *See* H.R.Report No. 95–997, 95th Cong., 2d Sess. (1978)(Honorable John J. LaFalce, Chairman); and

(4) Privately drafted model product liability legislation.

A bibliography of some of the major resources considered by the Department is set forth in Appendix A.

Criteria for the Act

The criteria[9] utilized in evaluating the provisions of the Model Law were:

Industry Study—PB 265–542, $21.25 (2 vol.)(1977)(Gordon Associates, Inc.).

Insurance Study—PB 263–600, $9.00 (1 vol.)(1977)(McKinsey, Inc.).

9. A more extensive discussion of these criteria appears in the "Task Force Report"

(1) *To ensure that persons injured by unreasonably unsafe products receive reasonable compensation for their injuries.*

Many proposed alternatives in product liability law are primarily justified by the fact that they contain "cost-saving devices" for product liability insurers or their insureds. However, these projected "cost savings" must be balanced against the responsibility of a product seller to provide reasonable compensation to persons harmed by unreasonably unsafe products. The cost of an accident should be shifted from a claimant to a product seller when there is a logical and articulated rationale for deeming it (as compared with the injured individual or society at large) "responsible" for the claimant's injuries.

(2) *To ensure the availability of affordable product liability insurance with adequate coverage to product sellers that engage in reasonably safe manufacturing practices.*

Product liability law should attempt to create a situation in which affordable product liability insurance is available to manufacturers that follow reasonably safe manufacturing practices. The law should not, however, be modified in order to provide such insurance to manufacturers who are unwilling or unable to follow reasonably safe manufacturing practices.

at VII–29. The criteria are also set forth in Subsection 103(C) of the Act and are discussed in the corresponding section-by-section analysis.

(3) *To place the incentive for loss prevention on the party or parties who are best able to accomplish that goal.*

Part of the product liability problem has been caused by unsafe manufacturing practices. Obviously, it is in the interest of all groups affected by the product liability problem to reduce the number of accidents caused by products. The Task Force study showed that product liability law can help bring about this goal. The threat of tort liability and product liability judgments has prompted manufacturers to make a greater effort to produce safe products. Nevertheless, existing state product liability law does not always place the incentive for loss prevention on the party or parties who can best achieve that goal.

The decision of where to place the incentive for loss prevention was not an easy one, and at least two factors helped determine the drafters' decision. One was based on pure economics—which party can prevent the loss at lowest cost? Economic analysis of preliminary drafts of this Act were helpful in this consideration.

A second factor focused on the question of who is in the best practical position to prevent a product-related harm. This consideration may be at counterpoint with pure economic analysis. Sometimes a product seller may be in a better practical position to implement a loss prevention technique although a product user could theoretically do so at a lesser cost.

(4) *To expedite the reparations process from the time of injury to the time the claim is paid.*

Delays in the reparations process do not serve any social interest. Seriously injured claimants can ill afford to endure long delays between the time of their injury and the time they are paid. Therefore, the Act has placed emphasis on arbitration and other means that will help expedite the reparations process.

(5) *To minimize the sum of accident costs, prevention costs, and transaction costs.*

The goal of minimizing accident, prevention, and transaction costs, while worthwhile, is not easy to fulfill within the tort-litigation system. For example, one can minimize "transaction costs" by abolishing trial by jury. However, this would be at the expense of other societal values which are particularly important in product liability cases, such as the need for the individualized judgment of cases and the experience of ordinary persons in making those judgments. Nevertheless, this consideration was significant enough to weigh in formulating the Act.

(6) *To use language that is comparatively clear and concise.*

Many product liability proposals that appear sound when stated in a broad and general manner break down when one focuses on the practicality of their implementation. In drafting the Act, practicality, together with conciseness and clarity of language, were important goals. The Act was drafted as a guideline for courts, not as a detailed legal contract between product seller and user.

Other considerations were utilized in the process of formulating each of the provisions. They are highlighted in the section-by-section analysis that accompanies the Act. Again, permeating the discussion of each provision is the concern that it is fair to all groups having an interest in the product liability problem.

It is important to understand the basic philosophy that underlies the Act. Product liability law is a branch of the law of torts. Its function is to shift the cost of an accident from a claimant to a defendant when the latter is deemed "responsible" for the claimant's injuries. This "responsibility" should be defined in terms that everyone can understand. Product liability law should indicate why a particular individual product seller was sufficiently blameworthy that it should bear the cost of that injury.

Tort law is not a compensation system similar to Social Security or Worker Compensation. A product seller should not, through the medium of tort law, be asked to pay merely because its product caused an injury. If a social judgment is made that product sellers are to bear the costs of all injuries caused by their products, it would be far more efficient to make purchasers of products third-party beneficiaries of product sellers' insurance policies as is the case with other compensation systems. Such systems also utilize cost-saving devices such as limiting recovery for lost earnings, eliminating recovery for pain and suffering, and abolishing the collateral source rule. In contrast, product liability law, with its full tort law recovery, reflects the social judgment that lia-bility should be imposed only when it is fair to hold the individual product seller responsible for an injury.

This proposal is offered in the hope that it will stabilize product liability law and benefit product sellers and users alike.

C.L. Haslam,

General Counsel, Department of Commerce.

Victor E. Schwartz,

Chairman, Task Force on Product Liability and Accident Compensation.

Uniform Product Liability Act

Code

Preamble

This Act sets forth uniform standards for state product liability tort law. It does not cover all issues that may be litigated in product liability cases; rather, it focuses on those where the need for uniform rules is the greatest. The principal purposes of the Act are to provide a fair balance of the interests of both product users and sellers and to eliminate existing confusion and uncertainty about their respective legal rights and obligations. The fulfillment of these goals should help, first, to assure that persons injured by unreasonably unsafe products will be adequately compensated for their injuries and, second, to make product liability insurance more widely available and affordable, with greater stability in rates and premiums.

* * *

Analysis

Preamble

The importance this Act places on increasing the degree of certainty in the product liability litigation process is tempered by the recognition that, even with nationwide adoption of a uniform code, its application may vary from state to state on some issues. One of the Act's goals, the development of a fair balance of interests, has been achieved by applying the general criteria set forth in Subsection 103(C) of the Act and by revising the first draft of the Act (*see* 44 FR 2996 (1979)) in light of the public comment it generated. A second goal is to promote a greater degree of certainty than exists under the present system. This can be achieved if the Act is adopted by the states in which a substantial majority of product liability claims are brought.

* * *

Code

§ 100. Short Title

This Act shall be known and may be cited as the "Uniform Product Liability Act."

Analysis

§ 100. Short Title

This is the customary "short title" provision. It may be placed wherever state legislative practice dictates. If a state legislature introduces parts of the "Uniform Product Liability Act" as separate measures, the short title should be adjusted accordingly.

* * *

Code

§ 101. Findings

(A) Sharply rising product liability insurance premiums have created serious problems in commerce resulting in:

(1) Increased prices of consumer and industrial products;

(2) Disincentives for innovation and for the development of high-risk but potentially beneficial products;

(3) An increase in the number of product sellers attempting to do business without product liability insurance coverage, thus jeopardizing both their continued existence and the availability of compensation to injured persons; and

(4) Legislative initiatives enacted in a crisis atmosphere that may, as a result, unreasonably curtail the rights of product liability claimants.

(B) One cause of these problems is that product liability law is fraught with uncertainty and sometimes reflects an imbalanced consideration of the interests it affects. The rules vary from jurisdiction to jurisdiction and are subject to rapid and substantial change. These facts militate against predictability of litigation outcome.

(C) Insurers have cited this uncertainty and imbalance as justifications for setting rates and premiums that, in fact, may not reflect actual product risk or liability losses.

(D) Product liability insurance rates are set on the basis of countrywide, rather than individual state, experience. Insurers utilize countrywide experience because a product manufactured in one state can readily cause injury in any one of the other states, the District of Columbia, or the Commonwealth of Puerto Rico. One ramification of this practice is that there is little an individual state can do to solve the problems caused by product liability.

(E) Uncertainty in product liability law and litigation outcome has added to litigation costs and may put an additional strain on the judicial system.

(F) Recently enacted state product liability legislation has widened existing disparities in the law.

* * *

Analysis

§ 101. Findings

Chapters VI and VII of the "Final Report of the Interagency Task Force on Product Liability" (hereinafter cited as "Task Force Report") provide support for most of the findings made here. Additional support comes from the Report of the Subcommittee on Capital, Investment, and Business Opportunities, "Product Liability Insurance," H.R.Rep. No. 95–997, 95th Cong., 2d Sess. (1978)(Honorable John J. LaFalce, Chairman)(hereinafter cited as "LaFalce Subcommittee Report"). Among other things, the "LaFalce Subcommittee Report" called for clarification and simplification of "present tort law relating to product liability by formulating Federal standards to be adopted by the States. . . ." *Id.* at 76.

Individual state studies on product liability conducted in Missouri (Report of the Senate Select Committee on Product Liability, 1977), Illinois (Judiciary I Subcommittee on Product Liability: Report and Recommendations—Part 1, undated), Georgia (Report of the Senate Products Liability Study Committee, 1978), Maine (Governor's Task Force, 1978), Michigan (Department of Commerce Task Force on Product Liability Insurance, 1978), and Wisconsin (Product Liability: An Overview, Wisconsin Legislative Council Staff, 1978) provide additional support for individual findings.

The Maine and Georgia reports emphasize that individual state tort reforms can do little to affect the product liability problem. This conclusion was reaffirmed in Governor Grasso's message vetoing a product liability tort bill passed by the Connecticut legislature in 1978, and Governor Brown's message vetoing a product liability tort bill passed by the California legislature in 1979. Both messages stressed that uncoordinated, individual state tort action will not stabilize product liability insurance rates.

More specific references to the findings of this Section appear in the following citations keyed to the various findings in each Subsection:

101(A)(1) "Task Force Report" at V–19, VI–27–28.

(2) "Task Force Report" at VI–28–32.

(3) "Task Force Report" at VI–2–26.

(4) "Options Paper on Product Liability and Accident Compensa-

tion Issues," 43 FR 14612–14 (1978); "Georgia Report", Appendix B; Johnson, "Products Liability 'Reform': A Hazard to Consumers," 56 "N.C.L.Rev." 677 (1978); Phillips, "A Synopsis of the Developing Law of Products Liability," 28 "Drake L.Rev." 317, 388 (1979); Comment, "State Legislative Restrictions on Product Liability Actions," 29 "Mercer L.Rev." 619 (1978). *See also* "Federal–State Product Liability Legislation for Client and Counsel," Federal–State Reports, Inc. (1977–79).

101(B) "Task Force Report" at I–26–28, VII–15–17; "LaFalce Subcommittee Report" at 72; "Michigan Department of Commerce Task Force on Product Liability Insurance Report" at 6 (1978).

(C) Task Force "Insurance Study" at IV–88 (citing uncertainty); "Task Force Report" at V–48–49 (relationship of premium to risk).

(D) "Task Force Report" at I–28; "Maine Report" at 23.

(E) "Task Force Report" at VII–214–16; *see also* Insurance Services Office, "Product Liability Closed Claims Survey" (hereinafter cited as "ISO Closed Claims Survey") at 118–30 (1977).

(F) *See* "Federal–State Product Liability Legislation for Client and Counsel," Federal–State Reports, Inc. (1977–79); "Product Liability Trends," at 97–98, 104–05, 157–58 (The Research Group, Inc., 1978); "Business Insurance," July 23, 1979 at 31; *see also* "Wisconsin Report" at 29–37 (describing 25 separate bills on product liability introduced in one legislative session).

* * *

Code

§ 102. Definitions

(A) *Product Seller.* "Product seller" means any person or entity that is engaged in the business of selling products, whether the sale is for resale, or for use or consumption. The term includes a manufacturer, wholesaler, distributor, or retailer of the relevant product. The term also includes a party who is in the business of leasing or bailing such products.

The term "product seller" does not include:

(1) A seller of real property, unless that person is engaged in the mass production and sale of standardized dwellings or is otherwise a product seller;

(2) A provider of professional services who utilizes or sells products within the legally authorized scope of its professional practice. A nonprofessional provider of services is not included unless the sale or use of a product is the principal part of the transaction, and the essence of the relationship between the seller and purchaser is not the furnishing of judgment, skill, or services;

(3) A commercial seller of used products who resells a product after use by a consumer or other product user, provided the used product is in essentially the same condition as when it was acquired for resale; and

(4) A finance lessor who is not otherwise a product seller. A "finance lessor" is one who acts in a financial capacity, who is not a man-

ufacturer, wholesaler, distributor, or retailer, and who leases a product without having a reasonable opportunity to inspect and discover defects in the product, under a lease arrangement in which the selection, possession, maintenance, and operation of the product are controlled by a person other than the lessor.

(B) *Manufacturer.* "Manufacturer" includes a product seller who designs, produces, makes, fabricates, constructs, or remanufactures the relevant product or component part of a product before its sale to a user or consumer. It includes a product seller or entity not otherwise a manufacturer that holds itself out as a manufacturer.

A product seller acting primarily as a wholesaler, distributor, or retailer of a product may be a "manufacturer" but only to the extent that it designs, produces, makes, fabricates, constructs, or remanufactures the product before its sale.

(C) *Product.* "Product" means any object possessing intrinsic value, capable of delivery either as an assembled whole or as a component part or parts, and produced for introduction into trade or commerce. Human tissue and organs, including human blood and its components, are excluded from this term.

The "relevant product" under this Act is that product, or its component part or parts, which gave rise to the product liability claim.

(D) *Product Liability Claim.* "Product liability claim" includes any claim or action brought for harm caused by the manufacture, production, making, construction, fabrication, design, formula, preparation, assembly, installation, testing, warnings, instructions, marketing, packaging, storage, or labeling of the relevant product. It includes, but is not limited to, any action previously based on: strict liability in tort; negligence; breach of express or implied warranty; breach of, or failure to, discharge a duty to warn or instruct, whether negligent or innocent; misrepresentation, concealment, or nondisclosure, whether negligent or innocent; or under any other substantive legal theory.

(E) *Claimant.* "Claimant" means a person or entity asserting a product liability claim, including a wrongful death action, and, if the claim is asserted through or on behalf of an estate, the term includes claimant's decedent. "Claimant" includes any person or entity that suffers harm.

(F) *Harm.* "Harm" includes: (1) damage to property; (2) personal physical injuries, illness and death; (3) mental anguish or emotional harm attendant to such personal physical injuries, illness or death; and (4) mental anguish or emotional harm caused by the claimant's being placed in direct personal physical danger and manifested by a substantial objective symptom. The term "harm" does not include direct or consequential economic loss.

(G) *Reasonably Anticipated Conduct.* "Reasonably anticipated conduct" means the conduct which would be expected of an ordinary reasonably prudent person who is likely to use the product in the same or similar circumstances.

(H) *Preponderance of the Evidence.* "A preponderance of the evidence" is that measure or degree of proof which, by the weight, credit, and value of the aggregate evidence on either side, establishes that it is more probable than not that a fact occurred or did not occur.

(I) *Clear and Convincing Evidence.* "Clear and convincing evidence" is that measure or degree of proof that will produce in the mind of the trier of fact a firm belief or conviction as to the allegations sought to be established. This level of proof is greater than mere "preponderance of the evidence," but less than proof beyond a reasonable doubt.

(J) *Reckless Disregard.* "Reckless disregard" means a conscious indifference to the safety of persons or entities that might be harmed by a product.

(K) *Express Warranty.* "Express warranty" means any positive statement, affirmation of fact, promise, description, sample, or model relating to the product.

* * *

Analysis

§ 102. Definitions

(A) *Product Seller.* "Product seller" includes any party in the regular commercial distribution chain. It does not include the occasional private seller. This is in accord with the "Restatement (Second) of Torts" Section 402A, Comment f (1965). The term also includes lessors (except finance lessors) and bailors of products, in accord with the majority of decisions that have addressed the issue. *See* Annot., 52 "A.L.R.3d" 121 (1973); "Francioni v. Gibsonia Truck Corp.," 472 Pa. 362, 372 A.2d 736 (1977)(finance lessor); Fraser, "Application of Strict Tort Liability to the Leasing Industry," 34 "Bus.Law." 605 (1979).

The Act excludes the seller of real property from its coverage, except for a builder-vendor engaged in the mass production and sale of standardized dwellings, including modular homes. *See* "Schipper v. Levitt & Sons," 44 N.J. 70, 207 A.2d 314 (1965); "Berman v. Watergate West, Inc.," 391 A.2d 1351 (D.C.App.1978)(extending "Schipper" to cooperative apartments); "Fuqua Homes, Inc. v. Evanston Bldg. & Loan Co.," 52 Ohio App.2d 399, 370 N.E.2d 780 (1977)(modular homes). *But see* "Wright v. Creative Corp.," 30 Colo.App. 575, 498 P.2d 1179 (1972)(rejecting "Schipper"). The potential liability of sellers of real property not engaged in such large-scale operations is left to each state's laws governing real property transactions. However, all sellers of building materials, furnishings, appliances, and other products made part of improvements to real property are not exempted from the coverage of the Act. *See* Maldonado, "Builder Beware: Strict Tort Liability for Mass Produced Housing, 7 Real Estate L.J." 283 (1979).

The Act also excludes from its coverage the provider of professional services when a product is utilized or sold as part of the rendition of such services. *Compare* "Barbee v. Rogers," 425 S.W.2d 342 (Tex. 1968), *with* "Newmark v. Gimbel's,

Inc.," 54 N.J. 585, 258 A.2d 697 (1969)(differentiating "sales-service hybrid transaction" of a beautician from "professional ministration" of a physician or dentist). The majority of current decisions look to the factual circumstances of each case and generally exclude persons exercising professional judgment within their legally authorized scope of practice. Thus, in the absence of any product preparation or modification, of any representation by service providers that the products are their own, or of warranty, the courts have generally not applied product liability doctrines where the provider is called upon to exercise such professional judgment. However, appropriate remedies may be available to injured parties under other theories of law, including malpractice. *See* "Batiste v. American Home Prods. Corp.," 32 N.C.App. 1, 231 S.E.2d 269 (1977).

Consequently, it is the intent of the drafters of this Act that professionals, such as pharmacists, physicians, optometrists, and opticians, should *not* be considered product sellers in those circumstances where they are selling a product while acting within their legally authorized scope of professional practice. *See* "Bichler v. Willing," 58 A.D.2d 331, 397 N.Y.S.2d 57 (1977); "Batiste v. American Home Prods. Corp.," *supra*. In addition, pharmacists or other professionals, employed by and working within the scope of their employment for a hospital or other health-related facility, would *not* be considered product sellers within this context since they would be rendering a part of the overall services of such facilities.

On the other hand, a pharmacist or other professional who is engaged in a commercial, non-professional sales transaction, such as the sale of perfume or photographic film, *would* be considered a product seller. Thus, the Act states that a party shall be considered a product seller when the sale of a product is the principal part of the transaction and when the essence of the relationship between the buyer and seller is *not* the furnishing of a professional skill or service. *See* Annot., 2 "A.L.R.3d" 1425 (1970).

With respect to non-professional services, when the sale of a product is the principal part of the transaction, and the essence of the relationship is not the furnishing of judgment, skill, or services, the non-manufacturer product seller is responsible under Section 105 of this Act. Therefore, when a non-professional service, such as application, installation, or dealer preparation, is an incidental part of the overall transaction of sale of a product, the provisions of Section 105 govern the entire transaction. *See* "Newmark v. Gimbel's, Inc.," 54 N.J. 585, 258 A.2d 697 (1969); "Winters v. Sears, Roebuck & Co.," 89 "A.L.R.3d" 196, 554 S.W.2d 565 (Mo.App.1977). However, when the non-professional service is the predominant element of the transaction, or when the service and sale elements are clearly distinguishable or contracted for separately, the Act does not apply to such non-professional service. Instead, it is governed by other applicable law of the state. *See* "Nickel v. Hyster Co.," 97 Misc.2d 770, 412 N.Y.S.2d 273 (1978). *See also* Brook, "Sales–Service Hybrid Transactions: A Policy Approach," 28 Sw. L.J. 575 (1975); and Greenfield, "Consumer Protection in Service Transactions—Implied Warranties and Strict Liability in Tort," 1974 "Utah L.Rev." 661.

It is also the intent of the drafters that this Act include manufacturers and other product sellers of new or remanufactured products, but not ordinary commercial sellers of used products. In this context, the commercial seller of used products is one who resells a product after it has been used by a consumer or other product user and is in essentially the same condition as when it was acquired for resale. Thus, the commercial seller of used products may be differentiated from sellers of fully rebuilt or remanufactured products that are included within the definition of "manufacturer" under Subsection (B). The slight majority of decisions indicate that product liability law does apply to sellers of used products; however, such sellers are not held to the same standards as are sellers of new products, due to the different nature and condition of the used product at the time of sale. Therefore, the issue of the potential liability of sellers of used products is left for resolution not under this Act, but rather under the other law of the state. *See* "Tillman v. Vance Equip. Co.," 596 P.2d 1299, 286 Or. 747 (1979); "Mickle v. Blackmon," 252 S.C. 202, 166 S.E.2d 173 (1969)(manufacturer); "Peterson v. Lou Bachrodt Chevrolet Co.," 61 Ill.2d 17, 329 N.E.2d 785 (1975)("as is" sale by dealer).

(B) *Manufacturer*. The term encompasses those product sellers who initiate and carry out the process of production. It also includes manufacturers of component parts, "private labelers" who hold themselves out to the public as manufacturers, and those product sellers who rebuild or remanufacture products for resale in "like new" condition. It does not include independent product designers whose services are contracted for by product sellers, if such designers are not otherwise engaged in the business of selling products. *See* Subsection (A)(definition of "product seller"). Unless they actually engage in some element of manufacture, traditional wholesalers, distributors, and retailers are excluded from the definition. However, if they do participate in the actual manufacturing process, they are deemed manufacturers, but only to the extent that they engage in such activity. They do not become manufacturers of the product as a whole.

This definition is drawn in part from Arizona's product liability law. *See* "Ariz.Rev.Stat.Ann." Section 12–681(1)(Supp.1978). Its greatest import within this Act is in regard to the responsibility of a manufacturer for defective products, as contrasted with that of other product sellers. *See* Section 105, "The Basic Standards of Responsibility for Product Sellers Other Than Manufacturers."

(C) *Product*. "Product" means property which, as a component part or an assembled whole, is movable, and possesses intrinsic value. Therefore, included are all goods, wares, merchandise, and their components, as well as articles and commodities capable of delivery for introduction into trade or commerce.

The definition follows existing case law by including movable dwellings, such as mobile homes, campers and similar vehicles. *See* "Morrow v. New Moon Homes, Inc.," 548 P.2d 279 (Alaska 1976)(mobile home). Also included are water, natural gas, and electrical energy provided by public utilities or other product sellers. *See* "Moody v. City of Galveston," 524 S.W.2d 583 (Tex.Civ.App.1975)(water); "Harris v. Northwest Natural Gas Co.," 284 Or. 571, 588 P.2d 18 (1978)(warnings regarding gas); "Ransome v. Wisconsin Elec. Power Co.," 87 Wis.2d 605, 275 N.W.2d 641 (1979)(electricity). However, human biologicals, such as blood and other bodily tissues or organs, are expressly excluded from the definition. In addition, representations of value, such as money or choses in action, are excluded, although the physical document and the ink or any other material used in printing the document do fall within the definition. *See* 72 *C.J.S.* "Product" (1951), and Sections 85–92 (Supp. 1975); 63 "Am.Jur.2d" "Products Liability" Section 5 (1972).

In a specific case, the particular product with which this Act is concerned is the "relevant product" which actually gave rise to the product liability claim. The "relevant product" may be the product as a whole or the particular component part or parts which gave rise to the product liability claim.

(D) *Product Liability Claim.* An important purpose of this Act is to consolidate product liability actions that have, at times, been separated under theories of negligence, warranty, and strict liability. This approach was suggested by the Task Force's "Legal Study" as well as by the "LaFalce Subcommittee Report." While an argument may be made that negligence theory is qualitatively different from strict liability and, therefore, should be preserved, product liability theory and practice have merged into a single entity and can only be stabilized if there is one, and not a multiplicity of, causes of action.

"Product liability claim" embraces express as well as implied warranty actions.

(E) *Claimant.* Living persons and those claiming through or on behalf of an estate in wrongful death or survival actions are both included within the meaning of the word "claimant."

Although the "Restatement (Second) of Torts" leaves open the question of whether persons other than product users should be included within the compass of product liability claims, subsequent case law has been almost uniform in ruling that such persons should be included. *See* "Giberson v. Ford Motor Co.," 504 S.W.2d 8 (Mo.1974)(collecting cases). *See also* Annot., 33 "A.L.R.3d" 415 (1970). The definition follows this line of decisions. *See* "Guarino v. Mine Safety Appliance Co.," 25 N.Y.2d 460, 255 N.E.2d 173, 306 N.Y.S.2d 942 (1969)(rescuer).

(F) *Harm.* Section 402A of the "Restatement" includes physical harm to persons and property. This Act provides that harm may manifest itself as damage to property, disability, including personal physical injuries and illness, death, and mental anguish or emotional harm attendant to such disability or death. It also includes mental anguish or emotional harm in circumstances in which the claimant is actually placed in personal danger, and the mental anguish or emotional harm is accompanied by substantial objective symptomatology. *See* "Wallace v. Coca–Cola Bottling Plants, Inc.," 269 A.2d 117 (Me. 1970).

The term also includes damage to the product itself. There is strong case law support for leaving direct economic loss cases to the field of commercial law. "Hawkins Constr. Co. v. Matthews Co., Inc." 190 Neb. 546, 209 N.W.2d 643 (1973); "Dennis v. Willys–Overland Motors, Inc.," 111 F.Supp. 875 (W.D.Mo. 1953); "Price v. Gatlin," 241 Or. 315, 405 P.2d 502 (1965). Courts that have allowed recovery in tort where the purchased property is "destroyed," but not where there is "mere loss of the bargain," have had difficulty applying this distinction where the product is wholly ineffective. *See* "Anthony v. Kelsey–Hayes Co.," 25 Cal.App.3d 442, 102 Cal.Rptr. 113 (1972); "States Steamship Co. v. Stone Manganese Marine Ltd.," 371 F.Supp. 500, 504–505 (D.N.J.1973)(collecting cases). For this reason and the fact that loss of the bargain damages are in essence a part of commercial law, claims for direct economic harm have been left to the "Uniform Commercial Code" ("U.C.C.").

The Act also does not include damages for consequential economic losses. Almost all courts have been in accord with "Seely v. White Motor Co.," 63 Cal.2d 9, 403 P.2d 145, 45 Cal.Rptr. 17 (1965), on this issue and have left claimants with whatever rights they have under the "U.C.C." Pursuant to Section 103, the Act follows the weight of authority in this regard, and does not preempt such recovery under the "U.C.C." *See* "Brown v. Western Farmers Ass'n.," 268 Or. 470, 521 P.2d 537 (1974); "Eli Lilly & Co. v. Casey," 472 S.W.2d 598 (Tex.Civ. App.1971); "Paul O'Leary Lumber Corp. v. Mill Equip., Inc.," 448 F.2d 536 (5th Cir.1971).

The insurance costs of extending consequential economic losses beyond parties to a contract would be enormous. It is much less expensive and more efficient for the product purchaser to obtain insurance against consequential economic losses caused by business stoppage. Also, most courts believe that a commercial purchaser should be charged with the risk that the purchased product will not match its economic expectations unless the manufacturer agrees that it will. *See* Note, "Economic Loss in Products Liability Jurisprudence," 66 "Colum.L.Rev." 917 (1966).

(G) *Reasonably Anticipated Conduct.* The definition is based in part on Arizona product liability law. *See* "Ariz.Rev.Stat.Ann." Section 12–681(4)(Supp.1978). "Anticipated" conduct includes occurrences which are expected, ordinary, usual, and familiar. The definition focuses on the class of persons which the product seller knows is likely to use the product. *See* "Thibault v. Sears,

Roebuck & Co.", 395 A.2d 843 (N.H. 1978). The concept of "reasonably anticipated conduct" should be contrasted with "foreseeable conduct." Almost any kind of misconduct with regard to products can be "foreseeable"—especially if the trier of fact is permitted to use hindsight, *e.g.*, that a soda bottle will be used for a hammer, that someone will attempt to drive a land vehicle on water, that perfume will be poured on a candle in order to scent it. *See* "Moran v. Faberge, Inc.," 273 Md. 538, 332 A.2d 11 (1975). This same conduct may not be reasonably anticipated by a potential product litigant, or by the trier of fact.

The Act's reliance on the concept of "reasonably anticipated conduct" places incentives for loss prevention on both product sellers and product users. It also helps to ensure that the price of products is not affected by the liability insurance costs that would spring from providing coverage for abnormal product use.

(H) *Preponderance of the Evidence.* Unless otherwise stated, the standard of evidence under this Act is the standard utilized in most civil litigation—a preponderance of the evidence. This standard requires a showing that it is more probable than not that a fact occurred or did not occur. *See* 30 "Am.Jur.2d" "Evidence" Section 1164 (1967).

(I) *Clear and Convincing Evidence.* Proof that is "clear and convincing" not only carries with it the power to persuade the mind as to its probable truth or correctness of fact, but also has an additional element of clinching such truth. The term is best understood in context.

It requires more proof than does the preponderance of the evidence standard (the ordinary standard under this Act), but does not require proof beyond a reasonable doubt. *See, e.g.,* "Aiello v. Knoll Golf Club," 64 N.J.Super. 156, 165 A.2d 531 (1960); "Cross v. Ledford," 161 Ohio St. 469, 120 N.E.2d 118 (1954); "Brown v. Warner," 78 S.D. 647, 107 N.W.2d 1 (1961).

(J) *Reckless Disregard.* As Prosser has indicated, "reckless disregard" occurs where the actor

> has intentionally done an act of an unreasonable character in disregard of a risk known to him or [one that was] so obvious that he must be taken to have been aware of it, and so great as to make it highly probable that harm would follow.

W. Prosser, "Torts" 185 (4th ed. 1971).

The term denotes aggravated conduct which represents a major departure from ordinary negligence.

(K) *Express Warranty.* This definition is based on its counterpart in the "Uniform Commercial Code" and includes any positive statement, affirmation of fact, promise, description, sample, or model relating to the product. *See* "U.C.C." Section 2–313; 63 "Am.Jur.2d" "Products Liability" Section 93 (1972). The product seller may give an express warranty orally or in writing, or through any other actions intended as a communication. *See* "Alan Wood Steel Co. v. Capital Equip. Enterprises, Inc.," 39 Ill.App.3d 48, 349 N.E.2d 627 (1976); "Larutan Corp. v. Magnolia Homes Mfg. Co.,"

190 Neb. 425, 209 N.W.2d 177 (1973). It should be noted that an action based on a violation of an express warranty must include the element of reliance, and the breach must relate to a misrepresentation of material facts. *See* Subsection 104(D).

* * *

Code

§ 103. Scope of This Act

(A) This Act is in lieu of and preempts all existing law governing matters within its coverage, including the "Uniform Commercial Code" and similar laws; however, nothing in this Act shall prevent the recovery, under the "Uniform Commercial Code" or similar laws, of direct or consequential economic losses.

(B) A claim may be asserted under this Act even though the claimant did not buy the product from, or enter into any contractual relationship with, the product seller.

(C) Whenever this Act does not provide a rule of decision, reference may be made to other sources of law, provided that such reference conforms to the intent and spirit of this Act as set forth in the following criteria used as guidelines for its development:

(1) To ensure that persons injured by unreasonably unsafe products receive reasonable compensation for their injuries;

(2) To ensure the availability of affordable product liability insurance with adequate coverage to product sellers that engage in rea-sonably safe manufacturing practices;

(3) To place the incentive for loss prevention on the party or parties who are best able to accomplish that goal;

(4) To expedite the reparations process from the time of injury to the time the claim is paid;

(5) To minimize the sum of accident costs, prevention costs, and transaction costs; and

(6) To use language that is comparatively clear and concise.

* * *

Analysis

§ 103. Scope of This Act

(A) The Act consolidates all product liability recovery theories into one. The approach taken is in accord with the Task Force's "Legal Study." While some have argued that for trial tactics purposes, it is useful to retain the negligence and breach of warranty causes of action as distinct from strict tort liability, a claimant's attorney can retain the essence of this utility by showing the basic wrongfulness of the product seller's conduct under Sections 104 or 105.

The Act explicitly preempts the "Uniform Commercial Code" ("U.C.C.") and similar laws in instances where such laws have governed matters within the Act's coverage. The purpose of this provision is to prevent conflicting product liability rules and remedies. *See, e.g.,* "Swartz v. General Motors Corp.," 378 N.E.2d 61 (Mass.1978). Although the Act eliminates breach of warranty as a separate cause of action in product liability cases, express warranties continue to play an important role in the Act. *See, e.g.,* Subsections 102(K), 104(D), 105(B), 106(B)(4), 107(E)(4), 110(A)(2), 110(B)(2)(a).

Because the Act does not provide remedies for purely economic losses, Subsection (A) ensures that the Act does not prevent recovery under commercial law for loss of the use of a product. Thus, product liability actions for personal injury, illness, death, or damage to property (other than the product itself) are governed by this Act. On the other hand, recovery under the "U.C.C." or similar law for economic losses is not precluded by this Act.

(B) The Act is in accord with the "Restatement (Second) of Torts" in that it is unnecessary for the claimant to be in contractual privity with the product seller in order to recover for harm. *See* "Restatement (Second) of Torts" Section 402A, Comment l.

(C) The Act and its accompanying commentary do not purport to be an exhaustive compilation of the entire subject of product liability law. Rather, they focus on subject matter areas that the "Task Force Report" suggested have created the most problems and are of major importance.

The interstices of the Act will be filled by statutory or common law additions of the individual states. Some of these interstitial issues will be pointed out in the section-by-section analysis. Others will be discovered in the course of litigation under the Act.

It is the intent of Subsection (C) that these additions of statutory or common law should enhance, rather than conflict with, the basic purposes of this Act. Those courts or legislatures that make such additions should keep in mind the "Criteria for the Act" set forth in this Subsection. A full explanation of the criteria is set forth in the Introduction to the Act. In regard to these criteria, it is essential to note that this Act does not intend to set up a compensation system similar to Worker Compensation. Rather, the purpose of the Act is to impose liability "only where it is fair to deem the product seller responsible for an injury." "Introduction," p. 14, *supra.*

* * *

Code

§ 104. Basic Standards of Responsibility for Manufacturers

A product manufacturer is subject to liability to a claimant who proves by a preponderance of the evidence that the claimant's harm was proximately caused because the product was defective.

A product may be proven to be defective if, and only if:

(1) It was unreasonably unsafe in construction (Subsection A);

(2) It was unreasonably unsafe in design (Subsection B);

(3) It was unreasonably unsafe because adequate warnings or instructions were not provided (Subsection C); or

(4) It was unreasonably unsafe because it did not conform to the product seller's express warranty (Subsection D).

Before submitting the case to the trier of fact, the court shall determine that the claimant has introduced sufficient evidence to allow a reasonable person to find, by a preponderance of the evidence, that one or more of the above conditions existed and was a proximate cause of the claimant's harm.

(A) *The Product Was Unreasonably Unsafe in Construction.* In order to determine that the product was unreasonably unsafe in construction, the trier of fact must find that, when the product left the control of the manufacturer, the product deviated in some material way from the manufacturer's design specifications or performance standards, or from otherwise identical units of the same product line.

(B) *The Product Was Unreasonably Unsafe in Design.*

(1) In order to determine that the product was unreasonably unsafe in design, the trier of fact must find that, at the time of manufacture, the likelihood that the product would cause the claimant's harm or similar harms, and the seriousness of those harms outweighed the burden on the manufacturer to design a product that would have prevented those harms, and the adverse effect that alternative design would have on the usefulness of the product.

(2) Examples of evidence that is especially probative in making this evaluation include:

(a) Any warnings and instructions provided with the product;

(b) The technological and practical feasibility of a product designed and manufactured so as to have prevented claimant's harm while substantially serving the likely user's expected needs;

(c) The effect of any proposed alternative design on the usefulness of the product;

(d) The comparative costs of producing, distributing, selling, using, and maintaining the product as designed and as alternatively designed; and

(e) The new or additional harms that might have resulted if the product had been so alternatively designed.

(C) *The Product Was Unreasonably Unsafe Because Adequate Warnings or Instructions Were Not Provided.*

(1) In order to determine that the product was unreasonably unsafe because adequate warnings or instructions were not provided about a danger connected with the product or its proper use, the trier of fact must find that, at the time of manufacture, the likelihood that the product would cause the claimant's harm or similar harms and the seriousness of those harms rendered the manufacturer's instructions inadequate and that the manufacturer should and could have provided the instructions or warnings which claimant alleges would have been adequate.

(2) Examples of evidence that is especially probative in making this evaluation include:

511

(a) The manufacturer's ability, at the time of manufacture, to be aware of the product's danger and the nature of the potential harm;

(b) The manufacturer's ability to anticipate that the likely product user would be aware of the product's danger and the nature of the potential harm;

(c) The technological and practical feasibility of providing adequate warnings and instructions;

(d) The clarity and conspicuousness of the warnings or instructions that were provided; and

(e) The adequacy of the warnings or instructions that were provided.

(3) In any claim under this Subsection, the claimant must prove by a preponderance of the evidence that if adequate warnings or instructions had been provided, they would have been effective because a reasonably prudent product user would have either declined to use the product or would have used the product in a manner so as to have avoided the harm.

(4) A manufacturer shall not be liable for its failure to warn or instruct about dangers that are obvious; for "product misuse" as defined in Subsection 112(C)(1); or for alterations or modifications of the product which do not constitute "reasonably anticipated conduct" under Subsection 102(G).

(5) A manufacturer is under an obligation to provide adequate warnings or instructions to the actual product user unless the manufacturer provided such warnings to a person who may be reasonably expected to assure that action is taken to avoid the harm, or that the risk of the harm is explained to the actual product user.

For products that may be legally used only by or under the supervision of a class of experts, warnings or instructions may be provided to the using or supervisory expert.

For products that are tangible goods sold or handled only in bulk or other workplace products, warnings or instructions may be provided to the employer of the employee-claimant if there is no practical and feasible means of transmitting them to the employee-claimant.

(6) *Post–Manufacture Duty to Warn.* In addition to the claim provided in Subsection (C)(1), a claim may arise under this Subsection where a reasonably prudent manufacturer should have learned about a danger connected with the product after it was manufactured. In such a case, the manufacturer is under an obligation to act with regard to the danger as a reasonably prudent manufacturer in the same or similar circumstances. This obligation is satisfied if the manufacturer makes reasonable efforts to inform product users or a person who may be reasonably expected to assure that action is taken to avoid the harm, or that the risk of harm is explained to the actual product user.

(D) *The Product Was Unreasonably Unsafe Because It Did Not Conform to an Express Warranty.* In order to determine that the product was unreasonably unsafe because it did not conform to an express warranty, the trier of fact must find that the claimant, or one acting on the claimant's behalf, relied on an express warranty made by the manufacturer or its agent about a material fact or facts concerning the product and this express warranty proved to be untrue.

A "material fact" is any specific characteristic or quality of the product. It does not include a general opinion about, or praise of, the product.

The product seller may be subject to liability under Subsection (D) although it did not engage in negligent or fraudulent conduct in making the express warranty.

* * *

Analysis

§ 104. Basic Standards of Responsibility for Manufacturers

No single product liability issue has generated more controversy than the question of defining the basic standards of responsibility to which product manufacturers are to be held. *See, e.g.,* Epstein, "Products Liability: The Search for the Middle Ground," 56 "N.C.L.Rev." 643 (1978); *see also* Vetri, "Products Liability: Developing a Framework for Analysis," 54 "Or.L.Rev." 293, 310 (1975); Henderson, "Judicial Review of Manufacturers' Conscious Design Choice: The Limits of Adjudication," 73 "Colum.L.Rev." 1531 (1973); Keeton, "Product Liability and the Meaning of Defect," 5 "St. Mary's L.J." 30 (1973); Wade, "On the Nature of Strict Tort Liability for Products," 44 "Miss. L.J." 825 (1973); Walkowiak, "Product Liability Litigation and the Concept of

Defective Goods: 'Reasonableness' Revisited," 44 "J. Air Law & Commerce" 705 (1978).

Much of the controversy appears to have sprung from the fact that the authors of Section 402A of the "Restatement (Second) of Torts" were focusing on problems relating to product mismanufacture or defective construction, and not on problems relating to defective design or the duty to warn. *See* "Restatement (Second) of Torts" Section 402A, Appendix (1965)(most cases cited deal with defects in construction cases); Wade, *supra,* 44 "Miss.L.J." at 830–32. In the 15 years following the publication of the "Restatement," courts have struggled to define standards of responsibility with respect to design and the duty to warn. *See, e.g.,* "Barker v. Lull Eng'r. Co.," 20 Cal.3d 413, 573 P.2d 443, 143 Cal. Rptr. 225 (1978); "Cepeda v. Cumberland Eng'r. Co.," 76 N.J. 152, 386 A.2d 816 (1978); "Phillips v. Kimwood Mach. Co.," 269 Or. 485, 525 P.2d 1033 (1974).

In the course of this struggle, courts appear to have drifted away from rationales for imposing liability and toward verbal formulae that attempt to distinguish between negligence and strict liability.

The drafters of this Act have focused on the basic rationale of product liability and made decisions that should make it easier for courts to decide these cases. It was determined that "strict liability" is justified in two product liability areas—defects in construction and breach of express warranty.

The "Task Force Report" concluded that strict liability for defective construction can be absorbed within the existing liability insurance system. There is a degree of predictability with regard to these defective products that is not found with respect to products that are defective in design or to failure to warn. Strict liability for defective construction has also been predicated on Section 402A of the "Restatement" and implied warranty claims under commercial law. These sources support the position that consumers have the right to expect that products are free from construction defects.

Strict liability cases involving breach of an express warranty can also be justified. If a manufacturer makes a specific representation about its product, it is fair to hold the manufacturer to that promise. Moreover, the consumer has the right to expect that a product will live up to the manufacturer's representations.

While some courts have indicated that strict liability should also be applied in design and duty-to-warn cases, it is difficult to find an adequate rationale to support that result. A few courts have sought to justify the result under a theory of "risk distribution" wherein the product seller distributes the costs of all product-related risks through liability insurance; however, this rationale breaks down in practice. The application of uncertain strict liability principles in the areas of design and duty to warn places a whole product line at risk; therefore, a firmer liability foundation is needed.

In terms of creating incentives for loss prevention, the approach of applying strict liability principles to design and duty-to-warn cases represents an "overkill;" a fault system will provide the needed incentive.

If the costs of product-related injuries are always to be distributed through the price of the product, the mechanism to bring about this result should be an appropriate compensation system with limited damages, not the tort-litigation system. The former is the approach taken in Worker Compensation and automobile no-fault reparations systems. While courts that have applied strict liability in design and duty-to-warn cases have often stated that they are not imposing "absolute" insurer liability, they have not been able to articulate why they draw a line short of that particular point. The reason for this is that the risk distribution rationale provides no stopping point short of absolute liability. Thus, a number of courts have plunged into a foggy area that is neither true strict liability nor negligence. The result has been the creation of a wide variety of legal "formulae," unpredictability for consumers, and instability in the insurance market.

In light of these facts, this Act places both design and duty-to-warn cases on a fault basis.

The Act utilizes the word "defective" as a generic term covering all four types of unreasonably unsafe products. A product cannot be proven defective unless the claimant shows that it is unreasonably unsafe under one or more Subsections under Section 104.[10]

This approach should not lead to problems of characterization. The claimant's pleading should indicate the theory on which it is based within the framework of Subsections (A), (B), (C), or (D). Of course, a product may be unreasonably unsafe in more than one way.

The manufacturer of a component part or parts is subject to liability under this Section for harms caused because that component part was defective. The manufacturer of a whole product is subject to liability under this Section for harms caused because the product, or any of its components, was defective.

The following commentary discusses each Subsection in turn.

(A) *The Product Was Unreasonably Unsafe in Construction.* The history of imposing strict liability for products which are unreasonably unsafe in construction goes back as far as 1913 when sellers of foods were first held liable for their failure to produce a product reasonably fit for its intended use. *See* "Mazetti v. Armour & Co.," 75 Wash. 622, 135 P. 633 (1913); Prosser, "The Assault Upon the Citadel (Strict Liability to the Consumer)," 69 "Yale L.J." 1099 (1960).

Subsection (A) imposes pure strict liability on the manufacturer in accordance with Section 402A of the "Restatement (Second) of Torts." *Cf.* "Pabon v. Hackensack Auto Sales, Inc.," 63 N.J.Super. 476, 164 A.2d 773, 783 (1960)(im-

plied warranty for defective ball bearing). The approach is also in accord with the overwhelming trend in case law in the United States. *See* Phillips, "A Synopsis of the Developing Law of Products Liability," 28 "Drake L.Rev." 317, 344–45 (1979).

In the course of its study, the Task Force found that most product sellers can absorb the financial impact of strict liability for products which are defective in construction. *See* "Task Force Report" at VII–17.

The approach taken here is subject to theoretical criticism because

> [A] standard which judges a manufacturer by his own rather than industry standards could penalize the manufacturer who goes out of his way to build into his product a high safety level not mandated or followed by the industry.

Twerski & Weinstein, "A Critique of the Uniform Product Liability Law—A Rush to Judgment," 28 "Drake L.Rev." 221, 225 (1979).

Nevertheless, this criticism overlooks the fact that the manufacturer's self-imposition of a higher standard will function as a shield against claims alleging liability in the more costly area of defective design. By adopting a higher standard, a manufacturer may occasionally be subject to liability under Subsection (A), while another manufacturer may not be, but the first manufacturer does not place its whole product line at risk of being found unreasonably unsafe in design.

---

10. Liability can be imposed on non-manufacturer product sellers under Section 105 when they have been negligent.

Not every minor variation from a standard will result in liability; rather, the variation must be a material one causing the claimant's harm.

In point of fact, there is no practical way to define defective construction except by the manufacturer's own standards. It is an optimal area for strict liability "because societal expectations are fairly well established with regard to such defects, and a ready gauge of acceptability exists by reference to like products that are non-defective." Phillips, "The Standard for Determining Defectiveness in Products Liability," 46 "U.Cin.L.Rev." 101, 104–05 (1977). Moreover, the imposition of strict liability with regard to defective construction is fair to the product user. Under a negligence system, the claimant would have the very difficult burden of showing that a manufacturer knew or should have known about a latent defect in one of thousands of mass-produced products.

(B) *The Product Was Unreasonably Unsafe in Design.* No court, in spite of some loose language that has been used, has imposed true strict or absolute liability on manufacturers for products which are unreasonably unsafe in design. *See* Henderson, "Manufacturers' Liability for Defective Design: A Proposed Statutory Reform," 56 "N.C.L.Rev." 625, 634–35 (1978). This is true because courts have appreciated the liability potential inherent in such cases—it is almost always possible to design a product more safely. Nevertheless, some courts in their instructions to the trier of fact have left juries "at sea." The jury is told to decide design cases by "considering" a number of factors; it is not given a guideline or formula for making the evaluation.

The approach taken here provides such a guideline. The trier of fact is instructed to impose liability if it finds that the product was unreasonably unsafe in design. The trier of fact is also given a formula to assist it in making this determination. The approach has its roots in the law of negligence[11] and has been put into modern and appropriate product liability terminology by some courts in their attempt to resolve the defective design dilemma. *See* "Hagans v. Oliver Mach. Co.," 576 F.2d 97, 99–100 (5th Cir.1978); "Dreisonstok v. Volkswagenwerk, A.G.," 489 F.2d 1066, 1071 (4th Cir. 1974); "Jeng v. Witters," 452 F.Supp. 1349, 1356 (M.D.Pa.1978).

Section 104 requires the court to make an initial determination as to whether the claimant has introduced enough evidence for the case to be considered by the jury. This requirement is especially important with respect to conscious design cases under Subsection (B). The dangers of the trier of fact introducing hindsight into the risk-utility analysis make it imperative for the court to apply its screening function carefully. *See* "Owens v. Allis–Chalmers Corp.," 83 Mich.App. 74, 268 N.W.2d 291 (1978); Henderson, *su-*

---

11. *See* "United States v. Carroll Towing Co.," 159 F.2d 169, 173 (2d Cir.1947)(the "Learned Hand formula").

pra, 73 "Colum.L.Rev." at 1531. *Cf.* Wade, *supra,* 44 "Miss.L.J." at 837–38 (suggesting that such formulae can *only* be applied by the court).

The formula set forth in Subsection (B) requires the trier of fact to balance two pairs of factors existing at the time of manufacture: (1) the likelihood that the product would cause the claimant's harm or similar harms, and the seriousness of those harms; against (2) the manufacturer's burden of designing a product that would have prevented those harms, and the adverse effect that alternative design would have on the usefulness of the product. *See* "Kerns v. Engelke," 390 N.E.2d 859, 865 (1979).

If the case is sent to the jury, the balancing formula should be placed in a jury instruction indicating that the claimant has the burden of showing, in light of the formula, that the product was unreasonably unsafe in design.

The Subsection also sets forth examples of important evidence that may be considered with respect to applying the formula.

First, warnings and instructions are important because, in an appropriate case, a product may be found not to be defective in design if the product seller has given an adequate warning about the product risk. *See, e.g.,* "Wagner v. Larson," 257 Iowa 1202, 136 N.W.2d 312 (1965); "Penn v. Inferno Mfg. Corp.," 199 So.2d 210 (La.App.) *aff'd,* 251 La. 27, 202 So.2d 649 (1967). There are limits to this possibility, however, since a product seller will not be shielded from liability for an unreasonably unsafe

product simply by indicating that the product "may be hazardous." Only a warning or instruction which, at the time of manufacture, substantially reduces the likelihood that the product would cause harm in the manner in which the claimant's harm was caused will affect the question of whether the product was defective in design.

Second, evidence relating to the technological and practical feasibility of designing and manufacturing a product which would have substantially served the expected user's needs, and would have also prevented the claimant's harm, addresses the side of the formula dealing with the manufacturer's burden. If an alternatively designed product which would have prevented the harm while preserving its usefulness could have been produced with a slight increase in cost, it is likely that the product is unreasonably unsafe. On the other hand, the manufacturer need not incorporate safety features that render a product incapable of performing some or all of the very functions that create its public demand. *See* "Hagans v. Oliver Mach., Inc.," 576 F.2d 97 (5th Cir.1978); "Dreisonstok v. Volkswagenwerk, A.G.," 489 F.2d 1066 (4th Cir.1974).

Third, it is important to consider evidence relating to the effect of the alternative design on the usefulness of the product. As learned scholars have observed, "it is virtually impossible to [evaluate a design defect case] without balancing risk and utility factors." *See* Twerski & Weinstein, *supra,* 28 "Drake L.Rev." at 229. *See also* "Phillips v. Kimwood Mach. Co.," 269 Or. 485, 525 P.2d 1033, 1038 (1974). It is important to note that this evidence is not directed to the general usefulness of the product in society, *i.e.,* the overall social worth of pharmaceuticals, lawnmowers, or other products.

Fourth, it is essential to consider evidence relating to the comparative costs of producing, distributing, selling, using, and maintaining the product as designed and as alternatively designed. This places the court and the trier of fact in the "real world" of design options.

Finally, if new or additional harms might have resulted if the product had been alternatively designed, the trier of fact should consider this factor in making its evaluation. Since this evidence will probably be introduced by the defendant manufacturer, it may be placed before the court and jury *after* the claimant's case has been presented.

In sum, Subsection (B) places the burden of proof on the claimant to show that in light of a balance of practical, objective factors, the product seller should bear the full cost of the injury and have the responsibility for attempting to distribute that cost through the price of its product. In light of the fact that the judgment is the equivalent of holding that the whole product line is defective, it is important that traditional tort law principles be followed and that the claimant retain the burden of proof. *See* Kalven, "Torts: The Quest for Appropriate Standards," 53 "Cal.L.Rev." 189 (1965). *But see* "Barker v. Lull Engineering, Inc.," 20 Cal.3d 413, 573 P.2d 443, 143 Cal.Rptr. 225 (1978).

Neither the formula nor the detailed list of the more important evidentiary items includes what has been called the "consumer expectation test." The reasons for not including it are rooted in both economics and practicality. As Professor Wade, Reporter for "The Restatement (Second) of Torts," has stated:

> In many situations, particularly involving design matters, the consumer would not know what to expect, because he would have no idea how safe the product could be made.

Wade, *supra,* "Miss.L.J.," at 829.

The consumer expectation test takes subjectivity to its most extreme end. Each trier of fact is likely to have a different understanding of abstract consumer expectations. Moreover, most consumers are not familiar with the details of the manufacturing process and cannot abstractly evaluate conscious design alternatives. This has been recently recognized by the Supreme Court of Texas. "Turner v. General Motors Corp.," 584 S.W.2d 844 (Tex.1979); *see also* Green, "Strict Liability Under Sections 402A and 402B: A Decade of Litigation," 54 "Tex.L.Rev." 1185 (1976).

(C) *The Product Was Unreasonably Unsafe Because Adequate Warnings or Instructions Were Not Provided.* A manufacturer may be held liable under Subsection (C) regardless of whether the product was found to be unreasonably unsafe in construction or design. Even where the lack of scientific knowledge or cost factors preclude the use of an alternative design, the manufacturer may still be required to provide a warning about the product's hazard or to provide adequate instructions about the product's use. *See* "Jacobson v. Colorado Fuel & Iron Corp.," 409 F.2d 1263, 1271 (9th Cir.1969).

It is important to note that Subsection (C) covers two arguably separate problems. First, was there a duty to warn or instruct about a particular matter? Second, assuming that a warning or instruction was given, was it adequate? While these two problems are theoretically separate, the underlying factors that must be taken into consideration in evaluating a manufacturer's duty with respect to them overlap; therefore, the two issues have been combined in Subsection (C). As will be indicated below, there may be a different evidentiary emphasis in the two types of cases.

The basic standard of responsibility for Subsection (C) is predicated on a fault basis. A "strict liability" base in this area creates unacceptable uncertainty within the tort-litigation system. This has recently been recognized by the Supreme Court of Michigan. "Smith v. E.R. Squibb & Sons," 405 Mich. 79, 273 N.W.2d 476 (1979).

Under Subsection (C), the trier of fact is to place itself in the manufacturer's position at the time the product was manufactured. In order to impose liability on the manufacturer, the claimant must prove that the probability that the product would cause the claimant's harm and similar harms and the seriousness of those harms rendered the manufacturer's instructions inadequate, and that the manufacturer

should and could have provided the warnings or instructions which claimant alleges would have been adequate. Obviously, where harms were likely to occur and unlikely to be recognized by the product user, the necessity of adequate warnings and instructions is correspondingly acute. On the other hand, the duty to provide adequate warnings and instructions cannot go beyond the technological and other information that was reasonably available at the time of manufacture. This concept is in accord with the overwhelming majority of court decisions. *See* "Robbins v. Farmers Union Grain Terminal Ass'n.," 552 F.2d 788 (8th Cir.1977)(collecting cases).

Unlike the basic formula for design cases, the utility of the product is not a consideration in deciding whether a warning is necessary. The focus is on the likelihood that the product would cause the claimant's harm, and the seriousness of that harm, the adequacy of the warnings that were provided, and the practical need for providing the warnings or instructions which claimant alleges would have been adequate.

Subsection (C)(2) lists examples of some of the more probative evidence that can assist the court and the jury in applying this formula.

Factor (a) focuses on the manufacturer's ability, at the time of manufacture, to be aware of the product's danger and the nature of the potential harm. This factor should not operate through hindsight.

Factor (b) involves evidence relating to the manufacturer's ability to anticipate that the likely product user would be aware of the product risk and the nature of the potential harm. The more serious the anticipated harm, the greater the duty to warn. *See* "Braniff Airways, Inc. v. Curtiss–Wright Corp.," 411 F.2d 451 (2d Cir.1969), *on rehearing,* 424 F.2d 427 (2d Cir.1970); "Davis v. Wyeth Laboratories, Inc.," 399 F.2d 121 (9th Cir.1968).

Factor (c), the technological and practical feasibility of providing effective warnings and instructions, may not be significant in many cases because warnings are often relatively inexpensive to provide. However, in some situations, it may not be feasible as a practical technological matter to provide a warning or the type of warning that the claimant suggests should have been provided.

Factor (d), the clarity and conspicuousness of the warnings or instructions, is material in cases where claimant alleges that the warnings given were not adequate. As Professor Phillips has noted:

> To be adequate, warnings must be reasonably conspicuous, strong and clear. They must describe the danger and, where pertinent, the means of avoiding it.

Phillips, *supra,* 28 "Drake L.Rev." at 351.

Also highly relevant to this issue is Factor (e), evidence relating to the adequacy of the warnings or instructions that were provided. Again, as Professor Phillips has noted:

> The effectiveness of a warning may be diluted by oth-

er supplier representations of safety that lull the user into a false sense of security. While little or no warning may have to be given to the expert user, a clear and strong warning is required for dangerous products which the supplier can reasonably expect to be used by inexperienced persons. *Id.* at 351–52.

Subsection (C)(3) sets forth a basic causation link for the Subsection. The claimant must show that if adequate warnings or instructions had been provided, the harm would have been avoided either because a reasonably prudent product user would have declined to use the product (a situation which may be most pertinent with respect to a pharmaceutical with a known risk), or because the product would have been used in a manner so as to have avoided the harm. *See* "Technical Chem. Co. v. Jacobs," 480 S.W.2d 602 (Tex.1972); *cf.* "Potthoff v. Alms," 583 P.2d 309 (Colo.Ct.App. 1978). While it has been suggested that no causation requirement should be required with respect to unavoidable pharmaceutical risks (*see* Twerski & Weinstein, *supra,* 28 "Drake L.Rev." at 236–37), the Act addresses itself to tort law, not the general public regulation of products. It is a basic requirement of tort law for the claimant to show that if the defendant had acted in a manner in which the claimant alleges was appropriate, then he or she would not have suffered harm. *See* W. Prosser, "Torts" at 236 (4th ed. 1971).

Subsection (C)(4) recognizes that a manufacturer should be able to assume that the ordinary product user is familiar with obvious hazards—that knives cut, that alcohol burns, that it is dangerous to drive automobiles at high speeds. Thus, the Act states that the manufacturer does not have to warn about dangers that are obvious. *See* "Kimble v. Waste Systems International, Inc.," 595 P.2d 569 (Wash.App. 1979). While it has been suggested that this approach may encourage the manufacture of "obviously dangerous" products, this is unlikely to occur under this Act, since the manufacturer of an unreasonably unsafe product may be subject to liability under Subsection (B).

Requiring a manufacturer to warn about matters that are obvious would tend to reduce the effectiveness of warnings. As experts in the field have observed, "Warnings, in order to be effective, must be selective." Twerski, Weinstein, Donaher, & Piehler, "The Use and Abuse of Warnings in Products Liability—Design Defect Litigation Comes of Age," 61 "Cornell L.Rev." 495, 514 (1976). It is recognized that, in some jurisdictions, there is an open-ended duty to warn about obvious dangers when they are highly likely to cause very serious injuries. *See* Marschall, "An Obvious Wrong Does Not Make a Right: Manufacturers' Liability for Patently Dangerous Products," 48 "N.Y.U.L.Rev." 1065 (1973)(collecting cases). Again, the Act approaches this problem by potentially subjecting a manufacturer of a patently dangerous product to liability for an unreasonably unsafe design.

Similarly, the product manufacturer is not under an obligation to warn about misuses or alterations of products that would not be expected by an ordinary reasonably prudent person who is likely to use the product in the same or similar circumstances. *See also* Section 112(C).

Subsection (C)(5) indicates that in the normal course of events, a manufacturer should place its warning or instruction in a place or in a form where it can be communicated to the actual product user. On the other hand, there are some situations in which this is impossible or impracticable. *See* "Bryant v. Hercules, Inc.," 325 F.Supp. 241 (W.D.Ky.1970). Therefore, the Subsection indicates that a warning or instruction may be given to a person who may be reasonably expected to assure that action is taken to avoid the harm, or that the risk of the harm is explained to the actual product user. By way of example, the Act sets forth situations where such a process is appropriate. Thus, communication to a using or supervising expert is explicitly stated to be adequate when the product—such as a prescription drug or a radioactive material—is one which may be legally used only by, or under, the supervision of such an expert. *See* "Carmichael v. Reitz," 17 Cal.App.3d 958, 95 Cal.Rptr. 381 (Dist.Ct.App.1971); "Terhune v. A.H. Robbins Co.," 90 Wash.2d 9, 577 P.2d 975 (1978).

The manufacturer of tangible goods sold or handled only in bulk or of other workplace products may communicate warnings or instructions to the employer of the claimant when that is the only practical and feasible avenue for making a warning. *See* "Reed v. Pennwalt Corp.," 22 Wash.App. 718, 591 P.2d 478 (1979).

Other situations not specifically pointed out in the Act may arise where it is permissible for the manufacturer to convey warnings to persons other than a product user, *e.g.,* warnings to the parent of a young child with respect to a food product. *Cf.* "Spruill v. Boyle–Midway Inc.," 308 F.2d 79 (4th Cir.1962).

Post–Manufacture Duty to Warn. Subsection (C)(6) recognizes a manufacturer's duty to warn after its product has been produced. The Subsection places an obligation on a manufacturer to act with reasonable prudence to learn about serious risks connected with products after they are manufactured. When it learns of such a risk, it is to act as a reasonably prudent manufacturer in the same or similar situation. This obligation is satisfied if the manufacturer makes reasonable efforts to inform product users or appropriate persons about the risk. The Subsection is in accord with basic negligence case law. *See* "Comstock v. General Motors Corp." 358 Mich. 163, 99 N.W.2d 627 (1959); "Schenebeck v. Sterling Drug, Inc.," 423 F.2d 919 (8th Cir.1970). The Subsection recognizes that in some situations, a general warning through an advertising medium may be all a manufacturer can provide. The standard is reasonableness, not absolute or strict liability.

(D) *The Product Was Unreasonably Unsafe Because It Did Not Conform to an Express Warranty.* When there has been an express warranty concerning the product, strict liability can readily be justified. The product seller has used specific words to induce the purchase of the product, and the Act indicates that it must be accountable for its representations. The term "express warranty" is separately defined in the Act in Subsection 102(K).

Since the case of "Baxter v. Ford Motor Co.," 179 Wash. 123, 35 P.2d 1090 (1934), courts have been virtually unanimous in imposing strict liability on product sellers when their statements about their products prove to be untrue. *See* W. Prosser, "Torts" at 652 (4th ed. 1971)("decisions to the contrary have been amazingly few").

Thus, where a product seller advertised that its pharmaceutical was "free and safe from all dangers of addiction" and claimant, because of a rare and totally unforeseeable susceptibility, became physically dependent on the drug, strict liability was imposed. "Crocker v. Winthrop Lab., Div. of Sterling Drug, Inc.," 514 S.W.2d 429 (Tex.1974); "Spiegel v. Saks 34th Street," 43 Misc.2d 1065, 252 N.Y.S.2d 852 (App.Term 1964), *aff'd,* 272 N.Y.S.2d 972 (App.Div.1966)(perfume advertised as "non-allergenic").

While many courts use the term "express warranty" to describe the cause of action set forth in Subsection (D), "warranty" is a term of commercial law which is appropriate in the ordinary sale of goods from an immediate buyer to an immediate seller. Here, the focus is solely on tort claims for personal injury and damage to property. In order to convey the tort basis of this cause of action, Section 402B of the "Restatement (Second) of Torts" (1965), utilized the term "misrepresentation" in place of the term "express warranty." Nevertheless, this parlance has not been generally accepted by courts, although they do appreciate the distinction between the tort action and commercial law. *See* "Drayton v. Jiffee Chem. Corp.," 591 F.2d 352, 359 (6th Cir. 1978)("sounds distinctly in tort"). In deference to this common usage, the term "express warranty," as defined in Subsection 102(K), has been utilized.

Subsection (D) applies only to representations or warranties made by the manufacturer or by a person for whom it is legally responsible. In general, the representation must have been made to the claimant, who must have relied on the warranty, and the harm must have resulted because of that reliance and because of the fact which was misrepresented. However, Subsection (D) does permit reliance by "one acting on behalf" of the claimant. Thus, if a wife purchases an automobile in reliance on a statement concerning its brakes and permits her husband to drive the car, this supplies the element of reliance although the husband, in fact, never learned of the statement. Otherwise, the Section is limited to consumers of products. *See* "Restatement (Second) of Torts" Section 402B, Comment j (1965).

The statement made by the product seller must be about a material fact or facts concerning the product. This does not include mere "puffing" or sales talk. Thus, the manufacturer of a grinding disk

that broke was not deemed liable for a breach of an express warranty after stating that the product was "stronger, sharper, and longer lived than ever before available anywhere." "Jakubowski v. Minnesota Mining & Mfg.," 80 N.J.Super. 184, 193 A.2d 275 (1963), *rev'd on other grounds,* 42 N.J. 177, 199 A.2d 826 (1964); *cf.* "Berkebile v. Brantly Helicopter Corp.," 462 Pa. 83, 337 A.2d 893 (1975)(helicopter "easy to operate"). In contrast, a manufacturer was deemed strictly liable when it advertised that a golf training device could be operated and the "ball will not hit player." A player of limited golfing ability was indeed hit by the ball, and the defendant was held liable. "Hauter v. Zogarts," 14 Cal.3d 104, 120 Cal.Rptr. 681, 534 P.2d 377 (1975).

* * *

Code

§ 105. Basic Standards of Responsibility for Product Sellers Other Than Manufacturers

(A) A product seller, other than a manufacturer, is subject to liability to a claimant who proves by a preponderance of the evidence that claimant's harm was proximately caused by such product seller's failure to use reasonable care with respect to the product.

Before submitting the case to the trier of fact, the court shall determine that the claimant has introduced sufficient evidence to allow a reasonable person to find by a preponderance of the evidence that such product seller has failed to exercise reasonable care and that this failure was a proximate cause of the claimant's harm.

In determining whether a product seller, other than a manufacturer, is subject to liability under Subsection (A), the trier of fact shall consider the effect of such product seller's own conduct with respect to the design, construction, inspection, or condition of the product, and any failure of such product seller to transmit adequate warnings or instructions about the dangers and proper use of the product.

Unless Subsection (B) or (C) is applicable, product sellers shall not be subject to liability in circumstances in which they did not have a reasonable opportunity to inspect the product in a manner which would or should, in the exercise of reasonable care, reveal the existence of the defective condition.

(B) A product seller, other than a manufacturer, who makes an express warranty about a material fact or facts concerning a product is subject to the standards of liability set forth in Subsection 104(D).

(C) A product seller, other than a manufacturer, is also subject to the liability of manufacturer under Section 104 if:

(1) The manufacturer is not subject to service of process under the laws of the claimant's domicile; or

(2) The manufacturer has been judicially declared insolvent in that the manufacturer is unable to pay its debts as they become due in the ordinary course of business; or

(3) The court determines that it is highly probable that the claimant would be unable to enforce a judgment against the product manufacturer.

(D) Except as provided in Subsections (A), (B), and (C), a product seller, other than a manufacturer, shall not otherwise be subject to liability under this Act.

* * *

Analysis

§ 105. Basic Standards of Responsibility for Product Sellers Other Than Manufacturers

Section 105 is derived in part from Tennessee law. "Tenn.Code Ann." Section 23–3706 (Supp.1978). The Section addresses the problem of excessive product liability costs for parties other than manufacturers in the distribution chain in a way that does not compromise incentives for loss prevention. It also leaves the claimant with a viable defendant whenever a defective product has caused harm.

The "ISO Closed Claims Survey" shows that manufacturers account for 87 percent of the total amount of product liability payments, while distributors, wholesalers, and retailers account for 4.6 percent. "ISO Closed Claims Survey," Report 3, at 35 (1977). Case law suggests that these non-manufacturer product sellers can usually shift their costs to the manufacturer through an indemnity suit. See, e.g., "Hales v. Monroe," 544 F.2d 331, 332 (8th Cir.1976); "Anderson v.

Somberg," 158 N.J.Super. 384, 386 A.2d 413, 419–20 (1978); "Litton Systems, Inc. v. Shaw's Sales & Serv., Ltd.," 119 Ariz. 10, 579 P.2d 48, 50 (1978).

Despite their relatively small role vis-a-vis manufacturers as product liability defendants, wholesalers, retailers, and distributors are frequently brought into a product liability suit. *See, e.g.,* "Tucson Indus., Inc. v. Schwartz," 108 Ariz. 464, 501 P.2d 936 (1972); "Vergott v. Deseret Pharmaceutical Co.," 463 F.2d 12 (5th Cir.1972); "Duckworth v. Ford Motor Co.," 320 F.2d 130 (3d Cir.1963). In light of ISO data showing that for every dollar of claims paid, at least 35 cents is spent in defense costs,[12] the net result is that wholesalers, retailers, and distributors are subject to substantial product liability costs in terms of both premiums and defense costs. These costs are added to the price of products and waste legal resources. *See* "Pender v. Skillcraft Indus., Inc.," 358 So.2d 45 (Fla.Dist. Ct.App.1978).

Under Section 105, product sellers other than manufacturers must exercise reasonable care in their handling of products. This obligation includes inspecting for hazards which a reasonably prudent product seller would have reason to discover. The focus of judicial inquiry will be on the opportunity the non-manufacturer product seller had to discover the hazard and on whether circumstances would permit a reasonable product seller to take corrective action. *See* "Edwards v. E.I. DuPont De Nemours &

Co.," 183 F.2d 165, 167 (5th Cir. 1950).

On the other hand, product sellers other than manufacturers are not liable for harms caused by products which are defective in construction or design, if those products were defective when they were received and the product seller had no reasonable opportunity to discover the defective condition. In addition, such product sellers are generally not liable for harms caused by breaches of the duty to warn or an express warranty unless the product seller's own conduct gave rise to the claim.

Subsection (A) provides that non-manufacturer product sellers are not subject to liability when they had no reasonable opportunity for product inspection which, in the exercise of reasonable care, would or should have revealed the existence of the defective condition. For example, if a retailer receives a defective product in a sealed container and there is no way for the retailer to be aware of the condition, the retailer will not be held liable. In general, Section 105 does not impose liability on non-manufacturer product sellers where there are defects in construction or defects in design that a reasonably prudent product seller would have had no opportunity to discover. The manufacturer can avoid many of these defects; the distributor or retailer cannot. However, a non-manufacturer product seller can waive the benefits of Subsection (A) through an express warranty that it makes or transmits to the product user. *Cf.*

12. *See* "ISO Closed Claims Survey," Report 14, at 118.

"Ky.Rev.Stat.Ann." Section 411.340 (Supp.1978). The term "manufacturer" is defined in Subsection 102(B).

Under Subsection (A), non-manufacturer product sellers are required to exercise reasonable care in their handling and storage of products and to pass along warnings from the manufacturer. Non-manufacturer product sellers are also responsible for defects introduced into the product by virtue of their own negligent conduct (*e.g.*, faulty product preparation or storage). Failure to fulfill their responsibilities will subject non-manufacturer product sellers to liability for their contribution to the harm which results.

Under Subsection (B), the non-manufacturer product seller is subject to the same liability as a manufacturer if the non-manufacturer product seller makes an express warranty. In these situations, such product seller has induced the purchase of the product by these specific words, and courts have been virtually unanimous in holding them responsible if the words prove to be untrue. *See* W. Prosser, "Torts" at 652 (4th ed. 1971).

Subsection (C) addresses the justifiable concern of Justice Traynor in "Vandermark v. Ford Motor Co.," 61 Cal.2d 256, 391 P.2d 168, 171, 37 Cal.Rptr. 896, 899 (1964), that:

In some cases the retailer may be the only member of that enterprise reasonably available to the injured plaintiff. In other cases the retailer himself may play a substantial part in ensuring that the product is safe or

may be in a position to exert pressure on the manufacturer to that end.

A majority of courts have followed the "Vandermark" case and have extended strict liability to retailers. *See, e.g.* "McKisson v. Sales Affiliates, Inc.," 416 S.W.2d 787 (Tex.1967); "Housman v. C.A. Dawson & Co.," 106 Ill.App.2d 225, 245 N.E.2d 886 (1969). *See also* "U.C.C." Section 2–314.

Section 105 responds to Justice Traynor's concern in cases in which it is necessary to do so. If the manufacturer is not subject to service of process or has been judicially declared insolvent, or if a court determines that it would be highly likely that the claimant would be unable to enforce a judgment against the product manufacturer, the retailer, wholesaler, or distributor has the same strict liability obligations as a manufacturer. Thus, the limited liability shield set forth in Subsection (D) only operates when the product manufacturer is reasonably available for suit by the injured claimant.

Some economists may criticize the exception to the general rule set forth in Section 105. Another approach is that of a recently enacted Nebraska statute which flatly exempts non-manufacturer product sellers from liability unless they have been negligent. *See* "Neb.Rev. Stat." Section 25–21, 181 (Supp. 1978). *See also* "Shainberg v. Barlow," 258 So.2d 242, 244 (Miss. 1972)(same result under case law). However, the Nebraska approach can leave a person injured by a *defective* product (as defined in Section 104) without compensation. The Act makes clear that in these situations, the party who actually sold or commercially leased the defective product should bear the loss.

Procedurally, if the claimant commences an action against the retailer, wholesaler, or distributor, and the action is based upon a theory other than the retailer's, wholesaler's, or distributor's own negligence—such as Subsection 104(A)—the defendant would make a motion for dismissal. At that time, the claimant must show that the manufacturer is unavailable under the provisions of Subsection (C). The court would then consider and make a determination regarding the three conditions listed in Subsection (C) concerning the manufacturer. If the claimant commences an action against the retailer, wholesaler, or distributor, and one of the claimant's theories is the negligent conduct of the defendant, the defendant may move to dismiss on the other theory, but the negligence theory will be litigated. If the action is dismissed against the retailer, wholesaler, or distributor under Section 105, the claimant retains the option to proceed against the manufacturer.

Subsection (D) makes clear that the Section sets forth the entire scope of liability of non-manufacturer product sellers.

However, it should be noted that retailers, wholesalers, distributors, or others can become manufacturers for the purposes of this Act to the extent that they design, produce, make, fabricate, construct, or remanufacture a product or component part of a product prior to sale. Such parties can also become manufacturers for the purposes of this Act if they hold themselves out as a manufacturer. *See* Section 102(B) ("manufacturer") and accompanying analysis.

In order for Section 105 to operate fairly toward claimants as well as non-manufacturer product sellers, it is suggested that:

(1) The non-manufacturer product seller be treated as a party for the purposes of discovery under the applicable procedural code. If this step is not taken, the Act may place an undue burden on the claimant in his or her attempt to prove the case; and

(2) The statute of limitation vis-a-vis the non-manufacturer product seller be deemed to have tolled in case the claimant is unable to enforce his or her product liability judgment against the manufacturer.

* * *

Code

§ 106. Unavoidably Dangerous Aspects of Products

(A) An unavoidably dangerous aspect of a product is that aspect incapable, in light of the state of scientific and technological knowledge at the time of manufacture, of being made safe without seriously impairing the product's usefulness.

(B) A product seller shall not be subject to liability for harm caused by an unavoidably dangerous aspect of a product unless:

(1) The product seller knew or had reason to know of the aspect and with that knowledge acted unreasonably in selling the product at all;

(2) The aspect was a defect in construction under Subsection 104(A);

(3) The product seller knew or had reason to know of the aspect and failed to meet a duty to instruct or warn under Subsection 104(C), or to transmit warnings or instructions under Subsection 105(A); or

(4) The product seller expressly warranted that the product was free of the unavoidably dangerous aspect under Subsection 104(D) or 105(B).

* * *

Analysis

§ 106. Unavoidably Dangerous Aspects of Products

Section 106 provides that, in general, a product seller will not be subject to liability for a product which is defective in design when a harm stems from an aspect of the product that is incapable of being made safe in light of the state of scientific and technical knowledge at the time of manufacture. The term "incapable" is meaningless unless it is placed in context. Therefore, Subsection (A) indicates that it applies when the danger cannot be avoided without seriously impairing the product's usefulness.

The approach taken in Section (A) recognizes that there may be circumstances in which a seriously injured person is left without compensation for an injury caused by an unavoidably dangerous aspect of a product; however, for reasons of policy that consumers can appreciate, Section 106 proposes that a product seller not be held responsible for harms that are simply unavoidable. *See* Johnson, "Products Liability 'Reform': A Hazard to Consumers," 56 "N.C.L.Rev." 676, 690 (1978). If the costs of unavoidable harms are to be shifted from the individual, they should be borne by society at large. The policy predicate underlying Section 106 is that it should help encourage research and development without unleashing unreasonably unsafe products on the public. It also makes clear to policymakers that the tort-litigation system is not the means for addressing injuries caused by all product hazards.

Section 106 is based on the "Restatement (Second) of Torts" Section 402A, Comment k (1965). *See also* "N.H.Rev.Stat.Ann." Section 507–D:4 (Supp.1978).

With the exception of one Illinois decision, "Cunningham v. MacNeal Memorial Hosp.," 47 Ill.2d 443, 266 N.E.2d 897 (1970), *subsequently overruled by* "Ill.Ann.Stat." ch. 91, Sections 181–84 (Supp.1979), this approach has been followed by the common law courts throughout the United States. *See, e.g.,* "Moore v. Underwood Memorial Hosp.," 147 N.J.Super. 252, 371 A.2d 105 (1977)(serum hepatitis contracted from blood supplied); "Dalke v. Upjohn Co.," 555 F.2d 245 (9th Cir. 1977)(tooth discoloration from tetracycline); "Chambers v. G.D. Searle & Co.," 441 F.Supp. 377 (D.Md.1975)(stroke allegedly from birth control pills); "Coffer v. Standard Brands, Inc.," 30 N.C.App. 134, 226 S.E.2d 534 (1976)(shell in nuts); "Hines v. St. Joseph's Hospital," 86 N.M. 763, 527 P.2d 1075 (1974)(blood transfusion).

Subsection (A) indicates that the time from which to judge the state of scientific and technological knowledge is the time of manufacture. See "Cochran v. Brooke," 243 Or. 89, 409 P.2d 904 (1966).

Subsection (B) indicates that the product seller shall not be subject to liability for harms caused by unavoidably dangerous aspects of products unless the claimant proves that one of four circumstances occurred.

The first circumstance involves the unusual situation in which the product seller knew or had reason to know of the unavoidably dangerous aspect and, with that knowledge, acted unreasonably in selling the product at all. An example is a product seller who markets a toy that is highly dangerous to children. This example can be contrasted with a pharmaceutical approved by the Food and Drug Administration, when both the government and the manufacturer know of the dangers connected with that product. In that situation, it is clear that this exception should not apply because it would not be unreasonable to sell the product.

The second circumstance deals with defects in construction. It is arguable that, even with the finest quality control, a product that is defective in construction can slip by inspection. Nevertheless, a judgment has been made by a majority of courts to impose strict liability on manufacturers for defects in construction. That judgment is preserved in this Act.

The third circumstance deals with the situation in which the product seller has failed to provide an adequate warning about an unavoidably dangerous aspect of a product. Section 106 is in accord with Subsections 104(C) and 105(A) and is predicated on a fault base—it is only to apply with respect to dangers which were known or could be discovered through the exercise of reasonable care. See "Dalke v. Upjohn," supra; "Chambers v. G.D. Searle & Co.," supra; "Toole v. Richardson–Merrell, Inc.," 251 Cal. App.2d 689, 60 Cal.Rptr. 398 (1967). As these cases reflect, the factual question underlying the legal issue of whether warnings or instructions were adequate is whether a product seller has met its duty to promulgate warnings and instructions commensurate with its actual knowledge gained from research and adverse reaction reports, and its constructive knowledge as measured by scientific literature and other available means of communication. See "Dalke v. Upjohn Co.," supra, 555 F.2d, at 248; "McEwen v. Ortho Pharmaceutical Corp.," 270 Or. 375, 528 P.2d 522, 528–29 (1974). Contra, "Bruce v. Martin–Marietta Corp.," 544 F.2d 442 (10th Cir.1976).

The Section's cross-reference to Subsections 104(C) and 105(A) makes clear that the product seller must meet its obligation to warn, instruct, or transmit warnings or instructions based on new information about an unavoidably dangerous aspect of a product that is discovered *after* the product has been manufactured. *See* "Love v. Wolf," 226 Cal.App.2d 378, 38 Cal.Rptr. 183 (1964); "Sterling Drug, Inc. v. Yarrow," 408 F.2d 978 (8th Cir. 1969). Only those harmed after the duty to warn arose would be entitled to a claim.

Finally, Section 106 makes clear that a product seller can be liable for an unavoidably dangerous aspect of a product if the product seller expressly warranted that the product was free from such aspect. *See* Subsections 104(D) and 105(B).

* * *

Code

§ 107. Relevance of Industry Custom, Safety or Performance Standards, and Practical Technological Feasibility

(A) Evidence of changes in (1) a product's design, (2) warnings or instructions concerning the product, (3) technological feasibility, (4) "state of the art", or (5) the custom of the product seller's industry or business, occurring after the product was manufactured, is not admissible for the purpose of proving that the product was defective in design under Subsection 104(B) or that a warning or instruction should have accompanied the product at the time of manufacture under Subsection 104(C).

If the court finds that the probative value of such evidence substantially outweighs its prejudicial effect and that there is no other proof available, this evidence may be admitted for other relevant purposes if confined to those purposes in a specific court instruction. Examples of "other relevant purposes" include proving ownership or control, or impeachment.

(B) For the purposes of Section 107, "custom" refers to the practices followed by an ordinary product seller in the product seller's industry or business.

(C) Evidence of custom in the product seller's industry or business or of the product seller's compliance or non-compliance with a non-governmental safety or performance standard, existing at the time of manufacture, may be considered by the trier of fact in determining whether a product was defective in design under Subsection 104(B), or whether there was a failure to warn or instruct under Subsection 104(C) or to transmit warnings or instructions under Subsection 105(A).

(D) For the purposes of Section 107, "practical technological feasibility" means the technological, mechanical, and scientific knowledge relating to product safety that was reasonably feasible for use, in light of economic practicality, at the time of manufacture.

(E) If the product seller proves, by a preponderance of the evidence, that it was not within practical technological feasibility for it to make the product safer with respect to design and warnings or instructions at the time of manufacture so as to have prevented claimant's harm, the product seller shall not be subject to liability for harm caused by the product unless the trier of fact determines that:

(1) The product seller knew or had reason to know of the danger and, with that knowledge, acted unreasonably in selling the product at all;

(2) The product was defective in construction under Subsection 104(A);

(3) The product seller failed to meet the post-manufacture duty to warn or instruct under Subsection 104(C)(6); or

(4) The product seller was subject to liability for express warranty under Subsection 104(D) or 105(B).

* * *

Analysis

§ 107. Relevance of Industry Custom, Safety or Performance Standards, and Practical Technological Feasibility

Subsection (A) adopts a fundamental principle of evidence law for the purposes of product liability cases. It excludes the showing of post-manufacture changes in the design of or warnings about a product, technological feasibility, "state of the art," or industry custom when evidence of those changes is offered to show that the product was defective at the time of manufacture. *See* Fed.R.Evid. 407 and Advisory Committee Commentary. The term "state of the art," as used in the listing of evidentiary items in Subsection 107(A), is a general, commonly used phrase whose meaning may include industry custom or the most scientifically advanced developments in the field. As will be indicated in the discussion of Subsections (B) through (E), the Act has generally eschewed the phrase because of its ambiguity. Nevertheless, it has been utilized in Subsection (A) in order to assure that all post-manufacture change is excluded from evidence.

The reasons underlying the rule on which Subsection 107(A) is based are twofold: first, subsequent changes are deemed irrelevant (all they show is that "as one gets older, one may get wiser"); and second, admission of such evidence may discourage the making of improvements or repairs. While the latter rationale has been challenged (*see* "Ault v. International Harvester Co.," 13 Cal.3d 113, 528 P.2d 1148, 117 Cal.Rptr. 812 (1974); Schwartz, "The Exclusionary Rule on Evidence of Repair—A Rule in Need of Repair," 7 "The Forum" 1 (1971)), the relevance of such evidence on the issue of defectiveness is of very limited value. On the other hand, the prejudicial effect of showing the subsequent change or repair—particularly one undertaken by the product seller itself—is quite substantial. *See* "LaMonica v. Outboard Marine Corp.," 48 Ohio App.2d 43, 355 N.E.2d 533 (1976); "Haysom v. Coleman Lantern Co.," 89 Wash.2d 474, 573 P.2d 785 (1978).

Subsection (A) permits the introduction of evidence which would otherwise be excluded under the Subsection, if that evidence is highly probative and necessary to prove a relevant matter other than the fact that the product was defective at the time of manufacture. Thus, evidence of such changes may be admissible to show that the product seller knew of the defect at a certain point in time after manufacture. In appropriate circumstances, this evidence may suggest that the product seller had a duty to take reasonable steps to warn product users about a newly discovered hazard. It may also be admissible when the product seller claims the product hazard was impossible to avoid. In cases of this kind, the court should make a finding that the probative value of the evidence substantially outweighs its prejudicial nature and that there is no other equally probative proof available. Allowing the introduction of evidence in these cases should *not* become a vehicle for avoiding the basic purpose of the rule.

Subsections (B), (C), (D), and (E) address one of the major issues that has divided product sellers and consumer groups concerned about product liability. Product sellers have vigorously argued that when their products comply with the "state of the art," it is unfair to deem them defective. Further, they contend that industry custom is likely to incorporate all cost-justified product safety features. They have received some support for this contention from members of the academic community, at least in regard to purchasers, as contrasted with nonpurchaser product users, of the product. *See* R. Posner, "Economic Analysis of Law" 71 (1972).

Consumer groups respond that it is inappropriate to allow product sellers to fix indirectly their own standard of liability. *See* Johnson, "Products Liability 'Reform': A Hazard to Consumers," 56 "N.C.L.Rev." 677, 680–81 (1978).

When the issue is carefully analyzed, there is less dispute between product sellers and consumer groups than appears on the surface. Part of the sound and fury is a debate over the ambiguous term "state of the art." The approach taken in Subsections (B), (C), (D), and (E) of not using the term "state of the art" eliminates that ambiguity and focuses on what is fair to each party.

Subsection (B) defines "custom" as the "practices followed by the ordinary product seller in the defendant product seller's industry or business." *See* W. Prosser, "Torts" at 166 (4th ed. 1971).

Subsection (C) indicates that compliance with industry custom is merely evidence that the trier of fact may consider in determining whether a product was defective under Subsections 104(B) and (C). There is strong support in the case law for this approach. *See, e.g.,* "Bruce v. Martin–Marietta Corp.," 544 F.2d 442 (10th Cir.1976); "Baker v. Chrysler Corp.," 55 Cal.App.3d 710, 127 Cal.Rptr. 745 (1976); "Maxted v. Pacific Car & Foundry Co.," 527 P.2d 832 (Wyo.1974); "Roach v. Kononen," 269 Or. 457, 525 P.2d 125 (1974); "Olson v. Arctic Enterprises, Inc." 349 F.Supp. 761 (D.N.D.1972).

Subsection (C) also permits introduction of evidence of non-compliance with custom—evidence likely to be introduced by a product liability claimant. While it might be argued that non-compliance with custom should indicate that the product was defective, situations may arise where a product seller followed an alternative procedure that was no less safe (perhaps even safer) than the custom in the industry. For that reason, non-compliance with custom does not create a situation where the trier of fact should consider the product defective *per se*.

Subsection (C) treats compliance or non-compliance with non-governmental product standards in the same manner as custom. Compliance or non-compliance with such standards is admissible in evidence when relevant to the issue before the court. Privately developed standards—for both design and performance—vary widely in their nature and quality. While almost all privately developed standards are labeled "minimum" (suggesting a standard below that which a product seller could reasonably achieve), some standards reach the best level that can be obtained as a practical technological matter. *See* "Task Force Report" at IV–13–17. On the other hand, some are clearly below the level of safety appropriate as a defense in a product liability case. *See* "Report of the National Commission on Product Safety" at 48 (1978)("chronically inadequate both in scope and permissible level of risk").

Compliance with standards that are rigorous and objective (in that they were developed through careful, thorough product testing and a formal product safety evaluation, and up-to-date in light of the technological and scientific knowledge reasonably available at the time the product was manufactured) suggests that a product was not defective. Failure to comply with such standards, especially performance standards, suggests that it was defective. Nevertheless, because of the variance in the nature and quality of privately developed safety standards, the Act has eschewed *per se* rules in this area. *See* "Poches v. J.J. Newberry Co.," 549 F.2d 1166 (8th Cir.1977).

Subsection (D), defining "practical technological feasibility," should be contrasted with Subsection (B)'s definition of "custom." The Subsection (D) definition contemplates a level of safety that was feasible, as a practical matter, at the time of manufacture. "Feasibility" includes economic considerations such as the ability of a product seller to price a product so that it is competitive, but excludes financial considerations peculiar to a particular product seller, such as its cash flow at the relevant time.

The definition's emphasis on *feasibility* addresses consumer concerns with "state-of-the-art" or "custom" defenses that could allow an industry or business to be shielded from liability when it has "negligently" lagged behind in both developing and utilizing safety technology.

Subsection (E) indicates that when a product seller proves by a preponderance of the evidence that it was not within practical technological feasibility to make the product safer, the product seller shall not be subject to liability. This is in accord with the great majority of case law. *See, e.g.,* "Olson v. Arctic Enterprises, Inc.," *supra;* "Wilson v.

Piper Aircraft Corp.," 282 Or. 61, 577 P.2d 1322, 1326 (1978)(" . . . plaintiff's *prima facie* case of a defect must show more than the technical possibility of a safe design"); "Bruce v. Martin–Marietta Corp.," *supra;* "Maxted v. Pacific Car & Foundry Co.," *supra;* "Roach v. Kononen," *supra. Cf.* "Ky.Rev.Stat. Ann." Section 411.310(2)(Supp.1978)(includes custom). *But cf.* "Colo.Rev.Stat." Section 13–21–403 (Supp.1978)("state of the art" presumption only).

Significantly, only a few intermediate appellate court decisions, primarily from one state, impose liability if the product was in accord with the technological, mechanical, and scientific knowledge reasonably feasible for use at the time of manufacture. *See, e.g.,* "Gelsumino v. E.W. Bliss Co.," 10 Ill.App.3d 604, 295 N.E.2d 110 (1973), and its progeny. *But see* "McClellan v. Chicago Transit Authority," 34 Ill.App.3d 151, 340 N.E.2d 61 (1975). *Compare* "Olson v. A.W. Chesterton Co.," 256 N.W.2d 530 (N.D.1977).

In order to meet appropriate consumer group concerns, Subsection (E) provides four exceptions to the defense. First, the defense will not apply if the product seller knew or had reason to know of the danger and, with that knowledge, acted unreasonably in selling the product at all. *See also* Subsection 106(B)(1) and analysis. This exception would only apply in very unusual situations. For example, a child's toy might comply with what was technologically feasible but, because of its danger, it would be unreasonable behavior to market the product for young children. Similarly, it would

be unreasonable to manufacture a home heating unit with a radium core unless technology had reached a point at which the inhabitants of the home (and others) would be protected from radiation.

Second, although the product was in accord with the "practical technological feasibility," it may be defective in construction. It is a basic principle of this Act to apply strict liability against the manufacturer in that case. *See* Subsection 104(A) and analysis.

Third, although the product complied with the "practical technological feasibility" at the time of manufacture, the product seller may have failed to meet its post-manufacture duty to warn or instruct under Subsection 104(C)(6).

Finally, although its product was in accord with "practical technological feasibility," a product seller cannot escape strict liability for express warranty under Subsection 104(D) or 105(B).

* * *

Code

§ 108. Relevance of Legislative or Administrative Regulatory Standards and Mandatory Government Contract Specifications

(A) When the injury-causing aspect of the product was, at the time of manufacture, in compliance with legislative regulatory standards or administrative regulatory safety standards relating to design or performance, the product shall be deemed not defective under Subsection 104(B), or, if the standard addressed warnings or instructions, under Subsection 104(C) or 105(A), unless the claimant proves by a preponderance of the evidence that a reasonably prudent product seller could and would have taken additional precautions.

(B) When the injury-causing aspect of the product was not, at the time of manufacture, in compliance with legislative regulatory standards or administrative regulatory safety standards relating to design or performance, the product shall be deemed defective under Subsection 104(B), or, if the standard addressed warnings or instructions, under Subsection 104(C) or 105(A), unless the product seller proves by a preponderance of the evidence that its failure to comply was a reasonably prudent course of conduct under the circumstances.

(C) When the injury-causing aspect of the product was, at the time of manufacture, in compliance with a mandatory government contract specification relating to design, this shall be an absolute defense and the product shall be deemed not defective under Subsection 104(B), or, if the specification related to warnings or instructions, under Subsection 104(C) or 105(A).

(D) When the injury-causing aspect of the product was not, at the time of manufacture, in compliance with a mandatory government contract specification relating to design, the product shall be deemed defective under Subsection 104(B), or, if the specification related to warnings

or instructions, under Subsection 104(C) or 105(A).

* * *

Analysis

§ 108. Relevance of Legislative or Administrative Regulatory Standards and Mandatory Government Contract Specifications

Product sellers have contended that it is unfair to deem a product defective when the challenged aspect of that product conformed to an applicable administrative or legislative regulatory standard. They note that considerable time and thought are spent in the development of such standards and that the standards are frequently subject to intense public scrutiny prior to the time of their official adoption. Product sellers point to legislative and administrative standards as a resource to provide some predictability within the scope of product liability law. They contend that it is unfair to allow lay jurors to reevaluate a standard that has presumably been drafted by government experts. Furthermore, some product liability loss prevention experts suggest that a defense based on compliance with standards will create incentives for manufacturers to comply with such standards. *See* Task Force "Selected Papers" at 266 (Remarks of Professor Alvin S. Weinstein).

On the other hand, some consumer groups maintain that government standards are often the result of compromise decisions—decisions that are sometimes unduly influenced by industry. These consumer groups point out that some government regulatory bodies may have insufficient personnel or expertise to make independent judgments. The general approach of courts, as well as that embodied in the "Consumer Product Safety Act," 15 "U.S.C." Section 2074(A)(1976) and the "National Traffic and Motor Vehicle Safety Act," 15 "U.S.C." Section 1391(2)(1976), is that government standards are only minimum standards, and that compliance should not be deemed an absolute defense in product liability actions. *See* "Roberts v. May," 583 P.2d 305, 308 (Colo.App.1978). In spite of this, some states have enacted statutes that grant this effect to such compliance. *See* "N.D.Cent.Code" Section 28–01.1–05(3)(Supp.1979); "Utah Code Ann." Section 78–15–6 (1977); "Colo.Rev.Stat." Section 13–21–403 (Supp.1978).

Nevertheless, case law also suggests that government safety standards are often deemed sound and appropriate for application to tort law claims. *See* "Jones v. Hittle Serv., Inc.," 219 Kan. 627, 549 P.2d 1383 (1976)(universally accepted standards for odorizing LP gas outweigh expert opinion); "McDaniel v. McNeil Laboratories, Inc.," 196 Neb. 190, 241 N.W.2d 822 (1976)(determination of the FDA prevails in absence of proof that the manufacturer furnished incomplete, misleading, or fraudulent information); "Simien v. S.S. Kresge Co.," 566 F.2d 551 (5th Cir.1978)(compliance with flammability standard); "Bruce v. Martin–Marietta Corp.,"

544 F.2d 442, 446 (10th Cir.1976)(claimants did "not present any more stringent standards which might have been applicable at the time of manufacture").

The approach taken in Subsection (A) is based on these cases and on the "Restatement (Second) of Torts" Section 288C (1965). When the specific injury-causing aspect of the product conformed to or was in compliance with the legislative or administrative regulatory standard, the product is deemed not defective under Subsection 104(B) when design is relevant, or under Subsection 104(C) or 105(A) when the duty to warn or instruct is relevant, unless the claimant proves by a preponderance of the evidence that a reasonably prudent product seller could and would have taken additional precautions.

This approach has enabled claimants to prevail when legislative or administrative standards did not meet an appropriate level of safety. For example, in "Raymond v. Riegel Textile Corp.," 484 F.2d 1025 (1st Cir.1973), the claimant was able to show that a standard promulgated under the "Flammable Fabrics Act" was outdated. *See also* "Burch v. Amsterdam Corp.," 366 A.2d 1079 (D.C.1976)(when manufacturer knows of greater dangers not included in a statutorily mandated warning, it should bring those precautions to the attention of product users). On the other hand, it recognizes that government safety standards *may* provide an adequate basis for evaluating safety in tort law.

Subsection (B) makes it clear that when the injury-causing aspect of the product did not conform or was not in compliance with a legislative or administrative regulatory standard, the product shall be deemed defective under Subsection 104(B), when design is relevant, or Subsection 104(C), when duty to warn is relevant, unless the product seller shows by a preponderance of the evidence that its failure to comply amounted to reasonably prudent conduct under the circumstances. *See* "Restatement (Second) of Torts" Section 286 (1965). A product seller may be able to prevail under Subsection (B) by showing that compliance would have created greater dangers than non-compliance would have. *Cf.* "Davison v. Williams," 251 Ind. 448, 242 N.E.2d 101 (1968)(violation of safety regulation may be justified in circumstances).

Subsection (C) addresses a highly specialized problem with respect to a product that had been manufactured strictly in accordance with mandatory specifications set forth in a government contract. When compliance with such a standard leads to an injury, the government, not the product seller, is the appropriate defendant. As the court in "Hunt v. Blasius," 55 Ill.App.3d 14, 370 N.E.2d 617, 621–22 (1977), indicated, "public policy dictates that bidders who comply strictly with governmental specifications should be shielded from liability in any respect in which the product complies." When enacting this provision, a legislature should ensure that its own state government bears financial responsibility (either through tort law or through a compensation system) for the harm it

has caused by directing that the product conform to contract specifications.

Subsection (D) provides a counterweight to Subsection (C). If the bidder fails to comply with a mandatory government contract specification, and this failure to comply caused the claimant's injury, the product seller will be deemed liable under Subsection 104(B) if the specification related to design, or under Subsection 104(C) or 105(A) of the specification related to instruction or warnings. If the manufacturer's compliance exceeded the government regulation and the product failed, liability should not be imposed under this Section—in that case, the technical "failure to comply" would not be the proximate cause of the injury that befell claimant.

* * *

Code

§ 109. Notice of Possible Claim Required

(A) An attorney who anticipates filing a claim shall notify all product sellers against whom the claim is likely to be made. The notice of claim shall:

(1) Identify the product as specifically as possible;

(2) State the time, place, circumstances, and events giving rise to the claim;

(3) Give an estimate of compensation or other relief to be sought.

(B) The attorney shall give notice of claim within six (6) months of the date of entering into an attorney-client relationship with the claimant in regard to the claim. For the purposes of Section 109, such a relationship arises when the attorney, or any member or associate of the attorney's firm, agrees to serve the claimant's interests in regard to the anticipated claim.

(C) If the claimant's attorney requests the information at the time the notice of claim is given, the product seller receiving the notice of claim shall promptly furnish the claimant's attorney with the names and addresses of each person whom the product seller knows to be in the chain of manufacture and distribution of the product, and who is likely to be subject to liability under Sections 104 or 105. Any product seller who fails to furnish such information may be subject to liability as provided in Subsection (E).

(D) A claimant who delays entering into an attorney-client relationship so as to delay unreasonably the notice of claim required by Subsection (A) may be subject to liability as provided in Subsection (E).

(E) Any party to the product liability claim or any attorney representing such a party who suffers a monetary loss associated with the litigation of the claim caused by the failure of a claimant or a claimant's attorney, or of a product seller or its attorney, to comply with the requirements of this Section may recover pecuniary damages, costs, and reasonable attorneys' fees from that party. Failure to comply with the requirements of Section 109 does not affect the validity of any claim or defense under this Act.

* * *

Analysis

§ 109. Notice of Possible Claim Required

The purpose of Section 109 is to inform product sellers at an early date that the products they produce may be defective. Under present law, a claimant can delay informing a product seller of a claim until the statute of limitation has nearly expired. In most jurisdictions, this period is two or three years. Although 77.8 percent of all bodily injury claims are reported within six months, the 22.2 percent that are not reported during this period are of concern because they represent about 68 percent of the claim payments. "ISO Closed Claims Survey" at 100 (1977).

A reasonable notice of claim requirement in product liability law promotes the interests of consumers and product users because it is a low-cost means of helping to assure product safety. Presumably, if informed about defective conditions at an early stage, a product seller is likely to take action to correct such conditions and thus prevent future injuries. This is why notice-of-claim provisions have been utilized in other contexts. *See, e.g.,* "U.C.C." Section 2–607 (warranty breaches); 18 E. McQuillan, "Municipal Corporations" Section 53.154 (3d ed. 1977)(suits against municipalities for injuries); 3 A. Larson, "Workmen's Compensation Law" Section 78.00 *et seq.* (1976)(notice of injury to employer). *See also* Comment, "Notice Requirement in Warranty Actions Involving Personal Injury,"

51 "Calif.L.Rev." 586 (1963); Phillips, "Notice of Breach in Sales and Strict Tort Liability Law: Should There Be a Difference?," 47 "Ind. L.J." 457, 468–69 (1972)(observing that requiring notice of claim may encourage defendants to make reasonable settlements).

This Section is adapted from the recently enacted "Minn.Stat. Ann." Section 604.04 (Supp.1978). It differs from analogous notice-of-claim provisions in that it does not provide that a claim or defense will be barred by the failure of the injured party to meet its conditions. As the court noted in "Greenman v. Yuba Power Prods., Inc.," 59 Cal.2d 57, 377 P.2d 897, 900, 27 Cal.Rptr. 697, 700 (1963), such a provision may

> become a booby trap for the unwary. The injured consumer is seldom "steeped in the business practice which justifies the rule." [James, "Products Liability" (pt. 2), 34 "Tex.L.Rev." 192, 197 (1955)]and at least until he has had legal advice it will not occur to him to give notice . . . .

Instead, Section 109 places a duty on the attorney to give the notice of claim. It imposes on the attorney the costs of investigation and other litigation expenses which stem from the failure to give notice.

Section 109 also places a burden on the product seller who is notified of an anticipated claim to provide the claimant's attorney with the names and addresses of others whom the product seller knows to be in the chain of manufacture and distribution of the product, and who

are likely to be subject to liability under Sections 104 or 105. The product seller is not obligated, however, to supply long lists of every supplier of a component part of its product or every possible wholesale and retail purchaser of it. Product sellers may also be held liable under this Section for litigation costs that stem from the failure to provide the required names.

Subsection 109(E) is limited to losses associated directly with the litigation of the claim in issue and does not apply to possible losses suffered by persons other than a party to the product liability claim or any attorney representing such a party.

Claims arising under Section 109 can be consolidated with the principal product liability claim brought under this Act.

* * *

Code

§ 110. Length of Time Product Sellers Are Subject to Liability

(A) *Useful Safe Life.*

(1) Except as provided in Subsection (A)(2), a product seller shall not be subject to liability to a claimant for harm under this Act if the product seller proves by a preponderance of the evidence that the harm was caused after the product's "useful safe life" had expired.

"Useful safe life" begins at the time of delivery of the product and extends for the time during which the product would normally be likely to perform or be stored in a safe manner. For the purposes of Section

110, "time of delivery" means the time of delivery of a product to its first purchaser or lessee who was not engaged in the business of either selling such products or using them as component parts of another product to be sold.

Examples of evidence that is especially probative in determining whether a product's useful safe life had expired include:

(a) The amount of wear and tear to which the product had been subject;

(b) The effect of deterioration from natural causes, and from climate and other conditions under which the product was used or stored;

(c) The normal practices of the user, similar users, and the product seller with respect to the circumstances, frequency, and purposes of the product's use, and with respect to repairs, renewals, and replacements;

(d) Any representations, instructions, or warnings made by the product seller concerning proper maintenance, storage, and use of the product or the expected useful safe life of the product; and

(e) Any modification or alteration of the product by a user or third party.

(2) A product seller may be subject to liability for harm caused by a product used beyond its useful safe life to the extent that the product seller has expressly warranted the product for a longer period.

(B) *Statute of Repose.*

(1) *Generally.* In claims that involve harm caused more than ten (10) years after time of delivery, a presumption arises that the harm was caused after the useful safe life had expired. This presumption may only be rebutted by clear and convincing evidence.

(2) *Limitations on Statute of Repose.*

(a) If a product seller expressly warrants that its product can be utilized safely for a period longer than ten (10) years, the period of repose, after which the presumption created in Subsection (B)(1) arises, shall be extended according to that warranty or promise.

(b) The ten–(10–) year period of repose established in Subsection (B)(1) does not apply if the product seller intentionally misrepresents facts about its product, or fraudulently conceals information about it, and that conduct was a substantial cause of the claimant's harm.

(c) Nothing contained in Subsection (B) shall affect the right of any person found liable under this Act to seek and obtain contribution or indemnity from any other person who is responsible for harm under this Act.

(d) The ten–(10–) year period of repose established in Subsection (B)(1) shall not apply if the harm was caused by prolonged exposure to a defective product, or if the injury-causing aspect of the product that existed at the time of delivery was not discoverable by an ordinary reasonably prudent person until more than ten (10) years after the time of delivery, or if the harm, caused within ten (10) years after the time of delivery, did not manifest itself until after that time.

(C) *Statute of Limitation.* No claim under this Act may be brought more than two (2) years from the time the claimant discovered, or in the exercise of due diligence should have discovered, the harm and the cause thereof.

* * *

Analysis

§ 110. Length of Time Product Sellers Are Subject to Liability

Perhaps more significant than any other single factor alleged to be the cause of the nationwide product liability insurance problem are the rules governing the responsibility of product sellers for older products. Most product liability policies include claims based not only on products manufactured or sold during the given policy year, but also on products manufactured or sold in the past. In the case of sellers of durable goods, this creates an "open-ended" liability situation.

The Supreme Court of Oregon summarized the general common law rule for products with the statement: "[P]rolonged use of a manufactured article is but one factor, albeit an important one, in the determination of whether a defect in the product made it unsafe.... " "Tucker v. Unit Crane & Shovel Corp.," 256 Or. 318, 473 P.2d 862 (1970)(boom crane manufactured in 1956, collapsed in 1965). *See also* "Gates v. Ford Motor Company," 494 F.2d 458 (10th Cir.1974)(24–year–old tractor); "Kaczmarek v.

Mesta Machinery Co.," 463 F.2d 675 (3d Cir.1972) (30–year–old pickling machine); "Mondshour v. General Motors Corp.," 298 F.Supp. 111 (D.Md.1969)(bus designed 17 years prior to accident).

Partly in response to this open-ended liability potential, a number of states have enacted statutes of repose that begin at the time a product is first sold and distributed. *See, e.g.,* "1979 Ala. Acts" No. 79–468, Section 3(b)("10 years after the manufactured product is first put to use"); "Ariz.Rev.Stat.Ann." Section 12–551 (Supp.1978)("12 years after the product was first sold for use or consumption ..."); "Fla.Stat.Ann." Section 95.031(2)(Supp.1979)("12 years after the date of delivery of the completed product"); "Ill.Ann. Stat." ch. 83, Section 22.2(b)(Supp.1979)(12 years from date of first sale or 10 years from sale to actual user-claimant—strict liability); "Ind.Code Ann." Section 33–1–1.5–5 (Supp.1978)("10 years after the delivery ... to the initial user"); "Neb.Rev.Stat." Section 25–224 (Supp.1978)(10 years after first sale); "Utah Code Ann." Section 78–15–3(1)(1977)(6 years after date of initial purchase; 10 years after date of manufacture).

The advantages of these statutes are that they: (1) establish an actuarially certain date after which no liability can be assessed; and (2) eliminate tenuous claims involving older products for which evidence of defective conditions may be difficult to produce. *See* "Order of Railroad Telegraphers v. Railway Express Agency," 321 U.S. 342, 348–49 (1944).

On the other hand, a fundamental problem with these statutes is that they *may* deprive a person injured by a product of the right to bring a claim based on a defective product before the injury has actually occurred. *See* Johnson, "Products Liability 'Reform': A Hazard to Consumers," 56 "N.C.L.Rev." 677, 689–90 (1978); "Victorson v. Bock Laundry Mach. Co.," 37 N.Y.2d 395, 335 N.E.2d 275, 373 N.Y.S.2d 39 (1975).

The limited available data show that insurers' apprehension about older products may be exaggerated. *See* "ISO Closed Claims Survey" at 105–08 (indicating that over 97 percent of product-related accidents occur within six years of the time the product was purchased and, in the capital goods area, 83.5 percent of all bodily injury accidents occur within ten years of manufacture). Nevertheless, as the "Task Force Report" indicated, the underwriters' concern about *potential* losses associated with older products may be an important factor in the recent increase in liability insurance premiums for manufacturers of durable goods. *See* "Task Force Report" at VII–21.

Section 110 attempts to provide insurers and product sellers with some security against stale claims, while preserving the claimant's right to obtain damages for injuries caused by defective products. It accomplishes this result through provisions on useful safe life, a statute of repose, and a statute of limitation.

(A) *Useful Safe Life.* The common law in most states is that "[t]he age of an allegedly defective product must be considered in light of its expected useful life and the stress to which it has been subjected." "Kuisis v. Baldwin–Lima–Hamilton Corp.," 457 Pa. 321, 319 A.2d 914, 923 (1974)(brake-locking mechanism on a crane failed after more than 20 years of use). The "Kuisis" court noted further that "in certain situations the prolonged use factor may loom so large as to obscure all others in a case." *Id.*

The basic problem has been the vagueness of the concept. Thus, while the "Task Force Report" noted that "if a useful life limitation were identified in statutory form, it might be expected that it would be given more serious attention by both judge and jury" ("Task Force Report" at VII–27), it also observed that "the concept would still lack specificity." *Id.* Subsection (A) is designed to define the concept with as much specificity as possible.

The Subsection was derived from "Minn.Stat.Ann." Section 604.03 (Supp.1978). It serves to remind the court and the trier of fact that a product seller may be held liable only for harms caused during the useful *safe* life of the product. It does not attempt to apply fixed useful safe life standards for all products. Such an approach is not possible as a practical matter. *See* Phillips, "An Analysis of Proposed Reform of Products Liability Statutes of Limitations," 56 "N.C.L.Rev." 663, 673 (1978). Rather, it identifies factors that will assist the court and the trier of fact in determining how long a product can reasonably be expected to perform or be stored in a safe manner.

Section 110 uses the term "useful safe life" (not "useful life," a term which has already acquired a meaning in the law of taxation), because the period in which the product can have some "utility" may be well beyond the period in which the product is "safe." For example, a driver may continue to "use" tires that lack sufficient treads for safety.

A product seller may raise the "useful safe life" of a product as an affirmative defense in a product liability claim. The period of time begins at the time of delivery of the product and extends through the time during which the product would normally be likely to perform in a safe manner.

"Time of delivery" is defined as the time of delivery of a product to its first purchaser or lessee not engaged in the business of either selling such products or using them as component parts of another product to be sold. "Time of delivery" is an important concept in the Act because it marks the last time a product seller has physical control of the product and the first time that the product is in the hands of someone other than a product seller. The useful safe life and repose periods of Section 110 begin to run from this point in time.

The Section then sets forth a series of factors that will be of assistance to the court and jury in determining whether the period of time has expired. The product seller need not introduce evidence with respect to each of the listed factors. Rather, each of the litigants in a product liability claim may introduce evidence on those factors listed which, they believe, will support their respective contentions. In some cases, evidence on one or a few of the factors may be regarded as dispositive of the "useful safe life" issue and, when this occurs, the lack of evidence on one of the other factors normally will not affect the outcome of the case. The product seller has the burden of proof upon the issue.

Factors (a) through (c) under Subsection (A) are basically self-explanatory. Factor (d) refers to the useful safe life stated *by the product seller*. A product seller can place some reliance on this provision when it has indicated that a product should not be used beyond a certain period of time. However, Subsection (A) does not give the product seller absolute power to limit a product's useful safe life. While this was suggested in "Velez v. Craine & Clark Lumber Corp.," 33 N.Y.2d 117, 305 N.E.2d 750, 350 N.Y.S.2d 617 (1973), almost all courts would insist on retaining judicial power to determine whether the product seller's limitation was a reasonable one. *Cf.* "Henningsen v. Bloomfield Motors, Inc.," 32 N.J. 358, 161 A.2d 69 (1960). Further, even the "Velez" court indicated that a product seller's limitation on useful life could not bind the rights of a non-purchaser claimant. Nevertheless, where the product seller imposes a reasonable limitation, made in good faith to protect the user, the trier of fact should give very serious consideration to this fact in determining whether the product was used beyond its useful safe life.

Factor (e), dealing with modifications of the product by users or third parties, relates to conduct that might shorten or lengthen the useful life of the product. While the Act treats product modifications in Section 112, they are also factors in determining whether a product has been used beyond its useful safe life.

(B) *Statute of Repose.*

(1) *Generally.* Statutes of repose differ from statutes of limitation in that they set a fixed limit after the time of the product's manufacture, sale, or delivery beyond which the product seller will not be held liable. The rationale of such statutes is threefold. First, the fact that a product has been used safely for a substantial period of time is some indication that it was not defective at the time of delivery. Second, if a product seller is not aware of a claim, the passing of time may make it extremely difficult to construct a good defense because of the obstacle of securing evidence. Although the burden of proof on the issue of defectiveness remains on the claimant under the Act, a jury, as a practical matter, may demand an explanation from a product seller when the claimant has suffered a severe injury. The third rationale is that persons ought to be allowed, as a matter of policy, to plan their affairs with a reasonable degree of certainty. This goes to the heart of the product liability insurance rate-setting problem. Even though past data show that 83.5 percent of bodily injury claims arise within a ten-year period,[13] there is no safeguard in the existing law that the past will portend the future. There is always the possibility that the number of claims for older products will in-

crease. *See* "ISO Closed Claims Survey" at 107.

On the other hand, consumers are justifiably concerned about overly broad absolute cut-offs of their right to sue. This provision recognizes consumer concerns in three basic ways:

(1) The term of the statute is ten years—beyond the term enacted or proposed in a number of states;

(2) The statute begins to run at the time of delivery, not the time of manufacture; and

(3) The statute does not contain an absolute cut-off, but rather a presumption that the product has been used beyond its useful safe life. Colorado law utilizes this approach. "Colo.Rev.Stat." Section 13–21–403(3)(Supp.1978). Most other state product liability statutes do not.

Consumer concerns are also addressed by three of the four additional restrictions contained in Subsection (B)(2).

(2) *Limitations on Statute of Repose.* This Subsection contains four key limitations on its scope of operation.

First, Subsection (B) does not apply when a product seller has expressly warranted or promised that a product can be used safely for a period longer than ten years. *See* Subsection 102(K)(definition of "express warranty").

Second, the statute of repose provisions do not apply when a product seller intentionally misrepresented facts about its product and

---

13.   Figure for capital goods.

this misrepresentation was a substantial cause of claimant's harm.

Third, Subsection (B) does not affect contribution and indemnity claims. Thus, an intermediate product seller will not have to absorb a liability loss that was the true responsibility of the original manufacturer. *See* Defense Research Institute, "Products Liability Position Paper" at 22 (monograph 1976); *see also* Phillips, *supra,* 56 "N.C.L.Rev." at 670–71 (1978).

Fourth, there is an exception for products that cause perceptible harm only through prolonged exposure (*see, e.g.,* "Michie v. Great Lakes Steel Div., National Steel Corp.," 495 F.2d 213 (6th Cir. 1974)), or that cause harms that take many years to manifest themselves. *See* "Sindell v. Abbott Laboratories," 85 Cal.App.3d 1, 149 Cal. Rptr. 138 (1978). An exception is also made for the unusual situation in which a product contains, at the time of delivery, a hidden defect that is not discoverable by a reasonably prudent product user and does not manifest itself until after a ten-year period has expired. *See* "Mickle v. Blackmon," 252 S.C. 202, 166 S.E.2d 173 (1969)(plastic used on gearshift lost its resiliency when exposed to sunlight).

If the ten-year presumption does not apply, a product seller can still prove that the product has been utilized beyond its useful safe life under Subsection (A).

(C) *Statute of Limitation.* Tort statutes of limitation traditionally begin at the time a person is injured. This Subsection follows that approach. Nevertheless, in accord with justified consumer concerns, Subsection (C) extends the limitation period beyond the time of harm in situations where the claimant would have no reason to know about the harm or the causal connection to a defective product (*e.g.,* the case of long-term pharmaceutical harms). This reflects a general trend in both statutory and case law. *See* Birnbaum, " 'First Breath's' Last Gasp: The Discovery Rule in Products Liability Cases," 13 "Forum" 279 (1977); and Annot., 91 "A.L.R.3d" 991 (1979). The two-year period represents the length of the traditional state statute of limitation based on claims for negligence. In light of the Act's adoption of the discovery rule, this is the maximum period that seemed to be appropriate.

The underlying philosophy of this Section is congruent with Sections 105 and 106, which shield product sellers from liability for risks that they would have no reason to discover at the time of manufacture.

* * *

Code

§ 111. Comparative Responsibility and Apportionment of Damages

(A) *Comparative Responsibility.* All claims under this Act shall be governed by the principles of comparative responsibility. In any claim under this Act, the comparative responsibility of, or attributed to, the claimant shall not bar recovery but shall diminish the award of compensatory damages proportionately, according to the measure of responsibility attributed to the claimant.

(B) *Apportionment of Damages.*

(1) In all claims involving comparative responsibility, the court, unless otherwise agreed by all parties, shall instruct the jury to answer special interrogatories or, if there is no jury, the court shall make findings, indicating:

(a) The amount of damages each claimant would be entitled to recover if the comparative responsibility of each party were disregarded; and

(b) The percentage of the total responsibility of all parties to each claim that is to be allocated to each claimant; defendant; third-party defendant; person or entity who misused, modified, or altered a product under Subsection 112(C) or (D), [or who voluntarily and unreasonably used or stored a product with a known defective condition under Subsection 112(B)]; and person released from liability under Subsection 113(E). Under this Subsection, the court may determine that two or more persons are to be treated as a single party.

(2) When the claimant's employer's or co-employee's fault is considered, damages shall be reduced in accordance with Subsection 114(A), if applicable, or by the percentage of responsibility apportioned to such employer or co-employee, if that amount is greater. When a person released from liability under Subsection 113(E) would otherwise be liable under this Act, damages shall be reduced by the percentage of responsibility apportioned to such person.

(3) In determining the percentages of responsibility, the trier of fact shall consider, on a comparative basis, both the nature of the conduct of each person or entity responsible and the extent of the proximate causal relation between the conduct and the damages claimed.

(4) The court shall determine the award of damages to each claimant in accordance with the findings and enter judgment against each party liable. For purposes of contribution under Section 113, the court shall also determine and state in the judgment each party's equitable share of the obligation to each claimant in accordance with the respective percentages of responsibility.

(5) Damages are to be apportioned severally, and not jointly, when a party is responsible for a distinct harm, or when there is some other reasonable basis for apportioning that party's responsibility for the harm. Otherwise, judgment shall be entered against each party liable on the basis of the rules of joint and several liability.

(6) When one or more parties made a substantial contribution to an indivisible harm, or for other reasons under the common law of the state is a joint tortfeasor, upon motion made not later than one (1) year after judgment is entered, the court shall determine whether all or part of a joint tortfeasor's share of the obligation is uncollectible from that joint tortfeasor.

If the court's finding is in the affirmative, the court shall reallocate any uncollectible amount among a claimant found to be responsible and other parties who are joint tortfeasors with the party whose share is uncollectible. The reallocation shall be made according to the respective percentages of responsibility of each party.

* * *

Analysis

§ 111. Comparative Responsibility and Apportionment of Damages

(A) *Comparative Responsibility.* Subsection (A) attempts to resolve existing legal uncertainty about the relevance of a claimant's conduct and the comparative responsibility of others who contributed to the claimant's harm. It applies principles of comparative responsibility to situations where more than one person has some responsibility for the product-related incident. *Cf.* "Uniform Comparative Fault Act" ("UCFA") Section 1. The consumer-oriented fairness of pure comparative responsibility is adopted, as compared with the "non-discriminating rough justice of the modified type. . . . " "Prefatory Note," "UCFA".

Although there is no assurance that the use of comparative responsibility principles will lower the cost of product liability claims, the inher-

ent fairness of such principles has led to their inclusion in the "UCFA" by the National Conference of Commissioners of Uniform State Laws. Section 111 borrows extensively from the "UCFA" and its accompanying commentary.

Some courts and commentators have voiced concern about the semantic and theoretical difficulties of mixing the "apples" of negligence with the "oranges" of strict liability. *See, e.g.,* "Kirkland v. General Motors Corp.," 521 P.2d 1353 (Okla. 1974); Robinson, "Square Pegs (Products Liability) in Round Holes (Comparative Negligence)," 52 "Cal. St.B.J." 16 (1977). Nevertheless, these concerns appear to be more theoretical than real.

The utility of comparative responsibility for product liability cases has been appreciated both by state legislatures[14] and courts.[15] It has also been recommended by a congressional subcommittee. "La Falce Subcommittee Report," *supra* at 76.

Section 111 places a strong incentive for loss prevention on the party who is best able to accomplish that goal. It also avoids burdening the careful product user with liability insurance costs assessed to persons who misuse or are otherwise at fault in their handling of products. While some economic analyses indicate that a comparative responsibili-

---

14. *E.g.,* "Ark.Stat.Ann." Section 27–1763–1765 (Supp.1977); "Me.Rev.Stat." tit. 14 Section 156 (Supp.1978); "Mich.Comp. Laws Ann." Section 600.2949 (Supp.1978), "Mich.Stat.Ann." Section 27A.2949; Conn. (1979 Conn.Pub.Acts 79–483, Section 4).

15. *E.g.,* "Thibault v. Sears, Roebuck & Co.," 395 A.2d 843 (N.H.1978); "Daly v. General Motors Corp.," 20 Cal.3d 725, 575 P.2d 1162, 144 Cal.Rptr. 380 (1978); "Busch v. Busch Constr., Inc.," 262 N.W.2d 377 (Minn. 1977); "Butaud v. Suburban Marine & Sport. Goods, Inc.," 555 P.2d 42 (Alaska 1976).

ty system creates a risk of economic inefficiency because of an overinvestment in safety, the drafters of the Act have made a value judgment that such an "overinvestment" is worth making.

(B) *Apportionment of Damages.* In order to apply comparative responsibility principles under this Act, it is necessary for the trier of fact to supply certain information in special interrogatories. Subsection (B)(1)(a), which is based on "UCFA" Subsection 2(A)(1), indicates that the trier of fact should set forth the amount of damages a claimant would receive if each party's comparative responsibility were disregarded. This helps assure that the trier of fact does not inflate or deflate the amount of damages claimant would receive if the claimant were free from responsibility.

Subsection (B)(1)(b), which is based on "UCFA" Subsection 2(a)(2), requires the trier of fact to indicate the percentage of responsibility allocated to each claimant; defendant; third-party defendant; and person or entity who has misused, altered, or modified products under Subsections 112(C) or (D). It also includes persons or entities who voluntarily and unreasonably used or stored a product with a known defective condition under Subsection 112(B)(2). As is noted in the analysis to that Subsection, this is an optional provision.

Although it is difficult to apportion the responsibility of an absent employer or co-employee who is immune from tort liability due to Worker Compensation laws, such an approach is necessary to ensure fairness to product sellers. It is also fair to employees because they have given up their right to sue in tort for harms caused by their employers' or co-employees' fault in exchange for their Worker Compensation benefits.

Subsection 111(B)(2) indicates that in cases of product misuse or alteration where an employer's or co-employee's fault is considered, damages should be reduced by the amount of Worker Compensation benefits the worker received or will receive in accordance with Subsection 114(A), or by the percentage of responsibility apportioned to such employer or co-employee, whichever is greater.

Thus, for example, in a case in which a manufacturer is found to have been 40 percent responsible, the injured employee's employer was 60 percent responsible, and Worker Compensation benefits constituted 15 percent of the damages, then the claimant's damages would be reduced by 60 percent, not 85 percent. On the other hand, if the manufacturer had been 80 percent responsible, the employer was 20 percent responsible, and Worker Compensation benefits constituted 30 percent of the damages, then the claimant's damages would be reduced by 30 percent, which was the amount of the Worker Compensation benefits and was greater than the employer's percentage (20 percent) of responsibility.

When a released party's fault is considered, the process is simpler. Damages are reduced according to the percentage of fault which the trier of fact attributes to that person or entity.

Subsection (B)(1)(b) also indicates that persons who have been released under Subsection 113(E) shall be included in the apportionment of responsibility. This approach is in accord with the "UCFA" and the majority of cases that have addressed this issue. Again, while it is difficult to apportion an absent person's fault, the approach helps to ensure that all releases are executed in good faith. *See* "Frey v. Snelgrove," ___ Minn. ___, 269 N.W.2d 918 (1978); "Bartels v. City of Williston," 276 N.W.2d 113 (N.D.1979); "Pierringer v. Hoger," 21 Wis.2d 182, 124 N.W.2d 106 (1963).

Subsection (B)(3), which is based on "UCFA" Subsection 2(b), provides a general guideline to assist the trier of fact in comparing responsibility among the parties. The "UCFA" comments (Section 2) indicate that in appropriate cases, the trier of fact may also consider:

(1) Whether the conduct was mere inadvertence or engaged in with an awareness of the danger involved;

(2) The magnitude of the risk created by the conduct, including the number of persons endangered and the potential seriousness of the injury;

(3) The significance of what the actor was seeking to attain by his conduct;

(4) The actor's superior or inferior capacities; and

(5) The particular circumstances, such as the existence of an emergency requiring a hasty decision.

"UCFA Comment" Section 2 ("percentages of fault").

"The extent of the proximate causal relation between the conduct and the damages claimed" refers to proximate cause as opposed to cause-in-fact. While, at times, the distinction may be a difficult one to draw, this Act is premised on apportioning responsibility only—pure causation in terms of cause-in-fact is irrelevant to that concept. *See* Malone, "Ruminations on Cause-in-Fact," 9 "Stan.L.Rev." 60 (1956). Proximate cause, on the other hand, is an important concept in this Section. In order for the product user's conduct to bring about a reduction or apportionment of damages, it must be a proximate cause of the harm.

The importance of the distinction between cause-in-fact and proximate cause as applied to this Section may be illustrated by the so-called "second collision case" in which the claimant sues the manufacturer for enhanced injuries due to an alleged defect in the automobile, although the initial impact of the accident was caused by the claimant's or another person's negligent driving. When the enhanced injuries caused by the "second collision" within the automobile can be reasonably separated from those injuries caused by the initial collision, damages should be approximately divided. Nevertheless, the negligent driving should not be compared with the manufacturer's conduct because it is not the proximate cause of the enhanced injuries, even though it is clearly a cause-in-fact. *See* "Austin v. Ford Motor Co.," 86

Wis.2d 628, 273 N.W.2d 233, 239 (1979).

On the other hand, there may be "second collision cases" in which the enhanced injuries and the initial impact injuries cannot be reasonably separated. Such a case might arise when an allegedly defective automobile was hit at high speed. *See* "Fietzer v. Ford Motor Co.," 590 F.2d 215 (7th Cir.1978). In such a case, the driver's conduct is considered a proximate cause of the harm for purposes of comparative responsibility.

Subsection (B)(3), which is based on "UCFA" Subsection 2(c), helps to assure that the mathematics of comparative responsibility will be correctly determined. The court must determine the award for each claimant according to the findings made under this Subsection.

Subsections (B)(4) and (5) indicate that the common law rules of joint and several liability continue to apply under this Act. In this connection, it is important for the court to determine whether the defendant *is* a joint tortfeasor, *i.e.,* if its tortious conduct was a substantial cause of an indivisible injury, or it is otherwise deemed to have that status (*e.g.,* persons acting in concert, express or implied; persons vicariously liable for the torts of another). *See* W. Prosser, "Torts" at 297–99 (4th ed. 1971). A defendant who caused only a divisible part of the claimant's harm is only severally liable for that portion. *See* "UCFA Comment" Section 4, and "Restatement (Second) of Torts" Section 433A (1965).

As with "UCFA" Subsection 2(c), the judgment for each claimant will also show the share of each party's total obligation to the claimant. This should save litigation costs and avoid the need for a special motion or a separate action on the issue.

Subsection (B)(5) follows "UCFA" Subsection 2(d) in providing for the reallocation of damages among the parties responsible when one of the parties' share is uncollectible. The reallocation procedure applies to claimants who are contributorily at fault and joint tortfeasors who have made a substantial contribution to claimant's harm.

* * *

Code

§ 112. Conduct Affecting Comparative Responsibility

(A) *Failure to Discover a Defective Condition.*

(1) *Claimant's Failure to Inspect.* A claimant is not required to have inspected the product for a defective condition. Failure to have done so does not render the claimant responsible for the harm caused or reduce the claimant's damages.

(2) *Claimant's Failure to Observe an Apparent Defective Condition.* When the product seller proves by a preponderance of the evidence that the claimant, while using the product, was injured by a defective condition that would have been apparent, without inspection, to an ordinary reasonably prudent person, the claimant's damages shall be subject to reduction. The procedural

principles governing reduction of damages are set forth in Section 111.

(3) *A Non–Claimant's Failure to Inspect for Defects or to Observe an Apparent Defective Condition.* A non-claimant's failure to inspect for a defective condition or to observe an apparent defective condition that would have been obvious, without inspection, to an ordinary reasonably prudent person, shall not reduce claimant's damages.

(B) *Use of a Product With a Known Defective Condition.*

(1) *By a Claimant.* When the product seller proves, by a preponderance of the evidence, that the claimant knew about the product's defective condition, and voluntarily used the product or voluntarily assumed the risk of harm from the product, the claimant's damages shall be subject to reduction to the extent that the claimant did not act as an ordinary reasonably prudent person under the circumstances. Under this Subsection, the trier of fact may determine that the claimant should bear sole responsibility for harm caused by a defective product. The procedural principles governing reduction of damages are set forth in Section 111.

* Optional Section

[(2) *By a Non-claimant Product User.* If the product seller proves by a preponderance of the evidence that a product user, other than the claimant, knew about a product's defective condition, but voluntarily and unreasonably used or stored the product and thereby caused claimant's harm, the claimant's damages shall be subject to apportionment. The procedural principles governing apportionment of damages are set forth in Section 111.]

(C) *Misuse of a Product.*

(1) "Misuse" occurs when the product user does not act in a manner that would be expected of an ordinary reasonably prudent person who is likely to use the product in the same or similar circumstances.

(2) When the product seller proves, by a preponderance of the evidence, that product misuse by a claimant, or by a party other than the claimant or the product seller, has caused the claimant's harm, the claimant's damages shall be subject to reduction or apportionment to the extent that the misuse was a cause of the harm. Under this Subsection, the trier of fact may determine that the harm arose solely because of product misuse. The procedural principles governing reduction or apportionment of damages are set forth in Section 111.

(3) Under this Subsection, subject to state and federal law regarding immunity in tort, the trier of fact may determine that a party or parties who misused the product and thereby caused claimant's harm should bear partial or sole responsibility for harm caused by the product and are subject to liability to the claimant.

(D) *Alteration or Modification of a Product.*

(1) "Alteration or modification" occurs when a person or entity other than the product seller changes the design, construction, or formula of the product, or changes

or removes warnings or instructions that accompanied or were displayed on the product. "Alteration or modification" of a product includes the failure to observe routine care and maintenance, but does not include ordinary wear and tear.

(2) When the product seller proves, by a preponderance of the evidence, that an alteration or modification of the product by the claimant, or by a party other than the claimant or the product seller, has caused the claimant's harm, the claimant's damages shall be subject to reduction or apportionment to the extent that the alteration or modification was a cause of the harm. Under this Subsection, the trier of fact may determine that the harm arose solely because of the product alteration or modification.

This Subsection shall not be applicable if:

(a) The alteration or modification was in accord with the product seller's instructions or specifications;

(b) The alteration or modification was made with the express or implied consent of the product seller; or

(c) The alteration or modification was reasonably anticipated conduct under Subsection 102(G), and the product was defective under Subsection 104(C) because of the product seller's failure to provide adequate warnings or instructions with respect to the alteration or modification.

The procedural principles governing reduction or apportionment of damages are set forth in Section 111.

(3) Under this Subsection, subject to state and federal law regarding immunity in tort, the trier of fact may determine that a party or parties who altered or modified the product and thereby caused claimant's harm should bear partial or sole responsibility for harm caused by the product and are subject to liability to the claimant.

* * *

Analysis

§ 112. Conduct Affecting Comparative Responsibility

(A) *Failure to Discover a Defective Condition.*

(1) *Claimant's Failure to Inspect.* Under common law, the product user had an obligation to inspect for defects; failure to do so could bar a claim. *See* "Palmer v. Massey–Ferguson, Inc.," 3 Wash.App. 508, 476 P.2d 713 (1970). However, under modern tort law, the product user is entitled to assume that the product is reasonably safe for its ordinary use. *See* "Restatement (Second) of Torts" Section 402A (1965); "Cepeda v. Cumberland Eng'r. Co.," 76 N.J. 152, 386 A.2d 816 (1978). Subsection (A) follows these cases and does not require the product user or consumer to inspect a product for a defect. *See* "Kassouf v. Lee Bros.," 209 Cal.App.2d 568, 26 Cal.Rptr. 276 (1962) (plaintiff, without inspection, ate a chocolate bar containing worms and maggots).

(2) *Claimant's Failure to Observe an Apparent Defective Condition.* Cases can arise where a defect

would be apparent, without inspection, to an ordinary reasonably prudent person. Subsection (A)(2) incorporates the Task Force's views in this area, permitting the trier of fact to consider this conduct and reduce claimant's damages. Under Comment n to the "Restatement (Second) of Torts" Section 402A, an individual who failed to discover an apparent defective condition would, theoretically, still be allowed a full claim. On the other hand, if that person knew about the defect and proceeded anyway, the claim would be totally barred. This approach has led to considerable litigation and expense over the issue of whether a claimant knew or did not know about a particular defect. *See* "Task Force Report" at VII–51–53; *see also* "Karabatsos v. Spivey Co.," 49 Ill. App.3d 317, 364 N.E.2d 319 (1977); "Teagle v. Fischer & Porter Co.," 89 Wash.2d 149, 570 P.2d 438 (1977); "Poches v. J.J. Newberry Co.," 549 F.2d 1166 (8th Cir.1977). The Act eliminates this distinction and focuses on the true responsibility of the product user.

Thus, if a claimant with good eyesight ate a candy bar that had bright green worms crawling over it, Subsection (A)(2) permits the trier of fact to find that the claimant should bear some responsibility for any ill effects suffered. This example involves a defective condition that can be discovered without inspection. *Cf.* "Auburn Mach. Works Co. v. Jones," 366 So.2d 1167 (Fla. 1979).

Subsection (A)(2) will not promote misconduct by product sellers. If they were aware of the defect in the goods at the time of sale, the punitive damages section of the Act (Section 120) would provide a strong incentive not to sell such a product.

(3) *A Non-claimant's Failure to Inspect for Defects or to Observe an Apparent Defective Condition.* When a product seller has sold a defective product and an intervening product user negligently fails to discover the defect or to take precautions against the possible harm, case law is uniform that the product user's conduct does not relieve the product seller of liability. *See* "Ford Motor Co. v. Matthews," 291 So.2d 169 (Miss.1974); "Boeing Airplane Co. v. Brown," 291 F.2d 310 (9th Cir. 1961); "Comstock v. General Motors Corp.," 358 Mich. 163, 99 N.W.2d 627 (1959). In this instance, the product seller is required to bear responsibility for the defective product it placed on the market.

(B) *Use of a Product With a Known Defective Condition.*

(1) *By a Claimant.* When it is clear that a claimant voluntarily and unreasonably used a product with a known defective condition, the claimant's damages are subject to reduction. Care must be taken not to allow recovery of a claim in a situation where individuals, in effect, have created their own product liability claim. In that regard, it should be noted that consent is a defense even to intentional wrongs. *See* W. Prosser, "Torts" at 101 (4th ed. 1971).

However, there may be cases where an individual voluntarily uses a product with a known defective condition, but the reasonableness of this conduct becomes a matter of dispute. For example, if a person

553

discovers a welt in a tire, should that person be required to stop immediately and call for assistance, or is it reasonable to proceed to a nearby gasoline station to have the tire repaired? The answer depends on the particular fact situation. Many cases arise in this shadowy zone. *See* "Henderson v. Ford Motor Co.," 519 S.W.2d 87 (Tex.1974); "Ford Motor Co. v. Lee," 237 Ga. 554, 229 S.E.2d 379 (1976). Subsection (B)(1) allows the trier of fact to consider the claimant's conduct in the particular fact situation and to reduce damages to the extent that it is appropriate to do so. From both the claimant's and the product seller's perspective, this mitigates the "all-or-nothing" approach that has arisen as a result of some court interpretations of Comment to Section 402A of the "Restatement (Second) of Torts."

(2) *By a Non-claimant Product User.* Subsection (B)(2) is placed in brackets as an optional section. It would apportion responsibility for injuries caused by a defective product between the product seller and a product user who voluntarily and unreasonably exposed the claimant to the product risk. Some case law and, perhaps, proper placement of incentives for loss prevention support this result. *Cf.* "Aetna Ins. Co. v. Loveland Gas & Elec. Co.," 369 F.2d 648 (6th Cir.1966); "Drazen v. Otis Elevator Co.," 96 R.I. 114, 189 A.2d 693 (1963). On the other hand, case law will not shift responsibility where the product was entirely unfit for its intended use,[16] and Subsection (B)(2) may create a situation in which a claimant injured by a defective product cannot bring a successful suit against anyone. This could occur when the Subsection shields the seller of the defective product, and an immunity (*e.g.,* Worker Compensation) shields the negligent third-party actor. Moreover, as Professor Phillips has observed,

> The third party rarely intends to cause the plaintiff injury. Where there is no such intent, the third party's failure to prevent the injury is attributable to his inadvertence, regardless of whether he actually knew or merely should have known of the danger.

Phillips, supra, 28 "Drake L.Rev." at 372.

In light of the very close balance of equities with regard to this Section, it has been bracketed and should be regarded as optional.

(C) *Misuse of a Product.* Subsection (C) provides for a reduction or apportionment of the liability of the product seller when an injury occurs, in whole or in part, because the product user misused the product in some way that the product seller could not reasonably anticipate. *See* "Netzel v. State Sand & Gravel Co.," 51 Wis.2d 1, 186 N.W.2d 258 (1971); "General Motors Corp. v. Hopkins," 548 S.W.2d 344 (Tex.1977). The definition of "misuse" is based on the Act's concept of "reasonably anticipated conduct." *See* Subsection 102(G) and analysis.

---

16. *See, e.g.,* "Clement v. Crosby & Co.," 148 Mich. 293, 111 N.W. 745 (1907); "Farley v. Edward E. Tower & Co.," 271 Mass. 230, 171 N.E. 639 (1930).

Damages are reduced or apportioned "to the extent" that the misuse caused the harm and, under Subsection (C)(2), the trier of fact may determine that the harm arose *solely* because of product misuse. "Helene Curtis Indus. v. Pruitt," 385 F.2d 841 (5th Cir.1967).

Subsection (C)(3) indicates that a third party who is not immune under state or federal law and who has misused a product may be subject to liability to the claimant.

(D) *Alteration or Modification of a Product.* Subsection (D) deals with the situation in which a person or entity other than the product seller has altered or modified the product and this has led to the claimant's harm. Alteration or modification (as contrasted with misuse) occurs when a claimant or third-party product user changes the product's design, construction, or formula, or modifies or removes instructions that accompanied or were displayed on the product.

Some courts have imposed liability on the product seller in this situation if the alteration or modification was in some manner "foreseeable." *See, e.g.,* "Blim v. Newbury Indus., Inc.," 443 F.2d 1126 (10th Cir.1971)(machine safety guard removed by co-worker). Courts that have held the original product seller responsible in these instances have bordered on imposing absolute liability. Thus, insurers have a just concern about the broad-scale imposition of liability where intervention by another party was the principal cause of the accident. As the American Insurance Association has noted:

It is difficult enough to calculate the risk associated with a given product even where there is access to knowledge about its basic inherent characteristics.... The task becomes impossible if the premium calculations must take into account not only the inherent properties of the machine, but also its transformation in the hands of others, and their neglect of repair and maintenance.

AIA, "Product Liability Legislative Package" at 16 (monograph 1977).

Moreover, if the law ignores alterations and modifications of products, it fails to place an incentive for loss prevention on those who might engage in such conduct.

The authors of the "Restatement (Second) of Torts" Section 402A, Subsection 1(b), recognized this fact and subjected the product seller to liability only when the seller's product reached "the user or consumer without substantial change in the condition in which it was sold." Comment g to that Section stated the matter more firmly:

The seller is not liable when he delivers the product in a safe condition, and subsequent mishandling or other causes make it harmful by the time it is consumed. The burden of proof that the product was in a defective condition at the time that it left the hands of the particular seller is upon the injured plaintiff; and unless evidence can be produced which will support the conclusion that it was then defective, the burden is not sustained.

Recently, a number of state legislatures have enacted the essence of this comment into law. "Ariz.Rev. Stat.Ann." Section 12–683(2)(Supp.1978); "Ind.Code Ann." 33–1–1.5 Section 4(b)(3)(Supp.1978); "Ky.Rev.Stat. Ann." Section 411–320 (1978); "N.H.Rev.Stat.Ann." Section 507–D:3 (Supp.1978); "R.I.Gen.Laws" Section 9–1–32 (1978); "Tenn.Code Ann." Section 23–3708 (1978); "Utah Code Ann." Section 78–15–5 (1977).

According to the statistics of the Insurance Services Office, product modification only occurs in approximately 13 percent of product liability cases. Of these cases, the largest number of the product modifications (39 percent) result from the conduct of employers. *See* "ISO Closed Claims Survey" at 140–41. This raises the main problem with rules that limit a product seller's responsibility for subsequent product alterations or modifications—often the injured worker cannot sue the one who is really at fault because of the "exclusive remedy" provisions of Worker Compensation statutes. However, it is fair to state that the destruction of a tort remedy against the employer

> should not of itself create a third-party remedy against the manufacturer or distributor of the product in question. If Worker Compensation is regarded as a proper remedy in other cases of an exclusive employer's wrong, then so too should it be where that wrong involves the product acquired from third-party defendants.

AIA, "Product Liability Legislative Package," *supra* at 15–16.

Nevertheless, Subsection (D) takes account of the hardship that can result from an overly broad liability limitation in cases of product modification or alteration. Thus, the provision is very narrowly drawn.

Subsection (D)(2) ensures that the principles of comparative responsibility are correctly applied by reference to Section 111. If an alteration or modification was made by the claimant, damages are subject to reduction in accordance with the claimant's percentage of responsibility. If a party other than the claimant is responsible for the modification or alteration, damages are to be apportioned in accordance with the parties' percentages of responsibility.

In the case of an employer or co-employee immune from tort liability or a released party under Subsection 113(E), the rules set forth in Subsection 112(B)(2) would apply with regard to reduction of damages.

Under Subsection (D)(2), a product seller may avoid liability to the extent it proves that claimant's harm was proximately caused by the alteration or modification. If the harm arose solely because of the product alteration or modification, the product seller will not be liable at all. On the other hand, the rule adopted ensures that the product seller will remain liable to the extent that it is responsible for the harm. *See* "Fincher v. Surrette," 365 So.2d 860, 863 (La.Ct.App. 1978). Subsection (D)(2) applies the comparative responsibility procedural principles set forth in Section 111.

As Subsections (D)(2)(a) and (b) indicate, the product seller cannot avoid responsibility for product alterations or modifications which the seller suggested (per instructions) or to which the seller expressly consented.

Subsection (D)(2)(c) indicates that the product seller may have a duty to warn against modifications or alterations of its product when it may reasonably anticipate that such conduct will occur on the part of persons who are likely to use the product. As Subsection 102(G)(definition of "reasonably anticipated conduct") indicates, this refers to conduct that would be engaged in by an ordinary reasonably prudent person.

Subsection (D)(2)(c) is not intended to encompass every type of act foreseeable by virtue of hindsight or otherwise. If alterations or modifications involve conduct which should have been reasonably anticipated by the product seller, such product seller will be responsible for harms that result if the failure to provide warnings against the type of alteration or modification at issue renders the product defective under Subsection 104(C). A general warning against any alterations or modifications will not suffice.

Subsection (D)(3) indicates that a third party who is not immune under state or federal law and who has negligently altered or modified a product may be subject to liability to the claimant.

* * *

Code

§ 113. Multiple Defendants: Contribution and Implied Indemnity

(A) A right of contribution exists under this Act between or among two or more persons who are jointly and severally liable, whether or not judgment has been recovered against all or any of them. It may be enforced either in the original action or by a separate action brought for that purpose. The basis for contribution is each person's equitable share of the obligation, including the equitable share of a claimant, as determined in accordance with the provisions of Section 111. For the purposes of this Act, contribution and implied indemnity are merged.

(B) If the proportionate responsibility of the parties to a claim for contribution has been established previously by the court, as provided in Section 111, a party paying more than its equitable share of the obligation may, upon motion, recover judgment for contribution.

(C) If the proportionate responsibility of the parties to the claim for contribution has not been established by the court, contribution may be enforced in a separate action, whether or not a judgment has been rendered against either the person seeking contribution or the person from whom contribution is being sought.

(D) Contribution is available to a person who enters into a settlement with a claimant only (1) if the liability of the person against whom contribution is sought has been extinguished by the settlement, and (2) to the extent that the amount paid in settlement was reasonable.

(E) A release, covenant not to sue, or similar agreement entered into by a claimant and a person liable discharges that person from all liability for contribution, but it does not discharge any other persons liable upon the same claim unless it so provides. However, the claim of the releasing claimant against the other parties is reduced by the amount of the released party's equitable share of the obligation, determined in accordance with the provisions of Section 111.

(F) If a judgment has been rendered, the action for contribution must be commenced within one year after the judgment becomes final. If no judgment has been rendered, the person bringing the action for contribution must have (1) discharged by payment the common liability within the period of the statute of limitation or repose applicable to the claimant's right of action against him and commenced the action for contribution within one year after payment, or (2) agreed while action was pending to discharge the common liability and, within one year after the agreement, have paid the liability and brought an action for contribution.

* * *

Analysis

§ 113. Multiple Defendants: Contribution and Implied Indemnity

Section 113 is based on Sections 4, 5, and 6 of the "Uniform Compar-

ative Fault Act" ("UCFA"). Here, however, contribution and implied indemnity are merged in one section. Express indemnity—where one party has agreed to hold the other harmless for damages arising out of product liability actions—is left to commercial and common law. *See* "Task Force Report" at VII–99–103.

There is clear precedent for the merger of contribution and implied indemnity. *See* "Safeway Stores, Inc. v. Nest–Kart," 21 Cal.3d 322, 579 P.2d 441, 146 Cal.Rptr. 550 (1978); "Skinner v. Reed–Prentice Division, Etc.," 70 Ill.2d 1, 374 N.E.2d 437 (1977), *cert. denied,* 436 U.S. 946 (1978); "Busch v. Busch Constr., Inc.," ___ Minn. ___, 262 N.W.2d 377 (1977); "Dole v. Dow Chemical Co.," 30 N.Y.2d 143, 282 N.E.2d 288, 331 N.Y.S.2d 382 (1972); *see also* "N.Y.Civ.Prac.Law" Section 1402 (1976). This approach avoids the "all-or-nothing" aspect of implied indemnity law. In most situations, fault will be apportioned among product seller defendants. However, a situation could arise where the trier of fact could find that one product seller in the distribution chain was entirely responsible for a product harm. In that regard, this Section should be read in conjunction with Sections 111 and 112.

Subsection (A), which is based on "UCFA" Subsection 4(a), establishes a right of contribution which may be enforced in the original action or in a separate action and provides that contribution will be determined by the proportionate responsibility of the defendants. The Subsection outlines the procedure for the trier of fact to make the appropriate determination.

Subsection (B), which is based on "UCFA" Subsection 5(a), outlines a simplified procedure whereby a party adjudged liable who has paid more than its proportionate share can recover from one who has paid less.

Subsection (C), which is based on "UCFA" Subsection 5(b), provides a mechanism for apportioning responsibility when all potential defendants were not parties to the original action. It indicates that if the court has not determined the proportionate responsibility of all parties in the original action, contribution may be obtained in a separate action.

Subsection (D), which is based on "UCFA" Subsection 4(b), makes it clear that a person who has settled a claim may seek contribution from another person. However, this Subsection limits the right of contribution in such a situation by requiring that the amount paid in settlement be reasonable and that the claimant's right to recover from the other person be extinguished by the settlement.

Subsection (E), which is based on "UCFA" Section 6, deals with the effect of the release of one or more, but not all, tortfeasors. Under this Subsection, a released person is free from liability for contribution, and the liability of other persons to the claimant is reduced by the released person's equitable share of the responsibility as determined in accordance with the provisions of Section 111. Although this provision "may have some tendency to dis-

courage a claimant from entering into a settlement, this solution is fairly based on the proportionate-fault principle." "UCFA Comment" Section 6. Furthermore, the provision that the liability of the non-settling persons is reduced by the settling person's percentage of the responsibility should discourage claimants from entering into collusive settlements with one defendant at the expense of the other parties.

The Act does not directly address the validity of "Mary Carter agreements." Such agreements are typically entered into between a claimant and one or more, but not all, of the product sellers. They are usually made in secret, and the agreeing product sellers remain as parties to the action. The agreeing product sellers' liability is decreased in direct proportion to the nonagreeing product sellers' increase in liability, and, in return, the agreeing product sellers guarantee the claimant a certain amount of money if the claimant does not obtain a judgment, or if it is less than a specified amount. While such an agreement appears collusive, some state courts currently regard "Mary Carter agreements" as valid. *See, e.g.,* Frier's, Inc. v. Seaboard Coastline Ry., 355 So.2d 208 (Fla.Dist.Ct.App. 1978). However, to the extent that a court chooses to regard a "Mary Carter agreement" as a *settlement,* Subsection (E) is intended to discourage such agreements.

Subsection (F) is based on "UCFA" Section 5 and sets forth the period of time in which an action for contribution may be brought.

* * *

Code

§ 114. Relationship Between Product Liability and Worker Compensation

(A) In the case of any product liability claim brought by or on behalf of an injured person entitled to compensation under a state Worker Compensation statute, damages shall be reduced by the amount paid as Worker Compensation benefits for the same injury plus the present value of all future Worker Compensation benefits payable for the same injury under the Worker Compensation statute.

(B) Unless the product seller has expressly agreed to indemnify or hold an employer harmless for harm caused to the employer's employee by a product, the employer shall have no right of subrogation, contribution, or indemnity against the product seller when the harm to the employee constitutes a product liability claim under this Act. Also, the employer's Worker Compensation insurance carrier shall have no right of subrogation against the product seller.

(C) When final judgment in an action brought under this Act has been entered prior to the determination of Worker Compensation benefits, the product seller may bring a subsequent action for reduction of the judgment by the amount of the Worker Compensation benefits, or for recoupment from the employee if the product seller has paid a judgment which includes the amount of such benefits.

* * *

Analysis

§ 114. Relationship Between Product Liability and Worker Compensation

The relationship between product liability and Worker Compensation is a major topic covered in depth in the "Task Force Report" at VII–85–113. Under current law in a number of states, the interaction of product liability and Worker Compensation law results in the manufacturer of a workplace product paying the entire out-of-pocket cost of a product-related workplace injury, plus damages for pain and suffering. This result occurs because the product manufacturer is unable to place a portion of the cost of that injury on an employer whose negligence may have helped bring about the claimant's injury. *See* "Seaboard Coast Line R.R. v. Smith," 359 So.2d 427 (Fla.1978); "Task Force Report" at VII–89–99.

After weighing many considerations, the Task Force and the United States Department of Commerce concluded that the development of Worker Compensation as a sole source of recovery in product-related workplace accidents would be the best solution to the problem, but only if the worker received additional benefits in the course of overall Worker Compensation reform. A model product liability law, however, is an inappropriate vehicle for making alterations of that dimension in Worker Compensation law.

The search for the next best solution is not an easy one. One approach is to permit a full contribution claim in all cases in which the employer is at fault. *See* "Dole v. Dow Chem. Co.," 30 N.Y.2d 143, 331 N.Y.S.2d 382, 282 N.E.2d 288 (1972); "Skinner v. Reed–Prentice Division, Inc.," 70 Ill.2d 1, 374 N.E.2d 437 (1977). This approach is in accordance with the principle of comparative responsibility, and it places strong incentives for loss prevention on the employer.

However, if full contribution or indemnity by the product manufacturer against the employer is permitted, the employer may be forced to pay an employee—through the conduit of the third-party tortfeasor—an amount in excess of the employer's statutory Worker Compensation liability. This thwarts a central concept behind Worker Compensation, *i.e.*, that the employer and employee receive the benefits of a guaranteed, fixed-schedule, no-fault recovery system, which constitutes the *exclusive* liability of the employer. The approach also increases transaction costs.

On the other hand, if contribution or indemnity is not allowed, the product seller might have to bear the burden of a full common law judgment, despite the possibly greater responsibility of the employer. As the Supreme Court of Minnesota recently noted, "[t]his obvious inequity is further exacerbated by the right of the employer to recover directly or indirectly from the third party the amount he has paid in compensation regardless of the employer's own negligence." "Lambertson v. Cincinnati Corp.," 257 N.W.2d 679, 684 (Minn.1977).

Equally troublesome is the fact that the present system dulls employer incentives to keep workplace products safe. The "ISO Closed Claims Survey" suggests that employer negligence is involved in 56 percent of product liability workplace cases. "ISO Closed Claims Survey," Report 10 at 81 (1978).

The purpose of the solution adopted in Section 114 is to sharpen employer incentives to keep workplace products safe without undermining the limited-liability concept that is central to the Worker Compensation system. The approach is based, in substantial part, on a proposal developed by the American Insurance Association (AIA). *See* AIA, "Product Liability Legislative Package" at 75–76 (1977). This approach has also been incorporated in the "National Workers' Compensation Standards Act of 1979," S. 420, 96th Cong., 1st Sess. (1979) and "Standards for State Product Liability Tort Litigation Act," H.R. 1675, 96th Cong., 1st Sess. (1979), and recommended by the "LaFalce Subcommittee Report" at 74.

Subsection (A) reduces the liability of a product seller by the total amount that has been or will be awarded in a state Worker Compensation proceeding. This Subsection operates regardless of whether the employer was, in fact, at fault. *See also* Subsection 112(B)(4) and accompanying analysis.

Subsection (B) abolishes the subrogation lien of the Worker Compensation carrier, or the right of a self-insuring employer to contribution or indemnity, in all workplace harm cases which are covered by this Act, except where the product seller has expressly agreed to indemnify or hold the employer harmless for harm caused by the product. As with Subsection (A), Subsection (B) operates regardless of the employer's fault or lack thereof.

Subsection (C) provides a procedural mechanism for reducing the product seller's liability when final judgment has been entered before the amount of Worker Compensation benefits has been determined.

The principal benefit of the approach adopted in Subsections (A) and (B) is a reduction in litigation transaction costs. Subrogation actions are not allowed. Furthermore, proceedings under this Act will be streamlined because in cases of employer negligence, there will be no three-party litigation as to the relative percentages of fault of employers and manufacturers. *See* AIA, "Legislative Package" at 67–68.

An additional benefit of the approach in Subsections (A) and (B) is that an injured employee will recover the same benefits received under the present system. At the same time, Section 114 cuts off the ability of the Worker Compensation carrier or self-insuring employer to shift its liability to the manufacturer. The employer, therefore, will have a greater incentive to provide a safe workplace than it has under the present system.

A third benefit is that the approach will also, to some degree, eliminate the harshness of the present system as it applies to manufacturers, by allowing product sellers to reduce their liability for workplace injuries. It will do this in all cases, even where the employer was not at fault.

While cases may arise where a product seller may pay more than its fair share under a comparative fault system, they are likely to be few in number under this Act. This is because an employer's misuse, or improper alteration or modification of the product, will in turn reduce the employee's award under Subsection 112(C). As the analysis to that Subsection indicates, this is also fair to employees because they agreed, within the context of their Worker Compensation system, to forego their right to sue when it is based on their employers' or co-employees' fault.

A closely related alternative approach to Section 114 was advanced by the Supreme Court of Minnesota in "Lambertson v. Cincinnati Corp.," *supra*. The court in that case held that the product manufacturer would be allowed limited contribution up to the amount of the Worker Compensation lien. This reduces the inequity against the product manufacturer, but preserves the employer's interest in not paying more than its Worker Compensation liability. The principal disadvantage of the "Lambertson" approach, as compared with Section 114, is that "Lambertson" does not reduce transaction costs.

Finally, it should be noted that any modification of the present tort and Worker Compensation systems, short of a sole source remedy, retains the multiple transaction costs of having two separate proceedings—the Worker Compensation proceeding and then the product liability claim—address a single injury. However, considering all the equities involved, Section 114 appears to offer the soundest solution apart from modifying Worker Compensation law to create a sole source remedy.

* * *

Code

§ 115. Sanctions Against the Bringing of Frivolous Claims and Defenses

(A) After final judgment has been entered under this Act, any party may, by motion, seek reimbursement for reasonable attorneys' fees and other costs that would not have been expended but for the fact that the opposing party pursued a claim or defense that was frivolous. A claim or defense is considered frivolous if the court determines that it was without any reasonable legal or factual basis.

(B) If the court decides in favor of a party seeking redress under this Section, it shall do so on the basis of clear and convincing evidence. In all motions under this Section, the court shall make written findings of fact.

(C) The motion provided for in Subsection (A) may be filed and the claim assessed against a party or a party's attorney or both, depending on which person or persons were responsible for the assertion of the frivolous claim or defense.

(D) Claims for damages under this Section shall be limited to expenses incurred by parties to the action or persons under a legal or contractual duty to bear the expenses of the action.

* * *

Analysis

§ 115. Sanctions Against the Bringing of Frivolous Claims and Defenses

The ISO data indicate that substantial product liability costs are incurred in the defense of product liability claims and lawsuits. "ISO Closed Claims Survey," Report No. 14 (1977)(defense costs equal about 35 percent of claim payments). Some have placed the blame for unnecessary defense costs and needless litigation on the contingent fee system. Nevertheless, as the plaintiffs' bar properly observes, the contingent fee brings no return to a claimant's attorney when the claimant is unsuccessful. On the other hand, some have argued that the contingent fee system has a negative impact on certain product liability cases to the extent that it causes insurers to settle non-meritorious claims because the cost of defending such cases may be greater than the amount of settlement.

Analysis of the countervailing arguments suggests that the best solution to reducing unnecessary litigation costs is to address the heart of the problem by discouraging frivolous claims and defenses.

Section 115 is based, in part, on "Ill.Ann.Stat." ch. 110, Section 41 (Supp.1979). It is also predicated on a proposal of the California Citizens Commission on Tort Reform advocating sanctions against "frivolous" claims or defenses. Report of the California Citizens' Commission on Tort Reform, "Righting the Liability Balance" at 146–47, 153–54 (1977).

The underlying purpose of Section 115 has broad support in existing statutes and court rules. For example, Rule 11 of the Federal Rules of Civil Procedure subjects an attorney to disciplinary action if the attorney knowingly files a pleading or defense where no grounds support it. *See* "Barnett v. Laborers' Int'l Union of N. Am.," 75 F.R.D. 544 (W.D.Pa.1977). Similarly, Federal Rule of Appellate Procedure 38 permits a court to award "just damages and single or double costs" to a party who has been subject to a "frivolous" appeal.

Additionally, Federal Rule of Civil Procedure 37(c) provides sanctions for an unreasonable failure to admit averments of fact or the genuineness of documents. In the federal courts, the above rules are supplemented by 28 "U.S.C." Section 1927 (1976)(imposing costs on an attorney who "multiplies the proceedings . . . to increase costs . . ."). *See* Annot., 68 "A.L.R.3d" 209 (1976).

The Section is not intended to affect the law relating to malicious prosecution.

Under Subsection (A), the statute may be invoked by either a product liability claimant or a product seller. Recovery is limited to reasonable attorneys' fees and other costs that would not have been expended but for the fact that the opposing party pursued a claim or defense that was frivolous.

In order to make a finding that the claim was frivolous, the court must conclude that the claim was without *any* reasonable legal or factual basis. Thus, this standard allows full room for bringing claims under novel legal theories.

Subsection (B) provides additional assurances that only those who bring frivolous claims will be penalized. First, the court may only impose damages under Section 115 on the basis of clear and convincing evidence, not merely a preponderance of the evidence. *See* "State of West Virginia v. Charles Pfizer & Co.," 440 F.2d 1079, 1092 (2d Cir. 1971)("clear showing of bad faith"). Second, the court must set forth its findings of fact in writing.

Subsection (C) gives the court latitude to impose costs on either attorney or client. As the "Task Force Report" noted, it is unlikely that many claimants will be financially able to respond to such a claim. "Task Force Report" at VII–62. It must be remembered that the attorney is in the best position to make a judgment about the reasonableness of bringing a claim or raising a defense. *See* "ABA Code of Professional Responsibility," DR 7–102(A)(1)(2); *cf.* "Acevedo v. Immigration & Naturalization Serv.," 538 F.2d 918, 921 (2d Cir.1976).

Subsection (D) makes clear that recovery under this Section is limited to expenses incurred by claimant or defendant or persons under a legal or contractual duty to bear the expenses of the action.

* * *

Code

§ 116. Arbitration

(A) *Applicability*.

(1) Any party may by a motion institute a pre-trial arbitration proceeding in any claim brought under this Act, if the court determines that:

(a) It is reasonably probable that the amount in dispute is less than $50,000, exclusive of interest and costs; and

(b) Any non-monetary claims are insubstantial.

(2) Arbitration may not be used if both the claimant and one or more defendants state that they do not want an arbitration proceeding.

(B) *Rules Governing*.

(1) *Substantive Rules*. The substantive rules of an arbitration proceeding under this Section are those contained in this Act as well as those in applicable state law.

(2) *Procedural Rules*. These are the procedural rules of an arbitration proceeding under this Section. If this Section does not provide a rule of procedure, reference may be made to the "Uniform Arbitration Act" or other sources of law. Any reference to other sources of law must conform to the intent and spirit of this Section.

* Optional Subsection

[(3) *Additional Rules and Administration*.

(i) The _____ (legislature to specify appropriate state agency or administrative body) is empowered to promulgate additional procedural rules for this Section.

(ii) The _____ (legislature to specify American Arbitration Association or similar organization) shall carry out the day-to-day administration of arbitration under this Section.]

(C) *Arbitrators*.

(1) Unless the parties agree otherwise, the arbitration shall be conducted by three persons: an active member of the state bar or a retired judge of a court of record in the state; an individual who possesses expertise in the subject matter area that is in dispute; and a layperson.

(2) Arbitrators shall be selected in accordance with applicable state law in a manner which will assure fairness and lack of bias.

(D) *Arbitrators' Powers*.

(1) Each arbitrator to whom a claim is referred has the power, within the territorial jurisdiction of the court, to conduct arbitration hearings and make awards consistent with the provisions of this Act.

(2) State laws applicable to subpoenas for attendance of witnesses and the production of documentary evidence apply in proceedings conducted under this Section. Arbitrators shall have the power to administer oaths and affirmations.

(E) *Commencement*. Arbitration hearings shall commence not later than thirty (30) days after the claim is referred to arbitration unless, for good cause shown, the court shall extend the period. Hearings shall be concluded promptly. The court may order the time and place of the arbitration.

(F) *Evidence.*

(1) The Federal Rules of Evidence [or designated state evidence code] may be used as a guide to the admissibility of evidence in an arbitration hearing.

(2) Strict adherence to the rules of evidence, apart from relevant state rules of privilege, is not required.

(G) *Transcript of Proceeding.* A party may have a transcript or recording made of the arbitration hearing at its own expense. A party who has had a transcript or recording made shall furnish a copy of the transcript or recording at cost to any other party upon request.

(H) *Arbitration Decision and Judgment.* The arbitration decision and award, if any, shall be filed with the court promptly after the hearing is concluded. Unless a party demands a trial pursuant to Subsection (I), the decision and award shall be entered as the judgment of the court. The judgment entered shall be subject to the same provisions of law, and shall have the same force and effect as a judgment of the court in a civil action, except that it shall not be subject to appeal.

(I) *Trial Following Arbitration.*

(1) Within twenty (20) days after the filing of an arbitration decision with the court, any party may demand a trial of fact or a hearing on an issue of law in that court.

(2) Upon such a demand, the action shall be placed on the calendar of the court. Except for the provisions of Subsection (3), any right

of trial by jury that a party would otherwise have shall be preserved inviolate.

(3) At trial, the court shall admit evidence that there has been an arbitration proceeding, the decision of the arbitration panel, and the nature and amount of the award, if any. The trier of fact shall give such evidence whatever weight it deems appropriate.

(4) A party who has demanded a trial but fails to obtain a judgment in the trial court which is more favorable than the arbitration award, exclusive of interest and costs, shall be assessed the cost of the arbitration proceeding, including the amount of the arbitration fees, and—

(i) If this party is a claimant and the arbitration award is in its favor, the party shall pay the court an amount equivalent to interest on the arbitration award from the time it was filed; or

(ii) If this party is a product seller, it shall pay interest to the claimant on the arbitration award from the time it was filed.

* * *

Analysis

§ 116. Arbitration

The "Task Force Report" suggested that mandatory non-binding arbitration may result in more accurate decisions, reduce overall litigation costs, and expedite the decision process in product liability cases. *See* "Task Force Report" at VII–229–39.

A synopsis of the basis for these conclusions is that: (1) cases will be decided more accurately because a small group, with a member who is an expert in the field, should be able to comprehend the esoteric details of product liability cases; (2) over time, the process will develop a resource bank of relatively neutral experts less easily misled in technical areas than a jury of laypersons; (3) arbitrators will be less affected by the emotional aspects of the case or by the artistry of counsel; and (4) the privacy of arbitration proceedings (as compared to judicial proceedings) will prompt more complete revelation of special manufacturing designs or processes. This, in turn, will permit more accurate judgments. *See* "Task Force Report" at VII–235.

The "ISO Closed Claims Survey" suggests further that arbitration will reduce accident reparation transaction costs. Even allowing for the fact that more substantial product liability claims are litigated to a verdict than are handled by arbitration, ISO data indicate that the average expense for attorneys and other allocated loss adjustment costs are considerably lower when the case is handled by arbitration as compared with a court verdict. *See* "ISO Closed Claims Survey," Report 14 at 120.

On the other hand, costs may increase under arbitration if there are numerous demands for trial following arbitration. This potential problem may not be as serious, however, as was once thought. Data collected by the Department of Justice show that appeal rates at the state level for a trial following arbitration

have ranged from 5 to no more than 15 percent of all cases arbitrated. Hearings before the Subcommittee on Improvements in Judicial Machinery of the Senate Committee on the Judiciary, 95th Cong., 2d Sess. 22 (1978)(Statement of Former Attorney General Griffin B. Bell). *See also* report of the California Citizens' Commission on Tort Reform, "Righting the Liability Balance" at 143 (1977).

Broader use of arbitration should expedite the reparations process. The "Task Force Report" showed that in the medical malpractice area, for example, the arbitration process had achieved a more expeditious resolution of claims than the jury system. *See* "Task Force Report" at VII–238.

Indeed, the benefits of arbitration have prompted the Department of Justice to recommend that mandatory non-binding arbitration be used in federal courts in all tort and contract cases. The Department of Justice reached this conclusion after its Office of Judicial Improvements made a thorough analysis of the matter in a study conducted wholly independently of the "Task Force Report."

Section 116 draws on portions of the Department of Justice's proposed bill on mandatory non-binding arbitration. *See* S. 373, 96th Cong., 1st Sess. (1979); H.R. 2699, 96th Cong., 1st Sess. (1979); the Statement of Former Attorney General Griffin B. Bell, *supra;* as well as state legislation on the topic of arbitration.

(A) *Applicability*. The Act provides for arbitration when the amount in dispute is less than $50,-000. This figure is to be determined by the court under a standard of reasonable probability. In this context, note that the sanctions imposed by Section 115 will apply to any party who delays the proceedings by making a frivolous assertion that the amount in dispute is above or below $50,000. Also, the proceeding is not mandatory if both the claimant and at least one defendant state that they do not want it.

The $50,000 figure is the same as that in the Department of Justice bill, and it should cover the bulk of product liability claims. In that regard, the ISO closed claims data, trended for severity, show that the average paid claim in bodily injury cases is $26,004. While some have suggested limiting arbitration to smaller claims, it is the larger claims that have been the greater transaction cost items in product liability cases. *See* "ISO Closed Claims Survey" at 113.

While there has been no state experience with cases at the $50,000 level, Former Attorney General Bell has noted that when Pennsylvania increased the jurisdictional amount for the state's arbitration program from $3,000 to $10,000, there was no increase in the appeal rate. Statement of Former Attorney General Griffin B. Bell, *supra* at 20.

It seems relatively certain that an arbitration procedure will help expedite and reduce costs connected with smaller claims. ISO closed claims data show that the large majority of product liability payments are relatively small (more than two-thirds are under $1,000—even when

trended for severity). *See* "ISO Closed Claims Survey" at 113.

(B) *Rules Governing.* Subsection (B)(1) indicates that arbitrators shall apply the product liability substantive law rules of this Act. Where the Act does not provide a rule of decision, relevant state law should be applied.

Subsection (B)(2) indicates that where a procedure is not provided in Section 116—*e.g.,* when a court can vacate a judgment—the "Uniform Arbitration Act" (enacted in a number of states), or another appropriate source of law, is to be used as a resource.

Subsection (B)(3), an optional section, permits the state to designate a supplemental source of procedural rules and to empower the American Arbitration Association or similar organizations to carry out the day-to-day administration of arbitration.

This Subsection leaves a great deal of room for the states to develop their own arbitration systems. The drafters of the Act have chosen to include only the most important procedural points concerning arbitration. The goal of substantive uniformity in product liability law will not be compromised by allowing individual states the freedom to choose the arbitration procedures that they find are the most efficient and workable.

(C) *Arbitrators.* The rules under Subsection (C) provide latitude for the parties to select a single arbitrator. Otherwise, the arbitration is to be conducted by three persons, one who is an active member of the state bar or a retired judge, one who has expertise in the subject matter area that is in dispute, and one who is a layperson. This provision differs slightly from the Department of Justice proposal in light of the needs of product liability. Having an individual who is familiar with the scientific nature of the subject matter involved will help expedite the case and serve as a deterrent to the presentation of biased expert testimony.

In addition, Subsection (C) provides for a layperson to be included to help assure that the consumer perspective regarding product safety is represented. The process of selecting a layperson should not be complicated. It is suggested that either normal jury rolls be utilized or that a list of laypersons be compiled for this purpose.

Aside from general guidelines regarding fairness and lack of bias, the Act does not outline the method of choosing arbitrators, but leaves that matter to the individual states. A state can help implement the general guidelines by requiring each arbitration panel candidate to disclose any personal acquaintance with the parties or their counsel and allow a *voir dire* examination. *See* "Mich. Comp.Laws Ann." Section 600.5045(1)(2)(Supp.1978). Some of the better procedures include:

(1) Having the American Arbitration Association select a pool of candidates according to its established selection procedures. Each party is allowed to reject certain candidates and rate the remainder in order of preference. Additional provisions take effect if this procedure fails to produce a panel. *See*

"Mich.Comp.Laws Ann." Section 600.5044(4)(5) (Supp.1978);

(2) Having the court appoint arbitrators. "Mass.Ann.Laws" ch. 231, Section 60(B)(Supp.1978);

(3) Having an arbitration administrator appoint arbitrators. "Wis.Stat.Ann." Section 655.02 (Supp.1979); and

(4) Having the parties and court combine to appoint arbitrators. "Neb.Rev.Stat." Sections 44–2840, 2841 (Supp.1978); "Ohio Rev. Code Ann." Section 2711.21(A)(Supp.1979).

(D) *Arbitrators' Powers.* These provisions are taken from the Department of Justice proposal on arbitration. They grant the arbitrators jurisdiction and also give them powers of subpoena.

(E) *Commencement.* This provision is also derived from the Department of Justice proposal. Its purpose is to help expedite the proceeding. The Act contains a slight modification of the Justice proposal in order to allow an extension for "good cause shown." This seems appropriate in light of the fact that some product liability cases are very complex. *Cf.* "Ariz.Rev.Stat.Ann." Section 12–567(C)(Supp.1978)(medical malpractice).

(F) *Evidence.* One method of expediting the process is to use informal means of proof. Nevertheless, some guidelines are needed. The Act follows the Department of Justice proposal in referring to the Federal Rules of Evidence as general guidelines. Strict adherence to rules of evidence is not required. *See* "Ariz.Rev.Stat.Ann." Section 12–567(D)(Supp.1978).

(G) *Transcript of Proceeding.* With respect to the provision of a transcript of proceeding, the Act generally follows the Department of Justice draft.

(H) *Arbitration Decision and Judgment.* The Act follows the Department of Justice proposal's provisions on decisions and judgment. The parties may request a trial on issues of law or fact. If they do not so request in a timely manner, the action is at an end—there is no appeal.

(I) *Trial Following Arbitration.* The Act follows the approach taken by a number of state medical malpractice arbitration statutes. It admits the results of the arbitration proceeding into evidence before the jury. This should act as a deterrent against seeking unnecessary trials. *See, e.g.,* "Ariz.Rev.Stat.Ann." Section 12–567(M)(Supp.1978); "Mass. Ann.Laws" ch. 231, Section 60(B)(Supp.1978). *Cf.* "Wis.Stat. Ann." Section 655.19 (Supp.1979)(excluding findings and order of arbitration panel).

The approach of Section 116 appears to be in accord with the Federal Constitution. *Cf.* "*Ex parte* Peterson," 253 U.S. 300, 309 (1920). Moreover, with the exception of two Ohio lower court decisions, state courts have upheld the constitutionality of provisions that do admit panel findings before the jury. *See* "Eastin v. Broomfield," 116 Ariz. 576, 570 P.2d 744, 750 (1977); "Attorney General v. Johnson," 282 Md. 274, 385 A.2d 57, 67–68 (1978) "Paro v. Longwood Hosp.," 373 Mass. 645, 369 N.E.2d 985 (1977); "Prendergast v. Nelson," 199 Neb. 97, 256 N.W.2d 657 (1977); "Stry-

kowski v. Wilkie," 81 Wis.2d 491, 261 N.W.2d 434 (1978), *contra* "Simon v. St. Elizabeth Medical Center," 3 Ohio Op.3d 164, 355 N.E.2d 903, 907–09 (C.P.1976); "Graley v. Satayatham," 74 Ohio Op.2d 316, 343 N.E.2d 832 (C.P.1976). *See generally* Reddish, "Legislative Response to the Medical Malpractice Insurance Crisis: Constitutional Implications," 55 "Tex.L.Rev." 759, 793 (1977); Lenore, "Mandatory Medical Malpractice Mediation Panels—A Constitutional Examination," 44 "Ins.Counsel J." 416, 422 (1977).

A possible drawback of this Section's approach is that a jury may have difficulty evaluating the conclusions of the panel where the jury is not privy to the prior fact-finder's qualifications and method of operation. Also, the jury may get sidetracked from the actual evidence in the case. *See* the observations of Judge Hinton in a classic comment, 27 "Ill.L.Rev." 195 (1932); Annot., 18 "A.L.R.2d" 1287 (1951). *But see* Fed.R.Evid. 803(22)(admitting felony convictions in a cognate civil case). Nevertheless, the benefits to be gained by a reduction in transaction costs outweigh these concerns and support the admission of the results of the arbitration proceeding into evidence at trial.

Subsection (I)(4) provides an additional deterrent against ill-considered appeals for trials following arbitration. If a party fails to obtain a judgment more favorable than the arbitration award, the court will assess the cost of the arbitration proceedings, including the amount of arbitration fees, plus interest, against that party.

In light of the fact that the present product liability system has created serious problems and the fact that mandatory non-binding arbitration has the potential for dealing with some of those problems, this slight incentive for retaining a sound arbitration award should not run afoul of constitutions in most states. *See* "Task Force Report" at VII–233. The Act does not enumerate grounds upon which a court may vacate an arbitration award. Guidance on this issue may be obtained from Section 12 of the "Uniform Arbitration Act."

* * *

Code

§ 117. Expert Testimony

(A) *Appointment of Experts.* The court may, on its own motion or on the motion of any party, enter an order to show cause why expert witnesses should not be appointed, and may request the parties to submit nominations. The court may appoint any expert witness agreed upon by the parties, and may appoint witnesses of its own selection. The court may consult with knowledgeable individuals or with professional, academic, consumer, or business organizations and institutions to assist with the selection process. An expert witness shall not be appointed by the court unless the expert consents to serve. An expert witness appointed by the court shall be informed of his or her duties in writing, a copy of which shall be filed with the clerk, or at a conference in which the parties shall have an opportunity to participate. An expert witness so appointed shall advise the parties of any findings; shall be available for deposition by any party; and may be called to testify by the court or any party. The court-appointed expert witness shall be subject to cross-examination by each party, including the party calling that expert as a witness.

(B) *Compensation.*

(1) Expert witnesses appointed by the court are entitled to reasonable compensation for their services in an amount to be determined by the court. The court, in its discretion, may tax the costs of such expert on one party or apportion them among parties in the same manner as other costs.

(2) In exercising this discretion, the court may consider;

(a) Which party, if any, requested the court appointment of the expert;

(b) Which party had judgment entered in its favor; and

(c) Whether the amount of damages recovered in the action bore a reasonable relationship to the amount sought by the claimant or conceded to be appropriate by the product seller or other defendant.

(C) *Disclosure of Appointment.* In the exercise of its discretion, the court may authorize disclosure to the jury of the fact that the court has appointed the expert witness.

(D) *Parties' Selection of Own Experts.* Nothing in this Section shall limit the parties in calling expert witnesses of their own selection.

(E) *Pre-trial Evaluation of Experts.* The court in its discretion may conduct a hearing to determine the qualifications of all proposed expert witnesses. The court may order a hearing on its own motion or on the motion of any party.

(1) *Need for Pre-trial Evaluation.* In determining whether to grant such a motion, the court shall consider:

(a) The complexity of the issues in the case; and

(b) Whether the hearing would deter the presentation of witnesses who are not qualified as experts on the specific issues.

(2) *Factors in Evaluation.* If the court decides to hold such a hearing, it shall consider;

(a) The background and skills of the proposed witness;

(b) The formal and self-education the proposed witness has undertaken relevant to the case or to similar cases; and

(c) The potential bias of the proposed witness.

(3) *Findings of Fact.* In making a determination as to whether a proposed expert witness is qualified, the court shall state its findings of fact to the parties.

(4) *Determination.* Based upon its findings of fact regarding the qualifications of any proposed expert witness, the court, in its discretion, may limit the scope of the witness' testimony, or may refuse to permit such witness to testify as an expert.

* * *

Analysis

§ 117. Expert Testimony

In General. The Task Force's "Legal Study" demonstrated that product liability cases are often compromised because of the lack of standards with regard to selecting and presenting expert testimony. *See* Volume IV, "Legal Study" at 153–155. One part of the problem is the biased expert; another is the unqualified expert.

Even if experts are properly qualified and objective, a jury of laypersons is often in a poor position to determine which expert is correct. For this reason, this Act gives the court power to make greater use of pre-trial arbitration where an unbiased, qualified expert will serve on the panel. *See* Section 116. Where arbitration is not used, however, this Section should promote the goal of presenting objective and sound expert testimony to the jury.

(A) *Appointment of Experts.* Subsection (A) is based on Rule 706 of the Federal Rules of Evidence and similar state rules. It indicates that courts have the power to appoint experts on their own authority. A number of courts have utilized this power even without the benefit of Fed.R.Evid. 706 or a similar state rule. *See* Annot., 95 "A.L.R.2d" 390 (1964). As the "Task Force Report" noted, the presence of a court-appointed expert "has a cautionary impact on the expert for hire whose theories at trial are subject to dispute not only by an adversary expert, but also by a neutral court-appointed one." "Task Force Report" at ·VII–43, *citing* Mitchell,

"The Proposed Federal Rules of Evidence: How They Affect Product Liability Practice," 12 "Duquesne L.Rev." 551, 557–58 (1974). *See also* 2 J. Wigmore, "Evidence" Section 563, at 648 (3d ed. 1940)(" ... this expedient would remove most ... abuses").

Subsection (A) also encourages the court to seek the assistance of various individuals, organizations, or institutions in making the selection of a court-appointed expert. The court may wish to utilize this opportunity to establish a panel of independent experts, recognized as such by their peers, from which selections for individual cases may be made. The court may also seek the assistance of these organizations to evaluate the credentials of expert witnesses nominated by the parties.

One problem with court-appointed experts is that the trier of fact may give them an aura of infallibility which they do not deserve. Under Subsection (A), this possibility is diminished because the experts are subject to cross-examination by *each* party. Also, Subsection (C) allows the court in its discretion to decline to disclose to the jury that the expert witness is, in fact, court-appointed.

(B) *Compensation.* Under Fed. R.Evid. 706 and similar state rules, compensation of experts is left to the judge's discretion. Subsection (B) goes a step farther and provides three guidelines for compensating experts. These guidelines should serve as an added inducement for attorneys to present objective expert testimony. The guidelines suggest that the court may impose the cost of the court-appointed expert on los-ing parties as well as on parties whom the court finds were substantially inaccurate in their estimation of damages.

(C) *Disclosure of Appointment.* Subsection (C) follows Fed.R.Evid. 706. In most instances, it is important for the trier of fact to appreciate that the witness is court-appointed. However, circumstances may arise in which the court believes disclosure of that fact will give the witness too much credence with the jury. Therefore, the court has the discretion to withhold the information when it is appropriate to do so.

(D) *Parties' Selection of Own Experts.* Subsection (D) also follows Fed.R.Evid. 706. Precluding the parties from introducing their own experts would vest too much power in court-appointed experts.

(E) *Pre-trial Evaluation of Experts.* A rule authorizing a court-appointed expert does not, in and of itself, provide guidance about who is properly qualified to testify in product liability cases. There are many approaches to that issue. One approach, used in some medical malpractice statutes, would require that an expert witness spend a substantial portion of his or her professional time in the actual practice of his or her area of expertise. While this approach may be appropriate in the area of medical malpractice, it was not followed here because a person may be well-versed in technical product liability matters even if he or she does devote substantial time to research or other endeavors other than actual practice. *See* "Task Force Report" at VII–44. Unfortunately, it is impractical to utilize a "standard test" for all experts in product liability cases. *See* Donaher, Piehler, Twerski & Weinstein, "The Technological Expert in Products Liability Litigation," 52 "Tex. L.Rev." 1303, 1325 (1974).

(1) *Need for Pre-trial Evaluation.* This rule gives some guidance to the trial court in deciding whether to conduct a pre-trial hearing on the qualifications of expert witnesses. It is not necessary or cost-efficient to utilize the procedure in *all* cases. It is appropriate to do so in more complex cases and also where the pre-trial hearings would serve as a deterrent to the presentation of witnesses who were not qualified. Such a deterrent should discourage parties from prolonging the litigation needlessly and, thus, encourage the expeditious resolution of claims under this Act. Either party may bring this matter before the court by motion.

(2) *Factors in Evaluation.* The factors in evaluation are drawn from Donaher *et al., supra,* 52 "Tex. L.Rev." 1303.

The court should examine the expert witness' background and skills and determine whether they are appropriate for the purposes of the case. The court should not only review the witness' formal education, but also whether the witness had undertaken specific preparation for the litigation before the court. Finally, the court should examine a witness for bias. A witness with marginal expert skills and a strong bias should be considered unqualified.

(3) *Findings of Fact.* If it seems clear to the court that the expert's background and experience do not qualify the expert to testify, it should state this conclusion in its findings of fact to the parties.

(4) *Determination.* This provision empowers the court to limit the scope of an expert's testimony to the witness' specific area of expertise. It also allows the court to refuse to permit the witness to testify as an expert when that individual is not qualified to do so.

* * *

Code

§ 118. Non-pecuniary Damages

(A) For the purposes of this Section, "non-pecuniary damages" are those which have no market value and do not represent a monetary loss to claimant.

(B) When sufficient evidence has been introduced, the amount of non-pecuniary damages shall be determined by the trier of fact. However, the court shall have and shall exercise the power to review such damage awards for excessiveness.

* Optional Subsection

[(C) Non-pecuniary damages under this Act shall not exceed $25,-000, or twice the amount of the pecuniary damages, whichever is less, unless the claimant proves by a preponderance of the evidence that the product caused claimant to suffer serious and permanent or prolonged (1) disfigurement, (2) impaired of bodily function, (3) pain and discomfort, or (4) mental illness.]

* Optional Subsection

[(D) Every third year following the effective date of this Act as stated in Section 122, the _____ Committee(s) of [each House of] the Legislature of this State shall review the monetary limitations contained in Subsection (C) to determine whether such limitations should be changed in view of the economic conditions existing at that time. Upon a finding that such change is warranted, said Committee(s) shall introduce legislation to amend the monetary limitations contained in Subsection (C).]

* * *

Analysis

§ 118. Non-pecuniary Damages

Claimant's "non-pecuniary damages" include awards for pain and mental suffering. They have no market value and, thus, are to be contrasted with pecuniary damages which compensate victims for lost wages, medical and rehabilitation costs, and other actual expenditures brought about by an unreasonably unsafe product.

According to the "ISO Closed Claims Survey," 70 percent of claims closed with payment include amounts in addition to a claimant's pecuniary loss. *See* "ISO Closed Claims Survey" at 54. Moreover, the average amount of payment above pecuniary loss increases significantly in the higher payment range. *Id.* at 54–55. A most important reason

for the difficulty in setting product liability rates is the "open-endedness" of damages for pain and suffering. *See* "Task Force Report" at VII–64–65. These escalating premiums have an inflationary impact on consumer prices as the product seller's insurance costs are passed on to the public. Damages that go beyond the amount necessary to ensure that the claimant receives reasonable compensation for the harm suffered represent an unwarranted cost.

The "Task Force Report" suggested that limits on awards for pain and suffering "would reduce uncertainty and thereby mitigate the 'apprehension factor' that has contributed to the rise in product liability insurance rates." *Id.* at VII–65. Nevertheless, such awards have deep historical roots and should not be limited in a manner that unreasonably curtails the rights of injured parties. Section 118 takes the position that a fixed limit on the amount of non-pecuniary damages is appropriate where claimant's harm is only temporary.

Section 118 is predicated on an examination of the weaknesses in the major rationales offered in support of awards for non-pecuniary damages. The award for non-pecuniary damages arose in early common law cases as a substitute for an injured claimant seeking personal "vengeful retaliation." *See* "Task Force Report," *id.* In those cases, the defendant usually committed an intentional wrong. This rationale has little application to cases arising under product liability. Under this Act, a product seller may be held liable for harm caused by products found to be defective in construction regardless of fault. The same result occurs when an express warranty is not true. In cases of harm caused by products found to be defective in design, or defective because of the absence of adequate warnings, the trier of fact must consider more sophisticated matters than would be applied under a general negligence standard.

A second rationale to support the award of damages for pain and suffering is that they have an important deterrent function. The "Task Force Report" found evidence that the general product liability problem caused manufacturers to devote more attention to product liability loss prevention techniques. *See* "Task Force Report" at VI–50. The approach taken in Section 118 retains this deterrent function while placing some reasonable limits on awards for pain and suffering.

A third rationale, supported by members of the plaintiffs' bar and some economic legal scholars, is that awards for pain and suffering are a reasonable attempt to reduce the serious discomfort endured by a claimant. *See* R. Posner, "Economic Analysis of Law" 82 (1972). On the other hand, studies have questioned whether monetary awards for pain and suffering do anything to alleviate the symptoms they are alleged to address. *See* J. O'Connell & R. Simon, "Payment for Pain & Suffering: Who Wants What, When & Why" (1972); Peck, "Compensation for Pain: A Reappraisal in Light of New Medical Evidence," 72 "Mich.

L.Rev." 1355 (1974). This Section adheres to the former assumption to the extent that when a claimant suffers serious and permanent or prolonged (1) disfigurement, (2) impairment of bodily function, (3) pain and discomfort, or (4) serious mental illness, the amount of non-pecuniary damages is left to the sound discretion of the trier of fact with appropriate review by the court in cases of abuse of that discretion.

However, when the claimant has not suffered such serious and permanent or prolonged harms,[17] non-pecuniary damages are limited to $25,000 or twice the amount of pecuniary damages, whichever is less.

An ample body of case law in the area of Worker Compensation and, more recently, automobile injury reparation statutes, provides guidance for the court to determine whether a harm is permanent or prolonged. *See, e.g.,* "Falcone v. Branker," 135 N.J.Super. 137, 342 A.2d 875 (1975)(collecting cases); "Vitale v. Danylak," 74 Mich.App. 615, 254 N.W.2d 593 (1977)(summary judgment under automobile no-fault act); "*In re* Requests of Governor and Senate, Etc.," 389 Mich. 441, 208 N.W.2d 469, 480 (1973)(term "permanent" supplies basis for legal interpretation).

Courts also have defined and explained the term "mental illness" in a number of contexts. "Carroll v. Cobb," 139 N.J.Super. 439, 354 A.2d 355 (1976)(voter registration requirements); "Sachs v. Commercial Ins. Co.," 119 N.J.Super. 226,

---

17. The Section does not address the question of whether non-pecuniary damages should be allowed or limited in wrongful death or survival actions.

290 A.2d 760 (1972)(insurance policy); "*In re* Humphrey," 236 N.C. 142, 71 S.E.2d 915 (1952)(incompetency proceedings); "Commonwealth v. Moon," 383 Pa. 18, 117 A.2d 96 (1955)(committal proceedings); "Interstate Life & Accident Ins. Co. v. Houston," 50 Tenn.App. 172, 360 S.W.2d 71 (1962)(insanity exclusion provision).

Objections to limits on awards for non-pecuniary damages take several forms. One is that such limits may violate due process or equal protection clauses of some state constitutions. *Cf.* "Wright v. Central Du Page Hosp. Ass'n.," 63 Ill.2d 313, 347 N.E.2d 736, 743 (1976)(restriction on amount of general damages in medical malpractice); "Graley v. Satayatham," 74 Ohio Op.2d 316, 343 N.E.2d 832, 836 (C.P.1976)(requiring list of collateral source benefits in medical malpractice). Another objection involves state constitutional prohibitions on damage limitations. *E.g.,* "Ariz.Rev. Stat.Ann.," Const. Art. 18, Section 6 (1956); "Ky.Rev.Stat.Ann.," Const. Section 54 (1891); "Penn.Stat. Ann.," Const. Art. 3, Section 18 (1969). An argument that Section 118 does not violate such prohibitions is that a strict product liability cause of action did not exist at the time the state constitution was adopted and is therefore exempt from its interdictions. *See* "Rail N Ranch Corp. v. State," 7 Ariz.App. 558, 441 P.2d 786, 788 (1968).

These objections notwithstanding, Section 118 can be supported. First, the common law rule will continue to operate where injuries are serious. *Cf.* "Rybeck v. Rybeck," 141 N.J.Super. 481, 358 A.2d 828, 836 (1976), *appeal dismissed,* 150 N.J.Super. 151, 375 A.2d 269 (1977)(limited court access for pain and suffering in no-fault—"the law is permitted to treat large problems differently from small problems if there is a rational basis for the difference"). Second, some ceiling or limit on damages for pain and suffering will reduce uncertainty in one of the greatest liability insurance ratemaking problem areas. Third, the limit will help assure that there is adequate insurance capacity to provide compensation for pecuniary losses caused by unsafe products.

Subsection (D) provides a mechanism for review and evaluation of the $25,000 limitation contained in Subsection (C). It is anticipated that the legislature may wish periodically to modify this limitation in light of significant changes in economic conditions.

Because of the facts that (1) the topic of pain and suffering goes beyond product liability and is applicable to all of tort law, (2) the limitation as drafted may raise transaction costs in regard to the issue of whether a harm is "serious, permanent, or prolonged," and (3) constitutional problems that may arise in some states, Subsections (C) and (D) are placed in brackets as optional sections.

* * *

Code

§ 119. The Collateral Source Rule

In any claim brought under this Act, the claimant's recovery, or that of any party who may be subrogated to the claimant's rights under this Act, shall be reduced by any compensation from a public source which the claimant has received or will receive for the same damages. For the purposes of this Section, "public source" means a fund more than half of which is derived from general tax revenues.

* * *

Analysis

§ 119. The Collateral Source Rule

The collateral source rule is a principle of tort law under which the defendant is not permitted to take "credit" for any money that an injured claimant received from another (collateral) source. The rule embraces both payments for loss of wages and medical expenditures.

The rule may permit double recovery by the claimant and may increase transaction costs. This Section recognizes these possibilities and provides for a limited modification of the collateral source rule when the claimant has received compensation from a public source for the same damages. Its approach is similar to that followed in medical malpractice by the states of Tennessee and Pennsylvania. See Volume V, "Legal Study" at 146.

There are two significant arguments against proposals to modify the existing rule. The first is that the "wrongdoer" should not have the benefit of a windfall. Proponents contend that it is better that the claimant have the benefit of a windfall than the defendant.

This argument can be rebutted in the context of product liability. Under Section 104 of this Act, a manufacturer may be held liable for defects in construction or breach of an express warranty on a strict liability basis. In other cases, a product seller's liability is based on fault, but not on gross negligence or intentionally wrongful conduct. Therefore, a selective modification of the collateral source rule in the context of product liability may be justified. Indeed, some states have upheld such selective abolition or modification where liability was predicated solely on a fault basis. See "Eastin v. Broomfield," 116 Ariz. 576, 570 P.2d 744, 751–52 (1977); But see "Graley v. Satayatham," 74 Ohio Op.2d 316, 343 N.E.2d 832 (C.P.1976)(holding unconstitutional selective abolition in medical malpractice context).

The second argument against modifying the collateral source rule is that a product seller should not be permitted to "externalize" the cost of an injury caused by its products. This argument is very strong when the injured claimant has purchased health and accident coverage. In that instance, the defendant product seller should not be able to benefit from the claimant's prior prudence. Nevertheless, some proposals have modified the rule in that situation. See "Neb.Rev.Stat." Section 44–2819 (Supp.1978); "Prendergast v. Nelson," 199 Neb. 97, 256 N.W.2d 657, 669 (1977); National Product Liability Council, "Proposed Uniform State Product Liability Act" Section 207 (undated). See also Comment, "An Analysis of

State Legislative Responses to the Medical Malpractice Crisis," 1975 "Duke L.J." 1417, 1447–50. The argument is less persuasive when the claimant has not directly contributed to the insurance fund as is the case with Worker Compensation.

When the claimant has received damages from a public source, the argument loses all of its force. The benefits received were not through the claimant's pre-accident financial planning or made a part of the claimant's remuneration as a condition of employment. Rather, they were derived from public tax funds that accumulated in part by contributions from the product seller. Since the product seller would be able to distribute the cost of a judgment that included this amount among consumers through product pricing, the public may be subjected to excessive, duplicative costs.

Section 119 defines a "public source" as a fund more than half of which is derived from general tax revenues. This would include welfare benefits and other forms of medical, hospitalization, and disability benefits which are funded by state or federal tax funds. It does not include Worker Compensation payments (which are specifically dealt with in Section 114), employee group insurance plans, or other similar sources. It also does not presently include payments received pursuant to the "United States Social Security Act." Although Social Security contributions are withheld from an employee's pay, they are not "general tax revenues." However, if the method of funding the Social Security system is changed, such payments might then come

within the operation of this Section. *Compare* the approach taken in Section 119 *with* the various approaches taken in state medical malpractice statutes. *See, e.g.,* "Tenn. Code Ann." Section 23–3418 (Supp.1978)(complete abrogation of collateral source rule expressly includes Social Security benefits); "Neb.Rev.Stat." Section 44–2819 (Supp.1978)(partial abrogation of collateral source rule does not include Social Security benefits).

A probable effect of Section 119 will be to reduce double expenditures for medical costs. The "ISO Closed Claims Survey" suggests that medical costs represent approximately 19.7 percent of product liability claims. "ISO Closed Claims Survey" at 57. Nevertheless, the cost savings generated by this Section will probably be modest. The ISO closed claims data, which were quite limited on this point, show that approximately 6.4 percent of claimants have been reimbursed by public collateral sources. *See* "ISO Closed Claims Survey" at 181. Collateral sources paid for 19.8 percent of the claims in those cases (this closely parallels the general percentage of medical benefits). Nonetheless, this Section should help reduce overall insurance costs. Liability insurers should take this matter into account when they formulate rates and premiums.

Section 119 also takes account of existing legislation that may authorize subrogation by public collateral sources. In order to reduce transaction costs and duplicative distribution costs, this Section prohibits such subrogation.

Finally, Section 119 does not alter existing law that prohibits the defendant from introducing into evidence the fact that the claimant has been indemnified by a collateral source. That alternative approach was rejected because it would leave the trier of fact in the role of balancing the delicate policy elements that surround proposals calling for abolition of the collateral source rule. This should be an issue of law for state legislatures or courts. Also, that approach would reduce the potential benefit of collateral source rule modifications in that it would increase transaction costs and lower predictability and consistency in the allocation of collateral benefits. *See* "Task Force Report" at VII–74–75. *Cf.* Defense Research Institute, "Products Liability Position Paper" at 44–45 (1976)(advocating modification of evidentiary rules to allow trier of fact to consider all collateral benefits).

* * *

Code

§ 120. Punitive Damages

(A) Punitive damages may be awarded to the claimant if the claimant proves by clear and convincing evidence that the harm suffered was the result of the product seller's reckless disregard for the safety of product users, consumers, or others who might be harmed by the product.

(B) If the trier of fact determines that punitive damages should be awarded, the court shall determine the amount of those damages.

In making this determination, the court shall consider:

(1) The likelihood at the relevant time that serious harm would arise from the product seller's misconduct;

(2) The degree of the product seller's awareness of that likelihood;

(3) The profitability of the misconduct to the product seller;

(4) The duration of the misconduct and any concealment of it by the product seller;

(5) The attitude and conduct of the product seller upon discovery of the misconduct and whether the conduct has been terminated;

(6) The financial condition of the product seller;

(7) The total effect of other punishment imposed or likely to be imposed upon the product seller as a result of the misconduct, including punitive damage awards to persons similarly situated to the claimant and the severity of criminal penalties to which the product seller has been or may be subjected; and

(8) Whether the harm suffered by the claimant was also the result of the claimant's own reckless disregard for personal safety.

* * *

Analysis

§ 120. Punitive Damages

Some product sellers and others have called for the abolition of punitive damages on the grounds that they serve no proper "tort law" purpose,[18] and at least one court has accepted these arguments in the area of product liability. *See* "Walbrun v. Berkel, Inc.," 433 F.Supp. 384–85 (E.D.Wis.1976); "Roginsky v. Richardson–Merrell, Inc.," 378 F.2d 832 (2d Cir.1967)(dictum).

Nevertheless, as Section 120 acknowledges, punitive damages serve an important function in deterring product sellers from reckless disregard for safety in the production, distribution, or sale of dangerous products. *See* "Toole v. Richardson–Merrell, Inc.," 251 Cal.App.2d 689, 60 Cal.Rptr. 398 (1967); "Gillham v. Admiral Corp.," 523 F.2d 102 (6th Cir.1975). At the same time, Section 120 recognizes and addresses punitive damages problems in the specific context of product liability.

While many product sellers have expressed great concern about the economic impact of punitive damages, the "ISO Closed Claims Survey" suggests that the number of cases in which such damages are imposed is insubstantial. "ISO Closed Claims Survey" at 183. Nevertheless, concern about punitive damages has caused some insurers to decline to provide insurance coverage for these damages. Also, a number of states and some insurers have declined to permit such coverage. They contend that a product seller should not be allowed to pass this cost on to an insurer. Transcending all of these concerns is the total lack of legal structure surrounding punitive damages. The approach taken in Section 120 is to provide such a structure, so as to reduce product sellers' reasonable concerns about punitive damages, while at the same time retaining the important deterrent function of punitive damages.

Subsection (A) addresses a basic argument against punitive damages—specifically that they apply a criminal law sanction to a civil law case, even though the defendant does not have the benefit of the constitutional protections that would be available under criminal law. Subsection (A) moves away from the ordinary "preponderance of evidence" test of civil cases and toward the criminal standard, but does not turn completely to a pure criminal standard of proof "beyond a reasonable doubt." Because the defendant is not subject to incarceration, and the "punishment" is more in the nature of a civil fine than a criminal sanction, the Act requires the claimant to prove by "clear and convincing" evidence that punitive damages are justified. *See* Subsections 102(H) and (I)(definitions of "preponderance of evidence" and "clear and convincing evidence").

Subsection (A) also requires that the claimant prove that the product seller's conduct demonstrated reckless disregard for the safety of others. The phrase "reckless disregard"—the traditional barrier that the plaintiff must cross in order to obtain punitive damages—means a conscious indifference to the safety of persons who might be

18. *See* "Proposed Uniform State Product Liability Act" Section 206 (National Product Liability Council)(undated); *see generally* Defense Research Institute, "The Case Against Punitive Damages" (monograph 1969)(marshalling arguments).

injured by the product. *See* Subsection 102(J)(definition of "reckless disregard"); *cf.* W. Prosser, "Torts" at 9–10 (4th ed. 1971). The "reckless disregard" standard is identified in statutory form to avoid any possible misinterpretation of this basic area of law. Thus, it should be clear that a product seller does *not* have to pay punitive damages under ordinary strict liability or negligence standards which fall short of reckless disregard.

Subsection (B) follows the current common law system in allowing the trier of fact to determine at its discretion whether punitive damages should be awarded. *See* Prosser, *supra* at 9. On the other hand, this Subsection draws upon a newly enacted Minnesota statute in having the court, rather than the jury, determine the amount of those damages. "Minn.Stat.Ann." Section 549.21 (Supp.1978). This approach is in accord with the general pattern of criminal law where the jury determines "guilt or innocence" and the court imposes the sentence. This is particularly appropriate in product liability cases where, under current law, product sellers are potentially subject to repeated imposition of punitive damages for harm caused by a particular product.

Subsection (B) provides guidelines for the court in determining the amount of punitive damages. The eight factors are derived from "Minn.Stat.Ann." Section 549.20(3)(Supp.1978). The drafters of that statute relied on a very thorough analysis of product liability punitive damages. *See* Owen, "Punitive Damages in Products Liability Litigation," 74 "Mich.L.Rev." 1257, 1299–319 (1976).

Factors (1) and (2) are self-evident. If the facts show that the product seller was actually aware of the specific hazard *and* its seriousness, *and* marketed it anyway, a higher award is in order.

Factor (3), profitability, recognizes that punitive damages may be used to attack directly the profit incentive that generated the misconduct.

Factor (4) is important regardless of the basic requirement that the product seller must have reckless disregard for the safety of others. If the product seller consciously concealed its activities, this fact argues for a higher award.

Factor (5) acknowledges that the product seller who was reckless in producing the product, but who acted quickly to remove the product from the market upon discovery of the hazard, should not be subject to as harsh a sanction as one who failed to act. Some have suggested that punitive damages should be awarded only where corporate management has either authorized, participated in, or ratified conduct that shows a conscious or reckless disregard for public safety. *See* "Task Force Report" at VII–79. Section 120 rejects that approach because it could foster legal disputes as to whether an individual stood "high enough" in the corporate structure to bear responsibility for punitive damages. Nevertheless, in circumstances where a non-management employee caused the harm and management acted quickly to mitigate that harm once it was discovered, a lower award is appropriate.

Factor (6) permits the court to consider the impact of the award on the product seller in light of its financial condition. This consideration has deep roots in common law. It is one that has been subject to criticism from product sellers and economists. Nevertheless, in light of the fact that the deterrence of wrongful conduct is the principal rationale for punitive damages, it is appropriate to consider the impact an award will have on a particular product seller.

Factor (7) is more important in product liability cases than in other liability cases because it addresses the problem of multiple exposure to punitive damages. This factor directs the court to consider both criminal and civil liability to which the product seller has been or may be subjected.

Factor (8) recognizes that the injury may also be attributable in part to the claimant's reckless disregard for personal safety. In such instances where the defendant can show such reckless disregard on the part of the claimant, punitive damages may be diminished proportionately according to the comparative responsibility of that claimant. The comparison, therefore, is between the reckless disregard on the part of the product seller and that of the claimant, and *not* between the reckless disregard of the product seller and mere negligence of the claimant. *See also* Section 111.

The Act indicates that the award of punitive damages goes to the claimant and not to the state.

While the argument that "since the damages are non-compensatory, they should go to the state" has some merit, the approach was rejected because of constitutional problems and the fact that it might place a claimant's attorney in a potential conflict of interest situation by forcing the attorney to represent both the claimant and the state. *See* "Task Force Report" at VII–79.

When the trier of fact determines that punitive damages should be awarded, one option available to the court is to limit the award to a multiple of the compensatory damages as is done in antitrust actions. While this approach has appeal, it is not appropriate in the case of product liability because this area of the law addresses a multiplicity of different kinds of wrongful acts. Antitrust law, on the other hand, addresses one basic kind of wrongful act: an antitrust violation. Under this Section, the defendant's wrongful conduct could range from that which merely could cause damage to property to conduct which could result in the deaths of many people. Antitrust law violations involve economic injury only, and rarely, if ever, result in serious physical injury or death. Thus, the punitive damages in product liability actions do not lend themselves to quantification in the same manner as do such damages in antitrust cases.

* * *

Code

§ 121. Severance Clause

If any part of this Act shall be adjudged by any court of competent jurisdiction to be invalid, such judgment shall not affect, impair, or invalidate the remainder thereof, but shall be confined in its effect to that part of this Act declared to be invalid.

* * *

Analysis

§ 121. Severance Clause

This Section makes clear that in the event any court of competent jurisdiction declares any part of this Act to be invalid, such action shall be confined to that part alone, and shall not affect the validity of the remainder of the Act. The source of this Section is "1976 N.Y.Laws," ch. 955 (12)(McKinney), which concerns medical malpractice.

* * *

Code

§ 122. Effective Date

This Act shall be effective with regard to all product liability claims filed on or after _____, 19__.

* Alternative Section

[This Act shall be effective with regard to all claims accruing on or after _____, 19__. It shall be prospective in operation, and shall only apply to a product-related harm occurring on or after this date. When the facts giving rise to a claim are discovered or should have been discovered after this date, this Act shall govern the claimant's action. When the facts giving rise to a product-related harm are discovered or should have been discovered prior to the effective date of this Act, the law of this State which was applicable at the time of such discovery shall govern the claimant's action.]

* * *

Analysis

§ 122. Effective Date

The issue of the effective date of a tort-related statute has not been given intense analysis in legal periodicals—perhaps because there have been relatively few legislative initiatives in the tort area. In an attempt to balance fairness to all parties against procedural convenience, the drafters of this Act have chosen to apply the statute to all claims *filed* after the effective date.

The shortcoming of this approach is that it may create a rush to the courthouse—or, conversely, a delay—by claimants' attorneys. Also, the new law will apply to some injuries that occurred *before* the effective date.

On the other hand, since the Act does not create new causes of action, but condenses, clarifies, and balances common law development, the approach taken is a fair one. Also, it allows claimants, product sellers, and insurers to know, with precision, what law will be applied to a claim. *See* "1979 Minn.Laws" ch. 81, Section 3; "Conn.Gen.Stat." Section 52–572 1 (rev. 1979); *cf.* "Peterson v. City of Minneapolis," 285 Minn. 282, 173 N.W.2d 353 (1969); "Godfrey v. State," 84 Wash.2d 959, 530 P.2d 630 (1975); *see also* Annot., 37 "A.L.R.3d" 1438 (1971).

Because state legislatures are likely to differ about the issue of effective date, an alternative approach has been drafted. The alternative provision would have the Act apply only to a harm actually sustained or causes of action discovered, or which should have been discovered (*e.g.,* latent disease) on or after the effective date. This approach makes the Act fully prospective in nature and recognizes that certain illnesses, such as malignancies, only become discoverable some time after the actual contact with the product. In the case of disease or other illness with delayed effects, the Act would apply if the harm or the cause thereof were discovered on or after the effective date. *See* Section 109(C); *see also* 73 "Am. Jur.2d" "Statutes" Sections 385 *et seq.* (1974).

A significant shortcoming of this alternative approach is that for many years it will leave claimants, product sellers, and insurance ratemakers with two potential sources of product liability law—existing common law and this Act. It should be noted that the phrase "the law of this State," as used in the alternative, includes a state's conflict of law rules as well as its substantive product liability law.

* * *

Appendix A—A Bibliography of Major Compendium Sources Reviewed in Connection With the Model Code

Final Report, Interagency Task Force on Product Liability (NTIS, 1977).

Product Liability Legal Study, Interagency Task Force on Product Liability (NTIS, 1977).

Product Liability Industry Study, Interagency Task Force on Product Liability (NTIS, 1977).

Product Liability Insurance Study, Interagency Task Force on Product Liability (NTIS, 1977).

Selected Papers, Interagency Task Force on Product Liability (NTIS, 1978).

Insurance Services Office, Product Liability Closed Claims Survey: A Technical Analysis of Survey Results (ISO, 1977).

Product Liability Insurance, A Report of the Subcommittee on Capital, Investment and Business Opportunities of the Committee on Small Business, H.R.Rep. No. 95–997, 95th Cong., 2d Sess. (1978).

"Impact on Product Liability": Hearings before the Senate Select Committee on Small Business, 94th Cong., 2d Sess., 95th Cong., 1st Sess. (1976–77).

"Product Liability Insurance": Hearings on S. 403 before the Consumer Subcommittee of the Senate Committee on Commerce, Science and Transportation, 95th Cong., 1st Sess. (1977).

Department of Commerce Task Force Report on Product Liability Insurance (State of Michigan, 1978).

Final Report of the Governor's Task Force on Product Liability (Maine, 1978).

Product Liability: An Overview, Wisconsin Legislative Council, Research Bulletin 78 (1978).

Illinois House of Representatives, Judiciary I Subcommittee on Product Liability, Report and Recommendations (1978).

Report of the Senate Product Liability Study Committee, State Capitol, Georgia (1978).

Report of the Senate Select Committee on Product Liability, Missouri Senate (1977).

American Law Institute, Restatement (Second) of Torts, Section 402A and Appendices (1965).

Defense Research Institute, Inc., Products Liability Position Paper (1976).

The Alliance of American Insurers, Product Liability Tort Reform Proposals (1976).

Proposed Uniform State Product Liability Act (National Product Liability Council).

American Insurance Association, Product Liability Legislative Package (1977).

The California Citizens' Commission on Tort Reform, Righting the Liability Balance (1977).

A review was also conducted of all enacted state product liability laws, all proposed federal product liability laws, and major proposed state product liability laws, as well as all law review and other related literature and major case law reported or published since the completion of the Interagency Task Force's seven-volume Legal Study in December 1976. That study reviewed case law and literature published prior to that date. Consideration was also given to pre–1976 sources that were not reviewed by the Legal Study.

COMMON SENSE PRODUCT LIABILITY LEGAL REFORM ACT OF 1996

104th Congress

2nd Session

House Rpt. 104–481

H.R. 956

CONFERENCE REPORT

House Rpt. 104–481

Mr. Hyde, from the committee of conference submitted the following.

The committee of conference on the disagreeing votes of the two Houses on the amendment of the Senate to the bill (H.R. 956), to establish legal standards and procedures for product liability litigation, and for other purposes, having met, after full and free conference, have agreed to recommend and do recommend to their respective Houses as follows:

That the House recede from its disagreement to the amendment of the Senate and agree to the same with an amendment as follows:

In lieu of the matter proposed to be inserted by the Senate amendment, insert the following:

SECTION 1. SHORT TITLE AND TABLE OF CONTENTS.

(a) SHORT TITLE.—This Act may be cited as the "Common Sense Product Liability Legal Reform Act of 1996".

(b) TABLE OF CONTENTS.—The table of contents is as follows:

SEC. 2.   FINDINGS AND PURPOSES.

(a) FINDINGS.—The Congress finds that—

(1) our Nation is overly litigious, the civil justice system is overcrowded, sluggish, and excessively costly and the costs of lawsuits, both direct and indirect, are inflicting serious and unnecessary injury on the national economy;

(2) excessive, unpredictable, and often arbitrary damage awards and unfair allocations of liability have a direct and undesirable effect on interstate commerce by increasing the cost and decreasing the availability of goods and services;

(3) the rules of law governing product liability actions, damage awards, and allocations of liability have evolved inconsistently within and among the States, resulting in a complex, contradictory, and uncertain regime that is inequitable to both plaintiffs and defendants and unduly burdens interstate commerce;

(4) as a result of excessive, unpredictable, and often arbitrary damage awards and unfair allocations of liability, consumers have been adversely affected through the withdrawal of products, producers, services, and service providers from the marketplace, and from excessive liability costs passed on to them through higher prices;

(5) excessive, unpredictable, and often arbitrary damage awards and unfair allocations of liability jeopardize the financial well-being of many individuals as well as entire industries, particularly the Nations small businesses and adversely affects government and taxpayers;

(6) the excessive costs of the civil justice system undermine the ability of American companies to compete internationally, and serve to decrease the number of jobs and the amount of productive capital in the national economy;

(7) the unpredictability of damage awards is inequitable to both plaintiffs and defendants and has added considerably to the high cost

of liability insurance, making it difficult for producers, consumers, volunteers, and nonprofit organizations to protect themselves from liability with any degree of confidence and at a reasonable cost;

(8) because of the national scope of the problems created in the civil justice system, it is not possible for the States to enact laws that fully and effectively respond to those problems;

(9) it is the constitutional role of the national government to remove barriers to interstate commerce and to protect due process rights; and

(10) there is a need to restore rationality, certainty, and fairness to the civil justice system in order to protect against excessive, arbitrary, and uncertain damage awards and to reduce the volume, costs, and delay of litigation.

(b) PURPOSES.—Based upon the powers contained in Article I, Section 8, Clause 3 and the Fourteenth Amendment of the United States Constitution, the purposes of this Act are to promote the free flow of goods and services and to lessen burdens on interstate commerce and to uphold constitutionally protected due process rights by—

(1) establishing certain uniform legal principles of product liability which provide a fair balance among the interests of product users, manufacturers, and product sellers;

(2) placing reasonable limits on damages over and above the actual damages suffered by a claimant;

(3) ensuring the fair allocation of liability in civil actions;

(4) reducing the unacceptable costs and delays of our civil justice system caused by excessive litigation which harm both plaintiffs and defendants; and

(5) establishing greater fairness, rationality, and predictability in the civil justice system.

TITLE I—PRODUCT LIABILITY REFORM

SEC. 101. DEFINITIONS.

For purposes of this title—

(1) ACTUAL MALICE.—The term "actual malice" means specific intent to cause serious physical injury, illness, disease, death, or damage to property.

(2) CLAIMANT.—The term "claimant" means any person who brings an action covered by this title and any person on whose behalf such an action is brought. If such an action is brought through or on behalf of an estate, the term includes the claimant's decedent. If such an action is brought through or on behalf of a minor or incompetent, the term includes the claimant's legal guardian.

(3) CLAIMANT'S BENEFITS.—The term "claimant's benefits" means the amount paid to an employee as workers' compensation benefits.

(4) CLEAR AND CONVINCING EVIDENCE.—The term "clear and convincing evidence" is that measure or degree of proof that will produce in the mind of the trier of fact a firm belief or conviction as to the truth of the allegations sought to be established. The level of proof required to satisfy such standard is more than that required under preponderance of the evidence, but less than that required for proof beyond a reasonable doubt.

(5) COMMERCIAL LOSS.—The term "commercial loss" means any loss or damage solely to a product itself, loss relating to a dispute over its value, or consequential economic loss, the recovery of which is governed by the Uniform Commercial Code or analogous State commercial or contract law.

(6) COMPENSATORY DAMAGES.—The term "compensatory damages" means damages awarded for economic and non-economic loss.

(7) DURABLE GOOD.—The term "durable good" means any product, or any component of any such product, which has a normal life expectancy of 3 or more years, or is of a character subject to allowance for depreciation under the Internal Revenue Code of 1986 and which is—

(A) used in a trade or business;

(B) held for the production of income; or

(C) sold or donated to a governmental or private entity for the production of goods, training, demonstration, or any other similar purpose.

(8) ECONOMIC LOSS.—The term "economic loss" means any pecuniary loss resulting from harm (including the loss of earnings or other benefits related to employment, medical expense loss, replacement services loss, loss due to death, burial costs, and loss of business or employment opportunities) to the extent recovery for such loss is allowed under applicable State law.

(9) HARM.—The term "harm" means any physical injury, illness, disease, or death or damage to property caused by a product. The term does not include commercial loss.

(10) INSURER.—The term "insurer" means the employer of a claimant if the employer is self-insured or if the employer is not self-insured, the workers compensation insurer of the employer.

(11) MANUFACTURER.—The term "manufacturer" means—

(A) any person who is engaged in a business to produce, create, make, or construct any product (or component part of a product) and who

(i) designs or formulates the product (or component part of the product), or

(ii) has engaged another person to design or formulate the product (or component part of the product);

(B) a product seller, but only with respect to those aspects of a product (or component part of a product) which are created or affected when, before placing the product in the stream of commerce, the product seller produces, creates, makes or constructs and designs, or formulates, or has engaged another person to design or formulate, an aspect of the product (or component part of the product) made by another person; or

(C) any product seller not described in subparagraph (B) which holds itself out as a manufacturer to the user of the product.

(12) NONECONOMIC LOSS.—The term "noneconomic loss" means subjective, nonmonetary loss resulting from harm, including pain, suffering, inconvenience, mental suffering, emotional distress, loss of society and companionship, loss of consortium, injury to reputation, and humiliation.

(13) PERSON.—The term "person" means any individual, corporation, company, association, firm, partnership, society, joint stock company, or any other entity (including any governmental entity).

(14) PRODUCT.—

(A) IN GENERAL.—The term "product" means any object, substance, mixture, or raw material in a gaseous, liquid, or solid state which—

(i) is capable of delivery itself or as an assembled whole, in a mixed or combined state, or as a component part or ingredient;

(ii) is produced for introduction into trade or commerce;

(iii) has intrinsic economic value; and

(iv) is intended for sale or lease to person for commercial or personal use.

(B) EXCLUSION.—The term does not include—

(i) tissue, organs, blood, and blood products used for therapeutic or medical purposes, except to the extent that such tissue, organs, blood, and blood products (or the provision thereof) are subject, under applicable State law, to a standard of liability other than negligence; or

(ii) electricity, water delivered by a utility, natural gas, or steam except to the extent that electricity, water delivered by a utility, natural gas, or steam, is subject, under applicable State law, to a standard of liability other than negligence.

(15) PRODUCT LIABILITY ACTION.—The term "product liability action" means a civil action brought on any theory for harm caused by a product.

(16) PRODUCT SELLER.—

(A) IN GENERAL.—The term "product seller" means a person who in the course of a business conducted for that purpose—

(i) sells, distributes, rents, leases, prepares, blends, packages, labels, or otherwise is involved in placing a product in the stream of commerce; or

(ii) installs, repairs, refurbishes, reconditions, or maintains the harm-causing aspect of the product.

(B) EXCLUSION.—The term "product seller" does not include—

(i) a seller or lessor of real property;

(ii) a provider of professional services in any case in which the sale or use of a product is incidental to the transaction and the essence of the transaction is the furnishing of judgment, skill, or services; or

(iii) any person who—

(I) acts in only a financial capacity with respect to the sale of a product; or

(II) leases a product under a lease arrangement in which the lessor does not initially select the leased product and does not during the lease term ordinarily control the daily operations and maintenance of the product.

(17) PUNITIVE DAMAGES.—The term "punitive damages" means damages awarded against any person or entity to punish or deter such person or entity, or others, from engaging in similar behavior in the future.

(18) STATE.—The term "State" means any State of the United States, the District of Columbia, Commonwealth of Puerto Rico, the Northern Mariana Islands, the Virgin Islands, Guam, American Samoa, and any other territory or possession of the United States or any political subdivision of any of the foregoing.

SEC. 102. APPLICABILITY; PREEMPTION.

(a) PREEMPTION.—

(1) IN GENERAL.—This Act governs any product liability action brought in any State or Federal court on any theory for harm caused by a product.

(2) ACTIONS EXCLUDED.—A civil action brought for commercial loss shall be governed only by applicable commercial or contract law.

(b) RELATIONSHIP TO STATE LAW.—This title supersedes State law only to the extent that State law applies to an issue covered by this title. Any issue that is not governed by this title, including any standard of liability applicable to a manufacturer, shall be governed by otherwise applicable State or Federal law.

(c) EFFECT ON OTHER LAW.—Nothing in this Act shall be construed to—

(1) waive or affect any defense of sovereign immunity asserted by any State under any law;

(2) supersede or alter any Federal law;

(3) waive or affect any defense of sovereign immunity asserted by the United States;

(4) affect the applicability of any provision of chapter 97 of title 28, United States Code;

(5) preempt State choice-of-law rules with respect to claims brought by a foreign nation or a citizen of a foreign nation;

(6) affect the right of any court to transfer venue or to apply the law of a foreign nation or to dismiss a claim of a foreign nation or of a citizen of a foreign nation on the ground of inconvenient forum; or

(7) supersede or modify any statutory or common law, including any law providing for an action to abate a nuisance, that authorizes a person to institute an action for civil damages or civil penalties, cleanup costs, injunctions, restitution, cost recovery, punitive damages, or any other form of relief for remediation of the environment (as defined in section 101(8) of the Comprehensive Environmental Response, Compensation, and Liability Act of 1980 (42 U.S.C. 9601(8))).

SEC. 103. LIABILITY RULES APPLICABLE TO PRODUCT SELLERS, RENTERS, AND LESSORS.

(a) GENERAL RULE.—

(1) IN GENERAL.—In any product liability action, a product seller other than a manufacturer shall be liable to a claimant only if the claimant establishes—

(A) that—

(i) the product that allegedly caused the harm that is the subject of the complaint was sold, rented, or leased by the product seller;

(ii) the product seller failed to exercise reasonable care with respect to the product; and

(iii) the failure to exercise reasonable care was a proximate cause of harm to the claimant;

(B) that—

(i) the product seller made an express warranty applicable to the product that allegedly caused the harm that is the subject of the complaint, independent of any express warranty made by a manufacturer as to the same product;

(ii) the product failed to conform to the warranty; and

(iii) the failure of the product to conform to the warranty caused harm to the claimant; or

(C) that—

(i) the product seller engaged in intentional wrongdoing, as determined under applicable State law; and

(ii) such intentional wrongdoing was a proximate cause of the harm that is the subject of the complaint.

(2) REASONABLE OPPORTUNITY FOR INSPECTION.—For purposes of paragraph (1)(A)(ii), a product seller shall not be considered to have failed to exercise reasonable care with respect to a product based upon an alleged failure to inspect the product—

(A) if the failure occurred because there was no reasonable opportunity to inspect the product; or

(B) if the inspection, in the exercise of reasonable care, would not have revealed the aspect of the product which allegedly caused the claimants harm.

(b) SPECIAL RULE.—

(1) IN GENERAL.—A product seller shall be deemed to be liable as a manufacturer of a product for harm caused by the product if—

(A) the manufacturer is not subject to service of process under the laws of any State in which the action may be brought; or

(B) the court determines that the claimant would be unable to enforce a judgment against the manufacturer.

(2) STATUTE OF LIMITATION.—For purposes of this subsection only, the statute of limitations applicable to claims asserting liability of a product seller as a manufacturer shall be tolled from the date of the

filing of a complaint against the manufacturer to the date that judgment is entered against the manufacturer.

(c) RENTED OR LEASED PRODUCTS.—

(1) Notwithstanding any other provision of law, any person engaged in the business of renting or leasing a product (other than a person excluded from the definition of product seller under section 101(16)(B)) shall be subject to liability in a product liability action under subsection (a), but any person engaged in the business of renting or leasing a product shall not be liable to a claimant for the tortious act of another solely by reason of ownership of such product.

(2) For purposes of paragraph (1), and for determining the applicability of this title to any person subject to paragraph (1), the term "product liability action" means a civil action brought on any theory for harm caused by a product or product use.

(d) ACTIONS FOR NEGLIGENT ENTRUSTMENT.—A civil action for negligent entrustment shall not be subject to the provisions of this section, but shall be subject to any applicable State law.

SEC. 104. DEFENSE BASED ON CLAIMANTS USE OF INTOXICATING ALCOHOL OR DRUGS.

(a) GENERAL RULE.—In any product liability action, it shall be a complete defense to such action if—

(1) the claimant was intoxicated or was under the influence of intoxicating alcohol or any drug when the accident or other event which resulted in such claimants harm occurred; and

(2) the claimant, as a result of the influence of the alcohol or drug, was more than 50 percent responsible for such accident or other event.

(b) CONSTRUCTION.—For purposes of subsection (a)—

(1) the determination of whether a person was intoxicated or was under the influence of intoxicating alcohol or any drug shall be made pursuant to applicable State law; and

(2) the term "drug" means any controlled substance as defined in the Controlled Substances Act (21 U.S.C. 802(6)) that was not legally prescribed for use by the claimant or that was taken by the claimant other than in accordance with the terms of a lawfully issued prescription.

SEC. 105. MISUSE OR ALTERATION.

(a) GENERAL RULE.—

(1) IN GENERAL.—In a product liability action, the damages for which a defendant is otherwise liable under Federal or State law shall

be reduced by the percentage of responsibility for the claimants harm attributable to misuse or alteration of a product by any person if the defendant establishes that such percentage of the claimants harm was proximately caused by a use or alteration of a product—

(A) in violation of, or contrary to, a defendant's express warnings or instructions if the warnings or instructions are adequate as determined pursuant to applicable State law; or

(B) involving a risk of harm which was known or should have been known by the ordinary person who uses or consumes the product with the knowledge common to the class of persons who used or would be reasonably anticipated to use the product.

(2) USE INTENDED BY A MANUFACTURER IS NOT MISUSE OR ALTERATION.—For the purposes of this Act, a use of a product that is intended by the manufacturer of the product does not constitute a misuse or alteration of the product.

(b) WORKPLACE INJURY.—Notwithstanding subsection (a), and except as otherwise provided in section 111, the damages for which a defendant is otherwise liable under State law shall not be reduced by the percentage of responsibility for the claimant's harm attributable to misuse or alteration of the product by the claimant's employer or any coemployee who is immune from suit by the claimant pursuant to the State law applicable to workplace injuries.

SEC. 106.   UNIFORM TIME LIMITATIONS ON LIABILITY.

(a) STATUTE OF LIMITATIONS.—

(1) IN GENERAL.—Except as provided in paragraph (2) and subsection (b), a product liability action may be filed not later than 2 years after the date on which the claimant discovered or, in the exercise of reasonable care, should have discovered—

(A) the harm that is the subject of the action; and

(B) the cause of the harm.

(2) EXCEPTION.—A person with a legal disability (as determined under applicable law) may file a product liability action not later than 2 years after the date on which the person ceases to have the legal disability.

(b) STATUTE OF REPOSE.—

(1) IN GENERAL.—Subject to paragraphs (2) and (3), no product liability action that is subject to this Act concerning a product, that is a durable good, alleged to have caused harm (other than toxic harm) may be filed after the 15–year period beginning at the time of delivery of the product to the first purchaser or lessee.

(2) STATE LAW.—Notwithstanding paragraph (1), if pursuant to an applicable State law, an action described in such paragraph is required to be filed during a period that is shorter than the 15–year period specified in such paragraph, the State law shall apply with respect to such period.

(3) EXCEPTIONS.—

(A) A motor vehicle, vessel, aircraft, or train, that is used primarily to transport passengers for hire, shall not be subject to this subsection.

(B) Paragraph (1) does not bar a product liability action against a defendant who made an express warranty in writing as to the safety or life expectancy of the specific product involved which was longer than 15 years, but it will apply at the expiration of that warranty.

(C) Paragraph (1) does not affect the limitations period established by the General Aviation Revitalization Act of 1994 (49 U.S.C. 40101 note).

(c) TRANSITIONAL PROVISION RELATING TO EXTENSION OF PERIOD FOR BRINGING CERTAIN ACTIONS.—If any provision of subsection (a) or (b) shortens the period during which a product liability action could be otherwise brought pursuant to another provision of law, the claimant may, notwithstanding subsections (a) and (b), bring the product liability action not later than 1 year after the date of enactment of this Act.

SEC. 107. ALTERNATIVE DISPUTE RESOLUTION PROCEDURES.

(a) SERVICE OF OFFER.—A claimant or a defendant in a product liability action may, not later than 60 days after the service of—

(1) the initial complaint; or

(2) the applicable deadline for a responsive pleading; whichever is later, serve upon an adverse party an offer to proceed pursuant to any voluntary, nonbinding alternative dispute resolution procedure established or recognized under the law of the State in which the product liability action is brought or under the rules of the court in which such action is maintained.

(b) WRITTEN NOTICE OF ACCEPTANCE OR REJECTION.—Except as provided in subsection (c), not later than 10 days after the service of an offer to proceed under subsection (a), an offeree shall file a written notice of acceptance or rejection of the offer.

(c) EXTENSION.—The court may, upon motion by an offeree made prior to the expiration of the 10–day period specified in subsection (b), extend the period for filling a written notice under such subsection for a period of not more than 60 days after the date of expiration of the period specified in subsection (b). Discovery may be permitted during such period.

SEC. 108.   UNIFORM STANDARDS FOR AWARD OF PUNITIVE DAMAGES.

(a) GENERAL RULE.—Punitive damages may, to the extent permitted by applicable State law, be awarded against a defendant if the claimant establishes by clear and convincing evidence that conduct carried out by the defendant with a conscious, flagrant indifference to the rights or safety of others was the proximate cause of the harm that is the subject of the action in any product liability action.

(b) LIMITATION ON AMOUNT.—

(1) IN GENERAL.—The amount of punitive damages that may be awarded in an action described in subsection (a) may not exceed the greater of—

(A) 2 times the sum of the amount awarded to the claimant for economic loss and noneconomic loss; or

(B) $250,000.

(2) SPECIAL RULE.—Notwithstanding paragraph (1), in any action described in subsection (a) against an individual whose net worth does not exceed $500,000 or against an owner of an unincorporated business, or any partnership, corporation, association, unit of local government, or organization which has fewer that 25 full-time employees, the punitive damages shall not exceed the lesser of—

(A) 2 times the sum of the amount awarded to the claimant for economic loss and noneconomic loss; or

(B) $250,000. For the purpose of determining the applicability of this paragraph to a corporation, the number of employees of a subsidiary or wholly-owned corporation shall include all employees of a parent or sister corporation.

(3) EXCEPTION FOR INSUFFICIENT AWARD IN CASES OF EGREGIOUS CONDUCT.—

(A) DETERMINATION BY COURT.—If the court makes a determination, after considering each of the factors in subparagraph (B), that the application of paragraph (1) would result in an award of punitive damages that is insufficient to punish the egregious conduct of the defendant against whom the punitive damages are to be awarded or to deter such conduct in the future, the court shall determine the additional amount of punitive damages (referred to in this paragraph as the "additional amount") in excess of the amount determined in accordance with paragraph (1) to be awarded against the defendant in a separate proceeding in accordance with this paragraph.

(B) FACTORS FOR CONSIDERATION.—In any proceeding under paragraph (A), the court shall consider—

(i) the extent to which the defendant acted with actual malice;

(ii) the likelihood that serious harm would arise from the conduct of the defendant;

(iii) the degree of the awareness of the defendant of that likelihood;

(iv) the profitability of the misconduct to the defendant;

(v) the duration of the misconduct and any concurrent or subsequent concealment of the conduct by the defendant;

(vi) the attitude and conduct of the defendant upon the discovery of the misconduct and whether the misconduct has terminated;

(vii) the financial condition of the defendant; and

(viii) the cumulative deterrent effect of other losses, damages, and punishment suffered by the defendant as a result of the misconduct, reducing the amount of punitive damages on the basis of the economic impact and severity of all measures to which the defendant has been or may be subjected, including—

(I) compensatory and punitive damage awards to similarly situated claimants;

(II) the adverse economic effect of stigma or loss of reputation;

(III) civil fines and criminal and administrative penalties; and

(IV) stop sale, cease and desist, and other remedial or enforcement orders.

(C) REQUIREMENTS FOR AWARDING ADDITIONAL AMOUNT.—If the court awards an additional amount pursuant to this subsection, the court shall state its reasons for setting the amount of the additional amount in findings of fact and conclusions of law.

(D) PREEMPTION.—This section does not create a cause of action for punitive damages and does not preempt or supersede any State or Federal law to the extent that such law would further limit the award of punitive damages. Nothing in this subsection shall modify or reduce the ability of courts to order remittiturs.

(4) APPLICATION BY COURT.—This subsection shall be applied by the court and application of this subsection shall not be disclosed to the jury. Nothing in this subsection shall authorize the court to enter an award of punitive damages in excess of the jury's initial ward of punitive damages.

(C) BIFURCATION AT REQUEST OF ANY PARTY.—

(1) IN GENERAL.—At the request of any party the trier of fact in any action that is subject to this section shall consider in a separate proceeding, held subsequent to the determination of the amount of compensatory damages, whether punitive damages are to be awarded for the harm that is the subject of the action and the amount of the award.

(2) INADMISSIBILITY OF EVIDENCE RELATIVE ONLY TO A CLAIM OF PUNITIVE DAMAGES IN A PROCEEDING CONCERNING COMPENSATORY DAMAGES.—If any party requests a separate proceeding under paragraph (1), in a proceeding to determine whether the claimant may be awarded compensatory damages, any evidence, argument, or contention that is relevant only to the claim of punitive damages, as determined by applicable State law, shall be inadmissible.

SEC. 109. LIABILITY FOR CERTAIN CLAIMS RELATING TO DEATH.

In any civil action in which the alleged harm to the claimant is death and, as of the effective date of this Act, the applicable State law provides, or has been construed to provide, for damages only punitive in nature, a defendant may be liable for any such damages without regard to section 108, but only during such time as the State law so provides. This section shall cease to be effective September 1, 1996.

SEC. 110. SEVERAL LIABILITY FOR NONECONOMIC LOSS.

(a) GENERAL RULE.—In a product liability action, the liability of each defendant for noneconomic loss shall be several only and shall not be joint.

(b) AMOUNT OF LIABILITY.—

(1) IN GENERAL.—Each defendant shall be liable only for the amount of noneconomic loss allocated to the defendant in direct proportion to the percentage of responsibility of the defendant (determined in accordance with paragraph (2)) for the harm to the claimant with respect to which the defendant is liable. The court shall render a separate judgment against each defendant in an amount determined pursuant to the preceding sentence.

(2) PERCENTAGE OF RESPONSIBILITY.—For purposes of determining the amount of noneconomic loss allocated to a defendant under this section, the trier of fact shall determine the percentage of responsibility of each person responsible for the claimant's harm, whether or not such person is a party to the action.

SEC. 111.   WORKERS COMPENSATION SUBROGATION.

(a) GENERAL RULE.—

(1) RIGHT OF SUBROGATION.—

(A) IN GENERAL.—An insurer shall have a right of subrogation against a manufacturer or product seller to recover any claimants benefits relating to harm that is the subject of a product liability action that is subject to this Act.

(B) WRITTEN NOTIFICATION.—To assert a right of subrogation under subparagraph (A), the insurer shall provide written notice to the court in which the product liability action is brought.

(C) INSURER NOT REQUIRED TO BE A PARTY.—An insurer shall not be required to be a necessary and proper party in a product liability action covered under subparagraph (A).

(2) SETTLEMENTS AND OTHER LEGAL PROCEEDINGS.—

(A) IN GENERAL.—In any proceeding relating to harm or settlement with the manufacturer or product seller by a claimant who files a product liability action that is subject to this Act, an insurer may participate to assert a right of subrogation for claimant's benefits with respect to any payment made by the manufacturer or product seller by reason of such harm, without regard to whether the payment is made—

(i) as part of a settlement;

(ii) in satisfaction of judgment;

(iii) as consideration for a covenant not to sue; or

(iv) in another manner.

(B) WRITTEN NOTIFICATION.—Except as provided in subparagraph (C), an employee shall not make any settlement with or accept any payment from the manufacturer or product seller without written notification to the insurer.

(C) EXEMPTION.—Subparagraph (B) shall not apply in any case in which the insurer has been compensated for the full amount of the claimant's benefits.

(3) HARM RESULTING FROM ACTION OF EMPLOYER OR COEMPLOYEE.—

(A) IN GENERAL.—If, with respect to a product liability action that is subject to this Act, the manufacturer or product seller attempts to persuade the trier of fact that the harm to the claimant was caused by the fault of the employer of the claimant or any coemployee of the claimant, the issue of that fault shall be submitted to the trier of fact, but only after the manufacturer or product seller has provided timely written notice to the insurer.

(B) RIGHTS OF INSURER.—

(i) IN GENERAL.—Notwithstanding any other provision of law, with respect to an issue of fault submitted to a trier of fact pursuant to subparagraph (A), an insurer shall, in the same manner as any party in the action (even if the insurer is not a named party in the action), have the right to—

(I) appear;

(II) be represented;

(III) introduce evidence;

(IV) cross-examine adverse witnesses; and

(V) present arguments to the trier of fact.

(ii) LAST ISSUE.—The issue of harm resulting from an action of an employer or coemployee shall be the last issue that is submitted to the trier of fact.

(C) REDUCTION OF DAMAGES.—If the trier of fact finds by clear and convincing evidence that the harm to the claimant that is the subject of the product liability action was caused by the fault of the employer or a coemployee of the claimant—

(i) the court shall reduce by the amount of the claimants benefits—

(I) the damages awarded against the manufacturer or product seller; and

(II) any corresponding insurers subrogation lien; and

(ii) the manufacturer or product seller shall have no further right by way of contribution or otherwise against the employer.

(D) CERTAIN RIGHTS OF SUBROGATION NOT AFFECTED.—Notwithstanding a finding by the trier of fact described in subparagraph (C), the insurer shall not lose any right of subrogation related to any—

(i) intentional tort committed against the claimant by a coemployee; or

(ii) act committed by a coemployee outside the scope of normal work practices.

(b) ATTORNEY'S FEES.—If, in a product liability action that is subject to this section, the court finds that harm to a claimant was not caused by the fault of the employer or a coemployee of the claimant, the manufacturer or product seller shall reimburse the insurer for reasonable attorneys fees and court costs incurred by the insurer in the action, as determined by the court.

TITLE II—BIOMATERIALS ACCESS ASSURANCE

SEC. 201. SHORT TITLE.

This title may be cited as the "Biomaterials Access Assurance Act of 1996".

SEC. 202. FINDINGS.

Congress finds that—

(1) each year millions of citizens of the United States depend on the availability of lifesaving or life enhancing medical devices, many of which are permanently implantable within the human body;

(2) a continued supply of raw materials and component parts is necessary for the invention, development, improvement, and maintenance of the supply of the devices;

(3) most of the medical devices are made with raw materials and component parts that—

(A) are not designed or manufactured specifically for use in medical devices; and

(B) come in contact with internal human tissue;

(4) the raw materials and component parts also are used in a variety of nonmedical products;

(5) because small quantities of the raw materials and component parts are used for medical devices, sales of raw materials and component parts for medical devices constitute an extremely small portion of the overall market for the raw materials and medical devices;

(6) under the Federal Food, Drug, and Cosmetic Act (21 U.S.C. 301 et seq.), manufacturers of medical devices are required to demonstrate that the medical devices are safe and effective, including demonstrating that the products are properly designed and have adequate warnings or instructions;

(7) notwithstanding the fact that raw materials and component parts suppliers do not design, produce, or test a final medical device, the suppliers have been the subject of actions alleging inadequate—

(A) design and testing of medical devices manufactured with materials or parts supplied by the suppliers; or

(B) warnings related to the use of such medical devices;

(8) even though suppliers of raw materials and component parts have very rarely been held liable in such actions, such suppliers have

ceased supplying certain raw materials and component parts for use in medical devices because the costs associated with litigation in order to ensure a favorable judgment for the suppliers far exceeds the total potential sales revenues from sales by such suppliers to the medical device industry;

(9) unless alternate sources of supply can be found, the unavailability of raw materials and component parts for medical devices will lead to unavailability of lifesaving and life-enhancing medical devices;

(10) because other suppliers of the raw materials and component parts in foreign nations are refusing to sell raw materials or component parts for use in manufacturing certain medical devices in the United States, the prospects for development of new sources of supply for the full range of threatened raw materials and component parts for medical devices are remote;

(11) it is unlikely that the small market for such raw materials and component parts in the United States could support the large investment needed to develop new suppliers of such raw materials and component parts;

(12) attempts to develop such new suppliers would raise the cost of medical devices;

(13) courts that have considered the duties of the suppliers of the raw materials and component parts have generally found that the suppliers do not have a duty—

(A) to evaluate the safety and efficacy of the use of a raw material or component part in a medical device; and

(B) to warn consumers concerning the safety and effectiveness of a medical device;

(14) attempts to impose the duties referred to in subparagraphs (A) and (B) of paragraph (13) on suppliers of the raw materials and component parts would cause more harm than good by driving the suppliers to cease supplying manufacturers of medical devices; and

(15) in order to safeguard the availability of a wide variety of lifesaving and life-enhancing medical devices, immediate action is needed—

(A) to clarify the permissible bases of liability for suppliers of raw materials and component parts for medical devices; and

(B) to provide expeditious procedures to dispose of unwarranted suits against the suppliers in such manner as to minimize litigation costs.

SEC. 203.   DEFINITIONS.

As used in this title:

(1) BIOMATERIALS SUPPLIER.—

(A) IN GENERAL.—The term "biomaterials supplier" means an entity that directly or indirectly supplies a component part or raw material for use in the manufacture of an implant.

(B) PERSONS INCLUDED.—Such term includes any person who—

(i) has submitted master files to the Secretary for purposes of premarket approval of a medical device; or

(ii) licenses a biomaterials supplier to produce component parts or raw materials.

(2) CLAIMANT.—

(A) IN GENERAL.—The term "claimant" means any person who brings a civil action, or on whose behalf a civil action is brought, arising from harm allegedly caused directly or indirectly by an implant, including a person other than the individual into whose body, or in contact with whose blood or tissue, the implant is placed, who claims to have suffered harm as a result of the implant.

(B) ACTION BROUGHT ON BEHALF OF AN ESTATE.—With respect to an action brought on behalf of or through the estate of an individual into whose body, or in contact with whose blood or tissue the implant is placed, such term includes the decedent that is the subject of the action.

(C) ACTION BROUGHT ON BEHALF OF A MINOR OR INCOMPETENT.—With respect to an action brought on behalf of or through a minor or incompetent, such term includes the parent or guardian of the minor or incompetent.

(D) EXCLUSIONS.—Such term does not include—

(i) a provider of professional health care services, in any case in which—

(I) the sale or use of an implant is incidental to the transaction; and

(II) the essence of the transaction is the furnishing of judgment, skill, or services; or

(ii) a person acting in the capacity of a manufacturer, seller, or biomaterials supplier.

(3) COMPONENT PART.—

(A) IN GENERAL.—The term "component part" means a manufactured piece of an implant.

(B) CERTAIN COMPONENTS.—Such term includes a manufactured piece of an implant that—

(i) has significant non-implant applications; and

(ii) alone, has no implant value or purpose, but when combined with other component parts and materials, constitutes an implant.

(4) HARM.—

(A) IN GENERAL.—The term "harm" means—

(i) any injury to or damage suffered by an individual;

(ii) any illness, disease, or death of that individual resulting from that injury or damage; and

(iii) any loss to that individual or any other individual resulting from that injury or damage.

(B) EXCLUSION.—The term does not include any commercial loss or loss of or damage to an implant.

(5) IMPLANT.—The term "implant" means—

(A) a medical device that is intended by the manufacturer of the device—

(i) to be placed into a surgically or naturally formed or existing cavity of the body for a period of at least 30 days; or

(ii) to remain in contact with bodily fluids or internal human tissue through a surgically produced opening for a period of less than 30 days; and

(B) suture materials used in implant procedures.

(6) MANUFACTURER.—The term "manufacturer" means any person who, with respect to an implant—

(A) is engaged in the manufacture, preparation, propagation, compounding, or processing (as defined in section 510(a)(1)) of the Federal Food, Drug, and Cosmetic Act (21 U.S.C. 360(a)(1)) of the implant; and

(B) is required—

(i) to register with the Secretary pursuant to section 510 of the Federal Food, Drug, and Cosmetic Act (21 U.S.C. 360) and the regulations issued under such section; and

(ii) to include the implant on a list of devices filed with the Secretary pursuant to section 510(j) of such Act (21 U.S.C. 360(j)) and the regulations issued under such section.

(7) MEDICAL DEVICE.—The term "medical device" means a device, as defined in section 201(h) of the Federal Food, Drug, and Cosmetic Act (21 U.S.C. 321(h)) and includes any device component of any combination product as that term is used in section 503(g) of such Act (21 U.S.C. 353(g)).

(8) RAW MATERIAL.—The term "raw material" means a substance or product that—

(A) has a generic use; and

(B) may be used in an application other than an implant.

(9) SECRETARY.—The term "Secretary" means the Secretary of Health and Human Services.

(10) SELLER.—

(A) IN GENERAL.—The term "seller" means a person who, in the course of a business conducted for that purpose, sells, distributes, leases, packages, labels, or otherwise places an implant in the stream of commerce.

(B) EXCLUSIONS.—The term does not include—

(i) a seller or lessor of real property;

(ii) a provider of professional services, in any case in which the sale or use of an implant is incidental to the transaction and the essence of the transaction is the furnishing of judgment, skill, or services; or

(iii) any person who acts in only a financial capacity with respect to the sale of an implant.

SEC. 204. GENERAL REQUIREMENTS; APPLICABILITY; PREEMPTION.

(a) GENERAL REQUIREMENTS.—

(1) IN GENERAL.—In any civil action covered by this Title, a biomaterials supplier may raise any defense set forth in section 205.

(2) PROCEDURES.—Notwithstanding any other provision of law, the Federal or State court in which a civil action covered by this title is pending shall, in connection with a motion for dismissal or judgment based on a defense described in paragraph (1), use the procedures set forth in section 206.

(b) APPLICABILITY.—

(1) IN GENERAL.—Except as provided in paragraph (2), notwithstanding any other provision of law, this title applies to any civil action brought by a claimant, whether in a Federal or State court, against a manufacturer, seller, or biomaterials supplier, on the basis of any legal theory, for harm allegedly caused by an implant.

(2) EXCLUSION.—A civil action brought by a purchaser of a medical device for use in providing professional services against a manufacturer, seller, or biomaterials supplier for loss or damage to an implant or for commercial loss to the purchaser—

(A) shall not be considered an action that is subject to this title; and

(B) shall be governed by applicable commercial or contract law.

(c) SCOPE OF PREEMPTION.—

(1) IN GENERAL.—This title supersedes any State law regarding recovery for harm caused by an implant and any rule of procedure applicable to a civil action to recover damages for such harm only to the extent that this title establishes a rule of law applicable to the recovery of such damages.

(2) APPLICABILITY OF OTHER LAWS.—Any issue that arises under this title and that is not governed by a rule of law applicable to the recovery of damages described in paragraph (1) shall be governed by applicable Federal or State law.

(d) STATUTORY CONSTRUCTION.—Nothing in this title may be construed—

(1) to affect any defense available to a defendant under any other provisions of Federal or State law in an action alleging harm caused by an implant; or

(2) to create a cause of action or Federal court jurisdiction pursuant to section 1331 or 1337 of title 28, United States Code, that otherwise would not exist under applicable Federal or State law.

SEC. 205.   LIABILITY OF BIOMATERIALS SUPPLIERS.

(a) IN GENERAL.—

(1) EXCLUSION FROM LIABILITY.—Except as provided in paragraph (2), a biomaterials supplier shall not be liable for harm to a claimant caused by an implant.

(2) LIABILITY.—A biomaterials supplier that—

(A) is a manufacturer may be liable for harm to a claimant described in subsection (b);

(B) is a seller may be liable for harm to a claimant described in subsection (c); and

(C) furnishes raw materials or component parts that fail to meet applicable contractual requirements or specifications may be liable for a harm to a claimant described in subsection (d).

(b) LIABILITY AS MANUFACTURER.—

(1) IN GENERAL.—A biomaterials supplier may, to the extent required and permitted by any other applicable law, be liable for harm to a claimant caused by an implant if the biomaterials supplier is the manufacturer of the implant.

(2) GROUNDS FOR LIABILITY.—The biomaterials supplier may be considered the manufacturer of the implant that allegedly caused harm to a claimant only if the biomaterials supplier—

(A)(i) has registered with the Secretary pursuant to section 510 of the Federal Food, Drug, and Cosmetic Act (21 U.S.C. 360) and the regulations issued under such section; and

(ii) included the implant on a list of devices filed with the Secretary pursuant to section 510(j) of such Act (21 U.S.C. 360(j)) and the regulations issued under such section;

(B) is the subject of a declaration issued by the Secretary pursuant to paragraph (3) that states that the supplier, with respect to the implant that allegedly caused harm to the claimant, was required to—

(i) register with the Secretary under section 510 of such Act (21 U.S.C. 360), and the regulations issued under such section, but failed to do so; or

(ii) include the implant on a list of devices filed with the Secretary pursuant to section 510(j) of such Act (21 U.S.C. 360(j)) and the regulations issued under such section, but failed to do so; or

(C) is related by common ownership or control to a person meeting all the requirements described in subparagraph (A) or (B), if the court deciding a motion to dismiss in accordance with section 206(c)(3)(B)(i) finds, on the basis of affidavits submitted in accordance with section 206, that it is necessary to impose liability on the biomaterials supplier as a manufacturer because the related manufacturer meeting the requirements of subparagraph (A) or (B) lacks sufficient financial resources to satisfy any judgment that the court feels it is likely to enter should the claimant prevail.

(3) ADMINISTRATIVE PROCEDURES.—

(A) IN GENERAL.—The Secretary may issue a declaration described in paragraph (2)(B) on the motion of the Secretary or on petition by any person, after providing—

(i) notice to the affected persons; and

(ii) an opportunity for an informal hearing.

(B) DOCKETING AND FINAL DECISION.—Immediately upon receipt of a petition filed pursuant to this paragraph, the Secretary shall docket the petition. Not later than 180 days after the petition is filed, the Secretary shall issue a final decision on the petition.

(C) APPLICABILITY OF STATUTE OF LIMITATIONS.— Any applicable statute of limitations shall toll during the period during which a claimant has filed a petition with the Secretary under this paragraph.

(c) LIABILITY AS SELLER.—A biomaterials supplier may, to the extent required and permitted by any other applicable law, be liable as a seller for harm to a claimant caused by an implant if—

(1) the biomaterials supplier—

(A) held title to the implant that allegedly caused harm to the claimant as a result of purchasing the implant after—

(i) the manufacture of the implant; and

(ii) the entrance of the implant in the stream of commerce; and

(B) subsequently resold the implant; or

(2) the biomaterials supplier is related by common ownership or control to a person meeting all the requirements described in paragraph (1), if a court deciding a motion to dismiss in accordance with section 206(c)(3)(B)(ii) finds, on the basis of affidavits submitted in accordance with section 206, that it is necessary to impose liability on the biomaterials supplier as a seller because the related seller meeting the requirements of paragraph (1) lacks sufficient financial resources to satisfy any judgment that the court feels it is likely to enter should the claimant prevail.

(d) LIABILITY FOR VIOLATING CONTRACTUAL REQUIREMENTS OR SPECIFICATIONS.—A biomaterials supplier may, to the extent required and permitted by any other applicable law, be liable for harm to a claimant caused by an implant, if the claimant in an action shows, by a preponderance of the evidence, that—

(1) the raw materials or component parts delivered by the biomaterials supplier either—

(A) did not constitute the product described in the contract between the biomaterials supplier and the person who contracted for delivery of the product; or

(B) failed to meet any specifications that were—

(i) provided to the biomaterials supplier and not expressly repudiated by the biomaterials supplier prior to acceptance of delivery of the raw materials or component parts;

(ii) (I) published by the biomaterials supplier;

(II) provided to the manufacturer by the biomaterials supplier; or

(III) contained in a master file that was submitted by the biomaterials supplier to the Secretary and that is currently maintained by the biomaterials supplier for purposes of premarket approval of medical devices; or

(iii) included in the submissions for purposes of premarket approval or review by the Secretary under section 510, 513, 515, or 520 of the Federal Food, Drug, and Cosmetic Act (21 U.S.C. 360, 360c, 360e, or 360j), and received clearance from the Secretary if such specifications were provided by the manufacturer to the biomaterials supplier and were not expressly repudiated by the biomaterials supplier prior to the acceptance by the manufacturer of delivery of the raw materials or component parts; and

(2) such conduct was an actual and proximate cause of the harm to the claimant.

SEC. 206. PROCEDURES FOR DISMISSAL OF CIVIL ACTIONS AGAINST BIOMATERIALS SUPPLIERS.

(a) MOTION TO DISMISS.—In any action that is subject to this title, a biomaterials supplier who is a defendant in such action may, at any time during which a motion to dismiss may be filed under an applicable law, move to dismiss the action against it on the grounds that—

(1) the defendant is a biomaterials supplier; and

(2)(A) the defendant should not, for the purposes of—

(i) section 205(b), be considered to be a manufacturer of the implant that is subject to such section; or

(ii) section 205(c), be considered to be a seller of the implant that allegedly caused harm to the claimant; or

(B)(i) the claimant has failed to establish, pursuant to section 205(d), that the supplier furnished raw materials or component parts in violation of contractual requirements or specifications; or

(ii) the claimant has failed to comply with the procedural requirements of subsection (b).

(b) MANUFACTURER OF IMPLANT SHALL BE NAMED A PARTY.—The claimant shall be required to name the manufacturer of the implant as a party to the action, unless—

(1) the manufacturer is subject to service of process solely in a jurisdiction in which the biomaterials supplier is not domiciled or subject to a service of process; or

(2) an action against the manufacturer is barred by applicable law.

(c) PROCEEDING ON MOTION TO DISMISS.—The following rules shall apply to any proceeding on a motion to dismiss filed under this section:

(1) AFFIDAVITS RELATING TO LISTING AND DECLARATIONS.—

(A) IN GENERAL.—The defendant in the action may submit an affidavit demonstrating that defendant has not included the implant on a list, if any, filed with the Secretary pursuant to section 510(j) of the Federal Food, Drug, and Cosmetic Act (21 U.S.C. 360(j)).

(B) RESPONSE TO MOTION TO DISMISS.—In response to the motion to dismiss, the claimant may submit an affidavit demonstrating that—

(i) the Secretary has, with respect to the defendant and the implant that allegedly caused harm to the claimant, issued a declaration pursuant to section 205(b)(2)(B); or

(ii) the defendant who filed the motion to dismiss is a seller of the implant who is liable under section 205(c).

(2) EFFECT OF MOTION TO DISMISS ON DISCOVERY.—

(A) IN GENERAL.—If a defendant files a motion to dismiss under paragraph (1) or (2) of subsection (a), no discovery shall be permitted in connection to the action that is the subject of the motion, other than discovery necessary to determine a motion to dismiss for lack of jurisdiction, until such time as the court rules on the motion to dismiss in accordance with the affidavits submitted by the parties in accordance with this section.

(B) DISCOVERY.—If a defendant files a motion to dismiss under subsection (a)(2)(B)(i) on the grounds that the biomaterials supplier did not furnish raw materials or component parts in violation of contractual requirements or specifications, the court may permit discovery, as ordered by the court. The discovery conducted pursuant to this subparagraph shall be limited to issues that are directly relevant to—

(i) the pending motion to dismiss; or

(ii) the jurisdiction of the court.

(3) AFFIDAVITS RELATING STATUS OF DEFENDANT.—

(A) IN GENERAL.—Except as provided in clauses (i) and (ii) of subparagraph (B), the court shall consider a defendant to be a biomaterials supplier who is not subject to an action for harm to a claimant caused by an implant, other than an action relating to liability for a violation of contractual requirements or specifications described in subsection (d).

(B) RESPONSES TO MOTION TO DISMISS.—The court shall grant a motion to dismiss any action that asserts liability of the defendant under subsection (b) or (c) of section 205 on the grounds that the defendant is not a manufacturer subject to such section 205(b) or seller subject to section 205(c), unless the claimant submits a valid affidavit that demonstrates that—

(i) with respect to a motion to dismiss contending the defendant is not a manufacturer, the defendant meets the applicable requirements for liability as a manufacturer under section 205(b); or

(ii) with respect to a motion to dismiss contending that the defendant is not a seller, the defendant meets the applicable requirements for liability as a seller under section 205(c).

(4) BASIS OF RULING ON MOTION TO DISMISS.—

(A) IN GENERAL.—The court shall rule on a motion to dismiss filed under subsection (a) solely on the basis of the pleadings of the parties made pursuant to this section and any affidavits submitted by the parties pursuant to this section.

(B) MOTION FOR SUMMARY JUDGMENT.—Notwithstanding any other provision of law, if the court determines that the pleadings and affidavits made by parties pursuant to this section raise genuine issues as concerning material facts with respect to a motion concerning contractual requirements and specifications, the court may deem the motion to dismiss to be a motion for summary judgment made pursuant to subsection (d).

(d) SUMMARY JUDGMENT.—

(1) IN GENERAL.—

(A) Basis for entry of judgment. A biomaterials supplier shall be entitled to entry of judgment without trial if the court finds there is no genuine issue as concerning any material fact for each applicable element set forth in paragraphs (1) and (2) of section 205(d).

(B) ISSUES OF MATERIAL FACT.—With respect to a finding made under subparagraph (A), the court shall consider a genuine issue of material fact to exist only if the evidence submitted by claimant would be sufficient to allow a reasonable jury to reach a verdict for the claimant if the jury found the evidence to be credible.

(2) DISCOVERY MADE PRIOR TO A RULING ON A MOTION FOR SUMMARY JUDGMENT.—If, under applicable rules, the court permits discovery prior to a ruling on a motion for summary judgment made pursuant to this subsection, such discovery shall be limited solely to establishing whether a genuine issue of material fact exists as to the

applicable elements set forth in paragraphs (1) and (2) of section 205(d).

(3)DISCOVERY WITH RESPECT TO A BIOMATERIALS SUPPLIER.—A biomaterials supplier shall be subject to discovery in connection with a motion seeking dismissal or summary judgment on the basis of the inapplicability of section 205(d) or the failure to establish the applicable elements of section 205(d) solely to the extent permitted by the applicable Federal or State rules for discovery against nonparties.

(e) STAY PENDING PETITION FOR DECLARATION.—If a claimant has filed a petition for a declaration pursuant to section 205(b)(3)(A) with respect to a defendant, and the Secretary has not issued a final decision on the petition, the court shall stay all proceedings with respect to that defendant until such time as the Secretary has issued a final decision on the petition.

(f) MANUFACTURER CONDUCT OF PROCEEDING.—The manufacturer of an implant that is the subject of an action covered under this title shall be permitted to file and conduct a proceeding on any motion for summary judgment or dismissal filed by a biomaterials supplier who is a defendant under this section if the manufacturer and any other defendant in such action enter into a valid and applicable contractual agreement under which the manufacturer agrees to bear the cost of such proceeding or to conduct such proceeding.

(g) ATTORNEY FEES.—The court shall require the claimant to compensate the biomaterials supplier (or a manufacturer appearing in lieu of a supplier pursuant to subsection (f)) for attorney fees and costs, if—

(1) the claimant named or joined the biomaterials supplier; and

(2) the court found the claim against the biomaterials supplier to be without merit and frivolous.

TITLE III—LIMITATIONS ON APPLICABILITY; EFFECTIVE DATE

SEC. 301.   EFFECT OF COURT OF APPEALS DECISIONS.

A decision by a Federal circuit court of appeals interpreting a provision of this Act (except to the extent that the decision is overruled or otherwise modified by the Supreme Court) shall be considered a controlling precedent with respect to any subsequent decision made concerning the interpretation of such provision by any Federal or State court within the geographical boundaries of the area under the jurisdiction of the circuit court of appeals.

SEC. 302. FEDERAL CAUSE OF ACTION PRECLUDED.

The district courts of the United States shall not have jurisdiction pursuant to this Act based on section 1331 or 1337 of title 28, United States Code.

SEC. 303. EFFECTIVE DATE.

This Act shall apply with respect to any action commenced on or after the date of the enactment of this Act without regard to whether the harm that is the subject of the action or the conduct that caused the harm occurred before such date of

And the Senate agree to the same.

JOINT EXPLANATORY STATEMENT OF THE COMMITTEE OF CONFERENCE

The managers on the part of the House and the Senate at the conference on the disagreeing votes of the two Houses on the amendment of the Senate to the bill (H.R. 956), to establish legal standards and procedures for product liability litigation, and for other purposes, submit the following joint statement to the House and the Senate in explanation of the effect of the action agreed upon by the managers and recommended in the accompanying conference report:

The Senate amendment struck all of the House bill after the enacting clause and inserted a substitute text.

The House recedes from its disagreement to the amendment of the Senate with an amendment that is a substitute for the House bill and the Senate amendment. The differences between the House bill, the Senate amendment, and the substitute agreed to in conference are noted below, except for clerical corrections, conforming changes made necessary by agreements reached by the conferees, and minor drafting and clerical changes.

The conferees incorporate by reference in this Statement of Managers the legislative history reflected in both House Report 104–64, Part 1 and Senate Report 104–69. To the extent not otherwise inconsistent with the conference agreement, those reports give expression to the intent of the conferees. (The conferees also take note of House Report 104–63, Part 1, which contains supplementary legislative history on a related bill.)

SHORT TITLE AND TABLE OF CONTENTS

The conferees, in section 1(a), modified the short title of the House bill to reflect the terms of the conference agreement. The conferees also decided that a table of contents would be helpful and therefore incorporat-

615

ed in section 1(b) the headings of the separate titles and sections of this legislation.

FINDINGS AND PURPOSES

H.R. 956 but not the Senate amendment included findings and purposes. The conferees decided it was important in the legislation itself to delineate the factual basis for congressional action and explain what Congress seeks to accomplish. The language adopted, contained in section 2, generally follows the House-passed bill with some modifications.

Paragraph (1) of the findings in H.R. 956 was not included in the conference agreement because the conferees decided that describing misuses of the civil justice system in very broad terms was unnecessary. That paragraph had been written at a level of generality exceeding other findings. The omission of the paragraph should not be interpreted as reflecting adversely on its accuracy.

Section 2(a)(9) of the conference agreement refers to two constitutional roles of the national government that are directly relevant to this legislation "to remove barriers to interstate commerce and to protect due process rights." Although the latter was not included in H.R. 956s findings, legislative history clearly conveyed the Houses recognition of the Federal governments due process related role. The report of the Committee on the Judiciary (House Report 104–64, Part 1) noted:

> Section 5 of the Fourteenth Amendment provides an independent constitutional ground for Congressional legislation limiting awards for punitive damages. Congress is given the authority, under section 5, "to enforce, by appropriate legislation" the provisions of the Fourteenth Amendment which include a proscription on state deprivations of "life, liberty, or property, without due process of law." (p. 8)

Including explicit reference to due process rights in the findings is appropriate if the findings are to more fully reflect our understanding of the constitutional underpinnings for this legislation.

The purposes of this legislation, as delineated in section 2(b), are "to promote the free flow of goods and services and to lessen burdens on interstate commerce and to uphold constitutionally protected due process rights. * * *" Upholding due process rights was an important objective the House sought to advance even though explicit reference to it did not appear in H.R. 956s statement of purposes. The Committee on the Judiciary's report (House Report 104–64, Part 1) on H.R. 956 stated: "The Committee acted to reform punitive damages not only to ameliorate adverse effects on interstate and foreign commerce but also to protect due process rights." (page 9) Adding the phrase "uphold constitutionally protected due process rights" to the purposes provides a more complete statement of congressional objectives.

DEFINITIONS

Section 101 defines 18 terms for purposes of Title I. One of these terms compensatory damages is not defined in either H.R. 956 or the Senate amendment.

APPLICABILITY; PREEMPTION

Section 102 addresses preemption, relationship to State law, and effect on other law.

LIABILITY RULES APPLICABLE TO PRODUCT SELLERS, RENTERS, AND LESSORS

Both the House bill and Senate amendment included liability rules applicable to product sellers. Section 103 of the conference agreement is designed to reduce consumer costs and provide fair treatment for product sellers defined to include those who sell, rent, or lease a product in the course of a business conducted for that purpose. To more fully reflect the application of this sections remedial provisions beyond sellers in the narrow sense of the word, the conference agreement refers to renters and lessors in section 103's title.

As a general rule, liability of product sellers can be predicated on harm resulting from a product sellers (1) failure to exercise reasonable care, (2) breach of its own express warranty, or (3) intentional wrong-doing. The failure to exercise reasonable care requirement for potential liability applies not only to products sold by the product seller as stated in H.R. 956 but also to products rented or leased by the product seller as stated in the Senate amendment. The conferees recognize that the unfairness of imputing manufacturer conduct to others applies regardless of whether a product is sold, rented, or leased and for that reason adopt the Senate language. That language is consistent with the intent of the House to make protections available in a sale situation also available in a rental or lease situation.

Both H.R. 956 and the Senate amendment set forth those limited circumstances in which a product seller can be treated as a manufacturer of a product. One covered situation involves a court determination that "the claimant would be unable to enforce a judgment against the manufacturer." In response to concerns raised after House consideration of the bill that claimants might not learn about such a judicial determination within the period of the statute of limitations and therefore would be barred unfairly from proceeding against the seller the Senate included a provision tolling the statute of limitations for limited purposes "from the date of the filing of a complaint against the manufacturer to the date that judgment is entered against the manufacturer." The conferees accept this provision because it safeguards a protection for claimants given expression in both bills. Since the conference agreement incorporates a uniform statute of limitations in section 106, the inclusion of this safeguard relating to the time bar is particularly appropriate.

The conference agreement clarifies that State law, rather than the provisions of section 103, govern actions for negligent entrustment. State law, for example, will continue to apply to lawsuits predicated on the alleged negligence involved in giving a loaded gun to a young child or allowing an unlicensed and unqualified minor below driving age to operate an automobile. Similarly, the potential liability of a service station that sells gasoline to an obviously drunk driver will be determined under State law. Section 103(d) gives expression to the interest of each State in setting standards for determining whether conduct within its borders constitutes negligent entrustment.

DEFENSES INVOLVING INTOXICATING ALCOHOL OR DRUGS

Both H.R. 956 and the Senate amendment provide a complete defense to a product liability action in situations in which a claimant, under the influence of alcohol or drugs, is more than fifty percent responsible as a result of such influence for the accident or event resulting in the harm he or she sustains. A society that seeks to discourage alcohol and drug abuse should not allow individuals to collect damages when their disregard of such an important societal norm is the primary cause of accidents or events.

The conference committee generally accepts the House formulation in section 104. The conferees did not incorporate the Senate reference to the defendant proving alcohol or drug related facts because the issue of who has the burden of proof on these issues is best left to State law. A requirement for the availability of the defense related to alcohol or drug use, under the Senate amendment, is that the claimant was "under the influence." The House language, which was adopted, is more broadly worded and refers to the claimant being "intoxicated or ... under the influence." The House provision was accepted because the conferees want to ensure the availability of the defense relating to alcohol or drugs in cases in which State law may consider an individual to be "intoxicated" but not necessarily "under the influence" perhaps because the latter term does not have legal significance in a particular jurisdiction.

The conferees specifically incorporate the Controlled Substances Act definition of controlled substance in the conference agreements delineation of what the term "drug" means following the House version in that respect. The Senate amendment was silent in this regard. The reference to the Controlled Substances Act will foster uniformity in decisions by State courts on whether particular substances constitute drugs. A substance that is taken by a claimant in accordance with the terms of a lawfully issued prescription, however, is not considered a drug for purposes of this section. The policy fostered is the denial of recovery to those whose accidents are primarily caused by the abuse of drugs.

Although the use of controlled substances in accordance with the terms of lawfully issued prescriptions can lead to accidents—in circumstances, for example, where ones ability to drive may be impaired—the conferees leave to individual States the responsibility of resolving whether potential recovery is defeated by such conduct. The conference agreement focuses on the most egregious conduct implicating Federal interests—noting the national market for illegal drugs and the transportation of illegal drugs across State lines and in international commerce.

The Senate provisions reference to a drug that "was not prescribed by a physician for use by the claimant" does not cover situations in which the terms of a lawfully issued prescription are disregarded perhaps by consuming excessive quantities. The conferees conclude, however, that individuals who abuse prescription drugs lack sufficient equities to recover for accidents primarily caused by their drug use and for that reason refer to any controlled substance "taken by the claimant other than in accordance with the terms of a lawfully issued prescription", thus opting for the broader House formulation.

Finally, the House version of this section is modified to cover controlled substances "not legally prescribed for use by the claimant" in addition to controlled substances "taken by the claimant other than in accordance with the terms of a lawfully issued prescription." The phrase "not legally prescribed for use by the claimant" makes unambiguous the requirement that the prescription be for the claimants own use. A claimant cannot cause an accident after using someone else's prescription, even in accordance with its terms, and recover damages.

The phrase "legally prescribed" is a variation on the Senate provisions reference to "prescribed by a physician." The change takes into account the fact that the right to prescribe medication is not limited to physicians in every jurisdiction. The potential applicability of defenses involving drugs should not depend on whether a legally issued prescription comes from a physician or non-physician particularly in view of the fact that physicians may not be available or accessible in some areas of the country.

MISUSE OR ALTERATION

Both H.R. 956 and the Senate amendment include an important reform—incorporated in section 105 of the conference agreement—designed to assure manufacturers and sellers that they can develop and sell products without undue concern about unknowable and unpredictable liability attributable to claims resulting from the misuse or alteration of their products.

Subsection (a)(1) of section 105 generally follows the House language. Damages will be reduced because of misuse or alteration, however, not only in cases of liability arising under State law—as H.R. 956 provides—but also in possible cases of liability arising under Federal law. Damages are reduced if the defendant establishes the requisite link between a certain percentage of the claimants harm and specified conduct.

Although the "preponderance of the evidence" standard will apply—as the House version explicitly states—the conference agreement deletes reference to this evidentiary standard in section 105(a) in order to avoid any possible negative inference from the fact that the legislation does not refer to "preponderance of the evidence" in other sections. Preponderance of the evidence is the usual standard in civil cases including product liability cases. The conferees intent is that courts apply the usual standard in all situations covered by this legislation except where another standard is explicitly mandated.

Subsection (a)(2) follows Senate language. Although this provision appears to state a self-evident proposition that a use intended by the manufacturer does not constitute a misuse or alteration it is included to alleviate concerns that some courts might reach a different result.

Subsection (b) follows House language and states the general rule that a claimants damages will not be reduced because of misuse or alteration by others in the workplace who are immune from suit by the claimant. The rationale is that Federal law should not mandate a reduction in damages for a claimant who cannot collect from an employer or co-employee for misuse or alteration. The conference agreement, however, carves an exception to the general prohibition against such reductions by specifying that damages will not be reduced "except as otherwise provided in section 111" of the conference agreement dealing with workers compensation subrogation.

The conferees intend that, consistent with normal principles of law, this section shall supersede State law concerning misuse or alteration of a product only to the extent that State law is inconsistent with this section. The deletion of language in the Senate amendment on this point was intended merely to avoid any possible inference that it is not intended to be the case in other sections of the legislation.

STATUTE OF LIMITATIONS

The fact that consumers generally do not live in the States in which the products they purchase and use are manufactured creates confusion and uncertainty for manufacturers when the law allows determinations of whether product liability actions are barred by a statute of limitations to vary from jurisdiction to jurisdiction. This uncertainty and unpredictability ultimately means higher prices for consumers. In addition, it is unfair to deny the potential for a remedy to an injured party living in one State that may be available to an injured party using the same product in another State. The conferees conclude that uniformity is needed and agree that two years is a reasonable limitation on the period of time for the filing of a lawsuit by an injured individual—regardless of where he or she may reside. This decision is reflected in the language contained in section 106(a).

The conferees expect that in most cases legal actions will be brought within two years of the accident or injury, because generally individuals have knowledge—or can be charged with knowledge—of the resulting harm and its cause at the time of an injury. An inflexible rule linking the running of the statute of limitations to the time of injury, however, would be unfair to those few injured parties who could not—despite the exercise of reasonable care—discover the harm and its cause. To address the exigencies of those situations, the conferees adopted the language of the Senate amendment referencing the date "on which the claimant discovered or, in the exercise of reasonable care, should have discovered" the harm and its cause.

STATUTE OF REPOSE

Both the House bill and Senate amendment included provisions to protect manufacturers against stale claims that arise many years after a products first intended use. A statute of repose would allow U.S. manufacturers to compete with foreign companies that have entered the American marketplace in recent years and face no liability exposure for very old products. Section 106(b) advances U.S. competitiveness, preserves and expands employment opportunities here at home, and protects American consumers from the higher prices for goods and services that result from excessive litigation related expenses, inflated settlement offers, and increased liability insurance rates.

The statute of repose contained in the conference agreement will, for durable goods, generally bar product liability actions that are not filed within 15 years of a products delivery. The time of delivery refers to the date that the product reaches its first purchaser or lessee who was not engaged in the business of selling or leasing the product or of using the product as a component in the manufacture of another product. The only exceptions to the statute of repose that courts appropriately can recognize are those explicitly provided for in section 106(b)(3) itself. The 15 year time period is taken from the House bill.

Section 106(b) adopts Senate language making the time bar applicable only to durable goods. Section 106(b)(2) is also language from the Senate amendment. It provides for deferring to State law time bars—on actions covered by this legislation—that are shorter than 15 years. The conferees believe that States should remain free to impose time limits of less than 15 years—a concept given expression in section 106(b)(2). Such State limitations are not inconsistent with the objectives of section 106(b)—including fostering a more conducive environment for U.S. companies to compete in the global marketplace. Furthermore, nothing in the conference agreement is to be interpreted to preempt state statutes of repose which may apply to goods other than durable goods as defined in this agreement.

Section 106(c) is a transition provision that permits product liability actions to be brought within one year of the date of enactment in situations in which the application of the statute of repose (or statute of limitations) shortens the period otherwise available under State law. The provision protects potential claimants by affording them a fair and reasonable opportunity to adjust to time limitations contained in section 106.

ALTERNATIVE DISPUTE RESOLUTION

Section 107 incorporates a provision of the Senate amendment dealing with alternative dispute resolution.

PUNITIVE DAMAGES

The requirement of "conscious, flagrant indifference to the rights or safety of others" in section 108(a) makes it clear that punitive damages may be awarded only in the most serious cases. Punitive damages are not intended as compensation for injured parties. Rather, they are intended to punish and to deter wrongful conduct.

The conferees understand that punitive damages can be awarded in cases of intentional harm. For this reason, it was not felt necessary to express the concept explicitly. Thus, the conference agreement does not retain the language contained in the House passed bill regarding conduct "specifically intended to cause harm."

Section 108(b) imposes a limitation on punitive damages with a special rule applicable to individuals of limited net worth and businesses or entities with small numbers of employees. The limitation on punitive damages cannot be disclosed to the jury. A punitive damage award may be appealed even if it falls within the limitation. Nothing in the bill prevents a trial court (and each reviewing court) from reviewing punitive damage awards individually and determining whether the award is appropriate under the particular circumstances of that case.

Although the conferees establish a mechanism for awarding additional punitive damages in limited circumstances ("egregious conduct" on the part of the defendant and a punitive damages jury verdict insufficient to punish such egregious conduct, or to deter the defendant), it is anticipated that occasions for additional awards will be very limited indeed. Findings of fact and conclusions of law relating to the award of additional punitive damages are designed both to ensure that judges carefully consider such decisions and to facilitate appellate review. The court may not enter an award of punitive damages in excess of the amount of punitive damages originally assessed by the jury. The additional award provisions do not apply in cases covered by section 108(b)(2) actions against an individual whose net worth does not exceed $500,000 or against entities that have fewer than 25 full-time employees.

Section 108(c)(1) clarifies that a separate proceeding on punitive damages pursuant to a bifurcation request of any party shall be held subsequent to the determination of the amount of compensatory damages. This order of proceedings, consistent with the intent of both the House and

Senate, is being made explicit to avoid any possible confusion. A determination of punitive damages first can adversely and unfairly influence financial markets and result in inappropriate pressure on defendants to settle. Punitive damages expressed as a multiple of compensatory damages to be determined later may not result in any liability if a different jury considering compensatory damages decides in favor of the defendant. This potential verdict for a defendant, however, may come too late because of the realities of the business world.

The conferees clarify in section 108(c)(2) that it is improper not only to offer evidence—but also to raise arguments or contentions relevant only to a claim of punitive damages in the compensatory damages proceeding, because of the potential prejudicial effects. The conferees objective is to avoid infecting determinations of liability—or the amount of compensatory damages with such irrelevant information.

LIABILITY FOR CLAIMS INVOLVING DEATH

Section 109 incorporates a provision of the Senate amendment designed to address a situation unique to one State.

SEVERAL LIABILITY FOR NONECONOMIC LOSS

The language of section 110 on several liability for noneconomic loss in product liability cases substantially follows the Senate amendment. The rule of several liability for noneconomic loss applies to all product liability actions nationwide.

The conference agreement, based on the Senate amendment, clearly states that in allocating noneconomic damages to a defendant,"the trier of fact shall determine the percentage of responsibility of each person responsible for the claimants harm, *whether or not such person is a party to the action*." [Emphasis added] The Senate formulation reflected here is fully consistent with the intent of the House as expressed in Report Number 104–64, Part 1: "[T]he trier of fact will determine the proportion of responsibility of each person responsible for the claimants harm, without regard to whether or not such person is a party to the action." pp. 13–14. Persons who may be responsible for the claimants harm include, but are not necessarily limited to, defendants, third-party defendants, settled parties, nonparties, and persons or entities that cannot be tried (e.g., bankrupt persons, employers and other immune entities).

The House passed version specified that the section "does not preempt or supersede any State or Federal law to the extent that such law would further limit the application of the theory of joint liability to any kind of damages." The conferees have not included this language in the conference report itself because it is superfluous and self-evident. Reference is made to it in the statement of managers, however, to rebut any possible negative inference from its omission. The quoted language itself reflects the conference agreements intent.

WORKERS COMPENSATION SUBROGATION

Section 111(a)(1)(A) provides that, in any product liability action involving a workplace injury, an insurer shall have a right of subrogation. Section 111(a)(1)(B) provides that, to assert a right of subrogation, an insurer must provide the court with written notice that it is asserting a right of subrogation. Section 111(a)(1)(C) states that the insurer need not be a necessary party to the product liability action. Thus, an employee can pursue a product liability action against a manufacturer without regard to the insurer's participation in the action. This section focuses on eliminating unsafe workplaces and is, therefore, applicable in all actions where employer or coemployee fault for a claimant's harm is at issue. Conversely, section 111 does not apply in cases where the product liability defendant chooses not to raise employer or coemployer fault as a defense.

Section 111(a)(2)(A) preserves the right of an insurer to assert a right of subrogation against payment made by a product liability defendant, without regard to whether the payment is made as part of a settlement, in satisfaction of a judgment, as consideration for a covenant not to sue, or for any other reason. "Claimant's benefits" is defined in section 101(3) and is a broad term which includes the total workers compensation award, including compensation representing lost wages, payments made by way of an annuity, health care expenses, and all other payments made by the insurer for the benefit of the employee to compensate for a workplace injury.

Section 111(a)(3) provides the mechanism for increased workplace safety. Under section 111(a)(3)(A), a product liability defendant may attempt to prove to the trier of fact that the claimants injury was caused by the fault of the claimants employer or a coemployee. The term "employer fault" means that the conduct of the employer or a coemployee was a substantial cause of the claimants harm or contributed to the claimant's harm in a meaningful way; it is more than a *de minimus* level of fault. Section 111(a)(3)(C)(i) provides that, if the trier of fact finds by clear and convincing evidence that the claimant's injury was caused by the fault of the claimant's employer or a coemployee, the product liability damages award and, correspondingly, the insurer's subrogation lien shall be reduced by the amount of the claimant's benefits. In no case shall the employees third-party damage award reduction exceed the amount of the subrogation lien. *Thus, the amount the injured employee would receive remains totally unaffected.* The Act merely provides that *the insurer* will not be able to recover worker's compensation benefits it paid to the employee if it is found by clear and convincing evidence that the claimant's harm was caused by the fault of the employer or a coemployee.

BIOMATERIALS

Title II of the conference agreement contains the "Biomaterials Access Assurance Act of 1996." A similar title passed both as a part of the House bill and the Senate amendment. Title II is intended to provide a defense to suppliers of materials or parts which are used to manufacture implantable medical devices. The definition of "medical device" in existing law, which is incorporated by reference into Title II, would limit this defense to a device which does not "achieve any of its principal intended purposes through chemical action within or on the body of man ...", in short, devices which do not contain drugs.

Newly patented devices, and others now in development, are manufactured from "parts" intended to be covered by Title II, but also contain an active ingredient or drug. The purpose of such devices is long term (up to one year) release of such materials into the body. Such devices can introduce medications affecting numerous bodily functions, previously only available by regular injections or oral dosages.

The conferees adopted a new definition which brings the "parts," but not the active ingredients, used in such "combination products" (as that term is used in section 503(g) of the Act) within the purview of this section. This will ensure that the development and availability of such devices will not be impaired because of the same liability concerns affecting the availability of materials for other types of implants.

COURT OF APPEAL DECISIONS

Section 301 describes the precedential effect of certain Federal appellate decisions. It is based on a provision of the Senate amendment.

FEDERAL CAUSE OF ACTION

Both H.R. 956 and the Senate amendment include provisions on preclusion. Section 302 incorporates the language of the House bill.

EFFECTIVE DATE

The effective date provision of H.R. 956 references actions commenced "after" the enactment date. Corresponding Senate provisions refer to actions "on or after" the date of enactment and clarify that the effective date is without regard to whether the relevant harm or conduct occurred before the enactment date. The conferees, in section 303, accept the "on or after" formulation and the clarifying clause from the Senate amendment.

From the Committee on the Judiciary, for consideration of the House bill, and the Senate amendment, and modifications committed to conference:

Henry Hyde, James Sensenbrenner, Jr., George W. Gekas, Bob Inglis, Ed Bryant,

>From the Committee on Commerce, for consideration of the House bill, and the Senate amendment, and modifications committed to conference:

Tom Bliley, Michael Oxley, Christopher Cox,

Managers on the Part of the House.

Larry Pressler, Slade Gorton, Trent Lott, Ted Stevens, Olympia Snowe, John Ashcroft, J.J. Exon, John D. Rockefeller,

Managers on the Part of the Senate.

PRODUCT LIABILITY REFORM ACT OF 1997

105th Congress   1997 S. 648

1st Session   105 F. 648

IN THE SENATE OF THE UNITED STATES
AS INTRODUCED IN THE SENATE

Be it enacted by the Senate and House of Representatives of the United States of America in Congress assembled,

SECTION 1. SHORT TITLE AND TABLE OF CONTENTS.

(a) SHORT TITLE.—This Act may be cited as the "PRODUCT LIABILITY REFORM ACT OF 1997".

(b) TABLE OF CONTENTS.—The table of contents is as follows:

SEC. 2. FINDINGS AND PURPOSES.

(a) FINDINGS.—The Congress finds that—

(1) our Nation is overly litigious, the civil justice system is over-crowded, sluggish, and excessively costly and the costs of lawsuits, both direct and indirect, are inflicting serious and unnecessary injury on the national economy;

(2) excessive, unpredictable, and often arbitrary damage awards and unfair allocations of liability have a direct and undesirable effect on interstate commerce by increasing the cost and decreasing the availability of goods and services;

(3) the rules of law governing product liability actions, damage awards, and allocations of liability have evolved inconsistently within and among the States, resulting in a complex, contradictory, and uncertain regime that is inequitable to both plaintiffs and defendants and unduly burdens interstate commerce;

(4) as a result of excessive, unpredictable, and often arbitrary damage awards and unfair allocations of liability, consumers have been adversely affected through the withdrawal of products, producers, services, and service providers from the marketplace, and from excessive liability costs passed on to them through higher prices;

(5) excessive, unpredictable, and often arbitrary damage awards and unfair allocations of liability jeopardize the financial well-being of many individuals as well as entire industries, particularly the Nation's small businesses and adversely affects government and taxpayers;

(6) the excessive costs of the civil justice system undermine the ability of American companies to compete internationally, and serve to decrease the number of jobs and the amount of productive capital in the national economy;

(7) the unpredictability of damage awards is inequitable to both plaintiffs and defendants and has added considerably to the high cost of liability insurance, making it difficult for producers, consumers, volunteers, and nonprofit organizations to protect themselves from liability with any degree of confidence and at a reasonable cost;

(8) because of the national scope of the problems created by the defects in the civil justice system, it is not possible for the States to enact laws that fully and effectively respond to those problems;

(9) it is the constitutional role of the national government to remove barriers to interstate commerce and to protect due process rights; and

(10) there is a need to restore rationality, certainty, and fairness to the civil justice system in order to protect against excessive, arbitrary, and uncertain damage awards and to reduce the volume, costs, and delay of litigation.

(b) PURPOSES.—Based upon the powers contained in Article I, Section 8, Clause 3 and the Fourteenth Amendment of the United States Constitution, the purposes of this Act are to promote the free flow of goods and services and to lessen burdens on interstate commerce and to uphold constitutionally protected due process rights by—

(1) establishing certain uniform legal principles of product liability which provide a fair balance among the interests of product users, manufacturers, and product sellers;

(2) placing reasonable limits on damages over and above the actual damages suffered by a claimant;

(3) ensuring the fair allocation of liability in civil actions;

(4) reducing the unacceptable costs and delays of our civil justice system caused by excessive litigation which harm both plaintiffs and defendants; and

(5) establishing greater fairness, rationality, and predictability in the civil justice system.

TITLE I–PRODUCT LIABILITY REFORM

SEC. 101.   DEFINITIONS.

For purposes of this title—

(1) ACTUAL MALICE.—The term "actual malice" means specific intent to cause serious physical injury, illness, disease, death, or damage to property.

(2) CLAIMANT.—The term "claimant" means any person who brings an action covered by this title and any person on whose behalf such an action is brought. If such an action is brought through or on behalf of an estate, the term includes the claimant's decedent. If such an action is brought through or on behalf of a minor or incompetent, the term includes the claimant's legal guardian.

(3) CLEAR AND CONVINCING EVIDENCE.—The term "clear and convincing evidence" is that measure or degree of proof that will produce in the mind of the trier of fact a firm belief or conviction as to the truth of the allegations sought to be established. The level of proof required to satisfy such standard is more than that required under preponderance of the evidence, but less than that required for proof beyond a reasonable doubt.

(4) COMMERCIAL LOSS.—The term "commercial loss" means any loss or damage solely to a product itself, loss relating to a dispute over its value, or consequential economic loss, the recovery of which is governed by the Uniform Commercial Code or analogous State commercial or contract law.

(5) COMPENSATORY DAMAGES.—The term "compensatory damages" means damages awarded for economic and non-economic loss.

(6) ECONOMIC LOSS.—The term "economic loss" means any pecuniary loss resulting from harm (including the loss of earnings or other benefits related to employment, medical expense loss, replacement services loss, loss due to death, burial costs, and loss of business or employment opportunities) to the extent recovery for such loss is allowed under applicable State law.

(7) HARM.—The term "harm" means any physical injury, illness, disease, or death or damage to property caused by a product. The term does not include commercial loss.

(8) MANUFACTURER.—The term "manufacturer" means—

(A) any person who is engaged in a business to produce, create, make, or construct any product (or component part of a product)and who

(i) designs or formulates the product (or component part of the product), or

(ii) has engaged another person to design or formulate the product (or component part of the product);

(B) a product seller, but only with respect to those aspects of a product (or component part of a product) which are created or affected when, before placing the product in the stream of commerce, the product seller produces, creates, makes or constructs and designs, or formulates, or has engaged another person to design or formulate, an aspect of the product (or component part of the product) made by another person; or

(C) any product seller not described in subparagraph (b) which holds itself out as a manufacturer to the user of the product.

(9) Noneconomic loss.—The term "noneconomic loss" means subjective, nonmonetary loss resulting from harm, including pain, suffering, inconvenience, mental suffering, emotional distress, loss of society and companionship, loss of consortium, injury to reputation, and humiliation.

(10) PERSON.—The term "person" means any individual, corporation, company, association, firm, partnership, society, joint stock company, or any other entity (including any governmental entity).

(11) PRODUCT.—

(A) IN GENERAL.—THe term "product" means any object, substance, mixture, or raw material in a gaseous, liquid, or solid state which—

(i) is capable of delivery itself or as an assembled whole, in a mixed or combined state, or as a component part of ingredient;

(ii) is produced for introduction into trade or commerce;

(iii) has intrinsic economic value; and

(iv) is intended for sale or lease to persons for commercial or personal use.

(B) EXCLUSIONS.—The term does not include—

(i) Tissue, organs, blood, and blood products used for therapeutic or medical purposes, except to the extent that such tissue, organs, blood, and blood products (or the provision thereof) are subject, under applicable state law, to a standard of liability other than negligence; or

(ii) electricity, water delivered by a utility, natural gas, or steam.

(12) PRODUCT LIABILITY ACTION.—The term "product liability action" means a civil action brought on any theory for harm caused by a product.

(13) PRODUCT SELLER.—

(A) IN GENERAL.—The term "product seller" means a person who in the course of a business conducted for that purpose—

(i) sells, distributes, rents, leases, prepares, blends, packages, labels, or otherwise is involved in placing a product in the stream of commerce; or

(ii) installs, repairs, refurbishes, reconditions, or maintains the harm-causing aspect of the product.

(B) exclusion.—The term "product seller" does not include—

(i) a seller or lessor of real property;

(ii) a provider of professional services in any case in which the sale or use of a product is incidental to the transaction and the essence of the transaction is the furnishing of judgment, skill, or services; or

(iii) any person who—

(I) acts in only a financial capacity with respect to the sale of a product; or

(II) leases a product under a lease arrangement in which the lessor does not initially select the leased product and does not during the lease term ordinarily control the daily operations and maintenance of the product.

(14) PUNITIVE DAMAGES.—The term "punitive damages" means damages awarded against any person or entity to punish or

deter such person or entity, or others, from engaging in similar behavior in the future.

(15) STATE.—The term "State" means any State of the United States, the District of Columbia, Commonwealth of Puerto Rico, the Northern Mariana Islands, the Virgin Islands, Guam, American Samoa, and any other territory or possession of the United States or any political subdivision of any of the foregoing.

SEC. 102. APPLICABILITY; PREEMPTION.

(a) PREEMPTION.—

(1) IN GENERAL.—This Act governs any product liability action brought in any State or federal court on any theory for harm caused by a product.

(2) ACTIONS EXCLUDED.—A civil action brought for commercial loss shall be governed only by applicable commercial or contract law.

(b) RELATIONSHIP TO STATE LAW.—This title supersedes State law only to the extent that State law applies to an issue covered by this title. Any issue that is not governed by this title, including any standard of liability applicable to a manufacturer, shall be governed by otherwise applicable State or Federal law.

(c) EFFECT ON OTHER LAW.—Nothing in this act shall be construed to—

(1) waive or affect any defense of sovereign immunity asserted by any State under any law;

(2) supersede or alter any Federal law;

(3) waive or affect any defense of sovereign immunity asserted by the United States;

(4) affect the applicability of any provision of chapter 97 of title 28, United States Code;

(5) preempt State choice-of-law rules with respect to claims brought by a foreign nation or a citizen of a foreign nation;

(6) affect the right of any court to transfer venue or to apply the law of a foreign nation or to dismiss a claim of a foreign nation or of a citizen of a foreign nation on the ground of inconvenient forum; or

(7) supersede or modify any statutory or common law, including any law providing for an action to abate a nuisance, that authorizes a person to institute an action for civil damages or civil penalties, cleanup costs, injunctions, restitution, cost recovery, punitive damages, or any other form of relief for remediation of the environment (as defined in section 101(8) of the Comprehensive Environmental Response, Compensation, and Liability Act of 1980 (42 U.S.C. 9601(8))).

(d) ACTIONS FOR NEGLIGENT ENTRUSTMENT.—A civil action for negligent entrustment, or any action brought under any theory of dramshop or third-party liability arising out of the sale or provision of alcohol products to intoxicated persons or minors, shall not be subject to the provisions of this act but shall be subject to any applicable State law.

SEC. 103.   LIABILITY RULES APPLICABLE TO PRODUCT SELLERS, RENTERS, AND LESSORS.

(a) GENERAL RULE.—

(1) IN GENERAL.—In any product liability action, a product seller other than a manufacturer shall be liable to a claimant only if the claimant establishes—

(A) that—

(i) the product that allegedly caused the harm that is the subject of the complaint was sold, rented, or leased by the product seller;

(ii) the product seller failed to exercise reasonable care with respect to the product; and

(iii) the failure to exercise reasonable care was a proximate cause of harm to the claimant;

(B) that—

(i) the product seller made an express warranty applicable to the product that allegedly caused the harm that is the subject of the complaint, independent of any express warranty made by a manufacturer as to the same product;

(ii) the product failed to conform to the warranty; and

(iii) the failure of the product to conform to the warranty caused harm to the claimant; or

(C) that—

(i) the product seller engaged in intentional wrongdoing, as determined under applicable state law; and

(ii) such intentional wrongdoing was a proximate cause of the harm that is the subject of the complaint.

(2) REASONABLE OPPORTUNITY FOR INSPECTION.—For purposes of paragraph (1)(a)(ii), a product seller shall not be considered to have failed to exercise reasonable care with respect to a product based upon an alleged failure to inspect the product—

(A) if the failure occurred because there was no reasonable opportunity to inspect the product; or

(B) if the inspection, in the exercise of reasonable care, would not have revealed the aspect of the product which allegedly caused the claimant's harm.

(b) SPECIAL RULE.—

(1) IN GENERAL.—A product seller shall be deemed to be liable as a manufacturer of a product for harm caused by the product if—

(A) the manufacturer is not subject to service of process under the laws of any State in which the action may be brought; or

(B) the court determines that the claimant would be unable to enforce a judgment against the manufacturer.

(2) STATUTE OF LIMITATIONS.—For purposes of this subsection only, the statute of limitations applicable to claims asserting liability of a product seller as a manufacturer shall be tolled from the date of the filing of a complaint against the manufacturer to the date that judgment is entered against the manufacturer.

(c) RENTED OR LEASED PRODUCTS.—

(1) Notwithstanding any other provision of law, any person engaged in the business of renting or leasing a product (other than a person excluded from the definition of product seller under section 101(13)(b)) shall be subject to liability in a product liability action under subsection (a), but any person engaged in the business of renting or leasing a product shall not be liable to a claimant for the tortious act of another solely by reason of ownership of such product.

(2) For purposes of paragraph (1), and for determining the applicability of this title to any person subject to paragraph (1), the term "product liability action" means a civil action brought on any theory for harm caused by a product or product use.

SEC. 104. DEFENSE BASED ON CLAIMANT'S USE OF INTOXICATING ALCOHOL OR DRUGS.

(a) GENERAL RULE.—In any product liability action, it shall be a complete defense to such action if the defendant proves that—

(1) the claimant was intoxicated or was under the influence of intoxicating alcohol or any drug when the accident or other event which resulted in such claimant's harm occurred; and

(2) the claimant, as a result of the influence of the alcohol or drug, was more than 50 percent responsible for such accident or other event.

(b) CONSTRUCTION.—For purposes of subsection (a)—

(1) the determination of whether a person was intoxicated or was under the influence of intoxicating alcohol or any drug shall be made pursuant to applicable State law; and

(2) the term "drug" means any controlled substance as defined in the Controlled Substances Act (21 U.S.C. 802(6)) that was not legally prescribed for use by the claimant or that was taken by the claimant other than in accordance with the terms of a lawfully issued prescription.

SEC. 105. MISUSE OR ALTERATION.

(a) GENERAL RULE.—

(1) IN GENERAL.—In a product liability action, the damages for which a defendant is otherwise liable under Federal or State law shall be reduced by the percentage of responsibility for the claimant's harm attributable to misuse or alteration of a product by any person if the defendant establishes that such percentage of the claimant's harm was proximately caused by a use or alteration of a product—

(A) in violation of, or contrary to, a defendant's express warnings or instructions if the warnings or instructions are adequate as determined pursuant to applicable State law; or

(B) involving a risk of harm which was known or should have been known by the ordinary person who uses or consumes the product with the knowledge common to the class of persons who used or would be reasonably anticipated to use the product.

(2) USE INTENDED BY A MANUFACTURER IS NOT MISUSE OR ALTERATION.—For the purposes of this Act, a use of a product that is intended by the manufacturer of the product does not constitute a misuse or alteration of the product.

(b) WORKPLACE INJURY.—Notwithstanding subsection (a), the damages for which a defendant is otherwise liable under State law shall not be reduced by the percentage of responsibility for the claimant's harm attributable to misuse or alteration of the product by the claimant's employer or any coemployee who is immune from suit by the claimant pursuant to the state law applicable to workplace injuries.

SEC. 106. UNIFORM TIME LIMITATIONS ON LIABILITY.

(a) STATUTE OF LIMITATIONS.—

(1) IN GENERAL.—Except as provided in paragraphs (2) and (3) and subsection (b), a product liability action may be filed not later than 2 years after the date on which the claimant discovered or, in the exercise of reasonable care, should have discovered—

(A) the harm that is the subject of the action; and

(B) the cause of the harm.

(2) EXCEPTION.—A person with a legal disability (as determined under applicable law) may file a product liability action not later than

2 years after the date on which the person ceases to have the legal disability.

(3) EFFECT OF STAY OR INJUNCTION.—If the commencement of a civil action that is subject to this title is stayed or enjoined, the running of the statute of limitations under this section shall be suspended until the end of the period that the stay or injunction is in effect.

(b) STATUTE OF REPOSE.—

(1) IN GENERAL.—Subject to paragraphs (2) and (3), no product liability action that is subject to this act concerning a product alleged to have caused harm (other than toxic harm) may be filed after the 18–year period beginning at the time of delivery of the product to the first purchaser or lessee.

(2) EXCEPTIONS.—

(A) A motor vehicle, vessel, aircraft, or train, that is used primarily to transport passengers for hire, shall not be subject to this subsection.

(B) Paragraph (1) does not bar a product liability action against a defendant who made an express warranty in writing as to the safety or life expectancy of the specific product involved which was longer than 18 years, but it will apply at the expiration of that warranty.

(c) TRANSITIONAL PROVISION RELATING TO EXTENSION OF PERIOD FOR BRINGING CERTAIN ACTIONS.—If any provision of subsection (a) or (b) shortens the period during which a product liability action could be otherwise brought pursuant to another provision of law, the claimant may, notwithstanding subsections (a) and (b), bring the product liability action not later than 1 year after the date of enactment of this Act.

SEC. 107. ALTERNATIVE DISPUTE RESOLUTION PROCEDURES.

(a) SERVICE OF OFFER.—A claimant or a defendant in a product liability action may, not later than 60 days after the service of—

(1) the initial complaint; or

(2) the applicable deadline for a responsive pleading; whichever is later, serve upon an adverse party an offer to proceed pursuant to any voluntary, nonbinding alternative dispute resolution procedure established or recognized under the law of the state in which the product liability action is brought or under the rules of the court in which such action is maintained.

(b) WRITTEN NOTICE OF ACCEPTANCE OR REJECTION.—Except as provided in subsection (c), not later than 10 days after the service of an offer to proceed under subsection (a), an offeree shall file a written notice of acceptance or rejection of the offer.

(c) EXTENSION.—The court may, upon motion by an offeree made prior to the expiration of the 10–day period specified in subsection (b), extend the period for filling a written notice under such subsection for a period of not more than 60 days after the date of expiration of the period specified in subsection (b). Discovery may be permitted during such period.

SEC. 108. UNIFORM STANDARDS FOR AWARD OF PUNITIVE DAMAGES.

(a) GENERAL RULE.—Punitive damages may, to the extent permitted by applicable state law, be awarded against a defendant if the claimant establishes by clear and convincing evidence that conduct carried out by the defendant with a conscious, flagrant indifference to the rights or safety of others was the proximate cause of the harm that is the subject of the action in any product liability action.

(b) LIMITATION ON AMOUNT.—

(1) IN GENERAL.—The amount of punitive damages that may be awarded in an action described in subsection (a) may not exceed the greater of—

(A) 2 times the sum of the amount awarded to the claimant for economic loss and noneconomic loss; or

(B) $250,000.

(2) SPECIAL RULE.—Notwithstanding paragraph (1), in any action described in subsection (a) against an individual whose net worth does not exceed $500,000 or against an owner of an unincorporated business, or any partnership, corporation, association, unit of local government, or organization which has fewer than 25 full-time employees, the punitive damages shall not exceed the lesser of—

(A) 2 times the sum of the amount awarded to the claimant for economic loss and noneconomic loss; or

(B) $250,000. For the purpose of determining the applicability of this paragraph to a corporation, the number of employees of a subsidiary or wholly-owned corporation shall include all employees of a parent or sister corporation.

(3) EXCEPTION FOR INSUFFICIENT AWARD IN CASES OF EGREGIOUS CONDUCT.—

(A) DETERMINATION BY COURT.—If the court makes a determination, after considering each of the factors in subparagraph (b), that the application of paragraph (1) would result in an award of punitive damages that is insufficient to punish the egregious conduct of the defendant against whom the punitive damages are to be awarded or to deter such conduct in the future, the court shall determine the additional amount of punitive damages (referred to in this paragraph as the "additional amount") in excess of the amount determined in accordance with paragraph (1) to be awarded against the defendant in a separate proceeding in accordance with this paragraph.

(B) FACTORS FOR CONSIDERATION.—In any proceeding under paragraph (a), the court shall consider—

(i) the extent to which the defendant acted with actual malice;

(ii) the likelihood that serious harm would arise from the conduct of the defendant;

(iii) the degree of the awareness of the defendant of that likelihood;

(iv) the profitability of the misconduct to the defendant;

(v) the duration of the misconduct and any concurrent or subsequent concealment of the conduct by the defendant;

(vi) the attitude and conduct of the defendant upon the discovery of the misconduct and whether the misconduct has terminated;

(vii) the financial condition of the defendant; and

(viii) the cumulative deterrent effect of other losses, damages, and punishment suffered by the defendant as a result of the misconduct, reducing the amount of punitive damages on the basis of the economic impact and severity of all measures to which the defendant has been or may be subjected, including—

(I) compensatory and punitive damage awards to similarly situated claimants;

(II) the adverse economic effect of stigma or loss of reputation;

(III) civil fines and criminal and administrative penalties; and

(IV) stop sale, cease and desist, and other remedial or enforcement orders.

(C) REQUIREMENTS FOR AWARDING ADDITIONAL AMOUNT.—If the court awards an additional amount pursuant to this subsection, the court shall state its reasons for setting the amount of the additional amount in findings of fact and conclusions of law.

(D) PREEMPTION.—This section does not create a cause of action for punitive damages and does not preempt or supersede any State or Federal law to the extent that such law would further limit the award of punitive damages. Nothing in this subsection shall modify or reduce the ability of courts to order remittiturs.

(4) APPLICATION BY COURT.—This subsection shall be applied by the court and application of this subsection shall not be disclosed to the jury. Nothing in this subsection shall authorize the court to enter an award of punitive damages in excess of the jury's initial award of punitive damages.

(c) BIFURCATION AT REQUEST OF ANY PARTY.—

(1) IN GENERAL.—At the request of any party the trier of fact in any action that is subject to this section shall consider in a separate proceeding, held subsequent to the determination of the amount of compensatory damages, whether punitive damages are to be awarded for the harm that is the subject of the action and the amount of the award.

(2) INADMISSIBILITY OF EVIDENCE RELATIVE ONLY TO A CLAIM OF PUNITIVE DAMAGES IN A PROCEEDING CONCERNING COMPENSATORY DAMAGES.—If any party requests a separate proceeding under paragraph (1), in a proceeding to determine whether the claimant may be awarded compensatory damages, any evidence, argument, or contention that is relevant only to the claim of punitive damages, as determined by applicable State law, shall be inadmissible.

SEC. 109. LIABILITY FOR CERTAIN CLAIMS RELATING TO DEATH.

In any civil action in which the alleged harm to the claimant is death and, as of the effective date of this Act, the applicable State law provides, or has been construed to provide, for damages only punitive in nature, a defendant may be liable for any such damages without regard to section 108, but only during such time as the State law so provides. This section shall cease to be effective September 1, 1997.

SEC. 110. SEVERAL LIABILITY FOR NONECONOMIC LOSS.

(a) GENERAL RULE.—In a product liability action, the liability of each defendant for noneconomic loss shall be several only and shall not be joint.

(b) AMOUNT OF LIABILITY.—

(1) IN GENERAL.—Each defendant shall be liable only for the amount of noneconomic loss allocated to the defendant in direct proportion to the percentage of responsibility of the defendant (determined in accordance with paragraph (2)) for the harm to the claimant with respect to which the defendant is liable. The court shall render a separate judgment against each defendant in an amount determined pursuant to the preceding sentence.

(2) PERCENTAGE OF RESPONSIBILITY.—For purposes of determining the amount of noneconomic loss allocated to a defendant

under this section, the trier of fact shall determine the percentage of responsibility of each person responsible for the claimant's harm, whether or not such person is a party to the action.

TITLE II–BIOMATERIALS ACCESS ASSURANCE

SEC. 201.   SHORT TITLE.

This title may be cited as the "Biomaterials Access Assurance Act of 1997".

SEC. 202.   FINDINGS.

Congress finds that—

(1) each year millions of citizens of the United States depend on the availability of lifesaving or life enhancing medical devices, many of which are permanently implantable within the human body;

(2) a continued supply of raw materials and component parts is necessary for the invention, development, improvement, and maintenance of the supply of the devices;

(3) most of the medical devices are made with raw materials and component parts that—

(A) are not designed or manufactured specifically for use in medical devices; and

(B) come in contact with internal human tissue;

(4) the raw materials and component parts also are used in a variety of nonmedical products;

(5) because small quantities of the raw materials and component parts are used for medical devices, sales of raw materials and component parts for medical devices constitute an extremely small portion of the overall market for the raw materials and medical devices;

(6) under the Federal Food, Drug, and Cosmetic Act (21 U.S.C. 301 et seq.), manufacturers of medical devices are required to demonstrate that the medical devices are safe and effective, including demonstrating that the products are properly designed and have adequate warnings or instructions;

(7) notwithstanding the fact that raw materials and component parts suppliers do not design, produce, or test a final medical device, the suppliers have been the subject of actions alleging inadequate—

(A) design and testing of medical devices manufactured with materials or parts supplied by the suppliers; or

(B) warnings related to the use of such medical devices;

(8) even though suppliers of raw materials and component parts have very rarely been held liable in such actions, such suppliers have ceased supplying certain raw materials and component parts for use in medical devices because the costs associated with litigation in order to ensure a favorable judgment for the suppliers far exceeds the total potential sales revenues from sales by such suppliers to the medical device industry;

(9) unless alternate sources of supply can be found, the unavailability of raw materials and component parts for medical devices will lead to unavailability of lifesaving and life-enhancing medical devices;

(10) because other suppliers of the raw materials and component parts in foreign nations are refusing to sell raw materials or component parts for use in manufacturing certain medical devices in the United States, the prospects for development of new sources of supply for the full range of threatened raw materials and component parts for medical devices are remote;

(11) it is unlikely that the small market for such raw materials and component parts in the United States could support the large investment needed to develop new suppliers of such raw materials and component parts;

(12) attempts to develop such new suppliers would raise the cost of medical devices;

(13) courts that have considered the duties of the suppliers of the raw materials and component parts have generally found that the suppliers do not have a duty—

(A) to evaluate the safety and efficacy of the use of a raw material or component part in a medical device; and

(B) to warn consumers concerning the safety and effectiveness of a medical device;

(14) attempts to impose the duties referred to in subparagraphs (A) and (B) of paragraph (13) on suppliers of the raw materials and component parts would cause more harm than good by driving the suppliers to cease supplying manufacturers of medical devices; and

(15) in order to safeguard the availability of a wide variety of lifesaving and life-enhancing medical devices, immediate action is needed—

(A) to clarify the permissible bases of liability for suppliers of raw materials and component parts for medical devices; and

(B) to provide expeditious procedures to dispose of unwarranted suits against the suppliers in such manner as to minimize litigation costs.

SEC. 203. DEFINITIONS.

As used in this title:

(1) BIOMATERIALS SUPPLIER.—

(A) IN GENERAL.—The term "biomaterials supplier" means an entity that directly or indirectly supplies a component part or raw material for use in the manufacture of an implant.

(B) PERSONS INCLUDED.—Such term includes any person who—

(i) has submitted master files to the Secretary for purposes of premarket approval of a medical device; or

(ii) licenses a biomaterials supplier to produce component parts or raw materials.

(2) CLAIMANT.—

(A) IN GENERAL.—The term "claimant" means any person who brings a civil action, or on whose behalf a civil action is brought, arising from harm allegedly caused directly or indirectly by an implant, including a person other than the individual into whose body, or in contact with whose blood or tissue, the implant is placed, who claims to have suffered harm as a result of the implant.

(B) ACTION BROUGHT ON BEHALF OF AN ESTATE.— With respect to an action brought on behalf of or through the estate of an individual into whose body, or in contact with whose blood or tissue the implant is placed, such term includes the decedent that is the subject of the action.

(C) ACTION BROUGHT ON BEHALF OF A MINOR OR INCOMPETENT.—With respect to an action brought on behalf of or through a minor or incompetent, such term includes the parent or guardian of the minor or incompetent.

(D) EXCLUSIONS.—Such term does not include—

(i) a provider of professional health care services, in any case in which—

(I) the sale or use of an implant is incidental to the transaction; and

(II) the essence of the transaction is the furnishing of judgment, skill, or services;

(ii) a person acting in the capacity of a manufacturer, seller, or biomaterials supplier;

(iii) a person alleging harm caused by either the silicone gel or the silicone envelope utilized in a breast implant containing silicone gel, except that—

(I) neither the exclusion provided by this clause nor any other provision of this act may be construed as a finding that silicone gel (or any other form of silicone) may or may not cause harm; and

(II) the existence of the exclusion under this clause may not—

(aa) be disclosed to a jury in any civil action or other proceeding; and

(bb) except as necessary to establish the applicability of this act, otherwise be presented in any civil action or other proceeding; or

(iv) any person who acts in only a financial capacity with respect to the sale of an implant.

(3) COMPONENT PART.—

(A) IN GENERAL.—The term "component part" means a manufactured piece of an implant.

(B) CERTAIN COMPONENTS.—Such term includes a manufactured piece of an implant that—

(i) has significant non-implant applications; and

(ii) alone, has no implant value or purpose, but when combined with other component parts and materials, constitutes an implant.

(4) HARM.—

(A) IN GENERAL.—The term "harm" means—

(i) any injury to or damage suffered by an individual;

(ii) any illness, disease, or death of that individual resulting from that injury or damage; and

(iii) any loss to that individual or any other individual resulting from that injury or damage.

(B) EXCLUSION.—The term does not include any commercial loss or loss of or damage to an implant.

(5) IMPLANT.—The term "implant" means—

(A) a medical device that is intended by the manufacturer of the device—

(i) to be placed into a surgically or naturally formed or existing cavity of the body for a period of at least 30 days; or

(ii) to remain in contact with bodily fluids or internal human tissue through a surgically produced opening for a period of less than 30 days; and

(B) suture materials used in implant procedures.

(6) MANUFACTURER.—The term "manufacturer" means any person who, with respect to an implant—

(A) is engaged in the manufacture, preparation, propagation, compounding, or processing (as defined in section 510(a)(1)) of the Federal Food, Drug, and Cosmetic Act (21 U.S.C. 360(A)(1)) of the implant; and

(B) is required—

(i) to register with the Secretary pursuant to section 510 of the Federal Food, Drug, and Cosmetic Act (21 U.S.C. 360) and the regulations issued under such section; and

(ii) to include the implant on a list of devices filed with the Secretary pursuant to section 510(j) of such Act (21 U.S.C. 360(J)) and the regulations issued under such section.

(7) MEDICAL DEVICE.—The term "medical device" means a device, as defined in section 201(h) of the Federal Food, Drug, and Cosmetic Act (21 U.S.C. 321(H)) and includes any device component of any combination product as that term is used in section 503(g) of such Act (21 U.S.C. 353(G)).

(8) RAW MATERIAL.—The term "raw material" means a substance or product that—

(A) has a generic use; and

(B) may be used in an application other than an implant.

(9) SECRETARY.—The term "secretary" means the Secretary of Health and Human Services.

(10) Seller.—

(A) IN GENERAL.—The term "seller" means a person who, in the course of a business conducted for that purpose, sells, distributes, leases, packages, labels, or otherwise places an implant in the stream of commerce.

(B) exclusions.—The term does not include—

(i) a seller or lessor of real property;

(ii) a provider of professional services, in any case in which the sale or use of an implant is incidental to the transaction and the essence of the transaction is the furnishing of judgment, skill, or services; or

(iii) any person who acts in only a financial capacity with respect to the sale of an implant.

SEC. 204. GENERAL REQUIREMENTS; APPLICABILITY; PREEMPTION.

(a) GENERAL REQUIREMENTS.—

(1) IN GENERAL.—In any civil action covered by this title, a biomaterials supplier may raise any defense set forth in section 205.

(2) PROCEDURES.—Notwithstanding any other provision of law, the Federal or State court in which a civil action covered by this title is pending shall, in connection with a motion for dismissal or judgment based on a defense described in paragraph (1), use the procedures set forth in section 206.

(b) APPLICABILITY.—

(1) IN GENERAL.—Except as provided in paragraph (2), notwithstanding any other provision of law, this title applies to any civil action brought by a claimant whether in a Federal or State court, against a manufacturer, seller, or biomaterials supplier, on the basis of any legal theory, for harm allegedly caused by an implant.

(2) EXCLUSION.—A civil action brought by a purchaser of a medical device for use in providing professional services against a manufacturer, seller, or biomaterials supplier for loss or damage to an implant or for commercial loss to the purchaser—

(A) shall not be considered an action that is subject to this title; and

(B) shall be governed by applicable commercial or contract law.

(c) SCOPE OF PREEMPTION.—

(1) IN GENERAL.—This title supersedes any State law regarding recovery for harm caused by an implant and any rule of procedure applicable to a civil action to recover damages for such harm only to the extent that this title establishes a rule of law applicable to the recovery of such damages.

(2) APPLICABILITY OF OTHER LAWS.—Any issue that arises under this title and that is not governed by a rule of law applicable to the recovery of damages described in paragraph (1) shall be governed by applicable Federal or State law.

(d) STATUTORY CONSTRUCTION.—Nothing in this title may be construed—

(1) to affect any defense available to a defendant under any other provisions of Federal or State law in an action alleging harm caused by an implant; or

(2) to create a cause of action or Federal court jurisdiction pursuant to section 1331 or 1337 of title 28, United States Code, that otherwise would not exist under applicable Federal or State law.

SEC. 205. LIABILITY OF BIOMATERIALS SUPPLIERS.

(a) IN GENERAL.—

(1) EXCLUSION FROM LIABILITY.—Except as provided in paragraph (2), a biomaterials supplier shall not be liable for harm to a claimant caused by an implant.

(2) LIABILITY.—A biomaterials supplier that—

(A) is a manufacturer may be liable for harm to a claimant described in subsection (b);

(B) is a seller may be liable for harm to a claimant described in subsection (c); and

(C) furnishes raw materials or component parts that fail to meet applicable contractual requirements or specifications may be liable for harm to a claimant described in subsection (d).

(b) LIABILITY AS MANUFACTURER.—

(1) IN GENERAL.—A biomaterials supplier may, to the extent required and permitted by any other applicable law, be liable for harm to a claimant caused by an implant if the biomaterials supplier is the manufacturer of the implant.

(2) GROUNDS FOR LIABILITY.—The biomaterials supplier may be considered the manufacturer of the implant that allegedly caused harm to a claimant only if the biomaterials supplier—

(A)(i) has registered with the Secretary pursuant to section 510 of the Federal Food, Drug, and Cosmetic Act (21 u.S.C. 360) and the regulations issued under such section; and

(ii) included the implant on a list of devices filed with the Secretary pursuant to section 510(j) of such Act (21 U.S.C. 360(J)) and the regulations issued under such section;

(B) is the subject of a declaration issued by the Secretary pursuant to paragraph (3) that states that the supplier, with respect to the implant that allegedly caused harm to the claimant, was required to—

(i) register with the Secretary under section 510 of such Act (21 U.S.C. 360), and the regulations issued under such section, but failed to do so; or

(ii) include the implant on a list of devices filed with the Secretary pursuant to section 510(j) of such Act (21 U.S.C. 360(J)) and the regulations issued under such section, but failed to do so; or

(C) is related by common ownership or control to a person meeting all the requirements described in subparagraph (a) or (b), if the court deciding a motion to dismiss in accordance with section 206(c)(3)(B)(i) finds, on the basis of affidavits submitted in accordance with section 206, that it is necessary to impose liability on the biomaterials supplier as a manufacturer because the related manufacturer meeting the requirements of subparagraph (A) or (B) lacks sufficient financial resources to satisfy any judgment that the court feels it is likely to enter should the claimant prevail.

(3) ADMINISTRATIVE PROCEDURES.—

(A) IN GENERAL.—The Secretary may issue a declaration described in paragraph (2)(B) on the motion of the Secretary or on petition by any person, after providing—

(i) notice to the affected persons; and

(ii) an opportunity for an informal hearing.

(B) DOCKETING AND FINAL DECISION.—Immediately upon receipt of a petition filed pursuant to this paragraph, the Secretary shall docket the petition. Not later than 180 days after the petition is filed, the secretary shall issue a final decision on the petition.

(C) APPLICABILITY OF STATUTE OF LIMITATIONS.— Any applicable statute of limitations shall toll during the period during which a claimant has filed a petition with the Secretary under this paragraph.

(c) LIABILITY AS SELLER.—A biomaterials supplier may, to the extent required and permitted by any other applicable law, be liable as a seller for harm to a claimant caused by an implant if—

(1) the biomaterials supplier—

(A) held title to the implant that allegedly caused harm to the claimant as a result of purchasing the implant after—

(i) the manufacture of the implant; and

(ii) the entrance of the implant in the stream of commerce; and

(B) subsequently resold the implant; or

(2) the biomaterials supplier is related by common ownership or control to a person meeting all the requirements described in paragraph (1), if a court deciding a motion to dismiss in accordance with section 206(c)(3)(B)(ii) finds, on the basis of affidavits submitted in accordance with section 206, that it is necessary to impose liability on the biomaterials supplier as a seller because the related seller meeting the requirements of paragraph (1) lacks sufficient financial resources to satisfy any judgment that the court feels it is likely to enter should the claimant prevail.

(d) LIABILITY FOR VIOLATING CONTRACTUAL REQUIREMENTS OR SPECIFICATIONS.—A biomaterials supplier may, to the extent required and permitted by any other applicable law, be liable for harm to a claimant caused by an implant, if the claimant in an action shows, by a preponderance of the evidence, that—

(1) the raw materials or component parts delivered by the biomaterials supplier either

(A) did not constitute the product described in the contract between the biomaterials supplier and the person who contracted for delivery of the product; or

(B) failed to meet any specifications that were—

(i) provided to the biomaterials supplier and not expressly repudiated by the biomaterials supplier prior to acceptance of delivery of the raw materials or component parts;

(ii)(I) published by the biomaterials supplier;

(II) provided to the manufacturer by the biomaterials supplier; or

(III) contained in a master file that was submitted by the biomaterials supplier to the Secretary and that is currently maintained by the biomaterials supplier for purposes of premarket approval of medical devices; or

(iii) included in the submissions for purposes of premarket approval or review by the Secretary under section 510, 513, 515, or 520 of the Federal Food, Drug, and Cosmetic Act (21 U.S.C. 360, 360c, 360e, or 360j), and received clearance from the Secretary if such specifications were provided by the manufacturer to the biomaterials supplier and were not expressly repudiated by the biomaterials supplier prior to the acceptance by the manufacturer of delivery of the raw materials or component parts; and

(2) such conduct was an actual and proximate cause of the harm to the claimant.

SEC. 206. PROCEDURES FOR DISMISSAL OF CIVIL ACTIONS AGAINST BIOMATERIALS SUPPLIERS.

(a) MOTION TO DISMISS.—In any action that is subject to this title, a biomaterials supplier who is a defendant in such action may, at any time during which a motion to dismiss may be filed under an applicable law, move to dismiss the action against it on the grounds that—

(1) the defendant is a biomaterials supplier; and

(2)(A) the defendant should not, for the purposes of—

(i) section 205(b), be considered to be a manufacturer of the implant that is subject to such section; or

(ii) section 205(c), be considered to be a seller of the implant that allegedly caused harm to the claimant; or

(B)(i) the claimant has failed to establish, pursuant to section 205(d), that the supplier furnished raw materials or component parts in violation of contractual requirements or specifications; or

(ii) the claimant has failed to comply with the procedural requirements of subsection (b).

(b) MANUFACTURER OF IMPLANT SHALL BE NAMED A PARTY.—The claimant shall be required to name the manufacturer of the implant as a party to the action, unless—

(1) the manufacturer is subject to service of process solely in a jurisdiction in which the biomaterials supplier is not domiciled or subject to a service of process; or

(2) an action against the manufacturer is barred by applicable law.

(c) PROCEEDING ON MOTION TO DISMISS.—The following rules shall apply to any proceeding on a motion to dismiss filed under this section:

(1) AFFIDAVITS RELATING TO LISTING AND DECLARATIONS.—

(A) IN GENERAL.—The defendant in the action may submit an affidavit demonstrating that defendant has not included the implant on a list, if any, filed with the Secretary pursuant to section 510(j) of the Federal Food, Drug, and Cosmetic Act (21 U.S.C. 360(j)).

(B) RESPONSE TO MOTION TO DISMISS.—In response to the motion to dismiss, the claimant may submit an affidavit demonstrating that—

(i) the Secretary has, with respect to the defendant and the implant that allegedly caused harm to the claimant, issued a declaration pursuant to section 205(b)(2)(b); or

(ii) the defendant who filed the motion to dismiss is a seller of the implant who is liable under section 205(c).

(2) EFFECT OF MOTION TO DISMISS ON DISCOVERY.—

(A) IN GENERAL.—If a defendant files a motion to dismiss under paragraph (1) or (2) of subsection (a), no discovery shall be permitted in connection to the action that is the subject of the motion, other than discovery necessary to determine a motion to dismiss for lack of jurisdiction, until such time as the court rules on the motion to dismiss in accordance with the affidavits submitted by the parties in accordance with this section.

(B) DISCOVERY.—If a defendant files a motion to dismiss under subsection (a)(2)(B)(i) on the grounds that the biomaterials supplier did not furnish raw materials or component parts in violation of contractual requirements or specifications, the court may permit discovery, as ordered by the court. The discovery conducted pursuant to this subparagraph shall be limited to issues that are directly relevant to—

(i) the pending motion to dismiss; or

(ii) the jurisdiction of the court.

(3) AFFIDAVITS RELATING STATUS OF DEFENDANT.—

(A) IN GENERAL.—Except as provided in clauses (i) and (ii) of subparagraph (B), the court shall consider a defendant to be a biomaterials supplier who is not subject to an action for harm to a claimant caused by an implant, other than an action relating to liability for a violation of contractual requirements or specifications described in subsection (d).

(B) RESPONSES TO MOTION TO DISMISS.—The court shall grant a motion to dismiss any action that asserts liability of the defendant under subsection (b) or (c) of section 205 on the grounds that the defendant is not a manufacturer subject to such section 205(b) r seller subject to section 205(c), unless the claimant submits a valid affidavit that demonstrates that—

(i) with respect to a motion to dismiss contending the defendant is not a manufacturer, the defendant meets the applicable requirements for liability as a manufacturer under section 205(b); or

(ii) with respect to a motion to dismiss contending that the defendant is not a seller, the defendant meets the applicable requirements for liability as a seller under section 205(c).

(4) BASIS OF RULING ON MOTION TO DISMISS.—

(A) IN GENERAL.—The court shall rule on a motion to dismiss filed under subsection (a) solely on the basis of the pleadings of the parties made pursuant to this section and any affidavits submitted by the parties pursuant to this section.

(B) MOTION FOR SUMMARY JUDGMENT.—Notwithstanding any other provision of law, if the court determines that the pleadings and affidavits made by parties pursuant to this section raise genuine issues concerning material facts with respect to a motion concerning contractual requirements and specifications, the court may deem the motion to dismiss to be a motion for summary judgment made pursuant to subsection (d).

(d) SUMMARY JUDGMENT.—

(1) IN GENERAL.—

(A) BASIS FOR ENTRY OF JUDGMENT.—A biomaterials supplier shall be entitled to entry of judgment without trial if the court finds there is no genuine issue concerning any material fact for each applicable element set forth in paragraphs (1) and (2) of section 205(d).

(B) ISSUES OF MATERIAL FACT.—With respect to a finding made under subparagraph (A), the court shall consider a genuine issue of material fact to exist only if the evidence submitted by claimant would be sufficient to allow a reasonable jury to reach a verdict for the claimant if the jury found the evidence to be credible.

(2) DISCOVERY MADE PRIOR TO A RULING ON A MOTION FOR SUMMARY JUDGMENT.—If, under applicable rules, the court permits discovery prior to a ruling on a motion for summary judgment made pursuant to this subsection, such discovery shall be limited solely to establishing whether a genuine issue of material fact exists as to the applicable elements set forth in paragraphs (1) and (2) of section 205(d).

(3) DISCOVERY WITH RESPECT TO A BIOMATERIALS SUPPLIER.—A biomaterials supplier shall be subject to discovery in connection with a motion seeking dismissal or summary judgment on the basis of the inapplicability of section 205(d) or the failure to establish the applicable elements of section 205(d) solely to the extent permitted by the applicable Federal or State rules for discovery against nonparties.

(e) STAY PENDING PETITION FOR DECLARATION.—If a claimant has filed a petition for a declaration pursuant to section 205(b)(3)(a) with respect to a defendant, and the Secretary has not issued a final decision on the petition, the court shall stay all proceedings with respect to that defendant until such time as the secretary has issued a final decision on the petition.

(f) MANUFACTURER CONDUCT OF PROCEEDING.—The manufacturer of an implant that is the subject of an action covered under this title shall be permitted to file and conduct a proceeding on any motion for summary judgment or dismissal filed by a biomaterials supplier who is a defendant under this section if the manufacturer and any other defendant in such action enter into a valid and applicable contractual agreement under which the manufacturer agrees to bear the cost of such proceeding or to conduct such proceeding.

(g) ATTORNEY FEES.—The court shall require the claimant to compensate the biomaterials supplier (or a manufacturer appearing in lieu of a supplier pursuant to subsection (f)) for attorney fees and costs, if—

(1) the claimant named or joined the biomaterials supplier; and

(2) the court found the claim against the biomaterials supplier to be without merit and frivolous.

SEC. 301.   EFFECT OF COURT OF APPEALS DECISIONS.

A decision by a Federal circuit court of appeals interpreting a provision of this Act (except to the extent that the decision is overruled or otherwise modified by the Supreme Court) shall be considered a controlling precedent with respect to any subsequent decision made concerning the interpretation of such provision by any Federal or State court within the geographical boundaries of the area under the jurisdiction of the circuit court of appeals.

SEC. 302.   FEDERAL CAUSE OF ACTION PRECLUDED.

The district courts of the United States shall not have jurisdiction pursuant to this Act based on section 1331 or 1337 of title 28, United States Code.

SEC. 303.   EFFECTIVE DATE.

This Act shall apply with respect to any action commenced on or after the date of the enactment of this Act without regard to whether the harm that is the subject of the action or the conduct that caused the harm occurred before such date of enactment.

BIOMATERIALS ACCESS ASSURANCE
ACT OF 1998

105th Congress   H. R. 872
2d Session

112 Stat. 1519, P.L. 105–230

August 13, 1998

(To be codified at 21 U.S.C. § 1601)

An Act to establish rules governing product liability actions against raw materials and bulk component suppliers to medical device manufacturers, and for other purposes.

Be it enacted by the Senate and House of Representatives of the United States of America in Congress assembled,

SECTION 1.   SHORT TITLE.

This Act may be cited as the "Biomaterials Access Assurance Act of 1998".

SEC. 2.   FINDINGS.

The Congress finds that—

(1) each year millions of citizens of the United States depend on the availability of lifesaving or life-enhancing medical devices, many of which are permanently implantable within the human body;

(2) a continued supply of raw materials and component parts is necessary for the invention, development, improvement, and maintenance of the supply of the devices;

(3) most of the medical devices are made with raw materials and component parts that—

(A) move in interstate commerce;

(B) are not designed or manufactured specifically for use in medical devices; and

(C) come in contact with internal human tissue;

(4) the raw materials and component parts also are used in a variety of nonmedical products;

(5) because small quantities of the raw materials and component parts are used for medical devices, sales of raw materials and component parts for medical devices constitute an extremely small portion of the overall market for the raw materials and component parts;

(6) under the Federal Food, Drug, and Cosmetic Act (21 U.S.C. 301 et seq.) manufacturers of medical devices are required to demonstrate that the medical devices are safe and effective, including demonstrating that the products are properly designed and have adequate warnings or instructions;

(7) notwithstanding the fact that raw materials and component parts suppliers do not design, produce, or test a final medical device, the suppliers have been the subject of actions alleging inadequate—

(A) design and testing of medical devices manufactured with materials or parts supplied by the suppliers; or

(B) warnings related to the use of such medical devices;

(8) even though suppliers of raw materials and component parts have very rarely been held liable in such actions, such suppliers have ceased supplying certain raw materials and component parts for use in medical devices for a number of reasons, including concerns about the costs of such litigation;

(9) unless alternate sources of supply can be found, the unavailability of raw materials and component parts for medical devices will lead to unavailability of lifesaving and life-enhancing medical devices;

(10) because other suppliers of the raw materials and component parts in foreign nations are refusing to sell raw materials or component parts for use in manufacturing certain medical devices in the United States, the prospects for development of new sources of supply for the full range of

threatened raw materials and component parts for medical devices are remote;

(11) it is unlikely that the small market for such raw materials and component parts in the United States could support the large investment needed to develop new suppliers of such raw materials and component parts;

(12) attempts to develop such new suppliers would raise the cost of medical devices;

(13) courts that have considered the duties of the suppliers of the raw materials and component parts have generally found that the suppliers do not have a duty—

(A) to evaluate the safety and efficacy of the use of a raw material or component part in a medical device; or

(B) to warn consumers concerning the safety and effectiveness of a medical device;

(14) because medical devices and the raw materials and component parts used in their manufacture move in interstate commerce, a shortage of such raw materials and component parts affects interstate commerce;

(15) in order to safeguard the availability of a wide variety of lifesaving and life-enhancing medical devices, immediate action is needed—

(A) to clarify the permissible bases of liability for suppliers of raw materials and component parts for medical devices; and

(B) to provide expeditious procedures to dispose of unwarranted suits against the suppliers in such manner as to minimize litigation costs;

(16) the several States and their courts are the primary architects and regulators of our tort system; Congress, however, must, in certain circumstances involving the national interest, address tort issues, and a threatened shortage of raw materials and component parts for lifesaving medical devices is one such circumstance; and

(17) the protections set forth in this Act are needed to assure the continued supply of materials for lifesaving medical devices, although such protections do not protect negligent suppliers.

SEC. 3.   DEFINITIONS.

As used in this Act:

(1) BIOMATERIALS SUPPLIER.—

(A) IN GENERAL.—The term "biomaterials supplier" means an entity that directly or indirectly supplies a component part or raw material for use in the manufacture of an implant.

(B) PERSONS INCLUDED.—Such term includes any person who—

(i) has submitted master files to the Secretary for purposes of premarket approval of a medical device; or

(ii) licenses a biomaterials supplier to produce component parts or raw materials.

(2) CLAIMANT.—

(A) IN GENERAL.—The term "claimant" means any person who brings a civil action, or on whose behalf a civil action is brought, arising from harm allegedly caused directly or indirectly by an implant, including a person other than the individual into whose body, or in contact with whose blood or tissue, the implant is placed, who claims to have suffered harm as a result of the implant.

(B) ACTION BROUGHT ON BEHALF OF AN ESTATE.—With respect to an action brought on behalf of or through the estate of a deceased individual into whose body, or in contact with whose blood or tissue the implant was placed, such term includes the decedent that is the subject of the action.

(C) ACTION BROUGHT ON BEHALF OF A MINOR OR INCOM-PETENT.—With respect to an action brought on behalf of or through a minor or incompetent, such term includes the parent or guardian of the minor or incompetent.

(D) EXCLUSIONS.—Such term does not include—

(i) a provider of professional health care services in any case in which—

(I) the sale or use of an implant is incidental to such services; and

(II) the essence of the professional health care services provided is the furnishing of judgment, skill, or services;

(ii) a person acting in the capacity of a manufacturer, seller, or biomaterials supplier; or

(iii) a person alleging harm caused by either the silicone gel or the silicone envelope utilized in a breast implant containing silicone gel, except that—

(I) neither the exclusion provided by this clause nor any other provision of this Act may be construed as a finding that silicone gel (or any other form of silicone) may or may not cause harm; and

(II) the existence of the exclusion under this clause may not—

(aa) be disclosed to a jury in any civil action or other proceeding; and

(bb) except as necessary to establish the applicability of this Act, otherwise be presented in any civil action or other proceeding.

(3) COMPONENT PART.—

(A) IN GENERAL.—The term "component part" means a manufactured piece of an implant.

(B) CERTAIN COMPONENTS.—Such term includes a manufactured piece of an implant that—

(i) has significant non-implant applications; and

(ii) alone, has no implant value or purpose, but when combined with other component parts and materials, constitutes an implant.

(4) HARM.—

(A) IN GENERAL.—The term "harm" means—

(i) any injury to or damage suffered by an individual;

(ii) any illness, disease, or death of that individual resulting from that injury or damage; and

(iii) any loss to that individual or any other individual resulting from that injury or damage.

(B) EXCLUSION.—The term does not include any commercial loss or loss of or damage to an implant.

(5) IMPLANT.—The term "implant" means—

(A) a medical device that is intended by the manufacturer of the device—

(i) to be placed into a surgically or naturally formed or existing cavity of the body for a period of at least 30 days; or

(ii) to remain in contact with bodily fluids or internal human tissue through a surgically produced opening for a period of less than 30 days; and

(B) suture materials used in implant procedures.

(6) MANUFACTURER.—The term "manufacturer" means any person who, with respect to an implant—

(A) is engaged in the manufacture, preparation, propagation, compounding, or processing (as defined in section 510(a)(1) of the Federal Food, Drug, and Cosmetic Act (21 U.S.C. 360(a)(1))) of the implant; and

(B) is required—

(i) to register with the Secretary pursuant to section 510 of the Federal Food, Drug, and Cosmetic Act (21 U.S.C. 360) and the regulations issued under such section; and

(ii) to include the implant on a list of devices filed with the Secretary pursuant to section 510(j) of such Act (21 U.S.C. 360(j)) and the regulations issued under such section.

(7) MEDICAL DEVICE.—The term "medical device" means a device, as defined in section 201(h) of the Federal Food, Drug, and Cosmetic Act

(21 U.S.C. 321(h)), and includes any device component of any combination product as that term is used in section 503(g) of such Act (21 U.S.C. 353(g)).

(8) RAW MATERIAL.—The term "raw material" means a substance or product that—

(A) has a generic use; and

(B) may be used in an application other than an implant.

(9) SECRETARY.—The term "Secretary" means the Secretary of Health and Human Services.

(10) SELLER.—

(A) IN GENERAL.—The term "seller" means a person who, in the course of a business conducted for that purpose, sells, distributes, leases, packages, labels, or otherwise places an implant in the stream of commerce.

(B) EXCLUSIONS.—The term does not include—

(i) a seller or lessor of real property;

(ii) a provider of professional health care services in any case in which—

(I) the sale or use of the implant is incidental to such services; and

(II) the essence of the professional health care services provided is the furnishing of judgment, skill, or services; or

(iii) any person who acts in only a financial capacity with respect to the sale of an implant.

SEC. 4. GENERAL REQUIREMENTS; APPLICABILITY; PREEMPTION.

(a) GENERAL REQUIREMENTS.—

(1) IN GENERAL.—In any civil action covered by this Act, a biomaterials supplier may—

(A) raise any exclusion from liability set forth in section 5; and

(B) make a motion for dismissal or for summary judgment as set forth in section 6.

(2) PROCEDURES.—Notwithstanding any other provision of law, a Federal or State court in which an action covered by this Act is pending shall, in connection with a motion under section 6 or 7, use the procedures set forth in this Act.

(b) APPLICABILITY.—

(1) IN GENERAL.—Except as provided in paragraph (2), this Act applies to any civil action brought by a claimant, whether in a Federal or

State court, on the basis of any legal theory, for harm allegedly caused, directly or indirectly, by an implant.

(2) EXCLUSION.—A civil action brought by a purchaser of a medical device, purchased for use in providing professional health care services, for loss or damage to an implant or for commercial loss to the purchaser—

(A) shall not be considered an action that is subject to this Act; and

(B) shall be governed by applicable commercial or contract law.

(c) SCOPE OF PREEMPTION.-

(1) IN GENERAL.—This Act supersedes any State law regarding recovery for harm caused by an implant and any rule of procedure applicable to a civil action to recover damages for such harm only to the extent that this Act establishes a rule of law applicable to the recovery of such damages.

(2) APPLICABILITY OF OTHER LAWS.—Any issue that arises under this Act and that is not governed by a rule of law applicable to the recovery of damages described in paragraph (1) shall be governed by applicable Federal or State law.

(d) STATUTORY CONSTRUCTION.—Nothing in this Act may be construed—

(1) to affect any defense available to a defendant under any other provisions of Federal or State law in an action alleging harm caused by an implant; or

(2) to create a cause of action or Federal court jurisdiction pursuant to section 1331 or 1337 of title 28, United States *1524 Code, that otherwise would not exist under applicable Federal or State law.

SEC. 5.   LIABILITY OF BIOMATERIALS SUPPLIERS.

(a) IN GENERAL.—Except as provided in section 7, a biomaterials supplier shall not be liable for harm to a claimant caused by an implant unless such supplier is liable—

(1) as a manufacturer of the implant, as provided in subsection (b);

(2) as a seller of the implant, as provided in subsection (c); or

(3) for furnishing raw materials or component parts for the implant that failed to meet applicable contractual requirements or specifications, as provided in subsection (d).

(b) LIABILITY AS MANUFACTURER.—

(1) IN GENERAL.—A biomaterials supplier may, to the extent required and permitted by any other applicable law, be liable for harm to a claimant caused by an implant if the biomaterials supplier is the manufacturer of the implant.

(2) GROUNDS FOR LIABILITY.—The biomaterials supplier may be considered the manufacturer of the implant that allegedly caused harm to a claimant only if the biomaterials supplier—

(A)(i) registered or was required to register with the Secretary pursuant to section 510 of the Federal Food, Drug, and Cosmetic Act (21 U.S.C. 360) and the regulations issued under such section; and

(ii) included or was required to include the implant on a list of devices filed with the Secretary pursuant to section 510(j) of such Act (21 U.S.C. 360(j)) and the regulations issued under such section;

(B) is the subject of a declaration issued by the Secretary pursuant to paragraph (3) that states that the supplier, with respect to the implant that allegedly caused harm to the claimant, was required to.—

(i) register with the Secretary under section 510 of such Act (21 U.S.C. 360), and the regulations issued under such section, but failed to do so; or

(ii) include the implant on a list of devices filed with the Secretary pursuant to section 510(j) of such Act (21 U.S.C. 360(j)) and the regulations issued under such section, but failed to do so; or

(C) is related by common ownership or control to a person meeting all the requirements described in subparagraph (A) or (B), if the court deciding a motion to dismiss in accordance with section 6(c)(3)(B)(i) finds, on the basis of affidavits submitted in accordance with section 6, that it is necessary to impose liability on the biomaterials supplier as a manufacturer because the related manufacturer meeting the requirements of subparagraph (A) or (B) lacks sufficient financial resources to satisfy any judgment that the court feels it is likely to enter should the claimant prevail.

(3) ADMINISTRATIVE PROCEDURES.—

(A) IN GENERAL.—The Secretary may issue a declaration described in paragraph (2)(B) on the motion of the Secretary or on petition by any person, after providing—

(i) notice to the affected persons; and

(ii) an opportunity for an informal hearing.

(B) DOCKETING AND FINAL DECISION.—Immediately upon receipt of a petition filed pursuant to this paragraph, the Secretary shall docket the petition. Not later than 120 days after the petition is filed, the Secretary shall issue a final decision on the petition.

(C) APPLICABILITY OF STATUTE OF LIMITATIONS.—Any applicable statute of limitations shall toll during the period from the time a claimant files a petition with the Secretary under this paragraph until such time as either (i) the Secretary issues a final decision on the petition, or (ii) the petition is withdrawn.

(D) STAY PENDING PETITION FOR DECLARATION.—If a claimant has filed a petition for a declaration with respect to a defendant, and the Secretary has not issued a final decision on the petition, the court shall stay all proceedings with respect to that defendant until such time as the Secretary has issued a final decision on the petition.

(c) LIABILITY AS SELLER.—A biomaterials supplier may, to the extent required and permitted by any other applicable law, be liable as a seller for harm to a claimant caused by an implant only if—

(1) the biomaterials supplier—

(A) held title to the implant and then acted as a seller of the implant after its initial sale by the manufacturer; or

(B) acted under contract as a seller to arrange for the transfer of the implant directly to the claimant after the initial sale by the manufacturer of the implant; or

(2) the biomaterials supplier is related by common ownership or control to a person meeting all the requirements described in paragraph (1), if a court deciding a motion to dismiss in accordance with section 6(c)(3)(B)(ii) finds, on the basis of affidavits submitted in accordance with section 6, that it is necessary to impose liability on the biomaterials supplier as a seller because the related seller meeting the requirements of paragraph (1) lacks sufficient financial resources to satisfy any judgment that the court feels it is likely to enter should the claimant prevail.

(d) LIABILITY FOR FAILURE TO MEET APPLICABLE CONTRACTUAL REQUIREMENTS OR SPECIFICATIONS.—A biomaterials supplier may, to the extent required and permitted by any other applicable law, be liable for harm to a claimant caused by an implant if the claimant in an action shows, by a preponderance of the evidence, that—

(1) the biomaterials supplier supplied raw materials or component parts for use in the implant that either—

(A) did not constitute the product described in the contract between the biomaterials supplier and the person who contracted for the supplying of the product; or

(B) failed to meet any specifications that were.—

(i) accepted, pursuant to applicable law, by the biomaterials supplier;

(ii) published by the biomaterials supplier;

(iii) provided by the biomaterials supplier to the person who contracted for such product;

(iv) contained in a master file that was submitted by the biomaterials supplier to the Secretary and that is currently maintained by the biomaterials supplier for purposes of premarket approval of medical devices; or

(v) included in the submissions for purposes of premarket approval or review by the Secretary under section 510, 513, 515, or 520 of the Federal Food, Drug, and Cosmetic Act (21 U.S.C. 360, 360c, 360e, or 360j), and received clearance from the Secretary if such specifications were accepted, pursuant to applicable law, by the biomaterials supplier; and

(2) such failure to meet applicable contractual requirements or specifications was an actual and proximate cause of the harm to the claimant.

SEC. 6. PROCEDURES FOR DISMISSAL OF CIVIL ACTIONS AGAINST BIOMATERIALS SUPPLIERS.

(a) MOTION TO DISMISS.—A defendant may, at any time during which a motion to dismiss may be filed under applicable law, move to dismiss an action against it on the grounds that the defendant is a biomaterials supplier and one or more of the following:

(1) The defendant is not liable as a manufacturer, as provided in section 5(b).

(2) The defendant is not liable as a seller, as provided in section 5(c).

(3) The defendant is not liable for furnishing raw materials or component parts for the implant that failed to meet applicable contractual requirements or specifications, as provided in section 5(d).

(4) The claimant did not name the manufacturer as a party to the action, as provided in subsection (b).

(b) MANUFACTURER OF IMPLANT SHALL BE NAMED A PARTY.—In any civil action covered by this Act, the claimant shall be required to name the manufacturer of the implant as a party to the action, unless—

(1) the manufacturer is subject to service of process solely in a jurisdiction in which the biomaterials supplier is not domiciled or subject to a service of process; or

(2) a claim against the manufacturer is barred by applicable law or rule of practice.

(c) PROCEEDING ON MOTION TO DISMISS.—The following rules shall apply to any proceeding on a motion to dismiss filed by a defendant under this section:

(1) EFFECT OF MOTION TO DISMISS ON DISCOVERY.—

(A) IN GENERAL.—Except as provided in subparagraph (B), if a defendant files a motion to dismiss under subsection (a), no discovery shall be permitted in connection with the action that is the subject of the motion, other than discovery necessary to determine a motion to dismiss for lack of jurisdiction, until such time as the court rules on the motion to dismiss.

(B) DISCOVERY.—If a defendant files a motion to dismiss under subsection (a)(3) on the grounds that it did not furnish raw materials or component parts for the implant that failed to meet applicable contractual requirements or specifications, the court may permit discovery limited to issues that are directly relevant to—

(i) the pending motion to dismiss; or

(ii) the jurisdiction of the court.

(2) AFFIDAVITS.—

(A) DEFENDANT.—A defendant may submit affidavits supporting the grounds for dismissal contained in its motion to dismiss under subsection (a). If the motion is made under subsection (a)(1), the defendant may submit an affidavit demonstrating that the defendant has not included the implant on a list, if any, filed with the Secretary pursuant to section 510(j) of the Federal Food, Drug, and Cosmetic Act (21 U.S.C. 360(j)).

(B) CLAIMANT.—In response to a motion to dismiss, the claimant may submit affidavits demonstrating that—

(i) the Secretary has, with respect to the defendant and the implant that allegedly caused harm to the claimant, issued a declaration pursuant to section 5(b)(2)(B); or

(ii) the defendant is a seller of the implant who is liable under section 5(c).

(3) BASIS OF RULING ON MOTION TO DISMISS.—The court shall rule on a motion to dismiss filed under subsection (a) solely on the basis of the pleadings and affidavits of the parties made pursuant to this subsection. The court shall grant a motion to dismiss filed under subsection (a).—

(A) unless the claimant submits a valid affidavit that demonstrates that the defendant is not a biomaterials supplier;

(B) unless the court determines, to the extent raised in the pleadings and affidavits, that one or more of the following apply:

(i) the defendant may be liable as a manufacturer, as provided in section 5(b);

(ii) the defendant may be liable as a seller, as provided in section 5(c); or

(iii) the defendant may be liable for furnishing raw materials or component parts for the implant that failed to meet applicable contractual requirements or specifications, as provided in section 5(d); or

(C) if the claimant did not name the manufacturer as a party to the action, as provided in subsection (b).

(4) TREATMENT OF MOTION AS MOTION FOR SUMMARY JUDGMENT.—The court may treat a motion to dismiss as a motion for

summary judgment subject to subsection (d) in order to determine whether the pleadings and affidavits, in connection with such action, raise genuine issues of material fact concerning whether the defendant furnished raw materials or component parts of the implant that failed to meet applicable contractual requirements or specifications as provided in section 5(d).

(d) SUMMARY JUDGMENT.—

(1) IN GENERAL.—

(A) BASIS FOR ENTRY OF JUDGMENT.—If a motion to dismiss of a biomaterials supplier is to be treated as a motion for summary judgment under subsection (c)(4) or if a biomaterials supplier moves for summary judgment, the biomaterials supplier shall be entitled to entry of judgment without trial if the court finds there is no genuine issue of material fact for each applicable element set forth in paragraphs (1) and (2) of section 5(d).

(B) ISSUES OF MATERIAL FACT.—With respect to a finding made under subparagraph (A), the court shall consider a genuine issue of material fact to exist only if the evidence submitted by the claimant would be sufficient to allow a reasonable jury to reach a verdict for the claimant if the jury found the evidence to be credible.

(2) DISCOVERY MADE PRIOR TO A RULING ON A MOTION FOR SUMMARY JUDGMENT.—If, under applicable rules, the court permits discovery prior to a ruling on a motion for summary judgment governed by section 5(d), such discovery shall be limited solely to establishing whether a genuine issue of material fact exists as to the applicable elements set forth in paragraphs (1) and (2) of section 5(d).

(3) DISCOVERY WITH RESPECT TO A BIOMATERIALS SUPPLI-ER.—A biomaterials supplier shall be subject to discovery in connection with a motion seeking dismissal or summary judgment on the basis of the inapplicability of section 5(d) or the failure to establish the applicable elements of section 5(d) solely to the extent permitted by the applicable Federal or State rules for discovery against nonparties.

(e) DISMISSAL WITH PREJUDICE.—An order granting a motion to dismiss or for summary judgment pursuant to this section shall be entered with prejudice, except insofar as the moving defendant may be rejoined to the action as provided in section 7.

(f) MANUFACTURER CONDUCT OF LITIGATION.—The manufacturer of an implant that is the subject of an action covered under this Act shall be permitted to conduct litigation on any motion for summary judgment or dismissal filed by a biomaterials supplier who is a defendant under this section on behalf of such supplier if the manufacturer and any other defendant in such action enter into a valid and applicable contractual agreement under which the manufacturer agrees to bear the cost of such litigation or to conduct such litigation.

SEC. 7. SUBSEQUENT IMPLEADER OF DISMISSED BIOMATERIALS SUPPLIER.

(a) IMPLEADING OF DISMISSED DEFENDANT.—A court, upon motion by a manufacturer or a claimant within 90 days after entry of a final judgment in an action by the claimant against a manufacturer, and notwithstanding any otherwise applicable statute of limitations, may implead a biomaterials supplier who has been dismissed from the action pursuant to this Act if—

(1) the manufacturer has made an assertion, either in a motion or other pleading filed with the court or in an opening or closing statement at trial, or as part of a claim for contribution or indemnification, and the court finds based on the court's independent review of the evidence contained in the record of the action, that under applicable law—

(A) the negligence or intentionally tortious conduct of the dismissed supplier was an actual and proximate cause of the harm to the claimant; and

(B) the manufacturer's liability for damages should be reduced in whole or in part because of such negligence or intentionally tortious conduct; or

(2) the claimant has moved to implead the supplier and the court finds, based on the court's independent review of the evidence contained in the record of the action, that under applicable law—

(A) the negligence or intentionally tortious conduct of the dismissed supplier was an actual and proximate cause of the harm to the claimant; and

(B) the claimant is unlikely to be able to recover the full amount of its damages from the remaining defendants.

(b) STANDARD OF LIABILITY.—Notwithstanding any preliminary finding under subsection (a), a biomaterials supplier who has been impleaded into an action covered by this Act, as provided for in this section—

(1) may, prior to entry of judgment on the claim against it, supplement the record of the proceeding that was developed prior to the grant of the motion for impleader under subsection (a); and

(2) may be found liable to a manufacturer or a claimant only to the extent required and permitted by any applicable State or Federal law other than this Act.

(c) DISCOVERY.—Nothing in this section shall give a claimant or any other party the right to obtain discovery from a biomaterials supplier at any time prior to grant of a motion for impleader beyond that allowed under section 6.

SEC. 8.   EFFECTIVE DATE.

This Act shall apply to all civil actions covered under this Act that are commenced on or after the date of enactment of this Act, including any such action with respect to which the harm asserted in the action or the conduct that caused the harm occurred before the date of enactment of this Act.

Approved August 13, 1998.

EEC DIRECTIVE ON LIABILITY FOR DEFECTIVE PRODUCTS

COUNCIL DIRECTIVE

of

25 July 1985 on the approximation of the laws, regulations and administrative provisions of the Member States concerning liability for defective products

(85/374/EEC)

THE COUNCIL OF THE EUROPEAN COMMUNITIES,

Having regard to the Treaty establishing the European Economic Community, and in particular Article 100 thereof,

Having regard to the proposal from the Commission,

Having regard to the opinion of the European Parliament,

Having regard to the opinion of the Economic and Social Committee,

Whereas approximation of the laws of the Member States concerning the liability of the producer for damage caused by the defectiveness of his products is necessary because the existing divergences may distort competition and affect the movement of goods within the common market and entail a differing degree of protection of the consumer against damage caused by a defective product to his health or property;

Whereas liability without fault on the part of the producer is the sole means of adequately solving the problem, peculiar to our age of increasing technicality, of a fair apportionment of the risks inherent in modern technological production;

Whereas liability without fault should apply only to movables which have been industrially produced; whereas, as a result, it is appropriate to exclude liability for agricultural products and game, except where they have undergone a processing of an industrial nature which could cause a defect in these products; whereas the liability provided for in this Directive should also apply to movables which are used in the construction of immovables or are installed in immovables;

Whereas protection of the consumer requires that all producers involved in the production process should be made liable, in so far as their finished product, component part or any raw material supplied by them was defective; whereas, for the same reason, liability should extend to importers of products into the Community and to persons who present themselves as producers by affixing their name, trade mark or other distinguishing feature or who supply a product the producer of which cannot be identified;

Whereas, in situations where several persons are liable for the same damage, the protection of the consumer requires that the injured person

665

should be able to claim full compensation for the damage from any one of them;

Whereas, to protect the physical well-being and property of the consumer, the defectiveness of the product should be determined by reference not to its fitness for use but to the lack of the safety which the public at large is entitled to expect; whereas the safety is assessed by excluding any misuse of the product not reasonable under the circumstances;

Whereas a fair apportionment of risk between the injured person and the producer implies that the producer should be able to free himself from liability if he furnishes proof as to the existence of certain exonerating circumstances;

Whereas the protection of the consumer requires that the liability of the producer remains unaffected by acts or omissions of other persons having contributed to cause the damage; whereas, however, the contributory negligence of the injured person may be taken into account to reduce or disallow such liability;

Whereas the protection of the consumer requires compensation for death and personal injury as well as compensation for damage to property; whereas the latter should nevertheless be limited to goods for private use or consumption and be subject to a deduction of a lower threshold of a fixed amount in order to avoid litigation in an excessive number of cases; whereas this Directive should not prejudice compensation for pain and suffering and other non-material damages payable, where appropriate, under the law applicable to the case;

Whereas a uniform period of limitation for the bringing of action for compensation is in the interests both of the injured person and of the producer;

Whereas products age in the course of time, higher safety standards are developed and the state of science and technology progresses; whereas, therefore, it would not be reasonable to make the producer liable for an unlimited period for the defectiveness of his product; whereas, therefore, liability should expire after a reasonable length of time, without prejudice to claims pending at law;

Whereas, to achieve effective protection of consumers, no contractual derogation should be permitted as regards the liability of the producer in relation to the injured person;

Whereas under the legal systems of the Member States an injured party may have a claim for damages based on grounds of contractual liability or on grounds of non-contractual liability other than that provided for in this Directive; in so far as these provisions also serve to attain the objective of effective protection of consumers, they should remain unaffected by this Directive; whereas, in so far as effective protection of consumers in the sector of pharmaceutical products is already also attained in a Member

State under a special liability system, claims based on this system should similarly remain possible;

Whereas, to the extent that liability for nuclear injury or damage is already covered in all Member States by adequate special rules, it has been possible to exclude damage of this type from the scope of this Directive;

Whereas, since the exclusion of primary agricultural products and game from the scope of this Directive may be felt, in certain Member States, in view of what is expected for the protection of consumers, to restrict unduly such protection, it should be possible for a Member State to extend liability to such products;

Whereas, for similar reasons, the possibility offered to a producer to free himself from liability if he proves that the state of scientific and technical knowledge at the time when he put the product into circulation was not such as to enable the existence of a defect to be discovered may be felt in certain Member States to restrict unduly the protection of the consumer; whereas it should therefore be possible for a Member State to maintain in its legislation or to provide by new legislation that this exonerating circumstance is not admitted; whereas, in the case of new legislation, making use of this derogation should, however, be subject to a Community stand-still procedure, in order to raise, if possible, the level of protection in a uniform manner throughout the Community;

Whereas, taking into account the legal traditions in most of the Member States, it is inappropriate to set any financial ceiling on the producer's liability without fault; whereas, in so far as there are, however, differing traditions, it seems possible to admit that a Member State may derogate from the principle of unlimited liability by providing a limit for the total liability of the producer for damage resulting from a death or personal injury and caused by identical items with the same defect, provided that this limit is established at a level sufficiently high to guarantee adequate protection of the consumer and the correct functioning of the common market;

Whereas the harmonization resulting from this cannot be total at the present stage, but opens the way towards greater harmonization; whereas it is therefore necessary that the Council receive at regular intervals, reports from the Commission on the application of this Directive, accompanied, as the case may be, by appropriate proposals;

Whereas it is particularly important in this respect that a re-examination be carried out of those parts of the Directive relating to the derogations open to the Member States, at the expiry of a period of sufficient length to gather practical experience on the effects of these derogations on the protection of consumers and on the functioning of the common market,

HAS ADOPTED THIS DIRECTIVE:

Article 1

The producer shall be liable for damage caused by a defect in his product.

Article 2

For the purpose of this Directive "product" means all movables, with the exception of primary agricultural products and game, even though incorporated into another movable or into an immovable. "Primary agricultural products" means the products of the soil, of stock-farming and of fisheries, excluding products which have undergone initial processing. "Product" includes electricity.

Article 3

1. "Producer" means the manufacturer of a finished product, the producer of any raw material or the manufacturer of a component part and any person who, by putting his name, trade mark or other distinguishing feature on the product presents himself as its producer.

2. Without prejudice to the liability of the producer, any person who imports into the Community a product for sale, hire, leasing or any form of distribution in the course of his business shall be deemed to be a producer within the meaning of this Directive and shall be responsible as a producer.

3. Where the producer of the product cannot be identified, each supplier of the product shall be treated as its producer unless he informs the injured person, within a reasonable time, of the identity of the producer or of the person who supplied him with the product. The same shall apply, in the case of an imported product, if this product does not indicate the identity of the importer referred to in paragraph 2, even if the name of the producer is indicated.

Article 4

The injured person shall be required to prove the damage, the defect and the causal relationship between defect and damage.

Article 5

Where, as a result of the provisions of this Directive, two or more persons are liable for the same damage, they shall be liable jointly and severally, without prejudice to the provisions of national law concerning the rights of contribution or recourse.

Article 6

1. A product is defective when it does not provide the safety which a person is entitled to expect, taking all circumstances into account, including:

(a) the presentation of the product;

(b) the use to which it could reasonably be expected that the product would be put;

(c) the time when the product was put into circulation.

2.   A product shall not be considered defective for the sole reason that a better product is subsequently put into circulation.

Article 7

The producer shall not be liable as a result of this Directive if he proves:

(a) that he did not put the product into circulation; or

(b) that, having regard to the circumstances, it is probable that the defect which caused the damage did not exist at the time when the product was put into circulation by him or that this defect came into being afterwards; or

(c) that the product was neither manufactured by him for sale or any form of distribution for economic purpose nor manufactured or distributed by him in the course of his business; or

(d) that the defect is due to compliance of the product with mandatory regulations issued by the public authorities; or

(e) that the state of scientific and technical knowledge at the time when he put the product into circulation was not such as to enable the existence of the defect to be discovered; or

(f) in the case of a manufacturer of a component, that the defect is attributable to the design of the product in which the component has been fitted or to the instructions given by the manufacturer of the product.

Article 8

1.   Without prejudice to the provisions of national law concerning the right of contribution or recourse, the liability of the producer shall not be reduced when the damage is caused both by a defect in product and by the act or omission of a third party.

2.   The liability of the producer may be reduced or disallowed when, having regard to all the circumstances, the damage is caused both by a defect in the product and by the fault of the injured person or any person for whom the injured person is responsible.

Article 9

For the purpose of Article 1, "damage" means:

(a) damage caused by death or by personal injuries;

(b) damage to, or destruction of, any item of property other than the defective product itself, with a lower threshold of 500 ECU, provided that the item of property:

   (i) is of a type ordinarily intended for private use or consumption, and

   (ii) was used by the injured person mainly for his own private use or consumption.

This Article shall be without prejudice to national provisions relating to non-material damage.

Article 10

1.   Member States shall provide in their legislation that a limitation period of three years shall apply to proceedings for the recovery of damages as provided for in this Directive. The limitation period shall begin to run from the day on which the plaintiff became aware, or should reasonably have become aware, of the damage, the defect and the identity of the producer.

2.   The laws of Member States regulating suspension or interruption of the limitation period shall not be affected by this Directive.

Article 11

Member States shall provide in their legislation that the rights conferred upon the injured person pursuant to this Directive shall be extinguished upon the expiry of a period of 10 years from the date on which the producer put into circulation the actual product which caused the damage, unless the injured person has in the meantime instituted proceedings against the producer.

Article 12

The liability of the producer arising from this Directive may not, in relation to the injured person, be limited or excluded by a provision limiting his liability or exempting him from liability.

Article 13

This Directive shall not affect any rights which an injured person may have according to the rules of the law of contractual or non-contractual liability or a special liability system existing at the moment when this Directive is notified.

Article 14

This Directive shall not apply to injury or damage arising from nuclear accidents and covered by international conventions ratified by the Member States.

Article 15

1.   Each Member State may:

(a) by way of derogation from Article 2, provide in its legislation that within the meaning of Article 1 of this Directive "product" also means primary agricultural products and game;

(b) by way of derogation from Article 7(e), maintain or, subject to the procedure set out in paragraph 2 of this Article, provide in this legislation that the producer shall be liable even if he proves that the state of scientific and technical knowledge at the time when he put the product into circulation was not such as to enable the existence of a defect to be discovered.

2.   A Member State wishing to introduce the measure specified in paragraph 1(b) shall communicate the text of the proposed measure to the Commission. The Commission shall inform the other Member States thereof.

The Member State concerned shall hold the proposed measure in abeyance for nine months after the Commission is informed and provided that in the meantime the Commission has not submitted to the Council a proposal amending this Directive on the relevant matter. However, if within three months of receiving the said information, the Commission does not advise the Member State concerned that it intends submitting such a proposal to the Council, the Member State may take the proposed measure immediately.

If the Commission does submit to the Council such a proposal amending this Directive within the aforementioned nine months, the Member State concerned shall hold the proposed measure in abeyance for a further period of 18 months from the date on which the proposal is submitted.

3.   Ten years after the date of notification of this Directive, the Commission shall submit to the Council a report on the effect that rulings by the courts as to the application of Article 7(e) and of paragraph 1(b) of this Article have on consumer protection and the functioning of the common market. In the light of this report the Council, acting on a proposal from the Commission and pursuant to the terms of Article 100 of the Treaty, shall decide whether to repeal Article 7(e).

Article 16

1.   Any Member State may provide that a producer's total liability for damage resulting from a death or personal injury and caused by identical items with the same defect shall be limited to an amount which may not be less than 70 million ECU.

2.   Ten years after the date of notification of this Directive, the Commission shall submit to the Council a report on the effect on consumer protection and the functioning of the common market of the implementation of the financial limit on liability by those Member States which have used the option provided for in paragraph 1. In the light of this report the Council, acting on a proposal from the Commission and pursuant to the terms of Article 100 of the Treaty, shall decide whether to repeal paragraph 1.

Article 17

This Directive shall not apply to products put into circulation before the date on which the provisions referred to in Article 19 enter into force.

671

Article 18

1.   For the purposes of this Directive, the ECU shall be that defined by Regulation (EEC) No 3180/78, as amended by Regulation (EEC) No 2626/84. The equivalent in national currency shall initially be calculated at the rate obtaining on the date of adoption of this Directive.

2.   Every five years the Council, acting on a proposal from the Commission, shall examine and, if need be, revise the amounts in this Directive, in the light of economic and monetary trends in the Community.

Article 19

1.   Member States shall bring into force, not later than three years from the date of notification of this Directive, the laws, regulations and administrative provisions necessary to comply with this Directive. They shall forthwith inform the Commission thereof.

2.   The procedure set out in Article 15(2) shall apply from the date of notification of this Directive.

Article 20

Member States shall communicate to the Commission the texts of the main provisions of national law which they subsequently adopt in the field governed by this Directive.

Article 21

Every five years the Commission shall present a report to the Council on the application of this Directive and, if necessary, shall submit appropriate proposals to it.

Article 22

This Directive is addressed to the Member States.

Done at Brussels, 25 July 1985.

For the Council

The President

J. POOS

†